A HISTORY *of* ENGLISH LITERATURE

A History of English Literature

WILLIAM VAUGHN MOODY
ROBERT MORSS LOVETT

EIGHTH EDITION BY *Fred B. Millett*

Charles Scribner's Sons   *New York*

PREFACE TO THE EIGHTH EDITION

In 1962, Moody and Lovett's *History of English Literature* celebrated its sixtieth birthday quietly. No other similar work in this field published in 1902 has had so long an active life. In this period of intense specialization in English studies, it is improbable that any one writer—or any two writers—will have the audacity to attempt to survey the whole range of English literature without the aid of learned collaborators.

Although one can only speculate as to the reasons for the longevity of this text, one of the reasons certainly was the expressive gifts of the original authors. The first version of this book was written by two brilliant young men who had recently joined the English Department of the new University of Chicago. When it was published, William Vaughn Moody was thirty-three years old, and Robert Morss Lovett, thirty-two. Apparently, they were happy collaborators, since one feels no marked diversity in style or tone as one moves from chapter to chapter of the original version. Readability is the secret of the long life of this book. In one case at least, this readability proved self-defeating. When I was engaged in preparing the Sixth Edition of this book (1943), one of my collaborators wrote me that a student of his had told him that she preferred reading Moody and Lovett to reading the literature it discusses.

William Vaughn Moody died in 1910. Before his death, he had become a well-known poet and dramatist. Robert Morss Lovett, who died in 1956, had a long and distinguished career as a critic and editor. To him were due the revisions that marked the editions up to the Sixth. When he and the publisher invited me to supervise the preparation of that edition, I turned, as I have indicated in its preface, to my former colleagues in the English Department at the University of Chicago and to scholars who had been trained at that institution. Their willingness to contribute generously and freely to the preparation of that edition grew, I believe, out of their admiration for the book and its authors and out of their sense of indebtedness and loyalty to the University of Chicago. They believed that they should do what they could to prolong the life of the book; they were challenged to meet the standard of readability that the original authors had set. The later history of the book is evidence of their success in meeting this challenge. To these circumstances, I believe, the book owes its unity of tone and style.

The changes in the Eighth Edition are limited to the bibliographies of the last two chapters which deal with English literature since 1900 and to the text of the final chapter, "The Twentieth Century: Convention and Revolt." It has interested me to observe the amount of critical attention that various writers have attracted in the past decade. In an ascending order, these writers are Lawrence, Conrad, Yeats, and Joyce. In the final chapter, I have attempted to bring up to date the accounts of writers who have been significantly productive since the Seventh Edition appeared. I have added comments on the following novelists: C. P. Snow, Lawrence Durrell, who appeared in the Seventh Edition as a poet, Kingsley Amis, Iris Murdoch, and Alan Sillitoe, on the following dramatists: Samuel Beckett, Harold Pinter, John Osborne, and Arnold Wesker, and on the movements in poetry and criticism during the late 1950's.

FRED B. MILLETT

PREFACE TO THE SEVENTH EDITION

IN THE SEVENTH EDITION, Chapter XVII, "Twentieth-Century Literature: Tradition and Experiment," has been revised in order to cover the significant writing that has appeared since the Sixth Edition was published. In the introduction to the chapter, the historical account has been extended to treat the effects on England of the Second World War and the problems created by it in the following decade. In the Novel section, three novelists who seemed less important than they appeared in the early 'forties have been dropped, and four novelists— Ivy Compton-Burnett, Evelyn Waugh, Graham Greene, and Henry Green—have been added. In the Drama section, T. S. Eliot's later plays are discussed, and comments on the work of Christopher Fry and Terence Rattigan have been included. The Poetry section has been extended by comments on the later work of T. S. Eliot, Edith Sitwell, C. Day Lewis, W. H. Auden, Louis MacNiece and Stephen Spender, and a brief account of the poets of the Second World War and of the spectacular poetic career of Dylan Thomas. Mrs. Cecil Woodham-Smith is now included among the biographers; Sir Osbert Sitwell, among the autobiographers, and F. R. Leavis and Sir Herbert Read are discussed as critics.

The Bibliographies have been revised to include all the scholarly and critical works that have appeared since the early 'forties that might prove of value to teachers and students using this book.

F. B. M.

PREFACE TO THE SIXTH EDITION

THE SIXTH EDITION of Moody and Lovett's *History of English Literature* aims to do for the student of the middle of the twentieth century what the first edition did for the student at the opening of the century. It gives an historical account of English literature, accurate in detail, attractive in style, and discriminating in its critical judgments. The last revised edition (1935) has been carefully edited page by page, and the account of English literature has been extended to 1940. The bibliographies have been re-worked from the beginning. The entire book has been re-set.

The initial plan for the preparation of a new edition of this book was a modest one. It involved the checking of the text for errors, the preparation of new bibliographies, and the reorganization and extension of the account of English literature from 1890 to the present day. As my work on the text began, however, it became clear that a much more searching revision would have to be made if the book were really to be brought up to date. The original text was written about 1900 and was first published in 1902. Between 1900 and 1941, important revaluations of authors, particularly those of the seventeenth, eighteenth, and nineteenth centuries, have been slowly taking place. It seemed increasingly desirable, accordingly, to extend the revision to include such modifications of interpretation and evaluation as would bring the book into line with the scholarship and criticism of the twentieth century. In consequence, there is hardly a page of the new text that has not undergone modification, frequently trivial, but sometimes drastic. It is hoped that none of the clarity and grace of the original edition has been lost in the attempt to embody in the new edition the results of contemporary scholarship and criticism.

From the first, this history of English literature has been a

ix

cooperative venture. As revision after revision appeared, Professor Lovett called on more and more of his colleagues and friends for advice and assistance. Thus, in the Preface to the 1918 edition, he wrote, "In this revision I have drawn, without the slightest reserve, on the learning of my colleagues of the English Department of the University of Chicago. To Professor Thomas A. Knott I am particularly indebted for a careful reworking of the first three chapters, and to Professor John M. Manly for the same service in the pages on the origin of the drama. Other portions of the book were read, with helpful criticism, by Professor C. R. Baskervill, Professor T. P. Cross, Professor J. W. Linn, Doctor G. W. Sherburn, and Doctor D. H. Stevens. Professor W. F. Bryan of Northwestern University gave me valuable suggestions based on his use of the book in the classroom. Mr. Padraic Colum furnished me with interesting notes on contemporary poets, and kindly contributed the sketch of the Irish literary movement."

I should not have ventured upon a thorough-going revision of this famous text if I had not felt certain that I could call on various specialists to give me the benefit of their unusual information and insight. Certain major obligations must be indicated in detail. I am profoundly indebted to Professor Martin M. Crow of the University of Texas for a detailed revision of Chapters I-III; to Mr. James D. Osborn of Yale University for a thorough reconsideration of the treatments of seventeenth-century literature in Chapters VIII-IX; to Professor George Sherburn of Harvard University for the new opening of Chapter X and many revisions throughout that chapter; to Professor Donald F. Bond of the University of Chicago for detailed editing of Chapters XI and XII; to Professor Carl H. Grabo of the University of Chicago for radical suggestions for the re-writing of Chapter XIII, a number of which I have endeavored to carry out; to Professor Morton Dauwen Zabel of Loyola University (Chicago) for numerous valuable leads in connection with Chapters XIV and XV. I have re-organized Chapter XVI with considerable care, and in Chapter XVII I have written an almost completely new account of English literature since 1914. To that chapter, the passages on Katherine Mansfield and Gerard Manley Hopkins have been generously contributed by Katherine Krusé.

The bibliographies for Chapters I-XVI have been prepared under my direction by Mr. Eugene Current-Garcia of Harvard University. They have been re-checked by Mr. Arthur R. Youtz of the staff of the New York Public Library. The material for the bibliography of Chapter XVII has been contributed by Mr. John Fall, General Assistant to the Director of the New York Public Library.

F. B. M.

Contents

A HISTORY *of* ENGLISH LITERATURE

CHAPTER I

The Anglo-Saxon Period

THE HEROIC AGE

I

ENGLISH literature had its beginnings at a time when the ancestors of the English people lived on the continent of Europe and spoke a tongue which, though the ancestor of modern English, is unintelligible to us without special study. Anglo-Saxon, or Old English, belongs to the low-German group of languages, of which Dutch is the best modern representative; and the men who spoke it lived, when history first discovers them, along the shores of the North Sea from the mouth of the Rhine to the peninsula of Jutland. They were divided into three principal tribes: the Saxons, dwelling near the mouth of the Elbe; the Angles, inhabiting the southwest part of Denmark; and the Jutes, extending north of the Angles into modern Jutland.

The Anglo-Saxon Tribes

How extensive these tribes were and how far into the interior their territories reached we do not know. That portion of them which concerns us dwelt along the sea; the earliest English poetry which has been preserved, even though it was composed three centuries later in England, gives glimpses backward into that almost unknown time—glimpses of wild moors and dense forests where lurked gigantic monsters half seen amid mist and darkness; glimpses of the stormy northern ocean filled likewise with shapes of shadowy fear. Whether from superstition or from the physical difficulty of the country, these tribes seem not to have penetrated far inland. Their two passions, war and

Their Home; War and Seafaring

1

wandering, urged them forth upon the sea. As soon as spring had unlocked the harbors, their boats sailed out in search of booty and adventure; sometimes to ravage or to wreak blood-feud on a neighboring tribe, sometimes to harry a monastery on the coasts of Roman Gaul or to plunder along the white cliffs of England, their future home. This seafaring life, full of danger and adventure, was a frequent inspiration of the poet. The sea, in the bold metaphors of their poetry, is the "seal-bath," the "swan-road," the "whale-path." The ship is the "swimming-wood," the "sea-steed," the "wave-house of warriors"; its curved prow is "wreathed with foam like the neck of a swan." The darker aspects of the ocean are also sung with fervor. The fatalistic Anglo-Saxon was fearless before the terror and gloom of the element which he loved most.

No actual poetry has come down to us from that earliest period, but the poetry of a subsequent age is filled with phrases and reminiscences of ancient pagan voyages and *Their* battles. This later poetry is nearly all Christian in *Religion* tone or in substance. But from other sources we know the primitive gods of the race: Tiu, a mysterious and dreadful deity of war; Woden, father of the later dynasty of gods and the patron of seers and travellers; Thor, the god of thunder; Frea, mother of the gods and giver of fruitfulness. These are commemorated in our names of the days of the week —Tuesday, Wednesday, Thursday, and Friday. The rites of Eostre, a mysterious goddess of the dawn, survive, though strangely altered, in the Christian festival of Easter. In studying the earlier poetry, Christian though it is superficially, we must put out of our minds as far as we can all those ideals of life and conduct which come from Christianity and remember that we have to do with men whose recently discarded gods were only magnified images of their own wild natures; men who delighted in bloodshed, in revenge, and in plunder, and were much given to deep drinking in the mead-hall, but who nevertheless were sensitive to blame and praise, were reared in an elaborate code of manners and endowed with chivalry and dignity, were passionately loyal to their king or lord, and were thrilled with a poetry that rang with heroic adventure.

Our Anglo-Saxon ancestors had in an eminent degree also that passion which gives the first impulse to literature among a primitive people—love of glory. When their first *Their* recorded epic hero, Beowulf, has met his death, *Singers* and his followers are recalling his noble nature, they say as their last word that "he was of all world-kings the most desirous of praise." It was not enough for such men as he that they should spend their lives in glorious adventures; they desired to see their names and their deeds spread among distant peoples and handed down to unborn generations. Hence the poet, who alone could insure this fame, was held in high esteem. Two classes of singers were recognized: first the gleeman, who did not create his own songs, but merely (like the Greek rhapsodist) chanted what he had learned from others; and, second, the scop, the poet proper, who took the crude material of legend and adventure which lay about him and shaped it into lays. Sometimes the scop was permanently attached to the court of an ætheling, or lord, was granted land and treasure, and was raised by virtue of his poetcraft to the same position of honor which the other followers of the ætheling held by virtue of their prowess in battle. Sometimes he wandered from court to court, depending for a hospitable reception upon his host's appreciation of the tales that he chanted to the harp.

Two ancient poems tell of the fortunes of the scop. The first of these, entitled *Deor's Lament,* stands almost alone in Old English poetry in that it is strophic in form with a *"Deor's* recurring refrain. In a tone of brooding, melan- *Lament"* choly fatalism the poet consoles himself for his eclipse by a rival scop, Heorrenda, and for the loss of his land-right and of the royal favor by recalling the misfortunes suffered by heroic persons of the long ago. After each tragic incident he says: "That was endured, this likewise can be." The frank utterance of personal grief, the grim, mournful stoicism, and, above all, the strophic structure and the refrain, give the poem extraordinary interest.

The second of these poems, entitled, from the opening word, *Widsith,* or *The Far-Wanderer,* is a glorification of the poet and of the generosity of his royal patrons. The poem begins:

"Widsith spake, unlocked his word-hoard; he who had travelled
throughout most of the tribes and nations in the world." Wid-
"Widsith"   sith is an imaginary poet who pictures himself as
having been at the courts of all the great kings
and emperors of both the Classical and the Germanic worlds.
The purpose seems to be to show the generosity with which rulers
and nations have always delighted to honor their poets. After a
long list of princes and peoples—"Attila ruled the Huns; Cæsar
ruled the Greeks; Offa ruled the Angles"—Widsith says: "Thus
through many a strange nation I travelled; therefore can I sing
in the mead-hall how kingly heroes honored me with gifts."
Then follows a series of nations—"I was with the Swedes, the
Danes, the Saracens, the Hebrews, the Assyrians, the Indians,
the Medes, and the Persians"—then a list of kings—Eormanric,
Eadwine, Wulfhere—many of whom are said to have honored
Widsith with gold and treasure. "Thus the gleemen roam thru
the wide world; they tell their need and say their thanks; always
south or north they visit a man prudent in speech, generous of
gifts, who wishes praise to be uttered before the warriors, noble
deeds to be performed, till light and life depart together; he
gains renown, he has long-lasting glory." Whether or not this
poem be as ancient as some scholars have thought, it reveals the
high position occupied by the scop and the gleemen in Germanic and especially in Anglo-Saxon society.

II

While Angles, Saxons, and Jutes were still unknown Ger-
manic tribes, their future island-home was being made into a
England   province of the Roman Empire. The very earliest
Before the   inhabitants of Britain, that mysterious race which
Anglo-   may have raised the huge circle of monoliths at
Saxon   Stonehenge, had given way—how early we do not
Invasions   know—to a Celtic-speaking people. Before the
Roman conquest this people spread over France,
Spain, and all the British Isles. The Celts were of an impetuous
character, imaginative, curious, and quick to learn. The Roman
historians tell us of their eagerness for news, of their delight in
clever speech and quick retort. Their early literature shows a

delicate fancy, a kind of wild grace and a love of beauty for its own sake, strikingly in contrast with the stern and stately poetry of the Anglo-Saxon scop. But this very quickness of sympathy and of intelligence proved fatal to their existence as independent peoples. When the Roman legions crossed from Gaul to Britain there was a brief period of fierce resistance, and then the Celts accepted, probably as much from curiosity as from compulsion, the imposing Roman civilization. Some of the more stubborn fled to the fastnesses of Wales and Scotland, but the greater part seem to have submitted to the Romans, as if by a kind of fascination, even to some extent giving up their own language for that of their conquerors. The Romans, like the English of modern times, carried wherever they went their splendid but somewhat rigid civilization, and by the end of the fourth century England was dotted with towns and villas where, amid pillared porticos, mosaic pavements, marble baths, forums, and hippodromes, a Roman emperor could feel at home.

This was the state of England when there began that remarkable series of movements on the part of the restless Germanic tribes which we know as the "migration." About the end of the fourth century, urged by a common impulse, tribe after tribe swept westward across the Rhine, and southward across the Danube; some came from the north by sea, to harry the coasts of Gaul and Britain; some scaled the Alps, and even the Pyrenees, to batter at the gates of Rome, or to plunder the rich lands and islands of the Mediterranean, and to found a kingdom in Africa. The Roman legions were recalled from Britain to guard the imperial city, the Roman officials withdrew, and the Celtic inhabitants, weakened by three centuries of civilized life, and accustomed to rely for defense on the strong sword of the Roman soldier, were left to struggle unaided against the savage raids of the Picts and Scots, and the pirate bands of Jutes, Saxons, and Angles, which appeared every spring in increasing numbers upon their coast. The Celts, however, did not submit themselves to the yoke of these savage Germanic invaders as they had done to the polished Romans. Not long after the year 400 the first band of Jutes landed on the island of Thanet at the invitation of the unwarlike Celts, to defend the latter against the Picts and Scots. Attracted by the

The Invasions

wealth and fertility of the country, and impressed with the help-lessness of its inhabitants, the Jutes ere long turned from allies to enemies far worse than those against whom they had been employed. During the following centuries, in steadily increasing numbers, they fought their way grimly from seacoast into interior, slaying or enslaving the Celtic population, or driving it before them into the western half of the island, or across the sea into Brittany, and obliterating all the monuments of civilization bequeathed by Rome. The Celtic and the Latin languages simply disappeared from the parts of the island occupied by the Anglo-Saxons, leaving scarcely a trace on the speech of the conquerors. A few river-names, Thames, Avon, Cam, are Celtic. Many place-names contain the Latin suffixes -chester, -caster, and -wich, -wick (Winchester, Lancaster, Greenwich, Berwick), transmitted from the Romans through the Celts to the English.

During these years of struggle there began to grow up about the person of an obscure Celtic leader that cycle of stories which *Celt and Saxon* was to prove fruitful of poetry both in France and in England—the legends of Arthur, founder of the Round Table, and defender of the western Britons against the weakening power of Rome and the growing fury of the barbarians. As the Angles and Saxons spread later over the western part of England, they seem to have absorbed the remaining inhabitants, who communicated to the conquering race its first leaven; they made it later more sensitive and receptive, and gave it a touch of extravagance and gayety, which, after being reinforced by similar elements in the temperament of the Norman-French invaders, was to blossom in the sweet humor of Chaucer, the rich fancy of Spenser, and the broad humanity of Shakespeare.

During the long period of ruthless conquest and unorganized settlement by the Angles, Saxons, and Jutes, there were growing slowly a number of little national groups among *Anglo-Saxon Civi-lization* the conquerors; and after the year 600, with the appearance of four great kingdoms in Kent, Northumbria, Mercia, and Wessex, each of which attained a temporary leadership, there followed more settled conditions, under which civilization and literature could flourish. Missionaries, schools, and monasteries not only com verted the pagan Anglo-Saxons to Christianity, but also made them familiar with both the religious and the secular literature which circulated on the continent; they may perhaps have made possible the composition of such a long and stately epic poem as the most remarkable literary relic of early Germanic literature, *Beowulf*. Further, the monastic scribe was the agent who for the first time could record and preserve both traditional and contemporary poetry, which till then had been only precariously transmitted through the memories of gleemen, and circulated only as they sang before the nobles in the mead-hall.

It was not till about 750 that the long poem entitled, from its hero, *Beowulf,* was composed. It is something over three thousand lines in length, and though consisting of two separate adventures, constitutes an artistic literary whole. *"Beowulf"*

Hrothgar, king of the Danes, has built near the sea a magnificent hall, named Heorot, where he sits with his thanes at the mead-drinking, and listens to the chanting of the gleemen. For a while he lives in happiness, and is known far and wide as a splendid and liberal prince. But one night there comes from the march- *Hrothgar and Grendel* land, the haunt of all unearthly and malign creatures, a terrible monster named Grendel. Entering the mead-hall he slays thirty of the sleeping Danes, and carries their corpses away to his lair. The next night the same thing is repeated. No mortal power seems able to cope with the gigantic foe. In the winter nights Grendel couches in the splendid hall, defiling all its bright ornaments. For twelve years this scourge afflicts the Danes, until Hrothgar's spirit is broken.

At last the story of Grendel's deeds crosses the sea to Gautland, where the stalwart Beowulf dwells with his uncle, King Hygelac. He determines to go to Hrothgar's assistance. With fourteen companions he embarks: "Departed then over the billowy sea the foamy-necked floater, most like to a bird." The next day *The Coming of Beowulf* the voyagers catch sight of the promontories of Hrothgar's land; and soon, from the top of the cliffs, they behold in the vale beneath them the famous hall, "rich and gold-variegated, mos:

glorious of dwellings under the firmament." The young heroes in their "shining war byrnies" (coats of ring-mail), and with their spears like a "gray ash-forest," are ushered into the hall "where Hrothgar sits, old and gray, amid his band of nobles." Beowulf craves permission to cleanse Heorot, and Hrothgar consents that the Gauts shall abide Grendel's coming in the hall that night. Meanwhile, until darkness draws on, the thanes of Hrothgar and the followers of Beowulf sit drinking mead, "the bright sweet liquor," and listening to the songs of the gleeman. The feast draws to a close when Wealhtheow, Hrothgar's queen, after solemnly handing the mead-cup to her lord and to Beowulf, and bidding them "be blithe at the beer-drinking," goes through the hall distributing gifts among the thanes. The king, queen, and their followers then withdraw to another building for the night, while Beowulf and his men lie down to wait for the coming of Grendel. All fall asleep except Beowulf, who "awaits in angry mood the fate of the battle."

The coming of the monster is described vividly: "Then came from the moors, under the misty hills, Grendel stalking. . . .

The Fight in the Hall The door, fast with fire-hardened bands, burst open. On the many-colored floor the foe trod; he went, wroth of mood; from his eyes stood a horrid light like flame. . . . He saw in the hall many warriors sleeping, a kindred band . . . . Then his heart laughed." He seizes one of the warriors, bites his "bone-joints," drinks the blood from his veins, and greedily devours him even to the hands and feet. "Nearer he stepped, seized a stout-hearted warrior in his bed." That warrior, the strength of thirty men in his hand-grip, seizes Grendel. Terror-stricken, the monster turns to flee, but is held by the strength of Beowulf. The other warriors, awakened by the combat and the "song of terror sung by God's adversary," try to help with their swords, but no mortal weapon can wound Grendel. At last the monster wrenches his own arm from its socket and flees to his lair to die, leaving Beowulf to nail the grisly trophy in triumph above the door of Heorot.

In the morning there is great rejoicing. The king, with the queen and her company of maidens, comes through the meadows to gaze in wonder on the huge arm and claw nailed beneath the gold roof of the hall. When the evening feast begins, Beowulf sits between the two sons of the king and receives the precious gifts—jewels, rings, and a golden necklace—which the queen presents to him. But after nightfall Grendel's mother comes to take vengeance for her son. She seizes one of Hrothgar's nobles, Æschere, and bears him away to her watery den.

Beowulf promises to pursue the new foe to the bottom of her fen-pool. With Hrothgar and a band of followers he marches along the cliffs and windy promontories which *The Fight* bound the moor on the seaward side, until he *Beneath* comes to Grendel's lair. It is a sea-pool, shut in by *the Sea* precipitous rocks, and overhung by the shaggy trunks and aged writhen boughs of a "joyless wood." Trembling passers-by have seen fire fleeting on the waves at night, and the hart wearied by the hounds will lie down and die on these banks rather than plunge into the unholy waters. The pool is so deep that it is an hour before Beowulf reaches the bottom. Snakes and beasts of the shining deep attack him as he descends. At last he finds himself in a cave where the "mere-wife" is lurking, and a deadly struggle begins. Once the giantess throws Beowulf to the ground, and sitting astride his body draws out her broad, short knife to despatch him; but his coat of ring-mail saves him, and with a superhuman effort he struggles up again, throws away his broken sword, and seizes from a heap of arms a magic blade, forged by giants of old time; with it he hews off the head of Grendel's mother, and then that of Grendel, whose dead body he finds lying in the cave. So poisonous is the blood of Grendel that it melts the metal of the blade, leaving only the hilt in Beowulf's hand. When he reappears with his trophies at the surface of the water, all except his own thanes have given him up for dead and have returned home. Great is the jubilation when the hero appears at Heorot with his companions and throws upon the floor of the mead-hall the huge head, which four men can hardly carry.

The second great episode of the poem is Beowulf's fight with the Dragon of the Gold-Hoard. Beowulf has been reigning as king for fifty years and is now an old man, when calamity comes upon him and his people in the form of a dragon, which flies by night enveloped in fire; and which, in revenge for the theft of a gold cup from its precious hoard, burns the king's hall. Old as he is, Beowulf fights the dragon single-handed. He slays the monster in its lair, but himself receives his mortal hurt.

The Fire-Dragon

The death of the old king is picturesque and moving. He bids his thane bring out from the dragon's den "the gold-treasure, the jewels, the curious gems," in order that death may be softer to him, seeing the wealth he has gained for his people. Wiglaf, entering the cave of the "old twilight-flier," sees "dishes standing, vessels of men of yore, footless, their ornaments fallen away; there was many a helm old and rusty, and many armlets cunningly fastened," and over the hoard droops a magic banner, "all golden, locked by arts of song," from which a light is shed over the treasure. Beowulf gazes with dying eyes upon the precious things; then he asks that his thanes build for him a funeral barrow on a promontory of the sea, which the sailors, as they "drive their foaming barks from afar over the mists of floods, may see and name Beowulf's Mount."

The Death of Beowulf

This is only a summary. The poem itself, however, has a solid background of detailed realism. We see vividly the courtly manners and customs of the royal and the noble personages, the engraved swords, the "boar-helmets" and the "woven ring-mail" of the warriors, the benches and tables of the "antler-broad hall," the servants pouring the bright mead; we hear the stately, eloquent speeches, the scop's clear song; we feel the high loyalty of thanes and of kinsmen to their lord, the faithfulness and generosity of the king to his retainers.

Life Reflected in "Beowulf"

Although the poem was composed in England about the middle of the eighth century, the subject-matter is not English. The places and the peoples are in Denmark and Sweden. The manners, the customs, the civilization, seem to be those of all the Germanic nations, as are also such historical and legendary allusions as Hygelac's raid on the Frisians and the minstrel's tale of Hnæf and Finn. These great persons and their heroic or

Other Anglo-Saxon Epics

tragic adventures, many of which are mentioned also in *Widsith,* are the heritage of all the Germanic peoples. That, besides *Beowulf,* other epic poems on these adventures were composed in Anglo-Saxon, we have direct evidence in the form of fragmentary poems, *Finnesburh* dealing with a story mentioned in *Beowulf*—the war between Finn and Hnæf—and *Waldere* consisting of two short passages from a poem of which we have several complete versions in continental languages.

The structure of Old English poetry is quite different from that of modern English poetry. The metrical unit is the single line, which regularly consists of four strongly accented syllables, with an unfixed number of unaccented syllables. This line is divided into two half-lines, each with two strong accents. Two or three of the accented syllables of the line begin with the same consonant sound—that is, they alliterate; the first accent of the second half-line is always alliterative. Rhyme is very rare. The following bit of vivid description (of Grendel's haunts) is taken from *Beowulf:* (ll. 1357–61)

Old English Verse-Form

hie dýgel lónd
*w*árigeath, *w*úlf-hleothu,   *w*índige naéssas,
*f*récne *f*én-gelad,   thaer *f*yrgen-stréam
under *n*aéssa genípu   *n*íther gewíteth,
*f*lód under *f*óldan.   Nis thaet *f*éor héonon.

[A secret land
They haunt, wolf-slopes,   windy headlands,
Fearful fen-paths,   where the mountain-stream
Under the shadows of cliffs   downward departs,
The flood beneath the earth.   That is not far hence.]

III

The immediate influence of the Romanized Celtic people and their civilization on the Anglo-Saxons was almost nothing. From such a poem as *The Ruin,* a melancholy lament over the crumbling towers and the fallen walls of an abandoned city, we may guess at the utter devastation wrought in the earlier period by the armies of the invaders. What influence the Celts exerted was indirect, and appeared chiefly in the fields of learning and religion.

Christianity came into England in two different streams, one from Rome, one from Ireland, which had been converted from

The Christianizing of England

heathenism several centuries before. The first stream began late in the sixth century, with the coming of Augustine to Kent. Little by little, after the advent of this great missionary in the south of England, the new creed drove out the old, winning its way by virtue of its greater idealism and the authority with which it spoke of man's existence beyond the grave. This stream of religious influence, which came from Rome, overran south and central England. It produced some schools of learning, but almost no English literature. The second stream of Christian influence swept into Northumbria through the labors of the Irish missionaries, who were carrying their creed at the same time into France, Spain, Germany, and Switzerland. Eventually, at the Synod of Whitby (664), the Celtic ecclesiastical usages of the north were discarded in favor of the Roman, and England was thus kept in close touch with the intellectual and religious life of the continent. It is, nevertheless, to the north and east that we must look for the first blossomings of Christian poetry in England.

Of all the monasteries which were founded in Northumbria by the Celtic missionaries from Ireland, two are most famous

Bede and Cædmon

because of their connection with literature—Jarrow and Whitby. At Jarrow lived and died Bæda, known as the "Venerable Bede," a gentle, laborious scholar in whom all the learning of Northumbria was summed up. He wrote many books, all but one in Latin, the most notable being *Historia Ecclesiastica Gentis Anglorum* (*Ecclesiastical History of the English People*). It is from a passage in this book that we learn the story of Cædmon, the earliest known poet of Christian England. He was a humble herdsman who lived near Whitby at the end of the seventh century. Bede tells us that at the feast, when the harp was passed round for each to sing in turn, Cædmon would rise and go to his house, because he knew nothing of the gleeman's art. But one night, when he had thus left the cheerful company and gone to the stable to tend the cattle, he fell asleep and had a wonderful dream. A figure stood beside him, saying: "Cædmon, sing to me." Cædmon answered: "Behold, I know not how to sing, and therefore I left the feast to-night." "Nevertheless, sing now to me," the figure said. "What shall I sing?" asked Cædmon. "Sing the beginning of created things," was the answer. Then in his dream Cædmon phrased some verses of the Creation, which in the morning he could remember. News of the wonderful gift which had been vouchsafed to the unschooled man was carried to Hild, the abbess of the convent, and she commanded portions of the Scripture to be read to him that he might paraphrase them into verse. So it was done; and from this time on Cædmon gave his life to the heaven-appointed task of turning the Old Testament narratives into song.

The poems which formerly were attributed to Cædmon (though not now regarded as his) consist of paraphrases of parts of Genesis, of Exodus, and of Daniel. Some- *Biblical* times, especially in dealing with a war-like episode, *Poetry* the poet expands his matter freely, treating it with all the vigor and picturesqueness of the Germanic poetry of war. In *Exodus,* for instance, the most vivid and original passages are those which tell of the overwhelming of Pharaoh's host in the Red Sea. The Egyptians and the Israelitish armies are described with a heathen scop's delight in the pomp and circumstance of battle, and the disaster which overtakes the Egyptian hosts is sung with martial vigor.

If we know little of Cædmon's life, we know still less of that of Cynewulf, a poet living a century later, who was perhaps the greatest of the Anglo-Saxon poets, if we except the unknown bard who composed *Beowulf.* We have, *Cynewulf* signed with Cynewulf's name in runes, two lives of saints, *Elene* and *Juliana,* and a poem dealing with Christ's ascension. One other poem has been ascribed to him with some probability, *Andreas,* a very lively and naïve story of a saint's martyrdom and final triumph over his enemies.

The Phœnix, a translation from the Latin, sometimes attributed to Cynewulf, is the only Anglo-Saxon poem of any length

"The Phœnix" which shows a delight in the soft and radiant moods of nature, as opposed to her fierce and grim aspects. In the land where the Phœnix dwells "the groves are all behung with blossoms . . . the boughs upon the trees are ever laden, the fruit is aye renewed through all eternity." The music of the wonderful bird, as it goes aloft "to meet that gladsome gem, God's candle," is "sweeter and more beauteous than any art of song." When the thousand years of its life are done, it flies away to a lonely Syrian wood, and builds its own holocaust of fragrant herbs, which the sun kindles. Out of the ashes a new Phœnix is born, "richly dight with plumage, as it was at first, radiantly adorned," and flies back to its home in the enchanted land of summer. At the end the history of the bird, which was traditionally treated as a symbol of the rising sun, is interpreted as an allegory of the death and resurrection of Christ, and of his ascent to heaven amid the ministering company of saints. The poem has a fervor and enthusiasm lacking in its Latin original, and is the work of a good poet. It has been pointed out that the fanciful description of the bird's home-land is remarkably reminiscent of the old Celtic tales about the Land of Eternal Youth; and certainly it is not difficult to see, in the bright colors and happy fancy of the poem, the working of the Celtic imagination, as well as the transforming touch of hope which had been brought into men's lives by Christianity.

One of the most curious and most interesting of the Anglo-Saxon poems is a collection of *Riddles,* which were erroneously

The Riddles attributed to Cynewulf. Riddles, which in the Middle Ages were considered a much more dignified literary form than they are today, when we relegate them to children and the "folk," had a wide European circulation. The Old English riddles are imaginative and picturesque. The new moon is a young viking, sailing through the skies in his pirate ship, laden with spoils of battle, to build a citadel for himself in highest heaven; but the sun, a greater warrior, drives him away and seizes his land, until the night conquers the sun in turn. The iceberg shouts and laughs as it plunges through the wintry sea, eager to crush the fleet of hostile ships. The sword in its scabbard is a mailed fighter, who dashes exultingly into the battle-play, and then is sad because women upbraid him over the fate of the heroes he has slain.

Besides the poetry attributed to Cædmon and to Cynewulf and their schools, there exist a few short poems, lyrics, or "dramatic lyrics," of the greatest interest. One of these, called *The Wife's Lament*, gives us a glimpse of one of the harsh customs of our ancestors. A *Love-Poems* wife, accused of faithlessness, has been banished from her native village, and compelled to live alone in the forest; from her place of exile she pours out her moan to the husband who has been estranged from her by false slanderers. *The Lover's Message* is a kind of companion piece to this. The speaker in the little poem is the tablet of wood upon which an absent lover has carved a message to send to his beloved. It tells her that he has now a home for her in the south, and bids her, as soon as she hears the cuckoo chanting of his sorrow in the copsewood, to take sail over the ocean pathway to her lord, who waits and longs for her. These are the earliest recorded English love-poems.

Three other poems require brief mention. In *The Seafarer* the poet, after describing the bitter misery of the sailor's life amidst winter storms, comes to the characteristic Anglo-Saxon conclusion that the charm of his perilous life outweighs all the attractions of a warm and comfortable home on the shore. *The Dream of the Rood* is an intensely emotional vision of the cross on which the Saviour died. The wonderful and glorious tree itself speaks, telling the story of the crucifixion, and the dreamer replies with a confession of the wretchedness of his sins, and of the redeeming power of the cross.

The longest and most perfect in form of these half-lyrical elegies or poems of sentiment is *The Wanderer*. It is a mournful plaint by one who must "travel o'er the water-track, stir with his hands the rime-cold sea, and struggle on the paths of exile," while he muses *"The Wanderer"* upon the joys and glories of a life that has passed away forever. "Often," he says, "it seems to him in fancy as if he clasps and kisses his lord, and on his knees lays hand and head, even as erewhile"; but he soon wakes friendless, and sees before him only "the fallow waves, sea-birds bathing and spreading their wings, falling hoar-frost and snow mingled with hail." Rapt away again by his longing, he beholds his friends and kinsmen hovering before him in the air; he "greets them with snatches of song, he scans them eagerly, comrades of heroes; soon they swim away again; the sailor-souls do not bring hither many old familiar songs." And at the close the Wanderer breaks out with a lament over the departed glories of a better time: "Where is gone the horse? Where is gone the hero? Where is gone the giver of treasure? Where are gone the seats of the feast? Where are the joys of the hall? Ah, thou bright cup! Ah, thou mailed warrior! Ah, the prince's glory! How has the time passed away . . . as if it had not been!" There is a wistful sadness and a lyric grace in this poem which suggests once more the Celtic leaven at work in the vehement Anglo-Saxon genius. It suggests, too, a state of society fallen into ruin, a time of disaster. Perhaps, before it was written, such a time had come for England, and especially for Northumbria.

While the Anglo-Saxons had been settling down in England to a life of agriculture, their pagan kinsmen who remained on *The Danish Invasions* the continent had continued to lead their wild free-booting life on the sea. Toward the end of the eighth century bands of Danes began to harass the English coasts. Northumbria, the seat and centre of English learning, at first bore the main force of their attacks. The very monastery of Jarrow, in which Bede had written his *Ecclesiastical History,* was plundered, and its inhabitants were put to the sword. The monastery of Whitby, where Cædmon had had his vision, was only temporarily saved by the fierce resistance of the monks. By the middle of the ninth century the Danes had made themselves masters of Northumbria, and the flourishing Anglo-Saxon civilization, the schools, the literature, were blotted out. The Danes were such men as the Angles, Jutes, and Saxons had been four hundred years before—worshippers of the old gods, ruthless assailants of a religion, literature, and society which they did not understand. In Wessex the heroism of King Alfred, who reigned from 871 to 901, turned back the tide of warlike invaders. The Danes, in accordance with the terms of their truce, settled thickly in the north and east, and three centuries later the language of those districts still contained many words borrowed from the Scandinavian settlers.

Until the Norman conquest, however, the only literature which remains to us was produced in Wessex. It is almost entirely a literature of prose; the best of it was the work of King Alfred himself, or was produced under his immediate encouragement. As a child King *King Alfred* Alfred had seen Rome, and had lived for a time at the great court of Charles the Bald in France; and the spectacle of these older and richer civilizations had filled him with a desire to give to his struggling subjects something of the heritage of the past. When, after long, desperate warfare, he had won peace from the Danes, he called about him learned monks from the sheltered monasteries of Ireland and Wales, and made welcome at his court all strangers who could bring him a manuscript or sing to him an old song. He spurred on his priests and bishops to write. He himself learned a little Latin, in order that he might translate into the West-Saxon tongue certain books which he believed would be most useful and interesting to Englishmen, putting down the sense, he says, "sometimes word for word, sometimes meaning for meaning, as I had learned it from Plegmund, my archbishop, and Asser, my bishop, and Grimbald, my mass-priest, and John, my mass-priest." He selected for translation a famous and influential philosophical work of the Middle Ages, the *Consolation of Philosophy* of Boethius; a manual of universal history and geography by Orosius; and a treatise on the duties of priests and learned men, the *Pastoral Care* or *Shepherd's Book* of Pope Gregory the Great, copies of which he sent to all his bishops in order that they and their priests might learn to be better shepherds of their flocks. More important still, he seems to have been the one who caused to be translated Bede's *Ecclesiastical History,* thus giving a native English dress to the first great piece of historical writing which had been done in England. Lastly, he appears to have directed the collection of the meager entries of the deaths of kings and

the installations of bishops which the monks of various monasteries were in the habit of making on the Easter rolls; these records were expanded into a clear and picturesque narrative, the
greatest space, of course, being taken up with the events of his
own reign. This, known as the *Anglo-Saxon Chronicle,* is the
oldest monument of English prose, and is, with one exception
(the Gothic *Gospels*), the most venerable piece of extended
prose writing in a Germanic language.

King Alfred does not seem to have succeeded in recreating
a vital native literature in England, but he prepared the way
Later Anglo-Saxon Literature for some important productions. The sermons or
Homilies of the eloquent and devoted Ælfric
(*c.* 1000) here and there rise to the rank of literature, by reason of the picturesqueness of some religious legend which they treat, by the fervor of their
piety, and by reason of their rhythmic, poetic style. The *Anglo-
Saxon Chronicle,* also, which continued to grow in the monasteries of Peterborough, Winchester, and Ely, here and there
records a bit of ringing verse. One of these poetic passages,
known as the *Battle of Brunanburh,* is entered under the year
937. Another late poem, the *Death of Byrhtnoth,* also called the
Battle of Maldon, bears the date 991. These are both accounts
of stubborn and heroic battles by the English against the Danes.
The latter is the swan-song of Anglo-Saxon poetry.

In passing judgment on Anglo-Saxon literature we must remember that the fragmentary survivals unquestionably repre-
Survival of Anglo-Saxon Literature sent only in the most imperfect way what must at
one time have been a rich and extensive literature.
Ancient poetry and prose could be preserved only
if written down, and then only if the manuscripts
themselves survived the ravages of accident and
time. The two centuries of devastation wrought by the Danes,
especially to the flourishing culture of Northumbria and Mercia,
devastation which was marked by the burning and plundering
of monasteries, almost the only safe and permanent depositaries
for manuscripts, resulted, as King Alfred complains, in the almost complete destruction of written literature. Six hundred
years later, at the dissolution of the English monasteries, their

libraries again were almost totally destroyed, and it was only through the activities of a few enthusiastic antiquaries that any of the literary monuments from the manuscript period were saved from vandalism. Only four manuscripts containing Anglo-Saxon poetry are extant—one in the cathedral at Vercelli, Italy; one in the cathedral at Exeter; one at Oxford, and one in London. For the most part we must reconstruct with the eye and ear of imagination the stately and heroic songs which thrilled the hearts of kings and warriors, of clerks and peasants, in every hall and hamlet of England for six centuries before the coming of the Normans.

CHAPTER II

The Norman-French Period

THE AGE OF CHIVALRY

THE NORMANS ("North-men"), a group of Scandinavian sea-rovers who settled in northwestern France about 900, were an extraordinary people. While many of their fellows were invading and settling in England, they appeared off the coast of France; and under their leader, Hrolf the Ganger (the "Walker"), they pushed up the Seine in their *The Normans* black boats, wasting and burning to the very gates of Paris. The French won peace by granting them the broad and rich lands in the northwest, known henceforth as Normandy. Unlike the other northern peoples, they showed a remarkable faculty for retaining their own individuality while assimilating the southern civilization. They married French women, and adopted French manners and the French tongue. In a little over a century they had grown from a barbarous horde of sea-robbers into the most polished and brilliant people of Europe, whose power was felt even in the Mediterranean and the Far East. They united in a remarkable way impetuous daring and cool practical sense. Without losing anything of their northern bravery in war, they absorbed all the southern suppleness and wit, all the southern love of splendor and art, and moreover developed a genius for organizing and conducting their government. Before the battle of Hastings in 1066 the Anglo-Saxons had been in cultural and literary contact mainly with the northern part of Europe. The intimate contact with the Scandinavian nations is reflected in the subject-matter of *Beowulf*, in the strophic form of several English poems, in the form and content of the *Runic Poem*. The political contact culminated in the long reign of Cnut, the Danish King who had transferred his court to England. From the moment Duke William overcame King Harold, however, English civilization, the government, and the Church were an integral part of the southern continental system. The Normans not only brought the terror of the sword and the strong hand of conquest but, more important still, became the transmitters to England of French culture and literature.

No one among the conquered people of England, however, could then have foreseen that the invasion was to prove a national blessing; for the sternness and energy *Effects* with which the Norman king and his nobles set *of the* about organizing the law, the civil government, *Norman* and the Church in the island involved much op-*Conquest* pression. Over the length and breadth of England rose those strong castles whose gray and massive walls still frown over the pleasant English landscape. Less forbidding than these, but at first no less suggestive of the foreigner, splendid stone abbeys and minsters gradually took the place of gloomy little wooden churches. Forest laws of terrible harshness preserved the "tall deer" which the king "loved as his life."

Within a half-century the Anglo-Saxon nobility and landed gentry had been completely displaced by Normans, while the English Church had been filled with French monks *Anglo-* and priests, so that all those classes which pro-*Norman* duced or read either polite or learned literature *Literature* were Norman-French. Furthermore, the constant and intimate contact of the Anglo-Norman nobility with France during the following two hundred years made them the medium through which England became thoroughly familiar with French literary material and literary forms. The Anglo-Saxon population, which placidly continued to employ only the English language, counted scarcely at all in literature and learning. In the court and camp and castle, in the school, in Parliament, and on the justice bench, French alone was spoken, while in the monastery and in the church, reading, writing, and even conversation were all carried on in Latin. It is small wonder that we find little English prose or poetry recorded before the year 1350. The literature which was in demand, and which consequently came to constitute the entire repertory of the minstrels—who had completely displaced the Anglo-Saxon scop and gleeman—

was exclusively in the French language, much of it composed by Normans and Frenchmen in England, much of it produced on the Continent and brought across the channel by wandering minstrels. These works in Anglo-French fall into two divisions: narrative and didactic. The former includes epics, romances, and tales; the latter, history, saints' lives and miracles, and a number of works which may be called utilitarian. Besides these, there are also preserved numerous lyrical and satirical poems, and some plays. The variety of works in Latin is wide. In the field of pure literature are satires and drinking-songs, love-songs, church hymns, and biblical and miracle plays. In the field of utilitarian writings are chronicles, legends, and miracles of saints, works on philosophy, logic, and theology, numerous sermons, and treatises on the natural sciences—astrology, mathematics, medicine, and law. Taken as a whole, the literature composed or circulated in England during the two and a half centuries after the battle of Hastings was rich, varied, and extensive; but unfortunately very little of it was in the English language.

If a prophet had arisen to tell the Norman barons and the great bishops and abbots of the twelfth and thirteenth centuries *Changes in English Speech* that neither French nor Latin, but English, was destined to be the standard speech of their descendants within one or two hundred years, he would undoubtedly have been laughed at. Nevertheless, incredible as it would have seemed, this is precisely what happened. Although not employed in written documents, the English tongue still was universally spoken by the lower classes, and even by the young children of the nobility, for we hear that the latter had to be taught their French in their childhood.

About 1200 English again began to appear in a few books, disputing a place by the side of the elegant language of the conquerors. Its reappearance, however, reveals it to be a greatly changed language. Even before the coming of the Normans the standard, conservative, literary language of the Anglo-Saxons had shown a tendency to simplify or discard the highly complicated Germanic inflectional endings. But the complete destruction of the English-using culture, and the relegation of English speech to illiterate peasants and serfs, removed every conservative influence, and changes followed in a rapid flood. The article "the," for example, had its nineteen forms reduced to one. From nine quite different noun declensions, each with seven or eight forms, the number shrank to one, with three forms. Thus, the noun dom (doom), which in Old English had the inflectional endings, -es, -e, -as, -a, and -um, in Middle English was reduced to the endings, -es, -e, and -en. Similarly, the noun ende (end), of another declension, had its inflectional endings reduced from -es, -e, -as, and -um, to -es, and -e. Grammatical gender disappeared. Verb inflection also was greatly simplified. The number of conjugations was lessened, strong ("irregular") verbs became weak ("regular"), personal endings became fewer. Prepositions, instead of taking the genitive, dative, or accusative, took only the accusative case.

By 1350, when English was again assuming the position of the speech of culture, its grammar was still further simplified, its inflectional endings were more nearly lost alto- *The* gether. Furthermore, the vocabulary was immensely *Result* enriched by the "naturalization" of thousands of French words. These are very largely words naming peculiarly French ideas, or at least ideas, objects, and institutions which were restricted principally to those social classes which had for two centuries spoken, read, and written only French. Very early we find in English documents such words as *castle, court, crown, tower, dungeon, justice, prison, sot* ("fool"), *peace, rent, charity, privilege*—almost every one of which reveals the comparative social positions of the French and the English-speaking classes. In spite of the subsequent loss of many words, in spite of many strange spellings and forms, the English of the thirteenth and fourteenth centuries is easily recognized as the same language which we speak today, the medium in which appeared the artistic and cultivated literary work of Chaucer, of Shakespeare, of Thackeray.

Mediæval literature was disseminated in two ways. The first and more permanent method was through copying by scribes. In every monastery one part of the cloister, or one *Mediæval* room, was dedicated to the labor of these copyists. *Literature* In this scriptorium, on wooden shelves, were kept the manuscript books of the monastery. The most skillful and competent members of the community spent hours of daily labor in the tedious task of copying these written books. Working with quill pen on sheets of sheepskin or calfskin, the scribe copied slowly and carefully, word by word and line by line, the page before him. The reproduction of literature, or of didactic or religious works, after this fashion was a slow and very costly process. The expensiveness of these manuscript books was often increased by the insertion of elaborate and beautiful drawings or illuminations. Naturally such books could be owned only by the wealthy. Sometimes a single manuscript would constitute the whole library of a castle. It would contain not only sermons, saints' lives, medical recipes, and a treatise on the seven deadly sins, but also songs, lyrics, hymns, and usually a number of metrical romances, the most popular form of literature in the Middle Ages.

The metrical romances, however, were circulated chiefly by the minstrels. These picturesque travelling entertainers were

The Minstrels
among the most popular persons in the Middle Ages. They journeyed from country to country, from city to city. The minstrels of lower degree entertained villagers, rustics, and townspeople with juggling tricks, dances, and songs, or by the recitation of long narratives of knightly or miraculous adventure. At the other end of the scale minstrels of great skill were attached to the courts of bishops, nobles, and even kings. Minstrels often organized their own guilds. The most skillful had a large repertory, constantly increased by new stories learned from their fellows. They themselves seem never to have recorded their tales, but most of the romances which we know they sang were written in manuscripts, either by monks or by other trained scribes who made a business of producing and selling books.

The metrical romances which composed the bulk of the minstrel repertory had flourished as a literary type in France (and

The Metrical Romances
in the French language in England) for two centuries before they began to appear in their English dress. These fascinating poetic tales—which remind us strongly of some of the narrative poems of Scott—were mostly accounts of the valiant or marvelous adventures of mediæval heroes—the outstanding figures in the

world of chivalry and romance—the warlike and courtly knights who loved "trouthe and honour, fredom and courtesye." The subject was most often the adventures of the knight against robbers, giants, or Saracens, or against the buffets of poverty, adverse love, or other misfortune. Against a background of feasts and wars and tournaments, of rich armor, gay dress, and horses, hawks, and hounds, these romances told of the thrilling, the extravagant, the supernatural. Above all, they emphasized the idealization and adoration of woman, which, originating in the intensely devotional cult of the Virgin Mary, had been secularized by the troubadours of Provence, and had become a vital part of the great creed of feudal chivalry.

The material of these richly bedecked tales came from three principal sources—the matter of Britain, the matter of France, and the matter of "Rome" as the trouvère Jean Bode said. From Britain came the tales of King Arthur and the Knights of the Round Table; from France the tales of Charlemagne and his twelve peers; from "Rome" came the tales of classical times and of more mysterious places—the story of Troy, the conquests of Alexander, and the marvels of the Orient. Of all these storehouses, the richest by far was the matter of Britain—Wales and Brittany—where for generations, perhaps for centuries, there had been growing up a mass of legend connected with King Arthur. A number of these Arthurian legends were gathered up, before the middle of the twelfth century, in a great Latin work called the *Historia Regum Britanniæ*, by Geoffrey of Monmouth, a Welsh writer who, though pretending to write a sober narrative of historical fact, was roundly denounced by many of his contemporaries for filling out his chronicle with the products of his own imagination. The book was immediately translated into French verse by Wace, of Jersey, and through this channel came, about the year 1200, into the hands of Layamon,[1] the first writer who treated this material in the English tongue.

Material of the Romances

---

[1] Though Layamon is the conventional spelling and pronunciation, the correct form is Laweman (Lawman). The name harks back to the period of dim antiquity when every little community had one member whose duty it was to act as a repository and interpreter of customary law in case of village disputes.

All that we know of Layamon, and of how he came to write his *Brut*, he tells himself in the quaint and touching words with which the metrical history opens:

"There was a priest in the land was named Layamon; he was the son of Leovenath—may God be gracious to him! He dwelt *Layamon* at Ernley, at a noble church upon Severn bank. *or* . . . It came to him in mind and in his chief *Lawman* thought that he would tell the noble deeds of the English; what the men were named, and whence they came, who first had the English land after the flood. . . . Layamon began to journey wide over this land, and procured the noble books which he took for authority. He took the English book that Saint Bede made;[1] another he took in Latin, that Saint Albin made and the fair Austin . . .;[2] the third book he took . . . that a French clerk made, named Wace. . . . Layamon laid these books before him and turned over the leaves; lovingly he beheld them—may the Lord be merciful to him! Pen he took with fingers, and wrote on book-skin, and compressed the three books into one."

The poem opens with an account of how "Eneas the duke," after the destruction of Troy, flees into Italy, and builds him a *Layamon's* "great burg." After many years his great-grandson, *"Brut"* Brutus, sets out with all his people to find a new land in the west. They pass the Pillars of Hercules, "tall posts of strong marble stone," where they find the mermaidens, "beasts of great deceit, and so sweet that many men are not able to quit them." After further adventures in Spain and France, they come at length to the shores of England, and land "at Dartmouth in Totnes." The verse has now run on for two thousand lines, and the story itself has just begun. But leisurely as Layamon is, he is seldom tedious; the story lures one on from page to page, until one forgets the enormous length. In treating the Arthur legends, Layamon is not content merely to transcribe the accounts of his predecessors. His own home was near the borders of Wales, where these legends were native;

---

[1] The Anglo-Saxon version of Bede's *Ecclesiastical History*.

[2] Probably the original Latin version of Bede, the authorship being mistaken by Layamon.

and he either first recorded or invented several additions of the utmost importance. The most notable of these are his story of the founding of the Round Table, and his account of the Celtic fays who are present at Arthur's birth and who carry him after his last battle to the mystic isle of Avalon. In the *Brut*, the figure of Arthur, to whose deeds a third of the poem is devoted, is treated in epic terms.

The publication, within a few years, in three languages, of a fascinating body of material available for literary treatment could not be overlooked by poets and minstrels. *Other* Within a few decades Arthur and his train of *Romances* great knights, Gawain, Lancelot, Tristram, and many others, had kindled the imagination of writers and audiences, and appeared as the leading figures in scores of courtly or popular romances in England, France, and Germany. Arthur became the incarnation of chivalry. Most of the romances received their first literary treatment in France, the centre of mediæval internationalism in culture and literature. Almost all the English romances of the thirteenth and fourteenth centuries are free renderings from French originals. This is true not only of those which mediævalize the legends of Troy and Thebes, or which deal with continental heroes, like Charlemagne and Alexander, or which tell a tale of continental origin, like *Amis and Amiloun* (a tale of sworn brothers-in-arms) and *Floris and Blancheflour* (a romantic love-story) ; but also of the Arthur stories, whose source was British, and even of the stories of purely English heroes, Bevis of Hampton, and Guy of Warwick. But of all the Arthurian romances in English of this period, such as *Sir Tristram, Arthour and Merlin, Morte Arthure,* and *The Awentyres* (adventures) *of Arthur at the Tarn Watheling* (Tarn Wadling in Cumberland), there is one, the best of all, and one of the most charming romances of the world. This is *Sir Gawayne and the Green Knight.* Its date is perhaps as late as the last quarter of the fourteenth century, but it is the culmination of the whole school of the preceding two centuries, and therefore is legitimately to be regarded as "Norman-French." Its closeness to the mediæval Irish romance, *The Feast of Bricriu,* suggests a possible Celtic origin.

When the poem opens, King Arthur and his court are gathered in the hall at Camelot to celebrate the feast of the New

"Sir Gawayne and the Green Knight" Year. The king, "so busied him his young blood and his wild brain," will not eat until some adventure has befallen. As the first course comes in, "with cracking of trumpets," and the "noise of nakers (drums), with noble pipes," there suddenly rushes in at the hall door a gigantic knight, clothed entirely in green, mounted on a green foal, and bearing in one hand a holly bough, in the other a great axe. He rides to the dais, and challenges any knight to give him a blow with his axe, and to abide one in turn. Gawayne, the king's nephew, smites off the head of the Green Knight, who quietly picks it up by the hair, and holds it out toward Gawayne, until the lips speak, giving him rendezvous at the Green Chapel on the next New Year's Day.

On All-Hallow's Day Gawayne sets out upon his horse Gringolet, and journeys through North Wales, past Holyhead into the wilderness of Wirral; "sometimes with worms (serpents) he wars, with wolves and bears," with giants and woodsatyrs, until at last on Christmas Eve he comes to a great forest of hoar oaks. He calls upon Mary, "mildest mother so dear," to help him. Immediately he sees a fair castle standing on a hill, and asking shelter he is courteously received by the lord of the castle, his fair young wife, and an ugly ancient dame.

After the Christmas festivities are over, Gawayne attempts to set forth again on his quest, but is assured that the Green Chapel is so near he may safely remain till the day of his appointment. His host now prepares for a great hunt, to last three days, and a jesting compact is made between them that at the end of each day they shall give each other whatever good thing they have won. While her lord is absent on the hunt the lady of the castle tries in vain to induce Gawayne to make love to her, and bestows upon him a kiss. Anxious to fulfill his compact, he in turn gives the kiss to her lord each night when the hunt is over, and receives as a countergift the spoils of the chase. At their last meeting the lady persuades Gawayne to take as a gift a green belt which will protect him from mortal harm. Thinking it "a jewel for the jeopardy" that he is to run at the Green

Chapel, he keeps the gift a secret, and thus proves false to his compact.

On New Year's morning he sets out with a guide through a storm of snow, past forests and cliffs, where "each hill has a hat and a mist-cloak," to find the Green Chapel. It proves to be a grass-covered hollow mound, in a desert valley, "the most cursed kirk," says Gawayne, "that ever I came in." The Green Knight appears, and deals a blow with his axe upon Gawayne's bent neck. But he only pierces the skin, and Gawayne, seeing the blood fall on the snow, claps on his helmet, draws his sword, and declares the compact fulfilled. The Green Knight then discloses the fact that he himself is the lord of the castle where Gawayne has just been entertained, that the ugly ancient dame who dwells with him is the fairy-woman, Morgain le Fay, who, because of her hatred of Guinevere, had sent him to frighten her at the New Year's feast with the sight of a severed head talking, and who has been trying to lead Gawayne into bad faith and untruthfulness, in order that she may grieve Guinevere, Arthur's queen. By his loyalty to his host Gawayne has been saved, except for the slight wound as punishment for concealing the gift of the girdle. Gawayne swears to wear the "lovelace" in remembrance of his weakness, and ever afterward each knight of the Round Table, and every lady of Arthur's court, wears a bright green belt for Gawayne's sake.

The picturesque and nervous language of the poem, its bright humor and fancy, its characterizations, the vivid beauty of its descriptions, as well as the skillful structure, and especially the pictures of English castle life in the Christmas holidays, and the detailed and lively accounts of the hunting of the boar, the fox, and the deer, all contribute to make this the most delightful example of English romance.

While the shimmering tapestry and cloth of gold of these bright romances were being woven to beguile the tedium of castle halls, a more sober literary fabric grew under the patient hands of monks and religious enthusiasts. The *Cursor Mundi*, the author of which *"Cursor Mundi"* is unknown, but the composition of which belongs to the first quarter of the fourteenth century, deserves particular comment. Though religious in aim and in matter, it shows a wholesome secular desire to be entertaining. The author, in beginning, laments the absorption of the readers of his day in frivolous romance, and proposes to compete against these vain tales of earthly love with an equally thrilling tale of divine love in honor of the Virgin Mary. He then proceeds to tell in flowing verse the story of God's dealings with man, from the creation to the final redemption, following in general the biblical narrative, but adorning it with popular legends, both sacred and secular, and with all manner of quaint digressions. The ambition of the author has really been accomplished; his book, which runs to 30,000 lines, is indeed a religious encyclopædia, and may well have caught the ear of such readers as were willing to be edified at the same time that they were entertained.

Of another religious writer whose work rises to the dignity of literature, the name and story have fortunately been preserved. This is Richard Rolle, the hermit of Hampole, in southern Yorkshire, who was born about 1300 and died in 1349. In his youth he went to Oxford, then at the height of its fame as a centre of scholastic learning, but the mysticism and erratic ardor of his nature made him rebel against the dry intellectuality of the scholastic teaching. He left college, made a hermit's shroud out of two of his sister's gowns and his father's hood, and began the life of a religious solitary and mystic. His cell at Hampole, near a Cistercian nunnery, was after his death visited as a miracle-working shrine, and cared for by the nuns. He wrote numerous canticles of divine love, many of which, though in prose, have an almost lyrical intensity. Of the many works attributed to Rolle, the most widely read was the *Prick of Conscience,* an account of the pains of life, death, and hell, and of the joys of heaven.

Richard Rolle of Hampole

But of all the religious writings of this period, by far the most beautiful are three poems, one lyric, one narrative, the third theological, which approach the subject of divine love, or wrath, from the personal side, and treat it with personal intimacy. The first is the famous "Love Rune" of Thomas de Hales, a monk of the Minor Friars. He tells us in the first stanza that he was besought by a maid of Christ to make her a love-

The "Love Rune" of de Hales

song, in order that she might learn therefrom how to choose a worthy and faithful lover. The monkish poet consents, but goes on to tell her how false and fleeting is all worldly love; how all earthly lovers vanish and are forgotten.

> Hwer is Paris and Heleyne
> That weren so bryght and feyre on ble?
> Amadas, Tristram, and Dideyne,
> Yseude, and alle the?
> Ector, with his scharpe meyne,
> And Cesar riche of worldes fee?
> Heo beoth iglyden ut of the reyne,
> So the scheft is of the clee.[1]

[Where is Paris and Helen, that were so bright and fair of face? Amadas, Tristram, Dido, Iseult, and all those? Hector with his sharp strength, and Cæsar rich with the world's fee (wealth)? They be glided out of the realm, as the shaft is from the clew (bowstring.)]

"But there is another lover," the poet continues, who is "richer than Henry our King, and whose dwelling is fairer than Solomon's house of jasper and sapphire. Choose Him, and may God bring thee to His bridechamber in Heaven." The poem is well-nigh perfect in form, and for rich and tender melody bears comparison with the best lyrical work of Shakespeare's age. It gleams like a jewel even among the great mass of skilled sacred —and secular—song of the time.

The second religious poem which deserves to be classed with this by reason of its beauty and its emotional appeal, is much longer, and written in stanzas with a complicated rhyme-scheme. It is called *The Pearl* and is usually assigned to the author of *Sir Gawayne and the* **"The Pearl"** *Green Knight.* The grief-stricken poet falls asleep on the grave of a young girl, "nearer to him than aunt or niece," whom he symbolizes as his "Pearl." In a dream-vision he sees her, and beholds the celestial country where she dwells. He dreams that he is transported to a wonderful land, through which a musical

[1] This treatment of the "Ubi sunt" formula should be compared with the quotation from the Anglo-Saxon poem, *The Wanderer*, on page 15.

river flows over pearly sand and stones that glitter like stars on a winter night. Around him are "crystal cliffs so clear of kind," forests that gleam like silver and ring with the melody of bright-hued birds. On the other side of the river, at the foot of a gleaming cliff, he sees a maid sitting, clothed in bright raiment trimmed with pearls, and in the midst of her breast a great pearl. She rises and comes toward him. Then the mourner tries to cross over, but being unable, cries out to know if she is indeed his pearl, since the loss of which he has been "a joyless jeweller." The maiden tells him that his pearl is not really lost, gently reproves the impatience of his grief, and expounds some of the mysteries of heaven, where she reigns as a queen with Mary. The mourner begs to be taken to her abiding-place; she tells him that he may see, but cannot enter, "that clean cloister." She bids him go along the riverbank until he comes to a hill. Arrived at the top, he sees afar off the celestial city, "pitched upon gems," with its walls of jasper and streets of gold. At the wonder of the sight he stands, "still as a dazed quail," and gazing sees, "right as the mighty moon gan rise," the Virgins walking in procession with the Lamb of God. The maiden is one of them.

> Then saw I there my little queen—
> Lord! much of mirth was that she made
> Among her mates.

He strives in transport to cross over and be with her, but it is not pleasing to God that he should come, and the dreamer awakes. The poem is usually regarded as an elegy, but some scholars consider it a spiritual autobiography or an allegory presenting religious and theological opinions.

The third religious poem, remarkable for its skilful structure and finished style, is the *Debate Between the Body and the Soul;* the subject is treated in almost every lan-**"Debate Between the Body and the Soul"** guage of western Europe, but the English version is markedly the best. It belongs to a popular mediæval genre—the *débat.* Other well known examples of the form are *The Owl and the Nightingale* and *The Flower and the Leaf.* The latter was once attributed to Chaucer. The poet, who has fallen into a deep slumber, sees lying on a bier the body of a proud knight, from which issues a dim shape, the soul, lamenting and bitterly reproaching the body for its pride, gluttony, and envy, which have sentenced the soul to eternal damnation. The body answers that the blame belongs to the soul, who has always been the master, and a debate ensues concerning the responsibility for the wretched plight of both. Finally a host of devils appear from hell:

> Thei weren ragged, rove, and tayled,
> With brode bulches on here bac,
> Scharpe clauwes, longe nayled;
> No was no lime withoute lac.
> On alle halve it was asayled
> With mani a devel, foul and blac;
> Merci crying litel availede,
> Hwan Crist it wolde so harde wrac.

[They were ragged, rough, and tailed, with broad bulges on their back, sharp claws, long nailed; no limb was without deformity. On every side it was assailed with many a devil foul and black; crying "mercy" little availed, when Christ wished it such hard vengeance.]

With horse and hounds the devils pursued the soul into a sulphurous pit; the earth locked itself again; and the dreamer awoke, cold with fear. The poem is notable for its vividness, as well as its phrasal and haunting lyric power.

The amalgamation of the English and French peoples and their cultures produced important results in the metre as well as in the vocabulary and literary content of the new language. Anglo-Saxon poetry had depended for its rhythmical effect upon two devices, alliteration and accent. The number of syllables in any given line could vary greatly, and the accents could fall anywhere in the line. The result was that the *Fusion of Saxon and French Metrical Systems* rhythm of Anglo-Saxon verse was exceedingly loose and pliable. Anglo-French verse depended upon two devices quite different from these—rhyme and a fixed number of syllables; the metrical system was therefore very definite and exact. When the fusion came there was a struggle as to which system should prevail in the new language. Some of the English poets, even as late as the authors of *Piers the Plowman*, stood out for the old system of accent and alliteration, without rhyme and without a fixed number of syllables; others imitated slavishly the French system of rhyme and uniform line-length; others, like the author of *Sir Gawayne and the Green Knight*, wrote stanzas in the looser alliterating metre, with rhyming verses at intervals. Still others wrote in the alliterating measure, but adopted more or less elaborate rhyme-schemes. The final outcome of the struggle, however, was that English verse gave up regular alliteration, retaining it only as an occasional decoration. The principle of accent, however, was retained; but, under the influence of French prosody, a system dependent on a fixed and regular number of syllables, with fairly regular alternation between accented and unaccented syllables, was adopted. Here again, as in the case of the vocabulary, the merging of Anglo-Saxon and French had a most happy result. It is by reason of this merging that English is capable of more subtle and varied lyrical effects than almost any other modern language.

Nor did the poets fail to show, even as early as the thirteenth century, their appreciation of what an exquisite instrument had

Lyric Qualities

fallen into their hands; for we possess several songs of that period, and a little later, which have in them more than a promise of Herrick and Shelley. They are mostly songs of love and of spring. The best known is perhaps the "Cuckoo Song," with its refrain of "Loude sing Cuckoo!"; but even more charming are the spring-song "Lent is come with love to town," and the love-song called "Allisoun," with its delightful opening:

> Bitwene Mersh and Averil
> When spray [1] begineth to springe.
> The little fowles [2] have hyre [3] will
> On hyre lud [4] to singe.

[1] Foliage.   [2] Birds.   [3] Their.   [4] Voice.

The England which finds utterance in these songs is a very different England from that which had spoken in *The Wanderer* and *The Seafarer*. It is no longer only the **Result** fierce and gloomy aspects of nature, but also her **of the** bright and laughing moods, that are sung. The **Norman** imaginations of men work now not only in terms **Conquest** of war but also of peace. England is no longer isolated; its culture is continental, international. Its intellectual and emotional life is rich and variegated. The Norman invasion has done its work. The conquerors have ceased to be a distinct and oppressive class, for foreign wars and centuries of domestic intercourse have broken down the barrier between men of Norman and men of Anglo-Saxon blood. The new language is formed, a new and vigorous national life is everywhere manifest. The time is ripe for a new poet, great enough to gather up and make intelligible to itself this shifting, many-colored life, and Chaucer is at hand.

CHAPTER III

The Late Middle Ages

THE AGE OF CHAUCER

I

GEOFFREY CHAUCER was born about 1340. His father, one of the Corporation of Vintners, was at one time a purveyor to King Edward III. It was probably through this business connection with the court that Chaucer, when about fourteen, became a page in the household of the King's daughter-in-law, the Duchess of Clarence. In 1359 *Chaucer's* he went with the King's army to France, where he *Early Life* saw unrolled the brilliant pageant of mediæval war, as the French chronicler Froissart has pictured it, at a time when chivalry and courtesy had flamed into their greatest splendor. He beheld the unsuccessful siege of the city of Rheims, was captured by the French, and was held as a prisoner of war until ransomed on March 1, 1360.

On his return to England he became an esquire of the King's Bedchamber, and spent the next ten years at Edward's court, then one of the most brilliant in Europe. The *Chaucer's* court of Edward still had all the atmosphere of a *French* French court, and Chaucer, although he decided *Period* to use his native tongue, became practically a French love-poet writing in the English language. Aside from the use of the eight-syllable line, rhyming in couplets, the conventions of the French school which are most evident in Chaucer's work are those which belong to the system of courtly love and those structural principles observable in the love-visions which preceded and were contemporary with Chaucer. The conventions of the system of courtly love, indeed, permeate

36

nearly all mediæval non-religious literature. The lover, compelled to be a faithful "servant" of his lady and of Dan Cupid, must languish in amorous pallor, toss sleepless on his couch, swoon, boast of his lady's beauty and wit, compose ballads in her honor, and fight for the glorification of her token. The lady must be cold as ice, must impose on her lover incredible trials of his courage and fidelity. After many years of hopeless service the lover may be accepted, not because of any merit of himself or of his deeds, but purely because of the lady's boundless compassion. These are the rules of conduct governing the actors in the love-visions—poems in which the lover, exhausted by the play of his emotions, falls asleep at dawn to the music of birds and the melody of brooks, amidst flowers and perfumes, and dreams of knights wooing their ladies. The most famous work of this French school was the *Roman de la Rose*, an elaborate allegory, placed in a dream-setting, of Love, the rose, growing in a mystic garden, warded by symbolic powers from the lover's approach, and provoking endless disquisitions, serious or satirical, such as the later Middle Ages loved to spend upon the subtleties of sentiment. Chaucer manifested his enthusiasm for this work by translating a portion of it into English verse. Less than two thousand lines of his translation have survived; indeed, the whole may never have been completed. But the *Roman de la Rose* and other poems of its school left a profound impression upon Chaucer's work, and for years he thought and wrote in the atmosphere which they created for him. During these years of French influence he wrote, for the knights and ladies of King Edward's court, those "ballades, roundels, virelays," by which his fellow-poet Gower says "the land fulfilled was over all." The most important work which remains to us from his purely French period, however, is the *Boke of the Duchesse,* written in 1369 to solace John of Gaunt, the King's fourth son, for the death of his wife, Blanche. Though working in the strict tradition of the French love-vision and borrowing freely from a poem by Guillaume de Machaut, Chaucer gave his elegy freshness and seeming sincerity.

Between 1368 and 1387 Chaucer made several journeys on official business to Flanders, to France, and to Italy. Although these journeys are not marks of special favor, Chaucer must have been fairly successful as a diplomat and certainly the

Chaucer's Later Life

opportunities afforded by wide travel for converse with many types of men, for observation of widely varying manners, and especially for becoming familiar with Italian literature, were of the utmost importance in his poetic education. During the remainder of his life, Chaucer—like many others of the King's esquires—held various official positions, some of which were probably in the nature of political sinecures, for much of the time his work was performed by deputies. From 1374 to 1386 he was controller of the customs on wool, leather, and skins at the port of London. For a while he was simultaneously controller of the petty customs at the same port. In 1386 he represented the County of Kent as "Knight of the Shire," a post he held for two years. In 1389 he was appointed clerk of the King's works at Westminster, the Tower, Windsor Castle, and other places. From 1391 until his death he apparently served as deputy forester of the royal forest of North Petherton. Most of the time during the last thirty years of his life we find him also drawing a pension from the national treasury, as well as the money equivalent of a daily pitcher of wine from the King's cellars. For several years he and his wife (whom he had married about 1366) also received pensions from John of Gaunt. Chaucer died in 1400.

The one event in Chaucer's life which probably produced the profoundest effect on his literary career was his first visit to

The Renaissance

Italy, in 1372. Italy was then approaching the zenith of her artistic energy, in the full splendor of that illumination which had followed the intellectual twilight of the Middle Ages, and which we know as the Renaissance, or "New Birth." Each of her little city-states was a centre of marvellous activity, and everywhere were being produced those masterpieces of painting, sculpture, and architecture which still make Italy a place of pilgrimage for all lovers of art. The literary activity was equally great, at least in Tuscany. Dante had been dead for half a century, but his poetry was just beginning to be widely recognized as one of the major efforts of the human imagination. Petrarch, the grave, accomplished scholar and elegant poet, was passing his closing years at his villa of Arqua, near Padua; Boccaccio, poet, tale-writer, pedant, and worldling, was spending the autumn of his life among the cypress and laurel slopes of Fiesole, above Florence. The world which lay open to Chaucer's gaze when he crossed the Alps was, therefore, one calculated to fascinate and· stimulate him in the highest degree.

From Chaucer's poems we get only an occasional glimpse of his life. One of these reveals his eagerness for study, which, after the day's work was done, would send him home, regardless of rest and "newe thinges," to sit "as domb as any stone" over his book, until his eyes were dazed. The unquenchable curiosity of the men of the Renaissance was his, more than a *Chaucer and the Renais- sance* century before the Renaissance really began to affect England. His, too, was their thirst for expression. The great books he had come to know in Italy gave him no peace until he should equal or surpass them. Among the works which he produced, very largely in emulation of the Italian masters, were the *Hous of Fame,* the *Parlement of Foules* (Birds), *Troilus and Criseyde,* and the *Legend of Goode Wommen,* one version of which was dedicated to the young Queen, Anne of Bohemia, whom Richard II had married in 1382.

Both the *Hous of Fame* and the *Parlement of Foules* are colored with Italian reminiscence; but the chief fruit of Chaucer's Italian journeys—aside from his in- creased literary power through his emulation of the Italian poets—was the long poem adapted from Boccaccio's *Filostrato* (The Love-Stricken *"Troilus and Criseyde"* One), entitled by Chaucer *Troilus and Criseyde.* The story of the love of the young Trojan hero for Cressida, and of her de- sertion of him for the Greek Diomedes, had been elaborated during the Middle Ages by Benoît de Sainte-Maure and Guido delle Colonne before Boccaccio gave it an animated but ornate treatment in facile verse. Chaucer, though prerending only to translate, radically changed the structure and emphasis of the story. Instead of an almost unmotivated recital of a mere intrigue, Chaucer has written a psychological novel in verse, analyzing minutely the action and reaction of character and situation upon the leading persons. In his hands the lovers' go-between, Pandarus, is transformed from a gilded youth of Troilus's own age and temperament to a middle-aged man, plausible, good-natured, full of easy worldly wisdom and materialistic ideas—a character as true to type and as vitally alive as Shakespeare's Pandarus in his cynical *Troilus and Cressida*. The growth of the love-passion in Cressida's heart is traced through its gradual stages with a subtlety entirely new in English poetry. The action, dialogue, and setting of the poem are all created with the magic realism of a master of narrative art. Though the scene is ancient Troy, though the manners and customs are those of mediæval knights and ladies, though the texture of the whole is stiffly brocaded with the conventions of courtly love, we seem, in many passages, to be looking at a modern play or reading from a modern novel, so intimate and actual does it appear.

The *Legend of Goode Wommen,* a kind of secular imitation of a collection of saints' lives, is chiefly interesting because of its prologue. In the body of the poem Cleopatra, **"Legend** Dido, Thisbe, and other famous women are cele-**of Goode** brated for their steadfastness in love, possibly as a **Wommen"** covert tribute to the wifely virtues of the young Queen. These stories are adapted from a Latin work of Boccaccio, *De Claris Mulieribus.* But the long prologue, original with Chaucer, is the most winning of his many passages of personal confession and self-revelation. In this poem, Chaucer uses the heroic couplet for the first time.

He represents himself as wandering in the fields on May-day, the only season which can tempt him from his books. The birds are singing to their mates their song of "blessed be Seynt Valentyn!" and Zephyrus and Flora, as "god and goddesse of the flowry mede," have spread the earth with fragrant blossoms. But the poet has eyes only for one flower, the daisy, the "emperice (empress) and flour of floures alle." All day long he leans and pores upon the flower; and when at last it has folded its leaves at the coming of night he goes home to rest, with the thought of rising early to gaze upon it once more. He makes his couch out of doors, in a little arbor, "for deyntee of the newe someres sake," and here he has a wonderful dream. He dreams that he is again in the fields, kneeling by the daisy, and sees approaching a procession of bright forms. First comes the young god of love, clad in silk embroidered with red rose-leaves and sprays of green, his "gilt hair" crowned with light, in his hand two fiery darts, and his wings spread angel-like. He leads by the hand a queen, clad in green and crowned with a fillet of daisies under a band of gold. She is Alcestis, type of noblest wifely devotion. Behind her comes an endless train of women who have been "trewe of love." They kneel in a circle about the poet, and sing with one voice honor to woman's faithfulness, and to the daisy flower, the emblem of Alcestis. The love-god then glowers angrily upon Chaucer, and upbraids him for having done despite to women, in translating the *Roman de la Rose,* with its satire upon their foibles; and in writing the story of Cressida, so dishonorable to the steadfastness of the sex. Alcestis comes to his rescue, and agrees to pardon his misdeeds if he will spend the rest of his life in making a "glorious Legend of Goode Wommen," and will send it, on her behalf, to the English queen. Chaucer promises solemnly, and as soon as he wakes betakes himself to his task.

In the *Hous of Fame,* where he sets out in search of "Love's Tidings," as well as in the *Legend of Goode Wommen,* Chaucer had apparently entered upon the task of constructing a work which would constitute a setting for a group of tales; but after starting, he left both these attempts unfinished. Yet the ambition to crown his life with some monumental work remained. The drift of his genius, as he grew older, was more and more toward the imaginative presentation of real *Influence of the New National Life on Chaucer* life. He had a wide experience of men of many ranks and conditions, and he had been storing up for years, with his keenly observant, quiet eyes, the materials for a literary presentation of contemporary society upon a great scale. Moreover, while Chaucer was growing up, England had been growing conscious of herself. The struggle with France had unified the people at last into a homogeneous body, no longer Norman and Saxon, but English; and the brilliancy of Edward III's early reign had given to this new people their first intoxicating draught of national pride. The growing power of Parliament tended to foster the feeling of solidarity and self-consciousness in the nation. As a member of Parliament, as a government officer, as an intimate member of the court, Chaucer felt these influences to the full. It must have seemed more and more important to him that the crowning work of his life should in some way represent the brilliant spectacle and complex culture of the actual society in which he moved.

With the happy fortune of genius he hit, in his *Canterbury Tales,* upon a scheme wonderfully adapted to the ends he had *Plan of* in view. Collections of stories, both secular and *the "Can-* sacred, articulated into a general framework, had *terbury* been numerous and popular in the Middle Ages, *Tales"* and the early Italian Renaissance, which inherited the taste for them, had enlarged their scope, and humanized their content. Boccaccio had furnished one example of throwing a graceful trellis-work of incident and dialogue about the separate stories of a collection. In his *Decameron* a company of aristocratic young people are represented as having taken refuge from the plague raging in Florence, in a villa on the slopes of Fiesole. They wander through the valleys of oleanders and myrtles, or sit beside the fountains of the villa gardens, and beguile the time with tales of sentiment and intrigue. Another Italian, Giovanni Sercambi, had pictured a pilgrimage composed of many classes of people, presided over by a leader or governor, and entertained on their journey with songs, dances, and the telling of tales by an official story-teller, who is Sercambi himself. As in the *Canterbury Tales,* the stories are linked together by transition passages, in which the tales are frequently the subject of comment. Chaucer, while adopting a similar framework, made his setting much more national and racy; individualized his characters so as to make of them a gallery of living portraits of his time; varied his tales so as to include almost all the types of narrative known to literature at the close of the Middle Ages; and, most important of all, put his tales into the mouths of the separate pilgrims.

He represents himself as alighting, one spring evening, at the Tabard Inn, in Southwark, a suburb at the southern end of London Bridge, where the famous Elizabethan play-houses, Shakespeare's among them, were afterward *The* to arise. Southwark was the place of departure and *Pilgrims* arrival for all south-of-England travel, and espe- *at the* cially for pilgrimages to the world-renowned *Tabard* shrine of Thomas à Becket, at Canterbury. A company bent on such a pilgrimage Chaucer finds gathered in the inn; he makes their acquaintance, and joins himself with them for the journey. Counting the poet, they are thirty in all. There is a Knight lately come from the foreign wars, a man who has fought in Prussia and in Turkey, jousted in Tramisene, and been present at the storming of Alexandria—a high-minded, gentle-man-nered, knightly adventurer, typical of the courteous, war-loving chivalry which was passing rapidly away. With him is his son, a young Squire, curly-haired and gay, his short, white-sleeved gown embroidered like a mead with red-and-white flowers; he is an epitome of the gifts and graces of the young courtly lover. Their servant is a Yeoman, in coat and hood of green, a sheaf of peacock-arrows under his belt, a mighty bow in his hand, and a silver image of Saint Christopher upon his breast; he is the type of that sturdy English yeomanry which with its gray goose shafts humbled the pride of France at Crécy and Agincourt. There is a whole group of ecclesiastical figures, representing in their numbers and variety the diverse activities of the mediæval Church. Most of them are satirical portraits, in their worldliness and materialism only too faithfully representative of the ecclesi-astical abuses against which Wyclif struggled. First of all there is a Monk, who cares only for hunting and good cheer; his bald head shines like glass, his bright eyes roll in his head; he rides a sleek brown palfrey, and has "many a dainty horse" in his stables; his sleeves are trimmed with fine fur at the wrists, his hood is fastened under his chin with a gold love-knot. As a com-panion figure to the hunting Monk, Chaucer gives us the gently satirized "Madame Eglantyne," the Prioress; she is a teacher of young ladies, speaks French "after the school of Stratford-atte-bowe," is exquisite in her table-manners, imitating as well as she can the stately behavior of the court. Other ecclesiastics are there,

hangers-on and caterpillars of the church: the Friar, intimate
with hospitable franklins, innkeepers, and worthy women, and
despising beggars and lazars; the Summoner, a repulsive person
with "fire-red cherubim face"; the Pardoner, with his bag full
of pardons "come from Rome all hot," and of bits of cloth and
pig's bones which he sells as relics of the holy saints. Chaucer's
treatment of these evil churchmen is good-natured and tolerant;
he never takes the tone of moral indignation against them. But
he does better; he sets beside them, as the type of true shepherds
of the church, a "poor Parson," such as, partly under Wyclif's
influence, had spread over England, beginning that great movement for the purification of the Church which was to result,
more than a century later, in the Reformation. Chaucer paints
the character of the Parson, poor in this world's goods, but "rich
of holy thought and work," with loving and reverent touch. The
Parson's brother travels with him—a Plowman, a "true swinker
and a good," who helps his poor neighbors without hire and
loves them as himself; he reminds us of Piers the Plowman, in
the wonderful Vision which is the antitype of Chaucer's work.
A crowd of other figures fill the canvas. There is a Shipman
from the west-country, a representative of those adventurous
seamen, half merchant-sailors, half smugglers and pirates, who
had already made England's name a terror on the seas and
paved the way for her future naval and commercial supremacy.
There is a poor Clerk of Oxford, a theological student, riding
a horse as lean as a rake, and dressed in threadbare cloak, who
spends all that he can beg or borrow upon his studies; he represents that passion for learning which was already astir everywhere in Europe, and which was awaiting only the magic touch
of the new-found classical literature to blossom. There is a
Merchant, in a Flemish beaver hat, on a high horse, concealing,
with the grave importance of his air, the fact that he is in debt.
There is a group of guild-members, in the livery of their guild,
all worthy to be aldermen; together with the merchant, they
represent the mercantile and manufacturing activity which was
lifting England rapidly to the rank of a great commercial power.
There is the Wife of Bath, almost a modern feminist figure,
conceived with masterly humor and realism, a permanent human

type; she has had "husbands five at church-door," and though "somdel deaf," hopes to live to wed several others; she rides on an ambler, with spurs and scarlet hose on her feet, and on her head a hat as broad as a buckler. These and a dozen others are all painted in vivid colors, and with a psychological truth which reminds us of the portraits of the Flemish painter, Van Eyck, Chaucer's contemporary. Taken as a whole they represent almost the entire range of English society in the fourteenth century, with the exception of the highest aristocracy and the lowest order of villeins or serfs.

At supper this goodly company hears from the host of the Tabard a proposition that on their journey to Canterbury, to beguile the tedium of the ride, each of them shall tell two tales, and on the homeward journey two more.[1] He agrees to travel with them, to act as master of ceremonies, and on their return to render judgment as to who has told the best story, the winner to be given a supper at the general expense. So it is agreed. The next morning they set out bright and early on their journey southward to the cathedral city. They draw lots to determine who shall tell the first tale. The lot falls to the Knight, who tells the chivalric romance of Palamon and Arcite. When it is finished the Host calls upon the Monk to follow. But the Miller, who is already drunk and quarrelsome, insists on being heard, and launches forthwith into a very unedifying tale about a carpenter. The Reeve, who had followed that trade in his youth, is so angry that he retaliates with a story of an unsavory intrigue in which a miller is badly worsted. The Host rises in his stirrups and calls on the Parson for a story, "by Goddes dignitee!" The Parson reproves him for swearing; whereupon the Host cries that he "smells a Lollard [2] in the wind," and bids them prepare for a sermon. This is too much for the Shipman, who breaks in impatiently. When the Host calls upon the Prioress, he changes his bluff manner to correspond with her

The Pilgrims on the Road

---

[1] Counting the Host and the Canon's Yeoman (who joins them on the road) the company consisted of thirty-two persons, making a total of a hundred and twenty-eight tales to be told. Less than a fifth of this number were actually written, and several of these were left fragmentary.

[2] The followers of Wyclif were called Lollards.

rank and her excessive refinement, speaking with polite circum-
locution, "as courteously as it had been a maid." The Prioress re-
sponds graciously, and tells the story of a little "clergeon," or
schoolboy, who, after his throat has been cut by the wicked
Jews, and his body thrown into a pit, still sings with clear young
voice his *Alma Redemptoris* to the glory of the Virgin. Overwhelmed with emotion, the company is riding silently along,
when the Host, to break the awe-struck mood, turns to Chaucer,
and begins to joke him upon his corpulency:

> "What man artow?" quod he;
> "Thou lookest as thou wouldest find an hare,
> For ever upon the ground I see thee stare.
> Approache near, and look up merrily.
> Now ware you, sirs, and let this man have place . . .
> He seemeth elvish by his countenance
> For unto no wight doeth he dalliance."

Chaucer, thus rallied, begins a travesty of those doggerel rhymes
of knightly adventure to which many of the romances of chivalry had in his day degenerated. The *Rhyme of Sir Thopas* is a
capital burlesque of the metrical romances which Chaucer himself had come to supplant. He has not got far before the Host
cries out upon the "drasty rhyming," and Chaucer meekly agrees
to contribute instead "a little thing in prose," a "moral tale";
and he proceeds with the long story of Melibeus and his wife
Prudence, a very tedious story indeed from the modern point of
view. The Squire's tale, as befits his years and disposition, is a
highly colored Oriental tale of love, adventure, and magic, in
which figure a flying horse of brass and other wonders. The
Pardoner, called on for "some merry tale or jape," but restricted
by the gentles to "some moral thing," preaches one of the sermons that he knows by rote—a startlingly vivid and vigorous
short story about three "rioters" who go in search of Death, and
who find him in a pile of gold.

So the stories continue, the transition passages constantly picturing the vivid dialogue and action of the pilgrims, at times
one theme being carried through several tales in succession.

The Wife of Bath, after a long prologue in which she describes
the vigorous measures by which she has ruled her five husbands,
tells a tale the point of which is that marital happiness results
only if sovereignty in marriage is vested in the wife. After the
Friar and the Summoner have told vulgar stories about each
other, the Clerk of Oxford resumes the theme introduced by
the Wife, with the story of the infinite, nay, incredible patience
of Griselda under the tests imposed by her husband Walter—a
tale borrowed from the Latin of Petrarch, who had translated it
from Boccaccio's *Decameron.* Finally, the Franklin tells a tale
of *gentilesse,* in which the husband and the wife, exhibiting mutual forbearance and courtesy, appear to solve the problem most
satisfactorily of all.

In the sixteenth century and later, when owing to the changes
in pronunciation (especially the loss of a final "e" from thousands of words and grammatical forms), the   *Chaucer's*
secret of Chaucer's versification was lost, he was   *Poetic Art*
regarded as a barbarous writer, ignorant of pros-
ody, and with no ear for the melody of verse. The exact contrary
of this was really the case. He was an artist in verse effects, who
not only wrote with a metrical accuracy, fluency, and variety
that have rarely been surpassed, but also paid constant and delicate heed to the niceties of rhythm and tone-color. In a half-
humorous address to his scrivener Adam, he calls down curses
upon that unworthy servant for spoiling good verses by bad
copying, and in *Troilus* he beseeches his readers not to "mis-
metre" his book. From his very earliest poems his work is almost
faultless and as he progressed in skill his music became constantly more varied and flexible. His early manner reaches its
height in the exquisite rondel, intricate in form but handled
with great simplicity of effect, which brings the *Parlement of
Foules* to a melodious close. A good example of his later music
may be found in the description of the Temple of Venus in the
Knight's Tale; or, as a study in a graver key, in the ballad
"Flee fro the Press," which marks so impressively the deepening
seriousness of Chaucer's mind in his last years.

Chaucer employed three principal metres: the eight-syllable
line, rhyming in couplets, as in the *Boke of the Duchesse;* the

ten-syllable line, also rhyming in couplets, as in the prologue to the *Canterbury Tales;* and the same line arranged in seven-line stanzas (known later as "rhyme royal"), as in *Troilus.* The heroic couplet he introduced into English verse; the rhyme royal he invented. In his shorter poems he made, however, endless metrical experiments, and showed a mastery of intricate verse-forms, remarkable even in an age when the French had made verse-writing a matter of almost gymnastic skill.

As for his material, Chaucer did not hesitate to take what suited him, wherever he found it; sometimes borrowing whole-
Sources sale without change, oftener adapting and rework-
of His ing his matter freely. Any such thing as "original-
Material ity," in the modern sense, was undreamed of in the
Middle Ages; the material of literature was com-
mon property, and the same stories were endlessly repeated. Whoever would learn the "sources" from which Chaucer drew must ransack the storehouse of mediæval fiction, and examine no little of mediæval science and philosophy. But what is more important is that Chaucer improved whatever he borrowed, and stamped it with his individuality of thought and style and struc-tural skill. That part of his work which we value most, how-ever, such as the prologues to the *Legend of Goode Wommen* and to the *Canterbury Tales,* was original in every sense, and some of the *Tales* have been so radically and vitally remodelled that they stand as genuinely original.

II

Chaucer lived and wrote in a world where the half-shadows of the Middle Ages were only beginning to scatter before the
Chaucer clear dawn-light of modern culture. He, first of all
and men in England, reacted to that stimulating and
Gower emancipating movement called the Renaissance, as
it stirred in the souls of men beyond the Alps; and
his artistic consciousness escaped from the rigid bonds, the cramping conventionalities, the narrow inhibitions of the Mid-dle Ages. From them he emerged into the world of living actu-alities that he exhibits in his powerful later work. In this he was

far beyond his age. The full force of his originality is most evident when he is compared with John Gower—the "moral Gower" to whom he dedicated his *Troilus*. Chaucer, in his mature work, looks forward to the England of the Tudors; Gower is still tramping in the treadmill of mediæval abstraction and prisoned thought.

John Gower (1330–1408) was an aristocratic, conservative, landed gentleman, with rich manors in Kent and elsewhere. He was known at court, where his poetry met with much appreciation. He was extremely pious; he became blind in his old age and resided in lodgings *John Gower* inside the priory of St. Mary Overy (now St. Saviour's) in Southwark, not far from the Tabard Inn which Chaucer had made famous. Here he spent his last days in devout observances; and here his sculptured figure can still be seen on his tomb, his head, crowned with roses, pillowed upon his three chief volumes. Each of these was written in a different tongue: the *Speculum Meditantis* in French, the *Vox Clamantis* in Latin, and the *Confessio Amantis* in English. This diversity in the choice of language shows clearly the opinion of the age—that the English tongue was not, as yet, obviously the one instrument of literary expression. For two centuries after his death, Gower was regarded as the equal of Chaucer and Lydgate. He was probably more truly representative of his age than Chaucer.

The *Speculum Meditantis,* or *Mirour de l'Omme,* consists of an elaborate allegory of the attacks of the seven deadly sins and their offspring upon mankind; a complete review of the state of the world and of its corruptions *The "Speculum Meditantis"* from the time of Rome, in which are vividly pictured the wickedness of London, its dram-shops, its cheating merchants and shopkeepers, its slothful monks and friars, its vulture-like lawyers, and its lazy and rebellious laborers; finally, there is presented a plan of salvation, consisting of the intervention of the Virgin Mary, whose history is narrated, together with the whole story of the gospel narrative. The work as a whole is systematically conceived and executed. The tone is one of moral earnestness, and the vignettes of contemporary life are painted with color and vigor.

The *Confessio Amantis,* like the *Canterbury Tales,* is a collection of stories. A lover makes confession to a priest of Venus, a

The "Confessio Amantis"

learned old man named Genius, and the stories are narrated by this priest for the purpose of illustrating the seven deadly sins. Though the design is occasionally marred by digressions, in general the structure of the poem is carefully planned and executed: each of the seven deadly sins, with five branches, is shown to be applicable to love and lovers, and one or more stories are told to illustrate and reprove each of the sins. Although the application of some of the tales is rather forced, the collection is noted for the number and variety of its excellent stories. The *Confessio Amantis* was Gower's most popular work, and still exists in three versions in forty-three manuscripts. In one version, Chaucer, who had dedicated his *Troilus and Criseyde* to "moral Gower," is urged "in his later age" to write a testament of love.

The *Vox Clamantis* is interesting for historical reasons. The second half of the fourteenth century was a time of revolution-

The "Vox Cla- mantis"

ary changes among the peasants of England. Four terrible attacks of the Black Death, the first in 1348, the last in 1375, swept over the country, destroying over a third of the population. For a long time the old feudal system known as "villeinage," according to which all agriculture was carried on for the lord of the manor by serfs bound to the land, had been in process of decay, giving way to a combination of renting to free farmers (like Chaucer's Plowman), and of hiring landless laborers, who wandered from district to district, wherever attracted by high wages. The destruction of such a huge number of laborers by the plague resulted in an enormous decrease in the production of food, and, as a result of the dislocation of the labor market due to the demand for workers, villeinage practically disappeared. The condition of the survivors, however, was not very greatly improved, for the short crops, the long periods of idleness between harvest and plowing, and especially the statutes, passed by Parliament, attempting to reduce wages to the scale prevailing before the plague, produced wide-spread hunger and discontent. The exactions of the Church, the extravagances of Edward III, and the heavy cost of his foreign wars added to the burden borne by the distracted peasantry. The fearlessness with which the Oxford reformer, John Wyclif, attacked the corruptions of the clergy and questioned the fundamental rights of property, was like flame to the fuel of discontent. In 1381 a nation-wide uprising of the peasants occurred, under the leadership of Wat Tyler, Jack Straw, and a socialist priest of Kent, named John Balle. They marched on London, sacked the Tower and the Savoy palace, and murdered an archbishop; it seemed as if the throne and the whole social order were about to be overturned. It was this state of things which prompted Gower to write his *Vox Clamantis*. As a landowner in Kent, he felt the full brunt of the disturbance. He writes from the aristocratic point of view, representing the common people as beasts, oxen, dogs, flies, and frogs, because of the evil magic of the time. But he does not hesitate to blame King Richard II for his neglect of his duties and he agrees on occasion with Wyclif and the Lollards, although he warns his readers against them. The poem is full of horror and dismay at the social volcano which had opened for a moment, threatening to engulf the nation.

John Wyclif (1320?–1384), the man who by his teaching had helped, though unintentionally, to foment the peasant rebellion, was primarily a theologian and religious reformer. His connection with English literature is, in *John Wyclif* a sense, accidental, but it is nevertheless very important. He attacked the temporal power of the church, advocating, partly in the interests of the overburdened poor, the appropriation by the state of all church property, especially of land. While waging a war of theory on this and other ecclesiastical questions, he planned and carried out a great practical movement, known as the Lollard [1] movement, for arousing the common people to a more vital religious life. He sent out simple, devoted men to preach the gospel in the native tongue, and to bring home to their hearers the living truths of religion which the formalism of the mediæval church had obscured. These "poor priests," dressed in coarse russet robes and carrying staves, travelled through the length and breadth of the land, as Wes-

---

[1] A satirical epithet, meaning the mumbling of prayers.

ley's preachers travelled four centuries later, calling men back to the simple faith of early apostolic times.

Wyclif and his Lollard priests began the great Protestant appeal from the dogmas of the church to the prime authority of

Wyclif's Bible

the Scriptures which culminated, in the sixteenth century, in Luther and the Reformation. In order to make this appeal effective with the masses, Wyclif not only wrote numerous tracts and sermons in homely, vigorous speech for the common people, but also urged the translation of the Bible into English. The task was completed by Nicholas of Hereford and a corps of assistants before Wyclif's death in 1384. The translation Wyclif had inspired was revised and rendered into more idiomatic language a few years later by John Purvey, and received its final form some time before the end of the century. It is one of the first great prose monuments in English, and its wide popularity, in spite of the occasional stiff and unidiomatic "translation-English," rendered it influential in gaining for the vernacular a position of dignity and honor.

The peasant rebellion and the Lollard agitation give us glimpses of an England which Chaucer, in spite of the many-

Chaucer and Langland

sidedness of his work, did not reveal. The *Canterbury Tales* contain few references to the plague, only one to the peasant uprising, and only one to Lollardry, and these references are casual or jesting. Chaucer wrote for the court and cultivated classes, to whom the sufferings of the poor were a matter of the utmost indifference. He is often serious, sometimes nobly so; but intense moral indignation and exalted spiritual rapture were foreign to his artistic, gay, tolerant disposition. In his graceful worldliness, his delight in the bright pageantry of life, he shows himself to be an adherent of the nobility, a follower of the Norman-French literary school; the other side of the English nature, its somber, puritanical, moralizing side, found expression in a group of poems which have until recently been ascribed to one author, William Langland, and which have been called the *Vision Concerning Piers the Plowman*. Although the question of the unity or diversity of authorship of these poems is still involved in controversy, the position of the adherents of the older view has been so seriously undermined that we are now obliged at least to discard completely the inferential biography of the author, which had been based solely on half-hints and imaginative details contained in the poems. The three poems comprise an original version and two successive revisions, the two latter being about three times as long as the former. It is profitable to consider the earliest version (1362) first.

The poem is a series of dreams or visions such as the *Roman de la Rose* had made fashionable. On a May morning, "weary forwandered," the poet leans beside a brook in the Malvern hills, and, lulled by the soft music of the waters, falls asleep. In a dream he sees a high Tower in the east, a dark Dungeon in a deep dale *"Piers the Plowman"* in the west, and in between a fair Field full of folk, working and wandering. Here are plowmen and wasters, proud ladies and gentlemen of fashion, hermits, peddlers, minstrels, lazy beggars, lying pilgrims, preaching friars, a fraudulent pardoner, absentee priests, unscrupulous lawyers, barons, townspeople, and serfs; some are good, some are wicked, most are greedy, lazy, rapacious. Suddenly a lovely Lady, Holy Church, descends from the mountain, and explains to the dreamer that the Tower is the abode of God the Father, who is the spirit of Truth. Truth, she says, consists in loving God and being charitable to men. From the Tower the dreamer turns to the Dungeon, from which streams a retinue of rascals in the train of Falsehood, the son of Wrong, who is the lord of evil. Falsehood is about to marry Lady Meed, the allegorical representative of the greed of the people in the Field, but Theology forbids the marriage, and in order to obtain leave Meed and Falsehood are required to go to the King's court. On their way the King orders the arrest of the mob of rascals, who disperse in a panic, and Lady Meed alone is brought to trial. Here she attempts to marry the King's greatest Knight, who is named Conscience, but the latter refuses until she obtains the consent of Reason. Before Reason can render judgment, Meed is caught red-handed in the act of bribing the King's officials to release a criminal, and in a stinging speech of denunciation by Reason is forever debarred from pleading before the King. Reason concludes with the assertion that the royal domain can be made righteous and happy only if he and Conscience rule over it. Immediately the dreamer sees Conscience and Repentance preaching to the Field full of folk, who, in the form of personified Deadly Sins, confess, repent, and promise to seek for Truth. But no one knows the way thither, not even a Palmer who has visited every shrine on earth, till Piers, the old, faithful Plowman, ventures to tell them how to find and follow the path. It leads through Meekness, Conscience, love of God and man, and the Ten Commandments (represented as almost impassable rivers, mountains, and forests), after which will be seen the Tower of Truth, surrounded by a moat of Mercy, and guarded by Grace. Entrance can be secured only through the Seven Virtues—the antitheses of the Deadly Sins. The pilgrims despair over the difficulties, and beg Piers to lead them, but he refuses until he has finished his plowing, sowing, and harvesting, and in the meantime commands them all to assist him. Many refuse to work, and Piers calls in Hunger, who beats them and feeds them only on beans, barley-bread, and water. At the harvest some become arrogant and refuse to work save for high wages, in spite of the renewed warnings of Hunger. Finally, Truth sends Piers a pardon, under the terms of which only those who aid him are to be admitted to the Tower. The pardon reads, "Those who do good shall enter eternal life, but those who do evil shall suffer in eternal fire." In a dispute over the meaning of the pardon, Piers and a priest jangle so loudly that the dreamer awakes.

Even to the shortest form of the poem as just given, several cantos were added, which, however, in vigor and structural *Later* power, fall far below the work of the first writer. *Versions* Twice afterward (1377, 1386–1398) the poem was augmented by many more cantos, and was extensively remodelled. A definitely planned allegory, with the systematic action of its living and moving figures, however, was beyond the power of the later writers. Nor did they see or understand the social abuses so clearly, nor could they propose so definite a remedy. Their work is full of poetic lines and of powerful short passages, but it lacks form and structure.

The name of Piers the Plowman was used as a rallying cry in the peasant uprising. But the poem aims, not at revolution, but at reform. Its remedy is neither physical violence nor an ascetic withdrawal from the social conflict, but the gospel of Truth, Love, Duty, and Work. *Spirit of the Poem* The poet's sense of equality of all men before God, his hatred of social falsities and hypocrisies, his belief in the dignity of labor, give an almost modern tone to his poem, in spite of its archaic metrical form and its mediæval allegorical machinery. His deep religious sense and the power of his feeling of social duty are neither ancient nor modern, but of all time.

The metrical form which this poet chose again contrasts him sharply with Chaucer. Chaucer threw in his lot from the first with the new versification imported from France, depending upon regular accent, a fixed number of syllables, and rhyme; and he developed this in such a way as to produce with it a rich and finished *Its Metrical Form* music. By his choice of the French system he puts himself in line with the future of English verse, even though the tradition he began was lost for a time in the fifteenth century. The author of *Piers the Plowman,* either because he knew that his popular audience would be more deeply moved by the ancient and traditional rhythms of the nation, or because these were more natural to himself, adopted the old system of native versification which depended upon a fixed number of accents (four) and alliteration for its metrical structure, and allowed great irregularity both in the position of stressed syllables and in the number of syllables in the line. The opening verses of the poem will serve as a specimen:

> In a *s*ómer *s*éason .   whan *s*óft was the *s*ónne,
> I *sh*ópe me in *sh*róudes .   as I a *sh*épe were
> In *h*ábit as an *h*érmit .   un*h*óly of workes;
> Went *w*íde in this *w*órlde .   *w*óndres to here.[1]

---

[1] The cæsura, or heavy pause in the middle of each line, is marked by a dot. The alliterative syllables, of which there are usually two in the first half, and one in the second half, are stressed. There are normally four stresses in the line.

This metre is, to a modern ear, somewhat monotonous and uncouth. It adapts itself much better to recitation than to read-*Its Poetic Quality* ing with the eye. However we account for it, the fact that the *Vision* is written in this antique and rapidly dying verse form, has told against it. From Chaucer, from France and Italy, flows the whole stream of later verse. *Piers the Plowman* has had no modern literary offspring, even though it was considered one of the most valuable pieces of literature in English and was imitated a number of times in its own and the following century.

But the work of the poet who wrote the earliest version has suffered most in modern criticism, because it has not been carefully distinguished from that of the later continuators and adapters. Their work is confused in plan, bewildered with detail, full of breaks and structureless transitions. Its total effect is majestic only because of the force of imagination behind it, but it is not artistic. It lacks the clear, firm outline and the harmonious proportion, which the first poet attained, and which likewise Chaucer's supreme artistic sense enabled him to attain in his later years. But it is probably the greatest piece of Middle English literature, except for the *Canterbury Tales*.

That Chaucer was far in advance of his time becomes clear when we note how persistently his fifteenth-century successors *Imitators of Chaucer and Gower* turned back to him for inspiration, as to their

Fader dere and maister reverent,

and found themselves unable to do more than awkwardly or pallidly imitate him. The chief among these imitators was John Lydgate, a monk of Bury St. Edmunds, who began making verses before Chaucer's death, and died before the outbreak of the Wars of the Roses. Lydgate, who was primarily a translator and compiler, was the most voluminous mediæval English poet. His major works were the *Troy-Book,* the *Falls of Princes,* the *Temple of Glass,* the *Pilgrimage of the Life of Man,* and the *Story of Thebes.* His *Story of Thebes,* based on Boccaccio and Statius, pretends to be told as one of the *Canterbury Tales;* the poet in his prologue feigns to have joined the pilgrims at Canterbury, and at the Host's request tells the story on the homeward journey. The device illustrates clearly the lack of originality of Lydgate and his brother poets. Lydgate's verse, moreover, is markedly halting and tuneless. But in his own day he was ranked with Chaucer and Gower as a brisk teller of stories. In this respect Thomas Occleve or Hoccleve (1370?–1450?) was a better disciple. He perhaps had the benefit of Chaucer's personal acquaintance and instruction, loved and mourned him deeply, and preserved, in the manuscript of his *Governail of Princes* or *De Regimine Principum* (written for the Prince of Wales, afterward Henry V), the well-known portrait of Chaucer as a gray-haired old man, hooded and gowned. This treatise on courtly morals and manners is probably his major work.

A third poet who continued the master's tradition (with a good sprinkling of Gower, to be sure) has lived in literary history as much by the picturesqueness of his personal story as by his poetry, which is nevertheless charming in its kind. This is the young Stuart prince, afterward James I of Scotland, who was captured by English sailors in 1405, and spent the next nineteen years in England, as a prisoner, in the Tower *James I of Scotland and "The King's Quair"* of London, Windsor Castle, and other strongholds. At the time of his capture he was a child of eleven. As he grew up in solitude, he turned for diversion to poetry and music—arts in which the Scottish kings were traditionally proficient. One day, from the windows of Windsor Castle, he saw a beautiful young girl walking in the garden below, as Palamon saw the fair Emilie in the *Knight's Tale*. The story of his love for Jane Beaufort and its happy outcome the young prince told with tenderness and fancy in his *King's Quair*. It is written in the seven-line pentameter stanza [1] invented by Chaucer and repeatedly used by him, though, in deference to the princely poet, it has since been known as "rhyme royal." Both the style and plan of the *King's Quair* are imitated from the artificial French poetry from which Chaucer more and more departed as he grew in original power, but from which neither Gower nor the Chaucerian imitators delivered themselves. It is significant of the failure of these imi-

[1] Rhyming, *a*, *b*, *a*, *b*, *b*, *c*, *c*.

tators to perceive the immense originality of Chaucer's later work, that they frequently put Gower on a level with him. In the Envoy of the *King's Quair* James recommends his "litel boke, nakit of eloquence,"

> Unto the ympnes (hymns) of my maisters dere,
> Gowere and Chaucere, that on steppis satt
> Of rhetorike whil they were lyvand here,
> Superlative as poets laureate,

and he brings the poem to a close with a prayer that their souls may together enjoy the bliss of heaven. When in 1424 the prince, on the eve of release from his long captivity, was married to the lady whom he had celebrated in the *King's Quair*, his reverence for Gower prompted him to have the wedding held in the church of St. Saviour's, where the old poet lay buried. James's assassination at Perth in 1437 is the subject of Rossetti's literary ballad, "The King's Tragedy."

The fifteenth century is often characterized as a period barren of poetic production. This is true only so far as it implies the absence of genius. Quantitatively the fifteenth cen-

Fifteenth-Century Poetry

tury was more prolific of English poetry (and prose) than any preceding century. The enormous growth of English commerce and industry, and the consequent rise of the middle classes in number, wealth, and leisure, resulted in a voracious public appetite for the output of literary mediocrity, a large part of which is purely utilitarian. The number of third-rate writers is very large—the works of over three hundred have been printed—and the quantity of their output is surprising. But the fact remains that the freshest and most spontaneous work is of popular origin. Songs and carols, ballads, and new and remodelled plays of all sorts constitute the finest literature of the century.

The English popular ballad used to be regarded as a variety of folk-art, communally produced. It was then defined as "a narrative poem without any known author or any marks of individual authorship, such as sentiment and reflection, meant in the first instance for singing, and connected, as its name implies, with the communal dance, but submitted to a process of oral tradition among people free from literary influences and fairly homogeneous." In recent years, scholars have emphasized the importance of the individual, though usually unknown, author and have minimized the communal element. These ballads appear to have flourished luxuriantly among the folk in the fourteenth and fifteenth centuries, after which their composition ceased. Over three hundred of them, in 1,300 versions, have survived, and have been collected and printed, the earliest collection being that in Bishop Percy's *Reliques of Ancient Popular Poetry,* the publication of which in 1765 aroused the keenest interest. These ballads in the main are of two different types, one presenting an emotional situation, often tragic, in short stanzas, with a refrain and with much repetition; the other, as in the case of the Robin Hood ballads, offering a rather extended narrative in stanzas of four lines, the second and fourth lines rhyming. The first type—the folk ballad—shows some signs of group composition although the originals were probably composed by individuals. The second type—the minstrel ballad—is certainly the result of individual composition. The former may be illustrated by the following:

> Lully, lulley, lully, lulley,
> The fawcon hath born my make [1] away.
>
> He bare hym up, he bare hym down,
> He bare hym into an orchard browne.   (*Refrain.*)
>
> In that orchard there was an halle,
> That was hangid with purpill and pall.   (*Ref.*)
>
> And in that hall there was a bede;
> Hit was hangid with gold so rede.   (*Ref.*)
>
> And yn that bed there lythe a knyght,
> His wowndis bledyng day and nyght.   (*Ref.*)
>
> By that bede side kneleth a may,[2]
> And she wepeth both nyght and day.   (*Ref.*)

[1] Mate.   [2] Maid.

One of the best known of the Robin Hood ballads, that entitled *Robin Hood and the Monk,* opens with the following musical and picturesque stanzas:

> In somer, when the shawes [1] be sheyne,[2]
> And leves be large and long,
> Hit is full mery [3] in feyre foreste
> To here the foulys [4] song.
> To se the dere drawe to the dale,
> And leve the hilles hee,[5]
> And shadow hem in the leves grene,
> Under the grenewood tre.

The ballad has a well-constructed plot, with fighting, imprisonment, disguise, and escape. Interest in the ballad is one of the features of the Romantic period, and from that period date most of the "literary" ballads, poems written consciously in the manner of the ancient ballad.

In prose the fifteenth century produced one work which has much of the elevation and imaginative splendor of great poetry,

Fifteenth-Century Prose
the *Morte d'Arthur* (The Death of Arthur) of Sir Thomas Malory. Malory was a knight, a gentleman of an ancient house, with its seat at Newbold Revell, Warwickshire. As a young man he served in France, in the military retinue of Richard Beauchamp, Earl of Warwick, a warrior in whom lived again the knightly ideal of a former age, and who was known by the romantic title of "Father of Courtesy." Malory himself seems to have had an unusually turbulent and contentious career, but it did not disqualify him for the task of combining in one great prose mosaic almost all the legends and tales of King Arthur and his knights of the Round Table, which had been richly elaborated by the poets and prose-writers of England and France. Here, in an enchanted realm, detached from actuality, we hear of the high deeds of love, loyalty, and revenge performed by the great personifications of chivalry—Gawain, Lancelot, Percival, and

---

[1] Groves.   [2] Beautiful.
[3] Pleasant.   [4] Little birds.   [5] High.

Galahad. Very largely by virtue of his imitating the style of his French originals, Malory became the master of a simple, flowing English, primitive in structure, but capable of considerable flexibility and falling into pleasant natural rhythms. The *Morte d'Arthur* was finished by 1470; it was printed in 1485, when Caxton, the first English printer, published it with an interesting preface from his own hand.

CHAPTER IV

The Renaissance

THE LITERARY decline that followed the death of Chaucer was due in considerable measure to political causes. The dispute in regard to the throne, which culminated in the Wars of the Roses, distracted the country, wasted its energy, and finally destroyed in large measure the noble families on whose patronage early literature and art were de-

*Period of
Decline
after
Chaucer*

pendent. The accession of Henry VII in 1485 brought about a period of quiet and recovery. As its power increased, the country resumed its position in the family of European nations, and began through them to feel the stimulus of the movement called the Renaissance.

The Renaissance was in essence an intellectual rebirth. It showed itself in the effort of the individual to free himself from

*The Ren-
aissance*

the rigid institutions of the Middle Ages, feudalism and the church; and to assert his right to live, to think, and to express himself in accordance with a more flexible secular code. As men gained this freedom they felt less inclined to assent to the mediæval view that this life should be sacrificed to the future; they turned more and more to the present world, to the problems of gaining mastery in it through wealth or statecraft, of discovering its secrets through exploration and scientific experiment, of heightening its enjoyments through art and literature.

One force of immense importance in the Renaissance was the new knowledge of the world of antiquity, which was obtained through the recovery of the writings and works of art of the classical period. The idea presented in the literatures of Athens and Rome, of life which should be lived for its opportunities of many-sided development and enjoyment, came to have a strong influence on men—an influence denoted by the term *Humanism*. Moreover, the perfect artistic forms achieved by classical poets, orators, sculptors, and architects became models on which the new taste for the beautiful formed itself. Naturally, Italy, as a seat of Roman civilization, possessed within herself a great store of the relics of the classical age, and was in the best position to receive more from the East. When the Turks conquered the Eastern Empire and captured Constantinople, in 1453, many Greek scholars betook themselves to Italy with their manuscripts. In this way Italian cities became centres of Greek study and of the classical culture on which the new intellectual impulse was nourished.

The Influence of the Classics

With all these advantages Italy became the teacher of Europe in philosophy, in art, and in classical scholarship. Other nations, however, supplied elements of the new world which was being created. Spain and Portugal gave the practical energy that sent Columbus to America and Vasco da Gama around Africa. Germany contributed the invention of printing, by which the new culture was diffused among the people; and Germany also took the lead in the movement which had for its object the emancipation of the conscience from the church. A beginning had been made in this direction by Wyclif; but the great forward step was taken when, in 1517, Luther nailed to the church door in Wittenberg his attack upon the power of the Pope. It is true, this Reformation, as time went on, produced a moral reaction against the worldly spirit of the Renaissance; but in the long run it made not only for religious liberty, but also for freedom of thought

Elements in the Renaissance

In the early Renaissance England lagged somewhat behind the more precocious nations, Italy and France. The English Renaissance can scarcely be said to begin until the reign of Henry VII, and it did not come to its full splendor until the latter days of Elizabeth. Even before the accession of Henry VII, however, we can discern signs of its coming. In 1476 Caxton set up his printing-press in London. Before this date one of the

Early Renaissance in England

colleges at Oxford had engaged an Italian teacher of Greek, and in the next few years William Grocyn and Thomas Linacre went to Italy to study with the Italian humanists. They returned to give Oxford an international reputation as the home of Greek studies, so that the greatest scholar of the time, the Dutch Erasmus, came there to study, thinking it no longer necessary for young men to resort to Italy.

These men of the new learning, especially the younger generation, Erasmus and his friends, John Colet and Thomas More, exemplify memorably the hopefulness and ideal-
The Oxford Reformers
ism that attended the early progress of the Renaissance. All three were reformers. Colet, who was afterward Dean of St. Paul's, set a model for the public-school system of England, in his famous St. Paul's School. Erasmus sketched the character of the perfect ruler in his *Institutes of a Christian Prince,* and More that of a perfect society in his *Utopia.* All three were interested in the reform of the church, and though they did not follow Henry VIII in his break with the Pope, they pointed the way toward the later alliance between the universities and the English Reformation.

Still more important than the universities as a centre of Renaissance influence was the court. Both Henry VII and Henry VIII ruled in the spirit of modern statecraft. Both
The Court of Henry VIII
encouraged trade and manufactures, and increased the wealth of the country. Both hastened the decline of feudalism by allowing men of low birth to rise to distinction, through personal service rendered to the sovereign. Thus the court became the field for the display of individual ambition. Henry VIII, indeed, in his own character resembled strongly some of the Italian princes of the Renaissance, who mingled the enlightenment of the statesman with the cruelty of the despot. The men who played for power in his service had need of the utmost address, in a game where the stakes were the highest, and defeat was fatal. The career of his great minister, Cardinal Wolsey, is a vivid illustration of the effect of the Renaissance in England. Of low birth, he rose to be the supreme figure in church and state. In diplomacy he

played the game that was taught by the Italian states, in the hope of securing for England the position of arbiter in the European balance of power. His policy tended to draw England nearer to the continental nations, and to give her a part in the new civilization. He seconded her sovereign's taste for art, learning, and magnificence. He founded Cardinal's College, now Christ Church, at Oxford, and built Hampton Court Palace, one of the best specimens of Tudor architecture. At his invitation the German painter Hans Holbein came to England and painted for us the faces and characters of the men of Henry's court, as Italian painters were doing of Florentines and Venetians. But Henry quarreled with Wolsey over the proposed annulment of his marriage with Katharine of Aragon, and stripped the prelate of his wealth and power.

The most attractive figure, both among the Oxford reformers and later at the court of Henry, is St. Thomas More (1478–1535). More separated from his early companions, *St.* threw himself into state affairs, became Lord Chan- *Thomas* cellor in succession to Wolsey, and, like him falling *More* a victim to the king's change of policy, was beheaded in 1535. He is remembered not only for his spiritual integrity but also for the union of his interests, intellectual and practical, which resulted in *Utopia,* written in Latin in 1516, and translated into English in 1551.

In this famous book a sailor returning to England holds a conversation with the author concerning the state of the realm, in the course of which it appears that many of the *"Utopia"* evils of government and wrongs of the people, of which the author of the *Vision Concerning Piers the Plowman* had complained, were still in existence. Then, in the second part, the sailor proceeds to give an account of a land beyond the sea, Utopia (Nowhere), where the people live by reason, and all poverty and injustice have been abolished. This sketch of an imaginary commonwealth owes much to Plato's *Republic,* and in turn became the ancestor of a whole class of fiction, of which Bacon's *New Atlantis* is an early and H. G. Wells's *Modern Utopia* a modern example.

More's *Utopia* represents the Renaissance interest in the state as a work of art, and its enthusiastic belief that not only human

"The Boke named the Governour"

society but human nature itself is capable of enormous improvement. Many other books of the time picture the individual life as a work of art, and emphasize the resulting gain to society. Such books are manuals of education, of manners, of personal ethics. One of the most important came to England from Italy, *The Courtier* (1528) by Baldassare Castiglione, a book which marks the evolution of the mediæval knight into the modern gentleman. *The Boke named the Governour* (1531), by Sir Thomas Elyot, was written to show how the culture of the individual should serve the state, its subject being the proper education of "the childe of a gentleman which is to have authority in a publike weale." It is largely concerned with the methods and benefits of study of the classics, but its English quality is seen in the author's enthusiasm for outdoor sports. "Wrastlynge," he naïvely tells us, "is a very good exercise . . . so that it be with one that is equal in strength or somewhat under, and that the place be softe so that in fallinge theyr bodies be not bruised." Bowling, however, "is to be utterly abjected of all noble men, in likewise foote balle, wherein is nothinge but beastly furie and extreme violence."

Both More and Elyot are to be regarded as writers for the aristocracy. Popular literature was stimulated by the theological

The English Reformation

controversies of the Reformation. The struggle for the emancipation of conscience from priestly control had begun in England nearly two centuries before, with Wyclif; and in spite of persecution the spirit of the Lollards had survived until the reign of Henry VIII. This spirit, strengthened by the example of the German and Swiss reformers, supplied the moral force which found in Henry's political separation from Rome in 1534, on the occasion of the annulment of his first marriage, an opportunity for radical theological reforms. This force went out through the country in the sermons of Hugh Latimer, the boldest among Henry's reforming bishops, and the most powerful preacher of the day.

He was of peasant birth; and his writings represent a development of popular English prose, straightforward, racy, simple as homespun.

The Reformation, and the controversies, religious and political, which grew out of it gave occasion for what we should call *journalism,* in the form of pamphlets, serious and satirical, in both prose and verse. It furnished also what came in course of time to be one of the strongest influences on the development of English style, in the translation of the Bible by William *The English Bible and Prayer Book* Tyndale and Miles Coverdale (1524–1539), of which the popular character is shown by the fact that 97 per cent of the words are Anglo-Saxon. A union between the Latin-English style of the educated classes and the simple every-day speech of the people is shown by another literary monument of the Reformation, the Book of Common Prayer, prepared under the direction of Cranmer, the Archbishop of Canterbury under Henry VIII and Edward VI. Here the sonorous Latin words, full of suggestion for the lover of the classics, are often followed by their Anglo-Saxon equivalents, the sentences falling with a rhythm which is in part caught from Hebrew poetry, in part, perhaps, from the artificial style which foreign models had introduced into England.

While English prose was thus developing in order to express the ideas of the time on the two important subjects, culture and religion, poetry was also taking on its modern form. The last poet of the old school of imitators of Chaucer was John Skelton (1460–1529). *The New Poetry* Toward the close of his life, however, he broke away from the tradition of his youth, and in such works as *The Tunning of Eleanour Rumming, Philip Sparrow,* and the *Garland of Laurel* adopted a rough, short metre, adapted to the energy of his satire, which sounded the popular cry against abuses in church and state. In his roughness and bitterness he affords a striking contrast to two poets of the close of Henry's reign, who relieved the poverty of English verse with forms imported from Italy, and thus began modern English poetry—Sir Thomas

Wyatt (1503–1542) and Henry Howard, Earl of Surrey (1517–1547).

The career of the former illustrates particularly the value to English literature of the close connection with foreign countries,

Sir Thomas Wyatt

which Henry VIII's ambition to take part in European affairs did much to restore. Wyatt was fre-quently abroad on diplomatic missions; like Chau-cer he visited Italy and also Spain and France. His poems are, for the most part, translations and imitations, both of Italian poetry, especially the love-sonnet, and of more serious and didactic Latin poems, such as satires and epistles.

The love-sonnet, in its origin, was the literary equivalent of that chivalry which led the knight of the Middle Ages to show

Wyatt's Sonnets

his devotion to his lady by fighting in field or in tournament for her protection and honor. The great examples of this chivalric love in poetic form had been given by Dante (1265–1321) in celebration of Beatrice, and by Petrarch (1304–1374) in praise of Laura. By the latter the sonnet was established as a strict form, a poem in two parts, one of eight lines (the octave) rhyming *a b b a a b b a,* and the other of six (the sestet) in which several arrangements of the *c d e* rhymes were permitted. With Petrarch's imitators the sonnet became a literary exercise, devoted to the expression of a love which might be entirely imaginary, or directed toward an imaginary person. Wyatt's sonnets, therefore, like those of his Italian masters, need not be regarded as having strict biographi-cal truth, though attempts have been made to find in them the history of a personal relation, and some have guessed that they were in part inspired by Henry's second queen, Anne Boleyn. At all events Wyatt's poetry suggests that even a conventional form was for him the means for a sincere expression of feeling; even his translations seem charged with his own temperament, and his rendering of the Penitential Psalms is touched with per-sonal religious emotion. Wyatt's effort to achieve the regularity and finish of his Italian models was not always successful; he makes bad rhymes, he fails to harmonize word and verse accent, he stumbles in scansion. Yet such lyrics as "Awake my lute" and "Forget not yet" are eminent examples of poetic power.

Wyatt's companion poet, Surrey, born in 1517 and beheaded in 1547, was younger than his master both in years and in spirit. In contrast to Wyatt's gravity he has all the exuberance of the age, a perpetual charm of youth and promise, as his brilliant figure passes through the sunlight and shadow of Henry's court, moving gracefully and carelessly to the scaffold which awaited him. Like Wyatt he imitated the Italian amorous poets; but more significant than his love-poems are those of friendship, the sonnets to Clere and to Wyatt, and the elegy on the Duke of Richmond, which are full of feeling, intimate, personal, sincere. Often, as, for example, in the youthful poem which begins "The soote season," he shows an interest in nature, and an eye for details of country life which remind us of Milton's "L'Allegro."

The Earl of Surrey

Surrey, like Wyatt, rendered his chief service to English literature by enriching it with foreign forms. He was the first English poet to use blank verse, in his translation of two books of the *Æneid*. Blank verse had been used in Italy a few years before in a translation of the same work, so that Surrey did not originate the form; but the happy skill with which he adopted it, and thus discovered to English poetry its most powerful and characteristic verse form, is worthy of all praise. He also adapted the sonnet to English use, making it a poem of three quatrains followed by a couplet, a form rendered immortal by Shakespeare.

Surrey's Poetry

Besides Wyatt and Surrey there were many courtiers of Henry VIII who used poetry as a sort of social accomplishment. Such verse was intended for private circulation in manuscript form. By the middle of the century, however, there had grown up a demand on the part of the reading public which publishers attempted to supply by volumes of miscellaneous verse. The most famous early collection *Songs and Sonnets,* commonly called *Tottel's Miscellany,* which contained the poems of Wyatt, Surrey, and several of their followers, appeared in 1557, a date which marks the public beginning of modern English poetry.

"Tottel's Miscellany"

The influence of Wyatt and Surrey is shown in the work which Thomas Sackville, afterward Lord Buckhurst (1536–

1608), contributed to a volume called *The Mirror for Magistrates* (1559). This book in general character looks back to an *Thomas Sackville* older fashion, being a collection of stories of persons who from their high place fell into tragic misfortune (it was, in fact, a continuation of a work of Lydgate called *The Falls of Princes*), but Sackville's "Induction" and "The Complaint of the Duke of Buckingham" are touched with the new spirit. He also wrote, in collaboration with Thomas Norton, the first regular English tragedy, *Gorboduc*. Both in his contributions to *The Mirror,* which are in Chaucer's seven-line stanza, and in *Gorboduc*, which is in blank verse, Sackville shows surprising mastery of his form. He has a sureness of touch and a freedom from technical errors which put him beyond Surrey and Wyatt, and his imaginative energy is suggestive of the great poets who were to follow.

The same sure advance in technical mastery is shown by George Gascoigne (1525?–1577). He, like Wyatt and Surrey, *George Gascoigne* drew largely on foreign sources. His comedy, *The Supposes,* came from the Latin (through the Italian form of Ariosto) and his tragedy, *Jocasta,* from the Greek. His *Steele Glas* was a highly imitative verse-satire. Against this product of imitation must be set his original verse, especially the "Lullaby of a Lover," which has all the lyrical and spiritual quality of Elizabethan song. It is noteworthy of his technical skill that he prepared a little treatise on versification, a text-book for other poets to follow, called "Notes of Instruction for the Writing of English Verse."

Except for the poets mentioned, however, English literature from the reign of Henry VIII through the early part of the reign of Elizabeth, gives little promise of the outburst which was to mark the closing years of the century. That outburst was the result of a sudden, overwhelming patriotism in which the whole nation shared. After the religious conflicts of the reigns of Edward VI (1547–1553) and Mary (1553–1558), when it seemed as if the country would be plunged again into civil war, the accession of Elizabeth brought back the unity and prosperity which England had enjoyed under the early Tudors.

The force of the Renaissance, which had been checked for a time by national hesitation, manifested itself anew and more widely. Many things combined to give distinction to personal character, and variety and color to life. *The Age of Elizabeth* The enlarged possibilities of the world, the new lands beyond the sea, offered unlimited opportunity for action. The diffusion of knowledge of the past, together with the freedom of thought which the Reformation had brought about, afforded opportunities as tempting for speculative enterprise and imaginative adventure. Altogether there appeared to men a new, wider, richer world; and with it came a clearer consciousness of the individual personality which that world seemed made to satisfy. This discovery of the new world and of man, as it has been called, coming to the nation in the time of joyful reaction from the uncertainty and peril of Mary's reign, set the whole mass into vibration; but the tendencies which made for purely personal and selfish advancement were both directed and kept in check by the growth of national feeling. Elizabeth's reign united the nation, and her personal presence gave it a visible sign of unity. Under her rule England passed through an experience as dramatic as that of Athens at Marathon; after a long period of suspense the strain was relieved by the wonderful repulse of the Spanish Armada in 1588. The patriotism, made so intense by danger and victory, shines through the literature of the time. The eager, instinctive response of the people found utterance in the choruses of Shakespeare's *Henry V.* The more conscious political virtue, which touched with something of high purpose the lives of Sidney, of Sackville, even of Essex and Ralegh, is reflected in Spenser's *Faerie Queene.*

It is easy to see how this spirit of the time finds expression in the drama and in lyric poetry—the more spontaneous and native types of Elizabethan literature. It is not so easy, but it is still interesting, to see it working itself out *Elizabethan Literature* in the more conscious and artificial forms. The patriotism which repulsed the Armada made men seek to create a literature in keeping with England's national greatness. It turned their attention first of all to their language.

Some held that English should be purified from words of foreign extraction; others that it should be enriched by coinages from the Latin and Greek. Questions of the structure and decoration of prose style brought into being a literature of rhetorical criticism. It was felt that the highest function of literature was to teach, and accordingly, to replace the romances and ballads which circulated among the people, authors sought to give serious employment to the printing-presses by providing them with works of instruction in all departments of knowledge. The poets seem instinctively to have felt the greatness of the future of English poetry, and to have taken conscious pride in their contribution to it. Like the prose writers, they were perplexed by many questions and theories. They suffered from the conception that dignified literature must be didactic, and hence produced interminable poems on historical, geographical, and philosophical subjects which might better have been treated in prose. They hesitated in the choice among foreign forms, and were troubled by the fact that classical poets did not use rhyme. But in all this writing, so much of which seems to us artificial and lifeless, there is the impulse of adventure and experiment, the faith in learning and culture, and the pride in national achievement which characterize the Elizabethan age alike in exploration, in trade, in social life, and in war.

The first works which should be mentioned in the Elizabethan period are those collections of material which served as mines

Stories and Histories
whence the crude ore was taken which was afterward smelted into the purer literary forms of poetry and drama. Such was the collection of *novelle,* or short stories, mainly from Boccaccio and other Italian writers, made by William Painter in his *Palace of Pleasure* (1566). Such stories were immensely popular and furnished the plots of many of the stories of Greene and plays of Shakespeare. Another collection, *Tragicall Discourses* (1567) by Geoffrey Fenton, was drawn in the main from a later Italian novelist, Bandello. Bandello's stories were chiefly of the horrors of the later Renaissance; they were used extensively by dramatists after Shakespeare, led by the public demand for sensation to provide plays of lust and blood. But England had a book of tragedies of its own—the *Acts and Monuments* (1563), com-

monly called the "Book of Martyrs" of John Foxe, filled with gruesome tales of the men and women who suffered martyrdom for their faith under Queen Mary. This book became the textbook of the Reformation, and to its heroic examples of constancy, as much as to any one influence, is due the severe, strenuous temper of English Puritanism. Another work of English history to which later poets and dramatists, including Shakespeare, were much indebted was the *Chronicle* (1578) of England, Scotland, and Ireland, by Raphael Holinshed. For Roman history they resorted to the translation of Plutarch's *Lives* (1579) by Sir Thomas North. And in this connection may be mentioned Richard Hakluyt's *Principal Navigations, Voyages and Discoveries of the English Nation* (1589).

The first concern of the Renaissance, it has been said, was with the individual—to enable him to realize the possibilities of life through training. It was the peculiar strength of the English Renaissance that this attitude was modified by the ideal of service to the state. This is well exemplified in the work of Roger Ascham (1515–1568), a famous scholar of the time and the tutor of the Princess Elizabeth. Of his two essays, the first, called *Toxophilus* (1545), was ostensibly written in praise of archery; but it is really a defense of a sound, well-balanced life, with due attention to field-sports, of which Elyot had called "the shotyng in a longe bowe" the chief.

The second, *The Schoolmaster* (1570), sets forth the theory of education as a humanizing process in which the pupil must work with the teacher. Ascham was a scholar, and in his style as in his substance he marks the reverence for classical authority which followed the revival of learning. His purpose obliged him to choose English and to write simply, but he declares that it would have been easier for him to write in Latin. His view of life, however, is thoroughly English; he praises learning not for its own sake, but because it furnishes discipline for character and examples for conduct. For him the aim of life is social usefulness; the private virtues and the service of the individual to the state go hand in hand. "In very deed," he says, "the good or ill bringing up of children doth as much serve to the good or ill service of God, our Prince, and our whole countrie, as any one thing beside."

Roger Ascham

As a Latinist and an Englishman he resented the strong influence of things Italian. He praises *The Courtier* of Castiglione which had been translated into English by Sir Thomas Hoby (1561), but he attacks such collections of Italian stories as those found in the *Palace of Pleasure,* "whereby many young willes and wittes, allured to wantonnes, do now boldly contemne all severe bookes that sounde to honestie and Godlines." Particularly he reprobates the practice among Englishmen of resorting to Italy for study or travel, and quotes an Italian proverb, *"Englese Italianato é un diabolo incarnato,"* or "An Italianate Englishman is a devil incarnate."

A more striking example of the literature of behavior is furnished by John Lyly (1554?–1606). Lyly was educated at Magdalen College, Oxford, where he seems to have gained the reputation of being a trifler—"the fiddlestick of Oxford," an enemy called him. His superficial cleverness, however, enabled him to write a successful account of the culture of the period, in *Euphues: the Anatomy of Wit* (1579), and its sequel, *Euphues and His England* (1580).

John Lyly

Euphues is first of all a work of fiction, founded upon the situation, common in mediæval story, of two friends in love with the same girl. Instead of using this situation as an opportunity to illustrate the chivalric devotion of friendship, however, Lyly allows his model Euphues to displace his friend in the affection of his lady, who then cynically accepts a third suitor. By virtue of this plot *Euphues* may claim to be the first of English novels. More important than the story, however, is the teaching of the book. The plot serves to connect a series of conversations, letters, and essays, on such subjects as love, social relations, education, religion. The ideal of a thoroughly and symmetrically developed personality is implicit in the title, which means literally "well shaped in growing." It is important to note that Lyly gives a place to religious influence in moulding character. After an impressive setting forth of the advantages of worldly culture, Euphues exclaims: "Vaine is Philosophy, vaine is Phisick, vaine is Law, vaine is all learning without that taste of divine knowledge."

"Euphues"

In this there may have been a design to court favor by appealing to all the interests of the day, those of the Renaissance and of the Reformation as well. The timeliness of the book is shown by its popularity and its influence as a manual of public and social conduct. It set both a fashion of speech and a code of manners; a dialect and an etiquette for polite usage. However indirect, wasteful, and artificial this fashion now appears, it was in its time an evidence and a cause of refinement. One of the distinguishing accomplishments of the Renaissance was the elevation of social life into a fine art; and of this result in England *Euphues* was the chief sign.

The artificial language which Euphues and his friends used, and which became a literary fashion, is the characteristic of the book for which it is remembered to-day. Among Lyly's stylistic devices the most remarkable is the *Euphuism* arrangement of words in antithesis, the contrast being marked by alliteration, thus: "Although I have *shrined* thee in my heart for a *trusty friend*, I will *shunne* thee hereafter as a *trothless foe.*" Another is his lavish use of similes drawn from what passed for natural history, as: "The milk of the Tygresse, that the more salt there is thrown into it the fresher it is." Euphuism was but one form of a widely diffused tendency in Renaissance literature, an attempt to prove the artistic value of prose by giving it some of the qualities of poetry. Mediæval Latin writers had made elaborate use of alliteration, balance, and antithesis. Earlier writers than Lyly, Ascham and Cranmer had shown traces of Euphuism, and English prose did not escape from its influence until well on in the next century. In Lyly's own generation, which was distinguished for its interest in all sorts of artistic experiments, other manifestations of the tendency to poeticize prose appeared, notably that introduced by the most charming and the most forceful of the literary dilettantes of the age, Sir Philip Sidney (1554–1586).

Philip Sidney was born in 1554, of one of the most distinguished families in England. He was sent to Shrewsbury school and to Oxford; and then spent some time abroad, in Paris, Vienna, and Italy, whence he returned to *Sir Philip* Elizabeth's court. There he represented the more *Sidney* elevated political conceptions of the time. His uncle, the Earl of Leicester, was the political chief of the Puritan party, which favored committing England to a definite alliance with the

Protestant states of Europe; and in furtherance of this policy Sidney was sent on a mission to Germany in 1577. He was also eagerly interested in the development of English power on the sea. In 1583 he obtained a grant of land in America, and two years later he made an unsuccessful attempt to escape from court and join Sir Francis Drake in one of his half-piratical expeditions against the Spaniards. This same year he accompanied the English army which was sent to help the Dutch Protestants against Spain; and in 1586 he fell in a skirmish at Zutphen.

Sidney's name, more than any other, suggests the greatness of national and personal ideals which we traditionally associate *"Astro-* with the age of Elizabeth. It is, therefore, some-*phel and* what disappointing to find his writing less eminent *Stella"* than his life. It must be remembered, however, that Sidney, like most men of position of his age, wrote not for the public but for himself and for a few friends. His works were published first in pirated editions, the *Arcadia* in 1590, and *Astrophel and Stella* in 1591. The latter is a collection of songs and sonnets, evidently addressed to one person, Lady Penelope Devereux, afterward Lady Rich. Sidney and Lady Penelope had been betrothed when the latter was a child. For some reason the match was broken off, and Lady Penelope married Lord Rich, with whom she lived for a while most unhappily. Whether Sidney actually loved her when it was too late, or whether he wrote love-sonnets as a literary exercise, addressing them to his old friend out of compliment and sympathy, it is impossible to say. On the one hand there is in his sonnets much of the conventional material of the Italian sonneteers; but on the other there are touches so apt to the situation of a man who loves too late, that one hesitates to ascribe them to mere dramatic skill. In none of the many sonnet cycles of the age, except Shakespeare's and Spenser's, do we find so much that has the stamp of personality upon it; surely in none except these so much that has the accent of great poetry.

Sidney's chief literary adventure was the *Arcadia,* which he began in 1580, when, in consequence of his opposition to the proposed marriage of the Queen to the Duc d'Anjou, he was banished from court. The writing of the *Arcadia* was merely a summer pastime, undertaken to please the Countess of Pembroke, Sidney's sister. The title of the work was suggested by romances, popular in Italy and in Spain, in which *The* the scenes are laid in a pastoral country like the *"Arcadia"* ancient Arcadia. The prose tale is interrupted at intervals by passages of verse, imitated from the eclogues of Virgil and Theocritus, in which the shepherds sing of love and the delights of rural life. This form of literature had an immense charm for countries which were becoming a little weary of the worldliness of the early Renaissance; and Sidney himself, in his banishment from court, doubtless felt the influence of this mood. It was, however, a passing one, for Sidney adopts as the prevailing model of his fiction the late Greek romances, which were then being translated into English, and which abound in adventures of all kinds connected by the most intricate plots.

In his attempt at enrichment of style, Sidney worked as consciously as Lyly. He frequently uses the antithesis and other mechanical devices, but his chief resource is in *The Style* prodigality of ornament and elaboration of figure. *of the* For example, one character is besought "to keep *"Arcadia"* her speech for a while within the paradise of her mind." Undressing is described as "getting the pure silver of their bodies out of the ore of their garments." This boldness of metaphor is characteristic of the spirit of the book. Sidney writes as if seeking adventures among words, with the enthusiasm that he might have thrown into a buccaneering expedition to the Indies, if fortune had been kind to him.

The verse passages which divide the several books of the *Arcadia* are interesting for their attempts at imitation of various artificial Italian forms. Sidney was, in verse as in *Sidney's* prose, an amateur and an experimenter. He was *Literary* interested in the plan of using Latin metres to the *Theories* exclusion of the rhyming verse natural to the English tongue. This attempt was in line with similar undertakings in France and Italy, and serves to show how strong and how dangerous an influence the revival of learning exerted upon the beginnings of modern literature.

Sidney subsequently shook himself partly free from such artistic vagaries. In 1579 Stephen Gosson published a pamphlet called *The School of Abuse,* in which, as a Puritan, he attacked the art of the age, especially the drama. Sidney replied with his *Defence of Poesie.* In this, one of the earliest pieces of English criticism, Sidney showed his classicism by his approval of plays built on the Latin model; but he defended English poetry, even the folk-ballad, exclaiming, "I never heard the old song of 'Percy and Douglas' that I found not my heart moved more than with a trumpet."

"The Defence of Poesie"

Sidney's *Arcadia* and Lyly's *Euphues* were the two most influential examples of prose fiction, and they were naturally the models for authors who depended upon the reading public. Apart from the writers who gathered about the court—amateurs like Sidney or those who, like Spenser, looked for support to the patronage of the rich and preferment from the Queen—there appeared in the reign of Elizabeth a group of men who lived directly on their literary earnings. These latter were often men of university education who had lost caste. As a class they showed the intense desire for sensual enjoyment, the violence of passion, the impatience of restraint, social or moral, that accompanied the assertion of individuality in the Renaissance. The irregularity of their lives, which ended often in misery or disgrace, has made them the heroes of stories famous among the tragedies of literature. Marlowe was stabbed to death by a political spy; Peele died of dissipation; Greene, as the story goes, from surfeiting; and Nashe, we are told, of starvation.

The Popular Writers

Such men turned chiefly to the theatre, as the most profitable market for literature; but they have left also a large body of miscellaneous writings, fiction, biography, pamphlets. They were not experimenters and innovators, like Sidney and his circle, but they were quick to test any literary theory or form by its adaptability to popular taste. Robert Greene (1560?–1592) began his career by imitating Lyly, in a number of euphuistic romances. After the *Arcadia* had begun to circulate in manuscript, he wrote *Menaphon*

Robert Greene

(1589), a pastoral tale in which he clearly imitated Sidney's style. Instead of the conventional eclogues, sung on the occasion of a rustic festival which interrupts the plot, he introduced songs as expressions of the true feeling of his characters at appropriate places in the story, just as Shakespeare did in his plays. Better known than *Menaphon* is *Pandosto* (1588), a somewhat similar narrative, on which Shakespeare based his *Winter's Tale*. Greene's most individual work was done in his realistic accounts of the arts of swindlers in London, and in the partly autobiographical narratives, *Greene's Repentance* and *Never Too Late*, in which he drew from his own life lessons of morality, possibly with a view to the growing Puritan element in the reading public.

Another writer who for some years belonged to the crew of literary adventurers was Thomas Lodge (1558?–1625). His romance, *Rosalynde* (1590), which furnished the story of *As You Like It*, is the most perfect bit of *Thomas* fiction of the time. In his subtitle, *Euphues' Golden* *Lodge* *Legacy*, Lodge recognized his obligations to Lyly; but his style is far less artificial than that of his prototype, and the exquisite pastoral setting (preserved by Shakespeare in his Forest of Arden) is to be set down rather to Sidney's influence. Lodge, like Greene and Nashe, had the lyrical gift of most of the writers of the time. His highest fame rests on the exquisite songs with which he interspersed his romances, such as "Love in my Bosom Like a Bee," and "Like to the Clear in Highest Sphere," from *Rosalynde*.

Thomas Nashe (1567–1600) was a journalist with a keen weapon of satire, whose pamphlets appealed to public interest in serious questions, such as the power of the bish- *Thomas* ops, and in private scandal, such as gathered about *Nashe and* his friend, Robert Greene. His chief importance is *Picaresque* due to his adoption of a new model for fiction. *Romance* The *Arcadia* and *Euphues* are both aristocratic, in that they tend to preserve the ideal of knightly virtue or to replace it by that of the cultivated gentleman. There was beginning to appear, however, a kind of story which set up the very opposite of this ideal; instead of a knight errant who goes on a quest to find the Holy Grail or to serve his lady, the author gives us the rogue errant who goes on a quest to satisfy his appetites. This sort of story, called picaresque, from the Spanish *picaro* or rogue, was very popular in Spain, whence examples were brought to England. Nashe imitated them in *The Unfortunate Traveller* (1594), which narrates the practical jokes, travels, and adventures of Jack Wilton, an English boy adrift on the Continent, enlivened by fictitious interviews with important persons, fictitious eye-witness accounts of striking events, and other journalistic tricks.

These writers represent the eccentric, ornamented, often loosely constructed prose of the Renaissance, a prose which was to be carried on by the writers of the next generation, and to become the typical style of the seventeenth century. Beside them, however, must be mentioned a writer who stands for a saner, more intellectual development of literary style. During the later years of Elizabeth's reign the country was distracted by a dispute between the Anglican bishops and the Puritans, who denied their authority. This dispute soon passed the bounds of literary controversy; and the refusal of the Puritans to attend the services of the Church of England, and the efforts of the government to compel them, made the matter one of politics. Before the break was irreparable, however, the argument for the authority of the church was stated with winning eloquence by Richard Hooker (1554?–1600) in his *Ecclesiastical Polity,* four books of which were published in 1594, a fifth in 1597, and three more after the author's death. As befits the subject, Hooker's prose is grave and regular, with something of the precision of classic style, as opposed to the willfulness and unconventionality of Sidney's romantic manner. Indeed, Hooker was the earliest writer who developed a very competent form of English prose to fulfill a serious intellectual purpose.

Richard Hooker

The development of a great prose literature in England was reserved for a later century; the chief glory of the English Renaissance was its poetry. The experiments and studies in foreign forms, made by Wyatt and Surrey, were the preparation for a period of wonderfully poetic achievement, in which two names stand clearly first. As in the drama there rises above earlier and later playwrights the single surpassing figure of Shakespeare, so in non-dramatic poetry stands pre-eminent Edmund Spenser (1552–1599), the poet of *The Faerie Queene.*

Spenser was born in London in 1552. He was sent to the Merchant Tailors' School, and then to Pembroke College, Cambridge, where he took his master's degree in 1576. In 1578 he was in London, in attendance on the ***Edmund*** Earl of Leicester, seeking to establish himself ***Spenser*** through the influence of his friends at court. After the publication of his *Shepherd's Calendar,* in 1579, preferment came to him in the shape of an appointment in Ireland, as secretary to the deputy, Lord Grey de Wilton. In Ireland Spenser was given office, and bought the Manor of Kilcolman, whither Sir Walter Ralegh came to visit him. Ralegh saw the first three books of *The Faerie Queene,* and on his advice Spenser went to London in the following year, to read them to the Queen and to publish them. The success of the poem was immediate, but the reward from the Queen, in whose honor it was written, was disappointingly small. Soon after its publication Spenser put forth a volume of poems styled *Complaints.* The circumstances of his journey to London he related, after his return to Ireland, in "Colin Clout's Come Home Again," in which he resumed the pastoral style of *The Shepherd's Calendar.* In the next few years Spenser was busy with his courtship and marriage, which seem to be commemorated in the sonnet series, the "Amoretti," and in his wedding-song, or "Epithalamion." He went to London again in 1596 to publish the second three books of *The Faerie Queene.* During this visit he wrote the "Hymn of Heavenly Love," and "Hymn of Heavenly Beauty," to accompany two earlier "Hymns in Honor of Love and Beauty." He also wrote in London the most exquisite of his shorter poems, the "Prothalamion." Soon after his return to Kilcolman; there broke out one of those frequent insurrections which marked British rule in Ireland. Spenser's castle, which stood in the path of the storm, was sacked and burned. He fled with his family to London, where, in 1599, he died.

Spenser's life was spent chiefly in three places, each of which left strong marks upon his character and work—Cambridge, London, and Ireland. At Cambridge he found the learning of the Renaissance, especially the philosophy of Plato, which appears clearly in *The Faerie Queene* and in the "Hymns." Here also he came to know the literature of France and Italy; his first published work consisted of translations from Petrarch and the French poet du Bellay. At Cambridge, also, he came into contact with the literary theories of the time, one of which was that English verse should be written according to Latin rules of prosody. This subject is discussed at length in the letters which passed between Spenser, after he removed to London, and his Cambridge friend, Gabriel Harvey. Spenser was too genuine a poet to be injured by such theories, but the influence of the environment where they were rife is seen in his scrupulous attention to the technical requirements of his art.

Spenser at Cambridge

Of this Cambridge period the typical product is *The Shepherd's Calendar,* a series of twelve pastoral poems or eclogues. The eclogue was a poem of pastoral life, in which shepherds were the speakers, rural nature and love their usual themes. The poet might introduce matter personal to himself or his friends, or might even discuss political affairs, but he kept the conventional framework. In Spenser's fifth eclogue, for example, Archbishop Grindal figures as the good shepherd Algrind. The poems of *The Shepherd's Calendar* show great variety in metre, for Spenser was clearly practising and experimenting. But most remarkable among their literary qualities is the diction, which he elaborated for himself with the design of giving a suggestion of antiquity and rusticity to his writing. The curious predilection for obsolete or coined words is but one manifestation of the experimentation in diction affected by the age. It is carried so far in *The Faerie Queene* that Ben Jonson could say of Spenser that he "writ no language."

"The Shepherd's Calendar"

In London Spenser was at the centre of the thrilling national life of England. Through Leicester and Sidney he was introduced to the two leading political conceptions of the time, England's leadership of the Protestant cause in Europe against Spain and Rome, and her expansion beyond the seas; ideas that were the result partly of fantastic chivalry, and partly of a broad view of world politics. Finally, in Ireland he saw the English race in passionate conflict with opposing forces. The chronically disturbed state of the country was aggravated by the intrigues of Philip of Spain and the Pope with the Irish chieftains, provoking those revolts which Lord Grey, strong in his belief that the Irish were the foes of God and of civilization, put down with savage fury. Out of the conception of the greatness of England's mission which Spenser found in London and struggled to realize in Ireland, and out of his chivalric devotion to this ideal and to the Queen who typified it, grew *The Faerie Queene*. It is the brightest expression of the ideal morality of the time, and in a sense is the epic of the English race at one of the great moments of its history.

Spenser in London and Ireland

Spenser and his contemporaries regarded moral purpose as essential to the greatest art; and with Spenser this purpose took the form of dealing with the old problem of the Renaissance—individual character in relation to the state. As he explained in his introductory letter to Ralegh, *The Faerie Queene* was to show forth the character of an ideal knight, in twelve books, each devoted to one of the twelve qualities of perfect chivalry. This exposition of private virtue was to be followed by a second poem, which should portray the virtues of the ideal knight as governor. In fact, Spenser wrote only six books, each of twelve cantos; and a fragment of a seventh. The first is given to the Red Cross Knight, who represents Holiness; the second to Sir Guyon, or Temperance; the third to Britomart, or Chastity; the fourth to Cambel and Triamond, or Friendship; the fifth to Sir Artegall, or Justice; the sixth to Sir Calidore, or Courtesy. These knights, as we learn from Spenser's introduc-

The Structure of "The Faerie Queene"

tory letter, are despatched on their various quests by Gloriana, Queen of Fairyland. In the course of their adventures appears from time to time the perfect knight, Arthur, who is himself in search of the Faerie Queene. The thread of the narrative is frequently interrupted by episodes. Moreover, the allegory, which should give unity to the whole, is inconsistent and complicated. It takes at times a political turn, and the characters, besides representing ideal qualities, refer directly to actual persons. Spenser explained: "In that Faerie Queene I meane glory in my generall intention, but in my particular I conceive the most excellent and glorious person of our soveraine the Queene." Belphœbe and Britomart also represent Elizabeth; Arthur is Leicester; the false lady Duessa is Mary Queen of Scots. In the fifth book the political state of Europe is presented at length, with Lord Grey as Artegall, France as Flourdelis, Henry IV as Burbon, Holland as Belge, and Philip II of Spain as Grantorto. This was but natural in an age in which politics were largely a matter of religion, and in which public and private conduct, like that of Sidney, Ralegh, and Essex, was still touched with something of the glamor of the chivalry which had passed away.

The moral seriousness which underlies the poem marks the great difference between *The Faerie Queene* and its Italian pro-

Spenser and Ariosto

totype. Spenser, like Wyatt and Surrey, was content to go to school to Italy, and he chose as the model for his great work the *Orlando Furioso* of Ariosto. Both Ariosto and Spenser deal with chivalry; but while Ariosto had merely the delight of the artist in the brilliant color which chivalry gave to life, with the easy contempt of the cynic for its moral pretensions, Spenser found in its persons and ideals a means of making goodness attractive. Ariosto pictures chivalric action because it is dramatic and exciting, not because he believes in it. Spenser deals with action because he must. His world is one which, according to the Platonic conception, is capable of being brought into harmony with an ideal. Naturally, to him the virtues which make for the effectiveness of the individual and the progress of the race are of supreme importance; and the opposing vices, idleness, gluttony, lechery, and, above all, despair, are the objects of his fiercest attack.

In details Spenser learned much from Ariosto; many passages he wrote in avowed imitation. His prevailing difference is in the greater richness and elaboration of his style, of which the verse form of *The Faerie Queene,* the Spenserian stanza, is typical. Ariosto wrote in *ottava rima,* that is, in stanzas of eight lines rhyming thus: *a, b, a, b, a, b, c, c,* Spenser used a more complicated stanza of his own, with rhymes arranged thus, *a, b, a, b, b, c, b, c, c,* the last line being an Alexandrine, a line of six feet. The brilliancy of the invention is shown by the fact that it adapts itself readily to the different demands of narrative, descriptive, and moral poetry; and that the poem sustains itself throughout its great length with little effect of monotony.

The Spenserian Stanza

Spenser had the great gift of the poet, the power to create the illusion of a different world, a world of magic where the imagination and the senses are satisfied. With all his morality, Spenser shared in the rich sensuous life which the Renaissance had thrown open to men. This immediate reliance upon the senses is one of the elements of reality which give greatness to his poem. *The Faerie Queene* is a long procession of figures, brilliant, fantastic, or terrible, which singly or in groups pass across an ever-varying, ever-wonderful landscape. And almost as marked as his feeling for form and color is his use of sound. His sensitiveness of ear is shown by the melody of his verse, so constant yet so varied; but there are also many passages in which he makes the music of nature an element of pleasure in his palace of art, notably in the description of the Bower of Bliss, in Book II, Canto XII. And more poignant sensuous appeal is not lacking. Altogether, Spenser has the resources of the whole world of sensation at command, and he never fails to heighten them with the illusions of his art. Of the color, the savor, the music of life, his poem is full—only the color is brighter, the taste sweeter, the music grander than any which mortal senses know.

Spenser's Art

And this world of imagined splendor is presented as the background of a steadily growing idea of righteousness, of heroic
goodness. The union of the two elements, sensuous
His and moral, seems at times to involve a naïve in-
Morality consistency. But Spenser belonged to an age when
it seemed not impossible that there should be some common
ground between the spirit of the Reformation and that of the
Renaissance. He was perhaps a Puritan; but, more fortunate
than Milton, he came before Puritanism had narrowed its view
of life to the single issue of salvation. There is, indeed, in
Spenser, as in many of his contemporaries, a note of melancholy, which suggests that the eternal contradiction of the joy,
of the present life by the threat of its hereafter was not unfelt.
The flowers are already lightly touched by the frost. But this
reminder that the time of free delight in the world of sense was
so short, its sunshine so threatened by the clouds of Puritanism,
makes its most signal product the more precious.

Spenser's latent Puritanism can be traced in the reserve with
which he usually treats passion. A franker, more unrestrained
abandonment to sensuous feeling marks such
George poems as Shakespeare's *Venus and Adonis* and
Chapman Marlowe's *Hero and Leander,* in which the tide of
Italianate eroticism reaches its height. Marlowe died before he
could complete the poem, which was finished by George Chapman (1559–1634). Chapman was one of the most considerable
literary men of the time. His appearance as a poet was somewhat late, his first important work being Ovid's *Banquet of
Sense* (1595). Three years later he published the last four
books of *Hero and Leander.* His famous translation of the *Iliad*
he completed in 1611, and the *Odyssey* two years later. Long
before this, in 1595, he had begun to contribute to the stage a
series of tragedies on subjects drawn from the history of France
during the time of Catherine de Medici's influence.

In his poetry, both original and translated, Chapman is rather
a man of the succeeding age than an Elizabethan. In him the
fulness and splendor of Elizabethan poetry, which had reached
their height in Spenser, tend to elaboration. conceit. and ob-

scurity, faults which unfortunately mar the greatest of his works, the translation of Homer. For the *Iliad* he chose the old English ballad metre. The sustained movement of this meas- *Chap-* ure gives it a certain likeness to Homer's hexameters; *man's* but, on the other hand, its facility and informality tend to produce a jog-trot familiarity in place of *Homer* Homer's rapidity and nobility. Moreover, Chapman is delib- erately indirect and fanciful, where Homer is direct and simple. Nevertheless, it was a circumstance almost as fortunate in its way for the English people as the series of happy accidents by virtue of which the English Bible became great literature, that the first translation of the noblest poetry of antiquity should have been made by one who, in spite of all his failings, was a true poet.

Spenser's *Faerie Queene* and Marlowe's and Chapman's *Hero and Leander* are perhaps the only long poems of the Elizabethan period which are still read. For the poets of that day, *Other* keenly interested as they were in artistic problems, *Poets* failed to solve the most essential of them; they never separated the proper subject-matter of poetry from that of prose. They versified not only history, but also politics, philos- ophy, geography, and science. Accordingly many of them, in spite of genuine poetic gift, have all but disappeared from view, hopelessly distanced in the race for immortality by reason of their bulk of unpoetical material. One of these leviathans is Michael Drayton (1563–1631). He devoted himself largely to history, his most characteristic work being his *Barons' Wars,* an account of the deposition of Edward II and the subsequent fall of Mortimer. Drayton was capable of gaining a genuine in- spiration from history, as is shown by his superb "Ballad of Agincourt," the ringing metre of which is preserved in Tenny- son's "Charge of the Light Brigade." Unfortunately he is known not by this spirited lyric, but as the author of *Poly- Olbion,* a huge poem in Alexandrines, containing a descriptive geography of England. Like Drayton, Samuel Daniel (1562– 1619) served the historical muse in a long narrative of the Wars of the Roses, and in his *Musophilus* attempted "A general defense of all learning." Among other poetic curiosities are William Warner's *Albion's England;* Lord Brooke's *Poems of Monarchy* and *Treatise on Religion;* Sir John Davies's *Nosce Teipsum,* a poem on human life and the immortality of the soul. Mistaken as such efforts in poetry seem to us, they must be thought of as part of that attempt already mentioned to give the English nation a literature worthy of its past and its high destiny.

It is not of these works, however, that we think when we speak of the glory of Elizabethan verse, but of the lyric quality which in nearly all the poets of the time flows some-

Lyric Poetry
where as a stream of living water, making glad even the waste places of their larger works. Almost every poet of note published his cycle of love songs and sonnets; besides Shakespeare's, Spenser's, and Sidney's sonnets, there are Daniel's *Delia,* Drayton's *Idea,* Lodge's *Phyllis,* and Constable's *Diana.* Many of them published series of eclogues in the manner of Spenser's *Shepherd's Calendar*—Drayton's *Shepherd's Garland* being among the most beautiful. But much more precious than this conventional and formal lyric art is the less premeditated singing of scores of poets, which was collected in the poetic miscellanies, such as *The Phœnix Nest, England's Helicon,* and Davison's *Poetical Rhapsody,* and in the song-books.

Many of the fugitive lyrics of the period are of doubtful attribution or altogether anonymous, but of the songs that can be assigned to any one writer a large share belongs to

Thomas Campion
Thomas Campion (1540–1613). Campion's verse is practically and honestly adapted to musical requirements, for the Elizabethan poet always conceived of a song as a thing to be sung. Like many of his contemporaries, Campion was stirred to rapture by sacred and profane love alike. Indeed, one of the peculiarities of the Elizabethan lyric poets is their mingling of sensuousness and piety—the latter not induced by fear of death, but by a trust in the Creator as frank and honest as was their delight in the world which He had made.

How common was the lyrical gift in the last years of Elizabeth's reign, is shown by the number of men of action who were also poets. The group of literary courtiers, of whom *The* Sidney was the chief, included a name as famous *Courtly* as his, that of Sir Walter Ralegh (1552?–1618). *Poets* Ralegh's place in literature belongs to him chiefly through his *History of the World,* one of the monuments of English prose in the next century; but the fragment of a long poem, *Cynthia,* the sonnet introductory to *The Faerie Queene,* and various lyrics like the reply to Marlowe's "Come, live with me and be my Love," and "The Lie," show that he possessed, in the words of a critic of the time, a vein of poetry "most lofty, insolent, and passionate." The tone of his poetry is on the whole singularly gloomy and bitter. His verses commemorate, for the most part, times of reaction and trouble in his checkered life, when he was thrown back by failure on the scepticism, distrust, and contempt that were fundamental in his nature.

Ralegh's rival both in glory and in misfortune, the Earl of Essex, the brother of Sidney's Stella, was himself a poet. Another member of the group of courtly poets was Sir Edward Dyer, a friend of Sidney's, who is remembered as the writer of the lines, "My mind to me a kingdom is." Still another was the Earl of Oxford.

The lyric and the drama must be counted as the great literary forms of the period, for these two represented truth to feeling and truth to life. Upon the rest of the literature of the sixteenth century, even including Spenser's wonderful poem, rested a blight of artificiality. The age was in the main one of conscious learning from masters, classical and foreign; of imitation; of uncertainty as to the principles and the uses of literature. The writers of the time were hampered by uncritical selection of material, by the requirements of conventions such as that which prescribed the pastoral, even by absurd theories such as that which tried to proscribe rhyme. Only in two directions, the lyric and the drama, did they win complete freedom, and in both they used it grandly.

CHAPTER V

The Renaissance

THE DRAMA BEFORE SHAKESPEARE

THE DRAMA was the most popular literary form of the Renaissance, as it was also the most powerful and spontaneous. It expressed, as no other literary product could have done, the manifold life of the Elizabethan age. Its chief glory is, of course, Shakespeare, but the school of dramatists from which Shakespeare proceeded was the result of a steady growth, prolonged through nearly four centuries. To trace the English drama from the beginning, we must go back even beyond the Norman conquest.

One familiar with the highly developed forms of tragedy and comedy which existed in ancient Greece and Rome might naturally presume that there was a continuous stream of plays derived from these throughout the Middle Ages; but this presumption would be entirely contrary to the facts. Both tragedy and comedy were native to Greece and flourished there with splendid natural vigor. In Rome, on the other hand, they were exotic, a literary fad or fashion introduced from Greece and cultivated only by a comparatively small circle of the upper classes. The popular stage entertainments of Rome were more like our revues, and as Roman culture decayed they became less and less dramatic and unspeakably indecent and immoral. As the Christian Church grew in power, its opposition to the stage became more effective. Plays were prohibited and actors proscribed in city after city throughout the Roman Empire.

The Decline of Roman Drama

Some three or four hundred years after the death of the Roman stage, there began to appear in the services of the church bits of drama, so brief and so simple dramatically that they may well have been composed with no clear appreciation of their significance. The earliest of these was a little scene representing the visit of the three Marys to the sepulchre of Christ on Easter morning, and their interview with the angels who are there to tell them that Christ has risen and will meet them in Galilee. The dialogue consists of only four sentences, but the little scene con- *Religious Source of the Drama* tains the essential elements of drama; it presents a story by means of actors who impersonate the characters of the story. Soon this scene was enlarged by the introduction of other characters and the expansion of the dialogue. Other scenes of Bible history were also dramatized as parts of the church service: the Visit of the Shepherds to the New-Born Babe at Bethlehem, the Visit of the Magi or Wise Men of the East, the Slaughter of the Innocents, and finally a whole series of scenes from the Old Testament. At first all these playlets were written in Latin and were sung as parts of the service of the church. But as they increased in number and in size they were first separated from the service, then translated into the language of the common people, and finally presented outside of the church—in the church porch, or the church yard, or some public square.

The earliest of these little plays was composed on the Continent about the year 900. The earliest of which we have any record in England belongs to the last third of the tenth century. The development of which we have just spoken occupied about four hundred years and *Cycles of Plays* by the beginning of the fourteenth century had resulted in vast plays or series of plays which were performed once a year in many of the principal towns of England. Four complete sets of these have been preserved to us. Three of these sets of plays— cycles they are commonly called—belonged to the cities of York, Wakefield, and Chester, from which they take their names. We have fragments also from Norwich, Newcastle-on-Tyne, and Dublin, and records of performances in many places. All these plays were alike in origin and structure and general content. They begin with the Creation and treat biblical episodes relating to the plan of salvation, including always the Creation and Fall of Adam and Eve, the Death of Abel, the Deluge, the Sacrifice of Isaac, the Prophecies of the Coming of Christ, the

Birth, Death, and Resurrection of Christ, and the Final Judgment. In their own day they were called Corpus Christi plays or Whitsun plays, from the time at which they were performed, or Craft plays, because they were performed by the crafts or trades-guilds of the towns. In France somewhat similar plays were called *Mystères,* and for the last hundred and fifty years it has been customary with scholars to call the English plays *Mysteries* or *Mystery Plays.*

In order to gain some idea of the appeal made by such plays to the audience for which they were intended, let us imagine *The Mystery Plays* ourselves for a moment in a provincial English town at the beginning of the fifteenth century, on the morning of Corpus Christi day. Weeks beforehand heralds have made the round of the city and the neighboring villages to announce the coming spectacle. The places where the cars or "pageants," which form both stage and dressing-room, are to stop, are crowded with the motley population of a mediæval city and countryside. The spectators of consequence occupy seats upon scaffolds erected for the purpose, or look on from the windows of neighboring houses, while the humbler folk jostle each other in the street. Soon the first pageant appears, a great box mounted on four or six wheels, and drawn by horses belonging to the masons' guild, which is charged with presenting the Creation of Eve and the Fall of Man. The curtain at the front and the side of the great box are drawn, revealing an upper compartment, within which the main action is to take place. On a raised platform sits enthroned a majestic person in a red robe, with gilt hair and beard, impersonating the Creator. Before him lies Adam, dressed in a close-fitting leather garment painted white or flesh-color. The Creator, after announcing his intention of making for Adam a helpmeet, descends and touches the sleeper's side. Thereupon Eve rises through a trapdoor, and Adam wakes rejoicing. Again the Creator ascends to his throne, and Adam withdraws to a corner of the pageant, leaving Eve to be tempted by a great serpent cunningly contrived of green and gold cloth, in which an actor is concealed. This monster, crawling upon the stage from below, harangues Eve with lengthy eloquence. Then follow the eating of the apple and the coming of God's angels, with gilt hair, scarlet robes, and swords waved and ridged like fire, to drive the pair from the garden into the wilderness, that is, into the lower compartment of the pageant, which is now uncovered to view. A trumpeter advances before the car, and sounds a long note in token of the conclusion of the play. The horses are re-harnessed to the car, and it moves off to the next station, to be replaced by others. These represent in turn Noah's Flood, given by the guild of water-merchants; the Sacrifice of Isaac, given by the butchers' guild; the Nativity, the Crucifixion, and so on in long procession, until the crowning spectacle of the Day of Judgment. The chief feature of spectacular interest in this last is Hell-Mouth, a great dragon's jaw belching flame and smoke, into which lost souls, dressed in black and yellow parti-color, are tossed by the devil—a most terrifying figure with a bright red beard, a hairy body, a hideous mask, horns, and a long forked tail.

Crude and even grotesque as much of this seems, the mystery play was, to the men of the Middle Ages, a very impressive thing. It not only appealed to their religious na- *Germs of* tures and to their love of spectacle; it also inter- *Regular* tested them profoundly from the human side. For *Drama* the authors were free to embellish the biblical story with episodes drawn from the common life of their own day. Even when these added episodes took a broadly farcical turn, nobody was shocked, any more than by the stone imps and monsters which grinned at them from the solemn shadows of their cathedrals. In the play of Noah's Flood, the patriarch causes first the animals to enter the Ark, then his sons and daughters-in-law; but when he comes to his wife, she objects. She does not relish being cooped up without her "gossips," and leaving these amiable women to drown. Remonstrances at last proving fruitless, Noah resorts to the argument of blows, and drives his scolding helpmeet into the Ark, to the great delight of the crowd. In the play of Abraham and Isaac, the yearning love of the old man for his little son, and the sweet, trustful nature of the boy, are brought home to us in such a way as to intensify the pathos of the moment when Abraham makes ready, at the Lord's command, to sacrifice the life which is dearest to him on earth. The pleading of the boy, the gradual overmastering of his fear of death by his pity for his father's anguish and his solicitude for his mother's grief, are rendered with touching truth.

> Therfor doo owr Lordes bydding,
> And wan I am ded, then prey for me:
> But, good fader, tell ye my moder no-thyng,
> Say that I am in another cunthre dwellyng.

In these episodes, and in many others which might be given, lie the germs of regular drama. Such humorous scenes as the quarrel of Noah and his wife constitute in reality crude little comedies out of which regular comedy could readily grow. In such tragic scenes as the Sacrifice of Isaac, the Slaughter of the Innocents, and the Crucifixion, the elements of noble tragedy were already present.

Another type of play very popular in England during the Middle Ages was the Miracle Play. It was a dramatization of

The Miracle Plays

the legend of some saint or martyr and presented either miracles performed by the saint or his relics or image, or the sufferings and death of the martyr. The earliest of these was the play of Saint Katharine, performed by the schoolboys of Dunstable about the year 1110, under the direction of their schoolmaster Geoffrey. The latest were perhaps the three performed at Braintree in Essex, from 1529 to 1533, to obtain funds for roofing the church. These plays must have given a better opportunity for free composition and for the development of realism in the presentation of character and incident than the Mysteries, but unfortunately no typical examples of this class of plays have come down to us, except the late fifteenth-century *Play of the Sacrament* and *The Life and Repentance of Mary Magdalen.*

Both Mysteries and Miracle Plays dealt primarily with the teachings of the church, theological or devotional. To complete

The Morality Plays

this teaching there was needed some exposition of the ethical side of religion, which deals with matters of conduct; and it was this ethical doctrine which the Morality Plays tried to bring home to men's minds. The Morality was a dramatized allegory. By means of personifications of such abstractions as the World, the

Flesh, Mankind, Mercy, Justice, Peace, the Seven Deadly Sins, Good and Bad Angels, Old Age, and Death, the Morality Plays attempted to represent, in a graphic way which would appeal to popular audiences, the conflict between sin and righteousness for the possession of the human soul. The early Moralities have an earnestness of purpose and a largeness of theme which make them no unworthy supplement to the mystery cycles. One of the most impressive is *Everyman,* which presents the soul (called Everyman) as summoned by Death to appear before God, and appealing to all the forces upon which he had relied in this life —Riches, Beauty, Strength, Friendship, Kindred—to go with and support him, but deserted by all except the despised Good Deeds. Little by little, however, their character changed: the treatment was narrowed so as to include only a single aspect of man's life; the characters became less and less abstract, and farcical matter was introduced to lighten the intolerably solemn tone. In most of the Moralities, from the middle of the fifteenth century onward, the principal character is one called by various names, but usually labelled the Vice. In some plays he is only a comic figure, dressed in the costume of a court-fool, carrying a sword of lath, and indulging in slapstick farce for the delectation of the crowd; but more often he has the additional function of master of all the intrigue, creating misunderstanding and strife by ingenious tricks or willful lies. By some critics he is supposed to survive in the fools of Shakespeare's plays, but these have little or nothing to do with the Vice; they are merely the court-fool or domestic fool of the time transferred to the stage. The Vice appears in such early plays as *Gammer Gurton's Needle* and *Ralph Roister Doister;* if he appears at all in the plays of Shakespeare and his successors, it is rather in the guise of the motiveless, intriguing villain than in that of the fool.

About the beginning of the sixteenth century, while the Moralities were yet in the height of their vogue, arose another form of play called loosely the Interlude—though *The Interludes* interlude was a term originally applied to a dialogue, and later to a play brief enough to be presented in the intervals of a banquet or other entertainment. These plays were very different in type and in origin. Some were derived from the Moralities themselves, some from French farces, some from *débats* (a French species of controversial dialogue) ; some from Latin school-plays, and some by the simple process of dramatizing an anecdote in prose or verse. In the late sixteenth-century play of *Sir Thomas More,* a band of strolling players is announced while Sir Thomas is dining, and they perform an Interlude before him and his guests. Usually these pieces had little action and required almost no stage-setting. For example, *The Four P's,* by John Heywood, "a newe and a very mery enterlude of a Palmer, a Pardoner, a Potycary and a Pedlar," is nothing more than an amusing series of speeches by the four characters, in which they vaunt their several callings, make themselves out very arrant rascals indeed, and by so doing satirize the society which they represent. The Interludes, as a whole, afford a curious illustration of the growing intellectual curiosity of the Renaissance, as well as of the popular devotion to the dramatic form.

Besides the Mysteries, Miracle Plays, Moralities, and Interludes, there were folk-plays of several kinds: wooing-plays and other jigs derived from ancient folk-customs; Robin Hood plays derived from the ballads; sword-plays and dances; and Christmas plays, or "mummings," faint survivals of primitive pagan religious ceremonies dating almost from the infancy of the human race, and still existing in remote corners of England, as may be learned from the charming account given in Thomas Hardy's *Return of the Native.*

Folk-Plays

Influences affecting the composition of plays as well as the costuming and staging of them flowed also from sources not strictly dramatic. From a very remote period, Christmas and other great festival seasons and occasions had been celebrated by elaborate and richly costumed disguisings, processions, tournaments, and other similar spectacles. As time passed these became more and more dramatic and in turn exercised a more and more powerful influence, direct and indirect, upon the drama and the stage.

Folk Festivals

In addition to these native elements in the formation of the drama, there was an important influence from without. This

influence was classical, and came from the great revival of
interest in Latin literature, which marked the beginning of the
Renaissance. It became the fashion in the sixteenth   *The
century for schoolmasters to present the comedies   Classical
of Terence and Plautus on the stages of grammar   *Influence:*
schools, with the students as actors. Before 1541   Comedy
Nicholas Udall, head master of Eton, wrote for his
boys a play, modelled after Plautus, called *Ralph Roister Doister,* the first regular English comedy. The importance of *Ralph
Roister Doister,* in furnishing English playwrights with an example of rapid dialogue and clear construction of plot, can
hardly be overestimated. The play is, however, an artificial production, with very little local color or truth to English life. The
next notable comedy, *Gammer Gurton's Needle,* was written by
an unidentified Mr. S. about 1560. Here the form of the Latin
model is still followed, but the main characters are manifestly
studied from real sixteenth-century peasants, and the background of English village life is given with much vivid realism.
Gammer Gurton's Needle is a great landmark in the history of
the drama in England, for it shows that English comedy had
been able to learn from classical models the lesson of clear construction and steady development of plot, without sacrificing
that broad and realistic comic spirit which had found expression
in the byplay of the Mysteries and Moralities, and which was
shortly to flower in such masterpieces of pure English humor as
Dekker's *Shoemaker's Holiday* and the tavern scenes in Shakespeare's *Henry IV.*

Upon tragedy the classical influence was even greater, and
the struggle on the part of the learned playwrights of the universities to impose the classical form upon English   *The
tragedy was more sustained. The classic drama-   Classical
tist selected for emulation was the Latin play-   *Influence:*
wright, Seneca. Between 1559 and 1581 ten trage-   Tragedy
dies of Seneca were freely translated. Coming into
the hands of English playwrights, just when they were eagerly
but blindly feeling their way toward a national type of drama,
these plays could not fail to impress them much, perhaps all the
more because the Senecan tragedy was directly opposed to that

kind of drama to which the English people naturally inclined.
Seneca's plays have very little stage action; important events,
instead of being directly represented, are merely reported on the
stage, by messengers or others. The tendency of English tragedy, on the other hand, was from the first to present everything
bodily on the stage, even the storming of cities, or battles between great armies, where the means at the disposal of the
actors were laughably inadequate to the demand. Latin drama,
again, is usually careful to preserve unity of time and place,
that is, to make all the action pass in a given locality, and to
cover no more than the events of a single day. English playwrights, on the contrary, had no hesitation in shifting the scene
to half a dozen different countries in the course of a single
play; and they thought nothing of introducing in the first act a
child who grew to manhood in the second act, and in the third
died and handed on the story, to be acted out by his sons in the
fourth and fifth. Classic drama also drew a very sharp line between comedy and tragedy, admitting no comic element into a
serious play. The English drama, on the contrary, from the
miracle plays down, set comedy side by side with tragedy; it
mingled the farcical with the august, the laughable with the
pathetic, as they actually are mingled in life.

University men and courtiers, while they shared the national
enthusiasm for stage-plays, were many of them repelled by the
"Gorboduc" crudities and absurdities of the native drama, emphasized as these were by the meager stage-setting.
They wished, therefore, to force the elegant but cold Senecan
model upon the public. In 1562 two young gentlemen of the
Inner Temple, Thomas Norton and Thomas Sackville, presented before Queen Elizabeth a play in blank verse called
Gorboduc, or Ferrex and Porrex, which was accepted as a kind
of manifesto on the part of the classicists, and as an example of
what could be done in handling a subject from British legend,
on the lines laid down by Seneca. *Gorboduc* has a chorus, made
up of four old men of Britain; messengers to report the action,
almost all of which takes place off the stage; and long epic and
lyric passages—what the French call *tirades*—to take the place
of stage action. It is a stately production, and deserves venera-

tion as the first regular tragedy written in English. Its classical form had little influence upon the native drama, just struggling into consciousness of itself, but its Senecan horrors were repeated *ad nauseam* in the learned and popular tragedies of the next generation.

In the end the native form won the day. It had on its side not only long tradition, but the overwhelming weight of popular taste. It was infinitely better suited to the robust imagination of the men of the English Renaissance, eager for excitement and craving strong sensations. Nevertheless, the apprenticeship of English playwrights to a foreign master, brief and incomplete *Effect of the Classical Influence* though it was, was invaluable. It taught them to impose some restraint upon the riot of their fancy; it showed them the beauty and artistic necessity of good structure; in a word, it brought form out of chaos. Nor did the influence wholly die, even when the battle had gone once for all in favor of the "romantic" drama. Marlowe, whose genius was intensely romantic, shows abundant traces of it; and the "Chorus" of *King Henry V, Romeo and Juliet,* and *Pericles,* is a slender remnant of the Senecan chorus. Ben Jonson, with a haughty disregard for popular applause, continued to wage a single-handed battle in favor of classicism, from the beginning of his career until twenty years after Shakespeare's death, when the Elizabethan drama was drawing near the end of its magnificent course.

We now stand on the threshold of those wonderful years (1580–1640) during which this course was run. England found herself, at the beginning of this period, quickened by three of the most potent influences which can *The Great Dramatic Period* affect the life of a nation: wide-spread intellectual curiosity, the beginnings of an intense religious ferment, and the pride of suddenly discovered national strength. The young "wits" who came up from the universities to London, tingling with the imaginative excitement of the age, seized upon the popular drama, crude though it then was, as capable of developing into a form of art concrete enough, flexible enough, exciting enough, to satisfy the life of the day with a reflection of its own diversity and splendor. The marvelously swift and many-sided dramatic development of the next thirty years (1580–1610) abundantly testifies to the sound instinct of the men who saw in the drama the best instrument for the expression of their swarming fancies.

The Elizabethan drama has been called "the drama of rhetoric," and from one point of view the description is exact.

The Drama of Rhetoric Not only were dramatists compelled by the meager stage-setting to indulge in long passages of description and soliloquy, but they also loved rhetoric for its own sake, as did their audiences. Nothing is more curious to our modern ears than the endless quibble and word-play, the elaborate conceits, the sounding and far-fetched phrase, in which all the Elizabethan dramatists, and Shakespeare as much as any, delighted to clothe their thought. Lyly's *Euphues* had a marked influence upon the early Elizabethan drama, for both good and evil. The taste for artificial language which it reflected and fostered filled the early drama with passages which are intolerably mannered; but, on the other hand, it refined poetic diction, and saved the drama from the rudeness by which a form of art popular in its appeal and humble in origin was naturally threatened.

As a dramatist Lyly occupies a peculiar position among Shakespeare's predecessors. He wrote, not for the regular dramatic companies, but for companies of child actors. These were choir-boys, one company attached to Saint Paul's Cathedral and known as the "Children of Paul's," the other attached to the Queen's chapel at Whitehall and known as the "Children of the Chapel Royal." To these child companies Lyly's tone and matter were admirably adapted. His plays are for the most part graceful adaptations of classic myths, so turned as to have a bearing upon some contemporary happening at court, yet moving always in an atmosphere of quaint and dream-like unreality. *Endymion* is an elaborate compliment to Queen Elizabeth, who appears in the play in the character of Cynthia, the virgin huntress. *The Woman in the Moon* is a veiled satire upon women in general, and Elizabeth in particular, written after

Lyly had been soured by years of fruitless seeking after court favor. Through the plays are scattered delightful lyrics, which Lyly was perhaps especially tempted to insert for the clear voices of the child players.

The child actors for whom Lyly wrote played at first exclusively in private—at court, or in the houses of the nobility. But the regular companies had already begun to establish themselves in the suburbs of London, and to erect permanent theatres. The first of these playhouses, known simply as "The Theatre," was built in Finsbury Fields, to the north of the city, by James Burbage, in 1576. It was at this playhouse *The Regular Companies and Their Theatres* that Shakespeare first found employment. Burbage's company, on the destruction of The Theatre, built the Globe, on the south bank of the Thames; and here, on the Bankside, other places of theatrical entertainment rapidly sprang up. Burbage built the Blackfriars as a winter theatre within the city limits. By the end of the century six theatres existed in the city and in the free lands or "liberties" adjoining, and there were five inns where plays were given.

Performances took place usually at three in the afternoon, and were announced by the hanging out of a flag and the blowing of trumpets. The theatres were round or octagonal structures, unroofed except for a shed or canopy over the stage. (The winter theatres, such as the Blackfriars, were entirely roofed in.) *Presentation of an Elizabethan Play* The stage extended out into the body of the house, was open on three sides, and was sufficiently elevated so that the main part of the audience, standing on the bare ground which formed the floor or pit of the theatre, could have a fair view. Persons who could afford to pay a higher price than the "groundlings" took advantage of the boxes built round the pit; and young gallants, for an extra fee, could have seats upon the stage itself, where they smoked their pipes, peeled oranges, cracked nuts, and often interfered with the performance by chaffing a poor actor, or by flirting ostentatiously with the fair occupant of a neighboring box. In accordance with the luxurious taste of the age in dress, the costumes of the actors were often very rich. All women's parts were played by boys; actresses were not seen in England until after the Restoration. It was long thought that the Elizabethans were practically without stage-setting, but there were certainly hangings painted to suggest the scenes of the play and more than adequate stage properties. It is true, however, that the dramatist was compelled, to a far greater degree than at present, to rely upon vivid poetic expression as the chief means of stimulating the imagination of his audience and of preserving the dramatic illusion.

While Lyly was at the height of his vogue, during the late eighties of the sixteenth century, a group of young dramatists were coming to the front whose appeal was not to the court but to the people, and whose plays were written for the popular theatres just described. The most important of these dramatists were Christopher Marlowe, Robert Greene, and George Peele, with Marlowe the undisputed leader. The non-dramatic work of these men has already been mentioned. Greene was by natural gift a prose romancer, Peele a lyric poet, and at least half of Marlowe's genius was of an epic kind. But the tendency of the age was so overwhelmingly in favor of drama that all three, in common with many of their fellows, were diverted into the channel of dramatic expression; and Marlowe achieved in this not wholly sympathetic medium all but the highest distinction.

Christopher Marlowe (1564–1593), one of the most striking figures of the English Renaissance, is the true founder of the

Christopher Marlowe

popular English drama, though he was himself an outgrowth of the long period of preparation which we have been traversing. He was born in 1564, two months before Shakespeare, in the old cathedral town of Canterbury. His father was a shoemaker; the boy was sent to Cambridge by a patron, who had noticed his quick parts. He graduated at nineteen; and four years later (1587) he astonished London with his first play, *Tamburlaine,* which he brought out with the Lord Admiral's Men, the rival company to the Lord Chamberlain's Men, whom Shakespeare joined.

In the brief and haughty prologue prefixed to *Tamburlaine*, Marlowe not only announced clearly the character of that play, but hinted at the program which he proposed to carry out in the future:

> From jigging veins of rhyming mother wits
> And such conceits as clownage keeps in pay,
> We'll lead you to the stately tents of war
> Where you shall hear the Scythian Tamburlaine
> Threatening the world with high astounding terms
> And scourging kingdoms with his conquering sword.

The "jigging veins of rhyming mother wits" is a sneer at the use of rhyme and awkward tumbling lines of fourteen syllables, which was customary with the popular playwrights of the time. For this "jigging vein" he proposes to substitute blank verse, which, though it had been employed since the example of Sackville and Norton, in *Gorboduc,* had not fully established itself. It is a sign of Marlowe's artistic insight that he should have recognized at once the value of blank verse for dramatic poetry; and we can see, beneath the surface of his words, a proud consciousness of his own power over this almost untried form of verse. Out of it he built that "mighty line" which astounded and fascinated his contemporaries, and his success with it fixed it firmly as the vehicle of serious drama henceforth. By his sneer at the "conceits" that "clownage keeps in pay," Marlowe showed his determination not to pander to the pit by means of vulgar comedy and horse-play, but to treat an elevated theme with seriousness. By the "stately tents of war," to which he promises to lead his hearer, he suggested the dignity and largeness of scope which he proposed to give to all his work. By the last three lines quoted above he foreshadowed his plan of giving unity to his dramas by making them revolve around some single great personality, engaged in some titanic struggle for power; and likewise of treating this struggle with the rhetorical splendor, the "high astounding terms," without which Elizabethan drama is now inconceivable. This program he carried out in the main with consistency.

Tamburlaine is a pure "hero-play." The Scythian shepherd conquers, one after another, the kingdoms of the East, forcing kings to harness themselves to his chariot, and carrying with him a great cage in which a captive emperor is kept like a wild beast. The huge barbaric figure of Tamburlaine is always before our eyes, and the action of the play is only a series of his triumphs. His character, half-bestial, half-godlike in its remorseless strength and confidence, dominates the imagination like an elemental force of nature, and lends itself admirably to those "high astounding terms" which fill whole pages of the play with thunderous monologues.

"Tam- burlaine"

Marlowe's second work, *Doctor Faustus,* is also a hero-play, but it is cast on more subtle lines. It is a dramatized story of the life and death oɪ mediæval scholar who sells his soul to the devil, in return for a life of power and pleasure. It embodied, in another form, the same aspiration after the unattainable which Tamburlaine had typified; and the story involved large questions of human will and fate, such as an imagination like Marlowe's loves to grapple with. It can hardly be said that the poet lived up to the possibilities of his subject. The play, as it has come down to us, is disfigured by comic passages of a coarse and tasteless sort, those very "conceits of clownage" which Marlowe had formerly declared war against. But even where the workmanship is poor, there is always something imposing in the design, and certain passages have hardly been surpassed for power and beauty. When Mephistopheles raises from the dead the spirit of Helen of Troy, Faustus utters one rapturous exclamation:

"Doctor Faustus"

> Was this the face that launched a thousand ships
> And burnt the topless towers of Ilion?

And at his death he starts up with the cry,

> Lo, where Christ's blood streams in the firmament!

These three lines alone stamp Marlowe as of the company of imperial poets.

Marlowe's third play, *The Jew of Malta,* is again a study of the lust of power—this time the power bestowed by great riches. Barabas, the old Jewish merchant of Malta, is the first vigorous sketch of which Shakespeare was to make in Shylock a finished masterpiece. The first two acts are conceived on a large scale, and carefully worked out; but after these Marlowe seems again to have fallen from his own ideal, and to have worked hastily and insincerely. Raw horrors accumulate on horror's head, and the play degenerates into melodrama of the goriest kind. Nevertheless, it shows a remarkable advance over *Tamburlaine* and *Doctor Faustus,* in the knitting together of cause and effect. Marlowe's growth in dramatic technic is still more strikingly apparent in his last play, *Edward II.* This is unquestionably his masterpiece, so far as play-making goes, though for the very reason that it discards rhetorical monologue for the rapid dramatic interchange of thought, it contains fewer quotable passages of pure poetry than any of the others. *Edward II* is an example of a form of drama which became very popular —the chronicle history. It served as a kind of text-book for a nation curious as to its past, and seeking therein lessons for its future guidance. One of the dangers most present to the mind of Englishmen of the sixteenth century was that of civil war; one of the mediæval themes that still fascinated the Renaissance mind was that of man highly placed in power, suddenly thrust down to misery and death. To these two facts we can attribute the interest of Marlowe and later of Shakespeare in the reigns of Edward II, Richard II, Henry VI, and Richard III.

"The Jew of Malta" and "Edward II"

Marlowe was killed in 1593, at the age of twenty-nine. There is something in the meteor-like suddenness of his appearance in the skies of poetry, and in the swift flaming of his genius through its course, that seems to make inevitable his violent end. He sums up for us the Renaissance passion for life, sleepless in its search and daring in its grasp after the infinite in power, in knowledge, and in pleasure.

A dramatist of whom little is known, but who is important as representing a type of drama which had great influence, is

Thomas Kyd. His plays, *The Spanish Tragedy*, acted about 1590, and the pre-Shakespearean *Hamlet*, are examples of

Thomas Kyd

what came to be called "the tragedy of blood." The appetite for crude bloodshed was persistent in Elizabethan audiences, and popular dramatists, in gratifying them, seem to have had a certain effrontery in defying the conventions of the classical drama in which untoward events take place off the stage.

Robert Greene was probably encouraged to write for the stage by Marlowe's success with *Tamburlaine*. Greene's best

Robert Greene

plays are *Friar Bacon and Friar Bungay* and *James IV*. The first of these has some country scenes, grouped about the character of Margaret, the fair maid of Fressingfield, which are in a fine healthy English tone. *James IV* has a clear and coherent development, unusual at this stage of the drama; one of its motifs, that of the persecuted woman who flees to the forest in the disguise of a page, was destined to become immensely popular in the later romantic drama, and to be used over and over again, with endless variations, by Shakespeare and Fletcher.

George Peele, like Greene, began his career by non-dramatic writing. His most characteristic early work consists of poems

George Peele

written for ceremonial occasions. One of these, "A Farewell to the Famous and Fortunate Generals of our English Forces," written on the departure of Drake and Norris, on the expedition to Portugal in 1589, is full of the new national spirit. Some of the lines have a superb ring of exultation and pride:

> You fight for Christ and England's peerless queen,
> Elizabeth the wonder of the world,
> Over whose throne the enemies of God
> Have thundered . . .
> O ten times treble happy men, that fight
> Under the cross of Christ and England's queen!

This passage well illustrates Peele's peculiar gift as a poet, that of making his lines *kindle* as they go. His best play, *David and Bethsabe,* is, considered merely as a play, poor enough; but it is full of passages, usually only a few lines long, which seem to take fire before a reader's eyes, and to burn with the softest yet most intense flame of the imagination. *David and Bethsabe* may be regarded as a late type of the mystery play, stripped of its sacred significance, and saturated with the sensuous grace and rich color of the Renaissance. Another play of Peele's, *The Old Wives' Tale,* is notable as having furnished Milton with the groundwork of *Comus.* It is a very crude but a very charming play; a sort of dramatized nursery-tale of giants, bewitched maidens, buried lamps, and magic wells, put forth with the occasional poetic grace and the aimless dreamy digression proper to the species.

Peele was out of place in drama, and never succeeded in writing a really good play. But his contribution to the development of dramatic style was nevertheless great. He succeeded in keeping much of the strength of Marlowe's "mighty line," while infusing into it a new tenderness and soft play of color. If Marlowe furnished the strength, Peele as surely furnished the sweetness, which went to make up the incomparable blend of Elizabethan drama at its great moment.

CHAPTER VI

The Renaissance

SHAKESPEARE

WILLIAM SHAKESPEARE was born on or about the 23rd of April, 1564, in the village of Stratford. He was the third child of John Shakespeare and Mary Arden. His mother was of gentle blood, and was possessed of some wealth by inheritance. His father, though a man of consideration in the

Shakespeare's Early Life

village, was of lower station, a dealer in various goods—corn, wool, meat, and leather. Until the age of fourteen the boy attended the Stratford grammar-school, where he picked up the "small Latin and less Greek," to which his immensely learned friend Ben Jonson rather scornfully refers. The better part of his education, a wonderfully deep and sure insight into nature, and a wide acquaintance with the folk-lore of his native district, he doubtless began to acquire in boyhood, by rambles through the meadows and along the streams of Warwickshire, stopping to chat with old crones over their cottage fires, or to listen to plowmen as they took their nooning. Only a few miles away was the picturesque town of Warwick, with its magnificent castle, to set him dreaming of the past. Within an easy day's walk lay Kenilworth Castle, the seat of Elizabeth's favorite, Leicester, and the historic town of Coventry, where one might still see mystery plays performed on certain festival days. Travelling companies of actors visited Stratford two or three times a year, and had to apply to Shakespeare's father for leave to play. At their performances young Shakespeare was doubtless sometimes present, drinking in his first impressions of the fascinating world of the drama. In these and other ways his mind found the food it needed, and stored up many a brave

108

image, which it should afterward evoke in the thick air of a crowded London theatre.

About 1578 the fortunes of his father began to decline, and Shakespeare was probably forced to leave school. In spite of the rapidly failing prosperity of the family, he was married at eighteen to Ann Hathaway, a young woman eight years his senior, the daughter of a peasant family of Shottery, near Stratford. That *Shake-speare's Marriage* the marriage was hasty and unfortunate has been conjectured from the general course of Shakespeare's life, as well as from various passages in the plays, which seem to have an autobiographic color. Certain it is that some time between 1585 and 1587 he left Stratford to seek his fortune in the capital. According to contemporary gossip, the immediate cause of his leaving was the anger of Sir Thomas Lucy, a local magnate, over a deer-stealing prank in which Shakespeare and other wild young blades of the village had engaged.

Outside the walls of London to the north, not far from where the road from Shakespeare's country entered the purlieus of the capital, stood the oldest of the London playhouses, called simply The Theatre. It had at the head of its company the famous actor James Burbage. Whether from accident or set intention, *Shake-speare in London* Shakespeare soon found himself connected with Burbage's company, where he made himself indispensable as actor and as retoucher of old plays. He continued with Burbage's company, as actor, playwright, and stockholder, when The Theatre was pulled down, and rebuilt as the Globe on the south bank of the Thames.

Of the external facts of Shakespeare's life in London we know few, and those few of small importance. We know of his friendship with the Earl of Southampton; of his friendly rivalry, in art and talk, with "rare Ben Jonson," the second dramatist of the age; of his careful conduct of his business affairs, and of his popularity as a playwright. Except for these few gleams of light, his external life is wrapped in mystery, and the very breadth and dramatic greatness of his plays prevent us from drawing any but the broadest inferences concerning his personal history.

The foundation of Shakespeare's substantial fortune may have been laid by a gift from his friend and patron, the young

His Return to Stratford; his Death
Earl of Southampton, to whom he dedicated his youthful poems, *Venus and Adonis* and *Lucrece;* but it was mainly by his earnings at the Globe and Blackfriars theatres that he was able to reinstate his parents in their old position of burgherly comfort, and to gain for himself a patent of gentility and the possession of the best homestead in his native village, with broad acres of land to add to its dignity. Hither, as he approached fifty, he retired, to spend the remainder of his life in country quietude, with his wife and his unmarried daughter, Judith. He died in 1616, at the age of fifty-two; and was buried in the old church by the Avon, where thousands of pilgrims have gone each year to read the words on his tomb, beseeching men to let his dust lie quiet in its grave.

The exact dates of production of Shakespeare's plays are often uncertain. The publication followed sometimes by years

The Dates of Shake-speare's Plays
the first appearance on the stage, and only seventeen of the thirty-seven were published in Shakespeare's lifetime. Sometimes there is external evidence in the form of a reference to the play in some contemporary document, or a reference in the text of the play to some contemporary event or publication. Certain peculiarities in Shakespeare's style tend to indicate the period of the work. For example, Shakespeare used rhyme much more freely in his earlier plays, and his blank verse was much more rigid. In his later plays he allows the thought to run on from one line to the next, admits extra syllables within the line, and sometimes concludes lines with small, unemphatic words. From these various indications it is possible to make out the chronology of Shakespeare's plays with approximate accuracy. Most critics divide his work into four periods: the first of experiment and external influence (1590–1594); the second of mature power in comedy and history plays (1595–1601); the

third of satire and tragedy (1601–1609), and the fourth of romance (1609–1611).

Shakespeare probably began his dramatic work, as has been said, by retouching old plays. The three parts of *Henry VI* are interesting specimens of his efforts in this direction. They also show so clearly the influence of Marlowe that it has been conjectured that he and *The First Period* Shakespeare worked together on the revision of the original plays. At all events, when Shakespeare essayed a history play of his own, in *Richard III,* he produced a portrait of elemental energy and evil pride which the creator of *Tamburlaine* and *Faustus* might have mistaken for his own handiwork. Another early play, *Titus Andronicus,* is written in a vein of raw horror calculated to outdo Marlowe at his hardest and cruellest, but Shakespeare's part in this crude melodrama is uncertain. Before this, however, he had made other experiments in quite different manners. His comedy, *Love's Labour's Lost,* sprang from his interest in the fanciful, artificial language to which Lyly's *Euphues* had given a tremendous vogue at Elizabeth's court and among all the young fashionables of London. Shakespeare's next play, the *Comedy of Errors,* was an experiment in still another direction. It is an adaptation of a Latin comedy, the *Menœchmi* of Plautus. The farcical plot turns upon the resemblance of twin brothers, in whose service are two clownish servants, also counterparts of each other. Shakespeare handles the intrigue with a skill which shows how rapidly he was growing in stage technic. Instead of following up his success in this kind, however, he turned immediately to try a new experiment, in the *Two Gentlemen of Verona.* This is a dramatized romance, adapted freely from one of the popular "novels" or love-romances of his day. The play, thin and youthful as it is, has more than a touch of real Shakespearean grace. The scene (Act II, sc. III) in which Launce, the clown, upbraids his dog for not joining in the family distress at his departure, is a piece of delightful nonsense, and the famous lyric, "Who is Silvia?" is the first of many exquisite songs which carry the spirit of the plays into the realm of music.

Shakespeare had now made rapid experiments in four directions: in *Richard III* he had essayed the chronicle or history
play, in *Love's Labour's Lost* the "conversation play,"
in the *Comedy of Errors* classical comedy, and in
Two Gentlemen of Verona romantic comedy. He
brought this first period of his work to a close with
two more efforts, wholly different in kind from the preceding
and from each other. These also are experimental, in the sense
that they enter realms before unknown to drama, but in both
conception and execution they are finished masterpieces. *A Midsummer Night's Dream* and *Romeo and Juliet* show that in several respects Shakespeare had now passed beyond his apprentice
state, and had attained the rank of master craftsman. The first
of these plays is thought to have been written in 1595; the
second, though it did not receive its final form until 1596 or
1597, was probably produced about the same time.

Earliest Master-pieces

A *Midsummer Night's Dream* is thought to have been written for some nobleman's marriage-festival, to take the place of
the masque or allegorical pageant traditional upon
such occasions. Theseus, Duke of Athens, and his
bride Hippolyta, in whose lofty figures the noble
bridal pair are perhaps shadowed forth, represent
love in its serene and lofty mood. About this central pair revolve three other groups, representing love in its
fanciful and grotesque aspects. The first group is made up of
the Athenian youths and maidens astray in the moonlight
woods, loving at cross-purposes, and played upon by Puck with
a magic liquor, which adds confusion to confusion in their
hearts. The second group consists of the fairy Queen Titania
and her lord Oberon; and here the treatment of the love-theme
becomes deliciously satiric, as it depicts the passion of the dainty
Queen for Bottom, the weaver with the ass's head. In the third
group, that of the journeymen actors who present the "tedious
brief scene of young Pyramus and his love Thisbe: very tragical
mirth," the love-theme is modulated into the most outrageous
parody. Then, poured over all, holding these diverse elements
in unity, is the atmosphere of midsummer moonlight, and the
aerial poetry of the fairy world.

"A Mid-summer Night's Dream"

A Midsummer Night's Dream, like the plays which preceded it, treats of love in a light and fanciful way, never more than half in earnest and usually frankly trivial. In *Romeo and Juliet* love ceases to be a mere sentiment, to be played with and jested over; it becomes a passion, tragical with the issues of life and death. Here for *"Romeo and Juliet"* the first time Shakespeare was really in earnest. The two young lives are caught in a fiery whirlwind, which sweeps them through the rapturous hours of their new love, to their death together in the tomb of Juliet's ancestors. The action, instead of being spread over months, as in the poem from which Shakespeare took the plot, is crowded into five days; and from the first meeting of the lovers until the end a sense of hurry, now ecstatic, now desperate, keeps the passion mounting in a swift crescendo. The play may not be a "tragedy of fate" in the Greek sense, but in it the poet for the first time draws characters with unerring deftness and power. The vulgar, garrulous nurse, the witty, hare-brained Mercutio, the vacillating yet stubborn Capulet, the lovers themselves, so sharply differentiated in the manner of their love, all these and a dozen minor figures have the very hue and gesture of life.

To this first period of production belong also Shakespeare's two longest poems, *Venus and Adonis* (1593) and *The Rape of Lucrece* (1594), both of which were dedicated to his patron, the young Earl of Southampton. They are both characteristic productions of the Renaissance, classical stories treated with an extravagant richness of decorative detail and a frank sensuousness for which Marlowe in *Hero and Leander* had *Shakespeare's Poems and Sonnets* given the model. To the same period probably belong most of the sonnets which were circulated in manuscript until their publication in 1609. In regard to their biographical significance there has been much the same sort of discussion as that attracted by Sidney's *Astrophel and Stella.* There is, however, this difference, that while the latter tells a straightforward story, whether true or not, Shakespeare's sonnets are addressed to several persons, and it is by no means certain that they make two, or even more, continuous sequences. They represent in part a relation of

the poet to two persons, "a man right fair," and "a woman colored ill," a relation marked by passion, jealousy, betrayal. Like
Sidney's sonnets, they show much of the artificial language of the
professional sonneteer, mingled with touches of such penetrating truth to human nature that they seem incontestably the result
of personal experience. Whatever their relation to the facts
of Shakespeare's outward life, they embody the emotion and
reflection of his inner world, expressed in lines of passionate pleading or protest, and again of grave, philosophical
eloquence.

Shakespeare's second period is marked by the success with
which he threw into dramatic form the rough masses of English
The　　　history which he found in the chronicle of Holin-
Second　　shed. In *Richard II* he returned to the subject of the
Period　　dispute for the crown among the descendants of Ed-
　　　　　ward III, and followed with three plays which contain some of his most remarkable work. These are *Henry IV* (in
two parts) and *Henry V*.

In planning *Henry IV,* Shakespeare followed the earlier
chronicle plays by interspersing the somewhat dry historic mat-
"Henry　　ter with scenes from the London tavern life of his
IV" and　　own day—a life full of racy humors fitted to afford
"Henry　　the desired comic relief. As the *genius loci* of the
V"　　　　tavern world, he created Falstaff, the fat old knight
　　　　　who helps Prince Hal (afterward King Henry V) to
sow his wild oats. The immortal figure of Falstaff holds the
prime place among the creations of Shakespeare's humor, as
royally as Hamlet holds his "intellectual throne." In *Henry V*
we see Shakespeare in a new and very engaging light; it is, indeed, hardly a figure of speech to say that we *see* the poet, for
in this play, as nowhere else in his dramas, does he speak with
the voice of personal enthusiasm. The manly, open character of
the King, and his splendid victories over the French, made him
a kind of symbol of England's greatness, both in character and
in achievement. The poet transfers to the battle of Agincourt
the national pride which had been kindled by the victory over
the Armada; and makes his play a great pæan of praise for the

island-kingdom. In the "choruses" introducing the several acts, and even in the speeches of the characters themselves, he expresses heart-felt patriotic emotion.

The schooling through which Shakespeare put himself in writing the English historical plays was arduous. He had to teach to the populace of his time the history of their country; it was therefore incumbent upon him to use the material without gross falsification, and at the same time to give it life and artistic form. To do this in the strictest of all forms, the drama, and with the meager resources of the Elizabethan stage, was a task which strengthened his art for the work he had still to do, especially for the four great tragedies, *Hamlet, Othello, Macbeth,* and *King Lear,* which mark the height of his achievement.

A further advance in Shakespeare's technical mastery is seen in *Julius Cæsar,* which was first acted in 1599. This play, falling in point of time between the "histories" and the *"Julius Caesar"* tragedies, partakes of the character of both. While Shakespeare keeps faithfully, even in details, to the story of the assassination of Cæsar and subsequent events, as he found it in Sir Thomas North's translation of Plutarch (1579), he imparts a large and vigorous movement to the dramatic action as a whole. The play might properly be called the tragedy of Brutus, since it closes with his death. On the other hand, even after the death of Cæsar in the third act, his spirit continues to animate the action, in the speech in which Antony calls on the very stones of Rome to rise and mutiny, in the apparition of the spectre which accosts Brutus in his tent, and in the fulfillment of its threat at Philippi. There are, indeed, two tragic figures in the piece—Cæsar, like Lear, conniving at his own ruin, but returning in the might of his indomitable personality to complete his work of subjugating the world; Brutus, like Hamlet, the instrument of a cause which he follows relentlessly through doubts, hesitations, public mistakes, and private griefs, until he is overwhelmed by forces which his own act has set in motion.

While writing the histories, Shakespeare had found time to

write the tragi-comedy *The Merchant of Venice,* and two brisk farces, *The Taming of the Shrew* and *The Merry Wives of Windsor.* The last, said to have been written at the request of Queen Elizabeth, who desired to see Falstaff in love, is a hasty and rather perfunctory piece of work, written mostly in prose. It is quite otherwise with the first-mentioned play. In *The Merchant of Venice* we see for the first time the presiding presence of the moral sense, and a fundamental seriousness, betraying itself even in the deeper and more religious harmonies of the verse, which mark the poet's advance over *A Midsummer Night's Dream* and *Romeo and Juliet.* Shylock was probably suggested by Barabas in Marlowe's *Jew of Malta,* but the subtle characterization in its humanizing of a figure usually regarded with mingled contempt and fear shows how far Shakespeare had transcended Marlowe's influence. In Portia Shakespeare drew his second great portrait of a woman. She is an elder sister of Juliet, less vehement, with a larger experience of life, a stronger and more practised intellect.

"The Merchant of Venice"

In the three comedies which followed, written between 1598 and 1601, he drew three other unforgettable female portraits, Beatrice in *Much Ado About Nothing,* Rosalind in *As You Like It,* and Viola in *Twelfth Night.* And, grouped around them, what a holiday company of delightful figures!—Benedick, "the married man," trying in vain to parry the thrusts of Beatrice's nimble wit; the philosophical Touchstone, shaking his head over the country wench Audrey, because the gods have not made her poetical; the meditative Jaques (a first faint sketch, it has been said, of Hamlet), with his melancholy "compounded of many simples"; Sir Toby Belch, champion of the ancient doctrine of cakes and ale, and ginger hot in the mouth; the ridiculous nincompoop Sir Andrew Aguecheek; the solemn prig and egotist Malvolio, smirking and pointing at his cross-garters; Maria, "youngest wren of nine"; and the clown Feste, with his marvelous, haunting songs. All these and more move here in a kaleidoscope of intense life, spiritualized by an indescribable poetic radiance.

The "Joyous Comedies"

It was for long the fashion to suppose that some time about 1601 Shakespeare passed from the happy, care-free mood, reflected in *As You Like It* and *Twelfth Night,* into a period of sorrow and gloom, expressed in the bitter, cynical comedies, *Measure for Measure* and *Troilus and Cressida,* and the great tragedies, *Hamlet, Macbeth, King Lear.* It was even plausibly suggested that the mysterious influence of the Dark Lady of the sonnets was the cause of this change. It is now clear that no such personal explanation is necessary for the change in the spirit of Shakespeare's work. A growing taste for satire and tragedy on the part of the playgoing public in the early years of the seventeenth century brought about similar alterations in the work of the other dramatists. The difference between the tone of the two periods, however, is so marked as to make the division a useful one. *The Third Period*

The note of the new period is struck by the comedies. In *Troilus and Cressida* Shakespeare drew a picture of faithlessness in love, a picture so cynical, so fierce in its bitterness, that it is almost impossible to think of it as the work of the hand which drew Juliet, Portia, and Rosalind. In *All's Well That Ends Well* he told in dramatic form a story from Boccaccio's *Decameron,* a typical Italian novella, showing how a woman by adroitness and enterprise—in short, by that supreme human force which the Italians called *virtu*—makes herself mistress of the person and then of the love of her husband. It is to be credited to Shakespeare's skill that the strong-minded heroine, Helena, has throughout the sympathy of the audience. In *Measure for Measure* Shakespeare struck at the hypocrisy of a man high-placed in office and posing as a severe moralist, who nevertheless yields to the very sin he punishes most ruthlessly in others. *The "Dark and Bitter Comedies"*

In *Hamlet,* the first of the four great tragedies which form the "captain jewels in the carcanet" of the master's work, we have the spectacle of a sensitive and highly intellectual youth, endowed with all the gifts which make for greatness of living, suddenly confronted with the *"Hamlet"* knowledge that his father has been murdered, and that his mother has married the murderer. Even before the revelation comes, Hamlet feels himself to be living in an alien moral world, and is haunted by dark misgivings. When his father's ghost appears to him, with its imperative injunction to revenge, Hamlet takes his resolution instantly. His feigned madness, an element of the drama retained by Shakespeare from the old story whence he drew the plot, is the first device which Hamlet hits upon to aid him in his dangerous duty. In spite of the endless debate concerning the reality of Hamlet's madness, there is no room for question in the matter. Not only is he perfectly sane, but his handling of the difficult situation in which he finds himself is in all points swift and masterful. He gives up his love for Ophelia because he cannot take her with him into the dark pass which he is compelled to enter; and the scathing satire which he pours out upon her when he fancies her in league with Polonius and the King to play the spy upon him, gathers its force from the greatness of the renunciation he has made. His scheme for proving the King's guilt beyond a peradventure, by means of the strolling players, is consummated with ingenious skill. His dealings with Rosencrantz and Guildenstern are those of a gifted man of action, to whose resolute will thought is a swift minister. His purpose is always firm; and it is one of the ironies of circumstance that Hamlet has come to stand in most minds for a type of irresolution. This misunderstanding of the character is largely due to the exaltation of excitement in Hamlet, which causes his mind, even in the moment when he is pursuing his purpose with most intentness, to play with feverish brilliancy over the questions of man's life and death; which makes his throbbing, white-hot imagination a meeting-place for grotesque and extravagant fancies; and which leads him, so to speak, to cover the solid framework of his enterprise with a wild festoonery of intellectual whim, to envelop it in fitful eloquence, swift and subtle wit, contemptuous irony, and mordant satire. Yet this is merely the byplay of his mind, the volatilized substance which escapes under the heat of excitement. In the midst of it he remains perfect master of himself and of his means, a supremely rational, competent, and determined being, a prince and master of men, dedicated irrevocably to ruin in the moral chaos where the "cursed spite" of his destiny has thrown him. With a miraculous art Shakespeare has depicted this character, not fixed in outline, but changing and palpitant as life itself, so that it constantly eludes our definition, and seems forever passing from one state of being into another, in the passion of its struggle.

Othello has a certain affinity to *Hamlet* in that here also the hero's soul is thrown into violent perturbation by the discovery of evil poisoning the very sources of his life. In Othello's case the pathos and the tragedy are *"Othello"* heightened by the fact that the evil exists only in the hero's imagination, into which we see the demon-like Iago pouring, drop by drop, the poison of suspicion. Othello is not by nature jealous; he everywhere shows himself "of an open and free nature," incapable of petty suspicion. But when Iago, working cautiously, with diabolic skill, has at last convinced him that Desdemona is false, the fatal rage which seizes him is a murderous reaction from the sickening blow of disillusion. The real centre of gravity in the play is Iago, with his "honest" manners, his blunt speech, his downright materialistic philosophy, his plausible zeal in his master's service; underneath it all his real nature lies coiled like a snake, waiting for a chance to sting.

King Lear is often put at the apex of Shakespeare's achievement, and by many judges at the head of the dramatic literature of the world. The story was as old as Geoffrey of *"King* Monmouth, the mediæval chronicler, and, like so *Lear"* many of the themes which Shakespeare handled, had already been made the subject of a play, a crude effort by some nameless playwright during the experimental stage of Elizabethan drama. Here, as was his constant custom, Shakespeare followed the main lines of the story given him, and incorporated into his grand edifice every bit of usable material from the building of his predecessor. Here, too, as always in Shakespeare, if we pierce to the core of his meaning, the real tragedy is a spiritual one. Lear is an imperious nature, wayward by temperament, and made more incapable of self-government by long indulgence of his passionate whims. At the opening of the play we see him striving to find a refuge from himself by surrendering all his wealth and power in exchange for absolute love. The heart of the old King demands love; love is the element upon which it subsists, and age, instead of abating this hunger, has made the craving more imperious. He demands love not only in the spirit but in the letter, and thrusts his youngest daughter, Cordelia, from him with cruel brusqueness, when she refuses to use the terms of extravagant hyperbole to describe her affection. This brusque and hasty spirit of the King precipitates upon his old head the enmity of his remaining daughters, Goneril and Regan. Before he has recovered from the shock of Cordelia's defection, this awful pair of daughters lay bare, little by little, their monstrous souls to their father's gaze. As in *Othello*, the result of the revelation is to unhinge for the sufferer the very order of nature. As if in sympathy with the chaos in Lear's soul, the elements break loose; and in the pauses of the blast we hear the noise of violent crimes, curses, heart-broken jesting, the chatter of idiocy, and the wandering tongue of madness. The sentimentalist's phrase, "poetic justice," has no meaning for Shakespeare. The ruin wrought in the old King's heart and brain is irreparable, and the tornado which whirls him to his doom carries with it the just and the unjust. The little golden pause of peace, when Lear and Cordelia are united, is followed by the intolerably piercing scene in which he bears her dead body out of the prison, muttering that they have hanged his "poor fool." The consequences of rash action, heartlessly taken advantage of, were never followed out to a grimmer end.

In *Macbeth* Shakespeare depicted the passion of ambition working in a nature morally weak, but endowed with an intense poetic susceptibility. Macbeth is a dreamer and a sentimentalist, capable of conceiving vividly the goal of his evil desires, but incapable either of resolute action in attaining them or of a ruthless enjoyment of them when attained. By the murder of the King, Macbeth is plunged into a series of crimes, in which he persists with a kind of faltering desperation, until he falls before the accumulated vengeance,

"Macbeth"

material and ghostly, raised up to punish him. As in *Antony and Cleopatra* we are shown the slow degeneration of the hero's character under the slavery of sense, so here we behold the break-up of a soul under the torture of its own sick imagination. The ghost of Banquo, shaking its gory locks at Macbeth from its seat at the banquet table, is a symbol of the spiritual distemper which results from the working of a tyrannous imagination upon a nature morally unprovided. The witch-hags who meet Macbeth on the heath are concrete embodiments of the powers of evil, summoned from the four corners of the air by affinity with the evil heart of the schemer. Shakespeare did not, of course, consciously strive after symbolism in these things. It does not seem impossible, indeed, that he believed in ghosts and witches, as did the great mass of men in his day, from King James down. It is certain that he was interested in his story, here and elsewhere, as a piece of life rather than as a moral symbol; his work is full of symbols simply because life itself is full of them.

Beside Macbeth Shakespeare has placed a woman who possesses all the masculine qualities which the hero lacks, but who is nevertheless intensely feminine in her devotion to her lord's interest, and in her inability to endure the strain of a criminal life after his support has been withdrawn from her. Her will, though majestic when in the prosperous service of her husband's ambition, collapses in sudden ruin when he fails to rise to the responsibilities of their grim situation. Macbeth's feebler moral substance crumbles piecemeal; but the firm structure of his wife's spirit, as soon as its natural foundation is destroyed, falls by instant overthrow.

Toward the conclusion of this period Shakespeare turned again to Roman history for subject-matter, treating it with the tragic force and the psychological insight that characterize the plays already discussed. In *Antony and Cleopatra* he showed the character of a great Roman general, crumbling before the breath of Eastern luxury and sensuality, personified in Cleopatra, "serpent of old Nile." In *Coriolanus* he explored the psychology of the aristo-

Later Roman Plays

cratic leader too proud to flatter "the mob," the fickle, many-headed multitude, and ultimately destroyed by them.

In two of the later plays of this period Shakespeare reverted to his early practice of working in collaboration. One of these, *Timon of Athens*, is thoroughly in the mood of this period, a kind of summing up of the pessimistic view of life in the person of Timon, the misanthrope, the character which constitutes Shakespeare's contribution to the play. The other play written in collaboration, *Pericles, Prince of Tyre*, anticipates in a measure the romantic character of Shakespeare's last work. The success of this piece, indeed, announced the rather general revival of romance on the London stage which succeeded the vogue of tragedy and satire.

"Timon" and "Pericles"

The plays which mark the closing period of Shakespeare's life are pure romances, conceived in a spirit of deep and lovely serenity, and characterized by a silvery delicacy, a tender musing touch, which is new in the poet's work. The first of the plays of the last period is *Cymbeline*, with its exquisite picture of Imogen and the woodland scenes between Arviragus and the young princes. Then followed *A Winter's Tale*, based upon Robert Greene's *Pandosto*—which, like Lodge's *Rosalynde*, had in part an Arcadian background. The wooing of Prince Florizel and Perdita has come, like the scenes in the Forest of Arden, to represent the very soul of pastoral romance. But the supreme exercise of the magic power of the master is seen in *The Tempest*. The background of the play was suggested by the wrecking of a vessel bound for Virginia, on the Bermudas, as narrated in *A Discovery of the Bermudas, otherwise called the Isle of Divels* (1610), and numerous other pamphlets. Thus Shakespeare had the greatest stimulus to the imagination of the age, the appeal of the new world beyond the sea, to work with. And to meet the possibilities of his theme he summoned all his powers: the grace that had created the fairy world of *Midsummer Night's Dream*, the lyric passion that had breathed through Juliet's lips on her bridal morning, the drollery and

Plays of the Fourth Period

wit that had set the laughter of centuries billowing about Falstaff, the titanic might that had sent a world crashing on the head of Lear—all meet together here, but curbed, softened, silvered down into exquisite harmony.

The Tempest was one of the plays acted at the wedding of Princess Elizabeth, daughter of James I, to Frederick, Elector Palatine, in 1613, and was long thought to have been written for that occasion. Although it was probably written a little earlier, and was followed by *Henry VIII*—a chronicle play in which Shakespeare collaborated with Fletcher—it may in a true sense be called Shakespeare's farewell to his art. When scarcely fifty years of age, with his genius at its ripest, and every faculty of his mind in full play, he laid down his pen forever—as Prospero, at the end, abjures his magic, breaks his wand, and drowns his book "deeper than did ever plummet sound." One is tempted to indulge the fanciful parallel still further, and to think of Ariel, the delicate and potent sprite whom Prospero sets free, as the spirit of Imagination, now released from its long labors in the master's service.

The common opinion that Shakespeare was unappreciated by his own generation is only partly true. If other evidence were lacking to prove the esteem in which he was held, *Appreciation of Shakespeare in His Day* his material prosperity would be sufficient to show his high popularity at court and with the theatregoing public. But there is witness that his genius was in tolerable measure recognized. His great antitype and rival, Ben Jonson, whose burly good sense was not prone to exaggeration, and who perhaps never quite conquered a feeling of jealousy toward Shakespeare, wrote for the first collective edition of the plays, published in 1623, a eulogy full of deep, in places even passionate, admiration; and afterward said of him in a passage of moving sincerity: "I did love and honor him, on this side idolatry, as much as any." The most significant hint we have of his personal charm is in the adjective which is constantly applied to him by his friends, "gentle," a word also often used to describe his art, in allusion evidently to its humanity and poetic grace.

The awe inspired by the almost unearthly power and richness of Shakespeare's mind is apt to be deepened by the knowledge that the noble plays to which English-speaking *His Care-* races point as their greatest single achievement, *lessness* were thrown into the world carelessly, and would *of Fame* have perished altogether if the author of them had had his way. During his lifetime they were printed only in cheap quartos, often pirated, sometimes taken down by shorthand from the lips of the players, or patched up from prompters' manuscripts dishonestly acquired. He does not mention his plays in his will. Not until seven years after his death did a collected edition appear (known as the First Folio), and then only because of the piety of two of his actor-friends. There are reasons for this apparent neglect. The printing of a play while it was still actable was disadvantageous to the company whose property it was, and Shakespeare had probably made over his plays to his company as they were produced. Notwithstanding these considerations, we are yet filled with astonishment. We see in the working of the master's spirit not only the vast liberality but the startling carelessness of nature, who seems with infinite loving pains to create her marvels, and then to turn listlessly away while they are given over to destruction.

CHAPTER VII

The Seventeenth Century

SHAKESPEARE'S CONTEMPORARIES
AND SUCCESSORS IN THE DRAMA

IN THE preceding chapter we considered Shakespeare alone in order that by isolating his work we might better see its absolute qualities. We must now turn to those playwrights who worked at the same time and in many cases side by side with him, and try to get some notion of the wonderful variety of the drama during its period of full bloom. And we must trace briefly the steps by which the drama declined, both by inner decay and outward opposition, until, in 1642, at the beginning of the Civil War, the doors of the theatres were closed, not to open again until the Restoration, eighteen years later.

The most commanding figure in the group of Shakespeare's dramatic contemporaries is Ben Jonson (1573–1637). Although brought up in humble surroundings—his stepfather was a bricklayer—he was sent to Westminster School *Ben* and possibly to Cambridge, and he ultimately became *Jonson* one of the most learned men of his time. As a young man he went upon one campaign with the English army in Flanders, where (as he afterward boasted) he fought a duel with a champion of the enemy in the sight of both armies, and in the classic manner took his arms from him. The incident is highly characteristic of Jonson's rugged and domineering character. As he served the Flemish soldier, he afterward served the luckless poets and poetasters who challenged him to a war of words.

After returning to England, he began to work for the theatres. His first important play was *Every Man in His Humour* (1598), in which Shakespeare is known to have acted. He engaged in a series of literary quarrels, in the course of which he wrote several elaborately satirical plays, *Cynthia's Revels, The Poetaster*, etc., to revenge himself upon his rather puny enemies. His four masterpieces appeared between 1605 and 1614. They are *The Silent Woman, Volpone, The Alchemist,* and *Bartholomew Fair*—all called comedies by him, though the second is biting satire, and the last pure farce. He also wrote *Sejanus* and *Catiline*, two massive tragedies learned and documented from Roman history. For many years after his appointment by James I as poet-laureate, he supplied the King with court-masques, mythological allegories delicate in fancy and rich in lyric tracery, which were acted at Whitehall by gorgeously costumed lords and ladies, amid magnificent stage-settings contrived by the King's architect, Inigo Jones, with the lyrics set to music by the King's musician, Ferrabosco.

Jonson came to the front as a dramatist at a time when one set of tendencies in the Renaissance, those in the direction

Jonson's Classicism

of imitation of the classics, were asserting themselves strongly against the practice of unlimited individualism and freedom in art which we call romantic. Sidney had already shown his scorn of plays on the native English model, and he was followed by a group of poets and critics who attacked all forms of romantic literature in satires and epistles, written in imitation of the Latin poets. By the beginning of the seventeenth century this reaction had gone so far that, as we have seen, Shakespeare was probably influenced by it to desert chronicle history and romantic comedy for tragedy and satire. Jonson led this movement in the drama. He took up the line of development which had been begun in *Gorboduc, Ralph Roister Doister,* and other plays written under the influence of Seneca and Plautus. The classical reaction was short-lived, and the romantic temper reasserted itself, as we see in the later plays of Shakespeare, but Jonson refused to bend. All his life he fought battles against what he judged to be the ignorant preference of the public for the romantic form. Not only did he stand out for the classical "unities" observed by Seneca, but he made war upon the fantastic and extravagant qualities of romantic imagination, and labored to supplant them by classical sanity and restraint.

In one respect at least the classical quality of Jonson's comedies gave them an interest that is permanent, and an influence that was far-reaching. One difference between the *Jonson's* romantic spirit and the classic is that the former *Realism* tends toward escape from the actual conditions of life, while the latter tends to work realistically within them. This appears when we compare *Twelfth Night* or *The Tempest* with *Every Man in His Humour* or *Bartholomew Fair*. Shakespeare's comedies are full of glancing imagination and irresponsible fancy; Jonson's move in the hard light of every-day London. This realism, the vivid picture of London life, makes his comedies among the most informative plays of the period. From Jonson's comedies alone it would be possible to reconstruct whole areas of Elizabethan society; a study of them is indispensable if one would know the brilliant and amusing surface of the most colorful era in English history. At least one of Jonson's comedies, too, gives this close and realistic study of manners with a gayety and grace fairly rivalling Shakespeare; *The Silent Woman* is one of the most sparkling comedies ever written, full of splendid fun, and with a bright, quick movement which never flags.

Another peculiarity of Jonson's art is hinted at by the title *Every Man in His Humour*. The word "humor" was a cant term in his day,[1] equivalent to "whim" or "foible." He *Jonson's* hit upon the device of endowing each one of his *Humors* characters with some particular whim or affectation, some ludicrous exaggeration of manner, speech, or dress; and of so thrusting forward this single odd trait that all others might be lost sight of. Every man, in other words, should be "in his humor." This working principle Jonson extended afterward in his two great comedies, *Volpone* and *The Alchemist*. In *Volpone* he studied, not a foible or whim, but a master-passion, the passion of greed, as it affects a whole social group; in *The Alchemist* he made an elaborate study of human gullibility.

[1] Note Bardolph's use of the word in *Henry IV* and *Henry V*.

There is doubtless something mechanical in this method of going to work according to a set program. Shakespeare also has devoted whole plays to the study of a master-passion—in *Othello* that of jealousy, in *Macbeth* that of ambition. But he does this in a very different way from Jonson; with much more variety, surprise, and free play of life. Jonson has, as it were, a thesis to illustrate, and exhibits one character after another, as a logician presents the various parts of his argument. In other words, he always, or nearly always, lets us see the machinery. But what he loses in spontaneity, he gains in intellectual unity and in massiveness of purpose.

Jonson's lyric gift, for its delicacy and sweetness, was conspicuous even in the Elizabethan age, when almost every writer was capable of turning off a charming song. The best known of his lyrics are "Drink to me only with thine eyes," and "See the chariot at hand here of love"; of both these the old-time music has fortunately reached us. Like Shakespeare, he inserted exquisite gems of song into the lively action of his plays. "Queen and huntress, chaste and fair," from *Cynthia's Revels*, is a perfect example of classic beauty in lyric form, in contrast with the romantic glamor of Shakespeare's "Take, oh, take those lips away," from *Measure for Measure*, or "Full fathom five thy father lies," from *The Tempest*.

His Lyric Gift

Jonson was also a critic of great sanity and force. His volume of short reflections upon life and art, entitled *Timber*, reveals the solidity, aggressiveness, and downright honesty of his mind. These qualities of aggressive decision and rugged honesty enabled him to hold for a quarter of a century his position of literary dictator and lord of the "tavern-wits." The tavern was for the seventeenth century what the coffee-house was for the eighteenth, a rallying-place for literary men; and Jonson is almost as typical a tavern figure as Falstaff. His "mountain belly and his rocky face," his bluff domineering personality, ruled by royal right the bohemian circle which gathered at "The Mermaid" or "The Devil and St. Dunstan," where the young fellows of the "tribe of Ben" heard words

Jonson as a Literary Dictator

So nimble and so full of subtle flame
As if that every one from whence they came
Had meant to put his whole wit in a jest,
And had resolved to live a fool the rest
Of his dull life.[1]

Here took place those famous wit-combats between Jonson and Shakespeare described by Fuller under the simile of a sea-fight; Jonson, slow of movement and "high built in learning," being likened to a great Spanish galleon, Shakespeare to an English man-of-war, swift to strike and dart away, confounding the enemy with agility and adroitness.

The qualities for which Ben Jonson demands admiration are rather of the solid than the brilliant kind. In an age of imaginative license he preached the need of restraint; in an age of hasty, careless workmanship he preached the need of sound construction and good finish. He was a safe guide; if the younger dramatists of his day had heeded him, the drama would not have gone on, as it did, deepening in extravagance and license until it died, so to speak, of dissipation.

In the dramatists next to be discussed we shall see the opposition between romantic and classical elements such as are represented in the works of Shakespeare and Ben Jonson. On the whole, the romantic forces were in *Decadence* the ascendant, but one classical legacy—the satiric *of the* presentation of real life in what is called the *Drama* Comedy of Manners—is due to Jonson's influence. This tendency grew stronger as the century advanced, and many of the Jacobean dramatists yielded to it in their later days. Both the romantic and the realistic elements were used in a way that justifies us in applying the term decadence to the drama of the period. There was a straining for effect, a deliberate search for sensation in the romance, and an unbelievable coarseness in the realism. And in both there were an absence of moral standards, a disregard of moral values, that marked a great falling off from the plane of Shakespeare and Jonson. It was in

[1] Verses entitled "Master Francis Beaumont to Ben Jonson."

part for this reason that the Puritans attacked the drama, and wholly for this reason that it had no strength to resist the attack.

Next to Shakespeare and Ben Jonson the most impressive body of plays is that which goes under the names of Beaumont and Fletcher, though in fact these two collaborated in only a few, the rest being the work of Fletcher alone or in partnership with others.

Beaumont and Fletcher

Francis Beaumont (1584–1616) and John Fletcher (1579–1625) are, in Lowell's phrase, among "the double stars of the heavens of poetry." Fletcher, the elder of the two, was the son of a Bishop of London. From the worldly circle in which his father moved, he gained an unusual insight into court life. None of Fletcher's fellows knew so well as he how to paint the hollow inside and the exquisite outer finish of courtly manners. The official residence of his father, the episcopal palace at Fulham, however, lay amid beautiful river and forest scenery. To the country memories gathered here in boyhood he gave expression later in the pastoral play of *The Faithful Shepherdess*, as well as in the songs with which his dramas are richly interspersed.

Their Intellectual Partnership

At the Mermaid tavern, among those "sealed of the tribe of Ben," he met the man whose name is inseparably linked with his own. Francis Beaumont, five years younger than Fletcher, was about twenty-one at the time of their meeting. After their partnership began, tradition says that they lived together on the Bankside, sharing everything, even their clothing, in common. They entered into a singularly effective intellectual partnership; one mind supplied what the other lacked, to produce a result of full and balanced beauty. Beaumont had the deeper and more serious imagination, and the greater constructive power; Fletcher excelled chiefly in lyric sweetness, rhetorical fluency, and many-colored sentiment. Beaumont died in the same year as Shakespeare (1616); his co-laborer lived until the accession of Charles I, in 1625.

Among the plays jointly written, the best are perhaps *Philaster* and *The Maid's Tragedy*, both produced about 1611. The theme of *Philaster* is a common one in the old drama, the same, for instance, as that of *Cymbeline*, namely, the unfounded jealousy of a lover, and the unswerving faithfulness of his lady, who follows him in the disguise of a page. The treatment shows the tendency of later romanticists to push a situation to extremes, beyond all credibility and reason, but the play contains perhaps more passages of pure poetry than any other by Fletcher and his collaborators. *The Maid's Tragedy* is dramatically more powerful. The soul of the hero is torn between his sense of personal honor and his sense of the inviolable divinity of the King who has shamefully wronged him. Here again there is that straining after intensity which marks the dramatic decadence. The search after intensity is, to be sure, often present even in the Elizabethan drama at its freshest and strongest. We have only to think of the typical characters and situations of Marlowe and Shakespeare to realize this fact. But the intensity of the later drama is more feverish and artificial. As the obviously "strong" situations began to be exhausted, dramatists made excursions into the strained and the exceptional in order to find novel matter. Of this tendency *The Maid's Tragedy* is an example, as well as of the moral laxity that marked much of these authors' work. The moral values are not preserved as in Shakespeare, but are apt to be blurred or distorted in the endeavor for piquancy and novelty. But it would be a great mistake to conceive of Beaumont and Fletcher in this merely negative light without holding in mind their great positive qualities. They are "absolute lords of a goodly realm of romance"; and the plays that go under their common name are perhaps not equalled in splendor and charm by any single body of Renaissance drama outside that of Shakespeare himself.

After Beaumont's death Fletcher collaborated with Massinger and others, his later work showing a tendency toward the comedy of manners enlivened by witty dialogue, for which his facile genius fitted him.

Of the life of Thomas Dekker almost nothing is known. He was born about 1570 and is lost sight of in 1632. He was one

Thomas Dekker of the dramatists whom Jonson attacked in *The Poetaster,* and he did not let the quarrel drop. He is, indeed, a central figure in the group of writers who, in the generation after Shakespeare, kept alive the bohemian tradition of his predecessors, with their scandals and quarrels, their freedom of life and art. But his individuality is so distinctly reflected in his plays that he seems one of the most definite figures of his time—a sunny, light-hearted nature, full of real, even if somewhat disorderly, genius. *The Shoemaker's Holiday,* written before 1599 and perhaps his earliest play, is his best. It is a study of London apprentice life, woven about a slender but charming love-story. The master-shoemaker, Simon Eyre, and his wife, Margery, are drawn with broad, exuberant humor. *The Shoemaker's Holiday* has in it all the morning gladness and freshness of the Elizabethan temper. Dekker wrote one other charming play, *Old Fortunatus,* a dramatized fairy-tale of the wishing-hat and exhaustless purse. It is a chaotic piece of work, but its incoherence rather adds to than detracts from the dreamy nursery-tale effect. The later work of Dekker, most of it done in collaboration with other playwrights, is much more serious, showing that he, too, felt the reaction from joyous romance which brought Shakespeare into his period of tragedy.

Thomas Heywood is another dramatist whose history is almost a blank. He was probably born about the same time as

Thomas Heywood Dekker, and seems to have been alive in 1641. His life therefore spans the whole period of the drama from Marlowe to Shirley. He was immensely productive, declaring himself to have had "a whole hand or a main finger in two hundred and twenty plays." He must in fairness be judged as a dramatic journalist, in an age when the theatre tried to do what the newspaper and the lecture hall now accomplish, rather than as a dramatist in the more dignified and permanent sense. In one direction, however, Heywood achieved mastery, namely, in the drama of simple domestic life. His most famous play of this nature is *A Woman Killed with Kind-*

ness. Here for once Heywood handled his subject with noble simplicity, with deep tragic effect, and with a truth and sweetness of moral tone which justify Charles Lamb's saying that Heywood is "a prose Shakespeare." In the drama of contemporary adventure, Heywood is also successful, though in a less supreme degree. Perhaps the best example of this type of play to be found among his works is *The Fair Maid of the West,* in which there are some capital vignettes of life in an English seaport town, as well as some delightfully breezy melodramatic sea-fighting.

Thomas Middleton (1570–1627) was a man of much larger powers. By his frank contact with life as it is, and by his continual effort to see life in its plainness and entirety, he attained at last to a grasp and insight which place him among the great names of the English stage. He had no university training, but was entered at Gray's *Thomas Middleton* Inn in 1596. His life about the law-courts gave him an intimate knowledge of the shady side of the metropolis, which was of great service to him when he began to write realistic comedies. Of these the best are *A Trick to Catch the Old One,* and *The Roaring Girl,* written with Dekker. His transition from comedy to tragedy is marked by the very interesting play *A Fair Quarrel,* in which the noble seriousness of certain scenes and the fine dramatic ring of the verse herald the approach of his complete maturity. It was between 1620 and his death in 1627, that is, when over fifty, that he wrote the two plays, *The Changeling* and *Women Beware Women,* in which his sturdy powers show themselves fully ripened.

Both *The Changeling* and *Women Beware Women* are unpleasant in plot, and marred by the obtrusion of crude horrors. They go back in fact to the type of drama called the "tragedy of blood," of which Thomas Kyd's *Spanish Tragedy,* Marlowe's *Jew of Malta,* and Shakespeare's *Tragedy of Blood* *Titus Andronicus* are examples. Indeed, *Hamlet* and *Lear* are really in plot tragedies of blood, though spiritualized out of all inner resemblance to the species. Middleton, however, uses horror for its own sake and for emphasis on situations already strained and painful. But both are studded with fine poetry, fine in feeling and supremely fine in expression. Middleton learned, better than any of Shakespeare's fellows, the secret of the master's diction. Without imitating the Shakespearean manner, he handles language, at his best, with the same superb confidence, in his comic prose as in his serious blank verse.

In John Webster we encounter the phenomenon of a really great poet—one who in sheer power of expression comes near-

John Webster

est to Shakespeare of all the men of that generation except Middleton—devoting himself to singularly repellent subjects and themes. His two greatest plays, *The White Devil* and *The Duchess of Malfi,* push the devices of physical horror to their farthest limit. They show the tragedy of blood in its most developed form, and employ all the grisly paraphernalia of the madhouse, the graveyard, and the shambles, as well as the agencies of moral terror, to wring from the drama all the crude excitement it is capable of giving. But his power of conceiving character and still more the surprising poetry, now wild and stormy, now tender and lyrical, now pungently epigrammatic, which he puts into the mouths of his people, have kept his fame intact. Of the two plays named above, *The Duchess of Malfi* is the finer. Webster not only shows in it a much firmer stagecraft than in his earlier effort, but also reveals powers of gayety and playfulness, and an understanding of the heart hardly to be looked for from one who voluntarily elected the tragedy of blood as his medium. At least two of the characters, the Duchess of Malfi and her husband Antonio, are robust and healthy figures, who even under the stress of torture keep their broad, quiet humanity.

In John Ford (1586–1640?) the search after abnormal situations reached its height on the moral and spiritual side, as it

John Ford

had done in Webster on the physical side. Ford was a man of means, not compelled to write hastily in order to gain an uncertain livelihood from the stage. His plays are good in structure and his blank verse is excellent. But while his work shows no sign of degeneration in respect to form, his deliberate turning away from the healthy and normal in human life, and the strange morbid melancholy which shadows his work, betray very plainly his decadent tastes. His best plays are *The Broken Heart, 'Tis Pity She's a Whore,* and the belated history-play, *Perkin Warbeck.*

Early in the history of the drama, war began between the actors and the Puritans. In 1576 we hear of strolling companies being kept out of London by Puritan law-makers; *War be-* and when the first theatres were erected they were *tween* placed in the suburbs to the north, and in the "lib-*Actors and* erties," or exempt lands, across the Thames in *Puritans* Southwark. Under Queen Elizabeth's protection the actors grew strong enough to enter the city; and as long as her hand was at the helm, the Puritans did not assert themselves very vigorously. But when James I came to the throne, with his lack of personal dignity, his bigoted dictum of the divine right of kings, his immoral court full of greedy nobles from Scotland and Spain, the Puritan party gained rapidly in aggressiveness. The thing which the Puritans hated most under the sun, after copes and crucifixes, was the theatre, because it was in the theatre that the "lust of the eye and the pride of life" found fullest expression. Naturally, therefore, as the Puritan disapproval grew more severe, the dramatists drew away from the London burgesses, and appealed in the tone and matter of their plays more and more to the taste of the court— a fact to which the deterioration of the drama was in considerable part due.

It has been thought from certain passages in the plays of Philip Massinger (1583–1640), as well as from their general tone, that he was at heart a Puritan, not in the nar-*Philip* row political sense, but as the term applies to men *Massinger* of high moral ideals, to whom the things that make for righteousness are the first concern, and the shows and passions of life, by comparison, unreal. By some ironic fate Massinger was born a dramatic poet at a time when the stage, to live at all, had to appeal to the jaded taste of a court. He spins his plots of worldly passion and ambition, but without real interest in them. When wickedness is required he forces his characters duly into wickedness, and in the effort to overcome the bias of his mind makes them very wicked indeed. But it is when he has a chance to treat some theme of self-sacrifice, of loyalty, of gratitude, of unworldly renunciation in the interest of an ideal, as in *The Great Duke of Florence, The Virgin Martyr,* and *The Maid of Honour,* that he shows himself to be a real poet, and handles his subject with placid dignity and power. He also achieved at least one great success in comedy, in his *New Way to Pay Old Debts.* The character of the miser and extortioner in this play, Sir Giles Overreach, holds a place among the classic figures of the English stage.

The great procession of dramatic poets which begins with Marlowe comes to an end with James Shirley (1596–1666). In

James Shirley him we detect a constant attempt to eke out his own scanty invention by imitating his predecessors. His work has, in other words, the "literary" quality, as distinguished from original inspiration. This criticism, however, applies chiefly to his tragedies. In comedy he followed the realistic type known as the comedy of manners, and brought it very near to the style of the Restoration. In *Hyde Park* (1637) it would take only a slight change here and there to convince us that we are among the gallants and dames of the time of Charles II, or even of Queen Anne. The dialogue is in prose, the language perfectly colloquial and realistic; instead of the long monologues and rhetorical passages of the earlier romantic comedy, there is a quick bandying of the shuttlecock of talk. The tone is that of a frivolous, gossipy age, not much in earnest about anything, and given over to the cult of fashion.

When we remember that *Hyde Park* was written on the eve of the most tremendous upheaval which English society has ever witnessed, this frivolity of tone becomes significant. It marks the point of extreme departure from the Puritan temper. So long as the dramatists were in earnest, even in the portrayal of those things which to the Puritan mind were abominations, there was a bond of sympathy. What the Puritan could not stand was the gay insincerity, the airy trifling with the essential facts of life, such as Shirley's comedies exemplify. After the election of the Long Parliament, the Puritan party quickly came to a reckoning with the theatre. In 1641 appeared a pamphlet called *The Stage-Players' Complaint,* which says pathetically: "The High Commission Court is down, the Star-Chamber is down, and some think Bishops will down; but why should not we then that are far inferior to any of these, justly fear that we should be down too?" In September of 1642 an ordinance of both Houses of Parliament closed the theatres throughout the kingdom. They were not reopened until eighteen years later, when the reins of power had fallen from the dead hand of Cromwell, and Charles II ascended the throne from which his father had been led to the scaffold.

CHAPTER VIII

The Seventeenth Century

NON-DRAMATIC LITERATURE BEFORE
THE RESTORATION

I

THE non-dramatic literature of the early seventeenth century shows in broad markings the same opposing forces which we discover in the drama—on the one hand, assertion of the right of the individual to do as he pleased in life and in art; on the other, insistence on the importance in both of order, restraint, and adherence to standards. On *The Seventeenth Century* the one hand the romantic impulse tended to outdo itself in a quest for novelty and excitement of experience; and on the other, a classic taste was gaining strength, partly by virtue of reaction from the excesses of the romanticists. It is characteristic of the confused and shifting currents of the time that there is little unity of practice between art and life. The Cavalier poets, some of whom, in conduct, were true children of the pagan Renaissance, tended toward the restrained and conscious artistry of Ben Jonson, while the religious poets, whose lives were saintly, wrote with an extravagance that seems the extremity of willfulness and whim. It was indeed an age of uncertainty and transition, both in literature and in political and social life.

There are many striking differences between this age and the great era which went before. In the first place, the national *Differences from the Age of Elizabeth* unity, of which devotion to Elizabeth was the symbol, was already impaired by the time of her death. But under her successor, the Scottish King, James I, party strife between the supporters of the Throne and those who maintained the rights of the people through Parliament, between those who held to the authority of the established church and its bishops and those who demanded a more democratic form of church government or even entire freedom of the individual in matters of conscience, increased, until in the next reign it resulted in civil war. In the second place, the great conceptions, philosophical, political, and social, that had marked the preceding age, gave way and disappeared. One of these was that of an ideal union between the interests of the Renaissance and those of the Reformation, between the claims of this world and those of the other, which, in the case of Spenser and Sidney, made for a complex though spiritualized humanism. Instead, we have in the seventeenth century, on the one hand, the gallant but light-hearted Cavaliers, and on the other the earnest but narrow-minded Puritans—followers of two utterly opposed views of life. In the absence of great conceptions, human ambition and human character became less splendid and unified. In place of Marlowe, Shakespeare, and Ralegh, we have Jonson, Bacon, and Donne. Milton and the great Puritans are obvious exceptions, but Milton illustrates the falling off from Spenser's generous views of life and character. Above all, the imaginative appeal of the new world beyond the sea had become dulled; America was no longer a field for Ralegh's search for Eldorado, or a background for *The Tempest,* but rather a place for colonization and trade. There were, it is true, compensations. If human character was less grandiose than among the Elizabethans, it was much more self-conscious and curious. If the men of the seventeenth century were less expansive, at least they left much fuller record of themselves, in biography and autobiography. If the world was less spacious and less inviting to bold exploration and speculation, it was, on the other hand, a tempting field for exploitation and patient investigation. If Eldorado disappeared, trade expanded, and while imagination grew weary, experimental science was rapidly developing. A deepening consciousness of unscrupulous economic and social competition is reflected in the harsh satirical comedies of Jonson, Middleton, and Massinger. Here again the transcendental vision of the Puritan and his absorption in the eternities are an obvious exception, but it is one of the paradoxes of the period that the Puritan, with all his intense concern with the other world, should have had so strong a practical sense of the values of this one.

A final difference between the two periods is apparent everywhere in the literatures of both, in drama, sermon, and song. The age of Elizabeth was full of enthusiasm and confidence in this world and the next. The early seventeenth century was overcast with shadows and forebodings, melancholy and depression. To pass from one to another is like passing from a plain bright with sunshine into the twilight of a forest. The clouds gathering in the political sky, the theology of Calvin and the Puritans, with its dark view of man's future, and the severe economic depression at the end of the century account sufficiently for this change, but it is perhaps further to be explained as one of those periodic reactions of human nature, which, weary and sated with joy and excitement, readily falls prey to melancholy and fear. The difference is easily seen in the late drama, where shapes of evil and horror haunted men's fancy, and in essays and sermons, where death challenges love as the theme calling out the highest eloquence. Even the attempts of comedians and Cavaliers to counteract this prevailing mood by hectic gayety and persistent trifling, are witnesses to its power, and often are followed by a reaction to religious contemplation, ecstatic or gloomy.

Of the two great transition figures who stand between the two periods, Ben Jonson has already been considered. The other, Francis Bacon, was born in 1561, three years before Shakespeare. His father was Lord Keeper of the Great Seal to Elizabeth, and his uncle was Lord Burghley, Elizabeth's prime

Bacon; His Life and Character minister. He was thus marked out by birth for a public career, and he threw himself into the strife for place with the keen intellectual zest and the moral ruthlessness characteristic of the Renaissance courtier. Owing to the opposition of his jealous uncle, he got little preferment under the Queen, but under James I he rose steadily through various offices to be Lord Chancellor, with the title of Viscount Saint Albans. In this position he supported his dignities by a magnificence of living altogether out of proportion to his legitimate income. In 1621 he was impeached before the House of Lords for bribe-taking and corruption in office, found guilty, and subjected to fine and imprisonment. He retired, a broken and ruined man, to his country seat of Gorhambury, and spent the remaining five years of his life in scientific and philosophic pursuits, still, however, keeping up a show of his former magnificence, with an unconquerable pride which caused Prince Charles to exclaim: "This man scorns to go out in a snuff!"

For Bacon's personal character it is impossible to feel much admiration. He exhibited nearly all the unworthy traits of the Renaissance politician—greed, ostentation, heartlessness, and lax public morality. But it is equally impossible not to admire his spacious and luminous mind and the devotion to pure thought which constituted his deeper life. In a letter written at the outset of his career he says proudly: "I confess that I have as vast contemplative ends as I have moderate civil ends, for I have taken all knowledge to be my province." In pursuance of this majestic program he sketched out a work which was to have been called the *Instauratio Magna,* the object of which was to present a complete view of knowledge as it existed in his day, and a guide for its further progress. Of the six books only one, the *Novum Organum,* reached anything like definite shape; the *Advancement of Learning* (written also in Latin as *De Augmentis Scientiarum*) was intended as an introduction to the whole. The instrument by which science was to complete its conquest was the application of the principle of inductive reasoning, by which the observation of specific facts leads up to the formulation of general laws. In the old scholastic system of deduction, general principles had been first laid down, and particular facts had been explained in the light of these principles. Since theory rested on an insignificant number of experiences, the explanations flowing therefrom had for the most part been fantastic and untrue. The change in method was due to come with the rise of the scientific spirit; it is Bacon's glory that he saw and expressed the vital need of change, before the scientific spirit had yet grown conscious of itself.

His Intellectual "Programme"; the Inductive System

All this marks Bacon as a man of the Renaissance, exulting in the grandest conceptions and undaunted by the most daring

"The New Atlantis" enterprises. This mood he never entirely lost. One of his last writings was a sketch of an ideal commonwealth beyond the sea, called *The New Atlantis*. It resembles Thomas More's *Utopia*, with perhaps this significant difference—that while the inhabitants of Utopia owe their happy state to the operation of reason, those of Atlantis owe theirs to study and research. The development of airplanes, submarines, telephones, and refrigeration is foreshadowed in their experiments. The centre of their commonwealth is a learned academy known as Solomon's House, and they despatch vessels yearly to bring them reports of inventions and discoveries throughout the world. A more practical Utopia this than St. Thomas More's, and yet a dream.

Bacon's interest in the world of human experience is shown by the *Essays*—"dispersed meditations," he calls them, or memo-

The "Essays" randa. As such they were first published (then ten in number) in 1597, in the author's thirty-sixth year. Fifteen years later they were issued again, with additions; and in 1625, a year before Bacon's death, they were put forth in final form, the essays now numbering fifty-eight, the old ones revised and expanded. It is clear that their charm grew upon Bacon, and lured him, half against his will, to put more and more serious effort into the manipulation of a language for which he had no great respect, yet of which he is one of the greatest masters.

Even in their finished state the *Essays* are desultory and suggestive, rather than coherent or exhaustive. They deal with

Their Subject-Matter many subjects, of public and private conduct, of statecraft, of the nature and value of human passions and human relations; and with these graver themes are intermingled others of a lighter sort, on building, on the planting of gardens, on the proper mounting and acting of masques and pageants. To a modern understanding those which deal with the deeper questions of human nature are apt to seem somewhat worldly-wise or even cynical. We get from them little real vision, few generous points of view; everywhere we find wit, keen observation, grave or clever mundane judgments. Now and again, to be sure, Bacon startles us with an altogether unworldly sentence, such as this: "Little do men perceive what solitude is, and how far it extendeth; for a crowd is not company, and faces are but a gallery of pictures, and talk but a tinkling cymbal, where there is no love." Some of the essays, such as that entitled "Of Great Place," show an unworldly wisdom which, if applied to Bacon's own life, would have made it a very different thing. Not seldom, too, he lifts the curtain upon that inner passion of his existence, the thirst for intellectual truth, which made him noble in spite of the shortcomings of his character. "Truth," he says, "which only doth judge itself . . . is the sovereign good of human nature." But for the most part their mood is one of practical and sometimes cynical worldliness. Of "Marriage and Single Life" he says: "He that hath wife and children hath given hostages to fortune."

Bacon shows himself in the *Essays* to be a consummate rhetorician. He made for himself a style which, though not quite flexible and modern, was unmatchable for pith and pregnancy in the conveyance of his special kind of thought. Though a devoted Latinist, and using a *Their Style* highly Latinized vocabulary, he saw the structural differences of the two languages so clearly that, when the bulk of English prose was being written in loose sentences of enormous length, he struck out at once a short, crisp, and firmly knit sentence of a type unfamiliar in English. He rejected the conceits and overcrowded imagery of the euphuists, but knew how to light up his thought with well-placed figures, and to give to it an imaginative glow and charm upon occasion, contrasting strongly with the unfigurative style of Ben Jonson, who represents in his prose the extreme revulsion from euphuism. For the student of expression Bacon's essays are of endless interest and profit; the more one reads them the more remarkable seem their compactness and their nervous vitality. They shock a sluggish attention into wakefulness as if by an electric contact, and though they may sometimes fail to nourish, they can never fail to stimulate.

A more thoroughly characteristic figure of the period is Jonn Donne (1572–1631). Born of a family with a strong Roman Catholic tradition, he was sent while very young to Trinity College, Cambridge, and later, as a member of Lincoln's Inn, read voraciously and lived gaily. He went with Essex on the expedition to Cadiz in 1596, an enterprise that ranked for daring with the repulse of the Armada, and later became secretary to Lord Keeper Egerton. Before this he had written a body of poetry which, though not published until after his death, circulated in manuscript, and like Wyatt's and Surrey's, had an immense influence on younger poets. Part of this poetry is in such classical forms as satires, elegies, and epistles—though its style has anything but classical smoothness—and part is written in lyrical forms of extraordinary variety. Most of it purports to deal with life, descriptively or experimentally, and the first thing to strike the reader is Donne's extraordinary frankness and penetrating realism. The next is the cynicism which marks certain of the lighter poems and which represents a conscious reaction from the extreme idealization of woman encouraged by the Petrarchan tradition. In his serious love-poems, however, Donne, while not relaxing his grasp on the realities of the love-experience, suffuses it with an emotional intensity and a spiritualized ardor unique in English poetry.

John Donne

This astonishing new poetry took the literary cliques of London by storm. But as striking as the novelty of subject-matter and point of view is that of its form. Instead of the unvarying succession of sonnets, Donne gives nearly every theme a verse and stanza form peculiar to itself; and instead of decorating his theme by conventional comparisons, he illumines or emphasizes his thought by fantastic metaphors and extravagant hyperboles. In moments of inspiration his style becomes wonderfully poignant and direct, heart-searching in its simple human accents, with an originality and force for which we look in vain among the clear and fluent melodies of Elizabethan lyrists. Sometimes the "conceits," as these extravagant figures are called, are so odd that we lose sight of the thing to be illustrated, in the startling

His Use of Conceits

nature of the illustration. With him love is a spider which, dropped into the wine of life, turns it to poison; or it is a cannon-ball:

> By him, as by chain'd shot, whole ranks do die;

or it is a devouring fish:

> He is the tyrant pike, our hearts the fry.

This fashion of conceitful writing, somewhat like euphuism in prose, appeared in Italy and Spain also. Its imaginative exuberance has its parallels in baroque architecture and painting.

About 1601 Donne fell passionately and seriously in love with the niece of the Lord Keeper, married her, and was imprisoned for a time by his angry father-in-law. *Donne's* For several years after his release he and his grow- *Later Life* ing family were dependent on friends and patrons; then, at the persuasion of influential admirers, he entered the church in 1615, where he rose rapidly to be Dean of Saint Paul's, and the most famous preacher of his time. After the death of his wife in 1617 he fell more and more under the shadow of a terrible spiritual gloom. Even in his early *Songs and Sonnets,* there are touches of macabre imagination, as in "The Relic":

> When my grave is broken up again
> Some second guest to entertain
>
> .   .   .   .   .   .
>
> And he that digs it spies
> A bracelet of bright hair about the bone,
> Will he not let us alone?

As his life drew near its close, he had himself sculptured in his winding-sheet, standing upright in his coffin, and this monument was placed above his grave in Saint Paul's.

Donne's religious poems and his magnificent sermons reached astounding heights of subtlety and intensity. The searchings of soul and the horrified fascination with which he contemplated the processes of dissolution and the awful event of death are rendered with amazing intellectual ingenuity and imaginative power. His prose style, involuted and ornate, cumulative and Ciceronian, is one of the more glorious monuments to the spirit of the early seventeenth century.

George Herbert (1593–1633), like Donne, published no poetry in his lifetime. After a youth spent in preparation for a court career, and some years of disappointed waiting for favors, he entered the Church. Once within the pale of the religious life, he felt the full force of that spiritual agitation and awe which sooner or later overtook many serious minds in the first half of the seventeenth century. After two years of devoted labor as a parish priest at Bemerton, near Salisbury, he was stricken with a mortal malady. On his death-bed he handed to Nicholas Ferrar a bundle of manuscript, asking him to read it, and then to use it or destroy it, as seemed to him fit. The volume was published in 1633 under the title of *The Temple,* in allusion to the scriptural verse, "In His temple doth every man speak in His honor." It is a winning account of the joy Herbert found in subjecting himself and his powers to the service of God.

George Herbert

Herbert pushed even further than Donne the use of conceits. Many of his poems are mere bundles of these oddities of metaphor, quaint and crabbed to the last degree; but he manages, by means of them, to express many pregnant and far-reaching thoughts. At times he shows an unusual power of direct and familiar phrasing. By means of sudden turns, emphatic pauses, lightning-like "stabs" of thought, he forces home his words into the reader's memory, and makes his quaint and daring conceitfulness interpret, rather than obscure, his meaning.

The pervading atmosphere of Herbert's poetry is one of moral earnestness and sincere piety, rather intellectual than impassioned. He is, therefore, the true poet of the Church of England. Richard Crashaw (1612?– 1649?), on the other hand, is a poet of Catholicism. His attitude toward divine things is not that of pious contemplation, but of ecstatic and mystical worship. Crashaw's early

Richard Crashaw

nurture was ultraprotestant because his father was a zealous antipapist preacher. At Cambridge, both as undergraduate and as fellow, however, he read deeply in the works of the early church fathers and in the lives of the saints, and he took part in the fasts and vigils of a religious brotherhood gathered about Nicholas Ferrar at Little Gidding, just outside Cambridge. His religious poetry, written at this time, recognizes the influence of George Herbert in the title *Steps to the Temple* (1646). As the struggle between the Church of England and the Puritan dissenters grew more and more bitter, he was ejected from his fellowship and fled for refuge to the arms of that venerable mother church of which his nature had from the first made him a member. After a time of bleak poverty in Paris, he was befriended by a brother poet, Abraham Cowley, and introduced to Queen Henrietta Maria, wife of Charles I, who had taken refuge at the court of France from the storms of civil war in England. Through her influence with a Roman cardinal, Crashaw was given a place in the Monastery of Our Lady of Loretto, in Italy; and he died shortly after, from the effect of a pilgrimage which he made on foot in the burning heat of the Italian summer—a fit end for a poet in whom lived again the mystical religious fervor of the Middle Ages.

Crashaw's poetry is excessively uneven. It contains the most extravagant examples of frigid conceitfulness to be found among all the followers of Donne, as in his description of the weeping eyes of Mary Magdalene in "The Weeper," as

> Two walking baths; two weeping motions;
> Portable and compendious oceans.

Yet side by side with these, often in the same poem, occur passages of noble distinction. His two most characteristic poems are perhaps "The Flaming Heart" and the "Hymn to Saint Teresa." He sings the raptures of the soul visited by divine love, in terms as concrete and glowing as any human lover has ever used to celebrate an earthy passion:

O thou undaunted daughter of desires!
By all thy dower of lights and fires,
By all the eagle in thee, all the dove,
By all thy lives and deaths of love,
By thy large draughts of intellectual day,
And by thy thirsts of love more large than they,
By all thy brim-filled bowls of fierce desire,
By thy last morning's draught of liquid fire,
By the full kingdom of that final kiss
That seized thy parting soul and sealed thee his,
By all the heav'ns thou hast in him,
Fair sister of the seraphim!
By all of him we have in thee,
Leave nothing of myself in me:
Let me so read thy life that I
Unto all life of mine may die.

Henry Vaughan (1622–1695), the third poet of this group, spent his youth among the romantic glens of the valley of the *Henry Vaughan* Usk, in northern Wales. Vaughan went up to Oxford in 1638, just as the quarrel between the King and the Parliament was drawing to a head. He fought for the King's cause, and when that cause was lost, retired to his native valley in Wales, to spend the rest of his long life as an obscure country physician. The death of his wife and his own severe illness awakened his religious nature, and under the influence of Herbert's *Temple* he wrote and published (1650) the first part of *Silex Scintillans,* that is, sparks struck by divine grace from a hard and sinful heart.

Vaughan's poetry, like Crashaw's, is very uneven. The reader must search long before finding the things of value, but when found they are worth the search. His best poems, such as "The World," "Departed Friends," and "The Hidden Flower," show an extraordinary insight into the mystical life of nature and the heart of childhood and a strange nearness to the unseen world. In "The Retreat" he anticipates not only the central theme but also the style of Wordsworth's great "Intimations" ode. Like William Blake he touched the deeper mysteries with childlike simplicity and unconsciousness in delicate and elusive music.

The poets just discussed may, by virtue of their kinship in style and in metrical form, be called the school of Donne. Another group may equally well be entitled the school of Spenser, since they employ a modification of the Spenserian stanza for narrative poetry, and otherwise resemble him in features of style, such as use of figures of speech, especially personifications and many conceits. *The School of Spenser: Giles Fletcher* Above all, they have the color and music of his verse. Of these the chief was Giles Fletcher (1588–1623), whose epic entitled *Christ's Victory and Triumph in Heaven and Earth* is, for all its quaintness of thought and phrase, no unworthy forerunner of *Paradise Lost*. It was published in 1610, when Milton was two years old. Signs of its influence upon Milton can be traced from his early "Hymn on the Nativity" to the *Paradise Regained* of his old age. The last canto, which deals with the resurrection and with the entrance of Christ into heaven, is the most beautiful part of the poem. It is a great Easter hymn, expressing the joy of earthly and heavenly things over the risen Redeemer. The sympathy with nature which it reveals is exquisite, resembling Chaucer's in its childlike delight and sweetness, but filled with a religious ecstasy which Chaucer's worldliness excluded.

An older brother of Giles, Phineas Fletcher (1582–1650), followed Spenser in writing a series of eclogues based on his life at Cambridge, but instead of introducing the conventional type of rustic, the shepherd, he made his characters fishermen, whence his title, *Piscatory* *Phineas Fletcher* *Eclogues*. Like Spenser he made his masterpiece an allegory, but instead of figuring forth the moral life of man he devotes himself to an endless account of man's physical and physiological nature under the metaphor of an island-city. *The Purple Island* is a stock example of the absurdities of the allegorical school. It suggests, also, the interest of the time in science. *The Purple*

Island represents the human body, its bones, the rocky founda‑ tion, and its veins and arteries, the rills and rivers.

William Browne (1591–1643) and George Wither (1588‑ 1667) continued the pastoral tradition of the school of Spen‑

Browne and Wither

ser; and like Spenser they vitalized the conven‑ tions of pastoral verse by breathing into them a sincere feeling for nature, and by making them convey, under a playful disguise, a certain amount of ethical and religious thought. Browne's *Britannia's Pastorals* gives us the homely sights and sounds of his native Devonshire in a way which makes his pages charming in spite of their senti- mentality, their false mythology, and their strained allegory. Wither's *Mistress of Philarete* is a celebration of Virtue, whom the poet personifies and praises exactly as if she were some lovely shepherdess of the plain. Both these poets passed be- yond the range of the Spenserian tradition. Browne was the author of the epitaph long attributed to Ben Jonson, and still regarded as an epitome of the classic qualities of seventeenth- century verse.

> Underneath this sable herse
> Lies the subject of all verse:
> Sidney's sister, Pembroke's mother:
> Death, ere thou hast slain another
> Fair and learn'd and good as she,
> Time shall throw a dart at thee.

And Wither is best known for the Cavalier gayety of the song:

> Shall I, wasting in despair,
> Die because a woman's fair?

A third group of poets may be called the school of Jonson, partly because they reflect his quality of careful workmanship,

The School of Jonson

but still more because they were of his personal following, "sealed of the tribe of Ben," and like him devoted to this world and its pleasures. The chief of them was Robert Herrick, who made of Jonson his patron saint and adopted his creed to live merrily and write good verses.

Robert Herrick (1591–1674) was apprenticed in boyhood to his uncle, a goldsmith in Cheapside. After some time spent at Cambridge he returned to London, in his thirtieth **Robert** year, and lived on his wits in the literary bohemia **Herrick** of the Inns of Court. In 1629, having taken orders, he was presented by King Charles to the vicarage of Dean Prior, in Devonshire, which, after London, he found dull and boorish. But with no duties to perform save the reading of a weekly sermon to a handful of sleepy parishioners, he had ample opportunity, during the next nineteen years, to develop his peculiar lyrical gift. His genius was of the kind which carves cherry-stones, not of the kind which hews great figures from the living rock. Left perfectly to himself, amid the flowers of his vicarage garden, with the pretty traditional ceremonies and merrymakings of country life to look at, he spent his days carving cherry-stones, indeed, but giving to them the delicate finish of cameos or of goldsmith's work. In poem after poem he enters with extraordinary zest and folk-feeling into the small joys and pageants of rural life—a bridal procession, a cudgel-play between two clowns on the green, a puppet-show at the fair, the hanging of holly and box at Candlemas eve. Perhaps the most exquisite of all is "Corinna's Going a-Maying." This little masterpiece is drenched with the pungent dews of a spring morning. As the poet calls his "sweet slug-a-bed" out-of-doors, and leads her through the village streets, already decked with whitethorn, toward the fields and woods where the May-day festivities are to be enacted, we feel that the poetry of old English life speaks through one who has experienced to the full its simple charm. But the note of sadness at the end, the looking forward to that dark time when Corinna herself and all her village mates shall "lie drowned in endless night," is an echo of classical stoicism.

When the parliamentary forces had gained the battle which they had been waging with the King's men, and **Herrick's** Herrick as a loyalist was ejected from his living, he **Religious** went back to London. The year of his return (1648) **Poetry** he published his poems under the title of *Hesperides and Noble Numbers*, the latter half of the title referring to the religious poems of the collection. There could be no more striking sign of the immense religious ferment of the time than these poems, emanating as they do from an epicurean and pagan nature, whose philosophy of life is summed up in his most famous song: "Gather ye rosebuds while ye may." In the wonderful poem called "The Litany," the masterpiece among Herrick's religious poems, we see how upon even his gay and sensuous nature there descended at times that dark shadow of religious terror which later found its final and appalling expression in the *Grace Abounding* of John Bunyan. In Herrick's case, however, this is only a passing phase of feeling. He is to be remembered as the poet of "Corinna's Going a-Maying," the "Night-Piece to Julia," and of a myriad other little poems in which he chronicles his delight in nature, and in the exquisite surface of life as he saw it.

The attempt, which is notable in Herrick, to escape from the seriousness of the age was characteristic of the court of Charles I and of the three poets, Carew, Lovelace, and *The Cava-* Suckling, who are known as the Cavalier poets. *lier Poets* Of the three, Thomas Carew (1595?–1639?) was the most sincere. His work is occasionally tinged with licentiousness, but much of it, on the other hand, has genuine beauty and dignity. He felt the influence of both Ben Jonson and Donne, and such a poem as "To His Mistress in Absence" has the sanity and finish of the one, mingled with the magnetic eloquence of the other. He is best known by his lighter efforts, such as his "Give me more love or more disdain," in which poem his felicity and courtly address display themselves at their height. He wrote also a striking court masque entitled *Cœlum Britannicum,* which was produced in 1634, with the greatest magnificence, as a kind of counter-demonstration to a recent Puritan onslaught upon the theatre. Carew died about 1639, just before the bursting of the storm which was to scatter the gay society of Whitehall, and bring to poverty, exile, and death the men and women who had danced the measures in his joyous masque.

Sir John Suckling (1609–1642) and Richard Lovelace (1618–1658) were young courtiers of wealth and great social bril-

liance, who practiced poetry much as they practiced swordsman-
ship; facility in turning a sonnet or a song being still, as in the
Elizabethan age, considered a part of a courtier's
education. Each of them wrote, almost spontane-   *Suckling*
ously, two or three little songs which are the per-   *and*
fection of melody, grace, and aristocratic ease. Suck-   *Lovelace*
ling's tone *is* cynical and mocking; the best songs of Lovelace,
on the other hand, "To Lucasta on Going to the Wars" and "To
Althea from Prison," breathe a spirit of old-fashioned chivalry,
of faithfulness to the ideals of love and knightly honor. Both
Suckling and Lovelace met with tragic reversal of fortune, and
the contrast between their careless, brilliant youth and their
later days has thrown about their names a romantic glamor
which has had perhaps as much to do with preserving their
fame as the tiny sheaf of lyrics they left behind.

Abraham Cowley (1618–1667) has been regarded as, next
to Donne, the chief exemplar of metaphysical poetry, but he
seems to have preferred the leadership of Jonson,
while his long religious epic might seem to connect   *Abraham*
him remotely with the followers of Spenser. Cowley   *Cowley*
was famous as a poet at fifteen, at thirty his name was one
to conjure with, and in his later years he was accepted by his
contemporaries as the crown and acme of the poets of all time.
His reputation decayed rapidly after his death, and he is now
a somewhat "frustrate ghost" in the corridors of fame. He has
all the mannerisms of the school of Donne, with little thought
or passion to redeem them. His greatest effort, *The Mistress,*
a series of love-poems, might, in Doctor Johnson's energetic
words, "have been written for hire by a philosophical rhymer
who had only heard of another sex"; and his once-famous
Davideis (1656), a heroic poem of the troubles of King
David of Israel, is now hopelessly dead. From any sweeping
condemnation of Cowley, however, must be excepted his earnest
and simple lines "On the Death of Mr. William Hervey," his
beautiful elegy on Crashaw, and a few of his *Pindarique Odes*
(1656), which last have at times a full and sonorous music.
The loose ode form, adapted by Cowley from the Greek of

Pindar, was used all the way down through the age of Dryden and Pope, and was almost the only relief which the classic age allowed itself from the monotonous beat of the heroic couplet. Cowley, as secretary to Queen Henrietta Maria in her exile, was associated with the men who carried to victory the banner of classicism and prepared the way for Dryden. In his own work he hung dubiously between the romantic and the classic schools; the romantic impulse in him was weak, and the classical instinct not spontaneous.

Cowley also wrote a group of essays (1668) which reflect the introspection of the time. He thus bridges the gap between the impersonal observation of Bacon and the genial, friendly tone of Steele and Addison. His last essay, "Of Myself," might have served as a model for the first essay in the *Spectator.*

Another poet who is eclectic in his tendency is Andrew Marvell (1621–1678). Marvell was among the first of English

Andrew Marvell poets to feel the charm of nature with romantic intensity, and at the same time with scrupulous realism. The bulk of his nature-poetry was written between his twenty-ninth and his thirty-first years, while he was living in country seclusion at Nun Appleton, as tutor to the young daughter of Lord Fairfax, commander-in-chief of the parliamentary forces. The principal record of these two years of poetic life is a long poem entitled "Appleton House"; besides this, the most beautiful of his country poems are perhaps "The Garden" and "The Mower to the Glow-worms." In these, and in his delicate little dialogues, he links himself with the pastoral school of Spenser; in other places, especially in the lines "To a Coy Mistress," he shows the influence of Donne. In his later life Marvell served for a time as assistant to Milton, then acting as Latin secretary to Cromwell's government. He helped Milton in his blindness, aided him to escape from his pursuers at the Restoration, and watched with mingled admiration and awe the progress of *Paradise Lost,* which began about 1658 to take shape, after twenty years' delay. In the noble "Ode to Cromwell," Marvell set an example, worthy of Milton himself, of simple dignity and classical restraint in the treatment of a political theme. And it is to this poem that we owe the description of Cromwell's opponent, Charles I, on the scaffold, in lines which, more than anything ever written, make him unforgettably the royal martyr:

> He nothing common did or mean
> Upon that memorable scene.

The characteristic prose of the mid-seventeenth century is nearer the romantic eccentricity and extreme individuality of the poetry of Donne and his school than to the *Seven-* classic precision of Jonson. It is extremely loose *teenth-Cen-* in structure, over-colored, elaborate, wayward. In *tury Prose* subject-matter the prose represents the self-consciousness and personal interest of the time. It was a period of autobiography, personal essay, biography, and history.

At the very outset we are confronted by the splendid figure of Sir Walter Ralegh, a prisoner in the Tower after the failure of his daring plans in America, launching himself *Sir Walter* on an enterprise equally characteristic of the confident *Ralegh* spirit of the Renaissance—*The History of the World*. Ralegh worked on this mighty task for years, with the assistance of Ben Jonson and others, and left six massive volumes completed. It is interesting to-day only because of the light which it throws on the conception of history in that time, and as a monument of English prose, much of it wearisomely pedantic and irritatingly loose and inefficient, but rising at times into sombre eloquence, as in its concluding sentence:

O eloquent, just, and mighty Death! Whom none could advise, thou hast persuaded; what none hath dared, thou hast done; and whom all the world hath flattered, thou only hast cast out of the world and despised; thou hast drawn together all the far-stretched greatness, all the pride, cruelty, and ambition of man, and covered it all over with these two narrow words, *Hic jacet!*

But Ralegh is a belated Elizabethan, and it was in such a
writer as Sir Thomas Browne (1605–1682) that the seventeenth-century "time-spirit" found curious but very
noble expression. His mind was deeply tinged
with melancholy, and he shared the prevalent
tendency toward religious mysticism. But these qualities are
oddly infused with scepticism flowing from his scientific studies,
a kind of dreamy, half-credulous scepticism, very different from
Bacon's clear-cut rational view of things, but more characteristic of an age in which mediæval and modern ways of thought
were still closely mingled together. After studying medicine at
Oxford, Montpellier, Padua, and Leyden, Browne settled as a
physician at Norwich, and there passed his life. In 1642 appeared his first work, *Religio Medici,* a confession of his own
personal religious creed. It is in essence a mystical acceptance
of Christianity. "Methinks," he says, "there be not impossibilities enough in religion for an active faith . . . I love to lose
myself in a mystery; to pursue my reason to an *O Altitudo!*"

*His Char-
acteristic
Mood*

This sense of solemn exaltation, this losing of himself in a mystery and an *O Altitudo*, is Browne's
most characteristic mood. He loves to stand before
the face of the Eternal and the Infinite until the
shows of life fade away, and he is filled with a passionate
quietude and humility. We see in him how far the temper of
men had departed from the Elizabethan zest of life, from the
Renaissance delight in the stir and bustle of human activity. "Methinks," he says, "I begin to be weary of the sun. . . .
The world to me is but a dream and mock-show, and we all
therein but pantaloons and antics, to my severer contempla-
tions."

While the mighty struggle which Lord Clarendon depicts
in his *History of the Rebellion* was shaking the earth with its
"drums and tramplings," Sir Thomas Browne was
quietly writing his longest work, *Vulgar Errors*
(1646), an inquiry, half-scientific and half-credulous, into various popular beliefs and superstitions. Twelve
years later he published the *Urn Burial,* a short piece suggested by the finding of some ancient Roman funeral-urns buried

*Sir Thomas
Browne*

*The "Urn
Burial"*

in the earth in the neighborhood of Norwich. The *Urn Burial* is ostensibly an inquiry into the various historic methods of disposing of the dead, but by implication it is a descant upon the vanity of earthly ambition, especially in its attempt to hand on mortal memory to future ages. It is Browne's most characteristic work and perhaps the supreme example of his style.

The grandeur and solemnity of this style, at its best, is hardly to be paralleled in English prose. Like almost all the writers of his age, Browne is extremely desultory and uneven; his "purple patches" come unexpectedly, but these occasional passages have a pomp and majesty ***Browne's Style*** which even Milton has not surpassed. His English is full of magniloquent words and phrases coined from the Latin, and the music of his periods is deep, stately, and long-drawn, like that of a heroic funeral march or the full-stop of a cathedral organ. The opening of the last section of the *Urn Burial* will serve perhaps to make these comparisons clear: "Now, since these dead bones have already outlasted the living ones of Methuselah, and in a yard under ground, and thin walls of clay, outworn all the strong and specious buildings above it; and quietly rested under the drums and tramplings of three conquests: what prince can promise such diuturnity unto his reliques?" The way in which Browne's imagination plays through his thought and flashes a sudden illumination of beauty over his pages may be suggested by these words, written one night when he had sat late at his desk: "To keep our eyes open longer were but to act our Antipodes. The huntsmen are up in America!"

A wide-spread national mood usually finds its analyst. The melancholy of the seventeenth century, its causes, its manifestations, and its cure, were exhaustively treated by ***Burton and the "Anatomy of Melancholy"*** Robert Burton (1577–1640) in his *Anatomy of Melancholy* (1621), a book into which he gathered the out-of-the-way learning and the dreamy speculation of fifty years of recluse life at Brasenose College, Oxford. So curious a mixture of pedantry, imagination, and quiet, brooding humor, covering in a sense the whole life and thought of man, could hardly have been produced in any other era of English literature as, indeed, no other era would have suggested "melancholy" as a theme for encyclopædic treatment. Burton's *Anatomy* may be described as a personal essay, the reflection of a single interest in a curiously self-centred, shut-in personality. Burton makes an exhaustive analysis of the causes and symptoms of melancholy and the treatments proposed for its cure; he studies especially the melancholy associated with love and religion. The style is discursive; the sentences are informal and long-winded. Innumerable quotations from the classical and modern languages, usually paraphrased, and pertinent allusions garnered in a lifetime of reading swelled the successive editions of the book until its final form reached almost half a million words. Sir William Osler described it as "the greatest medical treatise written by a layman."

Izaak Walton — A work of the same nature, but utterly different in tone and spirit, is Walton's *Compleat Angler* (1653). Izaak Walton (1593–1683) was a London linen-draper, who spent his working days in measuring cloth and serving his customers over the shop counter; but who passed his holidays in quite another fashion, roaming with fishing-rod and basket along the banks of streams, and gazing with unspoiled eyes at the unspoiled peace and gayety of nature. His book is a delightful medley in dialogue form of personal reminiscence and sportsman's dissertation on the haunts and habits of fishes and ways of taking them.

Biography and Autobiography — Walton contributed to the interest of the time in human life by writing his *Lives* of Donne, Herbert, Hooker, and others—the most charming pieces of contemporary portraiture which have come down to us. This interest manifested itself in a wide range, from sketches of types, called *Characters,* which were written in great numbers by Sir Thomas Overbury and others, to minute autobiographical studies. Of these we have two which are of extreme interest. Lord Herbert of Cherbury, elder brother of the poet, has recorded in his *Autobiography* the life experience of a Cavalier—and John Bunyan in his *Grace Abounding* that of a Puritan.

The interest in conduct and etiquette, which we saw manifesting itself so strongly in Elizabethan England, continued, but
takes in part a new form responsive to the deeper religious tone of the time. Jeremy Taylor (1613–   *Jeremy*
1667), who was a great preacher, a great contro-   *Taylor*
versialist on the Anglican side, and a master of sacred rhetoric,
wrote two manuals, *Holy Living* and *Holy Dying* (1650–1651),
of which Hazlitt says: "It is a divine pastoral. He writes to
the faithful followers of Christ as the shepherd pipes to his
flock. . . . He makes life a procession to the grave, but crowns
it with garlands, and rains sacrificial roses on its path."

Thomas Fuller (1608–1661), who was also a royalist
clergyman, in his *Holy State and Profane State* (1642) used
the generalized character sketch to define virtue and   *Thomas*
vice in various walks of life, and then drew concrete   *Fuller*
examples from biography. His *Worthies of England*
(1662) is a sort of biographical dictionary arranged by counties.
Such works as these have survived, not only because of their
intrinsic value, but because of the charm of their style, which
reflects the quaint or brilliant personalities of their authors.

II

John Milton, after Shakespeare the greatest of English poets,
was born December 9, 1608, in Bread Street, London. His
father was a scrivener (notary public), who had   *Milton's*
embraced the Puritan faith, but whose Puritanism   *Early Life*
was not of the hard and forbidding type. The boy
grew up in a home where music, literature, and the social
graces gave warmth and color to an atmosphere of serene
piety. During his boyhood England was still Elizabethan;
among the great body of Puritans, geniality and zest of life
had not yet given place to that harsh strenuousness which
Puritanism afterward took on. Milton was taught music, and
was allowed to range at will through the English poets; among
these Spenser, the poet of pure beauty, exercised over him a
charm which was to leave its traces upon all the work of his
early manhood. At Christ's College, Cambridge, whither he

proceeded in his seventeenth year, he began to prepare himself with earnestness and consecration for the life of poetry. He had already determined to be a poet, and that, too, in no ordinary sense. His mind was fixed on lofty themes, and he believed that such themes could be fitly treated only by one who had led a noble and austere life. The magnificent ode "On the Morning of Christ's Nativity" (1629), which deals with the signs and portents filling the world at the Saviour's birth, was written at twenty-one. It showed clearly, or might have shown to any one who had eyes to see, that another mighty poet had been given to England.

Two years later Milton left Cambridge and went to Horton, a little village west of London, whither his father had retired

At Horton to spend his declining days. Here, in a beautiful country of woods, meadows, and brimming streams, the young poet spent five quiet years. To the outward view he was all but idle, merely "turning over the Greek and Latin classics" in a long holiday. Really he was hard at work, preparing himself by meditation, by communion with nature and with the lofty spirits of the past, for some achievement in poetry which (to use his own words) England "would not willingly let die." Meanwhile he was writing very little, but that little perfect, thrice distilled. A sonnet sent to a friend on his twenty-third birthday shows that he was deeply dissatisfied with what he had done in verse before going to Horton; and indeed, if we except the Nativity Hymn, he had reason to be dissatisfied. The other poems of his college period are disfigured by the conceits, exaggeration, and tasteless ingenuity, peculiar to the seventeenth century. The Hymn itself is marred by the same faults, and even its beauties are some of them plainly imitative. But at Horton Milton's taste gradually became surer, his touch upon the keys of his instrument superlatively firm and delicate. He went back to purer models, and learned how to borrow without imitating. The result was three long poems and several short ones, absolutely flawless in workmanship, full of romantic beauty curbed and chastened by a classical sense of proportion and fitness. It is in these poems that we first see clearly what Milton stands for in the poetic art of the century. He is a child of the Renaissance, the last of that great romantic line of which Spenser, Sidney, Marlowe, Shakespeare, Donne, and Fletcher are scions; but he has drunk deeper than the others of the springs of antique art; there is in him a more austere artistic instinct, linked somehow with his austerer moral nature. The spirit of his art is romantic; its expression is, in the widest sense, classic.

The first product of Milton's Horton period, the poem in two parts, "L'Allegro" (the joyous man) and "Il Penseroso" (the meditative man), is in its nature autobiographical. *"L'Allegro"* The two parts of the poem paint the two sides of *and "Il* Milton's own temperament: the one urging out- *Penseroso"* ward, toward communion with the brightness and vivid activity of life; the other drawing inward, toward lonely contemplation, or musings upon the dreamier, quieter aspects of nature and of human existence. To represent these two moods he imagines two typical youths, living each through a day of typical thoughts and pursuits, in the midst of surroundings harmonious with his special tastes. Taken together the two little poems give a view of the life which Milton led during the five happy years of his preparation for the poetic ministry, wonderfully compressed, clarified, and fixed in permanent symbols.

The next two poems of this period were in masque form: one a fragment, *Arcades,* the other a complete masque, taking its title from the chief character, Comus, god of *"Comus"* revelry. *Comus* was written at the request of Milton's friend, Henry Lawes, a musician, who supplied the music and played the part of the Attendant Spirit when the masque was presented (1634) in the castle of Ludlow, on the Welsh border. The "plot" of *Comus* is simple and very effective, affording enough of the fantastic mythological element for scenic display, yet leaving the main interest of the piece to centre upon the rich, serious poetry which Milton puts into the mouths of his few characters. Two brothers and a sister, astray by night in the forest, become separated; the girl is taken captive by Comus, and is led to the place where he dwells, surrounded by strange half-bestial creatures whom he has transformed. He attempts to work upon her the same transformation.

She resists his effort, refusing to yield to the allurements of
sense, and is at length rescued by her brothers and an "attendant spirit," who takes the guise of their father's shepherd. It
was characteristic of Milton that he should have put a serious
moral lesson into a form of spectacular and lyric entertainment
usually of the most frivolous kind. Fortunately, his power as an
artist was so developed that he could charge the delicate texture of his masque with ethical doctrine, without at all marring
its airy beauty.

When *Comus* was written, the Puritans and the court party
were already drifting toward open conflict. The influences of
Deepening Seriousness of Milton's Work the Renaissance, for which the court party largely
stood, were losing force; and the moral enthusi-
asms flowing from the Reformation were meanwhile growing narrower and intenser, in that other
element of the nation, the Puritan party, where
they had taken deepest hold. An atmosphere of moral strenuousness, soon to deepen into sternness, and then into hard
fanaticism, had begun to spread over England, affecting in one
way or another the vital spirits of all men. In *Comus* this moral
strenuousness finds expression, though in the most unobtrusive
manner. In the last poem of Milton's Horton period, "Lycidas,"
written in 1637, there is sounded a sterner note, a note of
austere indignation and fierce warning against the corruptions
which had crept into the church.

"Lycidas" is an elegy upon the death of Edward King, a
college-mate of Milton's, drowned in the Irish Sea. King had
"Lycidas" been, in his way, a poet; and it was a fixed convention, among the poets of the pastoral school, to
represent themselves and their art under the guise of the shepherd life. When Milton, therefore, represents himself and his
dead companion as shepherds driving their flocks, and piping
for fauns and satyrs to dance; when he calls the sea-nymphs and
the gods of the wind to task for the disaster of his fellow-shep-
herd's death—he merely makes use of a literary mode bequeathed to him through Spenser, Fletcher, and Browne, by
Theocritus and Virgil. But he does not rest content with this;
he adds to it another kind of symbolism, not pagan but Chris-

tian. King, besides being a poet, had been preparing for the ministry. He was therefore not only a shepherd under Apollo, but a shepherd under Christ; a keeper of the souls of men which are the flocks of the Good Shepherd. This second symbolism Milton boldly identifies with the first, for to him the poet and the preacher were one in spiritual aim. Still more boldly, in the strange procession of classic and pseudoclassic divinities whom he summons to mourn over Lycidas, he includes Saint Peter, the bearer of the keys of the church; and he puts in his mouth words of solemn wrath against those "blind mouths," those worldly churchmen who,

> for their bellies' sake
> Creep, and intrude, and climb into the fold;

closing with a shadowy menace of the punishment which is soon to overtake the ecclesiastical corruption of the age. "Lycidas" gathers up all the iridescent color and varied music of Milton's youthful verse, indeed, of the whole Spenserian school; and at the same time, by virtue of the moral purpose which burns in it, it looks forward to the period of public combat into which the poet was about to plunge.

The twenty years of Milton's life as a public disputant we must pass over hurriedly. They were preceded by a period of travel abroad (1638–1639), chiefly in Italy, during which he may have met Galileo, was entertained by the Italian literary academies, and pondered much upon a projected epic or drama on the subject of King Arthur's wars, a subject suggested *Milton's Public Life: His Prose Writings* to him by the epics of Tasso and Ariosto. His return was hastened by news of King Charles's expedition against the Scots, a step whose seriousness Milton well knew. Once back in London, he was drawn into a pamphlet war on the vexed question of episcopacy. Then followed his ill-starred marriage into a Royalist family, and the writing of his pamphlets on divorce. These were received with astonishment and execration by his countrymen, who did not see that Milton was only bringing to bear, upon one issue of domestic life, that spirit of free inquiry everywhere being applied to public institutions, and everywhere spreading change through the social fabric of England. Another signal illustration of Milton's revolutionary questioning followed, in the shape of an attack upon the censorship of the press. The time-honored institution of the censorship he saw to be an intolerable hindrance to freedom of thought; in a pamphlet entitled *Areopagitica* (1644) he launched against it all the thunders and lightnings of his magnificent rhetoric. On the execution of King Charles I (1649) Milton was the first to lift up his voice, amid the hush and awe of consternation, in defense of the deed. His pamphlet *On the Tenure of Kings and Magistrates* (1649) was of such timely service to the Commonwealth party that he was appointed to the position of Latin secretary to Cromwell's government, his duties being to indite correspondence with foreign powers, and to reply to attacks by foreign pamphleteers of importance. In the midst of a controversy of this sort his eyes failed, and in a short time he was totally blind. He continued his duties, with Andrew Marvell as his assistant. After the Restoration in 1660, Milton was imprisoned for a short time and then forced to live in retirement in order to escape paying with his life for his fearless support of the ideals and actions of the Commonwealth party.

Ever since his college days Milton had been looking forward to undertaking some work of poetry large enough to give scope

"Paradise Lost" to all his power. By 1642 he had virtually decided upon the subject of the fall of Adam, though he at first intended to treat the subject in the form of a drama. During the eighteen years between 1642 and his dismissal from the Latin secretaryship in 1660, this subject was seldom long absent from his mind. In the midst of the "noises and hoarse disputes" into which he had thrown himself for patriotic service, the only poetic production which he allowed himself was a small group of sonnets, written at rare intervals and dealing for the most part with passing events. Except for these, he had hidden "that one talent which is death to hide," but he more than once turned aside in his pamphlets to throw out a proud hint concerning the work laid upon him by the "great Taskmaster," of adding something majestic and memorable to the treasury of English verse. Meanwhile his chosen subject lay in his mind, gradually taking form, and gathering to itself the riches of long study and reflection. When at last his duty as a patriot was done, he turned to his deferred task. Forced to seek shelter from the storm of the royalist reaction, he carried with him into his hiding-place the opening book of *Paradise Lost,* begun two years earlier. The poem was finished by 1665, and was published by an obscure printer in 1667.

The central theme of *Paradise Lost,* namely, the fall of Adam from a state of innocence into a state of sin, occupies a relatively small space in the whole scheme of the poem. In the approved epic manner, Milton opens his poem in the middle of the action, after the rebellious angels have been cast down into hell. *The Vastness of Its Scheme* The earlier events are given in retrospective narrative by the archangel Raphael and by Adam. The rebellion of Lucifer against the omnipotent ruler of heaven; the defeat of the rebel armies and their casting down into the dreary cavern of hell, which has been carved out of chaos to be their prison-house; the creation of the terrestrial universe and the setting of man in the garden of Eden to take the place of the apostate angels in God's affection; the expedition of Lucifer from hell to earth for the purpose of beguiling the innocent pair; the going and coming of God's messengers and sentinels—all this constitutes a vast drama of which the actual temptation and fall of Adam is the major climax. With the exception of Dante no modern mind has conceived an action so immense, or set a world-drama on a stage of such sublime dimensions.

In spite of this vastness of scheme, however, Milton's imagination does not take refuge in vagueness. His imagery is everywhere concrete, in places startlingly vivid and tangible. It may even be urged against the poem that some things are presented with an exactness of delineation which detracts from their power to awe the mind; but broadly speaking, the poet's *The Concreteness of Its Imagery* ability to evoke clear and memorable pictures of more than titanic size, and to make his cosmic drama as clear to our mental vision as are the natural sights of earth, gives to his work its most enduring claim upon our interest. Upon the theology of the poem time has laid its finger; a part of it thoughtful men now reject, or interpret in a far different sense from Milton's. The blind Puritan bard hardly succeeded, even to the satisfaction of his own day, in his avowed intention to

> assert Eternal providence
> And justify the ways of God to men,

for his religion was a special creed, made up in part of perishable dogmas. But by the imperishable sublimity of the pictures which he has given to our imaginations, he has asserted Providence in another sense, and justified God in the glory of the human mind He created.

The word "sublimity," so often abused, has in the case of Milton's later work real fitness. It was a quality which he attained only after years of stern experience; it was the reward of his long renunciation of his art in the interest of his country. There are suggestions of it in his youthful hymn on the Nativity, and one passage of "Lycidas" attains it:

Milton's "Sublimity"

> Ay me! whilst thee the shores and sounding seas
> Wash far away, where'er thy bones are hurled;
> Whether beyond the stormy Hebrides,
> Where thou perhaps under the whelming tide
> Visit'st the bottom of the monstrous world;
> Or whether thou, to our moist vows denied,
> Sleep'st by the fable of Bellerus old,
> Where the great Vision of the guarded mount
> Looks toward Namancos and Bayona's hold.

These lines, taken in their proper connection, achieve that synthesis of the majestic and the mysterious which we call sublimity. They show that the quality was native to Milton's mind. But it is highly probable that without those years of stern repression, when his imagination was held back by his will, gaining force like the dammed-up waters of a stream, he would never have attained that peculiar mightiness of imagery and phrase which causes *Paradise Lost* to deserve, as does perhaps no other work of English literature, the epithet sublime. Of course, this sublimity Milton gained only at the expense of some qualities of his youthful work which we would fain have had him keep. Grace, lightness, airy charm—these had gone from him forever when he took up his art again after his long silence. The art of "L'Allegro" and *Comus,* responsive and sinuous as the tracery of dancing figures about a Greek vase, had given place to an art as massive and strenuous as the frescoes of Michelangelo in the Sistine Chapel of the Vatican, depicting the solemn scenes of the creation and destruction of the world.

The change in the quality of thought and imagery is, of course, accompanied by a change in style. Milton deliberately chose blank verse as the most severe of English measures; having chosen it, he proceeded to build out of it a type of verse before unknown, admirably suited to the grandeur of his subject. The *The Verse of "Paradise Lost"* chief peculiarity of this Miltonic verse is the length and involution of period. The sense is held suspended through many lines, while clause after clause comes in to enrich the meaning or to magnify the descriptive effect; then the period closes and this suspended meaning falls upon the mind like the combing mass of a breaker on the shore. A second and scarcely less important device (though hardly so novel) is the extreme variety of pause; the sense comes to an end, and the suspended thought falls, at constantly varying places in the line, a device by which blank verse, monotonous when otherwise treated, becomes the most diversified of rhythms. In these and other ways Milton made for himself a noble verse-instrument to match the grandeur of his imagery and theme. The music of the Horton poems, compared with that of *Paradise Lost,* is like the melody of the singing voice beside the manifold harmonies of an orchestra, or the rolling chant of a cathedral organ.

In 1671, four years after the publication of *Paradise Lost,* appeared Milton's third volume of verse. (The college and Horton poems had been published in 1645.) It con *"Paradise Regained"* sisted of *Paradise Regained,* a supplement to *Paradise Lost;* and of *Samson Agonistes,* a drama in the Greek manner, on an Old Testament subject which Milton had first thought of treating nearly thirty years before. *Paradise*

Regained deals with Christ's temptation by Satan in the Wilderness. In his first epic Milton had shown how mankind, in the person of Adam, falls before the wiles of the Tempter, and becomes an outcast from divine grace; in his second he shows how mankind, in the person of Jesus, wins readmission to divine grace by withstanding the hellish adversary. By general consent *Paradise Regained* is given a much lower place than *Paradise Lost,* in spite of passages that rise to an impressive height. The poet's weariness is manifest; his epic vein seems exhausted.

"Samson Agonistes"   *Samson Agonistes,* however, a venture in a new field of poetry, shows Milton's genius at its subtlest and maturest. His desire was to bring over into English the gravity and calm dignity of the Greek tragedies; and, avoiding the lifeless effect of previous experiments of the sort, to give to his grave and calm treatment the passion, the conviction, the kindling breath without which poetry cannot exist. Two circumstances made this not only easy, but almost inevitable for him. In the first place his character, lofty and ardent to begin with, had now under misfortune and sacrifice taken on just that serene and melancholy gravity peculiar to the great tragic poets of antiquity. In the second place, the story of Samson was, in a sense, his own story. Like Samson he had fought against the Philistines with the strength of thirty men; he had taken a wife from among his enemies and suffered bitter loss at her hands; he sat now, blind and dishonored, amid.the triumph of the Cavaliers, as Samson among the festive Philistines. As he wrote, his own personal bitterness found veiled expression; and the grand choruses, with their dark and smothered music, pulsate with personal feeling.

Milton lived for three years after the publication of his last poems. Much of his patrimony had disappeared in the readjust-

Milton's Last Years   ments of the Restoration and in the great London fire of 1666, but he was still able to live in modest comfort. The painter Richardson gives us a glimpse of the poet during his last years, as he was led about the streets clad in a gray camblet coat, or as he sat in a gray coarse cloth coat at the door of his house, near Bunhill Fields, to receive visitors. "Lately," continues Richardson, "I had the good fortune to have another picture of him from an aged clergyman in Dorsetshire. In a small house . . . up one pair of stairs, which was hung with rusty green, he found John Milton, sitting in an elbow chair; black clothes, and neat enough; pale but not cadaverous, his hands and fingers gouty and with chalkstones." When we compare the figure thus suggested with the portrait painted in his twenty-first year, we realize how far and under what public and private stress, Milton had travelled from the world of his youth. In making himself over from Elizabethan to Cromwellian he had suffered much and renounced much; he had lost many of those genial human qualities which have won for less worthy natures a warmth of love denied to his austerity. But if we deny him love, we cannot help feeling an admiration mixed with awe, for the loftiness and singleness of aim, the purity and depth of moral passion, which make him conspicuous even among the men of those moving times. The deep voice of Milton rolled out its interrupted song more than a decade after the chorus of romantic poetry had been hushed, and men had turned away to listen to the new "classical" message of Dryden and the poets of precision.

In like manner the fervid and imaginative prose of the first half of this century survives into the Restoration period in the work of John Bunyan, a late but a very striking exponent of the religious revival which had begun more than a century before to stir the conscience of Northern Europe. Bunyan, the rude tinker of Elstow, who produced, without learning or literary example, one of the unique masterpieces of imaginative English prose, can be understood only by reference to another and greater literary phenomenon of the seventeenth century, the Authorized Version of the Bible. This version was made by order of James I; the work was divided *The King* among numerous biblical scholars appointed by *James* him, and was finished in 1611. The translators used *Bible* not only the original Hebrew and Greek texts and the Latin Vulgate, but also the various English translations, from Wyclif down. They succeeded in blending the peculiar excellences of all of these, with the result that in the King James Bible we possess a monument of English prose holding of no particular age, but gathering up into itself the strength and sweetness of all ages.

The influence of this mighty book upon the literature of the seventeenth century, although great, was restricted by two circumstances. In the first place, the Bible was early monopolized by the Puritan party; and biblical phraseology and imagery became associated with an ideal of life which, at least in the grim and ascetic form it assumed under James and Charles, was distasteful to most of the makers of literature. In the second place, Latin still held its established position as the language of learning, and writers went to that language for instruction, neglecting the ruder but more vital excellences abounding in the prose of the Bible. Bunyan, however, was at once a Puritan of the Puritans, an instinctive artist, and an unlearned man, to whom Latin was only a name. Hence the grandeur, simplicity, and force of biblical prose, acting without any interference upon his passionately earnest imagination, made him, all unknown to himself, a great writer.

John Bunyan (1628–1688) was born in the village of Elstow, Bedfordshire. His father was a tinker, a trade then considered little above vagabondage. After a slight schooling, *John Bunyan* and a short experience of soldiering in the Civil War, he married a wife as poor as himself, and took up his father's trade of pot and kettle mender. Before this, however, there had begun in him a spiritual struggle so terrible and so vivid, as we see it in the pages of his *Grace Abounding to the Chief of Sinners* (1666), that by contrast the events of his outer life are pallid and unreal. As he wrestled and played at tip-cat with his village mates on the green, or stood in the tower of the church to watch the bell-ringing, he was haunted by thoughts of sudden death, of the Judgment Day, and of his soul's damnation. He saw an awful face looking down from the clouds, and heard a voice asking whether he would leave his sins and go to heaven, or have his sins and go to hell. The tiles upon the house-roofs, the puddles in the road, spoke to him with voices of temptation and mockery. From this religious mania he was rescued by John Gifford, a local preacher, who gave him comfort and courage. Soon Bunyan himself began to preach, and a revulsion of feeling now lifted him to heights of ecstatic joy in the mercifulness of God and the beauty of holiness. He saw Christ himself looking down at him through the tiles of the house-roof, saying, "My grace is sufficient for thee," and the sense of salvation came like a "sudden noise of wind rushing in at the window, but very pleasant." In all this we see in its most intense form the religious excitement of the seventeenth century, and also the qualities of imagination and feeling which make Bunyan so powerful a writer.

At the Restoration, persecution of the nonconformist sects began. Bunyan was arrested for holding illegal religious meetings; and he spent most of the next twelve years in *"Pilgrim's* confinement, earning bread for his family by put- *Progress"* ting tags to shoe-laces, and keeping his mind awake by writing what he was no longer at liberty to speak. After his release in 1672 he was subjected to shorter terms of arrest, during one of which he expanded the trite metaphor of a journey to typify the Christian life into a book, and *Pilgrim's Progress,* one of the three great allegories of the world's literature,[1] was written. He published it in 1678. It furnished the simple Bedfordshire cottagers for whom it was written with a reflection of their own inmost struggles and aspirations, in a form which combined the fascinations of the novel, the fairy-tale, and the romance of adventure. Not only is the physical world through which Christian journeys from the "Wicket-gate" to the Land of Beulah pictured with the most familiar realism; but the wayfarers whom he meets are such as might have been seen in Bunyan's day on any English market road—portly Mr. Worldly-Wiseman, full of prudential saws; blundering, self-confident young Ignorance; "gentlemanlike" Demas, and sweet, talkative Piety. The landscape, the houses, the people, are all given with quaint, sturdy strokes which stamp them upon the

[1] The others alluded to are Spenser's *Faerie Queene* and Dante's *Divine Comedy.*

memory forever so that it is almost impossible for a reader of *Pilgrim's Progress* to think of the journey otherwise than as a real personal experience. And added to the charm which the book has as realism is its charm as romance. If, in one sense, it may be said to have anticipated the eighteenth-century novel, in another it may be said to have revived the mediæval romance, in which the hero was made to contend against dangers natural and supernatural, on the way to the goal of his desires. Giant Despair in his grim castle, the obscene devils creeping and muttering in the Valley of the Shadow, the dreadful enemy Apollyon, the angels and archangels who lead the way, with harpings and hosannas, from the dread River of Death to the shining gates of the Celestial City, are elements of marvel and adventure which immensely increase its appeal. If we add to these the charm of its style, quaintly graphic, humorously direct, tender and rich and lyrical when the author is moved by the beauty of his vision, it seems no matter for surprise that *Pilgrim's Progress,* before Bunyan's death, was read with delight, not only throughout England, but in France, in Holland, and in the far-off colonies of America.

Bunyan's later work included the Second Part of *Pilgrim's Progress* (1684), which narrates the journey of Christian's wife,

Bunyan's Later Work

Christiana, and her children to the Celestial City, under the guidance of Mr. Greatheart. He wrote also another allegory called *The Holy War* (1682), which represents the Christian life under the figure of warfare instead of a journey. Most notable, however, is the antitype of Christian presented in *The Life and Death of Mr. Badman* (1680). Here Bunyan adopts the form of a dialogue between Mr. Wiseman and Mr. Attentive. The former narrates the progress through sin to unhallowed death of an unregenerate boy and man, who from lying and Sabbath-breaking descends to fraudulent bankruptcy, drunkenness, and vice—a rogue story with a moral purpose, and a very real study of middle-class corruption in a provincial town like Bedford. It is this realism which makes the work a forerunner of the novels of Defoe in the next century.

As *Paradise Lost* is the epic of Puritanism in its external and theological aspect, *Pilgrim's Progress* is the epic of Puritanism in its inner and emotional phases. They are together the two great final products, one of that intellectual and artistic revival which we call the Renaissance, and the other of that religious revival which we call the Reformation. They mark the end of the stream of literature which flows down into

End of the Romantic Literature of the Century

the second half of the seventeenth century from its source in the later reign of Henry VIII and in the early Elizabethan age. We must now turn to consider a stream of literature of a very different kind, which began in a revolt against the extravagance and formlessness of the reigning "romantic" style, and which at the Restoration assumed an authority which it maintained uninterruptedly for nearly a hundred years.

CHAPTER IX

The Seventeenth Century

THE RESTORATION

THE DATE 1660 is one of the most significant in the history of English literature, as it is in the history of English politics. In that year Charles II was brought to the throne from which his father had been driven. The extravagant joy with which the King was received on his return from exile

The Restoration showed how closely this change of government from commonwealth to kingship corresponded to a change in the mood of the nation. The passionate absorption in other-worldliness, which was the essence of Puritanism, had, as we have seen, checked the frank Renaissance delight in this world and interest in the problem of living in it successfully. But the Puritan ideal, by its very nature, could appeal directly to comparatively few. Indirectly, indeed, by force of example, it influenced many, but the multitude at length grew weary of playing a part so exhausting and so difficult. During the latter years of the Commonwealth signs of a relaxed temper on the part of the public were not lacking; for example, licenses were given for operas to be performed in London. When at length the leaders of the Commonwealth forsook their own ideal and confessed their failure, the mass of the nation turned with relief to the pleasures and interests of the present world, ready to regard with complacency even the loose behavior of the court of Charles II.

The Restoration period must not be thought of, however, as a continuation of the interrupted Renaissance. Between them there is an important difference. In the age of Elizabeth, as in the age of Charles II and his successors, the ruling passion was indeed the development of physical and mental power on the stage of this world. The Elizabethan, however, thought of such

a life, not as limited and contracted by circumstances and conditions, but as unlimited in possibilities. Not only the geographical world, but the intellectual world, also,
was being enlarged and thrown open. The bounds   *Contrast*
of human thought, as well as those of human ac-   *of Res-*
tivity, seemed infinitely remote; the imagination, *toration*
dealing with power, as in Marlowe, or with knowl-   *with*
edge, as in Bacon, took wings to itself and flew.   *Renais-*
But in the greater part of the Restoration period   *sance*
there was awareness of the limitations of human experience,
without faith in the extension of the resources. There was the
disposition to accept such limitations, to exploit the potentialities of a strictly human world.

This sense of present fact, this identification of the real and
the material, as distinguished from the transcendentalism of
Renaissance and Puritan thought, is the chief characteristic of the mood of the century which suc-   *Character-*
ceeded the Restoration. In science it showed itself *istics of*
in an absorption in the details of investigation, as *the Res-*
opposed to the theoretical considerations of Bacon. *toration*
In politics it showed itself in the interest in actual *Period*
conditions, as opposed to dreams of theocracy. In all directions
it appeared as a disposition toward conservatism and moderation. Men had learned to fear individual enthusiasm, and therefore they tried to discourage it by setting up ideals of conduct
in accordance with reason and common sense, to which all men
should adapt themselves. Rules of etiquette and social conventions were established and the problem of life became that of
self-expression within the narrow bounds which were thus prescribed.

The literature of the period reflects these tendencies. On its
serious side it is largely concerned with politics, that is, with the
effort of men to organize the state, and to give it
power sufficient to restrain individual ambition.   *Restora-*
The lighter literature reflects the interest of men in *tion Liter-*
learning to live with one another. Naturally, it is *ature*
much concerned with life in London, and with details of dress
and manners which are important there. But the most note-

worthy evidence of the temper of the time in literature is the tacit agreement of writers, in both prose and poetry, upon rules and principles in accordance with which they should write. The acceptance of these literary conventions drawn from the practice of writers of the past is the most characteristic difference between the *classic* age of Dryden and Pope, and the *romantic,* individualistic epoch of Spenser and Shakespeare.

In this difference the influence of France counted for much. There the reaction against the poetic license of the Renaissance *The Influence of France* had set in somewhat earlier, at the time when Henry IV and Richelieu were laying foundations for the reconstruction of the French monarchy and through the French Academy establishing order and discipline in literature. Corneille and Racine had developed a drama on the lines of Latin tragedy, succeeding where the English classicists of the sixteenth century had signally failed, and Molière evolved, under the influence of classical examples, a type of social comedy, which ranged from hearty farce to the elegant comedy of manners. It must be remembered that many Englishmen of the class which cared for literature and the stage had spent years of exile in France, and naturally came to accept the French principles and standards. Through the new artistic conceptions brought back to England by the exiles, French influence upon English literature, especially upon the English drama, was strengthened. To their notions of refinement the license of the older dramatists seemed uncouth. "I have seen *Hamlet*," wrote Evelyn, "but now these old plays begin to disgust this refined century, since Their Majesties have been so long abroad." Altogether, though English literature of the Restoration is a genuine native growth in accordance with tendencies which can be discerned in the early seventeenth century, particularly in the work of Ben Jonson, yet the example of France, like that of Italy at an earlier period, was important in giving definiteness to movements which otherwise might have been tentative and hesitating.

The most striking way in which English poetry reflected the spirit of the new era was in its substitution of a single measurably perfect form for the metrical variety of Elizabethan poetry.

This form, the heroic couplet, consisted of two lines of rhyming pentameters. It had been used in earlier periods, for example by Chaucer; but in his hands the couplet had not been necessarily a unit since the thought had often been carried over in the succeeding pair of verses, with no pause at the rhyming word. And in the roman- *The Heroic Couplet* tic period which followed the eighteenth century the couplet was once more used with the old freedom. The metrical ideals of the Restoration, as contrasted with those of the ro- mantic school, may be illustrated by the comparison of a few lines from Keats, such as these from the beginning of *Endymion:*

> A thing of beauty is a joy forever:
> Its loveliness increases; it will never
> Pass into nothingness; but still will keep
> A bower quiet for us, and a sleep
> Full of sweet dreams, and health, and quiet breathing;

with these from *The Hind and the Panther* of Dryden:

> A milk-white hind, immortal and unchanged,
> Fed on the lawns, and in the forest rang'd;
> Without unspotted, innocent within,
> She fear'd no danger for she knew no sin.

In the first, it is clear, the couplet exerts little control over the thought; in the second the thought is limited and regulated by the acceptance of a precise and narrow form; and this limitation and regulation were of the essence of Restoration poetry.

Among the first writers to use the closed couplet consistently was Edmund Waller (1606–1687). As early as 1625, in lines on "His Majesty's Escape at Saint Andrew," he set the steady, measured pace which succeeding poets *Edmund Waller* were to follow with military precision for more than a century. His influence, however, became predominant only through the extraordinary energy and success of his follower, the greatest literary figure of the age of Charles II, John Dryden.

Dryden was born in 1631 at Aldwinkle, in Northampton-shire, of an upper middle class family with Puritan sympathies.

Dryden's Early Life

He was sent to Westminster School, and thence, in 1650, to Trinity College, Cambridge, where he remained seven years. During this time his father died, leaving him a small property. His first important poem was an elegy on the death of Cromwell, written in 1658. Two years later, however, Dryden, with the mass of Englishmen, had become an ardent Royalist and welcomed the return of Charles in a poem in couplets called *Astræa Redux.* In 1663 he married Lady Elizabeth Howard, a woman of higher rank than his own. In the meantime, he had begun to make a name as a play-wright, achieving success in both his heroic plays, like *The Indian Emperor* (1665) and his comedies, like *Sir Martin Marall* (1667). His next poem of importance was *Annus Mirabilis* (1667), a celebration of events in the preceding year, which had been distinguished by several victories at sea over the Dutch, and by the great London fire. In the following year, he published the "Essay of Dramatic Poesy," the finest piece of literary criticism that had been written in England.

In 1681 Dryden began the succession of political satires which are generally considered to be the finest political poems

His Satires

in English. The times were troubled. The court and the country were divided between the partisans of the King's brother, who, though Catholic, was recognized as the heir to the throne, and those of the King's illegitimate son, the Duke of Monmouth, whom certain persons zealous for the Protestant faith were disposed to set up as a rival candidate. The leader of the latter party was the Earl of Shaftesbury. In the biblical story of the revolt of Absalom against King David, Dryden found an apt parallel to existing circumstances in England, and his satire *Absalom and Achitophel* exposed with merciless humor the relations of Monmouth, the prince, and Shaftesbury, the evil counsellor. The poem became immensely popular and the next year Dryden followed it with a second blow at Shaftesbury in *The Medal.* In this year, also, Dryden extended his range into the field of religious controversy, with *Religio Laici*, a very temperate statement of a layman's faith in the Church of England. Three years after this confession of faith he became a Roman Catholic, and in 1687 published a political defense of the Church of Rome called *The Hind and the Panther.*

In 1668 Dryden was made Historiographer Royal and Poet Laureate, with a salary of two hundred pounds a year, later increased to three hundred pounds. These honors and emoluments he lost in consequence of the Revolution of 1688 and the accession of William III. He *His Later Works* was obliged to betake himself again to the stage as the most lucrative department of literature, and to undertake various jobs of translation for the publisher, Jacob Tonson. His production in these years added much to his fame. His later work includes his translation of Virgil; many of his translations from Horace, Ovid, Juvenal, Persius, and Homer; and his renderings into modern English verse of stories from Boccaccio and Chaucer, among which the *Palamon· and Arcite* is best known. These vigorous narrative poems were published in 1700, in a volume of *Fables.*

During these last years Dryden lived in London. The coffee-house of that day was the chief place of resort for literary men. At Will's or Button's the wits gathered for exchange of courtesies or for combat; there their admirers or patrons met them, and thence went forth the criti- *His Last Years* cism that made or marred the fortunes of rising men as surely as do the reviews in a modern literary journal. Dryden frequented Will's coffee-house, where he was as much a monarch as Ben Jonson had been at the Mermaid, or as, a century later, Samuel Johnson was at meetings of the Literary Club. It was to Will's that young Pope was brought to gaze on greatness and be inspired; and it was here perhaps that Dryden dismissed a youthful relative with the pitying "Cousin Swift, you will never be a poet."

It is not easy to arrive at a sound estimate of Dryden's poetry. To nineteenth-century critics, it seemed to lack elevation. In the first place the material of much of it is bor- rowed from other writers. But we must remember that in his long labors of translation and adapta- *Dryden's Poetry* tion, Dryden was fulfilling the requirements of his age. The time was one not of creation, but of criticism; one of steady assimilation of what earlier ages had produced. It was especially eager in its effort to diffuse and appropriate the ideals of Latin civilization, and in this diffusion the work of Dryden counted for much. In the second place, the subject-matter of his original poetry, the affairs of church and state, is remote from what is vulgarly regarded as poetic. But here again Dryden was responding to the demands of his age. In the days of Charles II men were weary of revolution. To them the kingship and the church, Anglican or Catholic, were interesting and beautiful, because they represented, for the mass of the nation, an ideal of individual restraint; just as to an earlier time the boundless self-assertion of Faustus and Tamburlaine had been interesting and beautiful for the opposite reason.

Not only the substance but the form of Dryden's verse has been a ground for detraction from his fame. Few major poets *The* have maintained such strict uniformity. With the ex- *Quality* ception of the lyrics in his dramas, several odes, two *of His* early poems in the heroic stanza, and the blank-verse *Poetry* of *All for Love,* Dryden cultivated steadily the heroic couplet. The heroic couplet appealed with irresistible force to an age weary of the conceits of the metaphysical poets, and desiring, above all, uniformity, precision, and regularity. It was, moreover, a vehicle strikingly adapted to the conveyance of the literary baggage of the time. When at the close of *Religio Laici* Dryden says,

> And this unpolished rugged verse I chose
> As fittest for discourse, and nearest prose,

his second line may be taken as referring to his poems in general. In them we look for the virtues of prose rather than for those of poetry, for the utilitarian qualities, neatness, clearness, energy, rather than for imaginative suggestion; we look for epigram in place of metaphor, for boldly marked rhythm instead of elusive harmony.

Although in the great body of his work Dryden kept to the couplet form, his odes, and the songs with which his dramas are strewn, show that he possessed power over a variety of metres. The two odes for Saint Cecilia's day, especially the second, called "Alexander's Feast," illustrate his skill in making his lines march to the measure of his thought. It is true, even in his lyrics Dryden's charm is rather one of line and general movement than of phrase or word. He has little of the magic and glamor that belong to poets of deeper, though perhaps less ample, inspiration. His best quality is artistic and literary, not imaginative.

Dryden was not only the foremost poet, but also the leading dramatist and the most distinguished critic of his time. The age of the Restoration was, as we have already noted, a period of assimilation rather than of creation, a time when men were interested in testing the product ***Dryden as Critic*** of earlier ages, and in winnowing the good from the bad. This interest accounts for the fact that to many of his works Dryden prefixed one or more critical essays in the form of dedications or prefaces, in which he discussed the leading artistic questions of the day. Among these essays the most important are "An Essay of Dramatic Poesy" (1668), "A Defense of an Essay of Dramatic Poesy" (1668), "Of Heroic Plays" (1672), the "Essay on Satire" (1693), and the Preface of the *Fables* (1700). It is to be noted that these writings were all "occasional," each put forth to further a particular purpose; and in the success with which they fulfilled their purpose they are one important sign of literary progress. The virtue of efficiency in prose style was strengthened enormously by Dryden's practice.

Dryden's prose lacks the personal eccentricity which we find in Burton, Browne, and their contemporaries; and it is usually without the artificial decoration which marks the style of Lyly and Sidney. He was chiefly occupied in ***Dryden's Prose*** securing its fitness for a well-defined end. Moreover, by his adoption of the modern sentence in place of the unit of great and unequal length used by Ralegh and Milton, Dryden carried out in prose a change exactly analogous to that accomplished in verse by his adoption of the couplet in place of the stanza. In other words, he did for prose what he did for poetry: he reduced the unit of treatment to manageable size; set an example of correctness; and finally, by his authority, did much to establish such a standard of taste as rendered impossible the eccentricities to which the preceding century had been indulgent.

In both his poetry and his prose Dryden represents the spirit of his age as it showed itself in dealing with its most important problems of life and art. He is at bottom a serious and intellectual master. For the more naïve and unconscious expression of the time we must turn to others. Like Elizabeth and Charles I, Charles II kept in some sort a literary court, of which lyric poetry and satire were the language. The courtly poets of the time, the successors of the Cavaliers, caught from the King an attitude of moral indifference and social flippancy. In their circles a very popular work was a fierce and scurrilous satire upon the Puritan, Samuel Butler's *Hudibras* (1663). Butler (1612–1680) was doubtless meditating his attack during the years of the Protectorate, when he was acting as private secretary to a Puritan squire. Three years after the accession of Charles II he published three cantos of a poem in which the vices of the Puritan period, hypocrisy, sanctimoniousness, and intolerance, are presented with savage exaggeration in the person of Sir Hudibras. *Hudibras* is in effect in the vein of that character writing which was popular in the seventeenth century and of which Butler left many examples. It is written in rough verse of four feet, with double rhymes for humorous effect, very different from the polished heroic couplet of Dryden's satire. Some of the more trenchant comments on Puritan defects have passed into proverbs, as:

Butler's "Hudibras"

> Compound for sins they are inclined to,
> By damning those they have no mind to.

It is also a mock heroic romance after the type of *Don Quixote.* Like their prototypes, Hudibras and his squire Ralpho fall into one ridiculous situation after another, which are continued in further instalments of the poem, published in 1664 and 1678.

While Butler and the Cavalier poets were embodying the mood of the aristocracy, Bunyan was writing his *Pilgrim's Progress* for the serious lower class, where Puritanism still survived. Between these extremes, however, we have an order that was to make its presence felt increasingly from this time on, the middle or burgher class; and as it happens, this class had, in the late seventeenth century, a

Samuel Pepys

representative figure almost as salient as Bunyan. Samuel Pepys (1633–1703) was a busy man of affairs, a clerk of the Navy Board, and later Secretary of the Admiralty under James II. Between 1660 and 1669 he kept a diary in cipher, which he left with his library to Magdalen College, Cambridge, where it lay undisturbed for over a hundred years. It was deciphered and published, though with important omissions, in the course of the nineteenth century, and was recognized at once as a personal document of great interest.

Pepys's diary is scarcely to be called literature. It is a transcript of the observations, doings, thoughts, and feelings of a commonplace burgher, all set down with the greatest fidelity. If Pepys goes on a picnic he mentions the time of starting, the constituents of the luncheon, *Pepys's Diary* the substance of the conversation by the way, the company he met, the sheep which he saw ("the most pleasant and innocent sight that ever I saw in my life"), the shepherd whose little boy was reading the Bible to him, the flowers, the glowworms which came out in the evening, and the slight accident by which he sprained his foot. In its detail it reflects the patient, industrious habits by which business and science were to thrive in the next century—for Pepys was a scientist and president of the Royal Society. In its uniformity of tone, its lack of emphasis and dramatic interest, so different from Bunyan's *Grace Abounding,* it illustrates again the sober modernity which the citizen's life was beginning to assume. In its worldliness, its reflection of perfectly unashamed delight in mere comfort, well-being, and success, it shows the bourgeois ideal of life. In its suggestions of moral laxity it perhaps testifies to the complacence with which even safe and honest burghers saw the natural life free itself from Puritan scruples. And finally, that pleasure in his own life which sustained the author in the mechanical toil of recording its phenomena, is analogous to the interest in human life generally which motivated the development of realistic fiction in the following century.

THE RESTORATION DRAMA

When the theatres were closed in 1642, the succession of great Jacobean dramatists had nearly come to an end, Shirley alone being alive. However, the drama retained its hold on the masses; even under Cromwell, the playwright Dave-
The
Heroic
Play
nant obtained permission to give a play with a musi-cal accompaniment, *The Siege of Rhodes* (1656). To this opera Dryden attributed the beginning of the dominant fashion of the time in tragedy, the heroic play, to which type many of Dryden's own dramas belong. To the most famous of them, *The Conquest of Granada,* he prefixed the essay, "Of Heroic Plays," in which he cites also the example of Ariosto, with his stories of love and valor, as contributing to his conception. The heroic play, though by no means an imita-tion of French tragedy, owed something to the example of Corneille, especially its heightening of characters to heroic pro-portions, and probably also its use of rhyme. Dryden defended the use of rhyme, in the dedication to one of his early plays, on the ground that "it bounds and circumscribes the fancy. For imagination in a poet is a faculty so wild and lawless, that like an high ranging spaniel it must have clogs tied to it lest it out-run the judgment." This psychological principle did not prevent Dryden's pushing his characters into unnatural extravagance of passion; a fault which, as it appears in *The Indian Emperor* (1665), and *The Conquest of Granada* (1670), was caricatured in *The Rehearsal* (1671), a famous mock-heroic drama by the Duke of Buckingham and others.

In the last of his heroic plays, *Aurengzebe* (1675), Dryden confesses in the prologue that he "grows weary of his long-loved mistress, Rhyme." Accordingly his next play,
Dryden's
Later
Dramas
All for Love (1678), a masterly treatment of the story of Antony and Cleopatra in the neoclassical form, he wrote in blank verse. The distinction of the play may be indicated by the fact that it is seriously com-parable with Shakespeare's magnificent tragedy. For the auda-ciously scattered scenes of the earlier play, and an action that moves freely around the ancient world, Dryden, accepting the principles of unity of time, place, and action, restricts the scene

to Alexandria and the time to the last day in the lives of the hero and heroine. Although the infinite variety of Shakespeare's Cleopatra is lost in Dryden's depiction of a royal intrigante, there is undoubtedly a tremendous gain in focus and momentum, lucidity and order, consistency and dignity. It deserves its reputation as the finest English tragedy on the neoclassical model. In addition to his tragedies, Dryden wrote a number of comedies in prose, and tragicomedies in a mixture of prose and verse, some of which are gratuitously gross.

A writer who on two occasions surpassed Dryden, Thomas Otway (1652–1685), was an unsuccessful actor who turned to writing plays. His *Don Carlos* (1676), written in rhymed couplets, won for him his first success. When *Thomas Otway* Dryden abandoned rhyme, the world of playwrights changed with him; and Otway's second important play, *The Orphan* (1680), was in blank verse. The situation, turning upon the love of two brothers for Monimia, the orphan ward of their father, is one which Ford might have created. In working it out, Otway is relentless; he has evolved from it one of the cruelest of English tragedies. In his power of deepening the horror by a lighter, simpler touch, pitiful as a strain of music, he reminds us again of the later Elizabethans, especially of Webster. Even more successful than *The Orphan* was *Venice Preserved* (1682), in which, as in *The Orphan,* Otway caught something of the greatness of handling characteristic of an earlier time. His plays have the genuine passion which Dryden often lacked, and they are not marred by the distortions of human life and character that abound both in Dryden and in the Jacobean dramatists. Except for the plays mentioned, the tragedy of the Restoration has, in the main, only a literary interest, as a survival of the great dramatic period, and as an illustration of influence of the neoclassical tragedy of France.

Restoration comedy, however, is a genuine reflection of the temper, if not of the actual life, of the upper classes of the nation; and as such it has a sociological as *Restoration* well as a literary interest. As practiced by Shake- *tion* speare, English comedy had been romantic in spirit. *Comedy* However seriously it had been concerned with the essentials of human nature, it had had comparatively little to do with the circumstances of actual human life. In Ben Jonson and Middleton, and especially in the latest of the Jacobeans, Shirley, we find more realistic treatment of the setting, the social surroundings, of the play. Following their lead, and stimulated by the example of Molière, the comedians of the Restoration devoted themselves specifically to picturing the external details of life, the fashions of the time, its manners, its speech, its interests. For scene they turned to the most interesting places they knew, the drawing-rooms, the coffee-houses, the streets and gardens of London. Their characters were chiefly people of fashion, and their plots, for the most part, were love intrigues, often borrowed from the French, both developed with clever dialogue. They represent the reaction of the playgoing public against Puritanism. They are antisocial, in that they represent social institutions, particularly marriage, in an obnoxious or ridiculous light; but they are not romantic or revolutionary. There is in them never an honest protest against institutions, never a genu, ine note of revolt. Conventions are accepted to be played with and attacked, merely by way of giving opportunity for witty raillery, or point to an intrigue.

The first of this school of comedians was Sir George Etherege (1634–1691), an Englishman who had been educated at Paris, *Wycherley and Congreve* and who there had seen the comedies of Molière. Etherege was followed by William Wycherley (1641–1715), whose best plays are *The Country Wife* (1673) and *The Plain Dealer* (1674). Both are borrowed in outline from Molière, but their moral atmosphere is that of the corrupt court of Charles II, where Wycherley was a favorite. William Congreve (1670–1729) was a far more brilliant playwright. His masterpieces, *Love for Love* (1695) and *The Way of the World* (1700), carry the interest of dialogue, of the verbal fence between character and character, to its extreme development.

Charles Lamb defended his delight in Restoration comedy on the ground that the world it represented was a "Utopia of gallantry, where pleasure is a duty, and the manners perfect freedom." Macaulay attacked this view with the argument that Restoration comedy reflected accurately the world it represented, and that the world was morally reprehensible. A balanced view of this school of comedy supports neither of these positions. Restoration comedies are more or less perfect works of art and must not be regarded merely as escapes from the bondage of morality or as sociological studies. They furnish the judicious reader with legitimate moral holidays, even though, in a world in which morality is constantly flouted, heroes and heroines are given a modest allowance of decency and virtue. With few exceptions, however, the characters are rakes or lights of love, but their wit is inexhaustible and their style irreproachable. No more brilliant comic dialogue exists than that of Congreve in *The Way of the World.*

It has been pointed out that one effect of the age that succeeded the Restoration was to organize society, to restrain the license of the individual. The antisocial influence of the plays of the time was clearly perceived, and protest was not lacking. It took time for the protest to gather force, in face of the spirit of wild reaction against all that savored of Puritanism; but *The Protest of Jeremy Collier* in 1698 a clergyman, Jeremy Collier, published his *Short View of the Profaneness and Immorality of the English Stage,* and Dryden, who was one of the dramatists particularly attacked, admitted the justice of the rebuke. Its immediate effect was not sufficient to do away with the coarseness of Restoration comedy, which appears to the full in Sir John Vanbrugh (1664–1726); but an improvement is noticeable in the works of George Farquhar (1678–1707), the last of the school; and in Steele's plays the drama is in full alliance with the forces which were making for morality and decent living.

CHAPTER X

The Eighteenth Century

THE REIGN OF NEOCLASSICISM

THE EARLY eighteenth century shows a continuation of the social and literary forces seen in the Restoration. It was less a period of imaginative creation than one of criticism of the moral, social, and political deficiencies of the time. By means of an elegant and incisive prose style, the century was to *General* show a great advance in the writing of essays and *Charac-* novels. In poetry, the tradition continued of brilliant *teristics* topical satire and of didactic poetry that frequently was more tedious than brilliant. Appeal was normally sought to what was variously called Reason, Nature (i.e., the "natural" thing), or Common Sense. Polish and elegance of form were of more importance than subtlety or originality of thought. Dryden had said

> The things we must believe are few and plain;

and Pope was to state the ideal subject-matter of literature as

> What oft was thought, but ne'er so well expressed.

It was an age of interest in society and institutions rather than in the individual. The trading classes, growing rich and influential, at times reaffirmed the Puritanical standards, which the Restoration, especially in the drama, had discarded. The protest of Jeremy Collier against the stage, in 1698, was typical of the attitude of the new century, which realized and feared the antisocial effect of vice. The tendencies to find the subject-matter of literature in common social experience, to aim at perfection of form, and to emphasize the social utility of letters are notably illustrated by the three chief literary figures of the age of Queen Anne—Swift, Addison, and Pope.

The first of them and the greatest, Jonathan Swift, was born in Ireland of English parents, in 1667. He was a posthumous son, and the consequent rôle of "poor relation" galled his excessive pride. He was sent to the University of Dublin, where, as he says, he was "stopped of his degree for dulness and unsufficiency; and at last hardly admitted in a manner little to his credit." In 1689 he left Ireland to take a position as secretary to a distant relative, Sir William Temple, with whom he remained intermittently for some years, reading aloud to his patron, writing at dictation, keeping accounts, and cursing his fate. While in this service he wrote *The Battle of the Books,* a contribution to the controversy which Temple was carrying on with Bentley, the great scholar, as to the comparative merit of ancient and modern writers. About this time, also, he wrote a satire on the divisions of Christianity, called *A Tale of a Tub.* Neither work was published until 1704. With Temple's help he entered the church, and after his patron's death he returned to Ireland as chaplain to Lord Berkeley, by whom he was given the living of Laracor.

Jonathan Swift

Then began the great period of Swift's life, the time of his political power. During the reign of William III party strife was bitter between the Whigs, who supported the King in his foreign policy of resistance to Louis XIV of France, and the Tories, who opposed him; and this struggle was continued in the reign of Queen Anne. Almost all the prominent literary men of the time were engaged on one side or the other. Swift, who after 1708 was much in London, engaged in promoting the interests of the Anglican church in Ireland, at first wrote on the Whig side; but in 1710 he joined the Tories, who were just coming into power and who were more friendly to the interests of the Church. The Tories were resolved to stop the war with France, and in defense of this policy Swift put out one of his strongest political writings, *The Conduct of the Allies.* His life during these years is reflected in his *Journal to Stella,* a series of letters which he wrote for his friend, Esther Johnson. Here we find

His Political Career

Swift playing the part in which he most delighted, that of a man of affairs, active, successful, and powerful. He records with gusto his hours spent with the members of the Queen's ministry; their politeness and his own proud familiarity; his ability to serve his friends and to punish his enemies. In 1713, as reward for his support of the Tory government, he was named Dean of Saint Patrick's in Dublin, a promotion little to his taste. The next year, upon the death of Queen Anne, the Tories went out of power, and Swift returned to Ireland, to live as a discredited Tory among violent Whigs.

Here his unconquerable activity found vent in defending the Irish, rather than the Englishmen who lived in Ireland, from *His Later* the careless tyranny of the London government. In *Life* his endeavor he published *The Drapier's Letters*, most of them in 1724, as a protest against debasing the Irish coinage. In 1726 he took the manuscript of *Gulliver's Travels* to London for publication, and the next year he returned thither to taste the pleasure of a great literary success. This, as all else in his life, seemed to turn only to disappointment. In 1728 Miss Johnson, the "Stella" of the *Journal*, died. Whether or not it is true, as some think, that Swift was secretly married to her, she was his closest friend, and her death left him desolate. As the years passed his hatred for the world grew more intense, and his satire more bitter. He had suffered during most of his adult life from giddiness and deafness and melancholia. In his seventy-fourth year his mind failed notably; he himself was most conscious of the failure, and suffered from the consciousness. After more than three years of painful mental incapacity and even insanity he died within a month of his seventy-eighth birthday.

It is evident from this narrative that, to a great extent, Swift's writings were occasional, and grew out of the circumstances of *Swift's* his life. With one or two exceptions, his works *Practical* were published anonymously. He was a man of *Nature* affairs, who became a man of letters because literature was a means by which affairs could be directed. His writings must be regarded, then, as one expression among others of energy turned to practical ends; as one evidence among others of his preternatural activity. For Swift lived hard. "There is no such thing," he wrote to a friend, "as a fine old gentleman; if the man had a mind or body worth a farthing they would have worn him out long ago."

This need of exercise shows itself not only in his serious preoccupation with the life of his time, but also in his gigantic sense of play. The anecdotes related of him by his earlier biographers are legion, most of them turning *His* upon the translation of some whim into practical *Activity* form, usually as a grotesque joke. The tale of his dispersing a crowd gathered to witness an eclipse, by sending a message that, according to the Dean's orders, the eclipse would be put off for a day; of his impersonating a poor usher at a reception, to draw the contempt of a rich fool; and of his disguising himself as a fiddler at a beggar's wedding, to discover the arts by which impostors live—all these bear testimony to that restlessness which could not be satisfied by work alone. With this lighter side of Swift's nature are to be connected the works by which he is chiefly known—his satires *A Tale of a Tub* and *Gulliver's Travels.*

Once, indeed, this love of a practical joke was directly responsible for some of Swift's most characteristic writings. A certain Partridge was in the habit of issuing an *The* almanac, with predictions of events to fall out in *Partridge* the next year. This impostor, partly because he was *Pre-* obnoxious to Swift's political friends, he exposed *dictions* and attempted to silence in a set of "Predictions for the year 1708," one of which was the death of Partridge himself, who, according to the prophecy, should "infallibly die upon the 29th of March, about eleven at night, of a raging fever." This pamphlet was published over the name Isaac Bickerstaff. On the 30th of March Swift published a letter supposed to be written by a revenue officer to a certain nobleman, giving an account of Partridge's last days and death. He also wrote "An Elegy of Mr. Partridge." Of course Partridge hastened in triumph to assure the world that he was not dead; but Swift promptly came back with "A Vindication of Isaac Bickerstaff," in which, after rebuking Partridge for his impudence, he proved by various logical demonstrations that Partridge certainly died "within half an hour of the time foretold."

This skit is broadly characteristic of the whole spirit and method of Swift's work. He hates wrangling and argument, and seldom bothers to use the weapons of logical controversy. He attempts, rather, with his almost unparalleled fund of ingenuity and caustic wit, to laugh his opponents off the stage—and he usually succeeds. In his writings there is a disconcerting intermingling of earnestness and play. In "A Modest Proposal for Preventing the Children of Poor People from being a Burden," the terrible suffering in Ireland is revealed in the mocking suggestion that the poor should devote themselves to rearing children to be killed and eaten. *A Tale of a Tub*, with its bitter reflections upon the spiritual history of man since the advent of Christianity, is on its face the story of three stupid brothers quarrelling over the inheritance of their father. *Gulliver's Travels* is, outwardly, a sort of *Robinson Crusoe;* yet it is full of satiric intention.

Swift's Method

Gulliver is shipwrecked first at Lilliput, where the inhabitants are six inches tall—except their emperor, "taller by almost the breadth of my nail than any of his court, which alone is enough to strike an awe into the beholders." Here the satire obviously consists in showing human motives at work on a small scale, and in suggesting, by the likeness of the Lilliputians to ourselves, the littleness of human affairs, and especially the pettiness of political intrigues. The arts by which the officers of the government keep their places, such as cutting capers on a tight rope for the entertainment of the emperor, remind us of the quality of statesmanship in both Swift's day and our own; the dispute over the question at which end an egg should properly be broken, which plunged Lilliput into civil war, is a comment on the seriousness of party divisions in the greater world. Gulliver's next voyage, to Brobdingnag, brings him to a people as large in comparison with man as the Lilliputians are small. Once more his adventures are a tale of wonder, behind which lurks Swift's contempt for man's meannesses. Gulliver tells the giant beings by whom he is surrounded, and in comparison with whom he is a mere manikin, of the world from which he has

"Gulliver's Travels"

come. Among other things, he tells of the invention of gun-
powder and the use of instruments of warfare. "The king was
struck with horror at the description I had given of those terrible engines. He was amazed how so impotent and grovelling
an insect as I (these were his expressions) could entertain such
inhuman ideas." The third voyage, to Laputa and other curious
places, embodies Swift's contempt for pedantry and for useless
"scientific" experiment. And, lastly, in the fourth voyage we get
a burning indictment of man's tortuous and sly reasoning as
compared to the noble inhabitants of Houyhnhnmland, who
within the shapes of horses embody "perfection of Nature." In
contrast to these beings into whose minds the light of pure
reason shines always and without diffraction, the beastly Yahoos
represent Swift's conception of man living in a degenerate state
of nature. The evil instincts of "civilized" man are here again
bitterly portrayed.

This double point of view, this combination of playfulness
and earnestness is seen in all Swift's best work and is· deeply
rooted in his mental constitution. He will not argue; he will,
with playful bitterness, dramatize the evils that man ought to
correct but either will not or cannot. One has only to examine
the half-dozen sentences scattered through Gulliver's voyages
that concern the content and methods of education to see that
Swift had a fine sense of values and that he had a relatively
simple program for promoting those values. But though he un-
ceasingly combatted man's follies, he had little or no confidence
that man would consistently fight for his own improvement.
All man seemed to want was an illusion of happiness—"the
serene peaceful state" (as Swift cried out) "of being a fool
among knaves." It was this despair of man that made Swift's
poetry the most realistic, the least idyllic or "romantic" that
was ever written. He refused the drug of illusion consistently.

It is the thoroughness of this pessimism, this complete distrust of the world, that gives to him his singularity and peculiar
impressiveness among English writers. In this pessi-   *His Dis-*
mism there is something stimulating, something   *tinction*
awakening. His keenness calls for answering alert-
ness in ourselves; his suggestiveness is tonic; even his coarseness
contains something of vigorous criticism that will not let us

rest in conventional opinions, but bids us prove all things and call everything by its true name.

The practical spirit which Swift brought to his writing, his intention to make it serve a turn and accomplish a purpose, is *His Style* reflected in his style. First among his merits as a writer is his incisive vigor. Further, his contempt for all kinds of sham led him to despise literary affectation; directness and simplicity are the virtues by which he sets most store. Indeed, if it had been unrelieved by his playfulness, his ironic ingenuity, it would perhaps have been too severe, too sternly practical, too reserved, too dry. It represents men and things in too hard a light, with too sharp an outline, without the softening and color which come from a sympathetic temperament. Yet with all this practical downrightness, Swift's style is full of finesse. A more subtle instrument, capable of more delicate persiflage, of more elaborate innuendo, it would be difficult to find. So little obvious are its devices, so persistent is its plainness, that we cease to suspect it; but the writer neither slumbers nor sleeps. Of obvious decoration, such as balance, rhythm, antithesis—the half-poetic qualities of earlier prose—Swift has little. Indeed, it is clear that the nakedness and simplicity of his style were necessary to the rapidity and address of his attack. In the heavy rhetorical panoply of *Euphues* or Jeremy Taylor he would have been as helpless as David in the armor of Saul. Absolute, unmitigated prose he wrote—the quintessence of prose.

The bulk of Swift's political writing appeared in pamphlets, but he used also the periodical form; he contributed to a paper *Periodical* in the Tory interest, called *The Examiner*, to which *Literature* Addison, the chief literary man among the Whigs, replied in the *Whig Examiner*. The idea of the periodical appearance of a party organ was suggested by the newspapers, of which the first had appeared in 1622, Butter's *Weekly News from Italy and Germany*. These early newspapers were at first little more than meager chronicles of events. Gradually they came to include discussion of lighter matters, at times in the form of answers to questions. *Defoe's Review* contained a separate department called "Advice from the Scandalous Club, being a weekly history of Nonsense, Impertinence, Vice, and

Debauchery." That province of journalism which lies between news and politics was not adequately possessed, however, until, in 1709, there appeared a periodical of which the object was to "observe upon the pleasurable as well as the busy part of man-kind." This was *The Tatler*, founded by Richard Steele (1672–1729), who was soon joined in the enterprise by his friend Joseph Addison (1672–1719).

The Tatler appeared three times a week. Each number con-sisted of several letters dated from the different coffee-houses of London; those from the Saint James being de- *"The* voted to foreign and domestic affairs, those from *Tatler"* Will's to poetry and the drama, those from White's to "gallantry, pleasure, and entertainment." There were also papers dated "From my own apartment," which dealt with mis-cellaneous topics, personal or social. It was in these last that the authors carried out most fully the object which they set before themselves, "to expose the false arts of life, to pull off the disguises of cunning, vanity, and affectation, and to recom-mend a general simplicity in our dress, our discourse, and our behavior." Although *The Tatler* appealed to the public with-out distinction of party, it was colored by Steele's Whig views. Accordingly, when the authors wished to avoid politics alto-gether they abandoned *The Tatler*, replacing it by *The Spec-tator* (1711), for which Addison wrote most of the best essays.

Although Addison and Steele are thus remembered for their effort to lead literature away from politics, both were party men. Addison first attracted notice while at Oxford by a *Joseph* Latin poem on the Treaty of Ryswick; in recognition *Addison* of this effort he received a pension of three hundred pounds a year, enabling him to travel abroad. After his return the Whigs needed a poet to celebrate the Duke of Marl-borough's victory of Blenheim, and the commission fell to Addison. His poem "The Campaign" gained for its author various honors and preferments, and until his death in 1719 he was almost constantly in office. Indeed, Addison's career affords the best example of the high rewards which the service of party offered in the early eighteenth century to literary men. Even his tragedy, *Cato,* which was presented in 1713, owed its great popularity to a supposed parallel between the struggles of parties at Rome and the contemporary political situation in England; and as neither party could allow the other to take to itself the platitudes about liberty with which the play is strewn, Whigs and Tories alike attended the performances, vying with each other in the violence of their applause.

No character in English letters is better known or more generally admired than Addison. This power of attracting admira-

Addison's Character
tion is largely due to a certain classic quality which showed itself in his literary ideals, in his pure, regular style, in the just appreciation of his criticism, and in his singularly correct sense of conduct. His taste was nearly faultless, and taste did for him what it should do for any one; it saved him from blunders and follies. In his life as in his writing, what he did was well done. Every stroke that went to the formation of his character seems to have been laid on with conscious care and conscious pride. The last touch of all, as he lay on his death-bed, and turning to his stepson bade him "See in what peace a Christian can die," expresses the mood in which his whole life was lived.

This mood colored most of Addison's writing. The papers which he contributed to *The Tatler, The Spectator,* and other

His Mission
periodicals are for the most part essays in the art of living. They illustrate the practical nature of his own culture, his easy, skilled mastery of life. Of the world of the eighteenth century, with its crudeness, its coarseness, its grotesqueness, as revealed in the drawings of Hogarth, Addison was as critical as Matthew Arnold of the later nineteenth century, with its materialism and its trust in machinery. Both were missionaries, Addison the more successful because the more tactful. His task too was simpler, to enforce ideals of civilization, and in particular to overcome the antisocial tendencies of both Puritan and Cavalier, preserving the zeal for conduct of the former without his gloom and intolerance, and the lightness and gayety of the latter without his license. Thus we find many of Addison's papers directed against the coarser vices of the time, against gambling, drinking, swearing, indecency of conversation, cruelty, practical joking, duelling. Others attack the triviality of life, special follies and foibles of dress, of manners, or

of thought; others, the lack of order and comfort in the life of the community. Addison cared also for the literary cultivation of his readers, as is shown by such papers as the famous series of criticisms on Milton. Finally, he made a novel contribution to literature in a series of sketches of character and contemporary types—of himself as the Spectator, of Sir Andrew Freeport the merchant, of Sir Roger de Coverley the country gentleman, of Will Honeycomb the man of fashion. These figures typified conveniently the interests of the public to which *The Spectator* appealed; but more than this they define themselves as persons, fitting members of the great company of characters who live in English fiction from Chaucer to George Meredith. One of them at least, Sir Roger de Coverley, to whose presentation both Addison and Steele contributed, is drawn with genuine affection, as an embodiment of healthy, kindly, natural virtue, touched with just enough humor to make the picture convincing and wholly winning.

In his treatment of these various subjects Addison displays the graces of style which are the expression of his character. He has perfect confidence in his position, and in his style ***His*** sureness goes hand in hand with absolute lightness ***Method*** of touch. His sense of humor saves him from putting himself on the defensive by overemphasis. Even such a serious subject as the separation between men on political grounds, he treats by a playful comparison with the fashion of ladies in wearing plaster patches of different shapes on their faces. This easy tone comes from Addison's moderation and reasonableness, and from his genuine good nature. Satirist though he is, he is never misanthropic. The difference between his satire and Swift's appears in the contrast between his bantering analysis of a "Coquette's Heart" and Swift's savage "Letter to a Young Lady."

Technically, Addison's style shows how rapidly English prose was approaching its perfection. For the more regular virtues, clearness, facility, grace, it has always been a model. ***His Style*** Its best encomium was pronounced by Doctor Johnson when he wrote: "Whoever wishes to attain an English style, familiar but not coarse, and elegant but not ostentatious, must give his days and nights to the volumes of Addison."

Despite the close connection between Addison and Steele, in friendship, political interests, and literary work, the two men *Addison and Steele* were very different. Addison's father was a clergyman. Addison himself intended to take orders, and throughout his life showed something of the remoteness and coldness of clerical culture. "He acted," as a contemporary said with some scorn, "like a parson in a tie-wig." Steele, on the contrary, was for some years a soldier, and never lost the bearing of his profession. He was Captain Steele and wore a sword to the end of his days.

Steele's life was a miscellaneous one, filled with all sorts of ventures, literary, political, and commercial. He left Oxford *Steele's Character* without his degree, to enlist as a soldier. He forsook the army to become an active pamphleteer and journalist in the interest of the Whigs, by whom he was given various government positions. He was elected to Parliament, but was expelled from the House for writing a political pamphlet. He wrote several plays, and was for a time director of Drury Lane Theatre. Altogether his life was a thing of fragments. His character, too, showed certain flaws and lapses, faults of a generous, spontaneous nature; and to these his writings in a measure served to call attention. While a soldier he wrote *The Christian Hero*, a thin volume designed to celebrate the superiority of Christian virtues over those noble Roman traits so valued in the neoclassical period; his plays were a bit superfluously moral; in *The Tatler* he appeared as a preacher. This discrepancy between his personal life and the tenor of much of his writing laid Steele open to gibe and sneer; but there is an honest human quality about his inconsistencies that gives him, after all, a charm which his greater contemporaries lack. Whether as Christian or as man of the world, Steele was always himself, and if he did not erect a palatial character like Addison's, he built a genial dwelling-place where all the world was welcome.

The inconsistency in Steele's life is reflected in his style. He *His Style* has two manners: one eminent, gracious, dignified, the style which corresponds to his moods of elevation and didacticism; the other careless, flexible, free, like his ordinary life. This second manner is best seen in his letters to his wife, which, in their delightful frankness and their abandonment to the feeling of the moment, show him in his most attractive aspect. They prove that the lightness and ease which mark *The Tatler* and *The Spectator*, qualities which in Addison were the fruit of cultivation, were entirely native to Steele.

Addison and Steele were moralists, and their doctrine is in a high degree characteristic of their time. It deals with the material and superficial aspects of living; it represents the effort of literature to support the conventions in accordance with which life was ordering itself. This attitude, however wholesome and necessary, involved a tendency to set an excessive value on outward behavior *Lord Chesterfield* as distinct from character, a tendency which becomes more marked in a writer of somewhat later date, Lord Chesterfield (1694–1773). The principles of good form, for which Chesterfield's name is a byword, he expounds fully in his *Letters to His Son*, which set forth a system of conduct based frankly upon scepticism as to the reality of morals. Historically Chesterfield represents the extreme swing of the pendulum that was set in motion by Steele and Addison. With him the decorum and urbanity inculcated by *The Spectator* have become the major ends of life, the chief business of a gentleman. Chesterfield typifies one aspect of the sceptical tendencies of his century, its refusal to go behind what was of obvious utility, to believe in what was technical or eccentric. Politeness can be seen, felt, valued; it lubricates social relations. Good manners, "the graces," may be an instrument of social as well as personal advancement; hence the wise man puts his trust in them, in the techniques of social success in the broadest sense. Chesterfield constantly preaches such doctrines of deportment in his *Letters*.

There is no sharp dividing line between the prose writers and the poets of the early eighteenth century. The practical spirit of the age, which limited the realm of art to the interests of actual life, made the material of prose *Prose and Poetry* and poetry much the same; and, because of the character of couplet verse, the typical virtues of poetry were not very different from those of prose. Of the writers already discussed, Swift and Addison were poets as well as writers of prose. The greatest poet of the period, however, the direct continuator of the tradition of Dryden, and the most brilliant man of letters of the early part of the century, was Alexander Pope.

Pope was born in 1688 of Catholic parents. By reason of the sweeping laws against the entrance of Catholics into public
Alexander Pope
service, he was shut out from the ordinary career of Englishmen in Parliament, the church, or the army. In consequence he was among his contemporaries almost the sole example of an author who was entirely a man of letters; the events of his life are altogether literary events. He began his career early. His *Pastorals,* written when he was seventeen, were published in 1709. The *Essay on Criticism* two years later attracted Addison's notice; and Pope's other early poems, "Windsor Forest," "Eloisa to Abelard," and above all *The Rape of the Lock,* of which the first draft appeared in 1712, added to his reputation. About 1713 he undertook the greatest venture of his life, the translation of Homer, which he did not complete until 1725. One important effect of the translation on Pope's own career and on the literature of the time is to be noted. From the publishers and from his sales to subscribers Pope obtained more than five thousand pounds for the *Iliad,* and two-thirds of this sum for the *Odyssey* (on which half of the work was done by others)—the greatest pecuniary reward which up to that time had been received by any English author. It made Pope independent of patronage and politics, and it marks a change in the social status of authors: they might now write frankly, for money, without losing caste.

The profits of his translation enabled Pope to buy a small place at Twickenham, on the Thames near London. This he
His Later Life
fitted up in the artificial style which the age affected in other things besides literature. He became a patron of the less formal style in landscape-gardening, which strove for intricacy and picturesque effects; he scattered statuary and temples about in artistic contrast to the woods and lawns; and as his crowning achievement he built his famous grotto, ornamented with mirrors and geological specimens. At Twickenham Pope lived the remainder of his life, secluded from the cares and struggles of the world, but very constantly occupied with his own relations to it. Here he entertained his

friends, among whom were the leading patrons and artists in painting, architecture, gardening, and music, as well as the best known literary men of his day—Swift, Arbuthnot, Gay, Young, and Thomson. Inferior, especially journalistic, writers envied his success, and provoked his wrath. As revenge for their attacks, he published, in 1728, a great satire entitled *The Dunciad*. At Twickenham also Pope saw much of Bolingbroke, and under his influence wrote the *Essay on Man*, published in 1733 and 1734. The remainder of his work consists of the *Moral Epistles* (satires in imitation of Horace), the "Epistle to Doctor Arbuthnot," which is Pope's chief defense of himself, and the "Epilogue to the Satires." These were published before 1739, after which date Pope wrote little. He died in 1744.

Pope's claim to the first place among the poets of his time cannot be gainsaid, but his true place among the poets of all time has been a matter of dispute. At the outset it must be recognized that certain sources of power *Pope's* were denied him, partly in consequence of the nature *Limi-* of the period in which he lived and its conception of *tations* the nature and function of poetry—so different from that of the nineteenth century or the present day. The poet's aim was not at all self-expression; he strove to utter "What oft was thought, but ne'er so well expressed." In other words, he avoided obscure private emotions and all highly particular personal experience. He valued the universal, and endeavored to give poetic fervor to the problems of man's moral nature. Unfortunately, universal truths are likely to be commonplaces and to lack any subtlety of appeal except through neat, polished diction and versification. The emotions involved are public property and so tend to lack poignancy.

But though certain qualities which we expect to find in poetry are necessarily absent in Pope, these were replaced, at least for his contemporaries, by others. First of all, he owed *His* his success to his marvelous skill in handling the *Poetic* heroic couplet. He declares that as a child he "lisped *Qualities* in numbers, for the numbers came." But he was not satisfied with precocious amateurism. One of his earliest friends and critics, William Walsh, pointed out to him that "though we had had several great poets, we never had any one great poet that was correct." Correctness, accordingly, Pope made his aim from the first. Correctness requires patience, and genius for taking pains Pope had in abundance. Nor did he sacrifice to mere exactness of metre and rhyme the other virtues of couplet verse, compression, epigrammatic force, and brilliancy of diction.

The importance of technical qualities in the eyes of Pope's public is attested by the success of the *Essay on Criticism*, in

The "Essay on Criticism"

which he set forth the artistic principles of the time with special reference to poetry. In this discussion he expresses the chief canon of the age in the direction to follow nature, but nature methodized by rules, for "to copy nature is to copy them." The substance of the poem is made up of commonplaces, for Pope and his readers believed that novelty was likely to be mere eccentricity; but these commonplaces are given the most apt, the most chiselled form, a form in which they are fitted to survive as part of the common wisdom of the race.

Pope's comprehension of the artistic demands of his time, and his rhetorical skill, fitted him admirably for the work which

Pope's Homer

took up most of the middle years of his life, that of translation. He translated from Ovid, Horace, and Statius; and he modernized Chaucer and Donne. But the most notable of all his attempts in this direction is his translation of Homer. The attitude of the eighteenth century toward the greatest of the classics is shown by a line in the *Essay on Criticism*, which declares that Homer and nature are the same, the highest object of study and imitation. Pope's own knowledge of Homer was amateurish and inaccurate; he was an indifferent Greek scholar, and was forced to depend on Latin, French, and English translations. But the impossibility of his making a literally faithful translation left him the freer to turn the material of the Greek poems into the form in which it was most fitted to become a part of the culture of his own time. Not only does Homer, in Pope's hands, become an eighteenth-century poet, by virtue of his submission to the literary fashions of the day—the heroic couplet, and conventional poetic diction

—but even the characters, the manners, the ethical ideals of primitive Greece are poured into eighteenth-century moulds. Just as to the cloudy mediæval imagination the heroes of Troy became knights, so to Pope's more enlightened understanding they are statesmen and party leaders, treating each other with parliamentary courtesy, and talking of virtue, patriotism, and fame as glibly and eloquently as Bolingbroke himself. In the loftier parts of Homer's poetry Pope's style has a certain appropriateness. It is in the level passages of narrative and description, where the simple material will not take the polish of brilliant diction and epigram, that Pope falls lamentably short of his original. Yet with all deductions, his Homer is an amazing performance, perhaps the most effective translation, or rather adaptation, in existence; a *tour de force* made possible by the definiteness and precision of eighteenth-century art, and by the confidence of the age in its own ideals.

The works of Pope thus far mentioned are chiefly remarkable for their literary qualities; they show him as the master of his form. But even more important is the group of poems in which, with no loss of artistic finish, he dealt directly with the life of his time. Of these *The Rape of the Lock* stands first. The poem was *"The Rape of the Lock"* suggested by a trivial occurrence, the rude behavior of Lord Petre in cutting a lock from the head of Miss Fermor. Only the excessive interest of the age in social matters, combined with the sympathetic genius of a poet, could have made such gossip as this outlast the centuries. Pope wrote first a rapid account of the card-party at Hampton at which the theft took place. Later he expanded the poem by introducing the sylphs who guard the lady's bed, make her toilet, and attend her in public—admirable suggestions of the artifice which directed each act, however trivial, of a belle of Queen Anne's day. *The Rape of the Lock* is not only a satire on society; it is also a witty parody of the heroic style in poetry. Even the verse form is treated humorously, especially through its tendency toward anticlimax, as in the lines,

> Here thou, great Anna! whom three realms obey,
> Dost sometimes counsel take—and sometimes tea.

In *The Rape of the Lock* the satire is general, and, on the whole, good-natured. Many of Pope's poems, however, are intensely personal, and grew out of the circum-

Pope's Character

stances of his life. As has been said already, his character was not a great one. We listen in vain in his poetry for the deeper notes of individual human experience. But his lack of absorption in his inner life made him morbidly sensitive in his superficial contact with the world. His biography is largely a record of his personal relations with Wycherley, Swift, Addison, Arbuthnot, and Bolingbroke; and of his literary enmities with men too numerous and generally too obscure for mention. During the last ten years of his life he brought about, by ingenious manipulation, the printing of his correspondence with many of his more famous literary friends. He did not wish to seem to publish these letters himself; hence the manipulation for which he has been excessively blamed. Though Pope was not a letter writer of the first rank, the publication of his correspondence had a great influence on letter writers after 1735.

Toward the close of his life his personal interests formed more and more the chief motive of his poetry. The *Moral*

His Later Satire

Epistles, though written ostensibly on general themes like "The Use of Riches," are crowded with particular allusions; and the "Imitations of Horace" are likewise made up of personal contemporary sketches. The "Epistle to Arbuthnot" contains Pope's revenge for Addison's support of a rival translation of Homer, the biting lines in which Addison is described as Atticus. Here, as in the best of all personal satire, the individual (Addison) becomes the stimulus for moral indignation of universal significance, for though Addison may or may not have been an envious, cold-hearted critic, there are always such in the world, and hence the satire has a certain universal validity. In the intense political animosity that arose at the end of the reign of Queen Anne, Pope by his Catholicism (which supposedly made him an enemy to the Hanoverian or Protestant succession), by his alliance with Swift, Arbuthnot, and others, was brought into collision with many anonymous journalists and with critics like John Dennis or like Theobald, a rival editor of Shakespeare, or like Bentley, who as a Greek scholar spoke disrespectfully of Pope's Homer.

These and countless other literary and personal grudges Pope paid off by the several editions of *The Dunciad*, an elaborate satire in which, after the fashion of Dryden in *MacFlecknoe*, the dullards, pedants, and bad poets are presented in ridiculous surroundings and attitudes. It should be remembered, however, that Pope, like Sir Philip Sidney before him, represented an aristocratic tradition in literature, part of which was the defense of poetry against those who through lack of skill or for mercenary reasons would do it wrong.

One of Pope's last friendships, that with Bolingbroke, proved the inspiration of the best remembered of his poems, the *Essay on Man*. Bolingbroke was the representative of a philosophy, thoroughly characteristic of eighteenth-century thought, to which the name Deism has been given. Deism was an effort to substitute natural for revealed religion. Indeed, Pope's *Essay* is rationalistic in that it finds satisfactory grounds for belief in God by the exercise of reason, unaided by revelation. The poem is in reality an application of common sense to the problems of the universe and to the life of man; and where common sense refuses to carry us, "beyond the flaming ramparts of the world," there Pope limits his inquiry. The first epistle is concerned with man's place in nature; the second with individual ethics; the third with the origin of society and politics; the fourth with the question of man's happiness. In all four appear the rationalism of the century, its satisfaction with things as they are, its dislike of those speculative differences which lead to fanaticism, its trust in downright utility. In short, the *Essay on Man* is a marvelous crystallization of the fluid popular thinking of his day. Some ideas are absurd; many are embodied in passages that seem permanent expressions of the ideas involved. The poem is not so systematic as Pope thought it, and more than once lines even contradict each other.

Pope was by personal inclination connected chiefly with the writers who gathered about Swift, and in Swift's absence in Ireland he was the centre of the group. His satellite of chief magnitude was John Gay (1685–1732). *John Gay* Gay, more than his greater friends, was a thoroughly good-natured, likeable man, whose bent was toward broad, genial humor rather than bitter satire. His earliest important poem, *The Shepherd's Week* (1714), was a burlesque treatment of the conventions of pastoral poetry. In *Trivia* (1716) he transferred his talent for humorous observation to the London streets, and this and the *Fables* (1727) show his happy faculty for easy comment and criticism of life. His fame in his own day rested perhaps chiefly upon *The Beggar's Opera* (1728), another burlesque centering about the adventures of Captain Macheath, a fascinating highwayman. Nearly all the songs were set to folk melodies long known in England. Indeed, Gay is now remembered chiefly for his lyrical gift, which produced the two famous songs, " 'Twas when the seas were roaring" and "Black-eyed Susan."

CHAPTER XI

The Eighteenth Century

THE DECLINE OF NEOCLASSICISM

I

THE DEATH of Pope in 1744 is conventionally regarded as marking the end of the period during which the classical ideal was dominant in literature. This ideal was now to give way gradually to what is called the Romantic Movement. Romanticism has already been referred to in connection with the Renaissance. It is essentially the emphasis upon the individual effort to escape from the world of conventions and social control. There are two great avenues of such escape—external nature and the imagination. The former appealed by contrast to the prevailing admiration of urban life; the latter led men's thoughts into the past, and to remote lands. Indeed, mediævalism became associated with the Romantic Movement somewhat as classicism with the Renaissance, because it provided writers with material and forms suitable to their mood. But romanticism looked toward the future also; in its reverence for the individual, it fostered sympathy for the oppressed, applauded resistance to institutions hostile to human rights, and looked forward to a more democratic social system. But it must not be thought that romanticism and classicism are mutually exclusive elements. Both impulses are present in every age. But while the classical movement was gaining strength throughout the seventeenth century and became dominant after 1660, the romantic tendency began to gather force early in the eighteenth century and came to full triumph early in the nineteenth.

The Romantic Movement

Even before Pope's death there were signs of reaction against the neoclassicism which he so perfectly typified. His success with the heroic couplet moved younger poets to try other forms, and

Early Romantic Tend- encies

in increasing number they returned to the great poems of his predecessors, Milton and Spenser, in blank verse and the Spenserian stanza. Moreover, his comparative neglect of external nature and the more extravagant aspects of human passion may have been a cause why men of originality should have entered these fields. At first this play of emotion manifested itself in a return to the great theme which had inspired so much seventeenth-century poetry and prose—death. The number of poems of the character of Thomas Parnell's "Night Piece on Death" (1721), and Robert Blair's "The Grave" (1743) gave rise to the term "graveyard poetry" to designate the school. The earliest poets to exemplify romanticism broadly, however, made use of the two avenues mentioned above—external nature and the past.

The first of this group of poets, James Thomson (1700–1748), was a Scotsman who came up to London in 1725. The

Thomson's "Seasons"

following year he published a section, "Winter," of a poem which he afterward continued under the titles "Summer," "Spring," and "Autumn," and which was published in 1730 as *The Seasons*. To a reader of to-day, accustomed to a subtler appreciation of nature than Thomson's, this poem seems a rather humdrum chronicling of the sights, experiences, and thoughts connected with the changes of the year; and the moral digressions, the compliments to patrons, the personifications, and the frequently stilted rhetoric, tend to obscure the real freshness and truth of Thomson's observation. But to the readers of his own day the novelty

Novelty of Thom- son's Nature- Studies

was great. For two generations the first-hand study of nature had been comparatively neglected. Literature had found its interests in urban life; or, if it ventured into the country at all, it was into the conventional, unreal country of the pastoral tradition. The Augustan age cared more for a formal garden in the Dutch or Italian style than for the sublimest natural landscape in the world; and when, by the necessity of their subject, Augustan authors had touched upon ordinary natural phenomena, they chose a style rich in literary connotation and appropriate to their rather formalized and "civilized" concept of nature. Accordingly, Thomson's poem seemed surprisingly simple and direct in its approach to outdoor nature. His views of English landscape, now panoramic and now detailed, his description of the first spring showers, of the summer thunderstorms, and of the terrors of the wintry night, showed an honest understanding and sensitivity. Thomson's popularization of scientific themes, particularly the concept of nature which Sir Isaac Newton had revealed, also contributed to the pleasure of the eighteenth-century reader. In the Hymn with which *The Seasons* concludes, a higher mood appears—a mood of religious ecstasy in the presence of nature, prophetic of Wordsworth, by whom, indeed, Thomson was highly valued:

> Ye forests, bend; ye harvests, wave to Him—
> Breathe your still song into the reaper's heart
> As home he goes beneath the joyous moon.

The Seasons is in blank verse. In *The Castle of Indolence*, published in 1748, Thomson adopted the Spenserian stanza. His allegiance to Spenser is more than formal. He succeeds in recapturing much of the master's rich, long-drawn music, and he steeps his allegory in the Spenserian atmosphere of mirage-like splendor. The embowered castle of the enchanter Indolence *"The Castle of Indolence"* and his captives, the "land of drowsy-head," with its "listless climate," where the plaint of stock-doves mingles with the sighing of the hillside pines and with the murmur of the distant sea, are described with an art which made *The Castle of Indolence* a fruitful influence in romantic verse, even as late as Keats.

As Thomson exemplifies the Spenserian influence at work in the eighteenth century, Collins, Young, and Gray mark that of Milton. Young reverted to Milton's blank verse; Collins and Gray abound in echoes, and indeed in literal borrowings, from Milton's earlier lyrical work. To Milton's example in *Influence of Spenser and Milton* "L'Allegro" and "Il Penseroso" is perhaps due the fact that both these poets, after they had abandoned other conventions of

neoclassic verse, persisted in the use of those lifeless personifications—"wan Despair," "brown Exercise," "Music, sphere-
descended Maid"—in which the Augustan age delighted.

William Collins (1721–1759) was a delicate, nervously irres-
olute spirit, who lived his life under the shadow of a constitu-

*Collins's
Odes*

tional despondency which deepened at last into
insanity. He was an ardent disciple of Thomson's,
and when he came up to London, he settled near
Thomson's house in Kew Lane, where the elder poet was illustrating his romantic tendencies by writing verse in the moonlight, while listening to the nightingales in Richmond Gardens.
In 1746 Collins published a slender volume of *Odes*, in which
we can trace, more surely than in Thomson's work, the recovery
of the more "romantic" qualities of poetry. The exquisite "Ode
to Evening" shows a sympathy with nature and an observation
of her aspects, subtler and more suggestive than that displayed
in *The Seasons*. The ode is unrhymed, and has a low, meditative twilight music. The famous "Ode on the Passions" is, on
the contrary, very rich and elaborate in its metrical form, and
illustrates the influence upon Collins of Milton's lyrical art.
The Passions here are shadowy personifications, and the effect
of the whole poem is rather cold, but it shows clearly that the
technical secrets of lyrical poetry were beginning to be redis-
covered.

Another ode of Collins's, "On the Popular Superstitions of
the Highlands" (written in 1749 but not published until 1758),

*"Ode on
Popular
Super-
stitions"*

is one of the most interesting landmarks in the history of the romantic revival. The purpose of the
poem is to recommend the native folk-lore of Scotland as poetic material. Collins lets his fancy play
over the folk-myths of water-witch, pygmy, and
will-o'-the-wisp, and over all the creatures of that fairy world
so real to the mediæval mind. With kindling imagination he
describes the wild Northern islands, whose inhabitants subsist
on birds' eggs found among the sea-cliffs, where the bee is never
heard to murmur; and he transports us to that mysterious region, where "beneath the showery West" the buried Kings stalk
forth at midnight

In pageant robes, and wreathed with sheeny gold,
And on their twilight tombs aerial council hold.

Here we see several of the leading traits of romanticism: interest in the mysterious and supernatural, in strange and remote conditions of human life, and in the Middle Ages as they appeared in vague chiaroscuro through a veil of dream.

Collins's constitutional melancholy found little expression in his verse; it appears only as a kind of romantic sensibility penetrating his best lyrics, such as the "Dirge in Cymbeline" and "How Sleep the Brave," and cast- *Young's* ing here and there a faint flush of warmth over *"Night* his odes. The funereal broodings and romantic *Thoughts"* despair, characteristic of the new movement, found their most striking expression in *The Complaint; or Night Thoughts on Life, Death, and Immortality* of Edward Young (1683–1765), published in 1742–1745, when the author was sixty. The *Night Thoughts* are a series of reflections upon the brevity and tragic uncertainties of life, leading to a view of religion as man's consoler. The poet dwells, sometimes with tragic force and gloomy magnificence of phrase, oftener with a hollow and pompous rhetoric, upon the solitude of the tomb and the grim circumstances of death. In the same year in which the *Night Thoughts* were begun, a far greater poet, Thomas Gray, began his famous "Elegy in a Country Churchyard," in which is revealed the same sombre view of man's life and destiny, though softened and broadened and humanized in a way to make the poem not only a perfect work of art, but a permanent expression of the mood it embodies.

Thomas Gray (1716–1771) lived the life of a scholar and recluse at Cambridge, where in his later years he held a professorship of history, but delivered no lectures. The *Thomas* range of his intellectual interests, as shown by his *Gray* letters, journals, and prose remains, was immense, including, besides ancient and modern literature, music, painting, architecture, and natural science. He was sensitive to all the finer influences of the time; and his development furnishes a kind of index to the spiritual forces at work, many years before they found a general outlet.

Gray's poetry, the bulk of which is very small, falls into three periods. His early odes, written about 1742, of which the best known are those "On Spring" and "On a Distant Prospect of Eton College," have much of the moralizing tone of Augustan poetry, though in their metrical form, in their sympathy with nature, and in their vague dejection, they show the romantic leaven at work. Gray's second period (1750–1757) includes the "Elegy in a Country Churchyard" (1751)[1] and his two most ambitious odes, "The Progress of Poesy" and "The Bard." "The Elegy," perhaps the most widely known and loved of English poems, is the finest flower of that "literature of melancholy" which Milton's "Il Penseroso," acting upon the

"The Elegy" awakening romantic sense of the second quarter of the eighteenth century, brought forth in remarkable profusion. A large part of the charm of "The Elegy" comes from the poet's personal, sensitive approach to his subject. He lingers in the churchyard, noting the signs of approaching nightfall, until the atmosphere of twilight musing is established, after which his reflections upon life and death have a tone of sad and intimate sincerity. In its recognition of the dignity of simple lives lived close to the soil, and in its sympathy with their fate, the "Elegy" looks forward to the humanitarian enthusiasm which marked the later phases of romantic poetry.

"The Progress of Poesy" "The Progress of Poesy" is a Pindaric ode, of the same type as Dryden's "Alexander's Feast," but more richly rhymed and more elaborate in construction. It has the elegance of diction and employs the neoclassic mythology of Queen Anne poetry, but in the richness of its music it shows the romantic temper. "The Bard" is more distinctly romantic, in both subject and treat-

"The Bard" ment. An ancient minstrel, the last of the Welsh singers, escaped from Edward's massacre, stops the King in a wild mountain-pass, and prophesies the terrors which are to gather over his descendants. This poem, with its imaginative rekindling of the passion of an ancient and perished people, shows, like Collins's ode "On the Superstitions

[1] Begun in 1742, but laid aside and not finished until 1750.

of the Highlands," that reversion to the Middle Ages for inspiration which soon became the leading feature of romantic art.

The third period of Gray's production shows how deep a hold mediævalism had already taken on him. He *Icelandic* mastered old Norse material, probably in trans- *and Welsh* lation, and studied Welsh. The fruits of these re- *Studies* searches were two powerful translations, as grim and picturesque as the most romantic heart could desire—"The Fatal Sisters" and "The Descent of Odin" (1768).

A great stimulus was given to the curiosity concerning mediæval literature by the appearance in 1765 of a ballad collection entitled *Reliques of Ancient English Poetry,* gathered together by Bishop Percy, an antiquarian scholar with literary tastes. These ballads had a great effect in quickening the romantic impulse, by virtue of their naïve feeling and simple, passionate expression. About the same time as the *Reliques,* appeared another book which, though not so genuine, had an even greater effect. This was an epic poem in irregular chanting prose, entitled *Fingal* (1761, dated 1762) purporting to have been originally written in the ancient Gaelic tongue of the *Ossian* Scotch highlands by Ossian, the son of Fingal, a Celtic hero traditionally said to belong to the third century. The figures of the story are shadowy and grand, the scenery wild, the imagery, at least to an uncritical reader, touched with a certain primitive sublimity and grandeur, and the whole pervaded by an atmosphere of melancholy which is emphasized in the sighing cadences of the style of which the following passage is characteristic:

By the side of a rock on the hill, beneath the ancient trees, old Ossian sat on the moss; the last of the race of Fingal. Dull through the leafless trees he heard the voice of the north. . . . Fair with her locks of gold, her smooth neck, and her breasts of snow; fair as the spirits of the hills when at silent noon they glide along the heath—came Minvane the maid. Fingal, she softly saith, loose me my brother Gaul. Loose me the hope of my race, the terror of all but Fingal. . . . Take thy brother, O Minvane, thou fairer than the snows of the north!

These "Ossianic" poems seem to have been in large part a clever literary fabrication, the work of a young Scotsman named Macpherson, who probably got his hint from genuine fragments of old Erse poetry. Their air of primeval sublimity was specious enough to make them pass current with an age which was weary of the classical traditions and eager for novel sensation; and their influence was enormous, not only in England but upon the Continent, in furthering the new taste for the mysterious past.

Less successful in attracting attention, but more significant because springing from a deeper artistic instinct, was the series
Chatter-ton's Mediæval Imitations of literary forgeries put forth by the "marvelous boy," Thomas Chatterton (1752–1770). His childhood was passed in the shadow of the church of Saint Mary Redcliffe, Bristol; and the beautiful old building, with its rich historical associations, threw upon his sensitive mind a spell which was almost a mania. Some old parchments from the archives of the church fell into his hands. While deciphering them, he conceived the daring scheme of composing poems and prose pieces in the mediæval style and diction, and of palming them off upon the good burghers of the town, as originals which he had unearthed in the muniment room of the church. Incredible as it seems, he began this work in his twelfth year. The first "historical" document which he submitted to his townsmen was a description of the opening of the old Bristol bridge. As this aroused some interest, he composed an elaborate series of poems and prose pieces grouped about the figure of William Canynge, mayor of Bristol under Henry VI, purporting to be the work of one Rowley, a fifteenth-century priest. Some of the poems, especially "Aella," "The Bristowe Trajedie," and the "Balade of Charitie," are of remarkable beauty and force; and when we remember that the author of them was scarcely more than a child, they become astonishing. After a proud struggle to make his living by his pen, Chatterton ended his morbid and amazingly precocious life by suicide in a London garret, before he was eighteen. He was a signal example of the romantic temper that was soon to spread through the nation. It was fitting that, when the battle

for the new poetry was fought and won, Keats should dedicate *Endymion* to his memory, and Shelley should place him in "Adonais" among the "inheritors of unfulfilled renown."

II

The new literary movement which we have been tracing was the work of a small coterie of men, for the most part comparatively obscure. They were the revolutionists, who had declared their independence of the reigning mode. But the conservative writers still had great authority, and the classical traditions continued to be widely accepted. In the third quarter of the century Samuel Johnson succeeded to that primacy in English literature which had earlier belonged to Dryden and to Pope; but it is significant of the effect the romantic revival was having on the hierarchy of eighteenth-century literary values that, though Johnson was of a more absolute temper than either of his predecessors, his sway was never so complete as theirs.

Persistence of the Classical Traditions

Johnson's life is typical of the social conditions under which literature was practiced, after it could no longer command high political reward, and was obliged to rely entirely upon the public. The reading public was of slow growth. The writers who depended upon it were compelled to live in a squalid bohemia—not unlike that inhabited by the popular group of authors in the age of Elizabeth—and to put forth masses of poetry, criticism, and journalism merely for bread. The name of the street where many of them lived, Grub Street, became a synonym for hack-writing and poverty. The aristocratic traditions of the profession were supported by men of the highest reputation, like Pope, who could approach the public directly through the subscription list; but for the ordinary writer there was no resource except servitude to the literary broker or bookseller. Under these hard conditions Johnson and his friends slowly made their way to distinction; from that Grub Street which Pope and Swift had scornfully lampooned, came their successors in power and reputation.

The Social Position of Writers

Samuel Johnson was born in 1709, the son of a Lichfield bookseller. He was at Oxford for a time, but his father's failure

Samuel Johnson

obliged him to leave the university, and after a brief period of earning his bread by teaching, he went up to London. Here he lived in a state of wretchedness which is reflected in his *Life of Savage,* a poet who was his companion in Grub Street misery. Often the friends walked the streets from dusk to dawn for want of mere shelter. One resource was, indeed, open to them. Following the success of *The Tatler* and *The Spectator,* had come the periodical magazine of miscellaneous literature, of which the *Gentleman's Magazine* (1731) and the *London Magazine* (1732) were the first. For some years Johnson reported the debates in Parliament for the *Gentleman's Magazine* and contributed a number of miscellaneous works to it. His first poem, "London" (1738), gave him some reputation, which was increased by "The Vanity of Human Wishes" (1749), and by his drama *Irene* (1749), a stiff classical tragedy, which was staged through the kindness of his friend and former pupil, David Garrick. He wrote also essays after the *Spectator* model, called *The Rambler* (1750–1752). But his pre-eminent position came to him after the publication of his *Dictionary of the English Language,* in 1755. When he had announced this work eight years before, Johnson had sought the support and patronage of Lord Chesterfield, but the latter had been contemptuously cold toward the project. When the work was about to appear, however, the nobleman let it be known that he would accept and reward the dedication of the work to himself; but it was Johnson's turn, and in his famous letter to Chesterfield he wrote for English literature its final declaration of independence from the institution of patronage.

The Dictionary made Johnson's fame. In 1764 he formed with Burke, Goldsmith, Gibbon, and others the famous Literary

His Later Life

Club, as chief member of which he held the unquestioned headship of contemporary letters in England. Still, Johnson was poor; and, until 1762, when King George III gave him a pension of three hundred pounds a year, he was forced to labor to support himself and the various persons who fell dependent upon him. The oriental apologue, *Rasselas*, appeared in 1759. He wrote another series of essays, *The Idler,* and contributed to *The Adventurer.* He edited Shakespeare. He undertook the preparation of a series of lives of the English poets, which appeared in 1779 and 1781. He died in 1784.

Both in his original writing and in his criticism of the writings of others, Johnson emphasizes dependence upon accepted models and attained results, as opposed to romantic experiment. In his poetry he followed *Johnson's* Pope's use of the heroic couplet. Like Pope, also, *Classicism* he modelled his poems on the works of Latin writers; his "London," for example, is a general attack upon the evils of society, in close imitation of Juvenal. His sympathy with classical ideals led him to observe the unities in his play *Irene.* In his prose he continued the work of Dryden and Addison. His two most important prose works, his "Introduction to Shakespeare" and his *Lives of the Poets,* illustrate the point of view in matters of art which Dryden had established; and his essays are modelled upon the form set by *The Tatler,* though Johnson's essays are longer, heavier, and duller than Addison's. His moral tone, too, is more serious, for he looked at morality from the point of view of character rather than from that of civilization. His essays on the "Necessity of Punctuality," on "Idleness," on "The Luxury of a Vain Imagination," are serious, though somewhat commonplace studies in the conduct of life. Indeed, the seriousness of Johnson's moral tone is everywhere pronounced; and in this respect, too, he is a genuine representative of the classic era, in its worthier aspects. His "Vanity of Human Wishes" is written in a strain of moral elevation. He accepted without question the classical dictum that works of art should both please and instruct; even his *Lives of the Poets,* he hopes, are "written in such a manner as may tend to the promotion of piety."

But although, in these particulars, Johnson illustrates the formally accepted point of view of the classical age, there are many signs in him of an individual reaction against it. It is true, he was a classicist in his insistence upon the universal in

taste as opposed to the individual. But at the same time his
sensible, reality-loving habit of mind led him to hit a sham
when he saw it, even such a venerable and rever-
*His
Reaction
Against
Classical
Tradition*
when he saw it, even such a venerable and rever-
enced sham as the unities of dramatic action. In
spite of his own conformity to classical require-
ment in *Irene*, he boldly points out, in his criticism
of Shakespeare, that the acceptance of any theatrical production as real, involves such concessions
from the imagination of the audience that it is not in common
sense to refuse license in minor matters. His attitude on this and
other points serves to illustrate the reason of the eighteenth century at war with the principles of art which had been long assumed to be the highest expression of that reason. His position
in the world of letters strikingly illustrates the approaching end
of the era which had begun with the Restoration. His sense of
the values of things, his freedom from cant, his independence of
character, his very prejudices, made broadly in the direction of
individualism as against authority in criticism and thus prepared
the way for the romantic reaction.

The Rambler essays show, perhaps more saliently than any
other of Johnson's writings, those peculiarities which have
made his style a byword for ponderosity. The dic-
His Style   tion involves a large proportion of Latin words,
perhaps, it has been humorously suggested, because Johnson
was then at work on his lexicon, and used his *Rambler* as a
track where he could exercise the words that had grown stiff
from long disuse. Moreover, Johnson doubles epithets, adds
illustrations, develops, expands, modifies, balances, repeats, and
exhausts the idea before he will have done with it. His sentences are thus complicated and weighty, full of inversions,
depending much on rhetorical artifices such as antithesis and
climax. But this elaborate manner is not always out of place. It
occasionally gives to Johnson's writing a sombre and splendid
eloquence, as in the opening passage of *Rasselas*. Moreover, he
could be simple and colloquial when he chose; and his later
works, possibly because they were written more hurriedly, are
much more terse and rapid. In general, Johnson's influence on
English style was a good one. While he confirmed the tradition

of order, correctness, and lucidity, which had begun with Dryden, he introduced a greater variety of effect, a more complex sentence structure, and a more copious diction. He showed how, even within the rules of composition defined in practice by Dryden and Addison, the richness and variety of Elizabethan prose might be attempted.

Johnson's character, which so greatly impressed his contemporaries, has been immortalized by the extraordinary zeal and ability of the greatest of all biographers, James Boswell, whose *Life of Johnson* (1791) is one of *Boswell's* the classics of the century. From the time when he *"Life of* first met Johnson in 1763, Boswell followed the *Johnson"* great man's doings and sayings with unwearied attention. In his effort to draw Johnson out and to make him expressive, he was deterred by no rebuffs, and he was not ashamed to offer himself as the butt of his master's wit. After an acquaintance of twenty years, during which Boswell was frequently in Johnson's company studying him, making notes, and keeping a journal, he was prepared, with the same cheerful sacrifice of his own dignity, to write the biography which still keeps Johnson in the place which he won, that of the most salient figure of his epoch. Of no man in the past is our perception so extraordinarily keen and first-hand. His bulky, awkward appearance, his brusque, overbearing manner, his portentous voice, his uncouth gestures and attitudes, his habits of whistling or "clucking like a hen" in the intervals of speaking, and of "blowing out his breath like a whale" when he had finished—all these have come down to us, together with the record of a great mass of his conversation and a vivid picture of his incisive and comprehensive mind. It is in conversation that Johnson's power and Boswell's skill are most strikingly manifested. Johnson wrote much, but nearly always under the spur of necessity; he talked spontaneously. Everyone knows such sayings as "Patriotism is the last refuge of a scoundrel," "When a man is tired of London, he is tired of life," or "A woman's preaching is like a dog's walking on his hind legs. It is not done well; but you are surprised to find it done at all."

To Boswell's *Life,* then, Johnson owes his latter-day reputation as an eccentric and as a sayer of good things. But there is another Johnson whom Boswell also portrays—the stricken,

Johnson's Character

hopeless, much-enduring, brave, pious soul, who exemplifies so much of what is wholly admirable in human nature. For Johnson suffered grievously in life, and the cast of his mind was sombre and melancholy to perhaps an abnormal degree. In *Rasselas* he deals honestly with the question of human happiness; and he finds that life is almost barren of joy, that escape from pain is the highest felicity. He made no attempt to blink the facts of existence; he had no imaginative coloring to give them; yet he faced life always with energy and courage. In spite of everything, in spite even of weakness in his own character, he believed in himself. In his strenuousness, his morality, his refusal to yield ground anywhere to the evils without or the foes within, in his resolve to draw inspiration from his own shortcomings, in all this Johnson is a great man, and for this he deserves his fame.

Johnson's so-called dictatorship of English letters was largely the result of his conversational supremacy in the Literary Club,

Oliver Goldsmith

which included nearly all the famous writers of the time. Next to Johnson himself its most notable figure was Oliver Goldsmith. Goldsmith was born about 1730 in Ireland, where his father had a small living. He was a dull boy at school, and had an undistinguished career at the University of Dublin. He then went to Edinburgh to study medicine, and afterward to Leyden; thence he begged his way over a large part of Europe, returning to London in 1756. After an unsuccessful attempt as a schoolmaster, he took to literature as it was practiced in Grub Street, and became a hack writer for various magazines. His papers called *The Citizen of the World* (1760–1761), which he wrote for the *Public Ledger,* consisted of observations upon English life written from the point of view of a Chinaman. About 1762 Johnson found him one day in his lodgings, the prisoner of his unpaid landlady, with the manuscript of *The Vicar of Wakefield* by him. Johnson sold the book, which appeared in 1766, after Goldsmith had published his first successful poem, *The Traveller.* His second venture into poetry, *The Deserted Village,* appeared in 1770. Meanwhile

Goldsmith had turned to the stage, producing *The Good-Natured Man* in 1768, and *She Stoops to Conquer* in 1773, the year before his death.

Goldsmith is almost as well known to us as Johnson, and largely through the same agency, the industry of Boswell. He is portrayed in the *Life of Johnson* as the second luminary of the club, the only member who dared persistently to provoke the wrath of the dictator. Again and again Boswell shows us Johnson and Goldsmith, the heavily armed soldier and the deft slinger. Occasionally Johnson bore down his opponent by sheer weight, but more often Goldsmith sent his stone to its mark and made good his retreat. Sometimes his success turned on a mere trick; but often his replies were compact of sense and salt, as when he doubted Johnson's ability to write a fable because he would inevitably make the little fishes talk like whales. Goldsmith's wariness in conversation did not accompany him into the more practical walks of life. He was invariably in difficulties, pecuniary or social, arising from his imprudence and a generosity like that of his own Good-Natured Man. For Goldsmith was, in one sense at least, the antithesis of Swift. He gave himself freely; he threw himself upon life with the imprudence of an incorrigible lover of adventure. Whether traversing Europe as a penniless student or selling his masterpieces, Goldsmith took no thought for the morrow. And with this confidence in his fellows went a great love for them, a love apparent in all the writings into which he put his real self. His papers in *The Citizen of the World,* though, like Addison's, often directed against the faults and absurdities of men, have a tenderness which goes beyond Addison's mildness, a note of kinship that is very different from *The Spectator's* aloofness. Goldsmith's poems are written in the metre of Pope, but in spirit they are far removed from Pope's satirical coolness. In place of the savage sketches of Atticus and Bufo in *The Epistle to Arbuthnot,* we have the village parson in *The Deserted Village.* And it is to be noted that, though Goldsmith had no personal sympathy with the rising romantic school, his interest in obscure and unfortunate phases of human life, his championship of the individual against the institution

Goldsmith's Character

which would crush him, in *The Deserted Village,* mark him as a precursor of the Romantic Movement.

Goldsmith invariably read the world in terms of his own idealism. This idealism gives its coloring to his novel, and also *"She Stoops to Conquer"* to his comedies. *She Stoops to Conquer,* the best known of them, presents us, soon after the opening of the play, with a riotous scene at the "Three Pigeons," led by the loutish squire, Tony Lumpkin. Two travellers appear, whom Tony directs to the house of his stepfather, Mr. Hardcastle, as to an inn. The travellers are young Marlow, whom Hardcastle is expecting as the suitor for his daughter, and his friend Hastings. Hardcastle recognizes them; but Marlow, and Hastings also for a time, believe themselves to be in a hostelry, think Hardcastle is the host and his daughter the servant, and behave accordingly. The situation, however, favors the love-affair between Miss Hardcastle and Marlow; for the latter, who has never been able to conquer his bashfulness with ladies of condition, finds his path easy with the supposed barmaid.

The play is a charming idyl, in which the rough edges of the world are ground smooth, in which faults turn out to be virtues, and mistakes to be blessings. At times the stage-land copies the actual world with fidelity, as in the scene at the "Three Pigeons," and in the simple country life in Hardcastle's home. Tony Lumpkin is a genuine child of the soil. But the magic of comedy is over all, a magic indeed much subdued from the brilliant romanticism of Shakespeare's day, but still potent. For the sober theatre of the late eighteenth century, *She Stoops to Conquer* is a kind of prose *Tempest,* the most victorious assertion in its age of the mood of the idyl.

Goldsmith's plays are a reflection of the idealism which was beginning to manifest itself in the realistic age. Opposed to him *Richard Brinsley Sheridan* is Richard Brinsley Sheridan (1751–1816), whose dramas are written in the mood of satirical observation of life which the eighteenth-century novel expressed, from Fielding to Miss Burney. Sheridan was born at Dublin of Anglo-Irish stock. After a romantic runaway marriage he settled in London; and when only twenty-four he produced *The Rivals* and *The Duenna* (1775). In 1777, after his assumption of the directorship of Drury Lane Theatre, he put on his best play, *The School for Scandal,* and in 1779 *The Critic.*

In *The Rivals* we have the immortal Mrs. Malaprop; her niece, Lydia Languish, the romantic heroine; and Lydia's lovers, Bob Acres, Sir Lucius O'Trigger, and Captain Abso-   *"The* lute, the last masquerading under the name Beverley. *Rivals"* Absolute thinks at first that he is loving in opposi- tion to his father's will, and when he finds that Lydia is the very bride picked out for him, he continues to maintain with her his character of Beverley, as an appeal to her romantic spirit. The plot involves some absurdities, but it is fertile in amusing situations, and the play abounds in clever dialogue.

The School for Scandal opens in the eighteenth-century world of fashion. In this corrupt society Lady Teazle has, for form's sake, provided herself with a lover, Joseph   *"The* Surface. Meanwhile Joseph, a cold-hearted hypo-   *School for* crite, has plans of his own, one of which is to marry   *Scandal"* Sir Peter Teazle's ward, Maria, and another to sup- plant his own brother Charles, a good-natured spendthrift, in their uncle's affection. The uncle, Sir Oliver, returns from India, introduces himself as a money-lender to Charles, whom he finds ready to sell even his family portraits, except that of Sir Oliver himself. This modest bit of loyalty serves to reinstate the prodi- gal in his uncle's good opinion; while Joseph, exposed on all sides, fades out of the play in disgrace.

It is evident that here we have an amusing mock world, where the principles, moral and social, on which human life is actually conducted are subordinated to the necessities of an in- trigue. The characters bear an amazing similitude to real people; indeed, many of them have long been accepted as exact delinea- tions of certain qualities and types; but we never forget while we are with them that we are in stage-land. At first sight *The School for Scandal,* with its opening scenes in which gossip runs wild, seems to revive the world of the Restoration drama, but there is a difference. Light, trifling, frivolous as is Sheridan's society, it is not fundamentally and flagrantly immoral. His people play with fire, but they are not burned. So much had the moral and social force of the century accomplished, in the years since Collier's attack on the stage.

It may have been owing to the development of the magazine that the work of the writers of Johnson's period was in general *Edward* of so miscellaneous a character. From this charge, *Gibbon* however, must be excepted Edward Gibbon (1737–1794), who is known for a single work. From his youth Gibbon believed in his destiny as a historian; and, like Milton, he sought long for a subject worthy of his powers. At last, while on a visit to Rome in 1764, he hit upon the idea of writing a history of the decline and fall of the empire. Four years later he began to work at this subject. In 1776 his first volume appeared, but it was not until after eleven years more of steady toil that the full six volumes were completed.

Gibbon is personally well known to us through his frank account of himself in his memoirs—a man with little dignity, or *His* presence, or passion, or heroism. Yet in the light of *Life and* his achievement his life takes on almost heroic pro-*Work* portions. To his great task everything in his career was subsidiary. He served for a time in the militia, and he remarks that the captain of the Hampshire Grenadiers was not useless to the historian of the Roman Empire. In like manner, he made his seat in Parliament merely a preparation for his work, "a school of civil prudence, the first and most essential virtue of an historian." It is this sureness of inspiration, this unity of accomplishment in Gibbon's life, that constitutes his claim to something more than the glory that belongs to literary success. In the light of his task his negative qualities become positive; his vices virtues. As an adaptation of means to end, Gibbon's life was a splendid performance.

The Decline and Fall of the Roman Empire treats the history of Rome from the second century to the end of the fifth, and *His Merits* then, with a more rapid method, follows the East-*and* ern or Byzantine Empire until the fall of Constan-*Defects* tinople. Of Gibbon's scholarship there can be no complaint. He was completely master of his authorities, and his treatment of them is so discriminating, so fair, so thorough that he cannot be superseded. Two serious faults in his work must be laid at the door of his century—his lack of philosophic insight and his lack of sympathy with spiritual movements. Like his contemporaries, he distrusted philosophy and disliked enthusiasm. Behind the facts, he did not care to penetrate; in the realm of emotion he was uncomprehending. Hence his dry, hard, inadequate treatment of Christianity, a treatment reflecting his own attitude and limitations. He had no spiritual interests; his point of view was consistently worldly.

Gibbon's style is of the elaborate type introduced by Johnson. It is massive, solid, and exhaustive. It substitutes courtliness for ease, elegance for charm. Its excessive polish gives an effect of insincerity, at times almost of mockery. *His Style* But, in the large, the effect of Gibbon's style is commensurate with the greatness of his theme. The rhythmic, unwearied march of the sentences, the flashing of antithesis, and the steady roll of the diction, are but pomp and circumstance befitting the stately procession of emperors and nations. Chief among Gibbon's literary qualities is his sense of structure, which shows itself in his faculty for handling large masses of material. He consciously composed by paragraphs, each one a unit, and each of just the right weight. "It has always been my practice," he wrote, "to cast a long paragraph in a single mould, to try it by my ear, to deposit it in my memory, but to suspend the action of my pen till I had given the last polish to my work." This sense of exact structure, of outline, of organic development, shows itself still more in the astonishing architectural merit of the whole work. The ruin of the Roman Empire is in political history what the fall of man is in theology, and Gibbon, like Milton, has realized the epic possibilities of his theme.

If Gibbon is a monumental example of a small personality becoming by training and economy fit for the greatest achievement, a corresponding case of a great man expending his powers with apparent fruitlessness on passing affairs is found in the career of Edmund Burke (1729–1797). Goldsmith's epigram,

> Who, born for the universe, narrowed his mind,
> And to party gave up what was meant for mankind,

expressed the opinion of contemporaries as to Burke's career. Yet so penetrating was Burke's thought, and so noble its presentation that its implications are of value to-day, irrespective of the occasions which called them forth.

Burke was a native of Ireland, and a Bachelor of Arts of Trinity College. He went to London as a student of law, but soon turned aside into literature. His first works *Edmund* were an ironical reply to Bolingbroke, called *A* *Burke* *Vindication of Natural Society* and *An Inquiry into the Origin of Our Ideas on the Sublime and the Beautiful* (1757). In 1761 he entered politics as secretary of the Lord Deputy of Ireland; later he became secretary to the Marquis of Rockingham and member of Parliament. Although he never held high office, he was for years the brain of the Whig party in its effort to limit the exercise of the royal prerogative, which George III, with the assistance of the Tory party, was determined to extend. This was indeed the old question which went back to the time of the Plantagenets; but there were involved in it new problems, arising from the growth of England as a colonial power both in America and in India. It is Burke's *His* peculiar distinction that he saw the dangers gather-*Views on* ing over England from all quarters, and strove to *America* avert them. He pointed out the one way of escape *and India* in the American situation. His speech on American taxation was delivered in 1774; his great speech on conciliation with America in 1775. When England emerged from the war against the coalition of European powers, with the loss indeed of America, but with victory in other quarters, Burke instantly began to press his inquiry into the circumstances of that triumph. The chief success of England had been in India, and the man who had won it was Warren Hastings. Against him Burke levelled his attack. Instead of thanking God that things had turned out so well, he asked why they had turned out well, on what principles the Indian Empire had been conquered and administered, and whether those principles were founded upon justice and humanity. In 1785 he delivered his great arraignment of English methods in India, in his speech on *The Nabob of Arcot's Debts,* and in the following year he moved the impeachment of Warren Hastings. Two years later he opened the case before the House of Lords, and he continued to manage it until the acquittal of Hastings in 1795.

Finally, when the dangers which Burke had apprehended from the internal state of England were exemplified in France, he threw himself toward the only safety which he could see, and led the opposition to the French Revolution. This attitude involved a separation from his party, but Burke took the step without flinching. His *Reflections on the French Revolution,* published in 1790, did much to check the rising sympathy with the movement in England and on the Continent. He followed this with *Thoughts on French Affairs* (1791), *Appeal from the New to the Old Whigs* (1792), and *Letters on a Regicide Peace* (1796–1797). In this opposition Burke took a larger point of view than that of mere insular prejudice. He believed that England had a world mission in stemming the tide of revolution, and in marshalling the forces of conservatism in Europe. Right or wrong, the struggle of England against France between 1794 and 1815 is a splendid act in the drama of nations. It is scarcely too much to say that the leading rôle which England played was cast for her by Burke. He wrote the lines which the cannon declaimed at Trafalgar and Waterloo.

His Views on the French Revolution

There are thus three periods in Burke's career, in which his writings concerned successively America, India, and France: a first period of Cassandra-prophecy, unheeded warnings, and despised advice; a second of vigorous pursuit of evil and vindication of justice; a third of courageous defense of the things he believed in, against the Revolution. In his first task he was almost utterly unsuccessful; in the second he won a qualified success amid apparent failure; in the third he was immensely victorious. Burke's conservative tendencies were the result of his character, and rested on the same practical philosophy that guided his thought in other matters.

For Burke was in character essentially moderate, conservative, and practical. His disposition was always to work with the materials which existed. He was opposed to doctrinaire theories, and to schemes of doubtful applicability. The French Revolution was, in one way, a manifestation of the rationalism of the eighteenth century; of the tendency to try all things in society by reason alone, and to work out by experiments in government the theories which

His Political Thought

had been expounded by speculative philosophers. The Revolution was conceived in the spirit of Voltaire's belief that "they are the most pestilent of all enemies of mankind who discrown sovereign reason to be the serving drudge of superstition and social usage." To Burke, on the contrary, reason was by no means an adequate measure of humanity. He took account of other elements, even of prejudice, the foe of reason. "Through just prejudice," he says, "a man's duty becomes part of his nature." He held that social usage, even that superstition, might be a part of the wisdom of the ages. And for that wisdom, expressed in concrete form as institutions, the embodied result of long experience, Burke had immense reverence. He held that if institutions were to change, it must not be by the mere arbitrary promulgation of law. On the contrary he says: "If a great change is to be made in human affairs the minds of men will be fitted to it, the general opinions and feelings will draw that way, every fear, every hope will forward it."

This reliance on the ultimate facts of human character, even its prejudices and weaknesses, this trust in life rather than in reason, mark a certain connection between Burke *His Con-* and the romantic school in literature. Still more is *nection* this connection emphasized by the imaginative *with the* power of Burke's sympathy; a sympathy which *Roman-* penetrated to the uttermost parts of the earth, mak-*ticists* ing the wrongs of the American colonists and the sufferings of the Hindus as real to him as the conditions under which he himself lived. Another point of contact between Burke and the romanticists is his power of investing with interest an d color the past experience of the race, and of making it appeal to the imagination. In short, Burke, like Scott and Wordsworth, was a romanticist in feeling, though often a classicist in expression.

It is the feeling behind his thought that gives to Burke's style its curious, far-reaching eloquence. His substance is solid, mas-*His Style* sive, full of fact, apparently most refractory and inert; yet it is constantly brought to a white heat by the flame of his passion. No such style as his had been seen in England. He formed it indeed on the model of Bolingbroke, but he has a range of effects to which his master was a stranger

—splendid imagery, irony, fervor, conviction; while in such technical matters as the articulation of his sentences and the direction of his paragraphs, Burke measured for the first time the rhetorical possibilities of English writing.

III

As Thomson, Collins, and Gray form a group of early romantic poets, so at the close of the century we find a similar group of later romanticists who illustrate the progress of the movement and the richer fulfilment of its promise, and mark the transition to the great period of romanticism in the nineteenth century. *Later Romantic Poets* They are George Crabbe, William Cowper, William Blake, and Robert Burns.

George Crabbe (1754–1832), although he used the couplet verse and considered himself a faithful member of the school of Pope, announces the advent of a new realism in the poetic treatment of human life. He was born in a poor fishing village on the North Sea, and in his best *George Crabbe* early poem, *The Village* (1783), he painted the life of the poor as he knew it, sternly and uncompromisingly—the steaming flats and stubbly commons, the damp and dirty houses, the hostile sea, from which only a wretched living could be wrung, the men and women degraded by harsh labor and coarse dissipation. Crabbe was generously *His Realism* befriended by Burke, at a time when he was in dire distress, and through Burke's influence he was admitted to holy orders. He settled in the country, and for twenty-two years after his first success was completely silent. When he came forward once more, with *The Parish Register* (1807) and *Tales of the Hall* (1819), it was to find himself in a changed world, in which singers and seers far greater than he had transformed the face of literature; so that his country sketches and tales, written still in the old-fashioned couplet, looked oddly stiff and belated. But his work, at its best, is as sterling as it is ungraceful, and the earlier portion of it belongs with the most vigorous and sincere poetry of the eighteenth century.

A more potent but equally involuntary work of revolution

was performed by William Cowper (1731–1800). He was a
life-long victim of nervous despondency, and to this weakness
William   was added an abnormal proneness to religious ter-
Cowper   ror. His early life was spent at Westminster School,
               and as a law student in London. Fits of gayety and
states of mystical exaltation were succeeded by terrible periods
of depression, and at last by insanity. At the age of fifty-two he
was living in the obscure village of Olney, where, under the
care of a widow, Mrs. Unwin, several years his senior, he was
spending a peaceful interval between two attacks of religious
melancholia. As an intellectual pastime he began to write verse,
in which he had some proficiency. At first he produced mere
essays, in the dullest abstract style. At the suggestion of one
Lady Austen, a bright and somewhat worldly woman who was
attracted by his shy, distraught personality, he began a long
poem in blank verse. The subject playfully suggested by Lady
Austen was "The Sofa," an article of furniture then novel.
Cowper dutifully "sang the sofa." But he did not cease there;
he proceeded to paint with animated realism the landscapes, the
changes of seasons, the human types and employments of the
rural world about him, as well as his own simple pleasures and
"The   occupations. The poem was published in 1785 as
Task"   *The Task*. A large portion of *The Task* is conven-
               tional enough, to be sure, and very dreary reading;
but here and there one comes upon little vignettes—the figure
of a teamster driving homeward in a snow-storm, a postman
hurrying through the village with his eagerly awaited bag of
news from the great world, ploughmen at work in the flat fields
by the Ouse—which are instinct with vivid natural life. The
amusing ballad of "John Gilpin" also belongs to this bright
period of Cowper's life. He afterward relapsed into melancholia, broken at intervals by a ray of poetic inspiration such as
that which produced his touching lines "On the Receipt of My
Mother's Picture Out of Norfolk," deservedly the best known
of his poems. His last poem, entitled "The Castaway," is a cry
of despair from the depths of visionary anguish into which he
was now hopelessly plunged.

While Crabbe and Cowper were at work, two other innovators, endowed with vast energy and working with superb self-

confidence, were already passing beyond them. One of these was William Blake, an obscure London engraver; the other was Robert Burns, a Scottish ploughman.

William Blake (1757–1827), though a poet and a mystic of the most extraordinary genius, had little or no influence on his generation. The greater part of his message was so *William* obscure, so wild, so incoherently delivered, that even *Blake* now, after much study, his commentators have succeeded 'r making clear only a portion of what he wrote. He belonged α that type of mind which in superstitious ages is called "possessed." When a very young child he one day screamed with fear, because, he said, he had seen God put *His* his face to the window. In boyhood he saw several *Mysticism* angels, very bright, standing in a tree by the roadside. In his manhood, the earth and the air were for him full of spiritual presences, all concerned with his fate or with that of his friends. The following extract from some verses, written in mature manhood during a country walk, are characteristic:

> With happiness stretched across the hills
> In a cloud that dewy sweetness distills;
> With a blue sky spread over with wings,
> And a mild sun that mounts and sings;
> With trees and fields full of fairy elves,
> And little devils who fight for themselves . . .
> With angels planted in hawthorn bowers,
> And God Himself in the passing hours;
> With silver angels across my way,
> And golden demons that none can stay;
> With my father hovering upon the wind,
> And my brother Robert just behind,
> And my brother John, the evil one,
> In a black cloud making his moan . . .
> With a thousand angels upon the wind,
> Pouring disconsolate from behind
> To drive them off, and before my way
> A frowning thistle implores my stay . . .
> With my inward eye, 'tis an Old Man grey;
> With my outward, a Thistle across my way.

With a metaphysical gift which made it natural for Blake to move in an ideal world, he combined a visual imagination of abnormal, almost miraculous power, which enabled him to give bodily form to abstractions, and to summon at any moment before him "armies of angels that soar, legions of demons that lurk." Outwardly he led a regular, quiet, laborious life, all the while pouring out poems, drawings, and vast "prophetical books" full of shadowy mythologies and mystical thought-systems, which show that his inward life was one of perhaps un-paralleled excitement and adventure. Aside from the prophetical works, such as *The Book of Thel* and *The French Revolution,* his fame as a poet rests chiefly on his *Poetical Sketches* (1783) and on his *Songs of Innocence and of Experience* (1789, 1794). These little volumes contain some of the simplest and sweetest, as well as some of the most powerful short poems in the language. At his best, Blake has a simplicity as great as Words-worth's, and a magic which reminds us of Coleridge, combined with a depth and pregnancy of meaning peculiar to himself. In him the whole transcendental side of the Romantic Movement was expressed by hint and implication, if not by accomplish-ment.

What Blake did toward reclaiming lost realms of the spirit and the imagination, Burns did, in more signal degree, toward *Robert Burns* reopening lost channels of feeling. He was born in a two-roomed clay cottage in Ayrshire, West Scotland, in 1759. His parents were God-fearing peasants of the best Scottish type, who worked heroically to keep the wolf from the door, and to give their children an elementary education. At fifteen Robert, the eldest, did a grown man's work in ploughing and reaping. Looking back upon his youth in after-years, he de-scribed it as "the cheerless gloom of a hermit and the unceas-*His Early Life and Poetry* ing toil of a galley-slave." But this is clearly an exaggeration, if not a total misrepresentation; for we have his youthful poems to prove him wrong. The youth who wrote the "Epistle to Davie," with its manly philosophy and genial temper, the "Address to the Deil," with its rich humor and fun, the "Cotter's Saturday Night," bathed in its tender light of fireside happiness, was neither a hermit nor a galley-slave, but a healthy, impetuous farm lad, with a warm heart, a rich nature, and a God-given genius for song. He had had a few books of poetry to read, and had heard, as every Scottish peasant hears, the floating ballad verse of the countryside. Then he had begun to rhyme, almost as spontaneously as a bird begins to sing, or, as he says himself, "for fun." Since his was a spontaneous, sincere, and absolutely original nature, the verses he strung together carelessly, as he followed his plough "in glory and in joy, along the mountain-side," were contributions to the world's spiritual experience; and since he was also a born master of words, they were contributions to the world's sum of beauty.

Between his twenty-third and his twenty-sixth year Burns wrote the larger portion of those poems which have made his name loved wherever the Lowland dialect is understood. In these he revealed with wonderful completeness the rural Scotland of his day, illuminated with a blended light of humor and tenderness the common experiences of his peasant world, not forbearing to treat its unedifying and even its scandalous phases with racy zest and laughing abandon. His large, genial nature embraces everything human in the world about him. He celebrates "Scotch Drink," holds up to laughter the praying hypocrite "Holy Willie," and paints the riotous games of Hallowe'en; but he can turn immediately to mourn over the "wee, modest crimson-tipped flower" uprooted in the furrow on the mountainside, and to find in a field-mouse whose snug home has been broken up by the ploughshare a thing to touch the springs of human pity.

By the time Burns had reached his twenty-sixth year his wild ways had got him into desperate trouble; his father was dead, and the hand-to-hand fight that he and his brother Gilbert were waging with poverty bade fair to end in absolute failure. Distracted and despairing, *His Later Life: Songs* Burns determined to go to the West Indies. In order to raise the passage money, some one suggested that he should publish the poems which lay in his desk in the cottage at Mossgiel. This he did, his friends getting enough subscribers from among the local gentry to make the venture pay. Neither the author nor any one else hoped for more than a local popularity. The little book was published at Kilmarnock in 1786, with the title, *Poems, Chiefly in the Scottish Dialect*. The few pounds brought in by the small edition were in his pocket, and his trunk was sent forward, when a letter from Edinburgh arrived which changed the whole face of his fortunes. It was from an eminent scholar and critic, who praised the book highly and called for another and a larger edition. Burns posted to Edinburgh, heralded and fêted on the way like a hero of romance. A winter in the Scottish capital followed, during which the ploughman-poet was petted and lionized; and another winter during which his great friends cooled toward him as an exploited attraction. Then he went back to Ayrshire, with an appointment as "gauger" (inspector of the liquor customs) in his pocket, married Jean Armour, and settled down to the task of combining farming and revenue service with poetry. His duties as gauger covered ten parishes, and compelled him to ride two hundred miles a week; what was worse, they threw him constantly into riotous company, where his wit and eloquence were always in uproarious demand. His farm naturally went to ruin, and he found time for little poetry except short snatches of song. With the exception of the "Jolly Beggars" and the immortal "Tam o' Shanter," Burns did no more sustained work. But in recompense he poured out hundreds of songs—drinking-songs, love-songs, songs of patriotism—some of which are among the eternal possessions of the race. Things went from bad to worse with him, and he died in 1796, at the age of thirty-seven, a self-defeated and embittered man. But he poured into the world a current of feeling, electrical and life-giving. He revealed, and made the heritage of all, the fountains of tenderness and passion, of natural tears and mirth; fountains never sealed to the simple and lowly, who are always "romantic" in any age and under any fashion of thought.

CHAPTER XII

The Eighteenth Century

THE NOVEL

S THE DRAMA was the characteristic and natural literary expression of the Elizabethan age, so the novel has been the prevailing type of popular literature in the last two centuries. For this change there have been assigned various reasons. In the first place, it is clear that the dramatist works within limitations. He must put his material before the *The Novel* public in a few hours and on a small stage. He *and the* must make his personages tell their story and re- *Drama* veal their characters, without appearing in his own person. The novelist, on the contrary, is practically unlimited in time, space, or method. He can assume omniscience in the conduct of his story, revealing his characters by selections from their acts, speeches, and thoughts; even from the life which lies beneath their conscious thought. And, above all, he can reveal his attitude toward life through his interpretation of the meaning of the events which he narrates. Naturally, therefore, the novel lends itself more easily to the treatment of the great mass of interests and problems which make up modern life. The drama, moreover, depends, to some extent at least, on the theatre. The English reading public in modern times has become so extensive and so scattered that it has far outgrown the possibility of being served by such an institution as the theatre of Shakespeare's time. Thus to the general causes for the predominance of the novel in the modern world must be added this physical reason, which applies with peculiar force to English literature.

To give a complete account of the modern novel we must go

back to the stories of the Middle Ages. These were in general of two kinds, adapted to two audiences, the nobles and the people. Of the first class were the romances clustering about such heroes as Charlemagne and King Arthur, and dealing with knightly adventure, mystical religious experience, and courtly love. These were told first in verse, later in prose. The *Morte d'Arthur* of Sir Thomas Malory (1470) is the most comprehensive example of the knightly epic in England. Written for people of leisure and culture, the romances of chivalry presented a highly imaginative, idealized view of life, in which strength, virtue, and passion were all of a transcendent and unnatural character. The fiction of the common people was decidedly more realistic. There were, first of all, moral tales, called *exempla,* many of them imported from the Orient, and collected for the use of the clergy in their sermons. The stories of knighthood were in part retold, often with the purpose of exhibiting in a cynical spirit the coarse human motives underlying chivalric achievement. A great parody on chivalric literature was the animal epic of *Reynard the Fox,* in which various animals replace the knights, and the fox by his cleverness triumphs over strength and valor. This element of trickery played a large part in popular fiction, being the motive of innumerable anecdotes turning on sharp answers and practical jokes. Sometimes the vices and follies of men were represented in short tales, in prose or verse; the hypocrisy of the clergy, for example, was a favorite subject. An idea of the range of mediæval popular fiction can be gained from Chaucer's *Canterbury Tales,* or from the collection of stories made by Boccaccio in the *Decameron.* These prose stories were called in Italy *novelle*, from which term is derived our word *novel.* The spirit of burlesque, aroused by the contrast between the ideals of chivalry and the affairs of actual life, led in Spain to the production of a form of story known as the picaresque romance. The typical Italian *novella* and the Spanish rogue story resembled each other in their realistic spirit, and their emphasis on natural human motives and to some extent on the manners of actual life. They are the source of the realistic novel of to-day, while the romantic novel looks back to the epic of chivalry for its beginnings.

Mediæval Fiction

English fiction of the Renaissance was largely derived from the sources just mentioned. There were great numbers of translations of the Italian *novelle* and some translations of the Spanish rogue stories. There were romances founded on the careers of popular heroes, such as Robin Hood and Guy of Warwick, The first landmarks in English fiction of the Renaissance were Lyly's *Euphues* and Sir Philip Sidney's *Arcadia*. The influence of all these may be seen in the work of Robert Greene, Thomas Lodge, and Thomas Nashe. This literature existed for the primary object of entertaining its readers, but according to the standards of the time it was furnished with a moral or useful purpose, which was in general to teach men to live successfully in the world. These two ends were kept in view with much adroitness by authors and collectors of stories. For example, Robert Greene, while amusing his readers with accounts of criminal life in London, points out how necessary it is for them to learn of the snares and dangers of such life in order to avoid them.

English Fiction of the Renaissance

In the seventeenth century the English readers of fiction were chiefly supplied from France, where there had arisen a school of writers who told at great length, and with much sentimental and imaginative embroidery, the stories of the Grand Cyrus and other half-historical heroes. Of these tales the best known are those by Mlle. de Scudéry. In their exaggeration of heroism and in their artificiality they resembled the romances of chivalry which they succeeded, and in turn contributed to the taste for the heroic play. Among the people the chief interest in the seventeenth century was the religious one; naturally, therefore, we find popular fiction of the period represented by the adaptation of the common type of story to the religious life. Bunyan's Pilgrim wanders through the world like the knight-errant or the Spanish rogue, meeting adventures. Like the knight he has a high purpose; like the rogue he mingles with people of every sort, and reflects in his journey the common sights and interests of English country life. Almost as notable a contribution to the development of modern fiction as *The Pilgrim's Progress* is Bunyan's autobiography, *Grace Abound-*

English Fiction in the Seventeenth Century

ing. One of the chief elements of the novel is the study of character, and in this study the novelist has often found his most genuine material in the literature of confessions; among such examples of personal analysis and recorded spiritual experience, Bunyan's account is one of the most naïvely convincing and powerfully rendered.

The real beginning of the English novel took place in the eighteenth century with the work of Daniel Defoe (1661?–

Daniel Defoe 1731). Defoe, like Bunyan, was a Dissenter, a thorough man of the people, a stranger to the ideals and refinements of aristocratic life. Moreover, in an age when the aim of the successful writer was to rise in the world and to gain aristocratic connections, Defoe seems to have been entirely willing to remain in his class, to serve it, and to write for it. He began life as a tradesman, but soon interested himself in politics, and held various offices under William III. In the early years of Queen Anne's reign he turned the arms of the Tories, who were in favor of a mild persecution of Dissenters, against themselves, by publishing a pamphlet, *The Shortest Way with Dissenters,* in which he ironically advised the severest punishments for religious nonconformity. With an art which he showed later in his novels he concealed his real personality, and his work passed as that of a genuine Tory. The trick was discovered, however, and Defoe was punished by being placed in the pillory and imprisoned. He was released to enter the service of the government as a secret agent, perhaps as a spy, which office he held under different ministries. In 1704 he founded a newspaper, *The Review,* and after its cessation in 1713 he continued his connection with the press. As a clever journalist he published the lives of various people of interest to the public: of Peter the Great, for one; of Jonathan Wild, a notorious criminal and thief-taker, for another; of Captain Avery, a notable pirate, for a third. His life brought him into contact with all sorts of adventurers; having a curious disposition and a retentive memory, he heard their stories and afterward wrote them out. When his material failed he drew upon his imagination; but he realized that he was writing for people who demanded fact, who perhaps thought it wrong to read fiction, and accordingly he tried to give every appearance of reality to his narratives.

The manner by which he turned from biography and history to fiction is illustrated by *A Journal of the Plague Year* (1722). In this work much of the material is authentic, gathered doubtless from many sources; but while a historian would have endeavored to base his account directly upon these various authorities, Defoe, as a story-teller, presents all his facts as the *"A Journal of the Plague Year"* continuous experience of an imaginary narrator. So cleverly is this done that the personality of this character comes to be the most authoritative thing in the book; we believe in the horrors of the plague because we believe that the imaginary spectator of them is truthful. In his power thus to produce a perfect illusion of reality, Defoe anticipates the later triumphs of great fiction. Many writers have used pestilence as one of the means of awakening terror in their readers; but Defoe has surpassed them, simply because he seems earnestly intent on telling the mere truth, with no care for literary effect.

While working on the border line between biography and fiction, Defoe was attracted by the story of a sailor, Alexander Selkirk, who had been wrecked on an island in the Pacific, and had remained there for many years. *"Robinson Crusoe"* This story suggested *The Life and Strange Surprizing Adventures of Robinson Crusoe*, which was published in 1719. Here again Defoe shows what a contemporary described as "the little art he is so truly master of, of forging a story and imposing it on the world for truth"; and here also the reason for his success is apparent. Defoe is always minute in his account of events and circumstances, and these circumstances, although not always the most important, are precisely those which the character who is telling the story would be likely to remember. In other words, Defoe is a master of the art of taking and keeping the point of view of his hero. Indeed, he seems to abdicate his rights as an author; to allow his hero to possess him. He throws himself completely into the situation of Crusoe, wrecked on the island. He foresees the dangers incident to such a situation, takes measures of precaution against them, indulges the

natural hope of escape, and makes the wonderfully human mistake of building a boat too heavy for him to launch. He is
absorbed in the trivial events of a solitary existence; he is filled
with satisfaction at his miniature conquest of nature, and with
horror at the frightful discovery of the human footprint in the
sand. In fact, so utterly did he merge himself in Crusoe that,
when his work was finished, he came to see in the struggles of
the York mariner an allegory of his own toilsome and dangerous experience of life.

    Crusoe proved so successful that Defoe followed it the same
year with the *Farther Adventures,* and in 1720 with the *Serious
Reflections of Robinson Crusoe.* In the next few
years he also published a series of stories of adventure: *Captain Singleton* (1720), a tale of piracy;
Moll Flanders (1722), the life of a thief and adven-
turess; *Colonel Jack* (1722), and *Roxana* (1724). These stories
are all picaresque in matter and in form. The hero, who is the
narrator, constitutes the chief element of unity; the other characters appear and pass away, no attempt being made to work
them into a plot. Defoe conceals his personality behind that of
his hero, as he had done in the case of Crusoe; yet his personal
attitude toward life appears in the purpose which each tale
clearly has. Defoe was a Dissenter; he wrote for the descendants
of Puritans, men in whom the interest in conduct and morality
was strong. Defoe's morality is that of the bourgeois. He incul-
cates the utilitarian virtues; his aim is social usefulness. *Robinson Crusoe* is a manual of the qualities that have won the world
from barbarism—courage, patience, ingenuity and industry. In
the minor novels these same practical virtues are exhibited, even
in the pursuit of evil ends. Further, as Defoe takes pleasure in
pointing out in his preface to *Moll Flanders,* it is well for good
people to know the devices of evil in order that
they may be on their guard against them. But beyond this Defoe has a moral ideal to which he
makes most of his characters conform, by regarding their lives
as warnings and subjects of repentance. This side of Defoe's
ethics is less sincere than the other, and its appearance is rather
an artistic blemish. In the case of Moll Flanders, who has been

*The
Minor
Novels*

*Defoe's
Morality*

a great sinner, repentance seems inadequate; in that of poor
Crusoe, who has done nothing worse than run away from home,
it seems forced. Yet in both cases Defoe bears witness to a prevailing demand for the moralization of literature, a demand
made by the English middle class for which he wrote, and of
which he was eminently a part.

One element of the modern novel Defoe's stories are without
—they lack plot. Like the Spanish rogue stories, they are merely
successions of adventures which befall the same *Richard-*
hero. The first great success in constructing a story *son's*
which should be guided throughout its course by a *"Pamela"*
single motive, the love of one person for another,
was *Pamela*, written by a London printer, Samuel Richardson
(1689–1761). Richardson was asked by a publisher to write a
series of letters which should serve as models for the correspondence and behavior of people in the lower walks of life.
He did so; and, to add interest, he wrote them as the connected
letters of a young serving-girl to her parents, telling the story
of her temptation by her master, a certain Mr. B., of her resistance, and of her final triumph in marrying him. The book appeared in 1740, and was so popular that Richardson wrote a
sequel, which described Pamela's experience as wife in a sphere
much above that of her birth, her lessons in behavior suitable to
that estate, and her plans for the education of her children. The
moral and social purposes of the book are therefore successfully
blended, though it must be admitted that Pamela's morality is
of a rather calculating type.

The success of *Pamela* encouraged the author to produce a
second work of fiction, *Clarissa,* which appeared in eight
volumes in 1747–48. This is the story of a young *"Clarissa"*
lady, Clarissa Harlowe, who is at the outset the unwilling object of the attentions of a certain Lovelace. A quarrel
has occurred between him and Clarissa's brother, and to keep
Lovelace from renewing the difficulty she continues to communicate with him. Her relatives, however, persist in distrusting
her, and to secure her final separation from Lovelace they introduce a second suitor, an impossible creature named Solmes;
and they resort to such measures of persecution to force her to

accept him that she finally decides to flee to the protection of a friend. Unfortunately, she accepts the assistance of Lovelace, who kidnaps and ruins her. After many chapters of suffering she dies, leaving a vast heritage of remorse to be divided among her relatives and Lovelace.

Like *Pamela, Clarissa* is told by means of letters which pass between the different characters. Obviously, this method is in its *Richard-* nature dramatic; that is to say, the reader holds com- *son's* munication directly with the characters. In other ways *Method* it is clear that Richardson thought of the novel as an elaborated drama. He calls *Clarissa* "a dramatic narrative"; and he does so very properly, for, as in a play, there is in *Clarissa* a definite catastrophe, every step toward which is carefully prepared for by something in the environment or the characters of the actors. Richardson could not, however, forego entirely the novelist's right to personal communication with his audience. He introduced footnotes in which he enforced his own view of the story, when he thought his readers likely to go astray. These comments were needed especially in reference to the two principal persons, whose characters show a degree of complexity to which the novel readers of that day were scarcely accustomed. In the case of Clarissa this complexity seems justified; in all her uncertainties, scruples, hesitations, still more in her humiliation and anguish, she appeals to us as a real woman; but Lovelace, though ingeniously constructed and consistent, is a mechanism.

This discrepancy is, after all, natural; for Richardson knew women better than men. As a youth he wrote love-letters for *Richard-* girls. As a mature writer he worked in close con- *son's* nection with the feminine part of his audience. *Character* His circle of admirers began with his wife and a young lady who was staying at his house while he was composing *Pamela*. It widened with his fame, until it included even great ladies of fashion, who in person or by letter communicated with the old printer about the progress of his tales. They petted him, flattered him, and debauched him with tea; until the good Richardson lost himself in the Avalon which they provided, and forgot the world of action outside. So se-

cluded did he become that at last he would communicate even
with the foreman of his printing-house only by letter. Because
of this seclusion Richardson's novels lack breadth and freshness.
They deal with a circumscribed world, a world of trifles and
scruples, of Puritan niceties of conscience, of feminine refinements of sentiment and casuistries of deportment.

The seriousness with which Richardson took himself as a
novelist appears most markedly in his third novel, *Sir Charles
Grandison* (1753–54), which deals with the love-
affair between the hero and a Miss Harriet Byron. ***His
Purpose***
Richardson, like Defoe, was of the middle class, and
distinctly wrote for it. Two serious preoccupations of the English
middle class at all times have been deportment and conscience.
The first, as we have seen, was a social interest of great importance in the early eighteenth century, when England was learning the lesson of civilization. Richardson began his work with
the humble design of teaching his readers to write, but his plan
broadened until it covered the essentials of the art of living.
Pamela lives a model life for servants; Clarissa is perfection in
a higher sphere; Sir Charles Grandison is an illustration of the
adaptation of aristocratic manners to middle-class instincts. But
in addition Richardson's characters are all involved in intricate
questions of conscience. Clarissa's course is determined only
after elaborate discussion of the right and wrong of each step.
In *Grandison*, it is only after the hero has dealt with a succession of difficult circumstances arising from the claims upon him
of his friend, his friend's children, his sister, his ward, and his
father's mistress, that he yields to his passion for Miss Byron.
Richardson surely did not exaggerate when he declared the inculcation of virtue to be his first object.

It was something like impatience with Richardson's moral
pretensions that led his contemporary, Henry Fielding, to enter
upon his career as a novelist. Fielding was of higher
birth than Richardson, his father being a soldier of ***Henry
Fielding***
some renown, and his grandfather the son of a
peer; he had, too, a far wider and more varied experience of
life. He was born in 1707, was educated at Eton, and afterward
went to Leyden to study law. In 1727 he returned to London,

where he supported himself for a while by writing plays. Deprived of his profession of playwright by the restrictions of the
licensing act of 1737, he betook himself again to the study of
law, meanwhile supporting his family by miscellaneous writing.
His wife died in 1744, leaving him with two children. He
struggled on until life was made somewhat easier for him by
his appointment as police magistrate in London, in which office
he was highly efficient. In 1754, broken in health, he left England for Portugal; he has left a pathetic account of this journey
in his *Voyage to Lisbon*. He died the same year.

It was while Fielding was earning his bread by various literary ventures that Richardson's *Pamela* appeared. Struck by the
sentimentality of the book, its narrow view of life,
"Joseph and the shallowness of its ethics, he began to write
Andrews" a burlesque upon it, in which he subjected Pamela's
(1742) brother, Joseph Andrews, to the same temptation
from his mistress that Pamela suffered from her master. Like
Pamela, Joseph resists; but unlike her he is turned out-of-doors,
and is left to make his way back to his home in the country.
Fielding soon lost sight of his narrowly satirical purpose in the
broader attempt to picture the rough English life of postroads,
inns, and country houses. He is not careful of the structure of
his story. The adventures of Joseph with his companion, Parson
Adams, do not all advance the plot; minor characters introduce
digressions, and the ending is merely a series of happy accidents. Yet, on the other hand, Fielding writes of real men and
women with a precision that comes from direct observation. His
pictures are often caricatures—as, for example, Mrs. Tow-
wouse, the innkeeper, and Trulliber, the hog-raising parson—
but they are caricatures that tell the truth.

Fielding's next novel, *Jonathan Wild* (1743), was a loose
narrative, suggested by the life of the famous rascal whom Defoe had celebrated, and written to burlesque the con-
"Tom ception of greatness held by ordinary writers of biog-
Jones" raphy. In his last two stories, however, *Tom Jones*
(1749) and *Amelia* (1751), Fielding developed genuine plots.
The former opens with the discovery of the hero as a new-born
baby in the house of a virtuous gentleman, Mr. Allworthy. Here

he grows up with Allworthy's nephew Blifil, who out of jealousy ruins Tom's reputation with his benefactor, and gets him turned out into the world. Meanwhile Tom has fallen in love with the daughter of a neighbor, Miss Sophia Western, who returns his love in spite of the opposition of her father. Tom travels to London, with many wayside adventures; he passes, not unscathed, through various temptations; and finally, by the discovery of the secret of his birth and the revelation of Blifil's villainy, he is advanced to his happy fortune, the favor of Allworthy and marriage with Sophia.

Although the hero travels from place to place and meets with a variety of adventures, *Tom Jones* is more than a picaresque story. Fielding very skillfully relates each character, each thread of plot, to the main theme, although he does not follow the more formal dramatic structure of Richardson. Even the brief critical essays with which he introduces each book and in which he discusses with the reader various problems of art and conduct—even these are integral to the steady progress of the story. In structure, in richness of characterization, in sanity and wisdom of point of view, *Tom Jones* stands unrivalled in the history of English fiction.

Amelia is the story of a good wife, who, in spite of temptation, remains faithful to a good-natured but erring husband, Captain Booth. But the tone of this novel is more serious. The fortunes of Amelia and Booth are set against the larger background of eighteenth-century London—a London in which bribery and political corruption are rife, a London in which success often goes to the least deserving. Against this background Fielding portrays the two sharply contrasted figures of Amelia and her husband, and with careful but unobtrusive art relates the fortunes of these two figures to the larger "epic" theme of his novel. *Amelia* is at once a searching criticism of contemporary society and a mature, soberly conceived story of everyday life, rich in incident and, like *Tom Jones*, remarkable for its insight into human character.

Fielding's great strength lies in the Rubens-like fertility with which he peoples his world. For the elaborate subtleties of Richardson he cared little. Fielding's vision is broader: like

Shakespeare he portrays all kinds of human character, and like Shakespeare he has a sympathetic yet maturely detached view of the human comedy. The forces which guide his characters are, for the most part, natural human needs, for it was these that Fielding knew best. His abounding physical vigor was one of the greatest of his gifts. It furnished him with unusual keenness of sense, and enabled him to apprehend and portray the primary facts of life with extraordinary vividness and frankness.

This physical keenness was the source of Fielding's realism, a realism that was in thorough keeping with the age. And with Fielding's realism must be connected his comic point of view, his wise, tolerant acceptance of things as they are. Of the smug, prudish morality of Richardson, Fielding would have nothing. He threw it aside and presented man full length as he found him. Yet though he portrayed men with no reservations, he never forgot that he was one of them. From this inborn sympathy comes his large tolerant way of looking at things, a view of life that often finds relief in raillery, but never in cynicism. He laughs, but his laughter is always ready to give place to tenderness and pity. For him the tragedy of life lay in the presence of virtue and innocence in a world of evil, cruelty, and deception. In his presentation of this tragedy Fielding is always direct, sincere, and simple. The scene in which Amelia prepares supper for Booth, and when he does not come puts aside the wine untasted to save a sixpence, while her husband is losing guineas at the gaming-table, is far more moving than are the complicated woes of Clarissa. It is this humanity, the most essential quality of the novelist, that makes Fielding's work permanently engaging and powerful.

It was in human sympathy that Fielding's successor was most notably deficient. Tobias Smollett (1721–1771) was a Scotsman, a physician who failed in his profession on account of his irascible temper, and who accordingly took up the practice of literature. His first novel was *Roderick Random* (1748), a tale of adventure, in which he made use of much of his own experience. He had been surgeon's mate on a man-of-war; accordingly, after describing Roderick's youth in Scotland, he sends him to sea, taking the opportunity to insert some vivid descriptions of

Smollett's "Roderick Random"

naval life. The hero also participates in the continental wars of George II, visits Paris, goes to South America, where he discovers a conveniently rich father, and returns to England to marry the waiting heroine, Narcissa.

Roderick Random is merely a succession of adventures, related by the hero. Of precisely the same type is Smollett's next novel, *Peregrine Pickle* (1751), except that the author tells the story. His third, *Ferdinand, Count Fathom* (1753), is more elaborate in plot, for there are two heroes, Ferdinand, a type of cruelty and mischief, and Renaldo, a type of colorless respectability. Smollett's last novel, *Humphry Clinker,* published in 1771, after his death, is in many respects his best. The element of plot is slight, since the story is little more than a series of mild adventures attending the journeys of a Welsh family through England and Scotland. These journeys, however, give Smollett an opportunity to describe men and things; and as a contemporary record and comment on life and manners the book is of decided interest. Moreover, the temper in which life is presented in *Humphry Clinker* is less harsh than in the earlier books.

Smollett's Later Novels

In general, however, Smollett lacked humor and geniality. Fun of a ferocious sort, cruel practical jokes, abound among his incidents, making us feel that the spirit which could find pleasure in them must have been a savage one. Furthermore, since such incidents frequently have no connection with the plot, and are introduced for their own sake, they must be set down as gratuitously unpleasant. Smollett's early heroes are cruel and passionate, but otherwise colorless, and always unsympathetic. His heroines are mere dolls. His best characters are his humors, men and women who stand each for a single quality or mannerism, and who respond to every stimulus in precisely the same way, like figures in a comic opera. Among the best of these humors are the characters in *Humphry Clinker*—Matthew Bramble, the irascible Welsh misanthropist, his sister Tabitha, Win Jenkins, the maid, who exhausts the possibilities of fun in English misspelling—and the sailor characters, Commodore Trunnion and Pipes in *Peregrine Pickle*, Bowling and Moyan in *Roderick Random*. Smollett's chief contributions to the novel were his enlargement of its area and the introduction of at least one special interest, the sea, as furnishing special types oi character and incident.

It is possible to classify the novels thus far mentioned accord-ing as they advance beyond, or revert to, the simple biographic *Laurence* story, in which the element of unity is the per-*Sterne* sistence of the hero. We next come to a book in which even this element of structure is lacking, which only by an extension of the term can be called a novel at all. The first two volumes of *The Life and Adventures of Tris-tram Shandy* appeared in 1759. The author, a clergyman, Lau-rence Sterne (1713–1768), wrote it, he says, in order to benefit the world "by ridiculing what I thought deserving of it." This ill-regulated book was a product of Sterne's disorderly existence. His father was a petty officer in the army, and he himself, born in barracks, spent his sickly youth in moving from one military station to another. He was sent to Cambridge, and thence drifted into the church, obtaining a small living in Yorkshire, where, he says, "books, fiddling, painting, and shooting were my chief amusements." *Tristram Shandy* made him famous. He was courted and flattered in London, promoted in the church, and well received at Paris, for *Shandy* was an international success. Meanwhile he continued his book, putting into it material of any sort which he happened to have on hand. His health failing, he spent a year in southern France. Part of the experiences of his journey he turned into the seventh volume of *Shandy,* part he saved for a book of travels called *A Sentimental Journey,* of which two volumes appeared in 1768, just before his death.

Tristram Shandy is not a novel in the proper sense of the word. Elements of the novel it has, characters and incidents, but *"Tristram* these are not bound together into a coherent story. *Shandy"* The book is without plan; without beginning, progress, or end. In the fourth volume the hero laments that though he is a year older than when he began to write, he has not got beyond his first day's life. The author shifts arbitrarily from one character to another, begins conver-sations in the middle, interrupts them with little essays full of odd learning, prepares for stories which are never told and scenes between his characters which are never acted. He introduces a new character, the Widow Wadman, with whom Tristram's Uncle Toby falls in love, by a blank page, on which the reader can write his own description. The style is given over to mannerism, abounds in trick and innuendo, and has none of the formal regularity which had marked written prose since the time of Dryden; it is full of the suggestiveness, the half-lights, of brilliant talk. Like Sterne's life, the book is an exaltation of whim. In his life and in his art he was without any sense of propriety, without respect for the conventions which the eighteenth century was so much interested in establishing. His moral tone is that of the Restoration; his style reminds one of the early seventeenth century. Altogether he represents a reaction from the rigid standards, moral and artistic, of Addison and Richardson.

Writing thus directly from his temperament, at the suggestion of his moods, Sterne is curiously subjective. For example, he treats passion, not because it exists as a cardinal *Sterne's* fact of life, but because he can draw from it a *Senti-* stimulus for himself and his readers. His humor, *mentalism* too, arises not from a broad vision of the world as comedy, but from a personal sense of the incongruous suggestions that hang about simple, commonplace, or even tragic circumstances. He sits down to weep beside the poor insane Maria, who stares alternately at him and at her goat. "Do you see any resemblance?" he asks. Again, his pathos is not the sympathy of the strong man who weeps because he must. His tears are not wrung from him by the tragedy of existence; on the contrary, he goes about seeking occasion for feeling. He is thus the chief of sentimentalists, of those who write not to picture the world as it is, but to draw from it suggestions for certain moods and feelings. This attitude, which became for a time a leading fashion in literature, found its model largely in *Tristram Shandy.*

But there is a stronger reason than this for Sterne's influence. He has a wonderful power of imparting humanity *His* to his characters, despite the eccentricities of their *Humanity* lives and surroundings. He makes no use of the ordinary material of the novelist—of men's desires, passions, political or religious beliefs, social relations, success or failure.

His characters live in a world of their own. Tristram's father is absorbed in curious learning and speculation; his Uncle Toby is occupied in acting out in his garden, with the aid of his servant, Corporal Trim, the battles and sieges that he has seen. And yet these characters live—live by virtue of the most adroit suggestion of humanity, in their speech, their appearance, their gestures and attitudes. With his usual self-consciousness Sterne calls attention to his method, a method new in eighteenth-century literature. "You perceive," he says, "that the drawing of my Uncle Toby's character went on gently all the time—not the great contours of it—that was impossible—but some familiar strokes and faint designations of it were here and there touched on, as we went along, so that you are much better acquainted with my Uncle Toby now than you was before." By this method Sterne gives to his characters an abiding reality and charm. With the characters of Cervantes and Shakespeare, with Quixote and Falstaff, they are among the very few "creations" of literature.

Sterne's habit of playing directly upon the sensibility of his readers was freely imitated. The most notable imitation is *The Man of Feeling* (1771) by Henry Mackenzie. This book also shows the influence of Sterne's loose structure, though Mackenzie explains the breaks in his story by the theory of a mutilated manuscript. The hero's faculty for finding tragedy in the lot of man, and his morbid emotion over it, connect the book with the "graveyard poetry" of the precursors of the Romantic Movement.

Mackenzie's "Man of Feeling"

Signs of a possibly conscious reaction in the direction of a more wholesome view of life than Sterne's are to be found in a book as famous as *Tristram Shandy*—Oliver Goldsmith's *Vicar of Wakefield* (1766). *The Vicar of Wakefield* is a perfect expression of homely English sentiment. That sentiment naturally gathers about the family life. The Vicar and his wife and children are thrown into poverty. Worse misfortune comes in the flight of the elder daughter, Olivia, who is lured away by an unworthy lover; in the burning of their poor house;

Goldsmith's "Vicar of Wakefield"

in the imprisonment of the father for debt. But through all these troubles shine the Vicar's love for his family and his confidence in life; and at the end his faith in the best of all possible worlds emerges triumphant. The Vicar is, it is true, the only character in the book. The Vicar's wife and children; young Squire Thornhill, and his uncle, Sir William Thornhill, who wanders through the book in an impossible incognito; the convenient Jenkinson, who has craftily made of Olivia's mock marriage a real one—all these are shadowy forms of which we get but glimpses as they cross the light of the Vicar's steady personality. The Vicar animates not only the characters but the spirit and purpose of the book. Goldsmith is not a realist. To him, as to Sterne, the positivism of the early century, with its demand for the presentation of life as it is, made no appeal. His world is an ideal one. Troubles and disasters accumulate like threatening clouds, but only to resolve themselves into beneficent showers. Suffering is not a problem; it is merely an artistic device to make the world seem more beautiful. Evil loses its essential quality; Olivia is married to a rake who does not love her, but we accept confidently his reform as a part of the happy outcome, so contagious is Goldsmith's optimism.

Goldsmith used one element of the Arcadian romance, and made of it a distinct contribution to the modern novel. The element of outdoor scene had been largely neglected by his predecessors. Richardson had shown care and skill *His Use* in the arrangement of his interiors; Fielding had *of Scene* given a few set pieces of description, showing the preference of eighteenth-century taste for artificial over natural beauty; but Goldsmith pictured nature with real feeling for it. He made it, especially in the early idyllic scenes of his novel, a happy reinforcement of his theme of domestic bliss and tranquillity; and it is, throughout the book, a symbol of the eternal goodness of the world, another reason for putting trust in life.

With the possible exception of lyric poetry, the novel is the form of literature which has been most successfully practiced by women. In the period before Defoe, the most popular writers of romance were women—Mrs. Behn and Mrs. Manley. Miss Sarah Fielding, sister of the novelist, wrote a story, *David*

Simple, which both Richardson and Fielding praised. Later in the century the line of realists, broken by Sterne and Goldsmith,

**Miss
Burney**

was continued by Miss Fanny Burney (1752–1840), whose first story, *Evelina*, appeared in 1778. Doctor Johnson, who was her father's friend, liked the book, and his support had much to do with its immediate success, though his influence on the style of her later books cannot be called happy. With an achieved literary reputation, Miss Burney, who had been glad to get twenty guineas for *Evelina*, sold her second book, *Cecilia* (1782), for £250. Soon after this she became a maid of honor to Queen Charlotte; and after escaping from the intolerable constraints of this situation she married General D'Arblay, by whose name she is sometimes known. At long intervals she followed her early works with two others, which are now forgotten, but her *Diary* remains one of the important documents of the time.

Evelina is the story of a young girl's introduction to the great world, told chiefly by herself in letters to her guardian. Her

**Her
Novels**

path is beset by rival suitors, and made doubtful by a mystery about her own birth; but her course is guided steadily by conscience and propriety. Indeed, both Evelina and Cecilia are of the family of Clarissa: both are a bit prudish, overscrupulous, oversensitive. The other characters are men and women drawn from nature, as Macaulay says, but not from life, each being developed in accordance with a single dominant passion or peculiarity. Like her model, Richardson, Miss Burney wrote to correct the evils of the time. Her minor characters were intended to make various faults and affectations contemptible or ridiculous, through an extravagant presentation of them. But as the element of truth is largely present in successful satire, it follows that Miss Burney's novels give us lively pictures of the age in which she lived. In *Evelina* we see reflected the uncouthness of the middle classes, the boorishness of their amusements, and their fondness for practical jokes; and in *Cecilia* the studies of contemporary life are still more detailed. Altogether Miss Burney's work will live, if not by its intrinsic interest, at least as a document of importance in the social history of England.

The novel of the eighteenth century from Defoe to Miss
Burney was, on the whole, conceived on realistic lines. The
novelists endeavored to deal with things as they *The*
were, though they usually claimed the purpose of *Romantic*
making them better. Toward the close of the cen- *Movement*
tury, however, a shift in emphasis may be perceived, as the novel exhibits various "romantic" tendencies.

As has already been noted, the Romantic Movement showed
its influence in a return to nature, in absorption in the remote
in time and space and a revelling in the attendant emotions of
awe and wonder, in emphasis on the individual, however
humble, and his defense against society. All of these forces are
reflected in fiction of the period. The new interest in nature
made scene an important element in the novel; the interest in
the past brought into being a new type of fiction, the Gothic,
the ancestor of the historical novel; the interest in the individual
gave rise to a considerable number of novels with a purpose.
Accordingly, therefore, we find at the close of the century three
types of fiction. In addition to the realistic novel, which dealt
with social life and manners, there was the romance, which
represented the purely emotional interest in nature and in the
past, and the humanitarian novel, which seriously undertook to
right the wrongs sustained by the individual at the hands of
society. These three objects, to paint life, to escape from life,
and to make life better, have defined three schools, the realists,
the romanticists, and the social novelists, which have continued,
with innumerable cross divisions, until the present time.

The long list of romances of the period begins with *The
Castle of Otranto*, published as early as 1764. It was the work
of Horace Walpole (1717–1797), one of the *Walpole's*
leaders of that fashion which, in its preference for *"Castle of*
the grotesque and barbarous instead of the classi- *Otranto"*
cally simple and civilized, was called "Gothic." In
The Castle of Otranto he tried to paint the domestic life and
manners of the feudal period, "as agitated by the action of
supernatural machinery such as the superstition of the time
might have accepted." With this excuse for the introduction
of supernatural elements, no explanation of them by rational

causes is needed, and none is attempted. A portrait steps from its panel and walks abroad, a statue sheds blood, a helmet of gigantic size crashes down into the courtyard, and gives symbolical accompaniment to the action of the story by dreadfully waving its plumes, all without the least apology from the author. His only effort is to give an air of reality to such impossibilities by making his characters natural, and by painting the manners of the time faithfully. In neither attempt was he highly successful. That he did succeed in arousing the emotions of horror and fear is proved by excellent testimony, for example, that of his friend Thomas Gray. For the rest, Walpole gave to the Gothic romance the elements on which it was to thrive for a generation to come—a hero sullied by unmentionable crimes, several persecuted heroines, a castle with secret passages and haunted rooms, and a plentiful sprinkling of supernatural terrors.

Another book of importance in the development of romantic fiction is *The History of the Caliph Vathek* (1786), written by William Beckford (1759–1844). This tale added *Other* to the attractions of remote time those of a distant *Gothic* and marvelous land; it substituted for the cre- *Romances* ations of mediæval superstition the mysteries of oriental necromancy; and it spiced the whole with a dash of eastern voluptuousness. Gothic romances were also produced by Matthew Gregory Lewis (1775–1818), whose *Monk* (1796) was the most popular book of its time, and whose *Bravo of Venice* (1804) has for its hero a distinct precursor of the Byronic type, an individual developed into a quite transcendent personality by feeding on his wrongs and crimes.

The most successful producer of Gothic stories was Mrs. Anne Radcliffe (1764–1823), who in the last decade of the century wrote five elaborate romances, of which *Mrs.* the most famous are *The Mysteries of Udolpho* *Radcliffe* (1794) and *The Italian* (1797). These have the faults and virtues of their type. They abound in mysterious incident, skillfully used; but they show an increasing tendency, toward finding a rational explanation for apparently supernatural occurrences. In plot they are carefully constructed to keep the reader guessing as to which of several possible explanations is the true one. They are decorated with elaborate set pieces of description, involving the romantic elements of Italian landscape, as treated by the painters, Claude or Salvator Rosa; but there is no accuracy in the local color, which is lavishly used, and no historical truth in the representation of manners and institutions of the past. The characters are either extravagantly false or mildly conventional. Of Elena, in *The Italian*, we are told that "her features were of the Greek outline, and though they expressed the tranquillity of an elegant mind, her dark blue eyes sparkled with intelligence." Beyond this the stereotyped formula can hardly go.

Although Walpole in his preface to *The Castle of Otranto* points a moral for his readers, the Gothic romance was written primarily to excite and entertain. A far more strenuous development of the novel was going on at the hands of the group of revolutionary ro- *The Revolutionists* manticists, of whom William Godwin (1756–1836) was the chief. With them the novel became a tract; it was put out simply as propaganda. The plot was arranged, and the characters were drawn, to expose a social evil or to show its remedy. Naturally, such books subordinated art to purpose, and for that reason few of them are remembered. A special class of such reforming novels was devoted to the bringing up of youth. This had been a leading theme in English prose literature from the time of the Renaissance, but whereas the early systems of education had been based on the study of the classics, as fitting a boy to take his proper place in formal society, the new education emphasized the place of nature and experiment in the child's development. In this "return to nature" the influence of the story *Emile* (1762) by the French philosopher Rousseau counted for much. A favorite plan of novelists devoted to this form of propaganda was to set in opposition two children, one brought up in the conventions of society, and the other in the freedom of nature, and show the advantage of the latter at all points. The chief of these educational novels are *The Fool of Quality* (1766) by Henry Brooke, *Sandford and Merton* (1783–1789) by Thomas Day, and *Nature and Art* (1796) by Elizabeth Inchbald.

Many other aspects of society—government, marriage, private property—were criticized by novelists in the period of the *Godwin's* French Revolution. The strongest book of this class *"Caleb* was William Godwin's *Caleb Williams* (1794). *Williams"* Godwin was one of the most earnest supporters in England of the French Revolution. He wrote *Caleb Williams* as a tract against the British Constitution and the ideals of aristocratic society, which Burke fought so hard to maintain. The real hero, Falkland, under great provocation has committed a murder, and in obedience to the false god of his class, Reputation, he has allowed a poor peasant to suffer the penalty for it. By accident his secretary, Caleb Williams, becomes possessed of the secret, and in self-preservation Falkland feels bound to crush him. The author gives a powerful account of the way in which an aristocrat like Falkland can use the forces of society and law against an individual of a lower class; and he presents movingly the sufferings of such an individual under this persecution. But more moving still is the picture of the ruin of a benevolent and elevated character by the possession of aristocratic power, and by subjection to aristocratic prejudices. The villain in the book is chivalry, and Falkland, even more than Williams, is its victim. *Caleb Williams* is an interesting example of the novel of propaganda, employed here to disseminate revolutionary ideas.

CHAPTER XIII

The Nineteenth Century

THE TRIUMPH OF ROMANTICISM

I

THE ROMANTIC MOVEMENT, of which the beginnings have been traced in the preceding chapter, was by no means confined to literature. In England the religious revival under John Wesley, in Germany the new philosophy put forth by Immanuel Kant, in France the immense social upheaval of the French Revolution, were symptoms, early or late, of the same great influence working for liberation. The French Revolution brought to Europe the hope of political freedom and social reconstruction, and though the hope was disappointed in the accession to power of Napoleon, its place was taken by the enthusiasm of the struggle of the nations against him in which England took the chief part. The first years of the nineteenth century were marked by the greatest national crisis which England had experienced since the days of Elizabeth. Then the country was confronted by Spain, under Philip II, seeking to become a world-power, and to impose its religious ideals on Europe; at the threshold of the nineteenth century she found herself face to face with France under Napoleon, seeking to gain a similar leadership and to impose a world-system. As the struggle with Spain led to an extraordinary outburst of patriotism, so did the war with Napoleon; and the apex of national glory reached in the destruction of the Armada was touched again at Trafalgar and Waterloo. And in both cases the falling off was rapid. The victory of Europe over Napoleon was attended by reactionary movements which threatened to undo all that the French Revolution had accomplished for the rights of man. Accordingly, we

The Romantic Movement

may distinguish two phases in the first third of the nineteenth century: one of enthusiasm, characterized by the work of Wordsworth, Coleridge, and Scott; and one of disillusionment and revolt, of which the younger group of romanticists, Byron, Shelley, and Keats, were in various ways typical.

The Romantic Movement has already been defined as an escape of the individual from social and literary conventions, a
Double Aspect of the Movement "return to nature," a welcoming back into life of all that was spontaneous and sincere; a reassertion of the right of man to indulge his impulses and emotions, even the wildest and most wayward. This reassertion naturally took two directions: one outward, toward whatever was remote. and unusual; one inward, into the heart of common things, which, when looked at closely, were found to be full of new meanings. These two impulses found expression in the work of the two poets in whom the English Romantic Movement first became conscious of its real aims—Samuel Taylor Coleridge (1772–1834) and William Wordsworth (1770–1850). A happy chance brought these two poets together in the impressionable period of their young manhood, when Coleridge was twenty-three and Wordsworth only two years older. Both had felt the storm and stress of the revolutionary age. Each brought to the other just that kind of stimulus needed to kindle his mind to creative activity; and together they gathered the diffused and uncertain rays of the new poetic illumination into an orb of steady splendor. In them the new poetry first found an adequate and unmistakable voice, and the little volume called *Lyrical Ballads,* which they published together in 1798, shows the two impulses of the new poetry in full play. Coleridge's contributions treat mysterious, supernatural subjects in such a way as to give to them an unparalleled illusion of reality; Wordsworth's treat simple, everyday themes of nature and human life in such a way as to reveal in them unsuspected elements of mystery and awe.

Coleridge was born at Ottery Saint Mary, Devonshire, in 1772. He had a precocious boyhood as a "blue-coat" at Christ's Hospital, the famous charity school in London. While at Cambridge he plunged, with his friend Robert Southey, then a student at Oxford, into the generous enthusiasms aroused by the French Revolution. After graduation the two young idealists, in their ardor for social reform, conceived a grand scheme of "pantisocracy," which they dreamed of realizing in the shape of a utopian community to be established across the ocean, on the banks of the Susquehanna. Preliminary to emigration Coleridge published a *Early Life of Coleridge* volume of juvenile verse, and married; by 1797 he had a young family on his hands, and had exchanged pantisocracy for a tiny cottage in the village of Nether Stowey, in the Quantock hills. In 1797 Wordsworth, together with his wonderful sister Dorothy, moved to Alfoxden, in order to be near Coleridge, whom he had met two years before. To Wordsworth the companionship meant much; to Coleridge it meant everything. Under the bracing influence of Wordsworth's hardy, original mind, supplemented by the quick sympathy and suggestiveness of Dorothy, Coleridge shot up suddenly into full poetic stature. In little more than a year (1797–1798) he wrote all his greatest poems, "Frost at Midnight," "France: an Ode," "Kubla Khan," "The Ancient Mariner," and the first part of "Christabel."

The rest of Coleridge's life, though he wrote a good deal of verse, has little importance in the history of poetry. He made a trip, in the Wordsworths' company, to Germany, and there became absorbed in the philosophy of Kant. So far as his later life had any definite purpose, it was spent in interpreting the principles of this philosophy to his countrymen. His bondage to the opium habit, added to an inherent weakness of will, made his life a heartrending succession of half-attempts and whole failures. He planned many books, and partly executed a few; but his chief influence was exerted through series of public lectures, in talk with his friends and with those young men who, as his reputation for transcendental wisdom increased, resorted to him as to an oracle of hope and faith, in the years which followed the failure of the French Revolution. By consent of all who heard him Coleridge was one of the most wonderful talkers that ever lived. His verse, fragmentary and of small bulk though it is, gives him rank as one of the world's great poets.

Coleridge represents perfectly that side of the romantic imagination which seeks to lose itself in dream and marvel; to con-

Character-istics of His Poetry jure up a world of phantasmal scenery and of supernatural happenings, illuminated by "a light that never was on sea or land." "Kubla Khan" paints an oriental dream-picture, as mysterious and as impalpable as the palaces and plunging rivers and "caverns measureless to man," which we sometimes see lifted for a moment out of a stormy sunset. "Christabel," which seems in its fragmentary form to have been planned as the story of a young girl fallen under the spell of an unearthly demon in woman's shape, moves in a mediæval atmosphere blended of beauty and horror—a horror poignantly vague, freezing the heart with its suggestion of all that is malign and cruel in the spirit world. "The Ancient Mariner," Coleridge's one finished masterpiece, stands almost alone in literature for the completeness with which it creates an illusion of reality while dealing with images and events manifestly unreal. Its great pictures of night and morning, of arctic and tropic seas; its melodies of whispering keel and rustling sails, and of dead throats singing spectral carols; its strange music, richer and more various even than that of "Kubla Khan," though not so grand and spacious—these elements make "The Ancient Mariner" a poem with scarcely an equal in its kind. It is manifestly a dream, but a dream caught in a magic mirror, which holds it spellbound in immortal freshness. "The Ancient Mariner" was Coleridge's chief contribution to *Lyrical Ballads*; in itself it represented a whole domain splendidly conquered for the reawakened imaginations of men.

William Wordsworth was born in 1770, at Cockermouth in Cumberland, and he received his early education at the country

Words-worth's Life grammar-school at Hawkshead, in the Lake region. He was a somewhat indifferent student at St. John's College, Cambridge, from 1787 to 1791. Late in the latter year he went to France, where he watched with enthusiastic hope the middle stages of the French Revolution, and shared in the ardent social enthusiasm which summed itself up in the motto of the revolutionists, "Liberty, Equality, Fraternity." He fell in love with a French girl, Annette Vallon,

and a daughter, Caroline, was born to them late in 1792. He
was in Paris before the awful excesses of the Reign of Terror
began, and he was on the point of throwing in his lot with the
revolutionists when a stoppage of his allowance compelled him
to return to England. The failure of his hopes and plans, personal and political, induced in him a profound despondency.
During this critical period, he says, his sister Dorothy's influence
kept alive the poet in him, by directing his mind toward the
sources of permanent strength and joy which lie in nature and
in human sympathy:

> She gave me eyes, she gave me ears;
> And humble cares, and delicate fears;
> A heart, the fountain of sweet tears;
> And love, and thought, and joy.

Their residence at Alfoxden, with Coleridge, 1797–1798,
marks the true beginning of Wordsworth's poetic career; for
up to this time, though he had written much, he had not found
his genuine matter and manner. In "We are Seven," "Expostu-
lation and Reply," "Lines Written in Early Spring," "Tintern
Abbey," and other pieces belonging to this period, the true
Wordsworth is apparent. During the winter in Germany which
followed, he added to these pieces some of his most characteristic poems, such as "She Dwelt among the Untrodden Ways"
and "Three Years She Grew in Sun and Shower." On his return
he settled with his sister in a cottage at Grasmere, on Lake Grasmere, and in 1802 he married. At Grasmere, and afterward at
Rydal Mount near the head of Lake Windermere, he lived for
fifty years among the Cumberland dalesmen, leading an existence as pastoral and as frugal as theirs, reading little and meditating much, looking with deep, unwearied delight upon the
mountains and skies and waters which had fascinated him in
boyhood. A small legacy from a friend, and later an appointment as distributor of stamps, made him independent, and left
virtually his whole time free for the pursuit of poetry, which was
for him, as for Milton, not only an art but a solemn ministry.
The heights of his poetic achievement are marked successively
by such pieces as "Michael" (1800); "Resolution and Inde-

pendence," the sonnets to Milton, to Toussaint L'Ouverture, "It Is a Beauteous Evening" and "Westminster Bridge" (1802); "The Solitary Reaper" and "Yarrow Unvisited" (1803); the "Ode to Duty," "To a Skylark," and *The Prelude* (1805); "The World Is Too Much With Us" and the "Ode: Intimations of Immortality" (1806); "Songs at the Feast of Brougham Castle" (1807), and *The Excursion* (1814). After this last date Wordsworth's genius gradually stiffened, and he produced little more poetry of the first order. This decline in poetic power in his later years was accompanied by a reaction from the social and political radicalism of his youth into a firm conservatism, which led him to uphold existing institutions of church and state in the spirit of Burke. For many years his poetry met with neglect and ridicule, but he gradually drew to himself the attention and veneration of the best minds. The crowd turned aside to follow first Scott, then Byron, and then Tennyson; but those whose suffrages were of most value rallied in increasing numbers about the "good old steel-gray figure" of the Cumberland poet; and before his death in 1850 he enjoyed a late but sure renown.

In Wordsworth the growing sensibility to natural phenomena, which we have traced from Thomson and Collins down to the *His Nature-Poetry: Its Sensitiveness* end of the eighteenth century, reached its height. He was gifted by nature with an eye and an ear marvelously sensitive to those slight and elusive impressions which most persons pass by without noticing at all. This sensibility was increased by a long life spent in the country, in a region full of charm and even of grandeur; and it was made efficacious by a remarkable serenity and patience, which enabled him to gather all the riches of the inanimate world, without haste and without disturbing excitement. Hence his poetry is full of exquisitely noted sights and sounds—the shadow of the daisy on the stone, the mist which follows the hare as she runs across a rain-drenched moor, the echo of the cuckoo's voice, the varying noise of waters, and the many voices of the wind. "To read one of his longer pastoral poems for the first time," it has been said, "is like a day spent in a new country." And all these sights and sounds are given with absolute fidelity to fact. There is no effect of heightening nature, of seeing her clothed in a light brighter or stranger than her own. Wordsworth writes "with his eye on the object," content to portray what he sees. He learned from Burns that "verse may build a princely throne on humble truth"; and everywhere he gives an impression of unquestioning, reverent faithfulness to the fact which his senses have perceived. It follows that the greater part of his nature-studies are in a low key; in the rareness of their grandeurs and glories, they breathe the modesty of nature. Especially noteworthy is the predominance in Wordsworth of broad elementary impressions—mere darkness and light, the silence of the sky, the moon looking "round her when the heavens are bare," the twilight with its one star, the breathlessness of the evening sea, the lonesomeness of upland fields, the "sleep that is among the lonely hills." It is the keenness of Wordsworth's sensibility to nature, his quiet, religious acceptance of her as she is, and his unwearied delight in her broadest and simplest phases, which together make him the first of her poets.

Its Truth

Its Breadth

This same sobriety and truth of tone, this same reverent regard for the great commonplaces of life, characterize also Wordsworth's treatment of human nature. He deals with the broad elementary passions, the every-day affections, occupations, and duties, in a state of society where man is simplest and nearest to the soil. In many of his best poems, indeed, the human beings whom he pictures seem almost a part of the landscape, an emanation from nature herself, like the trees or the rocks. The figure of the leech-gatherer on the moor in "Resolution and Independence" seems as much a part of the natural landscape as the pool by which he stands; the woman who speaks to the poet in "Stepping Westward" seems a part of the sunset, so blended is she with the scene; in "The Solitary Reaper" the singing of the girl comes out of the heart of the day, like the spirit of ancestral Scotland telling over its "old unhappy far-off things, and battles long ago"; she is hardly more of a human personality than the cuckoo or the nightingale to which the poet

His Treatment of Human Nature

compares her voice. Even when he looks closer at his human characters, and shows us their passions and the accidents of their life, they still partake of the simplicity and breadth of external nature, reminding us of biblical characters or the simple, tragic figures of the French peasant painter Millet. The story of Margaret, in the first book of *The Excursion*, and in a still better way "Michael" illustrate Wordsworth's power to give to the simple tragedies of the peasant world a monumental impressiveness. He is the poet of human life in its lowest terms, of that joy and sorrow which is "in widest commonalty spread." He looks to find the true significance of life on its simpler levels, as did Crabbe; but with far more sympathy, depth, and spiritual glow than Crabbe was able to bring to bear upon his subject. The best praise he can give his own wife is that she is a "being breathing thoughtful breath," in whose countenance meet sweet household records and promises. For Milton his best praise is that, although his "soul was like a star and dwelt apart," yet it laid upon itself "the lowliest duties" along "life's common way." With Wordsworth the doctrine of simplicity entered into his entire conception not only of art but of life.

Yet we should have but a very partial understanding of Wordsworth's personality and of his poetic meaning if we

His Mysticism

stopped here. There was in him, besides the realist and the moralist, the mystic. His pacific and serene temperament made it possible for him to ignore the callousness of nature, its lush fecundity, its terrifying demonstration of the struggle for existence, its carelessness of the individual life. Accordingly, nature is for him, even when he portrays her external aspect with the most naked truth, never merely a physical fact; nor has man, even when most blended in with her external features, merely a physical relation to her. On the contrary, nature is everywhere mystically transfused with spirit, and speaks mystically to the spirit in man, working

"Tintern Abbey"

upon him by the power of kinship and mutual understanding. Perhaps the most complete expression of this aspect of his thought is "Tintern Abbey," which appeared in the *Lyrical Ballads*. "Tintern Abbey" was written during a walking tour which Wordsworth took in

1798, in company with his sister, through a country familiar to him in earlier years. The well-remembered scenery of the River Wye calls up before his musing thought the picture of his boyhood, with its passionate absorption in nature, when the sounding cataract haunted him like a passion, and the rocks, the mountains, and the woods were to him "an appetite." He shows how the influences of nature, acting upon the plastic soul of youth, bear fruit in later life, in "sensations sweet felt in the blood and felt along the heart," and "little nameless unremembered acts of kindness and of love"; and how they lift the spirit which remembers them, to

> that blessed mood
> In which the burden of the mystery,
> In which the heavy and the weary weight
> Of all this unintelligible world
> Is lightened . . .
> While with an eye made quiet by the power
> Of harmony, and the deep power of joy,
> We see into the life of things.

And he suggests a metaphysical explanation for this strange power which nature has to soothe and ennoble the human soul, namely, that throughout nature there is diffused an active spirit living and working in her:

> I have felt
> A presence that disturbs me with the joy
> Of elevated thoughts; a sense sublime
> Of something far more deeply interfused,
> Whose dwelling is the light of setting suns,
> And the round ocean and the living air,
> And the blue sky, and in the mind of man:
> A motion and a spirit, that impels
> All thinking things, all objects of all thoughts,
> And rolls through all things.

"Tintern Abbey" gives us almost a complete program of Wordsworth's poetic career. In it we see marked out clearly the main paths which his mind followed during a long lifetime of contemplation. In many noble poems he developed the three themes presented here: the eternal beauty of nature, which waits everywhere about us "to haunt, to startle, and waylay"; the power of that beauty to heal, gladden, and fortify whoever gives it welcome; and the mystic source of this power, the spirit of Nature, hidden yet apparent in all the visible creation, building for itself a "metropolitan temple in the hearts" of simple and unselfish men. Perhaps the most exquisite expression he has given to the idea of nature's formative power upon the soul, and through the soul upon the body of man, is the poem beginning "Three years she grew in sun and shower."

The instinct to perceive nature and human life in transcendental terms was very early manifested in Wordsworth. In his school-days at Hawkshead the world would sometimes, he tells us, seem suddenly to dissolve, and he would fall into a transport of vision from which he had to bring himself back to reality by grasping at the wall by the roadside, or by stooping to pick up a stone. This habit of mind, sobered and strengthened by reflection, pervades all his poetry, and gives to it a peculiarly stimulating character. In reading him, we never know when the actual landscape and the simple human view will widen out suddenly into some vaster prospect, looking beyond space and time; so that he awakens in us a kind of spiritual apprehension or expectancy which forces us to look below the surface of his simplest poem, and to be on the alert for a meaning deeper than its primary one. The "Ode: Intimations of Immortality" is the poem in which the speculation is boldest. In this ode, which Emerson called "the high-water mark of poetry in the nineteenth century," the poet looks back with passionate regret to the lost radiance of his childhood, and tries to connect childhood reassuringly not only with manhood and old age, but also with a previous existence, whence it brings its aura of innocence and joy. The poem is a product of that majestic kind of metaphysical imagination which transcends space and time, and makes

His Metaphysical Imagination

"Intimations of Immortality"

Our noisy years seem moments in the being
Of the eternal Silence.

In the "Intimations" and other poems mystically conceived,
Wordsworth took the inheritance of the seventeenth-century
mystics, and of Blake, and gave it a clearer development, just
as in his nature poetry he carried to larger issues the work of
Cowper, Crabbe, and Burns.

Wordsworth's position and influence are due partly to the
fact that he greatly enlarged the boundaries of poetry, giving it,
as subject-matter, themes varying from the joys and *Words-*
sorrows of simple, homely lives, to the transcen- *worth's*
dental interests of the soul in communion with nature *Style*
and God; partly to his development of a poetic style
befitting such material. His first youthful verse was written after
the manner of Pope, in heroic couplets in the artificial diction
current in the eighteenth century. But with the poems he contributed to *Lyrical Ballads* (1798) he made a conscious change,
which he explained in the preface to the second edition in 1800.
The effort in Wordsworth's contributions to the volume was to
treat incidents from common life, and to relate them in a selection of language really used by men. He took as much pains to
avoid poetic diction as was ordinarily taken to employ it, and
relied for imaginative coloring on the passion which men would
express in the situations which he selected, and which would
give to their language dignity, variety, and metaphor. Clearly,
much depended on the poet's choice of the situation to be
treated, and Wordsworth was not uniformly happy in his selection. Common diction frequently remained commonplace, and
his language, in consequence, did not rise above sheer prose.
Besides, his lack of humor sometimes led him, as in "The Idiot
Boy," into manifest absurdity. In portraying his own life and
thought he fell into the same confusion through his inability to
distinguish between the supreme and the commonplace, and
accordingly he wrote in two styles, one inspired, the other pedes-
trian. His mind was, in ordinary moods, matter-of-fact, and it
worked slowly and stiffly. But just in proportion to the amount
of spiritual energy required to fuse this reluctant metal of his

mind into a plastic glowing state, is the beauty and permanency of the product of his highest creative moments; so that his finest poems seem as little subject to the touch of time, as immune from decay, as the mountains or the stars.

It has long been traditional to associate with Wordsworth and Coleridge, in the triad of "Lake Poets," the name of Robert

Robert
Southey

Southey (1774–1843), Coleridge's brother-in-law and colleague in the scheme of pantisocracy. Southey felt the impulse to escape from the present world into the regions of the past and the distant, the Orient, ancient Wales and Spain, and primitive Mexico, but with him this impulse was nourished rather by reading and study than by inward experience. He settled in the Lake country in 1803, and there gave himself largely to study and industrious writing of prose as well as poetry, for he had Coleridge's family to support in part, as well as his own. His romanticism found expression in long poems, *Thalaba the Destroyer* (1801), based on Mohammedan legend, and *The Curse of Kehama* (1810), on Hindu mythology. He is best remembered for such shorter poems as "The Battle of Blenheim," "My Days among the Dead are Past," and "The Cataract of Lodore," and for his admirable biographies of Nelson, John Wesley, and John Bunyan. He, like Wordsworth and Coleridge, shared in the political idealism of the early days of the French Revolution, and like them came to distrust popular government and became a strenuous defender of the institutions of the past. He holds his place as one of the Lake Poets, less by poetic quality than by personal association.

We have seen how the revolt against eighteenth-century actuality and "common sense" found expression in the wild phantasmagories of Blake, and in the strange dream-world of Coleridge. We have seen likewise how the reaction from the rigid

Romantic
Revolt
Sum-
marized

social aristocracy of the eighteenth century, and from its supercilious distaste for lowly human life, led, through the harsh realism of Crabbe, to Burns's passionate vindication of the primary instincts, and to Wordsworth's solemn revelation of the majesty of simple lives. We have seen, too, how the protest against eighteenth-century "urbanity" and absorption in the life of the town led, through Cowper's mild delight in rural things, to the piercing tenderness of Burns's "Mountain Daisy," and to the mystical insight of Wordsworth's "Tintern Abbey." In like manner, the revulsion from the Augustan indifference to the Middle Ages led, through the forgeries of Chatterton and the epic chants of the pseudo-Ossian, to Scott, for whom it was reserved to create the life of the past on a vast scale, and with an unparalleled illusion of truth.

Walter Scott was born in Edinburgh in 1771; his father was a lawyer, but was descended from a vigorous and warlike border clan. Scott developed early a passion for the ballad minstrelsy of his land; and he spent many days of his youth roaming over the country, gathering ballads and scraps of ballads from the lips of peasants. His collection was published as *Minstrelsy of the Scottish Border* in 1802–03. Except for a few ballads in the "grewsome" vein made popular by the "Lenore" of Bürger, the pioneer of German romanticism, Scott wrote no original poetry until his thirty-fourth year. In 1805 appeared *The Lay of the Last Minstrel,* in which a thread of Gothic supernaturalism is woven into a tale of Scottish border life in the Middle Ages. This was followed in 1808 by *Marmion. Marmion* exhibited in much greater measure the brilliant descriptive color, the swift and powerful narrative movement, and the ringing, energetic music, which had made the *Lay* instantly popular; and it showed a great advance over the earlier poem in lifelikeness and breadth. Scarcely more than a year later appeared *The Lady of the Lake,* a story softer and more idyllic than *Marmion,* yet not lacking in wild and stirring episodes; in it Scott came far nearer than he had done in his earlier poems to the broad, imaginative handling of mediæval Scottish life which he afterward gave in his prose romances.

Scott's Career as a Poet

These three poems, presenting many of the new romantic motives in popularly attractive form, took the reading world by storm. The diction employed in them was not, like the language of Coleridge and Wordsworth, so startlingly novel as a literary medium that it repelled the unaccustomed ear. The strong and buoyant metre appealed powerfully to a public weary of the monotonous couplets of the preceding age, but unable to appreciate the

Qualities of His Poetry

delicate melodies of the *Songs of Innocence and of Experience*
and the *Lyrical Ballads*. The romantic scenery, brightly and
firmly painted, but always kept subordinate to the action; the
character delineation, picturesque but not subtle; and the vigorous sweep of the story—all touched the popular heart. Scott
himself described the peculiar excellence of his poetry truly
enough, though with characteristic modesty, as consisting in a
"hurried frankness of composition which pleases soldiers,
sailors, and young people of bold and active disposition."

Scott's metrical tales did much to popularize romanticism in
its broader phases. He was, however, not much in earnest as a
poet; and when the public turned to the more lurid and extravagant verse-tales of Byron, Scott cheerfully resigned his place to
the younger man, and began his far greater work in prose.

The popular triumph of romanticism was also aided by another Scottish poet, Thomas Campbell (1777–1844). He began

*Thomas
Campbell*

his career as a follower of the Augustans, and was
known during his university career as the "Pope of
Glasgow." In Germany, where he went in 1799,
he fell under the influence of Bürger and the other early German romanticists, and in 1803 he published a volume of
poems in the new manner, among which "Lochiel's Warning,"
"Hohenlinden," and "The Last Man" attained and have held a
great popular esteem. His most ambitious narrative, *Gertrude
of Wyoming* (1809), is a highly romantic tale, in Spenserian
stanzas, of pioneer and Indian life in Pennsylvania. His famous
war-odes, "The Battle of the Baltic" and "Ye Mariners of England," full of martial energy and kindling enthusiasm, rank
with the best war-poetry of England, and are worthy of the race
which holds the dominion of the sea.

The group of poets who came to manhood when the French
Revolution was at its height reacted during the Napoleonic wars
into settled conservatism. Scott, indeed, by the accident of his
early surroundings, was conservative from the first. Southey and
Coleridge, after their youthful enthusiasm for revolutionary
utopianism, took refuge, the one in political Toryism, the other
in the complexities of German philosophy. Wordsworth, who
had felt the storm and stress of revolutionary ideas more than
any of the others, after a long period of wavering and disap-

pointment, finally intrenched himself behind the institutions of Church and state as he found them. The two poets whom we now approach, Byron and Shelley, took up the torch of revolution which had been kindled in France during their childhood, and carried it flaming into new regions of thought and feeling.

George Gordon, Lord Byron, was born in 1788, of a family of noblemen notorious for their passionate temper, their amatory adventures, and their thriftlessness. To his extraordinary physical beauty, his lameness added a touch of pathos. Personal fascination was his from the first. He mastered his little world of school-fellows at Harrow with the same power of personality which later took captive the imagination of Europe. His first volume of poems, *Hours of Idleness* (1807), an immature little book, was mercilessly ridiculed in the *Edinburgh Review*. Byron nursed his revenge, and in 1809 he published a vigorous onslaught upon his critics, entitled *English Bards and Scotch Reviewers*. This poem is written in the manner of Pope, for whom Byron always professed admiration, and is not unworthy of his school, either in mastery of the heroic couplet or in energy of satire. It is significant that Byron's first signal performance should have been conceived in a satiric vein, and educed by a blow to his personal pride.

Byron's Life and Writings

In the same year the young poet set off upon his travels, which he was to recount in the first two cantos of *Childe Harold* (1812). Not content with the conventional Grand Tour, he pushed on into Albania, Greece, and the islands of the Ægean: dining in the tents of robber chieftains, rescuing distressed beauties from death at the hand of harem slaves, and doing many other romantic things. The public, at any rate, was eager to ascribe all these adventures to him, incited thereto by the lurid verse-romances, *The Giaour* (1813), *The Corsair* (1814), *Lara* (1814), and others, which he now poured out with prodigal swiftness. These Oriental tales were crude and melodramatic, but they appealed enormously to the popular taste, and quite eclipsed Scott's saner and healthier muse.

On Byron's return to England, he was lionized by corrupt Regency society, and plunged into a series of notorious love-affairs. His marriage was quickly followed by a separation from his wife and by his final departure from his native country. The next years he spent in Switzerland and Italy, part of the time in company with Shelley. To this period belong his most important works, the later cantos of *Childe Harold* (1816–1818), the dramas *Manfred* (1817) and *Cain* (1821), and his satiric masterpiece, *Don Juan* (1819–1824). The romance of his life was crowned by a romantic and generous death. In 1824 he went to Greece, to put himself at the head of the revolutionary forces gathered to liberate that country from the tyranny of the Sultan. He was seized with fever in the swamps of Missolonghi, and died before he had had time to prove his ability as a leader.

In his Oriental tales and his dramas Byron presents under many names one hero—himself, or rather an exaggerated shadow of one side of himself. The Conrads and Laras of the tales are all proud and lonely souls in revolt; mysteriously wicked, infernally proud, quixotically generous, and above all melancholy. They all represent the individual in revolt against society. In *Manfred* and *Cain* these crude outlines became imposing silhouettes, thrown out sharply against a background half-real and half-supernatural. The scene of *Manfred* is the high Alps, where the hero lives in his castle in gloomy and bitter isolation, communing with unearthly powers, and scornfully accepting his dark fate. *Cain*, though imperfectly carried out, is superbly conceived. The earthly rebel and first shedder of human blood, under the guidance of Lucifer, the rebel angel, visits hell and chaos, and there finds grounds for the godless hatred that is in him. It was by these plays that Byron earned his title as founder and chief exemplar of the "Satanic school" of poetry. They are perhaps the most uncompromising expression of individualism and the most thoroughgoing negation of the social ideal to be found in our literature. Their popularity, which was instant and enormous throughout Europe, was largely due to historical causes. The French Revolution, the most daring reach which the human race had ever made after an ideal social state, had failed. Europe, under the rule of the monarchs who had overthrown Napoleon, had swung back from its eager dreams of freedom

The Eastern Tales

The Dramas: Reasons for Their Popularity

and fraternity into a reactionary mood, in the midst of which the still potent spirit of rebellion was forced to become personal, self-centred, and antisocial. Byron represented and justified to the European mind this recoil, and Byronism became a passion, a disease.

Childe Harold presents the Byronic hero in a more elegiac mood, as a pensive wanderer through Europe and the East. It is not until the later cantos that the verse rises into real magnificence. Among the lakes and mountain solitudes of Switzerland, the decaying glories of Venice, and the imperial ruins of Rome, the poet's imagination is genuinely kindled, and the passages which celebrate these scenes are among the triumphs of descriptive poetry in our language. Byron paints his pictures in free, bold strokes, and with a pomp of rhetoric well suited to his grandiose subjects. He makes up in broad impressiveness what he lacks in subtlety. His music, too, is loud and sonorous; without the heartfelt, searching beauty of greater melodists, but with an orchestral sweep and volume appropriate to the theme.

Byron as a Descriptive Poet: "Childe Harold"

In *Don Juan* Byron wrote his masterpiece, and it proved to be neither dramatic nor lyric, but satiric. *Don Juan* is a comprehensive satire upon modern society. The hero is a Castilian youth, a light-hearted, irresponsible pagan creature, who wanders through Turkey, Russia, and England, meeting all sorts of adventures, particularly such as are calculated to shock the moral sense, and to exhibit the social corruption hidden under the conventional veneer. The poem is, in effect, a long peal of scornful laughter flung at that peculiarly British variety of cant which Byron declared was in his day the "primum mobile" of his countrymen's life, both national and private. In his more serious work Byron is fatally subject to anticlimax. His imagination and his power of phrase are apt to fail him just when they are needed most. In *Don Juan* he turns this defect into a piquant virtue, by deliberately cultivating anticlimax for satiric ends. He drops with startling suddenness from the serious to the trivial, from impassioned poetry to mocking verse. The device is a simple one, but Byron uses it with a variety and zest truly won-

Byron as a Satirist: "Don Juan"

derful, and secures by means of it an effect of cynical noncha-
lance which is a triumph of its kind.

Byron's was a personality of immense force. To his age he
was a pillar of cloud by day and of fire by night, but one which
led only into the deserts of unfaith and negation.

*Byron's
Influence
and Style*

Such work as he had to do was a work of destruction; the age cried out for it, and he did it thoroughly. Of the higher powers of poetry he possessed few, and for them he cared little. He was a careless and
hasty worker. In his own words, if he missed his first spring he
went growling back to his jungle. That he was a great writer is
as certain as that neither by the soul nor the body of his art can
he take rank with the small company of supreme poets.

Among that company, Percy Bysshe Shelley is a presence so
bright and strange as to seem in truth one of those "spirits from
beyond the moon" of which he sang. He was born

*Shelley's
Life and
Poetic De-
velopment*

in 1792, just when the eyes of all Europe were
fixed in hope and fear upon France, and the stars
fought in their courses for the triumph of a new
order. At Eton, among the tyrannies and conventions of a great public school, his sensitive nature was thrown
into a fever of rebellion from which he never quite worked out
into spiritual sanity and health. "Mad Shelley" his schoolmates
called him, and in the judgment of the world he remained "mad
Shelley" to the end of his life. At Oxford, whither he proceeded
in 1810, he read the sceptical French philosophers, and deemed
it his duty to publish his religious views in a pamphlet entitled
"The Necessity of Atheism," for which he was expelled. An ill-
starred marriage with Harriet Westbrook followed, and after
that came a quixotic attempt to arouse Ireland to seek redress
for her national wrongs. The young couple carried on their mission by throwing from the windows of their lodging in Dublin
copies of Shelley's *Address to the Irish People,* "to every passer-
by who seemed likely." The curious mixture in Shelley of the
visionary and the serious thinker is sharply brought out by the
fact that the writings thus fantastically put in circulation are
often of grave and simple eloquence, wise in counsel and temperate in tone, and that most of the reforms which they advocate
have since been enacted into law.

An acquaintance with William Godwin, the revolutionary philosopher and novelist, author of *Political Justice* and *Caleb Williams,* led Shelley to write *Queen Mab,* a crude poem attacking dogmatic religion, government, industrial tyranny, and war. He separated from Harriet Westbrook in 1814, and united himself with Godwin's daughter, Mary, who after Harriet's suicide became his wife. His next poem, *Alastor, or the Spirit of Solitude* (1816), is a vaguely autobiographical account of a young poet's unsuccessful attempt to recapture his envisioned ideal. This was followed in 1818 by *Laon and Cythna,* which was at once suppressed and published later as *The Revolt of Islam,* a long narrative in Spenserian stanzas, proclaiming a bloodless revolution and the regeneration of man by love. In 1818 the Shelleys went to Italy, where his powers developed rapidly. At Rome, amid the tangle of flowers and vines which at that time covered the mountainous ruins of the Baths of Caracalla, he wrote his lyrical drama, *Prometheus Unbound.* The same year (1819) he finished *The Cenci,* a drama intended for the stage, and written in much more simple and everyday language than his other works. The short remainder of his life is marked by many great poems, some of considerable length, like the "Sensitive Plant" and "Adonais"; others shorter, among them the wonderful "Ode to the West Wind," and the best known of all Shelley's lyrics, the "Skylark." In 1822 the poet was drowned off Leghorn, in one of those swift storms which sweep the Mediterranean during the summer heats. His body was burned on the beach, and his ashes were placed in the Protestant cemetery at Rome, near the grave where, a few months before, Keats had been laid.

Shelley's most characteristic work, in both thought and style, is *Prometheus Unbound.* The subject was suggested by a lost drama of Æschylus, in which Prometheus, the heroic friend and lover of mankind, was unchained from a bleak precipice where the tyrant Zeus had hung him. In Shelley's treatment Prometheus represents, not a superhuman helper of mankind, but Mankind itself, heroic, just, gentle, sacredly thirsting after liberty and spiritual gladness, but chained and tortured by the ruler of Heaven. In the fulness of time Demogorgon (Necessity) hurls the tyrant from his throne; and

His Most Character- istic Work, "Prome- theus Un- bound"

Prometheus, amid the songs of Earth and the Moon, is united to Asia, the spirit of love in nature. Here, as elsewhere, Shelley shows himself a child of the French Revolution, in believing that it is only some external tyranny—the might of priests and kings, the weight of "custom," the dark creed of superstition— which keeps mankind from rising to his ideal stature. Here Shelley's faith in the inevitable elimination of evil from the world and its consequent domination by love receives transcendent expression. The nobility of mood and the heroic enthusiasm of the drama make it eternally inspiring. And for its spirit of revolutionary idealism the verse of the poem is a glorious vesture. The unearthly beauty of its imagery and the ethereal music of its songs and choruses make this not only Shelley's highest poetic achievement but his most powerful statement of his moral philosophy.

It is in its lyrics that *Prometheus* reaches its greatest altitudes, for Shelley's genius was essentially lyrical. In all his best songs and odes the words seem to be moved into their *His* places in response to some hidden tune, wayward and *Lyrical* strange in its movement, but always rounding into a *Genius* perfect whole. Such a poem as that beginning "Swiftly walk over the western wave" marks perhaps the extreme limit of the romantic divergence from eighteenth-century strictness of form; but it obeys a higher law than that of regularity, and with all its waywardness it is as perfect in shape as a flower. The rhythmical structure of the "West Wind" should be studied as a typical example of Shelley's power to make the movement of verse embody its mood. In this ode, the impetuous sweep and tireless overflow of the *terza rima*,[1] ending after each twelfth line in a couplet, suggest with wonderful truth the streaming and volleying of the wind, interrupted now and then by a sudden lull. Likewise in the "Skylark," the fluttering lift of the bird's movement, the airy ecstasy and rippling gush of its song, are mirrored in the rhythm in a thousand subtly varying effects.

Another main peculiarity of Shelley as a poet is what may be called his "myth-making" power. His poetry is full of "personi-

[1] Ten-syllable lines rhyming *a b a, b c b, c d c,* etc.

fications" which, although in origin not different from those which fill eighteenth-century poetry with dead abstractions like "smiling Hope" and "ruddy Cheer," are so vitally imagined that they become real spiritual presences, inspiring wonder and awe. Such are the "Spirits of the Hours" in *Prometheus*; such is the spirit of the west wind in the ode just mentioned, the latter a sublime piece of myth-making. It is in "Adonais," however, that this quality is perhaps best exhibited. To mourn over the dead body of Keats, in whose memory the elegy was written, there gather Splendors and Glooms, grief-clad Morning and wailing Spring, desolate Hours, winged Persuasions and veiled Destinies, and the lovely Dreams which were the exhalation of the poet's spirit, in life. It would be hard to find a more signal instance than these "personifications" afford, of the way in which a great poet can revivify an outworn and discredited poetic tradition. The elegy is of all Shelley's poems the one which would most have satisfied Keats's own jealous artistic sense. It is to be grouped with Milton's *Lycidas,* Tennyson's *In Memoriam,* and Arnold's *Thyrsis* as one of the four supreme threnodies [1] in English verse.

His "Myth-making" Power

Shelley's poetry seems to reflect a dream-world, peopled by ethereal forms and bathed in prismatic light. Even when he borrows imagery from nature it is from a nature heightened and rarefied by passage through his own imagination. He is at the other pole from Wordsworth's homeliness and large acceptance of nature as she is. But, despite the ethereal qualities of his poetry, he was not, as Matthew Arnold unhappily described him, "a beautiful and ineffectual angel, beating in the void his luminous wings in vain." Closer studies of Shelley's life and work have shown that he came nearer than any other poet of his period to assimilating the scientific findings of the age and that beneath the shimmering surface of his verse lie solid learning and comprehensive knowledge. The legendary "mad Shelley" has had to yield place to a greatly gifted man whose coherently purposive life was domi-

His Idealism

[1] Threnody, from two Greek words signifying "tear" and "song," *i.e.,* a song of grief for the dead.

nated by an ideal carefully grounded in science and philosophy. Furthermore, his passionate pleas for freedom, for justice, and for loving-kindness have never ceased to be potent in the deepening earnestness of the search after social betterment.

One effect of the revolutionary excitement of the age, and of the political agitation which it engendered, was to revive the *Revival of National Sentiment* sentiment of nationality, which had lost during the eighteenth century the lyric ardor given to it during the reign of Elizabeth. In Wordsworth's sonnets on national crises during the Napoleonic wars, and in Campbell's odes, this new national sentiment was expressed for England. In Scott's poems and novels it was expressed—in a broader, less political way—for Scotland. Ireland found a champion for her immemorial wrongs, and a reflection of her national peculiarities of temperament, in Thomas Moore *Thomas Moore* (1779–1852), the biographer and intimate friend of Byron. Moore's *Irish Melodies,* of which, beginning in 1807, he wrote an immense number, include a score or so really beautiful lyrics, where the bright fancy and vague, elusive melancholy of the Celtic nature find fit expression. Like the Elizabethan lyrist, Moore wrote for music, much of it of his own composing. He pays insincere tribute to the exotic variety of romanticism in his Oriental tale, *Lalla Rookh* (1817), which is as artificial in its candied sweetness and tinsel decoration as the Irish Melodies are, when at their best, genuine.

A link between the revolutionary poets, deeply imbued with the agitation of their time, and Keats, in whose work the re*Leigh Hunt* forming spirit counts for almost nothing, is furnished by Leigh Hunt (1784–1859). He was intimate with both Byron and Shelley, and shared their radicalism. In 1813 he was sentenced to two years' imprisonment for criticizing the Prince Regent. During his imprisonment he made an exhaustive study of the Italian poets, especially Ariosto; the chief fruit of this study in his own work was a narrative poem entitled "The Story of Rimini," suggested by Dante's account of the lovers Paolo and Francesca, in his *Inferno.* Hunt wrote a vast amount of critical and miscellaneous prose, among which his kindly spirited, mildly humorous, familiar essays are of especial interest. At least one of his shorter poems, "Abou Ben Adhem," has remained popular.

It was through Leigh Hunt that Keats, his friend and for a time his disciple, was led to the study of the Italians, from whom he derived, as Chaucer, Spenser, and Milton had done before him, a richness of tone and a glow of color that he could hardly otherwise have attained. The Romantic Movement has been called a "second Renaissance"; and it is a striking fact that the two great sources of literary inspiration in *Romantic Movement a "Second Renaissance"* the Renaissance, classical and Italian poetry, furnished to the later group of romantic poets invaluable aid. Byron and Shelley did their best work under Italian stimulus, supplemented in Shelley's case by the influence of Plato and the Greek dramatists. Keats formed his manner in the first place upon the Italian poets, and upon their greatest English imitator, Spenser; and in the old Greek myths he found the chief food for his imagination. Later he supplemented his training with a study of Shakespeare and of Milton, and their influence served to counteract his tendency to stylistic sensuousness.

John Keats was born in London in 1795, the son of a livery-stable keeper. He was apprenticed at fifteen to learn surgery, but he broke his indentures, and after studying medicine in the hospitals in London and passing his medical examinations, he gave up the profession for poetry. Leigh Hunt introduced him to a literary circle where his dawning talents found encouragement. In 1817 he published a little volume *Keats: His Life and Poetic Development* of verse, most of it crude and immature enough, but containing the magnificent sonnet, "On First Looking into Chapman's Homer," which reveals one source of his inspiration. From the first his imagination had turned to the old Greek world with instinctive sympathy; and he now chose as the subject for a long narrative poem the story of Endymion, the Latmian shepherd beloved by the moon-goddess. *Endymion* was published in 1818. The exordium of the poem, the Hymn to Pan in the opening episode, and a myriad other lines and short passages, are worthy of the Keats that was to be; but as a whole *Endymion* is chaotic, and cloyed with ornament. Nobody knew this better than Keats himself, as is indicated both by his letters and by the proudly humble preface in which he describes the poem as a "feverish attempt rather than a deed accomplished," and hopes that "while it is dwindling I may be plotting and fitting myself for verses fit to live."

To what purpose he plotted, the wonderful volume published two years later, in 1820, shows. It was entitled *Lamia, Isabella, The Eve of St. Agnes, and Other Poems;* besides the pieces named, it contained the great odes, "On Melancholy," "On a Grecian Urn," "To Psyche," and "To a Nightingale," and the heroic fragment, "Hyperion." Two years had done wonders in deepening and strengthening his gift. In turning from Spenser and Ariosto to the great masculine poets of the seventeenth century, Shakespeare, Webster, Milton, and Dryden, he had found the iron which was lacking in his earlier intellectual food, and had learned the lessons of artistic calmness and severity, without sacrifice of the mellow sweetness native to him; to charm he had added strength.

Before the 1820 volume was published, Keats was attacked by consumption, and had warning that another winter in England would prove fatal. In September of that year he sailed for Italy under the care of his faithful friend, Joseph Severn. Early in the spring of 1821 he died in Rome, and was buried in the Protestant cemetery by the Aurelian wall, where Shelley, also, was soon to be laid. On his tomb are carved, according to his own request, the words: "Here lies one whose name was writ in water." In a hopefuller time and in a mood of noble simplicity, he had said: "I think I shall be among the English poets after my death."

The essential quality of Keats as a poet is his sensitiveness to beauty, and the singleness of aim with which he seeks for "the principle of beauty in all things." He worships beauty for beauty's sake, with none of the secondary moral intentions of Milton, Wordsworth, and Shelley, but with the unreasoning rapture of a lover or a devotee. He tells of the "dizzy pain" which the sight of the Elgin marbles gave him, of the "undescribable feud" which they brought round his heart. He opens his second vol-

His Worship of Beauty

ume with the memorable line, "A thing of beauty is a joy forever"; and in his last volume, at the close of the ode "On a Grecian Urn," he declares that beauty is one with truth. In this last instance he attempts for once to rationalize his instinctive devotion; but it is as an overmastering instinct, not as a philosophic conception, that we find the worship of beauty everywhere operative in his work.

It is this passion for beauty, working through an æsthetic organism of extraordinary delicacy and power, which gives to Keats's poetry its sensuous richness, and which *Qualities* makes it play magically upon all the senses of *of His* the reader. The pure glow of his color reminds *Poetry* us of the Italian painter Giorgione; and the music of his best verse has a wonderful mellowness and depth, as if blown softly through golden trumpets. In the early poems the richness is indeed too great, the ornament excessive; but this is merely the eager lavishness of youth rejoicing in its abundance, and not yet disciplined by good taste. From the first his poetry had extraordinary freshness, energy, gusto. He revived old words, coined new ones, and put current ones to a new service, with a confidence and success unequalled by any other English poets except Chaucer, Shakespeare, and perhaps Spenser.

The sense of form, which is so conspicuous in Keats's later work, was a matter of growth with him. *Endymion* is formless, a labyrinth of flowery paths which lead nowhere. *His Sense* But the great odes, especially the "Nightingale" *of Form* and the "Grecian Urn," and the later narrative poems, "The Eve of St. Agnes" and "Lamia," have a wonderful perfection of structure, a subordination of part to part in the building up of a beautiful whole, which is the sign of the master workman. This is particularly true of "The Eve of St. Agnes," that latest and perhaps most perfect flowering of the old Spenserian tree. The story of Madeline's dream on the haunted eve, of its magical fulfilment through young Porphyro's coming, and of their flight from the castle, is set in a framework of storm and cold, of dreary penance and spectral old age, of barbarous revelry and rude primeval passion, which by a series of subtle and thrilling contrasts marvelously heightens the warm and tender radiance of the central picture; then, when the illusion

of reality is at the height, the whole thing is thrown back into
the dim and doubtful past by the words

> And they are gone; ay, ages long ago
> These lovers fled away into the storm.

Keats's strength, which we see in "The Eve of St. Agnes,"
"Lamia," and the odes, working in the service of perfect grace,
tempted him in "Hyperion" to attack a theme of epic
"Hy-
perion" dimensions, the overthrow of the old Titan sun-deity
Hyperion by the new sun-god Apollo. The subject
proved too large for his undeveloped powers, and he threw it
aside, on the ground that there were "too many Miltonic inversions in it." Probably the deeper reason was that he felt as yet
unequal to the task of imposing form upon his stupendous matter, and his artistic sense would no longer permit him to be content with formlessness. As the poem stands it is a superb fragment, an august portal to a temple which will never be built.

Although the body of Keats's work is unconcerned with prosaic human interests, it is a serious mistake to think of him as
indifferent to human affairs. His wonderful letters,
His
Humanity with their spirited humor, their quick human sympathy and solicitude, their eager ponderings upon
life and clear insight into many of its dark places, show a nature
vitalized at every point, and keenly alert to reality. In many of
his later poems, especially the great odes, the poignant human
undertone suggests that if he had lived he might have turned
more and more to themes of common human experience. Dying
as he did at twenty-five, after only three or four years of opportunity, he yet left behind him a body of poetry which is in its
kind unexcelled.

From the youthful work of Tennyson and Browning down to
the present day, the poetry of the Victorian age
His Place
in the has been deeply affected in form and color by
Romantic Keats's fascinating example. His importance in the
Movement romantic development which we have been tracing
is twofold. In the first place, no one in the line of
his predecessors had been endowed as was he to taste of all
earthly delights, to "burst joy's grape against his palate fine,"

and to convey in verse the wealth of his sensations. By describing life as it impinged upon his temperament, a temperament most rich and delicate, yet most robust, he greatly widened the sensuous realm of poetry. In the second place, he greatly enriched the texture of verse—its diction and melody—by importing into it new elements from Italian and Elizabethan poetry. In reclaiming the lost secrets of Renaissance verse, he did consummately what Thomson, Collins, Gray, and Blake had done falteringly.

II

The great development of poetry in these early years of the century was accompanied by an equally important movement in criticism. There had been great critics from the time of Elizabeth—Ben Jonson, Dryden, Samuel Johnson—but they had made their authority felt in personal intercourse, or in occasional publications, such as Dryden's prefaces, or Johnson's *Lives of the Poets.* *The Critical Magazines* The reviews and magazines were largely controlled by publishers, who employed hack writers to puff their wares and disparage those of others. The first great modern magazine to be established was the *Edinburgh Review* in 1802, of which Francis Jeffrey (1773–1850) soon became editor-in-chief. He and his coeditors insisted on entire freedom from publishers' influence, though political prejudice often colored their criticism. Jeffrey and his friends were Whigs; to offset the power which the rapid success of the *Edinburgh* gave them, the Tories in 1809 established *The Quarterly Review,* to which Southey was for long a chief contributor. In 1817 was founded *Blackwood's Edinburgh Magazine,* which was also Tory in politics, but more vivacious and less responsible than its contemporaries. For many years John Wilson (who wrote under the name Christopher North) was the leading spirit of *Blackwood's,* contributing to it the famous series of conversations which he called *Noctes Ambrosianæ.*

The criticism of Jeffrey may be taken as typical of that of the reviews in general. He was not an absolute monarch, ruling by divine right in accordance with an immutable standard set by the classics; he was rather the chief of an aristocracy of men of taste, and he admitted that the laws of taste varied and advanced. But as the spokesman of this aristocracy he was as positive and dogmatic as Doctor Johnson himself. The motto of the *Edinburgh Review,* "the judge is condemned when the guilty is acquitted," shows the spirit of judicial severity with which he exercised his functions. Each author, each book came before his court to be tried, and, if necessary for the public good, condemned. Wordsworth, Scott, Coleridge, Shelley, and Keats all fell under his ban.

Francis Jeffrey

In those days before the great modern reading public the critical reviews had immense power, and they used it often cruelly. A protest was made by Coleridge in his *Biographia Literaria,* in which he insisted that the function of the critic was to stand between the author and the public, to interpret, not to judge. But Coleridge did not restrict his critical activity to interpretation; he also evolved a number of important critical principles which make him the most energizing of the romantic critics. He illustrates the tendency of romantic criticism to stress the effect of art upon the critic's emotions and to regard art as a source of moral and philosophical wisdom. Although he was especially proud of his distinction between fancy and imagination, he enunciated more significant theories: that the right reading of poetry involves "a willing suspension of disbelief," and that the greatest poetry is that which achieves the most effective synthesis of elements, emotions, and attitudes. It was perhaps inevitable that Coleridge should not evolve an elaborate critical system, that he should be more successful in the less systematic work of interpretation. His sound taste and his powers of analysis made him a sympathetic but stern critic of Wordsworth's theory and practice of poetry. Sharing in the romantics' idolization of Shakespeare, he was at his best in his illuminating intuitions into the dramatist's characters and poetic processes. Whether his comments on Shakespeare are orderly or fragmentary, they are probably the finest fruits of English romantic criticism.

Coleridge as a Critic

Coleridge's critical activity was supplemented by the work of a group of writers who were all somewhat under the spell of his personality—Charles Lamb, William Hazlitt, Thomas De Quincey, and Leigh Hunt. This group of writers was distinctly urban; with the exception of De Quincey they lived in or near London. With- *The Romantic Critics* out the romantic resources of nature, they found compensation in literature, which they approached with sympathetic apprecia- tion and with romantic enthusiasm. They humanized literary criticism by introducing an autobiographic and personal ele- ment, by making it, in other words, the story of their own ad- ventures in the world of books, and an account of what they found there. Thus they abandoned the old dogmatic and judi- cial criticism, characteristic of the classical school, and ap- proached that modern method which we call impressionistic. They were especially drawn to a field which abounded in ro- mantic elements, and the chief service to letters in which they all shared was the recovery and interpretation of the Eliza- bethan and seventeenth-century poets and dramatists—an enter- prise to which Coleridge contributed his lectures on Shake- speare, Lamb his *Specimens of English Dramatic Poets,* and Hazlitt his series of lectures on *The Characters of Shakespeare's Plays* and *The Dramatic Literature of the Age of Elizabeth.*

Charles Lamb was born in London in 1775, and was brought up within the precincts of the ancient law-courts, his father be- ing a servant to an advocate of the Inner Temple. From the cloisters of the Temple he was sent to the *Charles Lamb* cloisters of Christ's Hospital, where he had for a classmate Coleridge, his lifelong friend.[1] At seventeen he be- came a clerk in the India House, and here he spent the working hours of the next thirty-three years, until he was retired on a pension in 1825.[2] His devotion to his sister Mary, upon whom rested an hereditary taint of insanity, has done almost as much as the sweetness and gentle humor of his writings to endear his name. He died in 1834, his sister outliving him and gradually

[1] See Lamb's "Recollections of Christ's Hospital" and "Christ's Hospital Five and Thirty Years Ago," in the *Essays of Elia.*
[2] See his essay, "The Superannuated Man."

sinking into that mental darkness from which his patience and tenderness had upheld her.

Lamb's first successful literary venture was his *Tales from Shakespeare* (1807), written in collaboration with his sister, and intended for children. The fineness of Lamb's critical gift, which was at least suggested in these rewordings of Shakespeare's plots, was brilliantly illustrated a year later by his *Specimens of English Dramatic Poets,* with critical comments. His reading in the Elizabethan drama was extensive, his appreciation of its qualities subtle and penetrating, and his enthusiasm for it unbounded. The book did much to revive the almost extinguished fame of the lesser dramatists grouped about Shakespeare. It is one of the earliest as well as one of the most significant products of the new romantic criticism.

His Literary Criticism

But it was not as a critic of literature but as a commentator upon life, as a gentle egoist, without a trace of vanity or self-assertion, recording his moods, his memories, his witty and tender observations, that Lamb was to fulfill his peculiar literary destiny. The *Essays of Elia,*[1] published at intervals in the *London Magazine,* were at length gathered together and republished in two series, the first in 1823, the second ten years later. They established Lamb in the title which he still holds, that of the most delightful of English essayists. They cover a great variety of topics, but the approach to the subject is always a personal one; and it is this intimate quality, communicating to us by some intangible suggestion the author's odd and lovable personality, which constitutes their chief charm.

"Essays of Elia"

Many of them are confessions of personal prejudice, such as the essay entitled "Imperfect Sympathies," where Lamb's dislike of Scotsmen and his taste for Quakers are made matters of delicious mirth. In "Old China" Lamb gives a winning picture of his home life with his sister, who appears here and elsewhere as "Cousin Bridget." In "Dream Children," a beautiful and deeply affecting essay, he

Their Matter

[1] The pseudonym Elia was borrowed by Lamb from an Italian clerk in the South Sea House named Ellia. The change of spelling has led to the broadening of the initial letter in pronunciation.

talks with two children conjured from nothingness to solace for an hour his lonely hearth. To turn from an essay like this to the famous extravaganza entitled "A Dissertation on Roast Pig," is to run the full gamut of Lamb's pathos and humor.

The style of these essays is curiously compounded of elements borrowed from older writers, especially from Robert Burton and Sir Thomas Browne. But in passing through Lamb's temperament these elements are *Their* fused into a style wholly new and individual, betray-*Style* ing its remote origin only by quaintness of phrase and verbal oddities. The Elia papers continue the traditions of essay writing fixed by Addison and Steele, but their range is wider, and their treatment of human life is marked by the more searching pathos, the more sensitive and flashing humor, which belonged to Lamb as a partaker in the romantic renaissance of feeling.

The romantic tinge of Lamb's mind is the more noteworthy because, like the eighteenth-century writers from whom he borrowed the idea of the essay, he cared little for natural beauty, and was essentially an urban spirit. London, its streets, its shops, its theatres, was the focus of his affection, and he has pictured many phases of its life with the vividness that comes from personal delight. In him we see, in a very curious and striking way, the increment of romantic sensibility infused into and transforming a nature belonging in many respects to the age of the Queen Anne wits.

Quite the opposite of Lamb in temperament, but like him a romantic essayist and critic, is William Hazlitt (1778–1830). Hazlitt's father was a Unitarian clergyman who held *William* several parishes in America after the Revolution. In *Hazlitt* 1798 he was, however, settled at Wem, in Shropshire, where Coleridge, at that time also a preacher of the same persuasion, came to visit him. Hazlitt has left a vivid portrait of Coleridge at that time in his essay "My First Acquaintance with Poets," and a still more vivid account of the stimulating influence of his conversation. It was under this energizing influence that Hazlitt became a critic of art, literature, and politics. He contributed much by his lectures to arouse interest in the Elizabethan writers; he championed the liberal cause in politics during the years of Tory reaction; he even wrote a eulogistic life of

Napoleon. But he is chiefly remembered for the miscellaneous essays, which he wrote with gusto on such subjects as "The Fight," "On Going a Journey," "On Actors and Acting," "On the Look of a Gentleman," "On the Pleasures of Painting." These he contributed to various periodicals and afterward collected in volumes, *Table Talk, The Round Table,* etc. They reveal the breadth and variety of his interests, and the energy with which he pursued them—a full-hearted zest quite different from the quiet humor of Charles Lamb.

Hazlitt carried the same energetic spirit into his enjoyment of literature. He often introduces us to authors and to books by

Hazlitt's Criticism

telling us the story of his own acquaintance with them, recalling with infinite verve the sensations which they gave him. Of *Tom Jones* he tells us: "It came down in numbers once a fortnight, in Cooke's pocket edition, embellished with cuts. I had hitherto read only in school-books . . . but this had a different relish with it—'sweet in the mouth,' though not 'bitter in the belly.' It smacked of the world I lived in, and in which I was to live—and showed me groups, 'gay creatures,' not 'of the element,' but of the earth; not 'living in the clouds,' but travelling the same road that I did. . . . My heart had palpitated at the thoughts of a boarding-school ball, or a gala-day at Midsummer or Christmas; but the world I had found out in Cooke's edition of the *British Novelists* was to me a dance through life, a perpetual gala-day." There is something spontaneous and contagious about such criticism; the reader is led on by the mood of the writer. It is in this impressionistic attitude toward literature that Hazlitt anticipates critics of a later generation, especially Stevenson.

Hazlitt chose the unpopular side in politics; he was unlucky in love and marriage, and he quarrelled furiously with his

Hazlitt's Personality

friends, even Charles Lamb and Leigh Hunt. He needed all the compensations that art and literature could give him. He is, indeed, in many ways quite the opposite of Charles Lamb, being somewhat coarse and boisterous where Lamb is refined and subtle; often harsh and repellent where Lamb is gentle and winning. His style is more obvious than Lamb's, with more direct emphasis and the embellishment of many quotations. Like Lamb's, however, it is eminently personal and intimate, and has often a true note of pathos in its revelation of the author's disappointed life. "So have I loitered my life away," he writes, "reading books, looking at pictures, going to plays, hearing, thinking, or writing on what pleased me best. I have wanted only one thing to make me happy; but wanting that have wanted everything."

In Thomas De Quincey the romantic element is even more pronounced, and displays itself not only in his writings but in the circumstances of his life. He was born in Man- *Thomas* chester in 1785, the son of a prosperous merchant in *De* the foreign trade. At sixteen he ran away from the *Quincey* Manchester grammar-school, and spent a summer wandering in North Wales, often sleeping on the open hills or in the tents of gypsies. When the cold weather came on, he made his way to London, where he led a wretched vagrant existence, until he was reclaimed by his family and sent to Oxford. He was one of the earliest converts to the "Lake poetry," and a year after leaving the university he established himself at Grasmere, in the neighborhood of Wordsworth and Southey. Here he lived for more than twenty years, reading prodigiously and consuming vast quantities of opium. By reason of some peculiarity of his constitution the drug was less fatal in its workings than is commonly the case; but the splendid and tumultuous dreams which it brought were paid for by periods of awful gloom and lassitude. In his thirty-first year De Quincey married. Forced to earn money by his pen, he published the famous *Confessions of an English Opium-Eater* in the *London Magazine* in 1821, and from this time forth he poured out magazine articles on almost every conceivable topic. In 1830 he removed, with his wife and children, to Edinburgh, where he resided until his death in 1859.

His best-known work is also his most characteristic, the *Opium-Eater* and its sequel, *Suspiria de Profundis.* *"Confes-* Only a small portion of the *Opium-Eater* deals *sions of an* with the subject of opium-taking. It is an extended *Opium-* autobiography covering the life of the author from *Eater"* early childhood to about the year 1819, when his bondage to opium became absolute, and he descended into the valley of the shadow, where he was to gather the dolorous matter of his *Suspiria*. The most powerful portion of the narrative, aside from the description of the sensations induced by opium, is that which tells of his life of vagrancy and deprivation in London, and of his nightly wanderings with "poor Ann" through the crowded desolation of Oxford Street. The *Suspiria de Profundis* (Sighs from the Depths) is made up mainly of dream-phantasies transcribed from the actual wanderings of his mind under the spell of opium, or suggested by them.

In such phantasmagoric imaginings as "Levana and Our Ladies of Sorrow," in the *Suspiria*, and the "Dream-Fugue" appended to the *English Mail-Coach*, De Quincey *His Char-* ventured upon a new domain of imaginative *acteristic* prose; a region audaciously won from verse, to *Style* which, by virtue of its impassioned and imaginative character, it properly belongs. His studies of Elizabethan prose-writers may have given him the hint; but he carried out as a deliberate experiment what with them had been an unconscious confusion of the categories of prose and verse. In doing so he revealed new possibilities in the English tongue. The following passage from the *Opium-Eater* will illustrate the poetical quality of his style. It describes a series of dreams suggested by the sight of a mysterious Malay, who appeared one day at De Quincey's door: "I brought together all creatures, birds, beasts, reptiles . . . that are found in all tropical regions. . . . I was stared at, hooted at, grinned at, chattered at, by monkeys, by paroquets, by cockatoos. I ran into pagodas, and was fixed for centuries at the summit, or in secret rooms; I was the idol; I was the priest; I was worshipped; I was sacrificed. I fled from the wrath of Brahma through all the forests of Asia; Vishnu hated me; Seeva lay in wait for me. I came suddenly upon Isis and Osiris: I had done a deed, they said, which the ibis and the crocodile trembled at. I was buried for a thousand years in stone coffins, with mummies and sphinxes, in narrow chambers at the heart of eternal pyramids. I was kissed, with cancerous kisses, by crocodiles, and was laid, confounded with all unutterable slimy things, amongst reeds and Nilotic mud." Upon this and similar passages of richly wrought, chanting prose, De Quincey's fame as a writer rests. The qualities of style exhibited in them have had a great influence upon the prose-writing of the century, an influence which can be traced in such widely different writers as Bulwer and Ruskin.

Two serious charges are to be brought against De Quincey as a writer—diffuseness and triviality. He cannot resist the slightest temptation to digress, and even in the most solemn pages of his *Confessions*, and in the midst of the touching story of Joan of Arc's childhood, he is capable of falling into a queer kind of "rigmarole" made up of pedantry and mirthless jesting. In reading him we are often visited by an uncomfortable sense of dealing with a nature not quite responsible and not quite human. He illustrates both the defects and the virtues of the romantic temper: its virtues in the enkindled splendor of his fancy and the impassioned sweep of his style; its defects in his extravagance, his unevenness, his failure to exercise adequate self-criticism.

His Defects as a Writer

A decided reaction from the romantic to the classic ideal is seen in Walter Savage Landor. In him this reaction is the more noteworthy because he began as a romantic poet, and wrote romantic dramas until a year or two before Byron's death; thereafter he cultivated the classical, dignified, restrained prose for which his name is famous.

Landor's life was a very long one. Born in 1775, he published an important poem, *Gebir,* in 1798, a short while before the *Lyrical Ballads* of Wordsworth and Coleridge heralded the triumph of the Romantic Movement. *Gebir* is a heroic narrative, conceived in a mood of romantic idealism such as only Shelley could rival; upon Shelley, indeed, the poem had a strong influence. If Landor had had, at this earlier period, greater artistic poise and sureness, *Gebir* and not the *Lyrical Ballads* might now be held to signalize the triumph of the new romantic poetry. But the poem is incoherent and immature, and in spite of many beauties is a failure. It lies outside Landor's characteristic work, as do likewise the efforts which he made during the next twenty-five years in the romantic drama. It was not until his forty-sixth year that he found his genuine manner, and began to produce work

Landor's Life

of permanent beauty. In 1815 he went to Italy and in 1821 settled near Florence, on the slope of Fiesole, in a beautiful villa, the garden of which, full of clouds of olive-trees and spires of cypress, commanded a magnificent view of the valley of the Arno and the far-stretching hills of Tuscany. Here he wrote most of those lofty and serene works by which he will be remembered, especially the *Imaginary Conversations* (1824–1829) and *Pericles and Aspasia* (1836).

The vitality of Landor's genius in old age is almost without parallel. At seventy he published a series of poems on subjects from old Greek life, which have all the freshness and spontaneous joy of youth. At least one of these, the "Hamadryad," should be read in connection with the loveliest of Landor's youthful lyrics, "Rose Aylmer," in order that the persistence of his freshness of feeling through a literary career of fifty years may be appreciated. He died in 1864, long after his early contemporaries had passed away, and a new generation of writers had arisen, with new aims and ideals. His literary life covered the immense span from the earliest work of Wordsworth to the *Atalanta in Calydon* of Swinburne. His personal life, in curious contrast with the serenity and classic poise of his best work, was one of constant storm, furious quarrels, and eccentric outbursts of temper. There is something pathetic in the unconscious irony of the opening line of the quatrain in which he took leave of earth:

> I strove with none, for none was worth my strife:
> Nature I loved, and next to Nature, Art;
> I warmed both hands before the fire of life;
> It sinks, and I am ready to depart.

Landor's most characteristic poetry has a more purely classical quality than any other English poetry save Milton's. Not only were many of his themes and characters classical, but his tone was restrained and calm, and his style highly polished and marmoreal. His most charming lyrics, half amorous, half courtly, are those inspired by various women in the family of Rose Aylmer and by the girl of whom he wrote under the name Ianthe. That Landor was the greatest English master of the epigrammatic quatrain is made clear by the series he wrote as he paced calmly past the many milestones on his way to a great, but amazingly productive, old age.

In the *Imaginary Conversations,* Landor brings together significant personalities, from all lands and all periods of history, sometimes in couples, sometimes in larger groups, and represents them in talk with one another. The Saxon earl Leofric talks with his bride Godiva as they ride into Coventry; Æsop, the Phrygian fable-writer, talks with Rhodope, a young Greek slave-girl, in the house of their Egyptian master; Henry the Eighth talks with Anne Boleyn in her prison; Dante talks with Beatrice in a Florentine garden in spring; the young Marcellus, wounded to death, confronts for a moment the conquering Hannibal. For the most part, the characters which Landor evokes are lofty and magnanimous ones. The dialogue shows no attempt at dramatic realism, but is always stately, pure, and exquisitely finished. Nothing is allowed to interfere with the classical precision and chaste rhythms of the style. In a sense, all the characters of the *Conversations* talk alike, using a diction and idiom removed from the realities of daily speech, and suggesting their individuality only by the more subtle differences of their thought and action. The aloofness and austerity in Landor's manner often repel the reader on first acquaintance, but, when once accepted, they add to his pleasure instead of lessening it. The purpose of the *Conversations* is usually as nobly and calmly serious as the style. It is these three characteristics, loftiness of character, dignity of style, and nobility of purpose, which make the *Imaginary Conversations* classic, in the broader sense of the word. After Milton's poetry, they are perhaps the best substitute afforded by English literature for a training in the Greek and Latin writers.

The "Imaginary Conversations"

In *Pericles and Aspasia* Landor substituted for the conversational manner the epistolary. In a series of familiar letters passing between the major and the minor characters of the book, we are told how Aspasia, a young woman of Asia Minor, comes to Athens, then at the height of its splendor under the wise rule of Pericles; how she meets the great leader, and comes to know, on terms of intimate friendship, Alcibiades, Socrates, and many

"Pericles and Aspasia"

other famous men of the age. We are given thus, in a delightfully natural and casual way, a picture of the intellectual life of the antique world in its heyday, a picture which makes the Athens of Pericles seem wonderfully near at hand and comprehensible. Aspasia, as she reveals herself in her letters, is a triumph of feminine portraiture. Her playfulness, her wit, her girlish adventurousness, her unpedantic delight in intellectual things, the womanly way in which her nature rises and sobers itself to meet the grave nature of Pericles, all combine harmoniously to make a woman such as Shakespeare might have created.

From the death of Byron in 1824 until the decisive appearance of Tennyson in 1842, there was a period of comparative exhaustion in English literature. Keats and Shelley were dead; Coleridge was lost in metaphysics, and Wordsworth had almost ceased to produce poetry of value; Scott died in 1832, and the best work of Lamb was done before that date. The first great wave of romanticism, which had begun to rise a century before, with Thomson and Gray, and which had reached its height in the first two decades of the nineteenth century, had passed by. During this period of lull, the new forces which were to go to the making of literature during the reign of Victoria were gathering head. We must now consider what distinctive elements went to the making of that literature, gigantic in bulk and almost infinite in variety, which places the era of Victoria beside that of Elizabeth.

Transition to the Victorian Era

CHAPTER XIV

The Nineteenth Century

THE VICTORIAN ERA

THE LITERATURE of the long reign of Victoria (1837–1901) presented the features natural in an era of great social change and intellectual advancement. Never before, not even in the troubled seventeenth century, had there been such rapid and sweeping changes in the social fabric of England; and never before had literature been so closely in league, or so openly at war, with the forces of social life. Among the many circumstances mak- *General* ing for change, the chief one was the growth *Charac-* of democracy. The Reform Bill of 1832 placed *teristics* the political power of England in the hands of the middle class, and after that date there was a gradual extension of the suffrage to the working classes. With the growth of democracy elementary education became generally accessible, and the number of readers increased rapidly. A vast body of people who heretofore had little or no access to literature were now reached by it, and in turn influenced its character. Almost all the great Victorian writers attempted to move, instruct, or inspire the huge, unleavened mass of society. The astonishing development of the practical arts, applied science, and machine-production, while it increased the comforts of living, led to deep-seated materialism against which nearly every great writer lifted his voice in protest and warning. The discoveries of science gave rise to a multitude of conceptions of the most revolutionary kind, unsettling many of the old bases of religious belief, and affecting literature in numberless ways. Epoch-making advances in geological and biological

295

studies disturbed profoundly traditional views of man's creation and of the length of his history on this planet. The application of the historical method to the study of the Bible resulted in the development of "the higher criticism," which not only had disquieting effects upon orthodox believers but also induced scepticism, if not pessimism, in many sensitive souls. Along with these changes there also began a restless search after some new form of society, or some modification of the old forms, by which the claims of all men to life and opportunity should be met. The humanitarian spirit that was an integral element in the Romantic movement was stirred by the hideous social and economic consequences of the Industrial Revolution, and reformers felt it their duty to publicize these horrors and to attempt to alleviate them by legislation. They set their faces sternly against the conservative believers in the doctrine of *laissez-faire,* with its assumption that if the economic instinct were given free play, the result would be, not the good of a single social class but the good of the whole social order. They also opposed the early Utilitarians who proposed as the goal of morality the greatest good of the greatest number but who also believed that this goal would be attained through the operation of the policy of *laissez-faire.* Social unrest was the great distinguishing feature of the Victorian era and the demand for social justice colored, in one way or another, the whole thought of the time.

It follows from all this that the most striking characteristic of Victorian literature was its strenuousness, its conscious purpose. Both poets and prose-writers worked under *Its Social Purpose* the shadow and burden of a conscious social responsibility. Almost all of them were makers of doctrine, preachers of some crusade, or physicians offering some cure for man's perplexities and despairs. Instead of the light-hearted interest in life which the Elizabethans showed, instead of the revolutionary idealism of the generation of Wordsworth, Coleridge, Shelley, and Byron, the prevailing mood was an earnest and often troubled facing of the momentous issues of life.

Nevertheless, the romantic impulse persisted. There were some minor reversions to classicism, but, taken largely, literature continued to be romantic, in the novelty and variety of its form, in its search after undiscovered springs of beauty and truth, in its emotional and imaginative intensity. This romantic impulse found expression particularly in the effort to bring to light the unusual and surprising elements in real and commonplace things, to startle men out of their acceptance of such things as typical and conventional. But Victorian romanticism was increasingly threatened by the rising tide of realism. The novel was coming more and more closely to grips with the problems of representing contemporary society without a romantic vesture, describing the manner of its high and low life, and interpreting its social and moral dilemmas. By the end of the century, realism had captured the novel and the drama, and had made serious inroads into the domain of poetry.

Its Romanticism and Realism

At the opening of the period stands a writer who represents perfectly the spirit in which the moderate reform of 1832 had been won, and the satisfaction with which its authors regarded their work. Thomas Babington Macaulay was born in 1800, of Scottish and Quaker ancestry. At Cambridge, in the midst of the political excitement which led up to the Reform Bill, he took a middle position between Tory and Radical, intrenching himself in the Whig principles of liberal conservatism, of which he was all his life a powerful and watchful champion. At college he distinguished himself as a writer and debater, and in 1825 he contributed his famous essay on Milton to *The Edinburgh Review,* and followed it with other essays which fastened attention upon him as a new force in literature. At thirty he entered Parliament, in time to take a conspicuous part in the passage of the Reform Bill. Four years later he went to India as legal adviser to the Supreme Council, returning in 1838 to play once more a leading rôle in Parliament, until his defeat in 1847. During these nine years several of his most famous essays appeared, notably those on the Indian proconsuls, Clive and Warren Hastings. In 1842 he published his *Lays of Ancient Rome,* sonorous and vigorous celebrations, in ballad verse, of the antique civic virtues, as shown in Horatius, Virginius, and other Roman worthies. In 1848, after long delay, he began to realize the dream of his life, in the publication of

Macaulay

the first two volumes of his *History of England*. He accomplished, in the five completed volumes of his history, only a fragment of the task which he had set himself. He died in 1859.

Gladstone bears witness that an announcement of Macaulay's intention to speak in Parliament was "like a trumpet-call to fill the benches." His power as an orator furnishes the key to what is most characteristic in his essays. In a speech the meaning must be so clearly stated, so aptly illustrated, so skillfully repeated and re-emphasized, that misunderstanding shall be impossible; and the flagging attention of the audience must be continually stimulated by strong contrasts, by striking antitheses, and by an illusion of rapidity, even where the movement is, by the necessity of the subject, slow. Suggestiveness, delicate shades of meaning of a sort to make the hearer hesitate and ponder, defeat the ends of parliamentary discourse; high imaginativeness, strong appeal to the more mystical and spiritual sides of man's nature, are here out of place. Everything must be explicit, sensible, emphatic. In all these respects Macaulay's essays are true to the ideal of parliamentary speaking. Probably no writer has ever been more skillful than Macaulay in making his whole meaning clear; none more successful in keeping the reader's mind awake, and his sense of movement agreeably satisfied. But, on the other hand, few writers of the century have been so limited to considerations of actual fact. He is always downright and positive, never in doubt, and never at a loss. Mystics like Plato, masters of pure thought like Bacon, sombre religious natures like Doctor Johnson, fare badly at his hands. But his defects served him perhaps as much as his virtues in his work of popularizing knowledge. From the stores of his capacious memory, one of the most marvelous on record, he presented in lucid and entertaining form a great mass of fact and opinion, the educative power of which was temporarily very great.

His Essays: Their Style and Matter

In his *History* he carried his popularizing zeal into a more difficult field, and scored an even more notable success. His aim was to write a history of England from the accession of James II to the end of George IV's reign, in a manner so concrete, picturesque, and dramatic that his narrative of actual events should have the fascination of romance; and, as he himself put the case, should have the power "to supersede the last fashionable novel upon the dressing-table of young ladies." The portion of the story *"History of England"* which he lived to complete is, in fact, presented with a wealth and minuteness of detail concerning particular persons, places, and events, such as a writer of fiction uses to embody the creations of his fancy. We do not find in Macaulay a profound view of underlying causes, that large intellectual interpretation of events which constitutes the "philosophy of history"; but in recompense he gives us a fascinating story, a broad and luminous canvas covered with firmly delineated pictures, which change before our eyes into new groupings, and give place to other spectacles, as in a magic diorama.

Macaulay's essays were chiefly written between 1825 and 1840, in the period of lull which followed the romantic outburst of the early part of the century. This was also the period of great industrial and commercial expansion, when material prosperity was bringing the middle class into power. The Reform Bill of 1832 gave this class a large share in the represent- *Macaulay's View of Life* ative government of England, and was regarded by many as a final step in accommodating the political institutions of the country to the legitimate demands of the people. Macaulay at heart was well satisfied with the results of his own time. In his complacent view of life, as well as in his pointed, emphatic style, he reflects the character of this period, when men were inclined to exchange the idealistic longings and aspirations of the previous era for a satisfied acceptance of the practical benefits which commerce, liberal government, and the mechanical sciences were bringing to English life. In his essay on Bacon he contrasts the aims of philosophy in the days of Plato and Seneca with that practical application of knowledge which it was part of Bacon's system to further. "The aim of Platonic philosophy," he says, "was to exalt man into a god. The aim of the Baconian philosophy was to provide man with what he requires while he continues to be man. . . . An acre in Middlesex is better than a principality in Utopia. The smallest actual good is better than the most magnificent promises of impossibilities. The wise man of the Stoics would no doubt be a grander object than a steam-engine. But there are steam-engines. And the wise man of the Stoics is yet to be born."

In all this Macaulay offers a striking contrast to the later social criticism of Carlyle, Ruskin, and Arnold, who united in bidding men ponder what their boasted progress was progress toward, and whether, in their zeal for worship of the steam-engine and the ballot-box, they were not perchance bowing down to heathen idols, forgetting the God of the spirit. Before considering their protest against materialism, however, we must take account of a somewhat earlier one in the field of religion, which had an important influence on literature—the Oxford Movement, led by John Henry Newman. The original inspiration of the movement, however, was given by John Keble (1792–1866), whose volume of devotional verse, *The Christian Year* (1827), like George Herbert's *Temple,* directed men's minds toward the source of poetry in the beliefs and practices of the church.

Newman was born in London in 1801. He went to Oxford, was elected a fellow of Oriel College, took orders in the Angli-

Newman and the Oxford Movement can Church, and became vicar of Saint Mary's Church in the university city. He was closely associated with a group of friends whose object came to be the overcoming of the scepticism and the doubt which had undermined the faith and lowered the morale of some of the best contemporary minds, the reclamation of the Church of England from the torpor and deadness into which it had fallen, and the restoration of the poetry, the mystic symbolism, the spiritual power, and the beauty of architecture, ritual, and service which had characterized the Catholic Church in the Middle Ages. In this respect the Oxford Movement was an outgrowth of the Romantic Movement. Newman himself states that it owed much to Scott, "who turned men's minds in the direction of the Middle Ages," as well as to Coleridge, Southey, and Wordsworth. Newman and his friends wished also to defend the Church, in view of its divine character, against the interference of the state, which was disposed to reform it along with Parliament and other institutions, curtailing its powers and revenues.

In 1833 Newman took a trip to Italy, in the course of which the vague feeling of his mission to redeem the English Church settled into a firm resolve. At Palermo, as he lay dangerously ill of a fever, he kept exclaiming: "I shall not die; I have a work to do." Sailing from Palermo to Marseilles in an orange-boat, he was becalmed in the straits of Bonifacio, and here he wrote the famous hymn, "Lead, Kindly Light." Upon his return he began a series of *Tracts for the Times,* the purpose of which was to define the position and beliefs of the English Church. From this title came the name Tractarian, by which his party was called. He expressed the inner meaning of the movement in sermons preached on Sunday afternoons at Saint Mary's, which drew the young men of Oxford to become his followers in this spiritual renaissance. The conception of the Church which Newman held gradually drew him toward Roman Catholicism; the famous "Tract 90," in which he tried to show that membership in the Church of England was not inconsistent with many beliefs and practices peculiar to the Church of Rome, was condemned by the University; Newman and his more ardent followers withdrew from Oxford to a semi-monastic establishment at Littlemore, whence in 1845 he was received into the Church of Rome. This step, separating Newman as it did from many of his friends and co-workers, is beautifully commemorated in his sermon, "The Parting of Friends."

Newman at Oxford

Newman's conversion was a great shock to the English Church. Some of his supporters followed him into the Catholic Church, the most famous being Henry Edward Manning (1808–1892). Others, such as James Anthony Froude, reacted violently into the liberalism and scepticism against which the Oxford Movement had been directed. Newman was himself bitterly accused of dishonesty and treachery. To such charges, especially those put forward by Charles Kingsley, he replied in his *Apolo-*

Newman as Catholic

gia pro Vita Sua (1864), in which he gave an account of his religious opinions, and of the Oxford Movement, so winning and so exquisite in its frankness and sincerity that he became from that time forth an object of veneration to his countrymen, almost a national saint. The *Apologia* represents Newman at his best, since it reflects his psychological subtlety, his tactical adroitness in meeting the attacks of his opponents, and his redoubtable combination of firmness and flexibility. His lucid and supple style and his warm oratorical tone have compelled the admiration of many readers who do not share his theological convictions. The work remains the most eloquent and appealing defense of religious faith produced in England in the nineteenth century. Before this he had been engaged in founding a university at Dublin, from which undertaking sprang his lectures on *The Idea of a University.* Aside from this the most notable of his writings as a Catholic are *A Grammar of Assent* (1870), in which he combats the scientific view of belief as depending on logical conclusions drawn from facts perceived by the senses; and *The Dream of Gerontius,* a poem of death and the rising of the soul to God. In 1879 he was made cardinal by Pope Leo XIII; eleven years later he died at the Oratory of Saint Philip Neri, Edgbaston, which he had established.

Newman was a writer in the service of his cause, not primarily an artist; yet he achieved very high distinction in English

*New-
man's
Style*

literature. His works include many volumes of sermons, theological treatises, church history, and two novels, as well as the essays, poems, and the spiritual biography already mentioned. Perhaps because of his singleness of purpose Newman's prose is characterized by wonderful transparency. He is as clear in handling subjects of extreme subtlety as Macaulay in those which he had reduced to extreme simplicity. Moreover, Macaulay's idea reaches us through a resisting medium; Newman's idea is one with the medium; his words convey his meaning as ether conveys light. Add to this the charm of Newman's personal, colloquial tone and the haunting melody of his cadences, and we see one source of his mysterious power, by virtue of which the Oxford Movement is remembered as one of the touchingly beautiful stories of human companionship and endeavor, comparable to that of Jesus and his disciples, or of Saint Francis and his order.

Macaulay represents belief in the world with its political and industrial progress; Newman, a return to faith in a church separated from the world, working under divine inspiration. There were many in these years who could not be satisfied with the first, nor accept the second, who yearned for some spiritual interpretation of the world which would save them from acquiescence in its materialism, and would give hope of social reform deeper than the improvement of governmental machinery. To such the writings of Thomas Carlyle came as a gospel.

Carlyle was born in 1795 at Ecclefechan, a village of the Scottish lowlands. After graduating from the University of Edinburgh, he rejected the ministry, for which he had been intended, and determined to be "a writer of books." In these early days of privation and loneliness, with dyspepsia "gnawing like a rat at the *Carlyle: Life and Writings* pit of his stomach," he fought the battle which he afterward described in *Sartor Resartus*. The "Everlasting No," the voice of unfaith denying God and the worth of life, he put from him; the "Everlasting Yea," the assurance that life could be made divine through labor and courage, he wrote on his banner, as he went forth to do battle against the selfish materialism and spiritual torpor of the age. Carlyle's *Life of Schiller* (1823) and his translations from the German got him a hearing with the publishers, but his earnings remained extremely small. After his marriage with Jane Welsh they went to live at Craigenputtock, a farmhouse amid miles of high, dreary moor, in a "solitude almost druidical." Here Carlyle passed six years (1828–1834). During this time he produced *Sartor Resartus,* the book in which he first developed his characteristic style and thought, and wrote several masterly essays, notably those on Burns and Boswell's *Johnson.* In 1834 he came to London, taking the house in Cheyne Row, Chelsea, where he spent the long remainder of his life. In 1837 he published *The French Revolution,* which turned the tide of public favor toward him. For more than thirty years after this he served as teacher and preacher to the people of England and America, thundering above them wrath, warning, and exhortation. The most notable works of this long period were *Chartism* (1839), an anti-democratic diatribe against the demands of the people for a "charter," or written constitution, involving, among other concessions, that of universal suffrage; *On Heroes; Hero-Worship, and the Heroic in History* (1841), a series of essays, exhorting the world to love, honor, and submit in childlike obedience to its heroic men, whether they appear as warrior, poet, or priest; *Past and Present* (1843), an account of how one strong man as abbot brought order out of confusion in the monastery of Saint Edmunds, with its lesson for modern England eloquently enforced; *Oliver Cromwell's Letters and Speeches, with Elucidations* (1845), a study of one of Carlyle's typical heroes as King; *Latter-Day Pamphlets* (1850); the *Life of John Sterling* (1851), a masterpiece of sympathetic biography; and the *History of Frederick the Great* (1858–1865), a vast picture of the life and times of the founder of the Prussian state. From 1865 until his death in 1881 the respect in which Carlyle's name was held steadily increased, though other teachers were rising to take his place, and some of the dogmas for which he stood were being undermined by time and criticism. In the twentieth century, some critics have found in Carlyle's doctrine of submission to the great man the seeds of modern theories of dictatorship.

The actual doctrines which Carlyle preached with such Hebraic intensity—his "Gospel of Work," his political dogma of "Government by the Best" (instead of "government by the worst," as he held democracy to be),

Underlying Spirit of His Work

and all the other shibboleths of his unending warfare with his age—are of less moment than the spirit which broadly underlies his writing. This spirit may be defined as an intense moral indignation against whatever is weak, or false, or mechanical; an intense moral enthusiasm for whatever is sincere and heroically forceful. From this point of view his most typical books are *Sartor Resartus* and *Heroes and Hero-Worship*. The first is an attack upon all those social shams and mechanisms which defeat the sincerity of life; the second is a pæan of praise for those chosen heroic spirits who join earnestness with power. *Sartor Resartus,* which is both destructive and constructive, is pre-eminent in doctrinal interest among all his books. It is also extremely ingenious in plan, and is written with a wonderful mingling of wild sardonic humor, keen pathos, and an almost biblical eloquence and imaginative elevation.

"Sartor Resartus" means "the tailor re-tailored," and its theme is clothes. It purports to be the fragment of a great "clothes-philosophy," the life-work of an eccentric German scholar and recluse, Herr Diogenes Teufels- *"Sartor* dröckh. This philosophy has been left in wild confu- *Resar-* sion, scribbled on scattered leaves, and stuffed helter- *tus": Its* skelter into twelve bags signed with the twelve signs *Plan* of the Zodiac. Carlyle represents himself merely as editor and expositor of this weltering mass of words, endeavoring desperately to extract order out of chaos, and to lighten a little, with much head-shaking and consternation, the dark and mystic abysses of the German professor's thought. This whimsical fancy of Carlyle's enables him to be both author and commentator; to state astounding paradoxes and then shrug his shoulders in sign of his own irresponsibility; to take the side of his opponents against what he, as a well-regulated editor, pretends to find extravagant and crazy doctrine, but what is really his own passionate heart's belief, however perversely expressed.

The book has a twofold meaning. In the first place, it is a veiled sardonic attack upon the shams and pretenses of society, upon hollow rank, hollow officialism, hollow cus- *Its* tom, out of which life and usefulness have de- *Meaning* parted. These are, Carlyle hints, the clothes which hide the real form of society, garments once useful, but grown by lapse of time to be mere fantastic frippery and stiff disfigurement, stifling the breath and health of the social body. Under the shield of this novel idea, he attacks the mechanical view of life, mechanical education, mechanical government, mechanical religion; and he preaches, now with drollery and paradox, now with fiery earnestness and prophetic possession, a return to sincerity in all things. In the second place, Carlyle applies the clothes-philosophy mystically to the universe at large; showing that as clothes hide the real man, and as custom and convention hide real society, so time and space hide the real spiritual essence of the universe. He gives us, as the climax of the book, a transcendental vision of all created nature as the garment of God; the same idea which Goethe put forth in his description of the earth-spirit in *Faust:*

> I sit at the roaring loom of Time
> And weave the living garment of God.

The fiction that he was translating from the German gave Carlyle an excuse for developing in *Sartor Resartus* a style of expression entirely without example, full of un-English idiom, of violent inversions, startling pauses, and sharp angularities—a style which he employed to rouse the attention of his reader as by a series of electric shocks. This extraordinary literary instrument he continued to use for the remainder of his life. It has been said that henceforth he wrote English no more, but "Carlylese," a style wonderfully well suited to his purpose of rousing a sluggish public out of mental and moral apathy into an alertness to great issues.

Its Style: "Carlyl-ese"

Sartor Resartus proved Carlyle to be, with all discount for the perversities of his style, a great literary artist. This title was broadened and confirmed by his historical masterpiece, *The French Revolution.* In this vast panoramic work, Carlyle furnished a specific example of a justifiably destructive historical process from which there emerged no hero spiritually great enough to impose order on the resultant chaos. Here we see to best advantage what Emerson calls the "stereoscopic imagination" of Carlyle, which detaches the figures from the background, and gives to the individual portraits unmatched vividness. The stupid, patient King, the "lion Mirabeau," the "sea-green incorruptible Robespierre," Marat the "large-headed dwarfish individual of smoke-bleared aspect"—not only these chief figures, but the minor ones, a multitude of them, stand out in the reader's memory unforgettably. The larger pictures are equally admirable: the storming of the Bastille, the Feast of Pikes, the long-drawn agony of the Night of Spurs. Above all, the unity and sweep of the story, reminding us of a play by Shakespeare or by Æschylus, acted by millions of figures on a

"The French Revolu-tion"

gigantic stage, make this the capital example in English of the dramatic portraiture of an historical era, and establish beyond question Carlyle's right to be considered a great constructive artist.

Carlyle poured into the swirling life of his time a stream of intense moral ardor and indignation which gradually raised the level of ethical feeling. He united in remarkable degree the artistic and the moral impulse; and he is in this respect typical of the Victorian era, during which, more than ever before, art was infused with moral purpose. But his nature was too extravagant, his tone too bitterly protesting, and his method too perverse, to allow him to become the supremely representative figure of the age. This position was reserved for Alfred Tennyson.

Carlyle's Service to His Age

Tennyson was born in 1809, at Somersby Rectory, Lincolnshire. His father was a vicar of the Church of England, holding several livings by gift from landed proprietors; so that Tennyson was from birth in close connection with the main conservative interests of England, ecclesiastical and economic. In 1830, while an undergraduate at Cambridge, he published his first independent volume, a group of little verse-studies in word-melody and word-picture. Two years later appeared a second volume, showing, in such poems as "The Lady of Shalott" and "The Lotus-Eaters," a control of both mediæval and classical story, and in certain others, like "The Palace of Art," giving indication of his ambition to be not a singer merely, but also a teacher. In "The Miller's Daughter" and "The May Queen," he began his long series of idylls of English life, short narratives richly pictured and melodiously tuned, with which he was destined to win the public, all the more easily perhaps because of their touches of sentimentality and unreality.

Tennyson's Early Life and Poetry

In 1836 Tennyson went to live near London, where he came into contact with Carlyle, and was stirred by his spirit of social protest. He also found in the latter's spiritual view of the universe a support for his religious faith, which was to be sorely tried by doubt. For ten years he published nothing, but brooded and worked away in his London lodgings until, in 1842, he came forth with two

"Locksley Hall"

volumes which took the critics and the world by storm. In these two volumes the range and variety of work was remarkable. Almost every province of poetry was touched upon, from the lyric simplicity of "Break, break, break" to the largely moulded epic narrative "Morte d'Arthur." In one of these poems, "Locksley Hall," he uttered the protest which young men like himself, of good though not noble birth, were feeling in the presence of class distinctions which subordinated love to rank, and of an industrial civilization which made gold the supreme test of success.

Five years later, in 1847, appeared *The Princess*. It was Tennyson's contribution to the question, then beginning to be *"The Princess"* widely discussed, of the higher education of women. The subtitle is "A Medley," and no description could be more just. In *The Princess* we see Tennyson's eagerness to touch the vital public questions of his time, in odd conflict with his pure poetic interest in picture and melody. The poem was an ill-conceived attempt to present a contemporary problem in fanciful guise. Its imperfect synthesis of matter and style impairs the effectiveness of the poem as a whole, although it does not dull the brilliance of such incidental lyrics as "The Splendor Falls on Castle Walls" and "Tears, Idle Tears."

In his next work, however, *In Memoriam* (1850), the poetry interpenetrates the theme, one which was just then engaging *"In Memoriam"* the minds of men more passionately than ever before in the world's history—the question of the immortality of the soul. The poem was written in memory of Arthur Hallam, a beloved friend and college-mate of Tennyson's, who had died in 1833. It consists of a hundred and thirty-one lyrics, "short swallow-flights of song," composed at intervals during seventeen years. In the beginning, the early phases of grief are touched upon, moods of stunned and bewildered sorrow.

> He is not here; but far away
>   The noise of life begins again,
>   And ghastly through the drizzling rain
> On the bald street breaks the blank day.

Gradually the personal pain merges itself into anxious speculation concerning the mystery of death and the hope of immortality.

> I stretch lame hands of faith, and grope,
>   And gather dust and chaff, and call
>   To what I feel is Lord of all,
> And faintly trust the larger hope.

Through states of doubt, despair, and anguished question, the poem slowly mounts into a region of firm though saddened faith, and ends in a full hymnal music breathing hope and fortitude of heart:

> O living will that shalt endure,
>   When all that seems shall suffer shock,
>   Rise from the spiritual rock,
> Flow through our deeds and make them pure.

When *In Memoriam* was written, Darwin's tremendous hypothesis of the evolution of human life from lower forms had not yet been given to the world,[1] but the idea was already in the air and in numberless ways science had begun to sap the old foundations of religious faith. Tennyson courageously faced the facts of science, as revealed in geology and biology; he envisaged clearly a Nature "red in tooth and claw"; but he succeeded in wringing religious consolation from the very things which were dreaded as a fatal menace to religion. In helping to break down the opposition between science and spiritual faith, *In Memoriam* did a great service to the age.

In 1850 Wordsworth, who had been poet-laureate after Southey, died; and Tennyson took the laurel. A government pension enabled him to marry and to settle in the *Tennyson as Laureate* Isle of Wight. From this time until his death, forty-two years later, in 1892, he stood as the spokesman of his people in times of national sorrow or rejoicing. In such poems as "The Charge of the Light Brigade," "The Revenge," and the "Ode on the Death of the

---

[1] The *Origin of Species* appeared in 1859, the *Descent of Man* in 1871.

Duke of Wellington," he ministered to national pride, stoked the fires of imperialism, and brought poetry nearer to the national life than it had been since Shakespeare. In the *Idylls of the King* he painted the character of the first English national hero, King Arthur, and gave a new meaning to the legends which had grown up in the Middle Ages about the knights of the Round Table. In no way does he illustrate more conspicuously his tendency to forsake pure romance for romantic treatment of present realities than in these poems, which are full of suggestions of modern moral and social problems. King Arthur's attempt to bring civilization to his realm through the devotion of his knights fails because of sins which Tennyson felt to be the peculiar danger of his own age. It was inevitable that he should interpret the Arthurian cycle in terms of his own personality and time. The *Idylls,* therefore, spoke more eloquently to Victorian than to modern readers, many of whom prefer the robust and barbarous mediæval originals to Tennyson's decorous moralistic versions of them. The poet's technical resourcefulness, his rich pattern of sounds and images, no longer veils the lack of passion and the presence of priggishness in these once famous tales.

Tennyson's later work consisted largely of the series of dramas, for the most part based on English history—*Queen Mary* (1875), *Harold* (1876), *Becket* (1884). He **His Later** was not highly successful in mastering the dramatic **Work** form, but his example recalled the former greatness and dignity of the drama and gave an early sign of its recovery. In "Locksley Hall Sixty Years After" (1886) his earlier, rather boyish mood of protest gave way to an arraignment of society for its sordid materialism, its vice, cruelty, and inefficiency, which reminds one of Carlyle in his bitterest mood. And then in a number of poems he recalled his old manner—in the classic beauty of "Demeter" and "The Death of Œnone"; in the allegory of noble striving toward the light in "Merlin and the Gleam"; in the instinctive and spontaneous trust of "Crossing the Bar." This poem, though not his latest, may be taken as his farewell word, spoken with solemn gladness as he put off into the mysterious sea of death.

The Victorian age is unlike certain other great periods of literature in that it had no one theme or body of subject-matter peculiarly its own, such as the mythology of Greece, or the Christian faith of Dante or Milton. On the contrary, it drew material for poetry from all ages. Tennyson is in this respect typical. Classical, mediæval, and Renaissance themes in his pages *Range and Finish of His Style* are mingled with stories drawn from his own day, such as "Dora" and "Enoch Arden." To meet these various demands his style shows equal variety. He essayed every kind of poetry, the song, the idyll, the dramatic monologue, the dialect poem, the descriptive or "pageant" poem, the ballad, the war-ode, the threnody, the epic narrative, and the drama. In all these, except the pure drama, he attained high, and in some the highest, excellence. Everywhere his style is one of exquisite finish, with a flawlessness of technic which it seems that no labor could improve. His is the best example in English of the "eclectic" style, made up of elements borrowed from many sources and perfectly fused, especially in his mature, vigorous, disciplined interpretations of such classical personalities and legends as those of "Ulysses" and "Tiresias."

The dominant element in Tennyson's thought is his sense of law. The thing which most impresses him is the spectacle of order in the universe. The highest praise which he *His Sense of Law* can give England is that she is "a land of settled government," where freedom is ever "broadening down from precedent to precedent." He is impressed by science because its office is to show law reigning everywhere, subduing all life to a vast harmonious scheme. A majestic movement is given to *In Memoriam* by the fact that it follows the year twice through its revolutions, so that the succession of day and night, the moon's changing phases, the circuit of the stars in their courses, the slow pageant of the seasons, seem at last to enfold with their large harmony and peace the forlorn heart of the mourner. This love of order also causes Tennyson to distrust individual whim and passion. The story of *The Princess* is the story of the overthrow, by a touch of nature, of all that is false in the heroine's plan for the enfranchisement of her sex; and the moral is that woman's place in life must be determined by the natural law of her being. In the *Idylls of the King* not only is the passion of Lancelot and Guinevere portrayed as the source of the moral ruin of Arthur's kingdom, but even the search for the Holy Grail is represented as contributing to this ruin, because it draws off Arthur's knights from their true work of establishing order and justice, and causes them to lose themselves in the extravagances of mystical religion. Tennyson is in constant protest, open or covert, against the individualism which the Victorian era inherited from the romantic revival. For the sake of peace and order, he was willing to make easy terms with forces with which he did not have the courage to deal squarely. His virtues and his vices combine to make him the most perfectly representative poet of his period.

Robert Browning, who disputes with Tennyson the first place among Victorian poets, is Tennyson's opposite in almost

Tennyson and Browning Contrasted

every respect but fame and length of years. His genius was pre-eminently dramatic; his interest lay, not in universal law, but in individual passion. And his style, instead of being eclectic and carefully elaborated, was highly individual, and often more intent on meaning than on form. Browning is strong where Tennyson is weak, weak where Tennyson is strong. Both shared almost equally in the Victorian tendency toward reflection, and toward·a didactic aim; but their reflection was exercised upon very different phenomena, and their teaching was widely opposed.

Browning was born in London in 1812. Mingled with the English and Scottish blood in his veins was a more distant strain

Browning: His Life and Poetic Career

of German and Creole, a fact of value in considering the cosmopolitan range of his imagination. He passed his boyhood and youth in the suburb of Camberwell, near enough to London to make the great smoky city on the horizon a constant reminder of the complex human life he was to interpret as subtly and deeply as any poet had done since the Elizabethan age. His first stimulus to poetic creation was given by a volume of Shelley which he picked up by chance on a London book-stall in his fourteenth year. His first long poem, *Pauline*, published in 1833, is a half-dramatic study of the type of spiritual life which Shelley's own career embodied; and Shelley's influence is clearly traceable both in its thought and in its style. After a trip to Russia and Italy, Browning published *Paracelsus*, in 1835. This, like *Pauline*, is the "history of a soul." In it Browning's wonderful endowments are already suggested: his knowledge of the causes of spiritual growth and decay, his subtle analysis of motive and counter-motive, his eloquence in pleading a cause, the enkindled power and beauty of his language when blown upon by noble passion. The hindrances from which he suffered are also only too clear, especially his tendency to lose himself in tangled thought and to grow harsh and obscure in pursuing the secondary suggestions of his theme. In *Sordello* (1840) these faults smother down the clear fire of poetry into a torpid smoke. In *Pippa Passes*, however (1841), he shook himself free from these faults of manner, and produced a dramatic poem of sustained beauty, as clear as sunlight, a work of simple, melodious, impassioned art. Between 1840 and 1845 Browning was chiefly occupied with attempts to write actable plays; of these the most interesting are perhaps *In a Balcony, Colombe's Birthday, A Blot in the 'Scutcheon,* and *The Return of the Druses.* He had also begun those short poems dealing with special moments in the lives of various men and women, historical or imaginary, which constitute the most important division of his work. These are now included under such collective titles as *Dramatic Lyrics, Dramatic Romances,* and *Men and Women.*

In 1846 Browning eloped with Elizabeth Barrett, whose poetic reputation was then far greater than his, and went to live in Italy. The pair settled in Florence, in the house called "Casa Guidi," from which was taken the title of Mrs. Browning's poem on the Italian Liberation, *Casa Guidi Windows.* Here Browning continued his great series of dramatic monologues. Here, also, after Mrs. Browning's death in 1861, he began *The Ring and the Book.* This is the crowning effort of his genius for the vastness of its scope and its grasp of human nature, though it lacks the spontaneous grace and charm which the best of his shorter pieces share with *Pippa Passes*, that perfect fruit of his youthful imagination. After the death of his wife, Browning spent most of his time in England. He wrote much, with a steady gain in intellectual subtlety, but with a corresponding loss of poetic beauty. He made a more and more deliberate sacrifice of form to matter, wrenching and straining the verse-fabric in order to pack into it all the secondary meanings of the theme. To the last, however, his genius continued to throw out bursts and jets of exquisite music, color, and feeling. Such, for instance, are the little pieces called "Wanting is —What?" and "Never the Time and the Place," written in his seventy-first year; and such is "Summum Bonum," written just before the pen dropped from his hand in 1889, in the seventy-seventh year of his age. He had had to wait long for recognition, but during the latter years of his life his fame overshadowed even that of Tennyson, and his works were studied and made a cult of, with an enthusiasm seldom accorded to a living poet.

Browning's earliest poem, *Pauline,* was, he tells us, intended as the first of a series of "mono-dramatic epics," each of which *His Interest in Soul-History: Illustrated by "Pippa Passes"* was to present the "history of a soul." Broadly viewed, the whole of Browning's work is what his youthful ambition dreamed of making it. In three forms—pure drama, dramatic narrative, and dramatic lyric—he gave the history of hundreds of souls; or if not their whole history, at least some crucial moment of it, when its issues trembled in the balance and dipped toward good or evil. In his earlier life he made many attempts to present these crucial moments in dramas intended for the stage, but the form was not perfectly suited to his peculiar task. In *Pippa Passes*, however, while keeping the dramatic form, he threw aside the demands of stage presentation, and presented four special moments of soul-history, connected with each other only by a slight thread. The germ of the poem came to him in youth, while listening to a gypsy girl singing in the Camberwell woods. He imagined some one walking alone through life, apparently too obscure to leave any trace behind, but unconsciously exercising a lasting influence at every step. This abstract conception he afterward connected with the personality of a little silk-winder in the silk-mills of Asolo, a mountain 'town which he had visited on his first journey to Italy. Pippa walks through Asolo on New Year's Day, her one holiday in the year, unconsciously dropping her divine songs into the lives of four groups of people, just at the moment when their fates are trembling between good and evil, courage and cowardice; and by the touching purity and gladness of her voice, or by the significant words she utters, she saves each in turn. At evening she goes back to her bare room and sinks to sleep with a final song on her lips, still ignorant of the service she has done to "Asolo's happiest four."

Pippa Passes illustrates the essential qualities of Browning's dramatic genius. He cannot throw, as could Shakespeare and his fellows, large and varied groups of people to- *Strength* gether, and make them act and interact through *and* the light and shadow of human motives. Nor has *Weakness* he the greater Shakespearean gift—the supreme *of His* dramatic gift—of forgetting and obscuring him- *Dramatic* self. In all the words which his characters utter we *Genius* seem to hear the ring of Browning's own voice; as an accompaniment to their actions there always runs, silent or expressed, his comment of blame or praise. He is less a dramatist than an exhibitor and interpreter of single dramatic situations, such as the four which are bound loosely together by Pippa's chance-heard songs. But in presenting these single situations Browning's power is absolute; here he works with the most graphic vividness, and with a compression of meaning which crowds into a few lines the implications of a lifetime.

It follows from the peculiar nature of Browning's dramatic gift that his most vital work is in his short poems, where he handles single situations or soul-states, growing *His Short* out of what has gone before and pointing toward *Poems:* what is to come after. In these not only does he *Peculiari-* select by preference a highly special moment in the *ties of His* life of the man or woman whose soul he wishes to *Method* show us in its working, but as a rule he views his theme from some odd and striking point of view. Another peculiarity of Browning's method in his short poems is that he throws the reader into the midst of the situation with startling suddenness, and then proceeds to reveal facet after facet of it, with a rapidity which is apt to bewilder a reader not in the secret of the method. There are no explanations, no gradual transitions; we are not allowed to guess at the whole intention until the end is reached. A capital example of this technique is the "Soliloquy of the Spanish Cloister," which has to be read to the end before we see it for what it is, the self-revealed picture of a narrow-minded, superstitious, sensual monk, stirred to hatred by a brother monk, whose mild, be-nignant ways and genuine piety we gradually discern through the speaker's jeers and curses. If we add to this method of organization the fact that Browning's best work is very com-pressed in style, we see why many persons have found obscure in him what is in reality clear enough, but is not to be under-stood without attention and alertness on the reader's part. Per-haps the poem which best illustrates all Browning's devices, harmoniously combined, is "My Last Duchess," a marvelous example of his power to give a whole life history, with a wealth of picturesque detail, in a few lines intensely compressed and heavily weighted with suggestion.

The range of Browning's imaginative sympathy is very great. In "Caliban upon Setebos" he has shown the grotesque imag-

His Wide Dramatic Sympathy   inings of a half-human monster, groping after an explanation of the universe. In "Childe Roland" he has shown the mystical heart of mediæval knighthood, fronting spectral terrors in its search after the stronghold of sin, the Dark Tower, where lurks the enemy of life and joy. In "Abt Vogler" and "A Toccata of Ga-luppi's" he has touched upon the inner meanings of music, and has painted for us convincing portraits of musical enthusiasts. In "The Grammarian's Funeral" he has shown the poetry and heroism hidden underneath the gray exterior of the life of a Renaissance pedant. In "Fra Lippo Lippi," "Andrea del Sarto," and "Pictor Ignotus" he has given the psychology of the painter's nature, and has illuminated those sources of success and failure in art which lie deep in the moral being of the artist. In "Balaustion's Adventure" he has revealed the inner spirit of Greek life in the fifth century before Christ. In "A

Death in the Desert" he has led us into the mystical rapture of the early Christians; and in "Christmas Eve" and "Easter Day" he has approached Christian faith from the modern position. In "Saul" he has shown us, against the splendid background of patriarchal Israel, the boy David singing, in the tent of the great King, songs of human joy which rise, in a sudden opening of the heavens of prophecy, into a song of the coming of the Messiah. In no one except Shakespeare can be found a mind more wide-ranging over the outer circumstances and the inner significance of man's life, or a more unwearied inquiry into its spiritual crises.

Browning's poetry is intensely charged with moral purpose. The world is for him, in Keats's phrase, the "Valley of Soul-making"; and every act, thought, and feeling of life is of concern only as it hinders or determines *His Teaching* the soul on its course. But he believes salvation to lie, not, as does Tennyson, in the suppression of individual will and passion, but in their strenuous exercise. It is the moments of high excitement in human life which interest him, because in such moments the great saving assertions of will and passion are made. Hence his interest in art, which embodies these moments of high excitement; and hence his indifference to science, which deals with impersonal law. To him love is the supreme experience and function of the soul, testing its temper and revealing its probable fate. In such poems as "Cristina," "Evelyn Hope," "The Last Ride Together," "My Star," "By the Fireside," and many more, he has presented love in its varied phases and has celebrated its manifold meanings not only on earth but in the infinite range of worlds through which he believes that the soul is destined to go in search after its own perfection. By the intensity and positiveness of his doctrine he influenced his age profoundly, and made his name synonymous with faithfulness to the human love which life brings, and through that to the divine love which it implies and promises.

The robustness of Browning's nature, its courage, its abounding joy and faith in life, make his works a permanent storehouse of spiritual energy for the race, a storehouse to which for a long time to come it will in certain moods always return.

In an age distracted by doubt and divided in will, he lifted his strong, unfaltering voice above the perplexities and hesitations of men like a bugle-call to joyous battle in which the victory is to the brave. But Browning's bequest to posterity was not merely his euphoric attitude toward life. Twentieth-century poets, who reacted against his somewhat jaunty optimism, were, nevertheless, able to profit by his psychological realism, his audaciously colloquial diction, his deliberately rough rhythms, and his extension of the domain of poetry to include cacophony and ugliness.

One of Browning's most perfect short poems, "One Word More," is addressed to his wife, Elizabeth Barrett Browning (1806–1861), and is a kind of counter-tribute to **Mrs.** her most perfect work, the *Sonnets from the Portu-* **Browning** *guese*, which contain the record of her courtship and marriage. Her early life was shadowed by illness and affliction; and her early poetry (*The Seraphim*, 1838, *Poems*, 1844) shows in many places the defects of unreality and of overwrought emotion natural to work produced in the loneliness of a sick-chamber. The best known of these early poems are perhaps "Lady Geraldine's Courtship," where she works under the influence of Tennyson's idylls, and "The Cry of the Children," where she voices the humanitarian protest against the practice of employing child-labor in mines and factories. After her marriage and removal to Italy her health improved, and her art greatly strengthened. Mrs. Browning was deeply interested in the struggle of Italy to shake off her bondage to Austria, as is shown by her *Casa Guidi Windows*, published in 1851. In 1857 appeared her most ambitious work, *Aurora Leigh*, a kind of versified novel of modern English life, with a social reformer and humanitarian, of aristocratic lineage, for hero, and a young poetess, in large part a reflection of Mrs. Browning's own personality, for heroine. *Aurora Leigh* shows the influence of a great novel-writing age, when the novel was becoming more and more imbued with social purpose. It attempts unsuccessfully to perform in verse the social function which Dickens, George Eliot, Kingsley, and others, strove to perform in prose. The interest in public questions also appears in Mrs. Browning's *Poems before Congress* (1860), and in her *Last Poems* (1862).

Mrs. Browning's technique is uncertain, and she never freed herself from her characteristic faults of vagueness and unrestraint. But her sympathy with noble causes, the elevation and ardor of her moods of personal emotion, and the distinction of her utterance at its best, tempt us to overlook her technical limitations. She shares her husband's strenuousness and optimism, but she speaks always from the feminine vantage-ground. Her characteristic note is that of intimate, personal feeling; even *Casa Guidi Windows* has been aptly called "a woman's love-making with a nation."

Browning's robust optimism in the face of all the unsettling and disturbing forces of the age is thrown into sharp relief by a somewhat younger poet, Matthew Arnold, in whom the prevailing tone is one of doubt and half-despairing stoicism. Arnold was born in 1822, *Matthew Arnold* the son of Thomas Arnold, the famous head-master of Rugby. He went up to Oxford just at the time when the religious revival, under John Keble and John Henry Newman, was stirring the university to its depths. The unsettling effect of this agitation, coming after the conventional religious teaching of Rugby, had much to do with determining Arnold's characteristic attitude of mind toward questions of faith. From his thirtieth year until shortly before his death in 1888, he held the position of inspector of schools. To the demands and responsibilities of this official position were added, in 1857, those of a professorship of poetry at Oxford. These outer circumstances were largely instrumental in turning his energies away from poetry, into the field of prose criticism, where, for the last twenty years of his life, he held the position of a leader, almost of a dictator.

Arnold may be described as a poet of transition. His bent as a poet was taken chiefly between 1840 and 1850, the period intervening between the first and the second outburst of creative energy in the century. Carlyle, Browning, Tennyson, and Newman were, each in his *Arnold a Poet of Transition* way, already building anew the structures of spiritual faith and hope; but to Arnold, as to many others, the ebbing of the old wave was far more clearly felt than the rising of the new one. Standing, as he says,

> between two worlds, one dead,
> The other powerless to be born,

he fronts life wearily, or at best stoically. He seeks consolation in the intellect; and his poetry, though penetrated with romantic sensibility, is marked by the self-control of the classically disciplined intelligence.

On the side of religion, Arnold's character led him to a melancholy reaction from the old faiths, and to a stoical rejec-

His Attitude Toward Life

tion of them as outworn things, "a dead time's exploded dream." He has expressed this view at least twice very movingly, in "Dover Beach" and "Obermann." This same scepticism applied to the facts of human intercourse breathes sadly but calmly through the series of love lyrics entitled "Switzerland." Just as he has felt compelled to surrender his faith in a personal God and a compassionate Saviour, so, as he regards the human heart and its destiny, he loses faith in the heart's promises as well. He sees the sad instability of mortal affection rather than its heroic constancy; he is pierced by a sense of the inevitable loneliness of each human soul. In the imperfections and unrealized ideals of life, in which Tennyson found cause to "faintly trust the larger hope," and in which Browning saw the "broken arcs" of heaven's "perfect round," Arnold found grounds for doubt, and he urged men to put away delusion and to expect in the future only what they see in the past. Other phases of this stoic dejection, and of the struggle which it wages with the restless craving for joy, are expressed in the pieces called "Self-Dependence" and "A Summer Night."

For his ideal of form, Arnold turned usually to the literature of Greece, abjuring romantic willfulness and vagueness in favor

His Ideal of Form

of classic lucidity and restraint. When he worked more deliberately in the Greek spirit and manner, his style was often cold and dry. In his long poems, especially, he was apt to sacrifice too much to his reverence for classical tradition. Only one of them, "Sohrab and Rustum," combines classic purity of style with romantic ardor of feeling. The truth of its oriental color, the deep pathos of the situation, the fire and intensity of the action, the strong conception of character, and the full, solemn music of the verse, make "Sohrab and Rustum" unquestionably the masterpiece among Arnold's longer poems. The same unity of classic form with romantic feeling characterizes his two shorter masterpieces, "The Scholar Gypsy" and "Thyrsis," which are crystal-clear without coldness, and restrained but powerful.

Arnold did not persist, in his poetry, in working through the period of dejection and doubt, and in following to their mature issues such hints of hope and faith as his poems show. Not even in "Thyrsis," the beautiful threnody in which he celebrated his dead friend Arthur Hugh Clough, did he find it possible to embrace any but the most shadowy consolation. In "Obermann Once More" he emerged for a moment into something like optimism; but when that piece was written his work as a poet was done. He seems to have felt that the practical work of regenerating society and reforming public faith could be better done in prose. He became a critic of poetry, of society, and of religion. *His Desertion of Poetry for Prose*

Arnold saw more clearly than Carlyle or Tennyson the problems created for the modern world by the immense mass of new knowledge—the result of scientific discovery—and by the vast increase of "people who counted"—the result of democracy. The first threatened to sweep away old bases of belief and morality; the second threatened to put an end to the kind of social control that had hitherto been the function of the upper class. Arnold's own profession, that of inspector of schools in the national system of education, brought him into practical contact with the situation. So, from 1860 on, he devoted himself chiefly to the writing of essays, in a style more urbane than Carlyle's but equally purposeful. He dealt with society itself in the papers composing *Culture and Anarchy* (1869); with the effect of scientific criticism on man's attitude toward the Bible and Christian faith, in *Literature and Dogma* (1873); and with the values of literature of the past to modern life in *Essays in Criticism* (First Series, 1865; Second Series, 1888). *Arnold's Prose*

Arnold's social message was more definite than Carlyle's gospel of work and hero-worship, though perhaps no easier for the mass of men to follow. It is expressed in his often-used term "culture," which he defines as "a pursuit of our total perfection by means of getting to know, on matters which most concern us, the best which has been thought and said in the world." It is easy to see that this idea of total perfection in life was in harmony with Arnold's classical ideal in poetry, an ideal of symmetry, of subordination of parts to whole. Carlyle had preached the value of conduct, the "Hebraic" element in life; Arnold set himself to preach the value of the complementary "Hellenic" element— open-mindedness, delight in ideas, alertness in entertaining new points of view, and willingness to examine life constantly in the light of new postulates. Wherever in religion, politics, education, or literature he saw his countrymen under the domination of narrow ideals, he came speaking the mystic word of deliverance, "culture." It is by culture that the Puritan dissenter shall be made to see the lack of elevation and beauty in his church forms; that the radical politician shall reach a saving sense of the rawness and vulgarity of his program of state; that the man whose literary taste is bad shall win admittance to the true kingdom of letters. In almost all his prose writing he attacked some form of "Philistinism," by which word he designated the narrow-mindedness and self-satisfaction of the British middle class.

His "Gospel of Ideas"

Just as Arnold was concerned with the problem of assimilating the masses into the civilization of the future, so also was he engaged in the task of assimilating new knowledge into the intellectual and moral life of mankind. The place of science in the education of the future he considered in "Literature and Science" (in *Discourses in America*). He wrote several books to show how the scientific criticism of the Bible left untouched the essentials of Christianity —the conception of God as a power "not ourselves which makes for righteousness," "the secret of Jesus," that "the kingdom of heaven lies within you." But perhaps his heart was most entirely

Arnold's Religious and Literary Criticism

in his essays in literary criticism. As professor of poetry at Oxford (1857–1867) he dealt with such themes as Celtic literature and translating Homer. He pointed out the value and methods of the study of poetry, and the peculiar contribution of poets like Wordsworth, Byron, and Keats to man's sense for beauty, which, with the sense for conduct and the sense for knowledge, makes up the sense for total perfection. Arnold was a more authoritative critic than any other of his day. He inherited classical standards and æsthetic methods of judgment, but on the whole he felt the function of criticism to be largely one of selection and interpretation. He defined it as "a disinterested endeavor to learn and propagate the best that is known and thought in the world," and thus emphasized its importance in the attainment of culture, both personal and social.

The total impression which Arnold makes in his prose is that of a spiritual man-of-the-world. In comparison with Carlyle, Ruskin, and Newman, he was worldly. For what he regarded as the disorderly æsthetics and morality of romanticism he substituted an ideal of balanced cultivation, the ideal of the trained, sympathetic, cosmopolitan gentleman. Yet in his own way he also was a prophet and a preacher, striving wholeheartedly to release his countrymen from bondage to mean things, and pointing their gaze to that symmetry and balance of character which has seemed to many noble minds the true goal of human endeavor.

The name of Arthur Hugh Clough (1819–1861) will always be associated with that of Matthew Arnold by reason of the threnody, *Thyrsis*. Clough was a fellow student of Arnold's at Rugby and at Oxford, during the years *Arthur* of Newman's influence, and his serious nature was *Hugh* stirred to its depths by the movement. He was, how- *Clough* ever, of too sceptical a nature to yield to authority in religion, and as the result of his intellectual honesty he resigned his fellowship, and after an attempt to settle in America, he became an examiner in the Education Office. He died in 1861.

Clough is typical of the young Victorians whose sense of the actual world and of the new scientific standards of truth made romanticism in life or in religion impossible for them. Like many of his contemporaries he was much influenced by Carlyle. He was a genuine poet, but the spiritual conflict in which he lived prevented his undertaking any large production. His longest poem is *The Bothie of Tober-na-Vuolich* (1848), the love-story, in hexameter verse, of an Oxford scholar and a girl in a Highland village or bothie, who is lovely to him as she appears doing the hard necessary field work of the farm. Through her he feels the attraction of reality, and abandoning his conventional academic career, he emigrates to New Zealand. Although Clough's confidence in life and in the spirit of man was expressed most vigorously in "Say Not the Struggle Nought Availeth," his most characteristic poems were lyrics which set forth his scornful refusal to content himself with conventional beliefs, despite his yearning for spiritual peace. His rejection of an easy compromise and his insistence on the necessity of dealing honestly with the causes of spiritual disquietude were to heighten the morale of younger poets who in a later age were to face the chaos of belief.

The new science, which was changing the intellectual outlook of mankind and threatening the traditional values enshrined in religion and education, produced a genuine *T. H.* man of letters in Thomas Henry Huxley (1825– *Huxley* 1895). Huxley was born at Ealing, May 4, 1825. His education was strictly scientific. In 1845 he took his degree in medicine at London University and was appointed assistant surgeon in the Royal Navy. He was attached for four years to a scientific expedition to the South Seas, and on his return to England was appointed lecturer in natural history at the School of Mines. In 1859 Darwin published his great collection of evidence in favor of evolution in *The Origin of Species*, and Huxley at once became an ardent advocate of the theory. He says in his *Autobiography* that he cared less for scientific research than for "the architectural and engineering part of the universe," that is, the explanation and defense of the scientific method and its application to human life in general. He wrote and lectured on many aspects of this theme, ethics, religion, education, and government. His essays on "Man's Place in Nature" (1863) and "On the Physical Basis of Life" (1868) set forth the general view of human life in the light of the account which science is able to give of its origins. The essays "On the Advisableness of Improving Natural Knowledge" (1866) and "A Liberal Education" (1871) deal with the importance of directing life in accordance with the dictates of science. In 1876 Huxley visited the United States to deliver the address at the opening of Johns Hopkins University. He died in 1895.

Huxley is the best representative in English literature of the influence of science and the scientific habit of mind, not only upon thought but also upon style. His *Autobiography* (1889) is a forthright statement of fact, which in its plainness and simplicity has a charm of its own. Huxley shows throughout all his writings a robust spirit, with no trace of the nostalgia with which many of his contemporaries looked back upon the traditional values threatened by the new science. With Matthew Arnold the contrast is particularly sharp. In reply to Huxley's vehement argument for scientific education, Arnold, in "Literature and Science," defended training in the classics. Where Arnold in *Literature and Dogma* sought to preserve the spiritual values of Christianity, Huxley fiercely attacked the historical evidence in a series of *Essays on Controverted Subjects*. In one of these on "Christianity and Agnosticism" he tells how he invented the latter term to describe the attitude of one who professes entire ignorance in regard to everything except the phenomena of the material world of which his senses bring him knowledge. Speaking for the scientist, he attacked the conviction "that authority is the soundest basis of belief; that merit attaches to readiness to believe; that the doubting disposition is a bad one and scepticism a sin. . . ." For him "scepticism is the highest of duties, blind faith the one unpardonable sin." He was the embodiment of the scientific conscience. He reflects the buoyancy and enthusiasm which characterized the followers of Darwin, who in the later nineteenth century looked to science with confidence for the ultimate solution of human problems. A corresponding difference is evident between the style of Huxley and that of the Oxford School of Newman and Arnold. All three were engaged in controversy, but while the latter are urbane in manner, insinuating rather than dictatorial, Huxley is assertive and assured, merciless in exposing the weaknesses of his opponents. In

Huxley's Attitude and Style

thought and style he is as completely representative of the values of knowing, as is Carlyle of those of conduct, and Arnold of beauty of life.

The dictatorship of taste which Arnold exercised in matters of literature was held in matters of art by John Ruskin, who, like Arnold, also extended his criticism into the region of social and moral ideals. His nature was more ardent than Arnold's; and his crusade against bad art, as well as against social and moral falsehood, partook of the Hebraic intensity of Carlyle, whose disciple, indeed, he acknowledged himself to be. He was born in 1819. His father, a London wine-merchant of wealth and liberal tastes, gave him every early advantage of education and travel. Family carriage trips through England, France, and Switzerland enabled him to gather those impressions of natural and of architectural beauty, which he afterward put to remarkable use in his critical writings. A boyish enthusiasm for the paintings of William Turner ripened with years into an ardent championship of that wonderful artist, then obscure and neglected. In the first volume of *Modern Painters*, published in his twenty-fourth year, Ruskin enshrined Turner as the greatest of English landscape-painters. The powers of analysis thus developed led him deep into the abstract theory of art; and in the remainder of the work, published at intervals during the next sixteen years, he examined many types and schools of painting, separating what he held to be true from what he held to be false, with haughty and uncompromising assurance. Meanwhile, in *The Seven Lamps of Architecture* (1849) and *Stones of Venice* (1851–1853), he made a similar examination of the principal types of European architecture, and attempted to establish similar underlying principles concerning their growth and decay, their worth and worthlessness. Many of Ruskin's judgments must of course be dissented from, but it cannot be questioned that in his writings art criticism was put for the first time upon a broad ethical basis. He believed the springs of art to lie deep in the moral nature of the artist, and in the moral temper of the age and nation which produced him. Latent or expressed, this is the pervading idea of all Ruskin's art criticism. By insistence upon this view,

Ruskin: His Early Life and Art Criticism

by eloquent illustration and fiery defense of it, he gradually led his readers to a new understanding of the ethical values in art, and awakened them to a new discrimination.

In 1860, at forty years of age, Ruskin finished *Modern Painters*, and practically closed that series of works which had made him the foremost art critic of the century. *Later Life:* From this time on he used art mainly as illustra- *Ethical* tion and text, by means of which to enforce some *and Eco-* ethical, economic, or religious lesson. He became *nomic* more and more absorbed in the problems of social *Teaching* life, as his convictions grew that all great art must be national and social, and must spring from healthy and beautiful conditions of life in the society where it arises. Modern art he held to be, with a few exceptions, debased; and he gradually came to believe that this debasement was due to the nature of industrial society. In two books, *Unto This Last* (1861) and *Munera Pulveris* (1872), he protested against the accepted theories of political economy. Wealth, for instance, he conceived to consist in *real* values as opposed to *exchange* values— in Tintoretto's damaged frescoes in Venice as against the lithographs sold along the Rue de Rivoli in Paris. Indeed, he held that the latter city was in effect so much the poorer because of the cost of producing intrinsically worthless things. Further, he held that the relationship between capital and labor is not economic but moral, and that the capitalist should be led to use his power, not to tax more and more heavily the labor of others, but to make them more independent. In short, he maintained that the aim of political economy, as distinct from "commercial economy," should be "the multiplication of human life at the highest standard."

His most popular book, *Sesame and Lilies* (1865) was in part a by-product of his thinking on political economy. In the first division of the book, entitled "King's Treasuries," *"Sesame* he held up to censure England's absorption in *and* worldly success, as opposed to spiritual success. To *Lilies"* the "gospel of getting on," which makes its appeal through the idea that money constitutes the only real "value," he opposed the gospel of spiritual wealth, especially as deposited in books, those King's Treasuries which are the real centre of the realm of "value." The second part, "Queen's Gardens," was Ruskin's contribution to the "woman problem" of the century, the theme being the same as that of Tennyson's *Princess*. *Sesame and Lilies* is written in a style of wonderful strength and richness. It affords perhaps the best single example of its author's mastery over the manifold chords of prose expression.

As he went on in years, Ruskin's sympathy went out more and more to the oppressed and unjustly treated of this world; *His Last Years* and he spent a large part of his energy and fortune in attempting to help the working classes by word and deed. To them he addressed a series of letters entitled *Fors Clavigera*,[1] beginning in 1871, which contain his views on economic, artistic, and religious subjects set forth sometimes with the most winning persuasion, and sometimes with furious invective. In 1875 he formed a society afterward called the Guild of Saint George, in which he attempted to put into practice his own economic, social, and spiritual ideals. The vows of the Guild enforced the virtues of obedience, industry, and unselfishness in a form suggesting knighthood. The order was, in fact, an attempt to restore a mediæval society through the diffusion of the ideals of chivalry among its members—to realize a Utopia on English soil. To this Guild, and to other experiments in housing and teaching the poor, he ultimately gave all his fortune. The terrible burden of arousing England to a sense of its responsibility in the face of monstrous social injustice weighed more and more heavily upon him. Attacks of brain fever interrupted his work, and between periods of mental darkness he wrote *Præterita*, a serene and pellucid account of his boyhood and youth. During his last years he lived at Brantwood among the English lakes, and there he died in 1900.

Ruskin combined many gifts and qualities: a subtle intellect, *His Style* a nervous system which vibrated intensely to impressions of beauty and ugliness, great moral ardor, marked impatience and dogmatism, and a marvelous prose style. His style is based on the prose of the English Bible,

[1] Ruskin points out that *Fors Clavigera* may mean Strength as Club-bearer, Strength as Key-bearer, or Strength as Nail-bearer, and that the title metaphorically suggests Strength of Deed, of Patience, and of Law.

modified by the religious writers of the seventeenth century, especially by the florid style of Jeremy Taylor; and it is enriched by a unique gift of description, lyrical in feeling and splendid in color. His elaborate description of Saint Mark's Cathedral in *Stones of Venice*, the Falls of Schaffhausen in *Modern Painters*, and the Rhone at Geneva in *Præterita*, are capital examples of ornate English prose. His style is as markedly romantic, in its emotional quality and its search after beauty, as Arnold's is classical in its subordination of emotion to intellect, and in its effort to secure clearness at any cost.

One of the important services of Ruskin as art critic was to defend to the public a group of young men who sought to bring back technical sincerity and spiritual truth to the arts of painting and poetry. They found *The Pre-* models for these qualities in the painters and poets *Raphael-* before Raphael, who had treated the most mystical *ite Move-* religious themes with simple-hearted realism, and *ment* thus called themselves Pre-Raphaelites. For subjects, as well as for inspiration, the Pre-Raphaelites went back to the Middle Ages. A mystical and intangible beauty of conception, together with a kind of naïve earnestness and simplicity of treatment, characterized their work in both painting and poetry. The founder of the Pre-Raphaelite Brotherhood was Dante Gabriel Rossetti; the first members were Londoners, like himself; but some of the most enthusiastic recruits of the Brotherhood were Oxford men, who saw in it an attempt to do in art and literature what Newman had tried to do in the Church. In this way the Pre-Raphaelite Movement is the child and heir of the Oxford Movement.

Dante Gabriel Rossetti was born in London in 1828. His father was an Italian patriot and exile; his mother of mixed English and Italian blood. In 1848 he definitely *Dante* adopted the career of painter, and in the same year *Gabriel* founded the Pre-Raphaelite Brotherhood. Before *Rossetti* 1850 he had produced such pictures as "The Girlhood of Mary" and "The Annunciation," which are representative of the early principles of the group. In that year the Brotherhood founded a little magazine called *The Germ*, which, though it ran for only four numbers, is famous as containing the poem which best illustrates the movement on its literary side, "The Blessed Damozel."

The Blessed Damozel, wearing the "white rose of Mary's gift," and holding the mystic lilies, leans from the "gold bar of *"The* heaven," yearning for her earthly lover, and pic- *Blessed* turing to herself the time when she shall lead him *Damozel"* with her among the celestial groves and by the liv- ing waters of God. The sights and sounds of heaven are imaged forth in the poem with a concreteness which would be startling if it were not solemnized by spiritual mean- ing and freighted with spiritual awe. From time to time, as the poem progresses, our minds are led out from among the shad- owy landscapes and the indwelling spirits of paradise, down through illimitable star spaces, to where upon earth the lover sits, hearing in the autumnal rustle of the leaves the feet of his beloved, as she tries to reach him down the echoing stairs of the sky.

The union of simplicity and concreteness with spirituality, which makes this poem typical of the Pre-Raphaelite aims in both poetry and painting, appears equally in another early poem of Rossetti's, "My Sister's Sleep." The strained stillness and sus- pense of a death-chamber, the anguish and fortitude of a mother in the presence of her loss, are given with passionate reserve and tender realism.

A considerable portion of Rossetti's verse was written in his early life, but only a few poems were then published. In his *Later Life* thirty-second year he married a Miss Siddall, whose *and* rare type of beauty he immortalized in the best- *Poetry* known of his pictures, the "Beata Beatrix." Two years after the marriage his wife died; and in despair at his loss, Rossetti placed in her coffin all his unpub- lished writings. They remained buried until 1869; then they were exhumed by his friends and published the following year. This memorable volume contained "Sister Helen," one of the finest of his literary ballads, many of the sonnets belonging to the *House of Life* sequence, and *Jenny,* a daringly realistic por- trait of a woman of the streets. Another volume published eleven years after and a volume of translations from the early

Italian poets, entitled *Dante and His Circle,* constitute the whole of Rossetti's poetical output. After his wife's death he withdrew more and more into himself, until he became a complete recluse. Intense brooding upon his loss, and the disastrous effects of the drug which he took as a relief from insomnia, made his life a tragedy relieved only by the creative play of his mind, which continued to embody itself in pictures and poems of strange and sometimes morbid beauty. He died in 1882.

Rossetti's work illustrates perfectly the romantic tendency to escape from the actual world. This tendency appears in his long poems in ballad form, "Sister Helen," "The Bride's Prelude," "Rose Mary," "The King's Tragedy." More subtly is it evident in such studies of love as "The Stream's Secret" and "Love's Nocturne," *Rossetti's Romanticism* where the poet strives to penetrate to the innermost and essential secret of that mysterious passion which swayed his life as it did that of his great name-poet Dante, but to such tragic destiny. The great memorial of this love is the sonnet sequence, *The House of Life.* This, in the final form which it took in the volume of 1881, consists of one hundred and one sonnets dealing with the history of the poet's love and loss. Rossetti's love poetry has a quality unique in English literature. It achieves a subtle synthesis of almost Oriental sensuousness, emotional intensity, and spiritual elevation. Because for him flesh and spirit were virtually indistinguishable, he wrought a more perfect fusion of sensuousness and spirituality than any other English poet had achieved since Donne.

As a whole, Rossetti's poetry is marked by a great picturesqueness and visual beauty. It is "painter's poetry," in that its appeal is constantly to the eye. Music it has, too, but the tendency to load itself with elaborate detail often defeats the music, and makes of the *Rossetti's Poetic Style* verse a kind of poetical tapestry, stiff with emblazoned images. Where it is not the poetry of a painter it is the poetry of a prisoner and a recluse. Outdoor nature and the common life of men seldom appear in it. In the main, its atmosphere is close and heavily perfumed, its emotion somewhat morbid and cloying. It is the poetry of a nature born for the

generous sunlight and color of Italy, and compelled to build a
dream-world amid the chill fog and bitter smoke of London.

In the earlier pictures of Rossetti appears the noble, serious
face of his sister Christina (1830–1894), who sat as his model
Christina   for the youthful Madonna. She also contributed
Rossetti   several lyrics to *The Germ.* Apart from her personal association with the Pre-Raphaelites, how-
ever, she holds a place of her own in English poetry. Her
longer poems, *Goblin Market* and *The Prince's Progress,* appeared in 1862 and 1866. These as well as her lyrics show the
lovely and naïve simplicity which was the essence of Pre-
Raphaelitism. As a religious poet she is the opposite of Clough.
Christina Rossetti was assured of her Anglican Catholic faith;
to it she gave up her life, with love and its promise of earthly
happiness. Her poetry, of both love and religion, is, therefore,
born of experience and has the truth of sacrifice.

One of the young Oxford men who was drawn to Rossetti by
kinship in interests was William Morris (1834–1896). Indeed,
William   before his acquaintance with Rossetti and the Lon-
Morris: don group, he and his friends, conspicuous among
Early   whom was the painter Edward Burne-Jones, were
Poems   showing the influence of the Oxford Movement,
and were absorbed in the study of religious architecture and mediæval literature. In 1856 Morris at his own expense established *The Oxford and Cambridge Magazine,* in
which appeared some of Rossetti's poems, as well as his own.
These last by 1858 had grown into a volume which he called
The Defence of Guenevere, from the opening poem in which the
sinful Queen throws back her hair from her cheek of flame to tell
Sir Gawaine and his knights that they lie. It is clear from this
first poem that we are in a different world from that of Tennyson's *Idylls of the King.* Here there is no note of modern meaning—only an attempt to give in utter sincerity the psychology of
the mediæval soul. Most of the poems deal with a later epoch
than that of King Arthur, especially the fourteenth century and
the great wars between the English and French. In "The Eve of
Crécy" and "The Gilliflower of Gold" Morris touches on the
joyous adventure of knighthood; in "Shameful Death" and

"The Haystack in the Floods" he dwells on the darker sides of mediæval life, its violence and terrible ferocity; "Sir Peter Harpdon's End" is the tale of the devoted knight who holds his castle for the English until he is taken and put to death. In "The Sailing of the Sword," "The Blue Closet," and "The Wind" he presents aspects purely picturesque and fanciful, sometimes mere flashes of color.

Nine years later (1867) Morris published his second volume of poetry, *The Life and Death of Jason*. It is in striking contrast to the first. We seem to emerge from a forest full of grotesque and terrible things upon a plain bright with sunshine; we pass from the world of the Holy Grail to the world of the Golden Fleece. *"The Earthly Paradise"* And yet the treatment of the myth is mediæval in that the poem is written in the same diffuse, soft-colored, gently flowing verse in which the Norman-French *trouvères* had sung the adventures of their knights and paladins. Shortly after *The Life and Death of Jason* Morris published the first part of a collection of similar tales, called *The Earthly Paradise*, which he completed in 1870. The narratives are held together by an ingenious scheme, analogous to that which Chaucer used in binding together his *Canterbury Tales*. A band of Northmen, sailing westward in their Viking ships, are cast ashore upon the Island of Atlantis, the earthly paradise of which the Greek poets dreamed. Here they find dwelling a fortunate race of men, who in times long past have come hither from Greece and Asia Minor. The newcomers remain through the changing seasons of a year, telling stories of their northern land, of "The Lovers of Gudrun" and "The Fostering of Aslaug," and listening to the tales which the islanders have brought from their ancient home, of "Atalanta's Race" and "The Love of Alcestis." But whatever are the sources of the stories, whether classical, northern, or Oriental, the style in which they are written is always that of the mediæval romances; even the metres employed are those familiar to Chaucer and the French *trouvères*. The philosophy, on the contrary, is pagan, with the pessimism peculiar to the Greek as he thought on the passing of youth and the brevity of life. The fear of death drives the wanderers forth on their voyage in

search of the earthly paradise; the thought of death casts
a shadow upon every tale. King Admetus would be happy
but

> That all those pageants soon should be passed by,
> And hid by night the fair spring blossoms lie.

Gregory, in "The Land East of the Sun," falls thinking

> Of what a rude and friendless place
> The world was; through what empty days
> Men were pushed slowly down to death.

At best life is

> A checkered day of sunshine and of flowers,
> Fading to twilight and dark night at last.

In this pessimism Morris reflected the mood which was spreading over England, as the result of the loss of the consolations
of religious faith, and doubt of the power of reform to deal
with the increasing misery of the poor—a mood from which by
no romantic device could he completely escape.

Literature was only one of Morris's many activities. His was
a life of ceaseless labor in many fields of industry. He began
Morris's life as an architect, abandoned this career for
Industrial painting, drifted at length into the designing and
Career manufacturing of furniture, wall-paper, and tex-
tile fabrics, and toward the close of his life turned
his inexhaustible energy into fine printing and bookbinding. He
always worked in the spirit of a mediæval master-craftsman, to
whom beauty and honesty of workmanship were a religion. His
sincerity, versatility, and skill revolutionized household decoration; as the impulse given by him came to be felt more and
more widely, the surroundings of ordinary domestic life were
beautified for multitudes. With all this business and industrial
life he continued to produce literature as a by-product, for, as
he said: "If a chap can't compose an epic poem while he's
weaving a tapestry he's no good at all." He produced a version
of the saga of Sigurd the Volsung, and translated other north-

ern stories, including *Beowulf,* as well as Virgil and Homer. Late in his life he produced a series of romances, in poetic prose, dealing with the primitive life of our north-

Prose-Romances

ern ancestors; the most notable are perhaps *The House of the Wolfings, The Roots of the Mountains,* and *The Story of the Glittering Plain.* In them he succeeded in importing into English literature the spirit of the northern saga, not, to be sure, without some artificiality, but nevertheless with great picturesqueness and romantic charm.

Morris's industrial experiences gradually led him to the conviction that the bases of modern commercialism were false, and he threw himself with heart and soul into the socialistic movement then beginning to gain head-

His Socialism

way in England. Two of his romances, *News from Nowhere* and *A Dream of John Ball,* are attempts to imagine a new organization of society; and some of his later poems are chants of prophecy and hope for the longed-for era of social justice. In the prelude to *The Earthly Paradise* he calls himself "the idle singer of an empty day"; but this "idle singer" was a man who spent the greater portion of his time and strength working in shop and designing-room to make the world as it is a more livable place, and who, as experience thus gained gave him prompting, tried with all earnestness to indicate what seemed to him a higher basis for the social life of man. Morris offers a striking instance of the synthesis of many, if not all, the interests manifested by the Victorian romanticists. His interest in classical antiquity and in mediæval and Scandinavian literature exemplifies their cultivation of the past. His venture into socialism and his activity as craftsman and designer illustrate their social idealism and their anti-materialism.

The pessimism characteristic of the concluding decades of the century found most poignant utterance in the *Rubáiyát of Omar Khayyám,* by Edward Fitzgerald (1809–1883). Although this is called a translation, it is really an original poem, based on the scattered fragments of the old astronomer-poet of Persia, who lived in the twelfth century. Fitzgerald published his poem

The "Rubáiyát of Omar Khayyám"

in 1859, but sold only a few copies. He continued to revise and enlarge it through several editions, and lived to see it one of

the most widely read books of the day. It popularized oriental-
ism as the Pre-Raphaelite movement had popularized mediævalism; it expressed in memorable form the questionings in regard
to the worth of life which were being asked more insistently. In
its frank acceptance of pleasure as the only justification and
alleviation of life, it prepared the way for a sort of neo-pagan-
ism by suggesting an escape from the burdens and problems of
society and from the moral seriousness which obsessed most
Victorian writers. The great vogue it ultimately achieved was
due to the grace and charm with which it expressed views and
values which most other Victorian poets did not entertain or
dared not utter. Its popularity is a measure of the extent to
which the Victorian view of life had been undermined.

Neo-pagan romanticism is illustrated clearly in the early
poetry of Algernon Charles Swinburne (1837–1909). Swin-

Algernon Charles Swin-burne
burne was at Oxford in 1857, and had some personal association with the Pre-Raphaelites, but his
genius was too eclectic to permit him to confine
himself to one school. In 1865 he published his
first experiment in classical tragedy, *Atalanta in
Calydon.* A year later he brought out the first series of *Poems
and Ballads.* In these he deliberately and ostentatiously repudiated those ideals of character and conduct which the modern
world cherishes as its hardest-won heritage from nineteen centuries of Christianity. He went back for his inspiration to paganism, and too often not to the vigorous early periods of paganism, but to its later ones, when men, callous or indifferent to
the moral issues of life, sought to lose themselves in feverish
self-indulgence, or in the quietism of pessimism; grateful

> That no life lives forever,
> That dead men rise up never,
> That even the weariest river
> Winds somewhere safe to sea.

This neo-pagan side, however, was but one of many in Swinburne's work. He, like Tennyson and Browning, was an eclectic,
drawing material from every storehouse. More than any other
poet he took his themes and inspiration directly from literature.

He expressed his literary judgments not only in prose criticism but in his memorial poems on the French romanticists, Charles Baudelaire and Theophile Gautier, and in *Swinburne's Themes* his sonnets on the Elizabethan playwrights, where the quality of the man, obscure save for his work, often is caught in unforgettable phrases. His fondness for an extreme and morbid variety of romanticism indicates Swinburne's essential decadence. It was in part, however, his literary idols' love of freedom and their youthful impatience of control that attracted him. No one has surpassed him in his praise of Shelley, or of Marlowe—

> With mouth of gold, and morning in his eyes.

Of political freedom and hatred of tyranny he sang gloriously. Perhaps this passion for freedom is in part responsible for his love of the sea, which he expressed in poetry of unexampled beauty and force. Otherwise, his picture of nature emphasizes morbidly the aspects of decay and death. On the other hand, he had an exquisite perception of the beauty and pathos of child-life. Besides his voluminous lyrical work, he essayed epic narrative in *Tristram of Lyonesse*; and he produced a number of dramas, some, like *Chastelard* and *Marino Faliero,* studies in the Elizabethan manner; others, like *Atalanta in Calydon* and *Erechtheus,* written on the model of Greek tragedy.

Whatever may be said of Swinburne's intellectual or moral limitations, as a technical master of verse, as a musician in words, he was very great. Especially in the more *His Verse Mastery* rapid and impetuous rhythms he was able to extend the boundaries of his craft, and to enter regions of verse-music unknown before. For a union of "splendor and speed" his poetic style is unequalled by any other poet of the Victorian age. His diffuseness and over-ornamentation result from his tendency to clothe trivial thoughts in sweeping and resounding phrase.

His excellences are present in the highest degree, and his faults almost absent, in his masterpiece, *Atalanta in Calydon,* a distinguished attempt to give in English verse the essential form and spirit of Greek drama. The subject of Swinburne's poem is the hunting of the wild boar in Calydon, the love of Meleager for the maiden-huntress Atalanta, and his death at the

"Atalanta in Calydon" hands of his mother. The action moves with stately swiftness, in obedience to the strict canons of Greek form; the pathos is deep and genuine; and the music, especially in the choruses, is splendid in range and sweep.

Walter Pater (1839–1894) represents the eclectic tone of the time in his conscious synthesis of elements, classical and roman-

Walter Pater tic, Christian and pagan. Pater was an Oxford man, a fellow of Brasenose College, where he spent much of his life in seclusion from the busy world and occupied with questions of beauty and taste. His first volume, *The Renaissance* (1873), is a series of studies of significant fig-ures in that movement, Leonardo da Vinci, Sandro Botticelli, Joachim du Bellay, and others. Another group of critical essays *Appreciations* (1889), contains studies of Coleridge, Words-worth, Rossetti, and others. Although Pater's criticism is frankly impressionistic in that he is satisfied to record his own reaction to works of art, his delicate sensitiveness to beauty in all forms makes these studies both subtly penetrating and illuminating. Pater used fiction as well as criticism, but fiction of a classical restraint, comparable to Landor's *Imaginary Conversations.* In *Marius the Epicurean* (1885) he gives us the life of a Roman youth in the age of the Antonines—an exquisite picture —and in *Imaginary Portraits* (1887) he sketched four figures which suggest the individual character and atmosphere of dif-ferent periods and countries. His interest in classical studies showed itself further in *Plato and Platonism* (1893) and *Greek Studies* (1895), essays collected after his death.

Although Pater's own work is classical in its control and fin-ish, he was hospitable to the romantic point of view. Indeed his

Pater's Philoso-phy of Life penetrating search for rare and strange forms of beauty led him to discover the romantic qualities and aspects of classical life and art, and the classi-cal elements in romantic periods. The Renaissance as the meeting-point of the two tendencies was peculiarly fascinating to him. Similar is his attitude toward the mingling of paganism and Christianity. In *Marius the Epi-*

curean he pictures most sympathetically the youthful Christianity in the age of Marcus Aurelius; in "Denys l'Auxerrois"
(*Imaginary Portraits*) he portrays the instinctive return to
paganism in the early Renaissance. His philosophy of life is a
scientific paganism. In the concluding chapter of *The Renaissance* he finds that physical life is a constantly changing combination of natural elements, "phosphorus, and lime, and delicate
fibres," and that the mental life also is a group of impressions,
"unstable, flickering, inconsistent . . . all that is actual in it
being a single moment . . . of which it may ever be more truly
said that it has ceased to be than that it is." Since this is the
case, the true use of these moments is to make each yield the
most poignant and exquisite sensation of which it is capable.
"Every moment some form grows perfect in hand or face; some
tone on the hills or the sea is choicer than the rest; some mood
of passion or insight or intellectual excitement is irresistibly
real and attractive for us—for that moment only." This is pure
paganism—a philosophic expression of "Gather ye rosebuds
while ye may." But it should be noted that Pater makes the final
test of a life so lived and trained in appreciation of this world,
the Christian one of willingness to sacrifice it. Marius lays down
his life that his Christian friend Cornelius may escape; Sebas-
tian van Storck (*Imaginary Portraits*) dies to save an unknown
child. These are, however, not examples of the Christian doctrine that "he who loseth his life for my sake shall, find it," but
rather fulfillments of the pagan conception in which the most
exquisite and noble emotion is felt in giving up that life for
others. But Pater's paganism proved a less permanent influence
than the example he set of highly sensitized observation, wide
critical sympathies, and fastidious expression of his subtle responses to a great variety of personalities and works of the
imagination.

CHAPTER XV

The Nineteenth Century

THE NOVEL

THE HISTORY of the novel in the nineteenth century presents exceedingly difficult problems in discrimination and clarification. An extremely large number of novels achieved wide popularity with an ever growing audience of readers. While certain well established types of novels continued to appear, numerous new combinations of the basic fictional elements—plot, character, and setting—and of the possible tones—realistic, romantic, satirical, and didactic—make classification difficult and the lines of development highly complex.

A first step toward elucidating the history of the nineteenth-century novel is the demarcation of three fairly distinct generations of novelists, the first, led by Austen and Scott, the second, dominated by Dickens and Thackeray, and the third, headed by Meredith and Hardy. Each of these generations can be distinguished from the others by the types of novels written, the degree of purity with which the types were preserved, and the extent to which novelists confined their activity to a specific genre or experimented with a number of forms of the novel.

During the first generation of the century, three distinct types of novels emerged—the romantic-historical novel, the novel of manners, and the realistic social novel or novel with a purpose. As the century passed, however, each of these types underwent modification, first, from one or another of the other types, and second, from external influences in the life of the period. The romantic novelist, for example, found in the increased knowledge of the past and of alien cultures material which the vogue of realism encouraged him to treat with something of the historian's cautious fidelity to fact. Similarly, the novelist of manners tended to abandon the treatment of the circumscribed lives of the upper-middle class or the aristocracy, and to extend his canvas to include the life of the army, the Church, politics, and industry. Under the influence of the social novelist, he frequently deepened his tone from irony to satire. Finally, the social novelist found rich material in the growing awareness of the economic evils of the time, in the attempt to eliminate them, and in the conflict between traditional belief and scientific scepticism. Since the zeal for reform had its roots in an essentially romantic conception of the relationship between moral man and immoral society, it is not surprising that many of the social novels contain a strong infusion of romanticism along with their avowed realism.

The work of Maria Edgeworth (1767–1849) not only forms a link between the eighteenth- and the nineteenth-century novels of manners but also illustrates the tendency of the novel of this type to develop a social purpose. *Maria Edgeworth* She was a follower of Miss Burney in the effort to paint contemporary society. Like her predecessor, she shared in the rather shallow social purpose of the eighteenth century; her general aim, as set forth in the introduction to her novel *Patronage* (1814), "the inculcation of simplicity and morality in an artificial and recklessly frivolous age," is one which Addison would have applauded. But her purpose was often more definite than this, and in several particulars her work suggested the course which the novel was to take in the future. Her long residence in Ireland interested her in social conditions in that island, and she wrote earnestly to improve them. *The Absentee* (1812) is both a satire against the Irish landlord who ruins himself in London society and a moving picture of the evils which his folly brings on his native land. In Ireland, too, Miss Edgeworth had an opportunity to study life in what to her readers were remote conditions. Her first and best story, the little masterpiece called *Castle Rackrent* (1800), is the account of the fortunes of a decaying family, as seen through the shrewd eyes and told by the witty Irish tongue of an old servant. It had the distinction of suggesting to Sir Walter Scott that true local color could be made as effective a background as false, and that the romantic interest could be united with an effort to portray life as it is.

The first generation of the nineteenth century produced in Jane Austen the supreme practitioner of the novel of manners. *Jane Austen*   Unlike Miss Edgeworth, whose novels represented a considerable range of social experience, Miss Austen exploited with unrivalled expertness the potentialities of a seemingly narrow mode of existence. From the outset she limited her view to the world that she knew and the influences that she saw at work. She was the daughter of a clergyman, and except for an occasional visit to a watering-place like Bath or Lyme, she spent her youth in a country parish. Her acquaintance included county families, clergymen, and naval officers—for her brothers were in the navy. The chief business of these people, as Miss Austen saw them, was attention to social duties; their chief interest was matrimony. This world Miss Austen represents in her novels; outside of it she never steps. And even in this petty world she takes account chiefly of its pettiness. The great things of life, passion, and moral purpose, the interests of the artist, the lover, the saint, may as well be presented on a small stage as on a large one, as well amid the society of a cathedral city as in London; but these things did not enter into Miss Austen's experience, and she did not have insight or imaginative sympathy enough to carry her beyond her own observation. There is scarcely any feeling for external nature in her stories, except in *Persuasion,* the latest of them. There is little passion; the language of emotion is usually forced and conventional. "Sense is the foundation on which everything good may *Her Limitations*   be based," she says in *Sense and Sensibility.* Her view of evil is superficial. One suspects that her estimate of life was not very different from that expressed by Mr. Bennet in *Pride and Prejudice:* "For what do we live but to make sport for our neighbors and to laugh at them in our turn?"

But if her range was thus limited, within it she was supreme. Absolutely sure of her material, undistracted by external interests, she wrote with a singular freedom from un-*Her Excellence*   certainty; and her novels have, in consequence, an exactness of structure and a symmetry of form which are to be found more often in French literature than in English. Of this precision *Pride and Prejudice* is an admirable example. Here the plot is the chief interest; simple, but pervasive; controlling every incident, but itself depending for its outcome upon the development or revelation of the principal characters. Surrounding these characters is the world of provincial folk which Miss Austen handled brilliantly—cynical Mr. Bennet and his fatuous wife; Mary Bennet the pedant, and Lydia the flirt; Mr. Collins the type of pretentious conceit, and Sir William Lucas of feeble dullness. These "humors" Miss Austen develops chiefly through her wonderful faculty for saying the thing appropriate to the character at the moment. Not only is the proper sentiment caught, but the turn of phrase, the manner, almost the modulation of the voice. In the sustained scenes between the more developed characters where the dialogue is more highly charged, Miss Austen shows dramatic power of a high order. One of the best of these scenes is that between Elizabeth Bennet and Lady Catherine de Burgh, in which Elizabeth like a good swordsman, light on her feet and ever ready, completely disarms her lumbering opponent. Miss Austen's later stories, *Mansfield Park* and *Emma,* are longer and slightly more elaborate than *Pride and Prejudice,* but in them the essentials of her art are still the same; a well-defined story, growing naturally out of the influence of character on character, and developed in the midst of a society full of the mild humors of provincial life.

Sir Walter Scott's tribute to his distinguished contemporary is still worth quoting: "That young lady had a talent for describing the involvements, feelings, and characters of ordinary life which is to me the most wonderful I have ever met with. The big bow-wow I can do myself like anyone going, but the exquisite touch which renders commonplace things and characters interesting from the truth of the description and the sentiment is denied me." His evaluation of his work, as well as of that of his rival, still holds. In the "big bow-wow" type of historical romance, Scott is still without a rival.

Scott, who was born in 1771, began his career as a novelist in middle life. It was not until he was forty-three that, finding his vogue as a poet threatened by Byron's popularity, he finished a tale that he had begun some nine years before. This was published anonymously in 1814 under the name *Waverley,* a title which was applied to the long series of novels which followed. Some of these, like *Guy Mannering* (1815), *Old Mortality* (1816), *The Heart of Midlothian* (1818), deal with Scotland; others, like *Ivanhoe* (1819), *Kenilworth* (1821), *The Fortunes of Nigel* (1822), are concerned with English history; several, like *Quentin Durward* (1823) and *The Talisman* (1825), transfer the scene to the Continent. In 1826 a printing-house, of which Scott was a member, failed for £130,000, the whole of which debt he felt bound to assume. He wrote his latest books to earn money to discharge this obligation, and had actually paid more than half when he died in 1832. The rest was paid by the sale of the copyrights on his earlier books.

Sir Walter Scott

Scott's life was a blending of the old and the new. He tried to be both a feudal lord and a modern business man, and both attempts are curiously connected with his literary career. He wrote partly for the pleasure of expressing in fiction the feudal ideal that he sought to realize in his life at Abbotsford, partly for the money with which to sustain that experiment. Some of his success in his own day may be attributed to the fact that his practical interests were those which his fellow men could comprehend. Scott was not a romanticist in the sense in which Coleridge was, or Shelley. He did not desire spiritual freedom; he was not conscious of the trammels of an ordered, conventional life; he had no dislike for the political and social world as it existed, no leanings toward revolution. But, on the other hand, he had in his blood an ardent love for Scotland, and an intimate sympathy with Scotsmen; he had, too, a fascinated view of the past. Thus he represented the simple, permanent elements of romanticism, the elements which his public were prepared to accept; and thus to an audience which neglected Wordsworth and flouted Shelley, Scott became the prophet of the new literary faith.

Scott's Romanticism

His native land and its people Scott learned to know at first hand, in his frequent journeys through the Border Country and the Highlands. He was the first British novelist to make a background actually studied from nature a pervasive and essential

element in his work. His descriptions of scenery are, it is true,
old-fashioned in method, unreasonably long, and over-detailed;
but they have an exact and vivid realism that goes
far to reward the reader's patience. Moreover, the   *His Use*
frequency with which the place determines the   *of*
event shows that in Scott's drama setting is a vital   *Setting*
element, not a mere decorative drop-curtain which interrupts
the action.

The natural background in Scott's work is, however, less
wonderful than the human. It is noteworthy that, even as early
as *Waverley*, his first novel, Scott recognized that
his chief strength lay in his knowledge of Scottish   *His Char-*
types. After some hesitation at the outset of the   *acters*
story, he starts his hero for Scotland, and plunges him into a
society composed of Baron Bradwardine, Laird Balmawhapple,
and Baillie Macwheeble, with David Gellatley and Old Janet
for dependents. These local types, which Scott drew so abundantly, are treated broadly for the humor and the pathos of
humanity warped by circumstances into a hundred fantastic
forms, but capable of sometimes throwing itself into an attitude of noble disinterestedness, of dignified endurance, or of
tragic despair. When the historic drama of the rising of 1745,
which draws Waverley into its sweep, has played itself out, and
the pale love-story has been tamely concluded, the figure that
remains with us as we close the book is that of Evan Dhu, the
humble follower of the Highland chief Vich Ian Vohr, standing at the condemnation of his master, and pledging himself
and six of the clan to die in his stead. "If the Saxon gentlemen
are laughing," he said, "because a poor man, such as me, thinks
my life or the life of six of my degree is worth that of Vich Ian
Vohr, it's like enough they may be very right; but if they laugh
because they think I would not keep my word, and come back
to redeem him, they ken neither the heart of a Hielandman nor
the honour of a gentleman." Among such types as these we look
for Scott's greatest characters: Edie Orchiltree in *The Antiquary*, Baillie Jarvie in *Rob Roy*, Peter Peebles in *Redgauntlet*,
and many more who stand out from the novels as complete and
substantive figures in which the race of Scotchmen has perma-

nently expressed itself. Only once, however, did Scott trust entirely to this element of native strength. In *The Heart of Midlothian* he dispensed altogether with the aristocratic heroine, threw aside the conventional plot, and wrote instead the story of Jeanie Deans, one of the most human women in all fiction.

It is, moreover, through indigenous types that Scott made his most impressive appeals to the sense of terror and mystery, already awakened in the reading public by the Gothic romancers. The fantastic figures which start out of the background, Madge Wildfire in *The Heart of Midlothian*, Meg Merrilies in *Guy Mannering*, and Norna of the Fitful Head in *The Pirate*, constitute far more powerful romantic elements than are afforded by his rather timid use of the supernatural.

The material which Scott gained at first hand from the Scotland of his own day he supplemented by a very diligent and
His Love of the Past human, if somewhat unscientific, antiquarianism. In his childhood he delighted to hear of the past from survivors of it. Of his mother's conversation he wrote: "If I have been able to do anything in the way of painting the past times it is very much from the studies with which she presented me." Later he drew on old books and letters to supply what family tradition failed to furnish. Such intercourse with the past widened his knowledge of men, and gave him material for his historical portraits. It also provided him with many of those incidents by means of which he gives to a character or to a scene its final reality. Scott was often slipshod in putting his stories together, but he was consummate in his power to place his characters in a picturesquely significant setting, and to draw from the interplay between his
His Use of Incident persons and his scene action so appropriate to the dramatic situation that it seems inevitable. A remarkable instance of this faculty occurs in *Old Mortality*, where Morton visits Burley in the cave reached by a single tree trunk bridging the chasm of a waterfall. As Morton approaches he hears the shouts and screams of the old Covenanter, in whom religious fury has become insanity; and at length he sees the fearful figure of Burley in strife

with the fiends which beset him. The effect of threatening
scenery and of the terror of madness is brought to a focus, as it
were, at the instant when Burley sends the tree crashing into
the abyss, leaving Morton to jump for his life.

Scott's stronghold was the period of Scottish history to which
a living tradition gave him access, that is, the century before his
birth. Here his historical portraits are wonderfully
definite; and his presentation of historical movements like that of the Covenanters or the Jacobites,
His Use of History
as seen in the high light of individual experience, is full of
insight and imagination. As he exhausted this material, or felt
the need of stimulating his audience with variety, he went farther and farther afield, and relied more and more on formal
history for his material. In his English and continental novels,
inspiration and research never quite took the place of what was
almost first-hand knowledge in the Scottish. Yet his treatment
of Richard's crusade in *The Talisman,* or of Louis XI's struggle
with Charles the Bold in *Quentin Durward,* or of Queen Elizabeth's coquetries in *Kenilworth,* testify to his power of using
history to give interest and significance to his action and characters, or, in other words, of making it contributory to the art of
fiction.

In the history of the English novel, the second generation of
the nineteenth century can be distinguished from the first generation by the increase in the number of major and minor novelists and by their eclecticism, since almost none of the writers to
be considered confined his work to a single type of fiction. In
this period, also, the historical novel declined in favor, and the
social novel and the novel of manners vied with each other for
the first place in the affection and esteem of readers. Whether
or not the decline in the popularity of the historical novel was
due to the overtowering figure of Scott, the mode was still so
attractive to both novelists and readers that nearly every major
novelist felt some compulsion to attempt at least once this difficult genre. One has only to recall such titles as Bulwer-Lytton's
The Last Days of Pompeii (1834), Thackeray's *Henry Esmond*
(1852), Kingsley's *Westward Ho!* (1855), Dickens's *A Tale
of Two Cities* (1859), Reade's *The Cloister and the Hearth*

(1861), and Eliot's *Romola* (1863), to realize the persistent appeal of historical fiction. But this list of familiar titles also suggests the modification the historical novel underwent during this period. Not only is it more carefully documented than many of the historical novels of the first generation, but it is likely to be combined—as in *Henry Esmond* and *Romola*, for example—with a subtle psychological or moral investigation.

Of the older novelists of the second generation, Benjamin Disraeli, Earl of Beaconsfield (1804–1881), cultivated most

Benjamin Disraeli

assiduously a single novelistic type, the social novel. Disraeli began his career with the publication of *Vivian Grey* (1826), in which a new type of hero is presented, the man of the world—a sign that the sinister, romantic rebel of Byron's tragedies had had his day. He continued to write novels of politics in which his own ambition is reflected and his later political program is expounded, as in *Coningsby* (1844) and *Sybil, or The Two Nations* (1845).

In *Coningsby,* Disraeli had a three-fold purpose: to satirize contemporary politics, to emphasize the importance of the Church to the development of England, and to defend the Jew. The book sets forth clearly his dislike of ultra-conservatism, on the one hand, and of whiggery and utilitarianism, on the other. The hero, Harry Coningsby, the orphan grandson of the Marquis of Monmouth, becomes a close friend of Oscar Millbank, the son of Monmouth's bitterest enemy. From his friend, Coningsby acquires political opinions so distasteful to his grandfather that he is disinherited. Launched on a career as a barrister, he is elected to Parliament through the influence of the elder Millbank, marries the latter's daughter, and is restored ultimately to his family fortune. The book is interesting not merely for its portraits of contemporary public figures and for its forceful political satire but also for its expression of Disraeli's political and social views. In *Sybil,* Disraeli painted a terrible picture of the lives of the contemporary working class as the background for the love-affair of a young aristocrat, Charles Egremont, and Sybil, the daughter of one of the leaders of the Chartist movement. Even after Disraeli was leader of the Conservative party and Prime Minister he used his leisure, when out of office, to write *Lothair* (1870), in which the effect of the Oxford Movement and the Catholic Reaction on English society is discussed, and *Endymion* (1880). With a large mixture of conventional romantic material, his novels contain social criticism of value and throw light on the political thought of the time.

Among the older novelists of the mid-century, Edward Bulwer-Lytton, Lord Lytton (1803–1873), was the most studiously eclectic. He moved freely over the fields of the romantic novel and the realistic social novel. **Edward** Although his first novel, *Pelham,* marks the re- **Bulwer-** action against Byronism, his other early novels il- **Lytton** lustrate the persistence of sensational elements inherited from the Gothic novels of the late eighteenth century. In *Pelham, the Adventures of a Gentleman* (1828), the hero is a young dandy, who learns worldly wisdom from a Chesterfieldian mother, and who, armed with unlimited conceit and self-possession, brings the world to his feet. According to Bulwer's view, society is too easily conquered to make rebellion worthwhile, and the success of his book proved him right.

In several of his novels, notably in *Pelham* and in *Lucretia* (1846), he plays upon his reader's sense of the terrible, by his pictures of criminal life. But he infuses these pictures with a definite purpose, treating his outlaws as victims of society. *Paul Clifford* (1830), for example, of which the hero is a highwayman, was written "to draw attention to two errors in our penal institutions, viz.:—a vicious prison discipline and a sanguinary penal code." Another sensational element in Bulwer's work is a pseudo-scientific use of the supernatural, of which *Zanoni* (1842) furnishes the most elaborate example.

A healthier romanticism is apparent in the series of historical novels that Bulwer wrote under the influence of Scott. In 1834, after elaborate preparation, he published *The Last* **His** *Days of Pompeii,* and later *Rienzi* (1835), *The* **Historical** *Last of the Barons* (1843), and *Harold* (1848). **Novels** In all of these he tried, much more consciously than Scott, to make the novel serve the purpose of the historian. *The Last Days of Pompeii* recounts the love affair of two

young Greeks, Glaucus and Ione, at the time of the great earth-
quake that destroyed the city. Their relationship is complicated
by the intrigues of Arbaces, Ione's villainous guardian, and by
the unrequited love of the blind girl, Nydia, for Glaucus. At
the time of the city's destruction Nydia saves the lives of the
lovers by leading them to the sea in safety. The book is noteworthy not only for its sharply contrasted characterization but
also for its accurate and detailed descriptions of ancient Greek
life and customs.

Under the influence of Thackeray's success Bulwer turned to
modern life in *The Caxtons, a Family Picture* (1849) and *My
Novel, by Pisistratus Caxton* (1853). *The Caxtons*
His Later is the chronicle-history of a large and prosperous
Works English family. Told by young Pisistratus Caxton,
it recounts his unhappy romance with Fannie Trevanion, his
stormy career at the University of Cambridge, and his accidental
discovery of old family secrets in which his father and uncles
are concerned. Its interest lies in its sensitive depiction of family
life and its incidental satire of English politics. There are effective characterizations of Pisistratus's father, Austin, a gentle
old scholar, who is devoting his life to the writing of a great
historical treatise, and of his uncles, Jack, an unsuccessful financial speculator, and Roland, a boastful military officer. Altogether, despite the affected, the sensational, and the sentimental
elements in Bulwer's novels, his versatility and his long-con-
tinued energy make him a useful sign of the shifting literary
currents during the middle years of the century.

Charles Dickens (1812–1870) must always be one of the most
striking figures in the history of English literature, on account
Charles of the dramatic nature of his success. He started
Dickens from the humblest position in life; when he was ten
years old he was at work in a blacking warehouse,
sleeping beneath a counter, and spending his Sundays with his
family in Marshalsea Prison, where his father was confined for
debt. Yet before he was thirty he was a great writer; and before he was forty, a notable public man. No writer in English
ever gathered with a fuller hand the rewards of the literary
calling. It is true, other writers have made more money, or have

won knighthood or the peerage; but none has had in his life-time so wide and intensely loyal a personal following; none has had in addition to money, friends, and fame, the peculiar tribute which came to Dickens from vast audiences gathered together, not once or twice, but hundreds of times, in scores of cities, to testify by "roaring seas of applause" to his personal triumph. In middle life Dickens began to give semi-dramatic public readings from his works, and these grew to be his chief interest. The strain and excitement wore him out. It is a circumstance perhaps as tragic in its way as that which shadows the close of Scott's life, that this personal triumph was the direct cause of Dickens's death.

Dickens's peculiar triumph calls attention to the prime fact in his authorship, his nearness to his public. He began his career as a reporter, the literary calling which is most im- *His* mediately of the people. He was later an editor of *Training* magazines, and even, for a short time, of a great daily newspaper. But though necessity made him a journalist, he wished to be an actor. As a young man he tried to get a position at Covent Garden Theatre. For years he was the leading spirit in a famous company of amateurs who played in various cities of England and, as we have seen, his chief interest came to be his readings. These two professional instincts account for much in Dickens's work. As a reporter and as an editor he studied his public; as an actor he taught himself to play upon it, through his writings and his dramatic readings from them, with incomparable skill.

It was while Dickens, then about twenty, was a reporter that he began to write sketches of London life for various news-papers. From his success with these came, in 1836, *"Pick-* an engagement to write the letterpress for a series *wick* of cartoons representing the humors of sporting *Papers"* life. For this purpose he invented the "Pickwick Club," which at once made a popular hit. The death of the artist who was engaged upon the drawings left Dickens free to widen the scope of the adventures of the club, and to add other characters without stint. The complete result was a great book, formless as to plot, crowded with humorous figures. These figures are given with broadly exaggerated traits, as if Dickens had always in mind the cartoon which was to accompany the text. They talk freely, not to say inexhaustibly, and all differently. But the author's chief resource is his faculty for bringing his caricatures into contact with the actual world, in situations that expose their oddities in high relief. Mr. Tupman as a lover, Mr. Winkle as a duellist or a sportsman, Mr. Pickwick in a breach-of-promise suit with the Widow Bardell, the Pickwick Club contending with a recalcitrant horse, the Reverend Mr. Stiggins drunk at a temperance meeting—these incongruities are narrated in a style always copious, but rapid and piquant.

In his later novels Dickens improved on his first attempts. He continued to be a caricaturist, to rely on distortions and *His Humors* exaggerations of feature or manner; but his range of effects became broader, and his figures more signifi- cant. Sairy Gamp, in *Martin Chuzzlewit* (1844), haunted by the mythical Mrs. Harris, Micawber, in *David Cop- perfield* (1850), "waiting for something to turn up," 'umble Uriah Heap, sanctimonious Pecksniff, cheerful Mark Tapley, all have distinct individuality, yet all illustrate so conveniently common attitudes and habits of mind that we use their names freely as categories.

In *Pickwick Papers* Dickens is purely a humorist; in the novels which followed he enlarged enormously the range of his *His Darker Characters* power over his audience. By the use of the method which he had employed in his humors, he created figures of a different sort, to excite not laughter but loathing and terror. In the portrayal of these types also he gained subtlety with practice. Fagin and Sykes in *Oliver Twist* (1838), Quilp, the dwarf, in *The Old Curiosity Shop* (1841), are examples of rather crude methods of exciting physical horror; monstrous as they are, they do not haunt the reader with the terrible suggestion of inhumanity that lurks be- hind the placid, smiling face of Mme. Defarge in *A Tale of Two Cities* (1859), as she sits in front of the guillotine, knit- ting, and counting the heads as they fall. In the novels just men- tioned Dickens showed again his fertility in inventing situa- tions, using his histrionic power as freely in melodrama as in

farce. The behavior of Fagin at his trial and in prison is the
creation of an actor, careful to make every gesture, every expression, tell on his audience.

A third type of character which Dickens developed, and
which in his time made immensely for his popularity, was that
of the victim of society—usually a child. The possibilities of childhood for romance or pathos had   *His*
been suggested by Shakespeare, by Fielding, and   *Humani-*
by Blake; but none of these had brought children   *tarianism*
into the very centre of the action, or had made them highly individual. In his second novel Dickens centred his story in a
child, Oliver Twist, and from that time forth children were
expected and necessary characters in his novels. Little Nell,
Florence Dombey, David Copperfield, stand out in celestial
innocence and goodness, in contrast to the evil creatures
whose persecution they suffer for a season. And further, they
represent in most telling form the complaint of the individual
against society. For with Dickens the private cruelty which his
malign characters inflict is almost always connected with social
wrong. Bumble's savage blow at Oliver Twist asking for more
food, Squeers's wicked exploitation of his pupils in *Nicholas
Nickleby* (1839), are carried back and laid at the door of society. The championship of the individual against institutions,
which had been a leading theme of later eighteenth-century
literature, had been checked by the reaction against the French
Revolution; but in Dickens's day the "redress of wrongs" had
again become a great public movement. This phase of romantic
political liberalism was reflected in a popular distrust of governmental methods, a deep-seated reaction against organized
authority. To this feeling Dickens constantly appealed. In
nearly all his books there is an attack upon some legal or social
evil: in *Oliver Twist* upon the workhouse; in *Bleak House*
(1853) upon the chancery courts; in *Little Dorrit* (1857) upon
imprisonment for debt. Undoubtedly there was something theatrical in Dickens's adoption of social wrong as a theme for fiction, but there was also much that was sincere. He had himself
known the lot of the persecuted; at the root of his zeal for reform was the memory of his own bitter childhood.

The types of character already discussed were sufficient to sustain the movement of Dickens's earlier books. These were usually simple in structure. His favorite authors were Smollett and LeSage, and he seems to have been disposed to build his own novels like theirs, on the picaresque plan. In most of them we begin with the hero in childhood, and follow his personal adventures into the thick of a plot involving the popular romantic material of the day, kidnapping, murder, mob-justice, and other incidents of criminal life. When the author needs the usual characters of the novel, a pair of conventional lovers, for example, he gives us figures as weak and unnatural as were many of Scott's titular heroes. In his later books, however, he gained the power of constructing elaborate plots, and of creating characters of heroic dignity and tragic intensity, such as Sidney Carton in *A Tale of Two Cities,* and Lady Dedlock in *Bleak House.* These are the most enduringly powerful of his novels, but they are not those upon which his fame rests. Dickens is remembered not as a dramatic artist in the novel form, but as a showman of wonderful resources. He is master of a vast and fascinating stage, crowded with farcical characters; with grotesque and terrible creatures, more devils than men; and with the touching forms of little children. The action is sometimes merry, sometimes exciting, sometimes pathetic. We have laughter, and horror, and tears; but the prevailing atmosphere is one of cheerfulness, as befits a great Christmas pantomime.

His Plots

Charles Reade (1814–1884) shines with the reflected light of Dickens. Like Dickens, Reade had the temperament of a romanticist; but beginning his career at a time when realism was the literary shibboleth, he made it his effort not only to discover the romantic elements in real life and to treat them in the romantic manner, but also to satisfy himself and his readers of their truth by elaborate documentary evidence. Reade had an immense fondness for the stage, chiefly, perhaps, because in the actor's life he found the romance which he was always seeking. He wrote numerous plays, and one of his best-known stories, *Peg Woffington* (1853), is a story of eighteenth-century stage life. His serious discipleship of Dickens appears in his social novels. *Put Yourself in His Place* (1870)

Charles Reade

is a story designed to reflect the wrongs which trades-unions inflicted upon the individual workman. In *A Terrible Temptation* (1871) he introduces a representative of himself, a novelist, a student of modern social conditions, to whom the oppressed have recourse, and who uses his power to enlist public sympathy in their behalf and to overawe the oppressor. Reade's masterpiece is *The Cloister and the Hearth* (1861), a novel of the period of the Renaissance, with the father of the great Erasmus as its hero. To the construction of this work Reade brought his laborious method of getting up his facts, but in spite of its learning the book is one of the three or four best historical novels since Scott.

Dickens and Reade had in common their essentially romantic temperaments, their tendency to seek literary effects of the sentimental kind, and their disposition to regard the novel seriously as a social instrument. A vigorous reaction against these practices was led by William Makepeace Thackeray (1811–1863). Thackeray *W. M. Thackeray* was an Anglo-Indian, born in Calcutta. After a short career at Cambridge, and some desultory art study, he turned to literature. His first work consisted of light essays, sketches of travel, and burlesques, in which the weaknesses of the romantic school are cleverly hit off in imitations of Scott, Bulwer, and Disraeli. His first long story, *Catherine* (1839–40), is the picture of a female rogue, drawn on the picaresque plan with unsympathetic realism, and intended as an antidote to the sentimental treatment of criminals like Bulwer's Clifford, and Dickens's Nancy in *Oliver Twist. Barry Lyndon* (1844), likewise a picaresque story, is a brilliant account of the exploits of an eighteenth-century adventurer.

Thackeray gave his realistic theories larger scope in *Vanity Fair,* written between 1846 and 1848. This, like most of his succeeding novels, he published in parts, seldom supplying the matter for the forthcoming chapter until the last possible moment. Naturally, the story is not a model of structure, but this rather loose method of working suited not only Thackeray's *The Structure of His Novels* temperament but also his artistic problem. For Thackeray's realism is that of the observer, not that of the analyst. He never isolates a single case and studies it with long, close patience. On the contrary, he sees life with the wide vision of a man of the world. To have confined his multitude of characters within the limits of a carefully built plot, would have introduced an element of unreality into his book. The action of *Vanity Fair* revolves about the heroines, Amelia Sedley and Becky Sharp. The two women in their opposition are admirable foils; Amelia mild and helpless—a parasite, the author calls her—living on the chivalrous protection of Dobbin; Becky, keen and competent, making her world for herself, levying tribute on every man who crosses her path. The two stories begin together, and Thackeray supplies a link between them later in Jos Sedley; but in the end he gives over the attempt to unite them, and lets the two sets of characters diverge in his novel as they would have done in life.

Thackeray's training was that of the essayist, and, like Fielding, he uses his story as a support for comment on human life *His Atti-* and nature. In *Vanity Fair* he introduces his char-*tude To-* acters as puppets whom he as showman can manip-*ward the* ulate as he pleases to illustrate his views. The scep-*World* tical persiflage with which he treats his characters indicates his attitude toward the world which he pictures. In the metaphor of the puppets lurks a gleam of the satire which Swift showed in his sketch of society as Lilliput. The title, too, *Vanity Fair*—Bunyan's fair, "where is sold all sorts of vanity, and where is to be seen juggling, cheats, games, plays, fools, apes, knaves, rogues, and that of every kind"— suggests something of contempt if not of bitterness. The roguishness and weakness of Thackeray's puppets have long been grounds for calling their showman a cynic, but Thackeray's cynicism is strongly tempered with tolerance and with pity. Dickens draws his pathos from the spectacle of ideal innocence exposed to the evils of the world; Thackeray makes no less pitiful the sorrows of men and women who are themselves sinful, weak, and stupid. Becky's husband, Rawdon Crawley, is not an admirable figure; yet we are sorry for him. George and Amelia are both in their way weak characters; yet the scene of their parting is suffused with tenderness. Thackeray is merciful toward the feeble, flawed souls that he portrays, because gentleness was a part of his nature. Disillusioned as to most of the pretentious virtues of the world, he still believed in goodness, in the instinctive kindness of one being to another. He exemplified this belief in his books as in his life.

The success of *Vanity Fair* showed Thackeray where his true power lay, and he lost no time in beginning a second novel to appear in numbers, *Pendennis*. Its appearance was interrupted by Thackeray's illness, however, and the book was not completed until the end of 1850. In *"Pendennis"* *Pendennis,* as in *Vanity Fair,* Thackeray is the moralist, but of a sterner sort. Instead of the figure of the puppet booth, he choses that of the morality play, representing his hero as passing through a series of temptations from the world, the flesh, and the devil, each of which constitutes an episode in the book, and as finally saved by the influence of two good women, his mother and Laura. Thackeray is entirely on their side, and yet he does not hesitate to show us the limitations of their virtue, in their suspicion and cruelty toward Fanny Bolton; and Fanny, pathetic in her renunciation, is reprehensible for the ease with which she consoles herself. Pendennis himself, though saved from the worst consequences of each temptation, is no less ready to fall into the next; and the best example of moral courage is given by the old worldling, Major Pendennis. Of such mixed materials are human nature and the moral life made.

The importance of the historical element in fiction after Scott is shown by the fact that even the petty world of *Vanity Fair* is disturbed by a great national crisis; but Thackeray, instead of using Waterloo to impose dignity and *His Use* splendor upon his story, characteristically gives us *of History* a "back-stairs" view of war. We follow the battle, not in the thought of Napoleon or of Wellington, but in the fears of wretched Jos Sedley, in the hopes of his servant Isidore, and in the calculations of Becky Sharp;—chiefly, but not wholly: for there is poor, almost abandoned Amelia "praying for George, who was lying on his face, dead, with a bullet through his heart." Thackeray is interested in famous events and persons because of the light they throw upon the common affairs of men Even in his historical novels he is a realist, seeking to recall the past, not in distant splendor, but in the actual forms in which it appeared to a contemporary. In *Henry Esmond* (1852), however, as in *Vanity Fair,* Thackeray's own temperament is to be reckoned with. His sympathy with the preceding century gives to his treatment of it a warmth and brilliance which touches the historical realism of this novel with the spirit of poetry.

In *Henry Esmond* we follow the hero's childhood at Castlewood, in the mysterious atmosphere of plotting Papists; and his *"Henry* youth in the London of Queen Anne, where the *Esmond"* persons and names of Addison, Steele, Prior, Swift, Fielding, Atterbury, meet us as casually as those of celebrities today. We see him take part in the victories of Marlborough, and in the daring game which the Pretender played for his crown. The vanished world lives for us in character and in episode; lives with a dignity and richness of conception and style which show Thackeray to have been, when he chose, the greatest artist among the English novelists. In his masterpiece he is writing, not as a careless, rather lazy master of a puppet-show, but in the person of the chivalrous Esmond. Every incident and description, then, must reflect his hero's character in some touch of nobility or of charm. In Esmond's revulsion from Marlborough, in his devotion to Castlewood and his son, in his passion for Beatrix, and in his love for Lady Castlewood, there is the constant revelation of an honorable and loyal man. When he is telling us of the quarrel between Marlborough and Webb, there is that in his manner which reminds us that it is a gentleman's story. When he surrenders his birthright, property, and name, he bears himself with a simplicity and a modesty which are in keeping with a great renunciation. The style itself, adroit in its technical approximation to the manner of the period, is still subtly expressive of Esmond's personality. When he leaves Castlewood or stands at his mother's grave, when he bends beside the body of his dear lord, run through by the villain Mohun, his utterance is perfect in its intimacy, its simplicity, its haunting rhythm. Even in a detail of the picture of Lady Castlewood vanishing from Esmond's sight in anger, Thackeray's distinction is evident. "He saw her retreating, the taper lighting up her marble face. her scarlet lip quivering, and her shining golden hair."

Thackeray's three later novels follow the lines of his earlier three. *The Newcomes* (1853–1855), like *Vanity Fair*, a large canvas of London society, and quite as successful, contains the most delightful of his heroines in Ethel Newcome and the most winning mixture of human weakness and chivalry in Colonel Newcome. *The Virginians* (1857–1859) is a sequel to *Henry Esmond*, and *The Adventures of Philip* (1861–1862) a diluted *Pendennis*.

In his return to realism Thackeray found an industrious follower in Anthony Trollope (1815–1882). The latter adopted his master's flippant view of the novel expressed in *Vanity Fair*, but, unlike Thackeray, he never succeeded as an artist in rising above it. A novel should be written, he says frankly, to amuse young people of both sexes, and there should be nothing too unpleasant in it; at least, he promises the reader that he will never let such a thing happen in a novel of his. Trollope's fame began with a series of novels dealing with clerical life in a cathedral city.

Anthony Trollope

In the first of these, *The Warden* (1855), the central figure is the Rev. Septimus Harding, precentor of Barchester Cathedral and warden of an ancient charitable institution called Hiram's Hospital. The latter position is a sinecure, customarily associated with the precentorship. Harding, a modest and conscientious widower, is considerably disturbed when the office itself and his administration of it are attacked by a public-spirited young doctor, John Bold, who is also the suitor of the younger of Harding's two daughters. In the face of newspaper attacks resulting from Bold's claims, Harding resigns. But when at the behest of Bold's fiancée, the young reformer withdraws his charges, the warden is restored to his position. Encouraged by the success of this novel, which was admired for its exhibitions of "the actuating motives, good and bad, of ordinary men and women," Trollope decided to follow it up with other novels, with the same setting and characters. In *Barchester Towers*, (1857) therefore, he continued his study of ecclesiastical life at Barchester. To the characters in the earlier novel, he added Mr. Proudie, the new bishop, Mrs. Proudie, his shrewish, practical wife, and Mr. Slope, his intriguing chaplain. The action centres in the maneuvers of Mrs. Proudie and Mr. Slope for the control of diocesan affairs. The prize at stake is the wardenship, for which Harding is again a candidate along with Mr. Quiverful, the father of a family of fourteen. Harding loses the election, but Slope's machinations are exposed and he is driven from the scene by the triumphant Mrs. Proudie.

Barchester Towers—generally considered his masterpiece—was followed by *Framley Parsonage* (1861), and by *The Last Chronicle of Barset* (1867). He also produced a series of political novels, and treated various aspects of English commercial and country life. In his wide survey of social conditions in the middle and upper classes of England, he comes nearer than any other English novelist to fulfilling the vast program of the French realists, Balzac and Zola. Trollope was a man of great industry, in every sense a professional novelist, writing a daily allowance, and often keeping two or three novels going at once. Much of his work is perfunctory, but at his best he has a power of creating figures which have an astonishing air of life. Of these Mrs. Proudie, the bishop's wife, who rages through several books, is the most notable.

Thackeray as a realist and moralist had an earnest sympathizer in a writer who was by circumstances a romanticist. Char-

Charlotte Brontë lotte Brontë (1816–1855) grew up in the Yorkshire parsonage of her father, with such experience as came from country boarding-schools, a year in Brussels, and her own family life with its terrible succession of tragedies—the death of her mother, the blindness of her father, the death of her sisters, and the ruin of her brother through dissipation. She and her sisters wrote for their own amusement, inventing scenes and characters to supplement the melancholy resources of the life that they knew.

The first of Charlotte Brontë's novels, *Jane Eyre* (1847), opens with a transcript from the author's own life at boarding-

Charlotte Brontë's Novels school, but the heroine soon passes beyond the world of the author's experience into the romantic realm of her longing and imagination. Undoubtedly, there is much that is second-rate in the story. The hero of Jane's adoration, Rochester, is an impossible character. His mad wife is a literary inheritance from Mrs. Radcliffe.

The incidents reveal almost pathetically Miss Brontë's ignorance of life and her lack of power to measure probability. But the heroine is a genuine woman. Psychologically she is a study of the author's inner life, and her romantic experience is symbolic of the attempt which Charlotte and her sisters made to enlarge and color their oppressive little world with the spaces and splendors of the imagination.

It was the honesty of Miss Brontë's romanticism that made *Jane Eyre* successful both with the critics and with the public. On the advice of critics, Miss Brontë abandoned Gothic machinery in her later books, *Shirley* (1849) and *Villette* (1853), and fell back on the material of her own life in Yorkshire and in Brussels. Nevertheless, these books bear constant witness to the lack of harmony between her artistic purpose and the means which her experience afforded her of carrying out this purpose with success. For while her experience in life was limited, and constantly tended to throw her back on romantic invention, she was in purpose a realist, bent on dealing with things as they are, and on making them better. She dedicated *Jane Eyre* to Thackeray, in terms which show the moral energy which she possessed. Unluckily her life did not bring her into contact with large projects of reform. As a moralist and as an artist it was her fortune to deal, in spite of all her efforts to the contrary, with the petty or the unreal. *Her Later Works*

In one direction Miss Brontë's experience was adequate—in her contact with nature. From her books one comes to know how largely in her life the clouds, the ragged hills, the wide spaces of the Yorkshire moors under sunset or moonlight, made up for the inadequacy of human society and interests. It is true, she has the Gothic trick of creating a sympathetic background to set off the incidents, but in a deeper sense nature enters into the warp and woof of her stories through the part which it plays in the most essential element in them, the inner life of her heroines. *Her Feeling for Nature*

An indisputable genius flowered in the undeservedly neglected poems of Charlotte's sister, Emily (1818–48), and in her single novel *Wuthering Heights* (1848). Despite the over-complicated plot and the awkwardness of having an elaborate and wildly passionate story told by a faithful housekeeper, the

Emily Brontë   novel has gradually come to be recognized as one of the major imaginative creations of the century. Its theme is the devastation wrought upon two generations of the Earnshaw and Linton families by the thwarted love of Heathcliff and Catherine Earnshaw. Heathcliff, a savage orphan, is picked up on the streets of Liverpool and brought to the Earnshaw household on the Yorkshire moors to be reared with the children, Hindley and Catherine. For the girl he develops an intense passion but by her brother Hindley he is humiliated and abused especially after the latter becomes master of the estate. Despite Catherine's deep response to Heathcliff's devotion, she cannot bring herself to marry him, and, stung by his ill treatment and her refusal, Heathcliff leaves Wuthering Heights. Three years later, his fortune made, he returns, to find Catherine married to her gentlemanly neighbor, Edgar Linton. Thenceforth Heathcliff is bent solely on avenging the wrongs he has suffered. He marries Edgar's sister Isabel and treats her shamefully. He precipitates Catherine's death by his violence. Years later, he forces marriage upon his sickly son Linton and Catherine's beautiful daughter, Cathy. But from the grave Catherine continues to call him, and at last in agonized madness he joins her in death. In the history of English fiction, this novel is unique for its dark and thunderous atmosphere and its powerful fusion of inordinately passionate love and hate.

Charles Kingsley (1819–1875) shared the Brontës' serious view of fiction but his position in the world was such as to con-

Charles Kingsley   nect him with larger issues. He was a clergyman, professor of history at Cambridge, a leader in the "Broad Church" movement, the friend of Tennyson, and Carlyle, of whose strenuous philosophy of life he was a sort of popular exponent. In his earlier novels, Kingsley gives a view of the problems which perplexed men's minds in the middle years of the century, the years of the Catholic revival and of Chartism; and he tries to point out a middle course between Catholicism and scepticism in religion, between Toryism and radicalism in politics.

Yeast (1848), Kingsley's first novel, is an account of the experiences of Lancelot Smith, a generous but wayward youth, and his relationships to a variety of "humor" characters. The tale recounts the young hero's loss of his fortune and his sweetheart and his passage into a life dedicated to religion. The book reflects the author's interest in the oppressed laboring class and in the Tractarian movement. Lengthy and somewhat static discussions of these movements delay the movement of the plot. In *Alton Locke* (1850), the tailor poet learns during his apprenticeship to sympathize with the plight of the laboring class. He becomes a Chartist leader, and for his part in a riot is sent to prison. He emerges from this experience a chastened and wiser man. The novel is noteworthy for its vivid pictures of the wretched life of the laboring class in the middle of the nineteenth century. Unfortunately, Kingsley was a disciple of Bulwer in his mingling of romance with realism, and his incidents, though dramatic, are often childishly unconvincing.

In his later work he imposed his social purposes on the historical novel. *Hypatia* (1853) is a study of the struggle between Christianity and paganism, in Alexandria, during the fifth century. *Westward Ho!* (1855) is a vigorous story of the times of Elizabeth, depicting the English contest with Spain by sea and in America. In both Kingsley makes a didactic use of the historical novel, presenting to his countrymen "New foes with old faces," and seeking to develop his ideal of Christian manhood, a union of physical energy and intellectual moderation to which he felt Catholicism was in some way a threat. His last story, *Hereward the Wake* (1866), illustrates the use of the historical novel to stimulate national consciousness. It is an account of the life of the last great English rebel against the Norman conqueror, and is a contribution to the rising tide of national feeling which expressed itself in emphasis upon the Anglo-Saxon heritage of the race.

The religious and social problems of England found a less passionate exponent in Mrs. Elizabeth Gaskell (1810–1865), the wife of a Unitarian clergyman in Manchester. Her life brought her into contact with the industrial and social difficulties growing out of the struggle *Mrs. Gaskell* between master and workman; and these she treated with great skill in *Mary Barton* (1848) and in *North and South* (1855).

Mary Barton is a painfully vivid picture of conditions among the working class during the economic depression which gave the decade the name of the "hungry forties." The heroine's father, a high-minded workman and ardent trade-unionist, shattered by the death from starvation of his wife and son, is further distressed by the unwelcome attentions paid his surviving daughter, Mary, by Henry Carson, the son of a wealthy mill-owner. When Carson is mysteriously murdered, Mary's other suitor, Jem Wilson, is accused of the crime, but he is finally acquitted through the efforts of Mary, to whom her father on his death bed has confessed his guilt. The book is notable for its realistic depiction of the wretchedness and poverty of the laboring class and its vigorous animus against the factory-owners and industrialists.

In *Cranford* (1853), her best-known book, she entered a different field, that of realistic observation for its own sake. *Cranford* is a series of carefully etched portraits and sketches of English village life. The focus of its action is the plight of Miss Matilda Jenkyns on the death of her sister and the loss of her property, and her attempt to earn her living by opening a tea-shop. Her struggle is brought to an end by the return from India of her long-lost brother, Peter, who is fortunately possessed of a modest fortune. The novel is justly famous for the picture it gives of gentlefolk in a sleepy Cheshire town in the early part of the century.

The intellectual and moral life of the period, reflected in the novels of Kingsley and Mrs. Gaskell, is revealed more fully

George Eliot in the work of Mary Ann Evans, or George Eliot. She was born in 1819 and grew up in the years when, under the influence of scientific speculation, the English mind was casting loose from its theological moorings. She was for a time assistant editor of the *Westminster Review*, the organ of the freethinkers; and in this position she met John Stuart Mill, Herbert Spencer, G. H. Lewes, and other liberals. Her irregular union with Lewes and her renunciation of formal Christianity were the two important events of her life, for they imposed upon her the responsibility of counteracting the view held by many that freedom of thought was naturally accompanied by moral laxity. They strengthened her already powerful ethical impulse. In 1857 she wrote: "If I live five years longer, the positive result of my existence on the side of truth and goodness will far outweigh the small negative good that would have consisted in my not doing anything to shock others."

Before this she had begun to experiment with fiction, her first story, "The Sad Fortunes of the Reverend Amos Barton," appearing in *Blackwood's Magazine* in 1856. She added to this story two others of moderate length, and republished all three in 1858 as *Scenes from Clerical Life*. The next year she published her first novel, *Adam Bede,* and it was evident that a new writer and a great one had appeared. Her next story, *The Mill on the Floss* (1860), turns on the refusal of her heroine, Maggie Tulliver, to break the social law for the sake of her own happiness. There followed *Silas Marner* (1861), *Romola* (1863), a historical novel of the time of Savonarola, *Felix Holt the Radical* (1866), *Middlemarch* (1872), and *Daniel Deronda* (1876). Besides these she wrote a number of poems, the longest being *The Spanish Gypsy* (1868). After the death of Lewes in 1878 she married J. W. Cross in 1880, the year of her death.

Her Novels

George Eliot's starting-point in *Adam Bede* was an incident in the life of her aunt, who once accompanied to the scaffold a poor girl condemned for infanticide. This aunt was the original of Dinah Morris, the woman preacher who rides in the hangman's cart with Hetty Sorrel. Hetty's aunt, Mrs. Poyser, is said to show some traits of George Eliot's mother; and Adam Bede was drawn from her father. Indeed, in her realism she was in large measure dependent on the material of her own early life in Warwickshire and Derbyshire. *The Mill on the Floss* abounds in charmingly humorous local types. The elder Tullivers, the Gleggs and the Pullets, and Bob Jakin are as distinct as Scott's minor characters, and as amusing as those of Dickens. In *Romola* she made a scholarly effort to reproduce the past faithfully, but the effort has not the reality of her earlier books. In *Middlemarch* she returned to the provincial life of the Midland counties and achieved conspicuous success with such characters as the Garths and the Vincys. The chief sign of decline in George Eliot's last novel, *Daniel Deronda,* is the attempt to re-

George Eliot as a Realist

place these vigorous living beings with badly imagined puppets like the Meyricks. She had used up the material of her youth, and found nothing in her brilliant life of culture and travel to take its place.

Adam Bede is the most natural of George Eliot's books, simple in problem, direct in action, with the freshness and

As a Psychologist

strength of the Derbyshire landscape and character and speech in its pages. Its successor, *The Mill on the Floss* (1860), shows signs of a growing perplexity on the part of the author, of a hesitation between her art and her message. For George Eliot was more than an observer; she was also a scientist and a moralist. She was not content to picture human life as it appears. She tried to pierce behind the shows of things, and to reveal the forces by which they are controlled. Accordingly she analyzes her characters. In the case of the simple types this analysis takes the form of comment, rapid, incisive, and convincing. She tells us, for example, that Mrs. Tulliver was like the goldfish who continues to butt his head against the encircling globe; and at once the type of cheerful incapacity to learn by experience is fixed before us forever. In the case of the more conscious, developed characters, her analysis is more elaborate and more sustained. For her heroines George Eliot drew largely upon her own spiritual experience, and this personal psychology she supplemented by wide reading, especially in the literature of confessions. In this way she gained an extraordinary vividness in portraying the inner life. Her most characteristic passages are those in which she follows the ebb and flow of decision in a character's mind, dwelling on the triumph or defeat of a personality in a drama where there is but one actor. Such a drama is that which Maggie Tulliver plays out in her heart, torn between the impulse to take her joy as it offers, and the unconquerable conviction that she cannot seek her own happiness by sacrificing others.

It is to be noted further that George Eliot never lets her case

As a Moralist

drop with the individual analysis. She always strives to make her case typical, to show that the personal action and the results for both the individual and society accord with general laws. Thus, in *Middlemarch,* Eliot illustrates through her account of the lives of two noble characters, Dorothea Brooke and Tertius Lydgate, the crushing of idealism by associations with mean-spirited or materialistic personalities. In both instances, their partners in marriage betray the high purposes ot the genuinely admirable characters. Tito's degeneration in *Romola* and Gwendolen Harleth's humiliation and recovery in *Daniel Deronda* are represented as occurring in obedience to laws of the ethical world, as immutable as those of the physical. This is George Eliot's chief function as a writer, the interpretation of the world in terms of morality. She does not deal with party questions, nor primarily with industrial or social problems. Her ethical motive is a broader one than the emancipation of thought or the formulation of a political program. It is to show how, in obedience to law, character grows or decays; how a single fault or flaw brings suffering and death, and throws a world into ruin; how, on the other hand, there is a making perfect through suffering, a regeneration through sin itself, a hope for the world through the renunciation and self-sacrifice of the individual. "It is a blind self-seeking," she tells us through Dinah Morris, "which wants to be freed from the sorrow wherewith the whole creation groaneth and travaileth," for, as she says again, "those who live and suffer may sometimes have the blessedness of being a salvation." It is this possibility of blessedness which in George Eliot's view is the compensation for evil; that we may

> Be to other souls
> The cup of strength in some great agony

in part makes up for the presence of that agony in the world. Whatever be the scientific value of a system of ethics which makes the service of humanity the highest reason for doing right, or whatever the disparity between the novelist's art and the presentation of such a system, George Eliot's work represents the most subtle and complex development of the novel with a purpose.

In the history of fiction the last generation of the nineteenth century can be distinguished from the first two generations by the comparatively small number of first-rate novelists it produced and by the virtual abandonment by such novelists of the types—the historical novel, the novel of manners, and the social novel—that, alone or in combination, had been popular since the opening of the century. Such novelists as Meredith, Hardy, and James developed complex forms of prose-fiction by skillfully fusing elements earlier novelists had left distinct. Thus, in Meredith and James elements from the novel of manners are combined imperceptibly with searching studies in psychology and morals, and in Hardy romantic elements from the regional novel are fused with a variety of philosophic pessimism. In consequence, the English novel in the third generation of the century attained heights of conscious artistry earlier novelists had rarely achieved.

Although the novels of George Meredith (1828–1909) have the unmistakably individual hall-marks of his philosophy and his style, they also show signs of the influence of his older contemporaries. The traditional novel of manners encouraged his brilliant depiction of upper-class characters, conventions, and conversation. George Eliot's elaborate studies in psychology and morals stimulated his investigations of these aspects of human behavior. The influence of the much-debated doctrine of evolution is apparent in his confident asseveration of man's identity with nature and harmony with it and in his romantic naturalistic ethics. His glowing renditions of natural beauty and his verbal brilliance show the influence of his long poetic apprenticeship.

For Meredith was a poet before he was a novelist, and he became a great one, although the public was very slow to recognize him. He was a personal friend of the Pre-Raphaelites, and from them took over the literary ballad, in which form "The Nuptials of Attila" is his best. His poems possess many of the qualities of his novels. In the "Ode to the Comic Spirit," which he calls "sword of the common sense," he sets forth the part of comedy in awakening the minds of men to the great issues of life. In "A Faith on Trial," with an optimism which reminds one of Browning, he asserts his belief in nature, which has evolved the mind of man from mere sentient life. His finest lyrical poem is "Love in the Valley." This is a genuine pastoral, the exquisite beauty and grace of a girl weaving itself through pictures of nature from dawn to noon and twilight and night, under sun

Mere-dith's Poetry

and rain and wind, amid flowers and birds and country sights and sounds, making a whole of infinite loveliness. Meredith's most remarkable poetic work is *Modern Love* (1862), a series of sixteen-line poems recounting the history of a tragically unhappy marriage. No English poet since Donne has set forth so powerfully the cross-currents of attraction and antipathy in the disastrous relationship of a gifted but mismated pair.

Meredith's first extended piece of prose fiction was an oriental extravaganza, *The Shaving of Shagpat* (1856). His first great novel, *The Ordeal of Richard Feverel,* appeared in 1859, and other works at intervals of two or three years. Of these, *Beauchamp's Career* (1876), *The Egoist* (1879), *Diana of the Crossways* (1885), *One of Our Conquerors* (1891), *Lord Ormont and His Aminta* (1894), and *The Amazing Marriage* (1895) are the most noteworthy.

Meredith, like George Eliot, is a psychologist and moralist. He chooses situations and events from actual life, and analyzes the reaction of his characters with great minuteness. Thus, in *Diana of the Crossways,* he takes a well-known case of a prominent literary woman who sold to a newspaper a political secret intrusted to her by her lover. Meredith boldly imagines all the mental states surrounding such an act, from temptation to retribution. Here, as in all his novels, he tests his characters by their response to the situation, which is often of an unusual, sometimes of a grotesque nature. Even when they fall, even when they suffer defeat, it may be that they show true mettle and are of heroic stuff. Like George Eliot, Meredith is concerned with sins of the self, but whereas George Eliot shows invariably the tragic results of selfishness, Meredith works also through comedy; the one scourges evil-doers; the other makes them ridiculous. *The Egoist* is a comedy in Ben Jonson's sense, as purging in its morality as classical tragedy. The novel is a protracted study of Sir Willoughby Patterne, whose consummate self-satisfaction is justified only in part by his wealth and social position. The plot arises from his attempts to find a wife in every way suitable to his condition. With various candidates, he makes considerable progress until his real nature is discovered. When in humiliation he turns to the intelligent but socially ineligible Laetitia

Meredith's Themes

Dale, she postpones her consent until he has learned to overcome the excessive egotism which has warped his basically admirable character.

Meredith was in open revolt against the realistic school of his day, which held that the object of art was to reproduce life with scrupulous minuteness. He shows this in his selection of unusual situations, in his suppression of detail, and in his emphasis upon the things that are truly significant. While George Eliot seeks to present a fully developed human society, and is at pains to make her characters talk with absolute realism, Meredith concentrates attention upon typical characters, and cares little whether his men and women talk naturally so long as they embody the essential, spiritual truth of humanity. His dialogue is more highly compressed, more heavily loaded with meaning, than it could be in actual life. The same pursuit of the essential makes him abrupt in structure; he shifts the scene suddenly, he drops the thread of his story and picks it up again where he wills, in such a manner as to render it difficult for any but a practiced reader to follow him. Like Browning, instead of presenting his tale in plain, clear narrative, he prefers to give it to us in flashes and half-lights, as it is seen from different points of view. He plays round his story, seeming to miss a hundred strong situations for which the reader actually hungers. But this is the strategy of novel-writing. After pages of skirmishing he at last brings his characters to battle in just that relation in which every force is available. Thus in vital moments Meredith does for his readers, more than any other novelist, what the artist should do—he gives a heightened sense of realities. He does not reproduce life; he does not decorate it; he does not idealize it; but he exemplifies it in types and situations of unusual meaning and power.

Meredith's Style

Like Meredith, Thomas Hardy (1840–1928) achieved a reputation both as novelist and as poet, although most of his poems were not given to the world until after his career as a novelist had ended. He published *Desperate Remedies* in 1871 and *A Pair of Blue Eyes* in 1873. *Far from the Madding Crowd* (1874) and *The Return of the Native* (1878) followed. His wider reputation began, however, with

Thomas Hardy

Tess of the D'Urbervilles (1891), and was established by *Jude
the Obscure* (1896). After that time he devoted himself to
poetry, writing a very large number of lyrics and ballads and a
long poem in dramatic form, *The Dynasts* (1903–1908), in
which he develops themes of the great world struggle centering
about Napoleon.[1]

Hardy's art is in sharp contrast to Meredith's, in both fiction
and poetry. In Meredith's view of life, man is all-important.
The works of man, his society, his consciousness,
and his expression of himself, are the great facts   *Contrast
of the world. Man is indeed held down and sacri-   with
ficed, by his own mistakes and by those of his   Meredith*
fellows; but he can rise against this human perverseness, attack
it, and overthrow it, or die valiantly in the attempt. The struggle
of humanity is one of a man with men, or of a woman against
a world of men, and is always capable of yielding glorious victory. This hope gives brightness to all of Meredith's books,
even to the most tragic. In Hardy's world, on the other hand,
man is of the smallest importance; man's intellect will never
bring him nearer to the secret of the universe, to the essential
reason or unreason of things. A man is not thwarted, and in-
sulted by his fellows only; his warfare is not chiefly with them;
the perversity of his lot is not chiefly of their making. It is rather
of the very nature of the world into which he is born, a world
full of the irony of circumstance. It is true, human beings are
often the vehicles of that irony, but Hardy's heroes are not
conquered by human opponents. They fall before they can come
to close quarters with the enemy.

Tess Durbeyfield meets mischance after mischance in a lot
which is not of her choosing. Again and again she is defeated
in her effort to make known to her betrothed what has befallen
her; and when at last on her marriage night she tells him, she is
met by a flat denial of her personality. "You were one person;
now you are another. . . . The woman I have been loving is
not you." Jude the Obscure, checked in his ambition for scholarship, cannot get near the man behind the system which damns
him. He can only write bitter words on the outside wall of the

[1] For a consideration of Hardy's poetry, see pages 412–414.

college which refuses him admittance. Thus Hardy's world is without the element of healthful, hopeful combat. Life is tragic by hypothesis; the irony of circumstance is a recognizable element in the metaphysical constitution of the world. Often the operations of this time-spirit are humorous, with a grim, contemptuous humor that is as bitter as its malice.

In contrast with the insignificance of man, Hardy presents the eternal reality of nature. With him the setting is an element *Hardy's* of first importance, essential in the development of *Use of* the story. Sometimes he treats it, especially in his *Setting* early work, in a poetic and idyllic fashion, as an escape from the tragedy of life—the pastoral escape. But more often he uses it with symbolical meaning, as when he makes the warped, misshapen, stunted trees in *The Woodlanders* suggest "the unfulfilled intention" in human life; or he represents it as the embodiment of the power not ourselves which works man's humiliation. Hardy chooses his human types from those who are closest to nature, those in whom the primitive impulses are strongest. Meredith draws his characters from the walks of life where men and women are most complex, where thought is most active. In Hardy's view, thought is as futile a road to truth as was the Tower of Babel to scale the heavens. Meredith, in his belief in the significant, is continually heightening the individual, pushing his characters beyond human limits. Hardy holds that nothing in man is significant except race, sex, and the great servitude to time and nature; and hence he chooses types that will present these realities most clearly.

Hardy began to write novels when George Eliot was at the height of her fame, and her influence is clearly to be seen in his *Hardy's* work. Like her he is a psychologist and a realist— *Philoso-* bolder, indeed, in his realism, since he had also be- *phy* fore him the examples of the French naturalists, Zola and Maupassant. He is also the product of a scientific age, though law in his universe becomes fatalism, the manifestation of a blind "will to live" which, from the human point of view, often seems malevolent caprice. It is not necessary to identify the pessimistic implications of Hardy's novels with a personal creed. It is enough to say that it was in harmony with the mood of the late nineteenth century, a mood of discouragement and disillusionment resulting in part from the decline of religious faith, and the account of the world and of man's position in it as given by science. Just as the influence of Kant and the romantic philosophers contributed to the romantic literature of the early part of the century, so the influence of Schopenhauer, with his presentation of life as the result of a blind "will to live" manifesting itself ruthlessly in defiance of man's conscious reason, counted for much in determining the realistic and pessimistic spirit of its close.

The fiction of Henry James (1843–1916) is closer in manner and spirit to Meredith's fiction than to Hardy's. Like Meredith, James was a past master of the novel of manners, although his concern was with not only British but cosmopolitan society. Like Meredith, also, he was *Henry James* constantly preoccupied, not only with society's manners but with its minds and its morals. Unlike Meredith, James showed relatively little concern with the larger philosophical problem of man's relation to nature and the universe. James was born in New York, and spent his early life in Cambridge, Mass., but during his maturity he lived almost entirely in England, and his associations and ideals were those of Europe rather than America. He began his career with essays and stories, publishing his first novel, *Roderick Hudson,* in 1876. This book dealt with a problem which came naturally to James, and which he made peculiarly his own—that of a young American brought into contact with the richer culture and more exacting civilization of Europe. This was the problem, also, of *The American* (1877) and *Daisy Miller* (1879). *The Portrait of a Lady* (1881) is the finest of his earlier works. Here a young American girl, infatuated by the atmosphere of Florence, marries an English resident of that city only to discover the real nature of her despicable husband but to remain faithful to him despite his vileness. *The Tragic Muse* (1890) deals with another problem, the opposition between the call of art and that of success in life through politics and family influence; and *The Awkward Age* (1899) with a still more subtle situation growing out of the presence of a young girl in the midst of a corrupt social environment.

Similar personal problems form the core of such later novels as *The Wings of the Dove* (1902) and *The Golden Bowl* (1904). *The Ambassadors* (1903), of his later masterpieces, returns to the case of the young American, a victim to the charms of Paris, whose family arrive like ambassadors from the new world to negotiate for his deliverance.

Henry James's titles represent works of various length. His exact sense of artistry, indeed, made him adjust the size of his

James's Shorter Stories

canvas to the demands of his material and the effect to be produced. Accordingly, we find his fictions varying from the sketch to two volumes. One form which he made peculiarly his own is that of the novelette or tale in which he treated problems of less magnitude than in his novels. Among his masterpieces in this form are *The Author of Beltraffio, The Madonna of the Future, The Lesson of the Master,* and *The Turn of the Screw.* In this less popular genre James achieved perfection more frequently than any other English practitioner of it.

Henry James early protested against the casual nature of the English novel, of which the typical form is a pseudo-biography,

James's Art

and strove to make it the object of more exact structure and technique. To this end he rewrote many of his earlier novels and stories, and supplied them with prefaces explaining his conception of the problems involved in treating the material. He is thus the chief technician among English novelists and his influence in this matter extends far beyond his immediate audience. James was in close contact with literary movements on the Continent, particularly in France, and wrote much admirable criticism, collected in *French Poets and Novelists* (1878) and *Partial Portraits* (1888), some of the most significant of which bore directly on the art of fiction. He, like Meredith, chose his material from the walks of life where consciousness is most acute, and, unlike the realists, he believed in psychological analysis of characters by the novelist. Accordingly, his novels lack external action. When, however, James's carefully developed situations rise to a climax, his art creates an emphasis that, as in the case of Meredith, satisfies the reader's demand for dramatic and vital action. James's style, like Meredith's, is an instrument skillfully adapted to its purpose, but its refinements and elaborations made little appeal to the larger reading public.

In a sense, then, James is a novelists' novelist. That is to say, among writers of English fiction, he considered the problems of imaginative narrative with the most unwavering seriousness, the most scrupulous discrimination. No other English novelist has devoted so much high thoughtfulness to the problems of point of view and structure, of the infinitely nice adjustment of substance and form, of the exhaustive exploitation of carefully defined themes. In English fiction James is the supreme technician. After him there could be no further development of the well-made novel. Consequently, successors who took seriously the problem of form in fiction were forced to seek by experimentation to find new forms expressive of significances debarred from the fastidious consciousness of Henry James.

CHAPTER XVI

The Nineteenth Century

THE END OF VICTORIANISM

THE VICTORIAN era did not end promptly and exactly with the death of the Queen in 1901. The system of ideas and values which the twentieth century has come to denominate Victorian had been sharply assailed long before the end of the century. Indeed, most of the nineteenth-century writers who are now regarded with admiration—writers as various as Carlyle, Ruskin, and Arnold—made their reputations, and retain them, by their hostility to the values commonly accepted in their time. On the other hand, such writers as Macaulay and Tennyson who accepted uncritically what T. S. Eliot has called the "cheerfulness, optimism, and hopefulness" of the nineteenth century have fallen tremendously in contemporary critical esteem because of the perfection with which they embodied the spirit of the age.

Carlyle, Ruskin, and Arnold had criticized their own time and country for materialism, smugness, æsthetic insensitiveness, and brutality in social and economic relations. As the century drew to its close, an increasing number of voices were raised in protest against one or another feature of the time-spirit. The last decade of the nineteenth century and the first decade of the twentieth can best be understood as a period in which attacks were made on Victorianism from every conceivable point of view. Novelists, dramatists, and poets joined in scrutinizing, criticizing, and usually condemning the great age that was passing. Some of these writers were merely destructive in their attacks; others—like Wells and Shaw—offered ground-plans for a new social order to replace the excessively defective Victorian scheme of things. The outbreak of the First World War and the war itself brought home poignantly to the contemporary consciousness the fact that nineteenth-century ways of life and thought were inadequate and outmoded. What was to take their place was in grave doubt. But, for better or for worse, the complacency and ease, the calm and comfort, the assurance and stability of the old days were gone, and after the war no one could possibly believe that they would ever be recovered.

FICTION

In the late nineteenth and early twentieth centuries, the novel exhibited two tendencies, each of which in some measure represents a reaction from Victorianism. The first of these tendencies —illustrated by such diverse writers as Stevenson, Barrie, Kipling, and Conrad—was motivated by the desire to restore the spirit of romance to the novel. The methods of these writers differed widely, but they were allied in their attempt to escape from the limitations of a drab and stuffy realism by seeking material or modes that would invest their novels with the aura of romance. The second major tendency in the novel is that illustrated by such conspicuous writers as Bennett, Galsworthy, and Wells. These writers regarded the novel as a social document, and in some cases as a medium for propaganda; their aim was to represent the life of their time, not only accurately but critically. For the social novel a distinguished tradition had been established by such nineteenth-century writers as George Eliot, Charles Reade, Charles Kingsley, and even Charles Dickens. But the novelists of the turn of the century differed from their literary ancestors in the severity of their criticism and the depth of their antipathy to the age in which they had grown up and which they chose to depict. On the whole, the social novel won a wider audience in this period and proved a more characteristic form than any of the varieties of romanticism attempted.

In fiction, the early leader in the revival of romantic fiction was Robert Louis Stevenson, who, by the charm of his personality, the elegance of his style, the cheerfulness of his view of life, no less than his gallant and adventurous novels, achieved a remarkable vogue before the close of the nineteenth century.

Stevenson was born in Edinburgh in 1850. After a brief attempt at the study of law he, like Scott, gave himself to literature. His first ventures were critical essays, in
Robert
Louis
Stevenson
which, following the romantic critics, he made
literature a happy hunting-ground for adventure.
He next sought experience of life in the same
spirit. A canoe trip along the rivers and canals of Belgium and
northern France gave him material for *An Inland Voyage*
(1878), and a trip through the Cévennes Mountains supplied
that for *Travels with a Donkey* (1879). A rapid journey across
sea and land to San Francisco to meet his future wife furnished
the subject-matter for *The Amateur Emigrant,* and some of the
sketches in *Across the Plains;* the fruits of his honeymoon in
the Sierras appeared in *The Silverado Squatters* (1883). Tuber-
culosis forced him into a long search for health at Davos Platz,
at Hyères, and in the Adirondacks, and instead of personal
adventure he was obliged to have recourse to imagination.
Treasure Island (1883) is a fascinating tale of piracy and
search for treasure; *Kidnapped* (1886) and *The Master of Bal-
lantrae* (1889) continue this vein. *The Strange Case of Dr.
Jekyll and Mr. Hyde* (1886) is a tale of spiritual adventure,
a scientific fantasy fraught with moral symbolism. In 1890 he
sailed from San Francisco for Samoa, where he spent the last
years of his life, finding in the South Seas new and strange
matter for the *Island Nights' Entertainments* (1893) and *The
Ebb-Tide* (1894). His imagination carried him back to his early
field, Scotland in the eighteenth century, and he wrote *David
Balfour* (1893), a sequel to *Kidnapped,* and was engaged on
two unfinished romances, *St. Ives* and *Weir of Hermiston* at the
time of his death in 1894.

Stevenson was not a novelist by accident. He tried his hand at
plays and poetry, as well as essays, but came to fiction by conscious choice. Not only did he seek for his mate-
Steven-
son's
Theory of
Fiction
rial, but by practice and study he evolved his style,
in the spirit of an artist. For he held the belief that
art, and especially the art of fiction, has a great
function to perform in life. He did not believe that
this function was to reproduce life. He repudiated the theory
that art can "compete with life," in Henry James's phrase, or

that it should be sacrificed to make life better, as in George Eliot's practice. He held that only by reaching its utmost attainable perfection can art perform its true service to life—by enabling men to escape from its superficial commonplace "realities," in which their daily existence must be passed, into realms of spiritual freedom. "Fiction," he maintained seriously, "should be to the grown man what play is to the child." "His life from without may seem but a rude mound of mud; there will be some golden chamber at the heart of it in which he dwells delighted." It is the function of romance to evoke that "golden chamber of a man's dreams."

Stevenson regarded incident as the most important element in fiction. But his practice in his later works shows that he did not satisfy himself with merely inventing surprising adventures and imagining exotic settings. With him human nature and human issues are at the *Steven-son's Art* centre of the developing web of event, and from the most romantic background human character disengages itself in strong, clear forms. Alan Breck on the Scottish moors, in *Kidnapped,* and Wiltshire, in "The Beach of Falesà," are both incontrovertibly actual. Stevenson's romanticism shows itself interestingly, also, in his technical adventuresomeness. His novels and tales are more various and daring in their method and technique than those of any of his predecessors; and on the whole his artistic experiments justify themselves. In firmness and clearness of structure, in devices of description and narrative, and in brilliancy of style, he marks the extraordinary technical advance which the novel has made since the days of Scott.

Stevenson owed his intimate friendship with his readers more perhaps to his essays than to his novels. He was a successor of the romantic essayists of the early century, reminding us of Hazlitt in the range of his subject-matter and the zest with which he reacted to books, cities, pictures, sports, experience of life, and the characters of his fellow men. Underlying all this there was a philosophy quite in harmony with his serious view of the function of romance, a philosophy most definitely stated in two essays in the volume *Across the Plains*—"Pulvis et Umbra," and "A Christmas Sermon." At the outset he accepts the scientific view of the world. "Of the Kosmos, in the last resort, science reports many doubtful things, and all of them appalling." The universe is "space sown with rotatory islands," made of "something we call matter," which "rots uncleanly into something we call life," which in turn preys on itself—"lives tearing other lives in pieces, cramming them inside themselves"

Steven-
son's
Idealism
until "our rotatory island is more drenched with blood . . . than ever mutinied ship." But in man, the final product of this fearful process, we find "one thought, strange to the point of lunacy; the thought of duty; the thought of something owing to himself, to his neighbor, to his God." Nay, the theory of evolution, emphasizing man's kinship with the lower animals, gives ground for believing that something of the same ideal animates all life. Thus he concludes, "God forbid it should be man that wearies in well-doing, that despairs of unrewarded effort, or utters the language of complaint." This is the end to which the religious faith of Tennyson and the moral sanctions of George Eliot have come; but Stevenson's assertion is made as confidently as theirs, though in lower terms, and represents as complete an answer to materialism and pessimism. Stevenson was, in effect, at one with Browning and Meredith in their optimistic striving, and his romantic art, like theirs, may be considered as the collection of instances of the manifestation of such idealism.

The revival of the romance which Stevenson had enthusiastically sponsored was carried forward by a group of fellow-

Sir J. M.
Barrie
Scotsmen of whom Sir James Matthew Barrie (1860–1935) was recognized as chief. Their name, the Kailyard School, that is, the cabbage-patch school, came from the fact that they caught romance in humblest forms, and were adepts in local color.

Barrie was born in 1860 in Kirriemuir. This neighborhood furnished him with material for the local sketches touched with sentiment, in *Auld Licht Idylls* (1888) and *A Window in Thrums* (1889). A bolder use of romance is seen in *The Little Minister* (1891). *Sentimental Tommy* (1896) and its sequel, *Tommy and Grizel* (1900), are psychological studies of a hero who illustrates Stevenson's thesis that the real life is in dreams. *Margaret Ogilvy* (1896) is a beautiful description of Barrie's

early home and a tribute to his mother. Barrie's wide appeal lay
in the fact that his novels illustrated the modulation of the stuff
of realism into the key of romance, even of the fantastic, with
overtones of irony.

A further example of the union between romanticism and
realism in fiction is furnished by Rudyard Kipling (1865–
1936). Kipling was born in India and began his *Rudyard*
career there as a journalist, an experience which *Kipling*
put him in possession of a vast amount of material
which appealed to the body of English readers as a storehouse
of romance, but which the author controlled with the detailed
knowledge of the realist. His first literary success was the result
of his short stories of army, civilian, and native life in India,
many of them originally published in Indian newspapers and
collected in 1888, under the titles, *Plain Tales from the Hills,
Soldiers Three,* and *The Phantom Rickshaw.* There followed
the collections called *Life's Handicap* (1891), *Many Inventions*
(1893), *The Day's Work* (1898), and *Actions and Reactions*
(1909).

Kipling understood thoroughly the art of the short story—
that concentration upon a total effect which distinguishes the
modern short story from the old-fashioned tale. *Kipling's*
His sketches of Indian life are single in purpose, *Art of the*
brief and vivid as flashes of lightning. Their appeal *Short*
is romantic by virtue of their remote material, stir- *Story*
ring the imagination by all that is strange and
haunting. For instance, "The Strange Ride of Morrowby Jukes"
and "The Mark of the Beast" surpass in horror the effects of the
eighteenth-century Gothic novel, and at the same time they are
told with the calm precision of the realist. Moreover, Kipling's
range of effects in these tales is very wide—horror in the two
just mentioned; pathos of childhood in "The Story of Muham-
mad Din," and of love in "Without Benefit of Clergy"; humor
in "My Lord the Elephant"; satiric comedy in "Cupid's Arrows."
In the short stories which followed, Kipling, while he enlarged
his canvas, always maintained complete unity of effect. In "The
Brushwood Boy" (*The Day's Work,* 1898) he entered the
realm of spirit life; in "The Maltese Cat" (*The Day's Work*),

that of animal psychology; in "With the Night Mail" (*Actions and Reactions,* 1909) he gives an imaginatively persuasive account of future communication by aviation. One theme he made peculiarly his own—that of human effort, the intensity of man's toil, the courage of his defiance of the elements, his miraculous achievements. In the stories of *The Day's Work* and in *Captains Courageous* (1897) he wrought the neo-stoic theme of human endurance imperishably into fiction.

Kipling's Longer Stories
Kipling's longer stories, which approach the novel in scope, are less distinguished for excellence in their field. His most successful works of larger dimensions are such books as *Captains Courageous* and *Kim* (1901), in which theme, background, and characters are maintained through a succession of episodes without close connection in plot. Such are his books for children—*The Jungle Books* (1894, 1895), those wonderfully penetrating excursions of the imagination into the field of animal life.

Joseph Conrad
Another example of romance fed by adventure in remote parts of the world is afforded by Joseph Conrad (1857–1924). Conrad was born in Poland, and spent his early life on the sea. He became by choice a writer of English rather than French, which he considered using, and began to turn into fiction the material acquired in his wanderings, especially in the South Seas. After working for some years on his first manuscript he published *Almayer's Folly* (1895), followed by *The Nigger of the Narcissus* (1897), *Lord Jim* (1900), and *Nostromo* (1904). Then, after a period of miscellaneous work, he returned to his true field of exotic adventure in *Chance* (1914) and *Victory* (1915).

Conrad's Art
Conrad's stories are distinguished for certain qualities of narrative art, notably a tendency, somewhat like Meredith's and James's, to postpone the crisis and defeat expectation. The result is to concentrate the force of the situation in a total effect of explosive intensity. This feature of the art of the short story has been adopted by the novelist, and in Conrad's case with extraordinary success. Again, he deals with characters of a powerful and bizarre originality, tested by strange conditions and extraordinary events.

Above all, he handles scene with wonderful effect to create that significant and influential medium which we call atmosphere. *Victory,* in its slow arranging of circumstances and human forces, its prolonged tension, and its final surprising and total catastrophe, is a typical example of Conrad's art in his longer work. "The Heart of Darkness" (the second story in the volume, *Youth*) is a magnificent example of atmosphere determining the unity and total effect of the short story. The heavy tropical air of equatorial Africa broods like a miasma over the monstrous and uncouth works of nature, twisting humanity itself into similar forms of atrocious inhumanity.

But Conrad's austerity of spirit, the refinement of his art, and his timelessness made him less characteristic of his period than many a realistic social novelist of much less æsthetic and intellectual distinction.

Samuel Butler, the author of *The Way of All Flesh* (1903), was only incidentally a novelist. Long before the posthumous publication of this frequently imitated work, he had **Samuel** revealed his antipathy to almost every manifestation **Butler** of Victorian thought and taste. He was born in 1835, the son of a clergyman, and as the result of his strong reaction against the evangelical religious circle in which he was brought up, he emigrated to New South Wales in 1857. Returning to London with a modest fortune, he devoted himself to painting, music, scientific experiment, and writing. One of his earliest and most important works is *Erewhon* (1872), the title of which is an anagram for Nowhere. The physical features for this Utopia of Butler's are drawn from New South Wales, but his traveler-protagonist finds a people much wiser than any whom Butler could have encountered there. The account of their society offers the cleverest satire on modern civilization since *Gulliver's Travels.* Butler finds occasion to attack the weaknesses of modern civilization, its treatment of crime, poverty, and sickness, in the Courts and the "straighteners"; its religion in the notion of Musical Banks issuing a currency which every one flaunted but nobody valued; its trust in machinery, which the Erewhonians banished for fear that it should become the master instead of the servant.

Butler defended the Lamarckian theory of evolution, as against the Darwinian, in such books as *Life and Habit* (1877) and *Unconscious Memory* (1880). After his death in 1902 there were published his *Note Books,* full of highly realistic comment on life, and his masterpiece of fiction, *The Way of All Flesh,* on which he had been engaged for some twenty years. This work, in which traces of Butler's evolutionary studies are evident, deals with the experience of Ernest Pontifex, brought up, as was Butler, under conventional religious influences, and his effort to shape for himself a life amid conditions of which he is pathetically ignorant. Ernest is not of heroic mould; his struggle is not only to overcome adverse circumstances, but also to build out of very ordinary material a character adequate to its environment. This narrative, with its air of being so genuine a record of experience as to be autobiographical, was the precursor of a long series of biographical novels.

"The Way of All Flesh"

The fame of George Gissing (1857–1903) was, like Butler's, mainly posthumous. Although Gissing wrote many novels to Butler's one, he was no more than Butler a novelist by vocation. Born in middle-class obscurity, he had the temperament of a scholar, and was driven only by severe necessity to turn out fiction. This aspect of his situation is developed in *New Grub Street* (1891). His poverty forced him to live among the poor and his realistic honesty made him write about them, but he despised the proletariat and admired the aristocracy. These aspects of his experience appear in *Born in Exile* (1892). Other studies of life among the poor are *Demos* (1886) and *Thyrza* (1887), done from exact observation. But Gissing's best work is in the vein of the psychological realism to which his own experience invited him. *The Private Papers of Henry Ryecroft* (1903) is the most popular of his works because it has something of the pleasure of life which was for the most part denied to Gissing himself. In truth, Gissing's fiction was a root out of dry ground, with little beauty of form, or amplitude of style, but urged upward by a stern, concentrated force of personality which carried it to a permanent place in English literature.

George Gissing

Butler and Gissing had attacked the Victorian fortress from within. George Moore (1852-1933) was to bring to the assault all the weapons he could borrow from foreign armories. In the role of "the English Zola," he set himself the task of shocking Mrs. Grundy into horrified silence and destroying English prudery. He was born in Ireland. In his early study of art, in London and Paris, he was drawn to the purely æsthetic attitude toward life, a phase which is represented by two volumes of verse, the second called *Pagan Poems* (1881). Later he was deeply affected by the French naturalistic school of fiction headed by Emile Zola, and when he definitely abandoned painting for writing he published a series of novels which show a boldness in dealing with life quite at variance with the Victorian tradition. The first of these, *A Modern Lover* (1883), was merely crude and vulgar, but some years later, in *Esther Waters* (1894), George Moore produced a masterly treatment of the English servant class. The heroine may be compared to Hardy's Tess of the D'Urbervilles as an example of utterly plastic human material, but while Hardy is under some suspicion of arranging his events to correspond with his view of a hostile universe, to Esther Waters things happen as naturally as leaves fall. Besides the novels there belong to this period Moore's first essay in confessional literature, *Confessions of a Young Man* (1888), and two volumes of criticism, *Impressions and Opinions* (1890) and *Modern Painting* (1893), in which he did great service by explaining and defending the impressionistic and realistic schools of French painting to English readers.

George Moore

The third phase of George Moore's activity began with his association with the Irish literary movement. He took up his residence in Dublin, and busied himself with the affairs of the Abbey Theatre, for which he wrote or collaborated in two plays, *The Bending of the Bough* (1900) and *Diarmuid and Grania* (1901). The most important influence of the Irish movement upon his work was the permeation of his novels by symbolism. The effect is apparent in *Evelyn Innes* (1898) and its sequel, *Sister Teresa* (1901), and still more in the beautifully

Moore and the Irish Movement

modulated tale, *The Lake* (1905). This is the shadowy love-story of an Irish priest, whose stagnant life is the result alike of his environment and character, which are represented and symbolized by the lake beside which he lives. The interest in religious experience apparent in the novels last mentioned is strongest in *The Brook Kerith* (1916) in which Jesus after the resurrection is the chief figure. Another result of Moore's residence in Dublin was to provide him with material for further literary reminiscences. His second volume of autobiography, *Memoirs of My Dead Life* (1906), concerned an earlier period, but the three volumes of *Hail and Farewell—Ave* (1911), *Salve* (1912), *Vale* (1914)—owe much of their piquant interest to his Irish associations. In his contributions to the literature of confession Moore does not, like the classical writers of autobiographies, present a personality inspired by a single aim or passion; rather he gives kaleidoscopic impressions of rapidly dissolving views of life, the vividness of the pictures equaled by the astonishingly frank account of his appearance in them.

George Moore is thus an important witness to the changing phases of literary interest and fashion during a whole generation. His style, detailed and matter-of-fact in his early novels, becomes in his later novels and confessions one of intimate association with the reader, an admirable vehicle for his highly conscious artistry.

Arnold Bennett (1867–1931), like George Moore, was to do his best work under French influences, in his case, the realism

Arnold Bennett of Balzac and Maupassant rather than the naturalism of Zola. He began his work as a professional purveyor of wares to the reading public. Only after years of apprenticeship did he emerge as a novelist of distinction. He took as his field the industrial region of The Five Towns, which contain the chief potteries of England, and proceeded to picture the limited lives of its inhabitants with a fidelity that reminds one of the French realism which Bennett had conscientiously studied. Into the everlasting monotony of this environment, however, Bennett introduced naturally romantic characters to whom all life is adventure, Helen of the High Hand and Denry the Audacious, in the books bearing their names. It is as if Bennett would have us understand that the

difference between realism and romanticism is that of temperament and attitude toward life.

Bennett's first widely successful novel was *The Old Wives'
Tale* (1908), in which he combines the two threads of realism
and romance by following the careers of two sis-
ters—Constance, who stays faithfully in her shop-   ***Bennett's***
keeping routine at Bursley, and Sophia, who elopes   ***Novels***
into the slightly more spacious career of the keeper of a *pension*
in Paris. In the trilogy, *Clayhanger* (1910), *Hilda Lessways*
(1911), and *These Twain* (1916), he again associates two
characters exhibiting opposite tendencies, the faithful realist,
Edwin, and the romanticist, Hilda, whose interrupted love-story
and subsequent marriage are narrated from the point of view of
each.

Bennett's social criticism may be regarded as incidental to his
main purpose, implicit rather than explicit, historical rather
than analytic. He presents in long perspective the
dull materialism, hypocrisy, and conventionality of   ***Bennett's***
Victorian provincialism as seen in the survivals of   ***Social***
it in The Five Towns—in Darius Clayhanger and   ***Criticism***
Auntie Hamps in the trilogy. Like Butler, he is severe in his
strictures on evangelical religion, and like Wells, he represents
the shams and shortcomings of education and of civilization,
both social and domestic, but he does so with the detachment of
the historian, not the ardor of the reformer.

John Galsworthy (1867–1933) is a subtler artist and more
penetrating critic of life than Arnold Bennett. Like Bennett, he
recognizes the shiftless arrangements which mankind
has made for its inhabitation of the earth, physically   ***John***
and spiritually, and which at their best go under the   ***Gals-***
name of civilization. Unlike Bennett, he does not con-   ***worthy***
ceal either his satire or his sympathy. Galsworthy recognizes the
separation of classes as the cardinal fact in the edifice of society.
His novels are chiefly occupied with the effect of class traditions
and loyalties upon individuals, and that of the inevitable conflict
of classes upon society as a whole. *The Country House* (1907)
presents the lower, and *The Patrician* (1911) the higher aristocracy, with their class consciousness growing out of possession
and position. *Fraternity* (1909) shows the pathetic impotence

of human will to break through the barriers of class, and *The Freelands* (1915), the tragic consequences of the blindness of the so-called intelligent class to the point of view of the other. His masterpiece is *The Forsyte Saga,* a family novel which began with *The Man of Property* (1906), and was continued in *In Chancery* (1920) and *To Let* (1921). The Forsytes are a business family, representative of the prosperous middle class, with its mind, its heart, and its conscience rooted in the idea of individual ownership.

In all English fiction, class has played an important part; from the time of *Pamela,* the novelist has shown us individual virtue or passion breaking its boundaries. The promotion of a character from a lower to a higher class by discovery of birth or by marriage has been a romantic motive constantly in use. Galsworthy, however, takes the fact of class much more seriously and scientifically. The rewards and the penalties of life are granted strictly within the limits defined by social distinctions. One situation that arises peculiarly out of class consciousness is scandal, and this Galsworthy uses in a number of his novels as a test of character. There is scandal in *The Country House,* the consequences of which Mrs. Pendyce averts from her family by acting according to her class instinct of an English lady, made strong out of her very weakness; and there is scandal in *The Man of Property,* the threat of which drives Soames Forsyte into a mad fury of possession—the only relation in life which is clear to him. There is scandal impending in *Fraternity,* between Hilary Dallison and the little model, but it cannot leap the barrier of class. On all who seek to pass beyond the bounds of class, whether they succeed or fail, there rests the curse of futility—upon young Jolyon Forsyte in *The Man of Property,* upon old Mr. Stone in *Fraternity,* and upon the young Freelands.

Galsworthy's Social Criticism

Galsworthy is a realist, both minute and delicate. For example, in *Fraternity,* the sense of smell is one factor that inhibits the human approach of the upper class toward the lower, although the ways in which individuals react to this element are subtly differentiated. He relieves the effect of detail, however, by giving it symbolic meaning, spiritual or social, beyond the fact

Galsworthy's Realism

itself. Even various "properties" of his characters serve to suggest or distinguish qualities or attitudes too delicate for phrasing. In this faculty Galsworthy suggests the deftness of Sterne and the spiritual penetration of Maeterlinck. On the whole, Galsworthy's view of mankind is pessimistic. In spite of ideal and heroic examples, his general conclusion is the inadequacy of man to cope with the problems of a complex social order, his impotence before the bonds of tradition and convention.

H. G. Wells, on the other hand, is incorrigibly hopeful of the improvement of relations between man and his environment. Wells was born in 1866 of a lower-middle class family. He obtained the really valuable part of his education in the Normal College of Science, and later in **H. G. Wells** sociological investigation. It was owing to a temporary period of ill health that he began the writing of fantastic romances based on imaginary developments of physical science, such as *The Time Machine* (1895) and *The Island of Doctor Moreau* (1896). He extended his field to serious sociological essays, such as *Anticipations* (1901), *A Modern Utopia* (1905), and *New Worlds for Old* (1908), in which the possibilities of greater happiness for man through his collective effort in improving his environment are attractively and ingeniously presented.

Wells began the writing of serious fiction with *Kipps* (1905), a treatment of the theme of the difficulty of changing from one social class to another, presented with the broad humor that Dickens would have employed. He continued the **Wells's Novels** study of middle-class life in the same caricatural style in *Tono-Bungay* (1909) and *The History of Mr. Polly* (1910). In *Ann Veronica* (1909) he explored the theme of woman's place in modern society, as determined by education, politics, and love when marriage is impossible. He continued to discuss the opposition between passion and social arrangements in *The New Machiavelli* (1911), *Marriage* (1912), and *The Passionate Friends* (1913). Wells's modernism did not permit him to solve the difficulty by invoking the Victorian motive of renunciation; instead, he devoted himself to studying the social consequences to his characters of acting in accordance with desire. The relation of instinct to intelligence, character, and man's work in the world is the theme of *The Research Magnifi-cent* (1915). In this book Wells abandoned the novel form for a loose narrative revealing the growth of a character through diaries and memoranda—somewhat as Carlyle did in *Sartor Resartus*. In *Mr. Britling Sees It Through* (1916) the form like-wise disappears before the terrible actuality of the substance— the life of an English family in the first year of the World War. All of Wells's work shows the journalistic quality of timeliness; in *Mr. Britling* it seems as if literature had for once kept pace with life, in its vivid, photographic reproduction of experience.

Pre-eminently a journalist, Wells is a conspicuous example of the reporter's skill in choosing material and adapting its form to the immediate needs of the public. He deals with sub-jects of immediate significance, in an alert, realistic manner. Through all his work runs the theme of a better world, to be realized through increasing control of nature and the liberating of man. He is the successor of the mid-nineteenth-century re-formers, Carlyle, Kingsley, Ruskin, and his differences from these masters in the details of his program serve to mark the trend of the age. His individual confession of faith in *First and Last Things* (1908) is an excellent starting point for such a comparison.

Wells is a clear example of the way in which biology and sociology have come to replace history as the background of knowledge in man's thought of the world. He *Wells's* shows the effect of the theory of evolution on the *Social* general mind. He regards human life as "a succes-*Criticism* sion of births, the race like a stream flowing through us" but with this cosmic view he has a definite concep-tion of the individuality of each man's experience. This latter perception perhaps explains his change of form from the socio-logical essay to the novel, which above all deals with the in-dividual man and woman. As has been said, he is an optimist; he believes in the intelligence and disinterestedness of men pro-moted by education. He is optimistic not only in regard to human nature but in regard to its environment. Unlike Carlyle and Ruskin, he has no hatred of machinery. His picture of modern society is as dark as theirs, but he believes that practical applications of physical and economic science will give man a worldly habitation worthy of the possibilities of his nature.[1]

DRAMA

The last decade of the nineteenth century witnessed a dramatic revival which seemed to promise the return of vitality to a literary form which through most of the century had been moribund. Most of the major Victorian poets had tried their hand at writing plays, without succeeding in doing more than add to the large number of poetic dramas unsuited to the stage. Tennyson's *Becket* (1893), as acted by Sir Henry Irving, had probably come closest to achieving the traditional association of poetry and the drama.[2] At the very beginning of the twentieth century, Stephen Phillips (1864–1915), a poetic follower of Tennyson's, with some experience of the stage, produced a series of verse-plays which seemed favorable auguries for the poetic drama. The most robust of his dramatic achievements was *Herod* (1900), a powerful presentation of the tyrant's morbid and murderous jealousy of his wife Mariamne. But Phillips's *Paolo and Francesca* (1902) now seems a decorous and anemic interpretation of the great legendary romance, and *Ulysses* (1902) is an enfeebled and devitalized chronicle play.

The really vigorous drama of the period took the form of the Ibsenesque domestic prose-drama. Its English pioneers were Henry Arthur Jones (1851–1929) and Sir Arthur Wing Pinero (1855–1934). In the eighties, Jones had written and lectured on the need for plays that should represent modern life accurately and investigate its values seriously, and, after the great financial success of his melodrama, *The Silver King* (1882), he was free to write plays of the kind he had demanded. His later plays fell fairly definitely into the categories of satirical comedies or social dramas. Of the latter sort, *Michael and His Lost Angel* (1896) and *Mrs. Dane's Defence* (1900) are the most memorable. Jones

---

[1] For comment on the novels written by Moore, Conrad, Bennett, Galsworthy, and Wells, after the First World War, see Chapter XVII.

[2] Throughout this section of this chapter, the dates are the dates of first performance and not the dates of first publication.

regarded the earlier play as his masterpiece, but to modern readers the presentation of the struggle between sensuality and spirituality seems laborious and pretentious. *Mrs. Dane's Defence,* despite its conventional moral judgments, is a theatrically adroit exposé of a sympathetically depicted woman with a past. Jones's more skilful plays, however, are satirical comedies of manners. *Saints and Sinners* (1884), though obvious in its moral distinctions and melodramatic in plot, had suggested the dramatist's keen eye for the insecure foundations of middle-class morality. In *The Crusaders* (1891), Jones satirized organizations bent on social reform; in *The Triumph of the Philistines* (1895) he paid his respects to British insensitiveness to the arts. With *The Masqueraders* (1894) and *The Liars* (1897) he cast a wider net, and caught in it the insincerities and hypocrisies inseparable from a complex and sophisticated social life.

Although Sir Arthur Pinero was less systematic in his social views than Jones, he was a more skillful craftsman and a finer

Sir Arthur Pinero dramatist. He began his career in the eighties with farces like *The Magistrate* (1885) and sentimental comedies like *Sweet Lavender* (1888), but it was only with the sensational production of *The Second Mrs. Tanqueray* (1893) that he became known as a serious dramatist. Though the social values made explicit in this bourgeois tragedy are purely conventional, the boldness of the theme—the attempted rehabilitation of a woman with a past—a theme which Jones was to take up seven years later in *Mrs. Dane's Defence,* the vigor of the rhetoric, and the ingenuity of the construction made this play a milestone in the history of the modern English drama. In later plays like *Iris* (1901) and *Mid-Channel* (1909), Pinero minimized the element of the thesis, and concentrated whole-heartedly on character drawing and action. There are few English social dramas as honestly circumstantial and as skillfully motivated as the latter play. Pinero's narrowly limited ideas and his somewhat old-fashioned technique soon gave him the status of a period-dramatist, and, although he attempted to adapt himself to the modes and manners of the post-war drama, he wrote little or nothing of interest after 1914.

To the social drama as established by Ibsen and exemplified

by Jones and Pinero, Sir J. M. Barrie (1860–1937) was opposed in temperament and principle. Theoretically he was
opposed to the technical limitations of "the well-made play," its
studiously realistic tone, and its dedication of dramatic art to
the demonstration of a thesis. Temperamentally he was opposed
to its elimination of those elements of sentiment, humor, fantasy, and pathos which were basic to his own na-   *Sir J. M.*
ture. It is in Barrie's experimental attitude to the   *Barrie*
potentialities of the theatre that he comes closest
to the spirit of the new drama. He regarded the theatre as an
ingenious toy the resources of which he would test to the limit
in his expression of his characteristic view of life. In material,
point of view, and range of feeling, the drama of Barrie is unmistakably individual. *The Little Minister* (1897), the dramatization of his novel, is willfully romantic; *Quality Street* (1903),
delicately sentimental. *Peter Pan* (1904), perhaps his most frequently revived play, is a recklessly gleeful dramatization of
that boyish imagination which Barrie never quite lost. *Alice Sit-
by-the-Fire* (1905) is sentimental comedy with an admixture of
good-natured satire of the problem plays of his contemporaries.
What Every Woman Knows (1908) is his finest comedy of
sentiment. With Scottish stubbornness, Barrie refused to swim
with the dramatic currents making for realism and social doctrine, and his personality was so attractive and his gifts so distinguished that he was rewarded by reaching the hearts of far
wider audiences than any of his serious rivals touched. But in
the world of the post-war drama he was to find himself an even
more solitary figure than in the dramatic world at the turn of
the century.

Under the influence of the social dramas of Jones and Pinero,
Oscar Wilde (1856–1900) somewhat half-heartedly built a
number of plays around some rather far-fetched problem in social relations, but *Lady Windermere's Fan* (1892) and *A
Woman of No Importance* (1893) are remembered, not for
their preposterous plots but for the epigrams Wilde lavished on
their lighter scenes. Once, in *The Importance of Being Earnest*
(1895), where he contented himself with an utterly farcical
plot, he achieved a minor masterpiece of paradoxical foolery,

just as in *Salomé* (1896), he attained perfection in a neo-romantic tragedy of decadence.[1]

George Bernard Shaw was not only as witty as Wilde but vastly superior to him in seriousness of purpose and intellectual significance. He was born in Dublin in 1856, but removed to London in 1876. He began his career as a novelist, then joined the Fabian socialist movement and, like Wells, devoted himself to social propaganda. Since his novels did not sell and since he could find no commercial producer for his early plays, he earned his living as a critic of music, art, and the theatre, showing his alertness to foreign influences by *The Quintessence of Ibsenism* (1891) and *The Perfect Wagnerite* (1898). His first play, *Widowers' Houses,* written in 1885, was not produced until 1892, and then with scant success. He followed this with *The Philanderer,* a satire on the emancipated woman, and *Mrs. Warren's Profession,* a treatment of commercialized vice which was refused performance by the censor. He reached dramatic maturity in *Arms and the Man* (1894), a brilliant satire on military glory, *Candida* (1897), a resolution of a triangular situation by Shaw's ideal woman, *The Man of Destiny* (1897), a mock-heroic skit on Napoleon, and *You Never Can Tell* (1900), a farcical treatment of the new woman. These seven plays were all distinguished by their attack upon some time-honored sham, their juxtaposition of reality and some pretentiously false view. Perhaps because of their slight success on the stage Shaw published them in two series, *Plays Pleasant and Unpleasant* (1898). In the elaborate prefaces to these volumes he commented on the technical and social qualities of the plays, and, further to guide his readers, expanded the stage directions into full descriptions, character sketches, and analyses, thus adapting the play to a public accustomed to the reading of novels. By this campaign in behalf of the printed play he helped to raise prose drama again to the status of literature.

Shaw's next plays were more immediately successful on the stage, but he continued to publish them as books, and by the aid

___

[1] For a consideration of Wilde's poetry and of his share in the decadent movement, see pages 405–406.

of prefaces to make them effective propaganda for his views on
the art of the theatre and on society. He attacked the illusions of
history in *Cæsar and Cleopatra,* and of romantic morality in *The
Devil's Disciple,* published in *Three Plays for Puritans* (1900).
In *John Bull's Other Island* (1904) he inverted the usual conceptions of Englishman and Irishman, depicting the former as a
soft-headed sentimentalist, the latter as a type of practical sense.
His arraignment of the British for atrocities in Egypt, which
occurs in the preface to this play, is one of the most powerful
polemical passages in modern English. In *Man and Superman*
(1905) he represented courtship as a war of the sexes and man
as the victim of woman, who is the incarnation of nature's purpose and the will to live. In *The Doctor's Dilemma* (1906) he
tilted against the professional humbug that surrounds medical
practice, and in *Getting Married* (1908) against the prudery
which conceals the true relation of the sexes. *Fanny's First Play*
(1911) is a satire on dramatic criticism, and *Androcles and the
Lion* (1912), on Christian martyrdom.

In the preface to *Man and Superman* Shaw explains that his
ideas, commonly attributed to Nietzsche, Wagner, Marx, and
Ibsen, came to him largely from Samuel Butler.   ***Shaw's***
Undoubtedly Butler's bold challenge of accepted   ***Theories***
shams and, in addition, the fashion, so popular in
the nineties, of the attack by paradox and hyperbole, are to be
accounted major influences in Shaw's development. In particular
Butler introduced him to the theory of evolution with which the
name of Lamarck is connected, according to which biological
changes have been not mechanical, but vitalistic, that is, they
are brought about in response to needs, in supplying which the
will of the individual is active. This faith is at the root of the difference between Shaw and Wells. The latter holds with Darwin
that environment plays a chief part in the modification of
species, and thus finds a basis for his belief in the advancement
of mankind through improving society by administrative measures abolishing waste and disorder. Shaw maintains that essential improvement of the race must come by way of breeding
individuals of higher capacity. Hence he attacks most vigorously
class distinctions which stand in the way of proper mating. No

more than Carlyle does he believe that democracy will work with such human material as we have at present, but while Carlyle trusted in the occasional hero, periodically to save and reanimate society, Shaw falls back on scientific breeding to beget a race of supermen. Like Carlyle, however, he sees in the will of the individual the only source of salvation. In *Major Barbara* (1905) he attacks such religion as the Salvation Army preaches, for its weakening effect on the poor, and declares that the hideous social disease of poverty will continue until the poor themselves refuse to suffer it longer, and abolish it. Among the other shams which Shaw attacks in the realistic spirit of Samuel Butler, or of Jonathan Swift, are the romantic conceptions of love, morality, and nationalism, the illusions and pretensions of all classes, aristocratic, bourgeois, and proletarian. He has a special contempt for men held fast by a professional code, such as physicians, lawyers, and soldiers. Some of his militancy may be attributed to personal prejudice and idiosyncrasy, more of it to ingenious journalism. Shaw possesses to a wonderful degree the power that Swift had, to startle men out of comfortable complacency, to force them to examine the views sanctioned by respectable leaders of society, and to think a little for themselves. This is the function especially of his writings on social organization—"The Revolutionist's Handbook," accompanying *Man and Superman*, and *The Intelligent Woman's Guide to Socialism and Capitalism* (1928).

Shaw's success in promoting his ideas is greatly advanced by his mastery of dramatic technique and his prose style. In respect to the former he is as revolutionary as toward other conventions. The conventional values of the theatre are no more to him than those of society. For the expected he is quite willing to substitute surprise, and for surprise, disappointment. Moreover, he disregards the principle that the life of a play is in action, and gives rein more and more freely to talk. Yet he carries out the theory of the drama of ideas by making his play an attack upon some accepted opinion and carrying a dramatic opposition into the minds of his audience. His skill in dialogue, in epigram, in verbal fence, makes for constant intellectual excitement. This dramatic style rises at times into genuine eloquence, with long rhythmical sen-

Shaw's Tech- nique

tences that remind one of Ruskin's. But while under stress of emotional intensity Ruskin's periods vibrate into poetry, Shaw's are deliberately pointed up by his polished wit. Like Swift, he writes the quintessence of prose.

Eleven of Shaw's plays were produced by Harley Granville-Barker (1877–1946) during his management of the Court Theatre between 1904 and 1907. To these alert and intelligent productions, Shaw owed the extension of his English reputation. Granville-Barker's intimate contact with the works of Shaw was the most important influence on his own writing of plays. He was a more fastidious artist than Shaw, but, like him, he was primarily concerned with the drama of ideas. His first full-length play, *The Marrying of Ann Leete* (1902) is a sensitive exhibition of the interplay of instinct and convention in a young woman's awakening to love. But *The Voysey Inheritance* (1905) depicts the conflict between personal morality and business ethics, *Waste* (1907), the tragic relationship between personal and political morality, and *The Madras House* (1910), the place of woman in modern society. In the plays published since the war—*The Secret Life* and *His Majesty*—the method of implication has been carried to such a point of refinement that only the most sensitive acting and the most perceptive audience could entertain the significances intended. Granville-Barker was the most subtle intelligence among the new playwrights, and his voluntary withdrawal from the theatre was one of the greatest losses the modern drama sustained.

Granville-Barker was responsible for the introduction to the English stage of such important early plays of John Galsworthy as *The Silver Box* (1906) and *Justice* (1910). *The Silver Box* is a revelation of the terrible disadvantage of the poor and friendless before the processes of justice which seek to be impartial. This is also the theme of his most powerful play, *Justice* (1910). *Strife* (1909) dramatizes a strike which after desperate struggle and suffering ends with masters and men in exactly the same position as before. Other phases of the influence of class are depicted in *The Pigeon* (1912), and *The Eldest Son* (1912). In *The Mob* (1914) Galsworthy anticipated the situation which was soon to become critical, of those who in war-time have scruples of reason or conscience against accepting the will of the majority, and become its victims. Galsworthy's plays are, on the whole, examples of the realistic treatment of social themes, which under the influence of Ibsen had become the chief type of European drama at the close of the nineteenth century. But like Ibsen in his latest work, Galsworthy relies on symbolism to convey intimations of his thought which are too subtle for direct expression. Not a great dramatist, Galsworthy must nevertheless be recognized as contributing to the task of restoring English drama to its old prestige as a medium for thought.[1]

In the nineties the ascendancy of the national drama of Norway under the leadership of Ibsen made a few Irish writers— *The Irish Drama* W. B. Yeats, George Moore, Edward Martyn— think of creating a national theatre for Ireland. They began by producing in Dublin for three successive seasons plays written by Irish writers but presented by English actors. This experiment closed unsuccessfully in 1901. Meanwhile the activities of the Gaelic League and other national societies had produced a company of Irish players. This company was ready to further any experiments that Yeats, the leader of the Irish dramatic movement, might make. A year afterward Yeats brought into the company the writer who was to prove the most gifted of Irish dramatists.

J. M. Synge (1871–1909) wrote six plays for the Abbey Theatre, five of which were produced—*The Shadow of the Glen,* *J. M. Synge* *Riders to the Sea, The Well of the Saints, The Playboy of the Western World,* and *Deirdre of the Sorrows,* the latter a powerful dramatization of the *Exile of the Sons of Usnech (Longes mac n-Usnig),* which forms one of the *Three Sorrows of Story-Telling* and has persisted in Irish tradition for at least a thousand years. Synge's genius consisted in his ability to give his characters a place in nature, and constantly to draw poetry from this surrounding nature—in *Riders to the Sea* there is the tragical poetry of the sea; in *The Shadow of the Glen* there is the poetry of desolate bogs and open spaces; in *The Well of the Saints* there is the simple poetry of spring-

---

[1] For a consideration of the dramas written by Barrie, Shaw, and Galsworthy, after 1914, see Chapter XVII.

time; in *Deirdre of the Sorrows* there is the poetry of wood and glen. With this lyrical poetry there is intense dramatic poetry also—the poetry that his characters themselves attain in their expression of resignation, exaltation, or disillusionment. His plays are masterpieces of construction, and *Riders to the Sea* is one of the best short tragedies ever written. His *Playboy of the Western World* is racial comedy in the sense that *Don Quixote* is racial comedy—it satirizes the Irish delight in romantic personality. Synge's is the most colorful and musical dramatic dialogue that any dramatist has attained in English since the Elizabethans; taking the actual speech of the Irish peasantry, he moulded it to a wonderful dramatic utterance.

William Butler Yeats (1865–1939) rendered service to the Irish drama, not only by his discovery and encouragement of Synge and by his share in organizing the Abbey Theatre but also by the writing of plays. Although *William Butler Yeats* Yeats's poetic gifts were lyrical, contemplative, and philosophical, and although he had no special gift for the drama of action, his contribution to the Irish drama was not only individual but distinguished. *The Land of Heart's Desire* (1894), his first play to be produced, has the qualities of an ethereal ballad. His next play, *The Countess Cathleen* (1899), was richer in human qualities and more stirring as drama. Probably his most effective play was *Cathleen ni Houlihan* (1902) which creates an impressive dramatic symbol for the ideal Ireland to which so many generous lives have been sacrificed. *The King's Threshold* (1903) made a moving defence of the high function of the true poet, but *The Shadowy Waters* (1904) proved tenuous and Maeterlinckian. Like almost every other Irish poet, Yeats drew upon the riches of the mediæval Irish heroic cycles—for tragedy, in *Deirdre* (1906), and for farce, in *The Green Helmet* (1910). Despite the distinct limitations of Yeats's plays as acting dramas, they did much to habituate both actors and audiences to the use of verse on the modern stage, and they fused verse and drama more successfully than any other modern playwright has done.[1]

[1] For a consideration of Yeats's poetic career before 1914, see below, pages 414–415. For his post-war career, see pages 458–459.

Lady Augusta Gregory (1859–1932) once said that she wrote comedy because that was what the Abbey Theatre needed. This remark is indicative of the spirit in which she con-

Other Irish Dramatists

tributed to the repertory which her friends Synge and Yeats were creating. Lady Gregory's forte was the writing of pure joyous comedy of a kind alien to the temperaments of the other members of the group. She was most successful in her treatment of the one-act farce-comedy, and of the many she wrote perhaps the most memorable are *Spreading the News* (1904), *Hyacinth Halvey* (1906), and *The Workhouse Ward* (1908). She had a genuine flair for devising fresh comic situations, but she was most gifted in the creation of comic dialogue. Her control over the Anglo-Irish dialect was perfect, even when she utilized it in her translations of Molière or in her folk-history plays, *The White Cockade* (1905) and *The Canavans* (1906). Her inability to construct a full-length play makes her work in this form less impressive, but her shorter pieces are classics in the repertory of the Abbey Theatre.

Two other Irish dramatists, who were not closely connected with the Abbey Theatre, represent the two important phases of modern drama, the neoromantic and the realistic. Lord Dunsany (1878–1957) has accepted the influences of Oriental and Greek literatures and also of Maurice Maeterlinck in evolving the type of play saturated with romance, fantasy, and decoration. Whatever symbolism Dunsany's writing holds is of secondary nature. In such plays as *The Gods of the Mountain*, and *King Argimenes and the Unknown Warrior* (1914), he transports his audience to a strange, colorful world somewhere between fairy-land and Valhalla, and, assuming this world to be actual, presents almost realistically the actions and struggles of the people who inhabit it. Much of his atmosphere is achieved by the rhythm of his dialogue. Most of his tales deal with this same world, offering a patent example of the literature of escape. Occasionally, in such plays as *The Glittering Gate* (1914), *A Night at an Inn* (1917), and especially in *If* (1922), he turns his potent fancy upon the humdrum world of here and now.

Another Irish playwright whose work has characteristics distinct from the poetic plays of the Abbey Theatre group and the fantasies of Lord Dunsany is the Ulsterman, St. John Ervine (1883–   ). In his early work, he attempted to do for Protestant Ireland what the Abbey Theatre playwrights were doing for Catholic Ireland. His first play, *Mixed Marriage* (1911), considers the complex relationships between religious sects in a country where social and political issues are inextricably entangled with religion. *John Ferguson* (1916), his most powerful play, is a somber study of Protestant fanaticism, marred by incursions of melodrama. *Jane Clegg* (1912), his most studiously realistic drama, is in the mode of rather grubby domestic drama popular in the provincial repertory companies before 1914. Ervine's post-war development has been in the field of the English comedy of manners, and all traces of his Irish origin and background have tended to disappear. Such exceedingly popular plays as *The First Mrs. Fraser* (1928) and *Anthony and Anna* (1935) are deft and ingenious, but they are hardly more than expert manipulations of familiar theatrical formulæ.

POETRY

In poetry, no less than in the novel and the drama, the late nineteenth century furnishes abundant evidence of the reaction against Victorian themes and techniques, although the poetic reaction took on somewhat less violent forms since poetry depends for much of its effect on the associations which themes and words have developed through generations of imaginative associations. But as Tennyson's prestige declined, one after another attempt was made to revitalize poetry by expressing new views and values or by utilizing unaccustomed or novel techniques.

Up to the First World War, however, it was still possible for poets working in the traditional modes to reach an audience and on occasion to achieve a considerable reputation or real distinction. Thus, the vogue of Stephen Phillips (1864–1915), whose poetic dramas have already been mentioned, illustrates the persistence of Victorian tastes almost to the verge of the war. His *Poems* (1897) are full of echoes of the great Victorians. Two poems in blank verse, "Christ in Hades" and "Marpessa,"

Stephen Phillips

the one Christian and the other Greek in subject, show Phillips's reliance on the past for inspiration; "The Wife," however, is a modern story of the streets of London, which suggests the boldness of the later realists in dealing with actual life. It is a somewhat pathetic fact that only in the late volume, *Lyrics and Dramas* (1913), did Phillips achieve any personal distinction of thought and style, and by that time his remarkable early vogue had passed.

Sir William Watson (1858–1935) was likewise content to go on in the paths of tradition, but while Phillips looked to

Sir William Watson

Tennyson as his master, Watson turned to the more austere and limited measures of Arnold and Wordsworth. Watson's best poetry was written in memory of his predecessors—"Lachrymæ Musarum" on the death of Tennyson, "In Laleham Churchyard" on the grave of Matthew Arnold, and "Wordsworth's Grave." Like Wordsworth he used the sonnet for comment on political affairs, and he had the independence and courage to protest against the resurgence of imperialism which showed itself in the conquest of the Soudan and the subjugation of the South African republics. His most famous poem, "The Woman with the Serpent's Tongue," was a bitter political satire, alleged to have been directed at Lady Margot Asquith. But such poetry as his was rapidly becoming outmoded. The *Selected Poems* (1928) seemed hopelessly anachronistic, and Sir William died in obscurity in 1935.

Of the poets whose work showed an advance in technical resources over the Victorians the greatest is Francis Thompson

Francis Thompson

(1859–1907). Educated at a Roman Catholic seminary, a student of medicine, and then for some years a wanderer and bohemian, he at length found refuge from the world in which he was as much a stranger as Shelley, in semimonastic seclusion. His greater poetry was published between 1893 and 1897.

Thompson represents the Christian and Catholic spirit in profound reaction from neopaganism and materialism. Like the
religious poets of the seventeenth century, he desired passionately to bring poetry once more into   *Thomp-*
the service of a heavenly instead of an earthly   *son's*
love. In "To a Poet Breaking Silence," he ex-   *Religious*
presses the ideal which George Herbert had set   *Poetry*
before himself.

> Teach how the crucifix may be
> Carven from the laurel-tree,
> Fruit of the Hesperides
> Burnish take on Eden trees,
> The Muses' sacred grove be wet
> With the red dew of Olivet,
> And Sappho lay her burning brows
> In white Cecilia's lap of snows!

In "The Hound of Heaven" he dealt with the theme of many
of Herbert's and Vaughan's poems, the pursuit of the human
soul by the love of God—but with a richness of imagery and a
sustained and swelling music that make his poetry compared to
theirs as a modern symphony to a Gregorian chant. "The Hound
of Heaven" is the best example of Thompson's immense technical resources. The poem, in the ode form, with lines of varying length and irregular rhyme scheme, is marvelous in the
adaptation of its movement to the rhythm of the life led by the
errant soul, with the refrain of the insistent pursuit always
nearer and more compelling. In contrast to the startling variety
of movement of "The Hound of Heaven" is the stark austerity
of the lines, "To the Dead Cardinal of Westminster," written
in memory of Cardinal Manning. In the former poem the theme
is the human soul in presence of God; in the latter it is the soul
in presence of a greater soul, an earthly captain, and in both the
attitude is that of pathetic humility, wholly and sincerely
Christian.

Thompson's love-poems deal with the subtleties of a passion,
unearthly yet not unreal. In *Sister Songs* its expression is intri-

cate and elaborate; in "The Poppy" it has a delightful simplicity. The touching effect which he gains from the mingled themes
of childhood and love, he draws still more poign-
His antly from those of childhood and death in "To
Love- Monica Thought Dying." To Thompson, as to his
Poetry predecessors, Vaughan and Blake, childhood is a mystery and a miracle far beyond woman.

Francis Thompson may be called a child of the early seventeenth century. Like the group of poets which included Vaughan
and Crashaw he made religion the major subject of his verse, and
like them he wrote of the themes of divine and human love, of
birth and of death, sometimes with the intimate simplicity of a
child, and again with the strange and ardent subtlety of the
philosopher. And like them he brought to the expression of
these mysteries profound intellectual concepts and a language
new to the uses of poetry. But as with these poets at their best,
this intellectual quality, this freighted language, does not exclude feeling, but is infused with it, sublimated into rare and
new forms of beauty.

That fresh and attractive effects could be secured in traditional poetic forms was made evident by the tremendous popu-
A. E. larity of A. E. Housman's *A Shropshire Lad,* which
Housman appeared unobtrusively in 1896 and attained perhaps as large an audience as any single volume of
verse in the period. Housman's seemingly simple lyrics, though
perfectly conventional in form, were products of a very complex
literary tradition, for Housman (1859–1936), one of the great
classical scholars of his time, was steeped in the lyricism of the
Greeks. His artistry, therefore, though direct and naïve in effect,
was highly conscious and polished. His vogue is explicable, on
the grounds, not merely of the transparency of his language and
the finish of his technique but also of the anti-Victorian values,
the stoical pessimism, and the rather joyless *carpe diem* philosophy of the poems. His *Last Poems* (1922) repeated many of
the notes and tunes of the earlier volume, but added nothing to
his range or his power.

The greatest of the post-Victorian traditional poets was undoubtedly Robert Bridges (1844–1930). It is significant that his

contribution to the technical resources of English poetry was made by imitating classical metres. In these experiments, which involve the application of the principle of quantity to English verse, he was more successful than Tennyson or Swinburne. Bridges was above all a scholarly poet; but this is not to say that he lacked originality. He reminds one of certain post-Elizabethans whose study of poetry as a conscious art did not exclude spontaneity. Indeed, the most accurate description of Bridges is as a belated classicist. But he went beyond the technique of the classicist, and in "Nightingales," "A Passer By," and "On a Dead Child," by relying on his sense of quantity in the language he uses, he wrote poems that have a new music.[1]

Robert Bridges

But though Bridges continued to demonstrate the potentialities of a sophisticated traditionalism, his poetry was by no means characteristic either of the nineties or the first decade of the twentieth century. The more typical poetry of the nineties was either decadent or muscular in tone. If the decadent movement is frequently regarded as synonymous with the nineties, the reason may be that so many of its adherents met with picturesque or violent deaths just before the close of the century. As a matter of fact, its roots go much farther back into the nineteenth century; Gilbert and Sullivan were satirizing the æsthetic movement in *Patience* as early as 1881. The sources of the æsthetic movement were complex: the mediævalism of Pre-Raphaelitism, the æstheticism of Walter Pater, the influence of various French *fin de siècle* writers, and such a movement as impressionism in painting.

The most famous figures in the æsthetic movement were Aubrey Beardsley (1872–1898), the great black and white artist, the perfectly appropriate illustrator of Wilde's *Salomé* and the incongruous illustrator of Malory's *Morte d'Arthur,* Ernest Dowson (1867–1900), whose lyric, "Cynara," expressed most perfectly the cynical hedonism of the group, and Oscar Wilde (1856–1900), easily its most famous and gifted representative.

Wilde was born in Dublin and educated at Dublin and Oxford. At the latter university he came under the influence of both

- For comment on the later work of Bridges, see pages 457- 458.

Pre-Raphaelitism and neopaganism, which are evident in his first volume of poems, published in 1881. It was to popularize

Oscar Wilde the pagan attitude toward life that he began to lecture, in the effort to enlist the public in the æsthetic movement, or cult of beauty in life. He continued his literary career by writing fiction, dramas, and essays—in a restless search for novelty characteristic of the end of the century. Not only did he enter all departments of literature, but in each his work is utterly various; it is as if in letters he were exemplifying Pater's doctrine of life as separate moments, to each of which should be given a value for its own sake, apart from those which precede and follow. In fiction he gives us the beautiful idyl, "The Happy Prince" (1888), and the study of morbid personality, *The Picture of Dorian Gray* (1891); in drama he presents the comedy of manners in *Lady Windermere's Fan* (1892), pure farce in *The Importance of Being Earnest* (1895), and neoromantic tragedy in *Salomé* (1896), in which the pagan and Christian strains are mingled in the sensual love of the daughter of Herodias for John the Baptist; in the essay he ranges from the brilliant paradoxes and whimsical defense of absurdities of the *Intentions* (1891) to a serious social study— "The Soul of Man under Socialism." Finally in poetry he passes from the artificial pagan and Pre-Raphaelite verse of his youth, with its imitation of emotion, to the terrible sincerity of "The Ballad of Reading Gaol" (1898). Written in simple ballad metre, it is one of the most poignant records of human suffering in all literature. This last, as well as *De Profundis,* a remorseful self-study in poetic prose, was written in prison, to which he was sentenced for sexual offences. This experience seemed for a time to bring into his life the sincerity that had been lacking.

But the æsthetic movement was to prove much less consequential in the history of modern English poetry than the movement initiated by William E. Henley (1849–1903), in an attempt to counteract by injections of healthy red blood the anemia which seemed to be destroying poetry. Poets, like Henley, Davidson, Kipling, and Masefield, despite their marked individualities, were alike in their insistence that poetry should possess virility, and that it should depict and interpret the lives and emotions of common men in diction selected from the language spoken by modern men.

Henley was a journalist and editor during many years when the new poetry could not obtain a hearing. As early as 1874, when an inmate of the Edinburgh hospital, he wrote a series of sketches in verse, which were published in *The Cornhill Magazine*. The experience of the patient as he passes under the anæsthetic, awakes in the clinic, and afterward lies on his bed of insomnia; his observation of figures around him and of the life of the hospital as it unfolds itself, are recorded with unflinching realism. The sketches are in various forms, from the sonnet to poems in unrhymed lines of irregular lengths. Later Henley wrote much verse in imitation of old French forms; but his true vehicle was the unrhymed, irregular, though rhythmical ode, approaching free verse, in which he wrote his realistic observations of city life called *London Voluntaries*. His first volume of poetry appeared in 1888 and his significant popularity belongs to the last decade of the century.

W. E. Henley

Henley as a critic reminds one of Hazlitt in his strong personal attitude and downright, defiant expression of it. His friendship with Stevenson, which began in the Edinburgh Hospital, is one of the beautiful episodes of his life, but he came to resent bitterly his friend's later pietism and what he regarded as the unworthy popularity which it brought him. His criticism of Stevenson after the latter's death was ill judged and in bad taste, but it was part of Henley's zeal for the real and his contempt for the conventional. In the same spirit he gave expression to the neo-stoic mood of the close of the century in his best-known poem, "Invictus":

Henley's Stoicism

> Out of the night that covers me,
>   Black as the pit from pole to pole,
> I thank whatever gods may be
>   For my unconquerable soul.

This personal mood provided an easy transition to the national mood of militarism. Henley's second volume of verse (1892) was called from its title poem *The Song of the Sword,* and later during the Boer War he was one of the most ardent imperialists. As editor of *The National Observer* he published the early poems of the later poet of imperialism—the *Barrack-Room Ballads* of Rudyard Kipling.

John Davidson (1857–1909), like Henley, had a long struggle for recognition. He began his career in Scotland by
John Davidson writing plays; then in 1890 he migrated to London, and published two novels. His first success came with *Fleet Street Eclogues* (1893), a series of conversations in verse in which the conventional pastoral speakers are replaced by journalists. He followed this with *Ballads and Songs* (1894), *New Ballads* (1897), and several additional volumes. He continued to work for the stage without marked success. He died, probably by suicide, in 1909.

Davidson's poetry contains elements both traditional and modern. "Old and new," he says, are ever "weltering upon the
David-son's Modernism borders of my world." For example, in "The Ballad of a Nun," he tells the mediæval story of the nun who deserted her convent and returned years later to find that the Virgin Mary had guarded her place—tells it with cruel realism and with its meaning changed from praise of asceticism to glorification of experience. In the same way the story of the knight who, sharing the joys of Venus, is pardoned by the Pope on the sign of the staff bursting into bloom, becomes a justification of license. This deliberate turning of Christian legend to pagan uses is characteristic of the spirit of revolt in which Davidson did his work. He is bitterly anti-Christian. His "Exodus from Houndsditch" is a deliberate arraignment of Christianity for its social failure. He is a convinced materialist. The soul for him is matter become self-conscious, chiefly through pain. The whole world process is toward the experience of more intense pain.

> The lowest struggling motion and the fiercest blood on fire,
> The tree, the flower, are pressing towards a future ever higher,
> To reach the mood august wherein we know we suffer pain.

Such is his answer to Tennyson's interpretation of the evolutionary process. The contrast between the great Victorian poet and this modern spirit may be further seen by comparing their accounts of the growth of a poet's mind, Tennyson's "Palace of Art" with Davidson's "Ballad in Blank Verse."

For the rest, Davidson deals in strong contrasts of both form and substance. Mediæval legend and modern industrialism mingle in his pages; the crude facts of city life with memories of nature; conventional lines, feeble and trite, with daring innovation. In "To a Street Piano" he takes, perhaps in a spirit of defiance, *Davidson's Contrasts* the most insistent of all the ugliness of life—the vulgar tunes that sing themselves into our minds,—and weaves them into a strain of beauty. Perhaps his most dignified individual work is in the dramatic monologues in blank verse, such as *The Testament of a Vivisector* and *The Testament of an Empire Builder,* in which, following the example of Browning, he put criticism of contemporary life into the mouths of its representatives.

The early fame of Rudyard Kipling (1865–1936) rested as much on his poetry as on his stories. His *Departmental Ditties* (1886) and *Barrack-Room Ballads* (1892) described in simple verse the characters and characteristics of army life in India. In them and in the *Kipling's Poetry* army tales Kipling made the modern British soldier a literary figure—and the value of his performance can be tested by comparing his pictures of military life with those of earlier military novelists, such as Charles Lever. Later in *The Seven Seas* (1896) and *The Five Nations* (1903), he became the poet of imperialism, of the larger conception of the Anglo-Saxon's place and function in the world that came to replace the insular patriotism of earlier national poets. Through his poems, stories, and journalistic writing, based on travel or residence in every part of the British dominion, Kipling became an important force in the creation of that imperial self-consciousness in which the communities of Anglo-Saxon blood have drawn nearer together, and he uttered the popular political philosophy of the time, for example, in "The White Man's Burden." Necessarily much of Kipling's imperial verse concerns the sea, the element in which Britain's colonies have grown into empire. It is interesting to see how the old themes of wandering by far ocean trails and seeking strange adventures, which we see in Anglo-

Saxon poetry, continue to animate this modern English poet, and how much they contribute to his conception of racial character and destiny.

It is not, however, as a political but as a human poet that Kipling will be best remembered. He has mingled poetry freely *Kipling's* with his prose, as head-notes to his stories or inter-*Humanity* ludes among them, in a manner almost Eliza-bethan, and with striking reinforcement to his themes. In these *Songs from Books* is distilled the essential humanity that is manifested in many new and telling forms throughout his fiction. One illustration will make clear the universal human quality of Kipling, "For to Admire an' for to See," in which the human inarticulateness and the lonely root-lessness of the Cockney soldier appear, rather than the political arrogance of the poetic imperialist.

> I see the sargeants pitching quoits,
> I 'ear the women laugh and talk,
> I spy upon the quarter deck
> The orficers and ladies walk.
> I thinks about the things that was,
> An' leans an' looks acrost the sea
> Till spite of all the crowded ship,
> There's no one left alive but me.

The early work of John Masefield reveals in its language, rhythm, and subject-matter the influence of Kipling. He was *John* born in 1878, and quite early in youth ran away to *Masefield* sea. In New York he found employment of various sorts, including both manual labor and tending bar. The fruits of this grim experience appear in a series of poems which owe their direct inspiration to Chaucer—*The Everlasting Mercy* (1911), *The Widow in the Bye Street* (1912), and *Dauber* (1913). These are narrative poems, full of physical violence and crude speech. With all their realism, however, they embody the romantic doctrine that man, however cruel and sordid, may become the vehicle of spiritual exaltation. This is, in fact, the theme of *The Everlasting Mercy. Dauber* is the story of a boy who shipped on a sailing vessel, hoping to find opportunity to paint pictures. The account of his suffering and death, in a situation utterly at variance with his temperament, is one of the most vivid realizations of life at sea in English literature. In the cruelty of its realism it reminds one of Smollett; in its art, of Stevenson. The style of these early narratives is of the simplest, reflecting the elemental qualities of human life. More sophisticated are *Reynard the Fox* (1919) and *Right Royal* (1920). The former brings together the characters of the countryside, portrayed with Chaucerian breadth and color, and then narrates the flight for life of the hunted fox with the tragic suspense which marked *Dauber*.

Masefield's true field is narrative poetry, with its wide opportunity for presenting outdoor scene and human action, a predilection which stamps him as a partisan of the strenuous life. But he also has a pronounced lyrical gift, shown in his sonnets, and particularly in "August, 1914," a simple, humbly beautiful elegy on the *Masefield's Dramas* thousands who were being led from England's shores to the slaughter. In dramatic poetry Masefield shows less sustained power than in narrative. *Philip the King* (1914) is the tragedy of the King of Spain, confronted with the failure of his life work and the ruin of his people. Masefield has tried to enlarge his canvas as well as to spiritualize his tragedy by introducing ghosts of the King's errors and crimes somewhat like the abstract forces in Hardy's *The Dynasts*. The suggestion of Hardy is also evident in the prose play, *The Tragedy of Nan* (1909), in which a story of woman's love defeated by human malevolence and ironical circumstance is told with the deepest power and intensity.

Masefield followed the example of contemporary men of letters in practicing many forms of literature. He wrote a number of romances, of which *Sard Harker* (1924) may be regarded as typical with its adventures of a boy in the cities and jungles of a highly imaginary Central America. If we may see in this something of Conrad's influence, it is rather Kipling of whom we are reminded in the short stories of *A Mainsail Haul* (1905), and several books for boys. As a critic, Masefield wrote interestingly of Shakespeare and of his personal friend, John M. Synge. He also gave a magnificent account of the British attempts to pierce the Dardanelles, in *Gallipoli* (1916).

Like Masefield, Wilfrid Wilson Gibson wrote most persua-sively of the lives of common men in the language of common

**W. W.
Gibson**

men. Born in 1878, he began to write poetry under the literary inspiration of the Pre-Raphaelites. Grad-ually the need of bringing poetry close to earth pos-sessed him, and in *The Stonefolds* (1907) he pictured the life of the shepherds of Northumberland. His form was still con-ventional blank verse, but in *Daily Bread* (1910), a series of sketches dealing with the inevitable theme of the poor—

> Daily bread, daily bread—
> Bread of life and bread of labour,
> Bread of bitterness and sorrow,
> Hand to mouth and no tomorrow,

he used a simple, quite colloquial, rhythmic form unrestrained by formal metre and rhyme. *Fires* (1912) presented the same simple material with more richness of color and imagination, and with the reinforcement of metre and rhyme. Gibson, like Masefield, found an opportunity for poetry in the war. In *Battle* (1915) he wrote of the experience of simple men, farm labor-ers, clerks, and artisans, thrown into the trenches to suffer and die, with a pathos which only the seeing eye of the poet can discern. His *Collected Verse* (1922) gives abundant evidence of the return to nature which certain poets of the early twen-tieth century achieved as strikingly as did their precursors a century earlier. Gibson died in 1962.

As a novelist, Thomas Hardy (1840–1928) belongs definitely to the nineteenth century, since his last novel *Jude the Obscure*

**Hardy's
Later
Career**

appeared in 1895. His prolific poetic activity after 1900 makes him one of the most powerful of twen-tieth-century poets. He had indeed written verse be-fore any of his fiction was published, and he con-tinued the practice throughout the years of his growing fame as a novelist. Some of these early verses were published as *Wessex*

Poems (1898), and *Poems of the Past and the Present* (1901). In these years Hardy was engaged on a historical drama, called *The Dynasts,* dealing with the struggle of Europe led by England against Napoleon. This vast work appeared in three parts, between 1903 and 1908. Thereafter he continued to write short poems, of which new collections appeared at intervals of two or three years. The last volume, *Winter Words,* was published after his death in 1928. No writer has shown more clearly the essential unity of a literary career, however various the forms which it assumes. The poems are simple expressions of experience drawn from the same countryside as the novels; *The Dynasts* is a profound and eloquent statement of the philosophy which lies behind his fiction.

The Dynasts, as history or poetic drama, is in close agreement with his earlier work. In the novels he had treated human experience through the men and women of Wessex, among whom he lived. In *The Dynasts,* he dealt with this experience on a grander scale, through *"The Dynasts"* nations and national leaders involved in the great European cataclysm of which memories lingered in the Wessex of his boyhood. An ancestor of Hardy's was captain of Nelson's flag-ship at Trafalgar. *The Dynasts* is a succession of dramatic scenes in verse and prose, divided into nineteen acts, with characters ranging from Napoleon and Wellington to peasants on the coast of Wessex, or citizens on the streets of Berlin. The scenes are presided over by spirits, supported by choruses, the Spirit of the Years, the Spirit of Pities, the Ironic Spirit, Rumors, Messengers and Recording Angels, who carry the interpretation which is in keeping with that of the novels—that an Unconscious Will, of which man is inevitably the victim, works behind all the activities of life. Only at the close does Hardy give us a note of hope that consciousness will develop to the point of becoming a guide to man in subjecting the immanent will to his own needs.

> But—a stirring fills the air
> Like to sounds of joyance there
> That the rages
> Of the ages

Shall be cancelled, and deliverance offered from the darts that were,
Consciousness the Will informing, till It fashions all things fair!

The titles of some of Hardy's later volumes, *Time's Laugh-ingstocks* (1909), *Satires of Circumstance* (1914), recall the
Hardy as Poet ironic attitude of his fiction. More than any other modern poet, Hardy demonstrated that poetry is not a question of special content but of special vision on the part of an author. His poetry grows out of his daily experi-ence—the desultory reading of Catullus or the daily newspaper, the meeting of some children in a country road, or the homely sorrows and amusements of his Wessex neighbors. His mind gives to these common themes a universality of interest, and the power and extraordinary versatility of his pen make them mem-orable. No poem of his, no matter how brief or how lightly handled, is trivial; had he wished, he might have developed many a situation inherent in them into another Wessex novel. He continued the dramatic monologue for which Browning is famous, but he converted it from the imaging of literary or his-torical characters to the presentation of characters who have no history, but whose destiny is tragic for all that. His tardiness in obtaining recognition as a great poet may be due to the fact that with his harsh, prosaic diction, and simple, often stark, metre, he wrote like nobody else, although he was indirectly of incal-culable effect on the younger generation.

The poetic career of William Butler Yeats (1865–1939) is marked by a dynamic capacity for development through a vari-ety of tones and styles. A book published in 1888
W. B. Yeats's Early Poetry contained "The Wanderings of Usheen," a narrative poem that at once made Yeats known. Based upon an eighteenth-century Gaelic lay and dealing with one of the most charming and most dramatic episodes in the Ossianic cycle of Celtic romance, "The Wanderings of Usheen" was the first poem written in English that had the real spirit of the mediæval Irish poetry—passionate delight in the appearance of nature, in strength, and in beauty; vehement lamentation for the facts of decay and death. Other poems about Ireland's heroic period appeared in Mr. Yeats's early books—notably the

superb "Death of Cuchulain." But there were also poems of homely Irish life—poems about fishers, fiddlers, huntsmen, and priests. It was evident that a poet had now appeared who could give to Irish tradition and Irish life a new and subtle beauty. But the volume of lyrics, *The Wind Among the Reeds* (1899), and the verse drama, *The Shadowy Waters* (1900), had an eso-teric content and Yeats gained the reputation of being the poet of mysticism. He wrote this esoteric verse from an intellectual impulse which urged him to create as the French symbolists were creating. The Irish mind is not mystical but intellectual, and Yeats's esoteric poems show the Celtic interest in what is remote and cryptic.

Yeats's early poetic achievement was twofold: he brought back the poetic drama to the theatre, writing, in *The King's Threshold* and *On Baile's Strand* (1904) and in *Deirdre* (1907), the first dramatic verse since Jacobean days that was really related to human impulse and expression and was not a mere decoration; he took the new Anglo-Irish poetry, with its tendency toward rhetoric and its gleams of racial imaginative-ness, and he gave it an æsthetic form that was to be the greatest influence on the next generation of Irish writers.[1]

Yeats's lifelong friend, George W. Russell (1867–1935), whose work appeared under the monogram "Æ," was, in the most profound sense, a mystic. Like many other mystics, he was content to express a single idea. In all his volumes of verse, in *Homeward,* in *The Earth Breath,* in *The Divine Vision,* he put into pregnant verse his all-sufficing thought. Men are the strayed heaven-dwellers—the angels who "willed in silence their own doom," the gods who "forgot themselves to men." Involved in matter, now they are creating a new empire for the spirit. He was drawn to the study of Celtic remains; the old Irish mythology seemed to him a fragment of the doctrine that was held by the Egyptians, the Greeks, and the Indians. He found it natural to allude to the Irish divinities as if they were as well-known as Zeus or Eros or Apollo. "Æ" took a large part in the public life of Ireland, and his prose, which is splendidly

"*Æ*"
(*George W. Russell*)

[1] For a consideration of Yeats's later poetic career, see pages 458–459.

eloquent, pleaded and pointed the way toward the creation of a new social order. He was also one of Ireland's few distinctive painters.

James Stephens (1882–   ), who was one of George W. Russell's "discoveries," has written one superb novel, *The Crock of Gold* (1912), and excellent poetry in various moods—earthy, fantastic, humorous, and poignant. *The Hill of Vision* (1912) and *Songs from the Clay* (1914) caused their author to be hailed as the successor to Yeats and Synge in carrying on the tradition of modern Irish literature. From the latter collection "The Rivals," "Deirdre," and "The Goat Paths" are typical of Stephens's subjects and style. In later years he has turned his attention increasingly to prose, revealing himself in *Deirdre* (1923) and *Etched in Moonlight* (1928) as one of the finest prose stylists of this generation.

PROSE-WRITERS

A number of distinguished prose-writers of the period remain to be considered, since they expressed themselves most persuasively in other literary forms than the drama, the novel, or the poem. It is this habit only that warrants grouping them, since in almost every other respect they show marked divergences. They may, however, serve to illustrate the diverse ways in which a number of gifted men reflected the age in which they lived or reacted against it.

W. H. Hudson (1841–1922), for example, reacted to his age by seeming to ignore it completely. Both temperament and experience unsuited him for life in modern industrial society. A genuine romanticist, he achieved his deepest intimacies with the living elements in nature. For this very reason, perhaps, he appealed strongly to a generation weary of its own civilization and eager to share with him an escape from it. Hudson was born in the Argentine where he acquired a peculiar knowledge of and affection for nature and animal life of which he was to write beautifully. An invalid, he lived in London and continued his studies of nature, especially of birds, and his exploration of the countryside by walking trips through the southern counties. Recognition as a literary artist of the first rank came to him only late in life. He was over fifty when he published *The Naturalist in La Plata* (1892) and *Idle Days in Patagonia* (1893). Then followed his narratives of journeys in England, of which *Hampshire Days* (1903) and *Afoot in England* (1909) may be mentioned as examples of sympathetic and imaginative absorption in the country world of nature and man. He had essayed fiction in *The Purple Land That England Lost* (1895), and in 1904 he published *Green Mansions,* a fantastic romance of the South American forest gorgeous in coloring. His true masterpieces, however, are the personal narratives, especially *A Little Boy Lost* (1905) and *Far Away and Long Ago* (1918), which recall his early life on the Pampas.

Like Hudson, Havelock Ellis (1859–1939) had an early experience of primitive life. As a youth Ellis was taken on a voyage to the antipodes, and remained for four years as a teacher in the wilds of New South Wales. This *Havelock* primitive life gave him an experience of reality *Ellis* upon which as a basis he constructed an edifice composed of scientific training and wide acquaintance with many aspects of modern culture. In 1890, his volume of critical essays, *The New Spirit,* and in 1897 *Affirmations,* reflected a scientifically liberalized attitude toward literature and literary men. Ellis's most significant reaction to his age appears in the series of scientific studies of sexual behavior which he published at intervals between 1896 and 1906. In these, he conscientiously tore away the veils with which Victorian prudery had concealed the human figure, and pioneered, despite censorious discouragement, for a more honest attitude toward sex. In 1914 he began to publish the charming *Impressions and Comments,* to which he added volumes in 1921 and 1924. These show that Ellis, through a scientific training, came to look upon æsthetic values as the most important in man's life, and upon the beautiful as the necessary synthesis of the true and the good. This philosophy is eloquently set forth in *The Dance of Life* (1923). Ellis was neither a great scientist nor an original thinker but he was a courageous pioneer and a brilliant popularizer. Much of his scientific work has already been superseded, but his exposition of life as a highly civilized art is likely to endure in interest.

Sir Max Beerbohm's relationship to his age is clearer than that of Hudson or Ellis. He was born in London in 1872, and **Sir Max Beerbohm** was at Oxford during the last years of Walter Pater's influence there. He began to write clever, paradoxical essays for the *Yellow Book* and other magazines which in 1896 he collected in a very thin volume entitled *The Works of Max Beerbohm*. This he followed by *More* (1899), *Yet Again* (1909), *And Even Now* (1920). He succeeded Bernard Shaw as dramatic critic of the *Saturday Review*, and in 1911 revived the humor of the nineties in *Zuleika Dobson, or an Oxford Love Story*, an extravaganza shot through with satire. Beerbohm's true vocation is caricature, in which field he has published several volumes of cartoons; and the spirit of parody is reflected in *A Christmas Garland* (1912), a series of delightfully humorous imitations of contemporary prose writers, against whose seriousness Beerbohm takes it upon himself to protest. His closest associations are with the decadents of the nineties. Like them, he found ridiculous the more pompous aspects of Victorianism. But his irony and wit made it impossible for him to ignore the absurdities of æstheticism. In consequence, the chief value of his work both in prose and in caricature lies in its record of the impressions made by the lesser follies of his age upon an urbane, sophisticated, and detached observer. Sir Max died in 1956.

The manner of G. K. Chesterton (1874–1936) is as light as Beerbohm's, but his basic seriousness is an exact counterpoise to **G. K. Chesterton** Beerbohm's affectation of frivolity. Chesterton caught the infection of satire and epigram during the nineties, but he used these weapons, not, like most of his contemporaries, for destructive criticism, but for the defense of conservative principles, old faiths and venerable institutions, especially the Catholic Church, and for laughing down the sweeping pretensions of science and modern thought. He tried his hand at fiction, the essay, biography, and poetry, but he made the sharpest impression on his audience in such books as *Heretics* (1905) and *Orthodoxy* (1908), in which he expressed with wit and vigor his disapproval of most aspects of modern unbelief and the necessity for a return to the faith that he himself had found.

CHAPTER XVII

Twentieth-Century Literature

CONVENTION AND REVOLT

THE PERIOD of twenty-five years (1914-1939) between the outbreak of the First World War and the beginning of the Second World War offered the sharpest possible contrast to the official serenity and complacency of the Victorian era. The First World War, with its almost overwhelming anxieties, sacrifices, and disasters, came as a terrific shock to a society that had felt itself permanently freed from the barbarousness of wholesale destruction of life and devastation of property. The hope and faith that this war was a war to end war and to save the world for democracy furnished the necessary moral justification for four years of suffering and sacrifice.

The military triumph achieved by England and her Allies in 1918 was, however, followed by a period of reaction, at first, hopeful and optimistic, and, later, sceptical and cynical. The end of the war created as many problems as it solved. The crusading idealism of the war-period gave way to nationalistic self-seeking and aggrandizement, and the peace-treaty signed at Versailles, while it brought to many small nations opportunities for political and economic self-determination hitherto denied them, was so harshly punitive that it contained within itself, as it is now evident, the noxious germs of an even more frightful world-disaster. Growing scepticism as to the nature of the peace and increased knowledge of the sinister forces that had led to the First World War deepened the sense of disillusionment and betrayal. The passing of the sacrificial mood of the war-period and the sense of release and escape from its horrors encouraged the continuance of the moral laxities inevitable in a social experience as devastating as wholesale warfare, and there developed a general tendency to question the ethical and social ideas and standards of pre-war society. The spurious commercial prosperity of the years immediately after the close of the war encouraged free spending and careless living and an exploitation of self-indulgence and sensuality.

At the end of a decade, the economic consequences of the First World War at last made themselves felt in the onset of an economic depression such as the modern world had never experienced. Taxes, greatly increased in order partially to defray the enormous costs of the conflict, mounted to such a height that they not only bore heavily on the salaried professional classes but threatened to wipe out the estates of all save the most favored of the aristocracy. An increasingly large number of collections of paintings and rare books appeared on the auction block, and found their way across the Atlantic into the great public or private collections made by American multimillionaires. With the onset of the depression came new social burdens and responsibilities. The collapse of the war-economy meant the incidence of unemployment on a scale hitherto unknown. Further tax-burdens had to be imposed in order to maintain hundreds of thousands of families on a dole-system that undermined their morale and threatened to create a permanent pauper class.

But the tremendous problems created for England by the First World War and its aftermath were intensified by political and economical developments elsewhere. The whole system on which the British Empire had been haphazardly constructed began to be challenged by new theories of the state and society, by Communism in Russia after 1917, Fascism in Italy after 1922, and Nazism in Germany after 1933. All these doctrines made inroads upon the English intelligentsia and served further to impair national morale. But the attempt of Hitler to create a new European order which Germany and not England should dominate brought about a gradual resurgence of English patriotism, the repression of critical political elements within, and the growth of a sturdy and courageous determination to defend the Empire and to put down Hitlerism.

The experience of England during the Second World War

(1939-1945) was far more catastrophic than that during the First World War, because in this conflict not only the military forces but the civilian population were intimately involved; it was not merely armed forces that paid heavily in what Prime Minister Winston Churchill tersely described as "blood, sweat, and tears." The almost unremitting attack on England made by the German Luftwaffe wrought not only the wanton destruction of Coventry and other provincial cities but the conversion of London itself into one of the major battle-fields of the war. As a result of a single air-raid in 1941, 1,436 persons were killed in London alone. In the last year of the war, a new horror was added to total war by the German invention of the robot-bomb. These new developments in modern warfare necessitated not only the evacuation to safe areas of government offices, of children and the aged, of precious art objects, rare books, and museum pieces, but also the organization of a vast system of civilian defense in which most able-bodied Englishmen and women played indispensable parts. By the end of the war in September 1945, England had suffered not only the loss of hundreds of thousands of young men but the devastation of wide areas in London and elsewhere and staggering blows to its economic system and its financial resources. The great conflict itself and its effects on English life and character, Sir Winston Churchill described with immense and intimate knowledge and sympathy in the six volumes of *The Second World War*, published between 1948 and 1953.

As a consequence of a resounding victory in the General Election of 1945, the Labour Party was faced with the immense task of dealing with the vast domestic and foreign problems created or intensified by the war. The Party had pledged itself to the public ownership of essential industries, a continuance of financial controls and rationing, an active housing program, and a scheme of national insurance and health benefits. By the most stringent controls of currency and of rationing, and despite the economic dislocations of the time, the Labour Party strove to create what came to be known as the Welfare State. The "austerity" program necessitated by the attempt at once to extend social benefits and to live within the nation's income demanded of the English stoicism hardly less heroic than that they had manifested during the war itself. The social consequences of the·program were spectacular; on the one hand, the liquidation of great fortunes by heavy inheritance taxes, the transference of many noble dwellings to the National Trust, the intensification of the dispersal of art treasures and rare books to museums or libraries in England and America, and the dimming of the brilliant life of the aristocrat, and, on the other hand, a great improvement in the health and economic circumstances of the lower classes, the gradual increase in and improvement of housing, and the opening up of private schools and universities to promising youngsters whose economic condition had hitherto denied them the privileges of education of high quality. The return of the Conservative Party to power in 1951, with Sir Winston Churchill as Prime-Minister, could not halt or fundamentally modify the social and economic revolution that followed the Second World War.

These striking internal changes in English life were matched by equally dramatic changes on the international scene. The outbreak of war in Indo-China in 1946 and the division of Germany between Russia and its erstwhile allies in 1948 symbolized the start of a "cold war" that was to have repercussions on the political and intellectual life not only of England but of the rest of the world. The interminable international debates that characterized the meetings of the United Nations only slightly mitigated the tensions that developed between the Free World and Russia and its Communist satellites, and the French war in Indo-China (1949–1954) and the Korean War (1950–1953) were tragic manifestations of the profound political sickness of the world in the mid-twentieth-century.

Although the rise of the Welfare State improved conspicuously the living-conditions and the health of the less privileged classes in English society and brought about what has been called the biggest revolution in England's social history since the freeing of the serfs, the effect of this revolution on literature and the fine arts took unexpected and surprising forms. One of the major results was the development of overt tension between the representatives of the country's traditional upper-middle class culture with its adherence to the established order and writers and artists from the lower-middle class or the working class whom the privilege of a university education had made vocal. These writers voiced with satirical humor or exacerbated exasperation their frustration and resentment at discovering that a university education did not make them free of the privileges of upper-class society or insure them a way of life superior to that of the class from which they had emerged.

Popular journalism denominated the conflicting forces, the Angry Young Men and the Establishment. The rebels were also referred to as "the kitchen-sink school" because of their preoccupation with the drabber and grubbier features of the less privileged modes of living. The Establishment consisted of those social, political, and religious forces that, despite the social revolution, still maintained control of superior appointments and conspicuous rewards. The rebellion expressed itself, with varying degrees of intensity, in the different literary genres. In fiction, novels emerging from the hitherto generally inexpressive classes extended the range of scrupulous and informed descriptions of working class life to include vigorous attacks on the upper reaches of the social order. Even more conspicuously, young playwrights wrought innovations in the substance and form of drama that exposed the emptiness and banality that had come to mark the conventional drawing room play about aristocratic or upper-middle class life. In poetry, the rebellion took the form of a rejection of the complex stylistic modes introduced into English poetry by the Americans Ezra Pound and T. S. Eliot and the creation by young poets of a style devoted to a deflationary observation of the familiar world. In criticism, there was a marked reaction against the microscopic readings recommended by the New Critics and the fastidious but dogmatic eclecticism of Eliot and F. R. Leavis.

PROSE FICTION

Of the major post-Victorian novelists who had made their reputations before the outbreak of the First World War, almost

CONVENTION AND REVOLT

none showed any marked development in attitudes **Survivors**
or techniques during the remaining years of their
activity. The rich, tapestry-like style which George Moore
(1852-1933) had attained in *The Brook Kerith* (1916) he utilized with even greater success in *Héloïse and Abélard* (1921),
which re-created lovingly the Paris of the twelfth century, with
its harsh physical and ample intellectual life, followed the
famous lovers on a springtime journey through Brittany, and
included a moving account of the Children's Crusade. After
this masterpiece in his later personal style, *Ulick and Soracha*
(1926) and *Aphrodite in Aulis* (1930), which he completed
with difficulty during a serious illness, did not add to his reputation. None of the post-war novels of Joseph Conrad (1857–
1924) equalled the moral probings of *Lord Jim* (1900), the
generous vitality of *Nostromo* (1904), or the superbly oblique
love-story of *Chance* (1913). His most noteworthy post-war
novel was *The Arrow of Gold* (1919), a highly romantic re-
creation of what was apparently an episode in his own young
manhood. Both *The Rover* (1923) and *Suspense* (1925), his
final novel, were completed with more than the usual self-tor-
ture, and show signs of the struggle to force himself to complete them. None of the later novels of Arnold Bennett
(1867–1931) measured up to the solidity and penetration of
The Old Wives' Tale (1908). The trilogy, powerfully initiated
with *Clayhanger* (1910) and *Hilda Lessways* (1911), faltered
to an ineffective conclusion with *These Twain* (1915), and was
continued in a perfunctory wartime effort with *The Roll-Call*
(1918). Probably the best of his post-war novels is *Riceyman
Steps* (1923), the grimly realistic story of the love affair and
married lives of a middle-aged book-seller and the keeper of a
little shop. Although in this novel, Bennett's preoccupation
with drabness and decrepitude comes perilously close to Bal-
zacian parody, the grimness is relieved by the loving kindness
of the illiterate maidservant, Elsie, who reappeared as the
heroine of an excellent short story, "Elsie and the Child"
(1924). In *Lord Raingo* (1926) and *Imperial Palace* (1930),
his assiduity in documentation failed to offset the thinness

and lifelessness of the characterization and the feebleness of the action.

Of the older generation of novelists, John Galsworthy (1867–1933) was the only one who did not attain his full stature before the beginning of the First World War. It was only with the publication of *In Chancery* (1920) and *To Let*
John Galsworthy (1921) that he brought to completion *The Forsyte Saga,* which he had initiated as early as 1906, with *The Man of Property.* This trilogy is Galsworthy's most substantial achievement, a critical creation of the life of the class he knew best, the upper-middle class, and of its spiritual decadence in the last generation of the nineteenth century. The two trilogies he wrote thereafter, *A Modern Comedy* (1929) and *End of the Chapter* (1934) revealed more and more clearly the limitations of his point of view and his powers. The first of these trilogies follows the fortunes of the Forsytes in the post-war world. Galsworthy attempted to explore the manners and morals of "the younger generation," but it was obvious that he did not understand them fully nor approve of them. His tendency to revert to the standards of the generation from which he had temporarily escaped is apparent in the admiration expressed for Soames in *A Modern Comedy* in contrast to the violent revulsion he had shown toward him in *The Man of Property.* With *End of the Chapter,* his reversion to type was complete. He accepted without question the mores of his socio-economic group. Their code of honor, their snobbishness, their distrust of passion and beauty received implicit condonation. The sensitiveness of feeling that had motivated Galsworthy's revolt from his class proved too unsubstantial a thread to guide him through the spiritual chaos of the post-war world. Though he realized that loyalty to one's class or profession was not enough, he failed to discover just what was to take the place of such loyalty. But as the social historian of the passing of Victorianism, Galsworthy is still without a serious rival.[1]

For H. G. Wells (1866–1946), the First World War was a shocking but an exceedingly stimulating experience; it acceler-

[1] For a consideration of Galsworthy's drama, see below, pages 452–453.

ated his creative processes to such a degree that his productivity during the war years far exceeded that of any of the novelists of his own generation.

H. G. Wells

His own painful adjustment to the inescapable facts of the war was set forth skillfully and appealingly in *Mr. Britling Sees It Through* (1916), certainly the most telling presentation in English fiction of the effects of the early years of the conflict upon liberal thought and feeling. In the early post-war period, he was inclined to decrease the fictional content of his novel and to increase the expository element. This tendency, apparent in *Joan and Peter* (1918), is more conspicuous in *The World of William Clissold* (1926), where his favorite novel form, the biographical novel, is strained to the breaking point to include a series of essays expressing the hero's prolific ideas on a great number of important matters. Though Wells continued to produce novels, almost automatically, his most significant activity, after the mid-twenties, was the popularization of knowledge, of history in *The Outline of History* (1920), biology in *The Science of Life* (1929–31), economics, politics, and sociology in *The Work, Wealth, and Happiness of Mankind* (1931). In *The Shape of Things to Come* (1933), where he attempted to dramatize his conception of future history, fact and fantasy are characteristically though bewilderingly combined. Wells was the only major Edwardian novelist to live to see the outbreak of the Second World War, an event which provoked him to a fury of pamphleteering for a world view of political and economic problems. But by that time, Wells's voice, like that of Shaw, seemed as insignificant as those of the old men on the walls of Troy watching the conflict in which they were too feeble to engage.

A number of novelists, somewhat younger than Wells, were more contented than he was with the resources of the traditional novel-form and worked effectively within its limits. Of these, the oldest, Somerset Maugham (1874–   ), had begun his career in 1897 with

Somerset Maugham

a studiously drab realistic novel, *Liza of Lambeth*. He did not achieve a critical reputation, however, until the publication of his powerful biographical novel, *Of Human Bondage,* in 1915.

Of the type made popular by Samuel Butler's *The Way of All Flesh* (1903), this novel has its own virtues of relentless honesty and solid characterization, and it is one of the most powerful of the numerous "young man" novels produced in the first two decades of the century. It depicts with remarkable sensitiveness the fumbling attempts of his physically handicapped hero to find himself, emotionally and professionally. Maugham's later novels did not quite achieve the vitality of his masterpiece, but certain of them showed the technical brilliance and resourcefulness developed through long years of productivity in the field of high-grade magazine fiction. Probably the most memorable of these later novels are *The Moon and Sixpence* (1919), a sardonic interpretation of the career of the French painter, Gauguin, and *Cakes and Ale* (1930), a *tour de force* of satire, pointing out the feet of clay of the last great Victorian man of letters. In later years, Maugham tended to cultivate the short story at the expense of the novel, and here his great technical competence served admirably to communicate his sophistication, cynicism, worldly wisdom, and Odysseus-like observations of men and cities in many exotic parts of the world. Throughout his career as novelist, short-story writer, and dramatist, Maugham was willing to turn his very real gifts to something less than the most serious uses, but, at his best, he was an artist whom it would be unwise to ignore.[1]

The attack on realism which was the major objective of the "high-brow" novelists of the period was foreshadowed in the distinguished work of E. M. Forster (1879–   ).

E. M. Forster
Although he did not reach a wide audience of readers until the publication of his masterpiece, *A Passage to India* in 1924, his work had begun quietly with *Where Angels Fear to Tread* two decades earlier. The surface manner of Forster's novels is realistic, but his impatience with realism is apparent in his introduction into his plots of sudden acts of violence or accidents and in his willful juxtaposition of a romantic figure and a realistic environment, as in *The Longest Journey* (1907) or a realistic figure in a romantic environment,

[1] For a consideration of Maugham's work as a dramatist, see below, pages 454–455.

as in *A Room with a View* (1908). Forster's favorite theme—
the conflict between a sensitive unconventional character and
the world of insensitive unimaginative convention—gave free
play to his delicate perceptions and his taste for cruel ironies.
But his earlier novels impress one as experiments that have not
completely succeeded. With *A Passage to India,* however, he
passed far beyond the experimental stage, and this infinitely
perceptive study of inter-racial psychology and attitudes is his
chef d'œuvre. His work proved stimulating to a number of
younger novelists who were to go far beyond him in their assault upon the ascendancy of realism in English fiction.

The attack on realism made by the major novelists of the
generation that followed the First World War took on a number of different guises. The motivation for the attack was the
growing awareness of the limitations of realism as a literary
mode and impatience with the results of a thoughtless sub-
servience to it. For the doctrine of realism implied views not
only of the nature and technique of art but of the nature of man
and society. To its critics, realism seems to exclude elements in
human nature which art could not afford to ignore and to discourage the use of the technical forms and styles necessary for
the expression of such elements. The major limitation of realism arose from its definition of reality as objective and material
physical experience. This conception of reality, underlying the
work in fiction of such writers as Bennett, Galsworthy, and
Wells, was vigorously attacked by Virginia Woolf in an important essay, *Mr. Bennett and Mrs. Brown* (1924). To Mrs.
Woolf, reality was not objective and material but subjective and
psychological. Life was not a matter of physical and chemical
elements but an awareness of experiencing consciousness. To
her it seemed that the older realistic novelists had failed to
communicate to their readers this sense of fluid shapeless awareness. Even before Mrs. Woolf's attack on the theory of realism
was launched, a number of important anti-realistic novels had
already suggested the soundness of her views.

To an assault on the psychological and aesthetic limitations
of realism, D. H. Lawrence (1885–1930) devoted his turbulent

D. H.
Lawrence

but prolific life. To him realism was primarily objectionable because of the support it gave to the sterility of contemporary materialism, commercialism, and nationalism. Lawrence, like the great anti-Victorians Carlyle and Ruskin, believed that modern life would remain sterile until man experienced a conversion which should lead him to spiritual rebirth and harmony. He therefore devoted his very great gifts to attacking the forces that he believed were corrupting and destroying man and to setting forth the way to a more harmonious and creative kind of life. He held that man would achieve harmony only if he came to terms with his deepest instincts and brought those instincts and his intelligence into adjustment with each other. Not a little of his work, in consequence, was concerned with exposing the deep-seated conflicts in the relationships between complex modern men and women. In his attack on prudishness, he was encouraged by his preoccupation with the doctrines of psychoanalysis, although he converted orthodox Freudianism to his own meanings and purposes. In his hostility to the modern social-political order, he represented the anti-intellectualism, the cultivation of the instinctive so marked in other artists of the twentieth century.

For the effective expression of what he felt most needed saying, Lawrence found the mode of realistic fiction almost utterly inadequate. To him it seemed that realism was forced by its very nature and assumptions to deal with only the periphery of man's experience. He felt himself driven, accordingly, to experiment with means to bring to light those unconscious elements in man's nature which were far more influential agents than superficial consciousness. The task that faced him was that of devising a language in which the unconscious could be expressed. This language he found in metaphor and symbol, and, although his way to success was not without misadventures, he succeeded beyond any writer of his time in giving the unconscious adequate and powerful voice.

Since Lawrence was constantly experimenting in the hope of achieving a perfect medium for the expression of his ideas, his major novels mark the stages of his unending quest. At first, *Sons and Lovers* (1913) seems to be a "young man" novel of the type of Samuel Butler's *The Way of All Flesh* (1903) and Somerset Maugham's *Of Human Bondage* (1915). But this study of the psychological roots of the hero's difficulty in adjusting to the demands of adult life goes far beyond either of these distinguished novels. With *The Rainbow* (1915) and *Women in Love* (1920), Lawrence carried even further his searching revelation of the complex relationships between men's and women's conscious and unconscious minds. Finally, in *Lady Chatterley's Lover* (1928), he stated in the most explicit terms what he felt it most important to say, the deep need of modern men and women to face all the elements in their natures if they were not to live frustrated and incomplete lives. The novel lends itself easily to gross misinterpretation, but Lawrence's unusual explicitness is only a means of expressing his basically mystical view of relations between the sexes.

Lawrence's rejection of modern civilization encouraged him to cultivate the idea that he himself might be the founder of a new and vital social order. But when this fantastic scheme failed, he did not cease to attempt to discover a primitive people who might manifest the naturalness, the unselfconsciousness, and the instinctive honesty he coveted in human relationships. Again and again, he thought that he had found such a people, in the American Indians, in the Mexicans, and, finally, in the Etruscans. Possibly this last discovery was the most satisfying, since there were no living Etruscans to challenge his re-creation of them in the light of his own ideal.

For his age, Lawrence was important as a liberator and a healer. But despite the inadequacy of his ideas, he, as all creators of imaginative literature must, will survive as an artist. Lawrence's artistry is profoundly romantic; it is spontaneous, uncalculated, and experimental. Such art has obvious defects of form and style. But no other contemporary novelist was Lawrence's equal in communicating an extraordinarily vivid sense of living things and beings. Huxley described Lawrence himself as "an upspringing fountain of vitality," and his works are living water from such a fountain.

Lawrence's close friend, Aldous Huxley (1894–1963), was as deeply convinced as Lawrence that modern man and society

Aldous Huxley

were in a perilous state, but his reaction to the situation tended to be negative or only faintly positive where Lawrence's was emphatically positive. Huxley's apprehension of life and its problems was intellectual where Lawrence's was intuitive and mystical. Lawrence was both critical and creative; Huxley was primarily critical. His novels revealed an increasingly hostile reaction to the life they represent. The earlier novels—*Crome Yellow* (1921) and *Antic Hay* (1923)—were lightly and sophisticatedly satirical. The discord on which *Antic Hay* ends deepened through *Those Barren Leaves* (1925) and came to its overpowering climax in *Point Counter Point* (1928), his most thorough exposure of the moral and spiritual chaos of the modern world. The novels he wrote in the 'thirties—*Brave New World* (1932), *Eyeless in Gaza* (1936), and *After Many a Summer* (1939)—were a series of attempts to find some positive faith that might lead him and his readers out of the labyrinth in which they were lost. In the first of these novels, Huxley, defrauded of the hope his grandfather had felt that science would create a new and better world, protested the obliteration of all human values by a society completely controlled by science. With the later novels, the goal toward which the Huxleyan hero was striving became slightly more discernible. Huxley's spokesman, in these novels, pleaded for a renunciation of the world, for passive resistance to its violences, and for the cultivation of contemplation freed from desire. He continued to be obsessed with speculations as to the future of mankind. In *Brave New World Revisited* (1958), he showed that many of the fantastic prophecies he had made in *Brave New World* had come true and predicted a society quite as grim as he had forecast earlier. In *Island* (1962) he described the utopian lives of the inhabitants of a South Sea island named Pala as seen through the eyes of a disillusioned English journalist. But Huxley's account of the sources of the hero's unhappiness had a more compelling immediacy than his description of the earthly paradise, and the paradise itself was not spared the inescapable inner threats of pain and death and the final prospect of destruction from external violence. In Huxley, the wheel had come full circle from the religious

agnosticism and scientific optimism of his grand-father, Thomas
H. Huxley, to social pessimism and anti-scientific mysticism.

Huxley, like Lawrence, rejected the realistic novel as inadequate to his purposes. For the cumulative interest of plot, he
substituted the juxtapositions of assorted characters more or less
artificially assembled and grouped. For a carefully sustained
tone, he substituted violent and sometimes wilfully shocking
contrasts. In his masterpiece of structural ingenuity, *Point
Counter Point,* he attempted to apply to fiction the composi-
tional principles of symphonic music. His style was also a manifestation of his intellectual eclecticism. His vocabulary was
probably richer than that of any other modern novelist, since he
had drawn freely on his encyclopedic learning for the rendition
of his account of an inexhaustibly complex modern culture in
which he had difficulty in finding a meaning.

But Huxley's intellectual dexterity is dwarfed by the cultural
orientation, linguistic equipment, and stylistic audacity of James
Joyce (1882–1941). At first glance, the works of
Joyce seem to defy the discovery of any principle   *James
of growth or continuity. What was clear, however,   Joyce*
in such early work as *Chamber Music* (1907) and *Exiles*
(1918) was that Joyce had a remarkable capacity for assimilating a variety of styles, since the manner of the collection of
poems was that of the seventeenth-century classical lyricists and
the mode of the drama was Ibsenesque. But while this capacity
for stylistic assimilation grew steadily in Joyce's later career, the
more important principle of development was the more and
more audacious reaction against realism, from *Dubliners*
(1914) to *Finnegans Wake* (1939). *Dubliners,* to be sure, is
realism of an apparently familiar variety, but realism attuned
to the communication of psychological states. Behind the writing was a deeply sensitive and subjective personality that would
not long remain content with the limits of realism. The direction the reaction was to take was clearly indicated by *A Portrait
of the Artist as A Young Man* (1916), the most revolutionary
of the "young man" novels that followed in the wake of Butler's *The Way of All Flesh* (1903). Joyce's novel, however,
possesses an artistry far beyond that of Butler's awkwardly man-

aged narrative, and the audaciously masculine revelations are comparable only to the equally feminine exposures that Dorothy Richardson was undertaking in the *Pilgrimage* series, the first volume of which was launched a year before the publication of Joyce's novel. But, while Miss Richardson continued to be satisfied with the persistent notation of her introspective introverted heroine's psychological experience, Joyce, who, in the *Portrait,* had carried the rendition of conscious psychological activity as far as possible, felt the need of discovering, as D. H. Lawrence during the same years was discovering, technical means for the exploitation of the unconscious and for the elevation of particularity to the plane of universality.

The result of these experiments was *Ulysses* (1922), the most complex piece of fiction the modern world has produced. But the complexity is one, not of structure but of style and symbol. The plot of *Ulysses* seems almost negligible; it recounts the trivial experiences of Leopold Bloom, a solicitor of newspaper advertising, in Dublin, on the day and night of June 16, 1904. The most important events are his meeting with Stephen Dedalus, the young artist of the *Portrait,* and his reconciliation with his wife, Molly. But what happens is far less important than the manner in which events are narrated and the symbolic significance that is given them. For the great variety of styles, not only in different sections but within certain sections, seems purposeless until one realizes that, as *"Ulysses"* the title suggests, the trivial personalities and events are being given significance through an elaborate parallelism between them and characters in Homer's *Odyssey.* Thus, Leopold Bloom is equated with Odysseus, Molly Bloom with Penelope, and Stephen Dedalus with Telemachus. Furthermore, each of the major events in the *Odyssey*—such as the encounter with the Cyclops, Calypso, and the Sirens, the home-coming, and the slaying of the suitors—has its more or less obvious parallel in the events narrated in *Ulysses.* In this principle of parallelism is to be found the clue to the variety of styles in which the book is written. For Joyce has seen fit to attempt to heighten the effect of each episode by composing it in a style most appropriate to it. Thus, Leopold Bloom's encounter with Gerty Macdowell—the modern equivalent of the princess Nausicaa—is written in a style that parodies that of the sentimental novelette, and the episode in the maternity hospital is told in a style that parodies the genetic development of English prose. The technical complexity is further increased by the emphasis, in some of the episodes, on a particular organ of the body and a particular art or science. The problem of the function of this stylistic and symbolical complexity is not one that it is easy to solve conclusively. The import of the basic parallelism seems, however, unquestionable. The Homeric parallel furnished an heroic frame of reference by which the modern characters are seen to be at once petty and sublime. One's impression of their pettiness arises from the contrast between the banality and triviality of their actions and language and the dignity and beauty of those of the epic characters; the sense of sublimity arises from the identification of the modern characters with the heroic characters, as they manifest the same emotions, impersonate the same immortal longings, and act out the perpetual human drama. It thus becomes possible to catch the significance of the emphasis on a particular bodily organ or a particular art or science in each major section of the work. Since *Ulysses* affirms the oneness of all life, and since Odysseus and Bloom are facets of the same life, seen under different lights, life, as represented in *Ulysses,* is one, just as the different organs of the body compose one body, and just as the arts and sciences make the composite unity of human culture.

The intricate process of unification illustrated by *Ulysses* is carried even further in *Finnegans Wake,* a work the progress of which had been signalized by a series of fragmentary publications beginning in 1927. If *Ulysses* is devoted to demonstrating that all life is one, *Finnegans Wake* would seem to be concerned with demonstrating that not only all life but all language is one. Here both the hero and the style are protean. For the novel would seem to be the account of the dreams of a man of Scandinavian origin, who lives with his family in a modern Irish city, but who in his dream-life assumes the natures of various Germanic deities and in these guises manifests primitive tendencies long repressed by civilization. But the content of

the novel can be discerned only dimly through a language contrived with Olympian playfulness out of the many languages
Joyce knew. It is as though he were bent on suggesting the
essential unity of all language by showing repeatedly the almost
imperceptible line between the meaning of a word in one lan-
gauge and the very different meaning of a similarly sounding
word in another language. The more obvious purposes of *Finnegans Wake* are not difficult to distinguish; like *Ulysses,* it is
concerned with the psychological adjustments of the hero to
the eternal elements in the family constellation. But the book is
linguistically so intricate that to all but a very few patient and
learned readers it is likely to remain an insoluble puzzle. At
the very least, however, it can be taken as representing the
utmost remove from the kind of realism with which Joyce began
his career as a writer of fiction, in *Dubliners.*

No fact about twentieth-century fiction is more striking than
its indebtedness to a very considerable number of gifted women
Women   writers. Their number is so large and their gifts so
Novelists   various that at least in the 'thirties they seemed to
                 threaten the feminization of fiction. Their promi-
nence was probably due in some measure to the fact that many
of the men who might have been their rivals during this decade
had been killed during the First World War or were prevented
by their experience in it from arriving at creative maturity. In
any case, the success of the feminist movement almost certainly
encouraged many more women to attempt careers as writers
than the man-made Victorian world permitted. The women
novelists work in so many forms as to permit very few unquali-
fied generalizations about their contributions to twentieth-
century fiction. One admirable common quality is their tendency
to represent the world from the point of view of women. They
have obviously felt less compulsion than such nineteenth-century
women-novelists as George Eliot and George Sand to assume a
masculine disguise and to write with masculine authority, although one of them, Henry Handel Richardson, found some
sort of reassurance in a male pseudonym. With this general
shedding of a masculine disguise, these women faced deliberately the neglected task of presenting the world in feminine

terms and of rendering both men and women characters from the special vantage point of womankind. This procedure has brought a new sensitiveness to English fiction, and has, so to speak, added a new dimension to it. Furthermore, although women novelists have perhaps been more inclined than their masculine rivals to content themselves with the traditional well-made novel, several of them—notably Dorothy M. Richardson, Katherine Mansfield, and Virginia Woolf—have made brilliantly successful experiments with the form and style of fiction.

It is probably significant that Henrietta Richardson (1870–1946) should have published all her novels under the pseudonym, Henry Handel Richardson, for her work neither asks nor requires special consideration on *Henry* the grounds of its femininity. Miss Richardson's *Handel* major interests were her native land, Australia, *Richard-* and music, of which she had been a close student *son* and impassioned admirer. Both these subjects she viewed with an objectivity rather masculine than feminine. Her career as a novelist began with a remarkably fine novel about a musical genius, *Maurice Guest* (1908), a subject to which she returned somewhat less happily in *The Young Cosima* (1939). Her most impressive work was the biographical trilogy, *The Fortunes of Richard Mahony,* which she published between 1917 and 1929. This elaborate study of the misadventures of the physician-hero in the pioneering era in Australia is remarkable for its vigorous handling of both character and setting. Though the self-pitying hero may not seem quite worthy of the skill and the detail with which his unhappy lot is presented, the trilogy has more solidity and virility than any similarly extensive work by a contemporary woman novelist.

With *Pointed Roofs* (1915), Dorothy M. Richardson (1882–1957) embarked upon a literary project of great significance for twentieth-century fiction. This novel was the first of a series devoted to depicting the objective *Dorothy* and subjective adventures of a young woman, *M. Rich-* whose name, Miriam Henderson, is significantly *ardson* identical in rhythm with Miss Richardson's. The distinction of the method of the *Pilgrimage* series is that the life-history of the heroine is set forth from within the mind of the woman herself. This method differs from that of Henry James and the older psychological novelists in that it is descriptive rather than analytical. The medium of communication is a psychic stream of which the elements are sense-impressions, bodily sensations, emotions, observations, thoughts, and ideas. This psychic stream is pictured with untiring fidelity to the processes by which the human mind works. But, despite the psychological accuracy and the great technical interest of the *Pilgrimage* series, it suffers as a piece of creative art from the fact that the heroine is almost too introverted and introspective a character to hold one's interest throughout a dozen volumes. But probably no woman of the period has come so close as Miss Richardson to writing a completely feminine novel, to reporting with astonishing fidelity the mysteries of feminine psychology. On women writers, this courageous experiment in fiction has had an effect comparable to that of James Joyce on men novelists.

The reputation of Katherine Mansfield (1888–1923) as a writer of peculiarly evocative short stories was based on five *Katherine* volumes of short stories written during a period of *Mansfield* slightly over ten years. Of these stories, a consider-able number show both perfection in technique and maturity of vision. The type of story she practiced is the plotless variety exemplified by Chekhov, whose work Miss Mansfield admired inordinately. Dealing less than he with universals and more with fragile moods of tenderness and irony, she too was primarily an impressionist. The significant moment in a human relationship, the curious and subtle spiritual adventure, the poignant ironies of contrasting human emotions, she strove to mirror with increasing objectivity. Her painfully developed insight into human experience led her to deal almost exclusively with inner rather than outer events, but, unlike Dorothy Richardson and Virginia Woolf, who are almost exclusively autobiographical, Miss Mansfield observed and understood characters widely divergent from herself in both temperaments and accidentals. An almost excessively conscious and conscientious artist, she attempted to work out her own æsthetic. "Life and art," she wrote, "are two things indivisible. It is only by being true to life that I can be true to art. And to be true to life is being good, sincere, simple, honest."

From the first, she exhibited an astonishing assurance in technique and in control of her subject matter. Her touch was unerring. By the suppression of non-essentials and the unfaltering selection of telling details, she built up to the intensification of a single emotion, mood, or psychological situation. Her growth was in the direction, not of a more perfectly expressive technique, but of intensity of feeling and maturity of vision. She progressed from a rather jaundiced and smug view of people to one of pity and piercing sympathy. From a rather broad and sometimes crude satirist, she developed into a master of irony. Her depth of feeling and subtlety of insight, together with her delicately sensitive prose, imparted a poetic lyricism to subjects that otherwise might have seemed sentimental or mawkish. She always wielded the gleaming blade of irony. She was at her best in the delineation of young children, adolescent girls, and old women, perhaps because the experiences and observations of her own adult life were too close to her to view in perspective. In any case, "Prelude," "At the Bay," and "The Garden Party," which draw on her more youthful experiences, have a tremulous beauty rare in stories concerned with her later life. From her experiences in later life, the best stories are "The Daughters of the Late Colonel," "The Fly," "Mr. Reginald Peacock's Day," and "Je ne Parle Pas Français." Her stories range from the dewy childish awareness of family life in New Zealand, through the wearinesses and frustrations of her English life to the sad and sometimes bitter loneliness of dwelling in the strange land of the Continent.

The major purpose of Virginia Woolf (1882–1941) was the communication through fiction of a sense of reality, but her conception of reality differed fundamentally from the realism of such novelists as Arnold Bennett and John Galsworthy. She was persuaded that *Virginia Woolf* reality, as distinct from realism, is an inward subjective awareness, and that to communicate a sense of it the novelist must abandon the attempt to construct an external world brick by brick and devote himself to the building up of character through the complexity of consciousness. Mrs. Woolf, like Miss Richardson, saw consciousness, as all but the behavioristic psychologist sees it, as a complex of sensations, feelings, emotions, and ideas, and she attempted, through her rendition of this complex, to create the sense of being alive. That sense no other novelist of the period—not even Dorothy Richardson, who may be said to have initiated the method in English—was so skillful in communicating. For Mrs. Woolf brought to her work highly individualized gifts—hypersensitivity on the sensory side, refined observation of the process of thought and feeling, and a deep and tender response to the pathetic evanescence of the reality she devoted herself to adumbrating through her fiction.

On the technical side, likewise, Mrs. Woolf had remarkable powers. Like Huxley and Joyce, she usually abandoned plot as too restrictive a principle of structure, but since she realized that the stream of consciousness must be supplied with banks if it were not to inundate both writer and reader, she tried various means of giving the stream both form and movement. In *Jacob's Room* (1922) the integrating principle, the personality of the hero, proved inadequate to bind together the disparate subjective and objective impressions of him, but in *Mrs. Dalloway* (1925), the same principle was used triumphantly, since the personality of the not too profound but singularly charming woman is kept sufficiently steadily in the centre of the reader's interest to furnish a point of reference for the other persons in the novel, even though they touch the life of Clarissa Dalloway only fleetingly. Even more daringly in *To the Lighthouse* (1927), Mrs. Woolf focussed this remarkably poignant picture of human transience on a single personality. For Mrs. Ramsay is seen not merely as the selfless center of her own existence, but (not only in her life but after her physical death in her spiritual persistence) as the focus of a concentric series of existences more or less intimately involved with hers. *The Waves* (1931) was the highwater mark of Mrs. Woolf's experimentation. Concerned from the beginning with the nature of personality and convinced of its fluid formlessness, she suggested here that personality has no existence apart from the society in which it develops, that the so-called individual existence is really no more than a facet of the existence of a group. She illustrated this conception of personality in *The Waves* by presenting the lives of a closely knit group of seven characters in a series of poetically stylized dialogues or interior monologues. The basic unity under the appearance of diversity is emphasized by the fact that all the characters express themselves in the same style, a highly imagistic, deeply rhythmical utterance that is constantly on the verge of becoming poetry. The least easily approached of Mrs. Woolf's novels, it is also her most brilliant and original creation. In contrast to it *The Years* (1937), her first popular success, seemed like a vulgarization of the method she had worked out for herself in the earlier novels.

Perhaps the most assured talent among the younger women novelists is that of Elizabeth Bowen (1899–   ), whose first novel, *The Hotel* (1927), has been followed by a series of distinguished works of fiction. Miss *Elizabeth* Bowen's impeccably accurate and lucid style re- *Bowen* minds one of Katherine Mansfield's, but her canvases are larger and her range wider. At first, her work gives an impression of somewhat bewildering variety, since her novels have a greater range of milieu than those of most of her contemporaries: the Riviera in *The Hotel*, Irish country-house society in *The Last September*, Paris in *The House in Paris*, and London in several other novels. The diversity of setting tends to obscure her allegiance to a theme similar to that favored by E. M. Forster, the eternal conflict between sensitivity and insensitivity, between coarseness and fineness of feeling and emotion. She is especially adept in her treatment of young girls of unblemished innocence and rare sensibility attempting to adjust themselves to a life that is neither innocent nor sensitive. In *The Hotel*, she traces the tragi-comic line of development of the friendship between her young heroine and an ambiguous widow. In *The Last September* (1929), against the refreshingly unfamiliar background of Irish country-house life in the years of the "Trouble," the gauche young heroine's first love affair reaches a tragic conclusion when her lover, an English officer, is shot from ambush. The focus of interest in *The House in Paris* (1935), is a precocious boy who gradually becomes tensely aware of the complex web of emotions and circumstances of which he is the helpless center. *The Death of the Heart* (1938) contrasts the natural responses of a young orphaned girl with the selfish and sophisticated attitudes of the social group in which she is forced to move. In *The Heat of the Day* (1949) Miss Bowen reflected the political tensions of the time in her study of the topical subject of political treason, and, although the end of the novel was somewhat unsatisfactorily inconclusive, it displayed anew her masterly creation of subtle personalities in complex and ambiguous relationships. *A World of Love* (1955), which developed a plot out of the effects on a closely related group of the discovery of a dead hero's love-letters, reworked in a curiously oblique style two of her favorite themes: life in an Anglo-Irish country-house and a young girl's initiation into love. Although Miss Bowen's descriptions are almost too poetic for prose and although her wit is a little exhausting, her work rises above that of many of her competent contemporaries by reason of the shrewdness of her observations, the sensitiveness of her responses to the atmosphere of places, and the depth of her understanding pity for those sensitive souls who face the world without armor.

The mordant and searching wit of Ivy Compton-Burnett (1892–   ) allies her with the tradition of brilliantly stylized dialogue of Congreve's Restoration comedies, for her novels are, almost without exception, conversation-pieces; they contain little in the way of descriptions of setting, characters, or actions. Not only a few specially favored characters but the children and servants express themselves in the identical epigrammatic style *Ivy* and in incredibly swift repartee. The usual setting *Compton-* is a country-house at about the turn of the century; *Burnett* her characters, an ingrown family, their knowing servants, and their duller neighbors. Although her sometimes complicated plots, developed entirely in dialogue, have melodramatic elements, their tragic potentialities are turned into high comedy by her wit and wisdom. Her favorite themes are domestic tyranny and the futile struggle to oppose it and the inexhaustible tragi-comedy of the self-deceived. Her first novel, *Dolores* (1911) was an inconsequential youthful effort, and it was only with *Pastors and Masters* (1925) that her characteristic technique and point of view declared themselves. Of the succeeding novels, perhaps the most noteworthy are *Daughters and Sons* (1931), a study of the family relations of a matriarch, who "seldom spoke anything but evil of any human being," *Bullivant and the Lambs* (English title, *Manservant and Maidservant,* 1947) in which the tyranny of a father is echoed below stairs, *Two Worlds and their Ways* (1949), setting forth parallel chicaneries in the two worlds of school and home, and *The Present and the Past* (1953), in which with somewhat mellowing temper she makes comedy out of the plight of a weakling caught in the web wrought by his first and second wives. *Mother and Son* (1955) worked out the destructive influence of a dominating mother on her husband and their middle-aged son. *A Father and His Fate* (1957) struck a somewhat more humane note, since her depiction of the sufferings of an erring woman were suffused with unusual pity. In *A Heritage and Its History* (1959) the author's familiar mixture of secret sin, family hostilities, and overpowering greed were made tolerable by her unfailing wit and her wisdom about the seamier sides of human nature.

Despite the radical innovations wrought on the content and form of the novel by experimenters like Lawrence, Joyce, and Mrs. Woolf, twentieth-century fiction continues to show the widest possible range of modes from realism and naturalism to romanticism and sentimentalism. It is evidence of the vitality and amplitude of modern fiction that it should manifest a varied and abundant life. *Varieties of Modern Fiction*

One of the clearest illustrations of contemporary realism can be found in such novels of Sean O'Faolain as *A Nest of Simple Folk* (1933), and *Bird Alone* (1936). In O'Faolain, the romanticizing lyrical impulse present in most Irish writers seems repressed, and the result is a sharpened unflinching particularity that within its limits is highly effective. Dissatisfaction with the repressions and reticences of such traditional realism has driven James Hanley (1901–   ) to practice a naturalism so bold and brutal that it would have horrified the English Zola, George Moore. His novels of life at sea—*Boy* (1931) and *Stoker Bush* (1935)—retain no vestige of landlubber romance: instead, they represent the lives and work of sailors as coarse and brutal, violent and ugly. In the trilogy, which began with *The Furys* (1935), he follows unflinchingly the fortunes and grim misfortunes of a lower-class family in a waterfront city, during the first two decades of the century.

Such scrupulously objective naturalism as Hanley's had already proved inadequate to the purposes of Liam O'Flaherty (1897–   ). His fiction illustrates the tendency of the modern naturalist to pierce below the surface of naturalistic objectivity and to explore more and more deeply the more inaccessible psychological levels of experience, while remaining as faithful to psychological fact as the earlier naturalists were to objective fact. O'Flaherty's special power is the imaginative re-creation of the constantly intensifying series of emotional states experienced by his central character during a brief but crucial period. Thus, in *The Informer* (1925), *Mr. Gilhooley* (1926), *The Assassin* (1928), and *The Puritan* (1931), he follows the relentless course of his heroes on their way to disaster by setting forth the stages of their increasing emotional violence and psychological disorientation. Despite the repetitious pattern of O'Flaherty's more important novels, he is the unrivalled master of the type of psychological realism he has made his own.

The tendency of naturalism to ally itself with other modes is apparent in the fiction of T. F. Powys (1875–1953). His favorite theme is one that recurs among novelists of his generation, the destruction of innocence and purity by lust and brutality. Despite the realistic setting and language, the characters are simplified to such a degree that they tend to become figures in a moral allegory. He further heightened the symbolic significance of his work by utilizing in some of his best novels—*Mr. Weston's Good Wine* (1927) and *Unclay* (1931) —unmistakably allegorical figures. In his horrified revolt against man's brutality and cruelty, he sometimes carried brutality—as in *Mr. Tasker's Gods* (1925)—beyond the limits of æsthetic effectiveness. In the massive and highly individualized novels of his older brother, John Cowper Powys (1872–1963), the vein of naturalism is almost hidden by a complex combination of neo-romantic elements. Nature plays an important part in all his novels—from *Wolf Solent* (1929) to *Owen Glendower* (1940)—but it is nature seen, not with Wordsworthian or Tennysonian eyes, but with the eyes of almost primordial vision. Both in nature and in man as a part of nature, vast forces making for good and evil are contending for mastery. The evil forces in particular are invested by Powys's imagination with an aura of fascinated horror. He has an acute sense of place and a tendency to indulge in windy and pretentious philosophizing. The combination of these elements produces a highly complex variety of neo-romanticism.

Of novelists who initiated their literary careers just after the first quarter of the twentieth century, Evelyn Waugh (1903–   ), Graham Greene (1904–   ), and Henry Green (1905–   ) have won very considerable reputations. The earliest of Waugh's novels, *Decline and Fall* (1928) and *Vile Bodies* (1930) signalized the appearance of a satirist as high-spirited as the earlier Aldous Huxley, and even more mordant. But these brittle and apparently insouciant novels implied a moral or ethical standard by which man's follies and weaknesses could be condemned. Waugh's conversion to Catholicism in 1930 furnished him an explicit base for his moral judgments, and, although his novels are far less obviously Catholic than the serious fiction of Graham Greene, *Brideshead Revisited* (1945), despite its superficial air of worldliness, had its religious overtones. Similarly, his satire on totalitarianism in *Scott-King's Modern Europe* (1947) and on Californian funeral rites in *The Loved One* (1948) had moral implications for those who read between the lines of his satirical extravaganzas. A more substantial achievement was the trilogy initiated by *Men at Arms* (1952), continued in *Officers and Gentlemen* (1955), and completed with *Unconditional Surrender* (American title, *The End of the Battle*, 1962). The first of these novels

showed the central figure, Guy Crouchback, a Catholic aristocrat, beginning his participation in the Second World War
with something of the idealism of a mediæval crusader. *Officers
and Gentlemen* recounted his experiences in training with the
Haldberdiers regiment in Scotland, his active service in the
disastrous Cretan expedition, and his disillusionment at the
discovery that not all officers are gentlemen. The concluding
volume of the trilogy set forth not only Crouchback's resigned
acceptance of things as they are but also his efforts to accomplish some good in the world by his fumbling attempt to aid
some Jewish refugees while serving with the Partisans in
Yugoslavia and, on the personal plane, by re-marrying his
estranged wife in order to give her illegitimate child a name.

Graham Greene (1904–   ) is, like Waugh, a convert to
Catholicism, and both his light and his serious fiction implies
his preoccupation with the tenets of his faith. Greene himself
classifies his fiction as "entertainments"—like the expert thrill-
ers, *This Gun for Hire* (1936) and *The Ministry of Fear*
(1943) and "novels." In both these categories, however, he is
concerned obviously or subtly with evil and its endless conflict
with righteousness. In *Brighton Rock* (1938), although the
Graham action is violent, the atmosphere grubby, and the
Greene characters unsavory, he suggests the possibility of
the extension of grace to even a vicious believer.
Similarly, in *The Power and the Glory* (1940), a Mexican
priest, who falls far short of being an ideal character, is a force
for good by reason of his unwavering faith. *The Heart of the
Matter* (1948) studied the effect on a conscience-ridden Englishman of an adulterous affair into which he drifts largely
out of pity and of his final attempt to escape from his unbear-
able spiritual dilemma by the theologically dubious method of
suicide. Less successfully, in *The End of the Affair* (1951),
Greene attempted to show the conversion of an adulterous
woman as the result of her lover's apparently miraculous restoration to life. *The Quiet American* (1955), a political novel
set in Indo-China in wartime, showed its hero as not only
crassly materialistic but dangerously innocent by reason of his
failure to understand other peoples. A more impressive novel,

A Burnt-Out Case (1961) told the story of a famous but utterly disillusioned architect's quest for some justification for living. Seeking refuge in a leper colony in Africa, he seems about to achieve a degree of religious enlightenment when evil forces in others—an unscrupulous journalist and a petty jealous husband—bring him to an untimely death. Greene also tried his hand, if less successfully, at the drama. His first play, *The Living Room* (1953), showed an innocent girl as the victim of a struggle between her lover, a rationalistic psychologist, and her priest, in an environment marked by morbid religiosity.

Greene's preoccupation with sin and the subtlety with which he has explored its ramifications perhaps account for the fact that he had been studied more seriously by French critics than any other mid-twentieth-century English novelist.

Although there are striking analogies between the novels of Henry Green (1905–   ) and those of Ivy Compton-Burnett, the differences are sufficiently significant to give his work the distinction of individuality. Both of these rarely gifted writers build their novels chiefly out of conversation, tend to restrict each novel to a relatively limited milieu, and turn into high comedy situations that less witty writers might find tragic. But Green's dialogue is far less stylized than Miss Compton-Burnett's; speech is subtly adjusted to each of his characters. Furthermore, Green ranges far beyond the limited world of country-house gentry for his themes and his characters. If Miss Compton-Burnett's favorite theme is domestic tyranny, Green's is the inroads of fear upon personality, the subtly demoralizing fear of loss of love, loss of position, loss of reputa- **Henry** tion. In *Living* (1929), Green, drawing wisely **Green** from his own life-long experience in industry, wrote a richly informed and human story of working-class life. *Caught* (1943) dealt with his own and his countrymen's experiences in wartime civilian defense. In *Loving* (1945), Green made high comedy out of the ravages of love among English masters and servants who had taken refuge from the war in an Irish country-house. *Concluding* (1948) played sardonically with the intrusion of totalitarian personalities upon personal liberty. In *Doting* (1952) he made sport with the shabby subterfuges of middle-aged dalliance. Although Green's imagination shuns the depths of tragedy, his wisdom about human nature, his limitless wit, and his great technical skill give his novels rare distinction.

In the Nineteen-Fifties, a number of writers produced distinguished fiction that demonstrated the continued vitality of the novel. Closest to the tradition of the novel as social history were the works of C. P. (Sir Charles Percy) Snow (1905–   ). Trained as a physicist and experienced as an influential civil servant during the Second World War, Snow had access to material denied to most novelists, and of this material he took every advantage. In a series of novels entitled *Strangers and Brothers,* he not only recounted the personal and professional history of Lewis Eliot in *Time of Hope* (1950) and *Homecoming* (1956) but also utilized Eliot as the observer-narrator in novels in which he was not the central figure. From Eliot's observations of Cambridge University, three novels derived their materials. In *The Light and The Dark* (1947), Eliot observed sympathetically the life and destructive career of a brilliant but unstable Fellow, Roy Calvert. *The Masters* (1951), a neatly rounded and malicious comedy of academic life, focussed on the election of a Master by the Fellows of a College.

C. P. (Sir Charles Percy) Snow

The Affair (1960) concerned the innocence or guilt of a young scientist who had been accused of faking scientific evidence. The ultimate triumph of the accused to which Eliot significantly contributed was delayed not only by the scientist's unpleasant personality and leftist views but also by the lack of enthusiasm for justice of some of the Fellows. *The New Men* (1954) dealt impressively with the new world of the atomic scientist and the ethical conflicts the destructive power of science aroused in Eliot's younger brother, Martin. In *The Conscience of the Rich* (1958), Eliot witnessed the rebellion of son against father in an aristocratic Anglo-Jewish family before the Second World War. Recurrent themes in Snow's novels were the conflict between personal ambition and the individual conscience and the temptations that power, personal and professional, brought with it. Snow used with admirable effectiveness his wide experience of men and affairs. He was an excellent observer and a sound, if unexciting, craftsman. He was more perceptive of men in their professional and political relations than in their more personal and intimate concerns.

The novels of William Golding (1911–) belonged to the genre of the philosophical apologue rather than the novel as social history. Golding's central concern was the problem of evil and its threats to individual and social existence. His novels had a stark spare *William Golding* quality that was classical rather than romantic. Perhaps the most successful of his novels was *Lord of the Flies* (1954) in which he traced with horrifying persuasiveness the emergence of destructiveness in a group of well-bred English boys marooned on a tropical island during the atomic war. *The Inheritors* (1955) was a stylistic *tour de force,* since the central figures, a few survivors of an ancient race, are so primitive that they are hardly capable of articulate speech; ultimately, they are destroyed by a more civilized but more successfully destructive people. In *Free Fall* (1960), Golding was concerned with an artist's attempt to discover where in the past he had chosen the path that turned the good in his life into evil.

If the tone and manner of Golding were classical, those of Lawrence Durrell (1912–) were extravagantly but sophisticatedly romantic. In the first three of a group of novels known as the *Alexandrian Quartet, Justine* (1957), *Balthazar* (1958), and *Mountolive* (1958), Durrell from three different points of view gave three different interpretations of the complex erotic and political contemporaneous relations of characters of various cultural backgrounds in modern Alexandria. The action in *Clea* (1960), the final volume of the series, occurred at a later time and showed what the lapse of years had done to the major characters and gave a final and definitive interpretation of their personalities and their motives. Durrell's style was lush and baroque; his elaborate set-pieces of narrative were brilliant; if his characters and plot did not contribute conspicuously to his announced intention of conducting "an investigation of modern love," the novels constituted a series of lyrical hymns of homage to Alexandria and evoked powerfully its corrupt and fascinating atmosphere.

The widely varied voices of a slightly younger generation were heard in the novels of Iris Murdoch, Kingsley Amis, and Alan Sillitoe. The novels of Miss Murdoch (1919–   ) were curious but at their best effective blends of wit, eroticism, fantasy, and symbolism. The eroticism, however, had the moral and almost disembodied quality of the love-making in Restoration Comedy. *The Bell* (1958) depicted tragi-comically the disintegration of a lay religious community under the impact of uncontrollable erotic urges. Although *A Severed Head* (1961) had the surface appearance of a modern comedy of erotic manners, beneath the surface lay an obscure pattern carrying more profound symbolic significances. *An Unofficial Rose* (1962), out of the design made by the characters' unstable amorous relations, developed the theme that love is a fatality of which the consequences in most cases fall far short of satisfactory fulfilment. Kingsley Amis (1922–

Kingsley Amis   ) objected to being considered a leader of the Angry Young Men, perhaps because he responded with extravagant humor rather than indignation to the frustrations of the over-educated but socially under-privileged. The hero of *Lucky Jim* (1954), however, became as archetypal a figure of revolt as the Jimmy Porter of John Osborne's *Look Back in Anger,* but Amis made riotous farce out of this young intellectual's personal and professional misadventures in a red-brick provincial university. *That Uncertain Feeling* (1955) recounted divertingly the hapless amorous adventures of a lower-class Welsh librarian in upper-class provincial society. *Take a Girl Like You* (1960) established Amis' leadership among the comic novelists of his generation. Here, the exuberant farce contrived out of the pursuit of a determinedly innocent girl by a high-principled delinquent was deepened by touches of bitter wisdom. In Alan Sillitoe (1922–   ), the contemporary English working class found an eloquent spokesman. In the title-story of the volume, *The Loneliness of the Long-Distance Runner* (1959), the under-privileged hero expresses his defiance of the forces that would control him by willed self-defeat. The brothers who are the heroes of his novels *Saturday Night and Sunday Morning* (1959) and *Key to the Door* (1961) are completely antisocial in their urges and behavior. The earlier novel depicted brilliantly the self-regarding demands and the casual physical satisfactions of its hero. The later novel described the hero Brian Seaton's experiences during the Depression and during his military service in Malaya; it rejected in thought and action the official goals and values that the Establishment found in a conflict in which he was determined to play as negative a role as possible.

DRAMA

On the whole, the English drama in the first generation after the First World War did not equal in distinction or variety that of the period from 1890 to 1914. That renaissance of the drama for which Henry Arthur Jones called and for which he worked manfully in the 'nineties reached its peak in the early years of the twentieth century, and although the repertory theatres in provincial England and in Ireland continued their work, they produced no writers comparable in power to those of the earlier generation, and the new art-theatres in London and Dublin, although they made intelligent and courageous productions, brought no very impressive talents to light. Again, one is tempted to wonder whether among the countless victims of the war there were not young men whose talents would have brought vitality to the theatre. In any case, there were many indications that dramatists and their audiences were reverting to the trivial conception of drama as entertainment which had made the nineteenth-century drama a byword for emptiness and vacuity.

Certain writers whose careers in the theatre were well advanced by 1914 continued to write plays during the war and after it. Of these, Barrie, Galsworthy, and Shaw demand attention here.

Barrie developed no new attitudes or values in the post-war period, but his long experience in the theatre stood him in good

Sir J. M. Barrie stead until within a few years of his death in 1935. Always stoutly inimical to the realism and intellectualism prevalent in the drama of the period, he continued to cultivate the vein of sophisticated sentiment in which he had been conspicuously successful in *What Every Woman Knows* (1908) and earlier plays.[1] The war had a relatively slight influence on Barrie's writing for the stage. The incidental war-motifs in *A Kiss for Cinderella* (1916) are handled in terms of delicate sentiment, and the play, as a whole, is a shrewd combination of realism and fantasy. Other war motifs occur in *The Old Lady Shows Her Medals* (1917) and *A Well-Remembered Voice* (1918). The first combined humor and pathos with Barrie's customary adroitness, but the latter wrings the last tear-drop from the spectacle of the homely communication between a bereaved father and the spirit of his son who has been killed in battle. In *Dear Brutus* (1917) Barrie was on somewhat safer ground; the basic pessimism which underlay his cultivation of sentiment did not destroy or belie the wisdom of his demonstration of the changelessness of human nature. In the creation of the dream-daughter, Margaret, Barrie is in his happiest vein. With *Mary Rose* (1920), fantasy and sentiment again combine; here the pathos is intensified through the heroine's ultimate discovery of the incompatibility between her own immortality and the mortal and therefore mutable and forgetful world. Barrie's final effort, *The Boy David* (1936), was one of the most eagerly anticipated and one of his most completely unsuccessful plays. The presentation of David as a winsome Peter-Pan-like figure seemed a failure in understanding and taste. Although from the beginning of his career, Barrie stood aside from the main stream and the tributaries of the modern drama, he won a wide audience through his remarkable gift for giving his slightly cynical sentimentalism dramatic form and body.

Although no play that John Galsworthy (1867-1933) wrote after 1918 equalled certain of his earlier plays in vigorous real-

[1] Throughout the drama section of this chapter, the dates are those, not of publication, but of first production. The earlier dramatic work of Barrie, Galsworthy, and Shaw is discussed in Chapter XVI.

ism, he produced a number of successful and skillful plays in his later life. Both *The Skin Game* (1920) and *Loyalties* (1922) give evidence of his reaction from the idealistic mood of the period of the war. *John Galsworthy* The earlier play is a harsh and unlovely study of the struggle for social position between an old county family and that of a rising industrialist. Although at the beginning of the play certain of the characters manifest admirable traits, by the end of their conflict they have all deteriorated as a result of the parts they have played in it. The play might very well be taken as a wry allegory of the fate of the contestants in the war that had recently ended. The second play, *Loyalties,* is probably the finest of Galsworthy's later dramas. Inspired by the martyred Edith Cavell's dictum, "Patriotism is not enough," Galsworthy has shown here a group of characters involved in a social-moral dilemma, to which each reacts in accordance with the particular narrow loyalty by which he has been conditioned; again, each participant in the contest is worsened by it. Here Galsworthy is apparently pointing rather hopelessly to the need for a higher loyalty than one to race, social class, or profession. In *Escape* (1927), the sentimentality that weakened his later novels also attacked his drama, for this series of scenes representing the reaction of very different characters to their confrontation by an escaped convict is deprived of any real moral significance by the fact that the escaped man is innocent of the crime for which he has been imprisoned. The problem then is the relatively easy one of whether or not the convict's unwilling hosts shall obey the letter or the spirit of the law.

Although George Bernard Shaw (1856-1950) developed no new ideas of very great importance after 1914, he continued to engage incessantly in dramatic activity, and produced several plays of great interest and effectiveness and a number of others in *George Bernard Shaw* which he set forth his increasingly perverse views on the most controversial issues of the day. Aside from his one-act play, *O'Flaherty, V.C.* (1918), which unmasks a hero as he had done years before in *Arms and the Man,* Shaw's most important dramatic reaction to the First World War was *Heartbreak*

House (1920), in which he depicted the spiritual bankruptcy of pre-war Europe and its desperate need for some sort of regeneration. His most astonishing production during his later period was the series of plays, *Back to Methuselah* (1921), which he described as a metabiological pentateuch, and in which he reconstructed the history of the world, past, present, and future, on his own terms. Despite some tedious topical political satire, this series of plays is an impressive dramatization of Shaw's Lamarckian doctrine, his thesis that what man wills determines his future. The figure of Lilith, Adam's legendary first wife, is an eloquent spokeswoman for the usually repressed romantico-mystical aspects of Shaw's doctrine. The most effective of Shaw's later plays, *Saint Joan* (1923), is a highly sympathetic rendition of the career of the Maid of Orleans; characteristically, she becomes not a religious mystic but the first of the great proponents of Protestantism. *The Apple Cart* (1929), *On the Rocks* (1933), and *Geneva* (1938) are hardly more than lively talkative dramatizations of political pamphlets, in which Shaw set forth his views of the increasingly desperate conflict between democratic and totalitarian ideas. The flagging of Shaw's unconquerable spirit is apparent in his despair of the ability of democracy to solve its own problems and in his defense of some variety of dictatorship. On the outbreak of the Second World War, Shaw reverted to his old role of devil's advocate.

Alone among the playwrights who had established themselves before 1914, Somerset Maugham showed some genuine development in the later period. His earlier plays **Somerset** had been delightful examples of the comedy of **Maugham** manners which Oscar Wilde had assisted in reviving, but they had little substance and less bite. Although the most popular of his later plays, *The Constant Wife* (1927), is a perfect example of his earlier dramatic manner, his more serious plays contain elements new to his writing for the stage. *Our Betters* (1917) is a virulent attack on aristocratic English decadence and on social-climbing Americans; *The Circle* (1921) is a worldly-wise demonstration of the eternal appeal of love outside the bonds of matrimony, and *For Services Rendered* (1932) is one of the bitterest of the plays on the theme of the futile sacrifices of the war heroes. Maugham's more serious plays may lack the perfect deftness and assurance of his comedies of manners, but they are important indications of the changes wrought upon him with the passage of the years.[1]

Lennox Robinson (1886–1958), a native of County Cork, made a local reputation as an Abbey Theatre playwright before 1914, but his wider fame belongs to his later years, spent first as manager and then as producer at the *Lennox* Abbey. Between his early and his later plays, there *Robinson* are marked differences. The earliest ones—*The Clancy Name* (1908), *The Cross Roads* (1909), and *Harvest* (1910)—belong to the mode of determinedly grim realistic tragedy, affected by the English repertory theatres of the decade and memorably illustrated by Masefield's *The Tragedy of Nan* (1908). Robinson gradually learned, however, to emphasize his thesis less obviously and to be less insistent on precipitating tragedy at the cost of psychological probability or æsthetic persuasiveness. His later plays show a wide range in type and manners. His most popular successes have been comedies of Irish manners like *The Whiteheaded Boy* (1916), *Crabbed Youth and Age* (1922), and *The Far-Off Hills* (1928), but his more serious studies of Irish problems—from the historical portrait of the patriot, Robert Emmet, in *The Dreamers* (1915) to the consideration of the fate of the Anglo-Irish gentry under the Irish Free State, in *The Big House* (1926)—are perhaps of greater interest. His most challenging later plays, however, are those which show some tendency to break away from the limitations of realism and to indulge in non-realistic effects. Some of these suggest the influence of the Italian playwright, Luigi Pirandello, in their preoccupation with the problem of reality and with the divergencies between life and art. The first of these plays, *The Lost Leader* (1918), like Pirandello's *As You Desire Me,* weighs delicately the evidence for and against the identification of a mysterious person, in this case that of a strange old man, Lucius Lenihan, as the secretly surviving statesman, Parnell. The plays that concern the relationship between life and art are *Is Life Worth Living?* (1933), played in America as *Drama at*

[1] For a consideration of Maugham as a novelist, see pages 427–428.

Inish, which treats humorously the effects of a steady diet of Ibsen on simple Irish village folk, and a one-act play, *Church Street* (1934), which reminds one of the central theme and method of Pirandello's *Six Characters in Search of an Author.*

Of the playwrights who emerged shortly after 1914, it is noteworthy that the most significant ones were not English but Irish or Scottish. No English playwright appeared who had *Noel* anything new to say or who discovered new tech- *Coward* niques for the embellishments of old truths. Noel Coward (1899–   ) will serve to illustrate the technical agility and the intellectual vacuity of the work of most of the post-war English playwrights. His early play, *The Vortex* (1924), is a sardonic delineation of the superficial brilliance and the underlying callousness of the intelligentsia in the post-war social and artistic world. *Easy Virtue* (1926) is interesting chiefly as marking the complete reversal of the Victorian moral standards upheld in Pinero's *The Second Mrs. Tanqueray* (1893). Although the theme of these two plays is identical—the relations between a woman of easy virtue and "respectable" society—in Coward's play, as distinct from Pinero's, the dice are heavily loaded in favor of the proudly erring heroine. Despite such spectacular successes as his one-man revue, *This Year of Grace* (1928), and his nostalgically sentimental *Bitter Sweet* (1929), Coward reached his most characteristic expression in *Private Lives* (1930) and *Design for Living* (1933). The earlier play has grace and wit and the vestigial remains of decency; the latter play is devoid of both wit and decency. *To-night at Eight-Thirty* (1936), a series of nine one-act plays, was a remarkable demonstration of Coward's almost unfailing technical resourcefulness and adroitness. But, despite the calculated patriotic emotion of *Cavalcade* (1931), Coward's work generally illustrates the irresponsibility with which most twentieth-century playwrights regarded life and the drama in the first two decades after the First World War.

The most vigorous talent to emerge from the ranks of the *Sean* Abbey Theatre playwrights since the death of *O'Casey* Synge in 1909 is the proletarian playwright, Sean O'Casey (1880–   ) who made his reputation as a writer of naturalistic tragi-comedies on the swarming life of the Dublin tenements in which he had been brought up. His first play, *The Shadow of a Gunman* (1923), had as its background the strife between the Irish Republican Army and the English Black and Tans in May, 1920. It found its focus in the character of a poet, Donald Davoren, whose high pretensions to courage and heroism are utterly riddled by his cowardly behavior during the action of the play. *Juno and the Paycock* (1924), a more substantial performance, is one of the finest plays written during the postwar period. The nucleus of the plot is the time-worn comic device of a legacy that turns out to be non-existent, but the banality of this central theme is concealed by the richness of the characterization of Captain Boyle, "The Paycock," the boastful ne'er do well, and his evil crony and toady, Joxer, Johnnie, his crippled informer son, and Mary, the betrayed daughter. But the finest of the characterizations is that of the Captain's wife, who, like Maurya in Synge's *Riders to the Sea,* rises indomitably above the disasters that fall upon her family. In this play, O'Casey's powers were revealed to the full: his gift of racy, exuberant Dublin speech, imaginative but without the poetic elevation of Synge's Aran dialect, and his audacious but somehow successful sudden alternations between the most extreme moods—from tragedy to comedy, from melodrama to farce, from pathos to humor. These same powers were equally apparent in O'Casey's next play, *The Plough and the Stars* (1926). The tragedy of the young wife, Nora, who fails in her attempt to keep her husband from joining the Easter Rebellion of 1916, gives coherence and form to a rich series of earthy, humorous, or tragic portraits of persons affected in one or another way by the course of the civil strife. One of O'Casey's most audacious effects comes at the close of the play, where, after Nora has gone mad, and an innocent bystander, trying to protect her, has been shot by a sniper, two British soldiers enter the empty room and consume the tea Mrs. Grogan had made for Nora, as they join their off-stage companions in singing "Keep the Home Fires Burning." O'Casey's tragi-comic treatment of the events connected with the Easter Rebellion provoked a demonstration at the Abbey Theatre similar to that occasioned by the first performances of Synge's *The Playboy of the Western World*, and these disturbances may have had something to do with the directors' refusal to produce O'Casey's next play, *The Silver Tassie* (1929), an anti-militaristic play, which marks O'Casey's break with the naturalism characteristic of the earlier dramas. Most of this account of the experiences of an Irish soldier before, during, and after the First World War was rendered in the familiar naturalistic technique, but in the second act, the influence of German expressionism made itself apparent in the stylized poetic litany to the guns which the soldiers intone on the battle field. In this experimental play, the different methods are not so successfully fused as the very diverse styles—poetic, realistic, satirical, and allegorical—were in *Within the Gates* (1934), a modern morality play, satirizing various aspects of bourgeois urban society and hymning the joy of life through the lips of a prostitute. O'Casey's plays since *Within the Gates* have not added perceptibly to his reputation. *The Star Turns Red* (1940) was an ill-timed radical drama of the life of a city on the verge and in the early stages of a class war. Here, as in *Within the Gates,* the characters are allegorical types rather than individuals, and the range of styles is much wider than in the dramatist's earlier works. *Purple Dust*, which was published in 1941, was a broadly satirical farce on the contrast between the English and the Irish character. Though there is some comic invention in the play, both characters and episodes are so extravagantly treated as to have the effect of crude caricature. The English dilettantes, Stoke and Poges, are men of straw, and the Irish peasants speak in a dialect that sounds like an unhappy imitation of Synge's. But, despite the disappointing later plays, O'Casey was the most forceful of the new men writing for the English theatre.

Among the younger playwrights associated with the Abbey Theatre, the Ulsterman, George Shiels (1885–   ), was the most popular. Although he attempted serious psy-

George Shiels

chological drama in *The Passing Day* (1936), and the problem play in *The Jailbird* (1936), his most characteristic vein is the comedy of modern Irish village life. In this genre, his most notable successes have been *Paul Twy-*

ning (1922), *Professor Tim* (1925), and *The New Gossoon* (1930). The two earlier plays are built around stock comic situations, the first, that of the itinerant stranger who sets things right in a household at loggerheads, and the second, that of the good man who tests his relatives by returning to them in an unattractive disguise. Shiels's gift of comic characterization and dialogue tends to conceal the conventionality of these plot devices. *The New Gossoon,* one of his most popular comedies, is a comedy of village intrigue, of which the manipulator is Rabit Hamil, a richly humorous poacher, whose objective is a good marriage for his daughter. But the special value of the comedy is its contrast between the older generation of Irish farm-folk and the new generation, seemingly corrupted by "petrol and pictures and politics and jazz and doles and buses and bare legs and all sorts of foreign rascalities," but, for all these, sound at heart. Though one missed in Shiels the poetic imagination of Synge and the geniality of Lady Gregory, he probably represented as faithfully as they had done, one aspect of the spirit of the new Ireland.

The work of several of the more experimental Irish playwrights was fostered and encouraged by the Dublin Gate Theatre, which was founded in 1928 by Hilton Edwards and Michael MacLiammoir, two of its leading actors. The ideal of the Gate Theatre was not to compete with the activities of the Abbey Theatre but to supplement them. To this end, it devoted itself to presenting experimental Irish plays and European dramas for which there was no place in the Abbey repertory. During the first seven years of its existence, the Gate Theatre produced more than ninety plays, among them some of the most important examples of classical and modern drama. It gave, for example, Ibsen's *Peer Gynt,* Shaw's *Back to Methuselah,* and a new version of the *Oresteia* of Aeschylus.

All the early plays of Denis Johnston (1901–   ), with the exception of *The Moon in the Yellow River* (Abbey, 1931), were first produced at the Gate Theatre. Although Johnston wrote plays like *Storm Song* in the technique of the realistic drama, his most significant work was expressionistic. Attempting no direct realistic representation of life, his plays use what-

ever means—poetic, colloquial, stylized, symbolical, allegorical—will communicate most tellingly what he
Denis   thinks it important to say. His first play, *The Old*
Johnston   *Lady Says "No"* (1929), has all the apparently incoherent waywardness and uncontrolled imagination of August
Strindberg's *Dream Play.* In essence, this dramatic phantasma-
goria is an answer to Yeats's *Cathleen ni Houlihan,* since the
Old Lady of Johnston's play is a degraded and disreputable figure, symbol of an Ireland unworthy of the sacrifices she has
demanded. The play, like Yeats's, is concerned with attitudes
toward Ireland, and in the semi-conscious delirium of the actor
who has been knocked out while impersonating the Irish patriot,
Robert Emmet, in a romantic play, Johnston dramatizes the conflict between kinds of patriotism and comments disapprovingly
on most of the known varieties. His next play, *The Moon in
the Yellow River* (1931), continued the discussion of political
issues. Here, the conflict is between two types of revolutionary
—the romantic and the scientific—and it is obvious from the
way in which the conflict is worked out that Johnston approves
of neither. In *A Bride for the Unicorn* (1933), Johnston dramatizes in the phantasmagoric form of the earlier plays the life
experience of the young idealist, John Foss, and his catastrophic
discovery that his life-quest has been a disguised quest for death.
Here, again, Johnston's attack on romantic idealism is renewed.
The theme of *Storm Song* (1934), technically his most conventional play, is the artist's supreme obligation to his art. But the
theme emerges rather fitfully from a satirical presentation of
the personalities closely or remotely concerned with the making
of a documentary film of the nature of Robert Flaherty's *Man
of Aran.* Johnston's plays draw so heavily on all the technical
resources of an experimental theatre that it is difficult to estimate their quality from their appearance on the printed page.
But there seems little question that in him Ireland developed
a dramatist of genuine poetic and satirical gifts, one who
perhaps came closer to the vision and power of Yeats than any
other contemporary Irish playwright.

One of the most gifted of the younger playwrights to reach
a London audience by way of various provincial theatres, and

particularly the Malvern Festival, was the Scottish physician who wrote under the pseudonym James Bridie (1888–1951). A useful clue to his lively dramatic activity is his contention that, since there "are not, and cannot be, any new stories" to serve as plots for plays, the dramatist has three courses open to him. "He may distort an old story; he may decorate it in some original way," or he may "look for new meanings or aspects of the stories and throw the spotlight of his talent upon the parts of the story that make those aspects or meanings credible." This theory will help explain *James Bridie* Bridie's choice and treatment of well-known legends in *Tobias and the Angel* (1930), *Susanna and the Elders* (1937), and *Jonah and the Whale* (1938). Bridie reveals the influence of Shaw in his high-handed but intuitive treatment of the legends he dramatizes, in the freshness of his interpretations of traditional characters, and in his audacious juxtapositions of serious and comic moods and scenes. He is perhaps less interested in ideas and more interested in persons than Shaw, as he is also less inclined to indulge in non-dramatic, though intellectually exciting, discourses. *Tobias and the Angel* draws its material from the apocryphal *Book of Tobit,* and traces serio-comically the evolution of the character of Tobias under the tutelage of a companion who, it turns out, is the Archangel Raphael. Despite the young hero's original vacillating timidity, he achieves strength of character and attains worldly success under the angelic guidance. *A Sleeping Clergyman* (1933) is a study in heredity that betrays the influence of Bridie's scientific training and medical experience. The action of the play covers two generations, and shows how, from a stock that is weak and vicious, characters may unpredictably emerge that attain stability, dignity, and worth. The scientific optimism of this play is a far cry from the pessimistic determinism many earlier writers had gleaned from Darwinism. *Susanna and the Elders* follows fairly closely the biblical story. Here, Bridie is less interested in the characters of Susanna and her Greek lover than in those of the elders, who, despite their lust and their lies, are shown to be capable of both virtue and generosity. As in earlier plays, Bridie carried out his determination to emphasize fresh aspects or significances in stories that habit has accustomed us to accept for their conventional values. Although Bridie's most popular stage success was *Storm in a Teacup* (1936), an Anglo-Scottish version of Bruno Frank's comedy, *Sturm im Wasserglas,* his original plays gave clear evidence of the appearance of a fresh point of view and a vigorous talent in the English theatre.

Two poets—T. S. Eliot (1888–   ) and Christopher Fry (1907–   )—have been conspicuous leaders in a movement to revive the poetic drama. Eliot's interest in the problems of a modern poetic drama was made manifest by his essay, "A Dialogue of Poetic Drama" (1928) and his fragmentary Aristophanic melodrama, *Sweeney Agonistes* (1932), but it was not until he contributed the choruses to the pageant play, *The Rock* (1934), that he faced the demands of the modern stage seriously. His first full-length play, *Murder in the Cathedral* (1935), which blends curiously but rather effectively a mediæval saint's legend and comic relief that takes the form of contemporary satire, treats of the conflict between the claims of the world and the claims of the spirit. The central figure, Thomas à Becket, and his fate are impressive, but, since the hero's conflicts are almost completely resolved before the play begins, it is difficult to develop much suspense. In fact, the play is not, in any sense, a tragedy; it is a dramatized saint's legend. In *The Family Reunion* (1939) Eliot modernized the old Greek theme of Orestes pursued by the Furies. In this case, the hero may or may not be guilty of a crime, but he is tormented by the burden of the will to criminality. The play traces the process of his spiritual evolution and final escape from the burden of his sense of guilt through his discovery of its sources in himself and in his inheritance and his willing acceptance of the processes of repentance, penance, and retribution. Despite a stylistic complexity that makes effective performance difficult, this is perhaps Eliot's most powerful play. These experiences led him to consider, both theoretically and practically, the problem of creating a type of poetry that would at once serve the purposes of the modern drama and at the same time give the drama, on occasion, an elevation of which even the best prose was incapable. The first of these

T. S. Eliot

experiments was *The Cocktail Party* (1949), in which the characters were modern upper-class Londoners, and the dominant tone was worldly and sophisticated. But the theme of the play, the distinction between the life possible for the average person and the life possible for the saint gave the poet an opportunity to create spires of poetic utterance high above the level of worldly cocktail-party chatter. If this play lacked some of the poetic richness of *The Family Reunion,* and if its symbols seemed a little contrived, it gained in humanity, even though its success in formulating the conditions of saintliness and in depicting a modern saint may not have been complete. In *The Confidential Clerk* (1953) Eliot went even further in the direction of a style that would not disturb an audience habituated to prose; in consequence, this play had even fewer high poetic passages than *The Cocktail Party.* But this process of stylistic dilution, it might be argued, was appropriate to a play whose complicated plot, inspired by Euripides' *Ion* and involving the identity of three "foundlings," seemed more appropriate to farce than to what was really comedy of sentiment. *The Elder Statesman* (1958), remotely inspired by Sophocles' *Oedipus at Colonus,* treated Eliot's now familiar theme of an old sin brought to light and acknowledged and the consequent spiritual release. Despite an increased warmth of feeling, the characters seemed anemic, and the play proved less impressive than the earlier works. Whatever may be said of the soundness of the theories set forth in *Poetry and Drama* (1951) and exemplified in Eliot's later dramas, there is no question that the plays belong to the most distinguished drama of our time, and have exerted a potent influence on younger poets.

The earlier dramatic practice of Christopher Fry indicated clearly that he did not share Eliot's views that poetry should adjust itself radically to the demands of the acted drama. *The Lady's Not for Burning* (1948) dazzled its audiences with an exuberance of language suggestive of the less restrained Elizabethans. This mediæval comedy concerned the successful attempt of a professional soldier weary of life to save from burning a young woman charged with being a witch, but the skill shown in the creation of plot, character, and atmosphere was less impressive than the utterly uninhibited display of fresh and startling metaphors. *Venus Observed* (1950), a modern comedy of the rivalry between a worldly scientist and his son for the favors of various ladies, was appropriately clothed in less gaudy poetic apparel. The concern with religious issues that Fry shares with Eliot and that he had exemplified in such early plays as *A Boy with a Cart* (1939) and *Thor with Angels* (1948) was made more overt in *A Sleep of Prisoners* (1951), where four English soldiers imprisoned in a bombed church re-enact in their dreams four biblical stories in which force and violence are set over against tolerance and love. With *The Dark Is Light Enough* (1954) Fry again tried his hand at comedy, and devoted his powers and sympathies to portraying a noblewoman whose profound feeling for the human value of even a base person ultimately induced in him some degree of nobility. *Curtmantle* (1962), an historical drama of the reign of Henry II, challenged comparison with T. S. Eliot's *Murder in the Cathedral* and Jean Anouilh's *Becket*. Written in a less spectacularly decorative style than his earlier plays, it failed to make vital any character save that of the King.

Terence Rattigan (1911–   ) has been called "the most consistently successful of modern English playwrights," and the record of his successes in the theatre justifies this superlative. In the prefaces to his *Collected Plays* (1953), Rattigan set forth the goals and the principles that have guided his achievement. A significant clue to his practice and perhaps to his popularity is his outspoken hostility to the use of the drama as a means of disseminating ideas. His aim is entertainment, light or serious; his goal, the creation of what used to be called "the well-made play," with the modifications inevitably induced by contemporary taste; he believes that the most powerful effects can be secured by means of under-statement and suggestion. Of Rattigan's lighter efforts, *French without Tears* (1936) and *O Mistress Mine* (English title, *Love in Idleness*, 1944) have been extremely successful. The earlier comedy is a delightfully fresh picture of the vagaries of young love against a foreign setting; the later juxtaposes knowingly a worldly mother, the mistress of a cabinet minister, and her solemnly moralistic son. Probably the best of his serious plays to date are *The Winslow Boy* (1946) and *The Deep Blue Sea* (1952). The earlier of these plays deals movingly with a father's sacrificial attempts to clear the name of his son wrongly charged with theft; the later play depicts relentlessly the deterioration of a middle-aged married woman hopelessly infatuated with a caddish ex-fighter pilot. Among his later plays, the most successful was *Ross*. In this piece, based on the life of T. E. Lawrence, Rattigan set forth a plausible explanation of his hero's passionate quest for anonymity but was not altogether successful in fusing the play's epic and psychological themes.

Against the essentially conventional drama of which Rattigan was the most conspicuous mid-century representative, there developed in the late 1950's violently opposed currents. Of these, it was possible to distinguish both native and international strains, but representatives of both these strains manifested their vitality in the ease with which they moved freely among the dramatic media: stage, television, and radio. In some instances, writers, after serving their apprenticeship in radio and television, turned to writing for the stage.

The native strain in the anti-conventional drama took the form of social realism, with or without a political message. Of the writers in this mode, John Osborne (1929–   ) attracted the widest attention. Jimmy Porter, the vituperative anti-hero of his *Look Back in Anger* (1956), came to serve as the archetype of the Angry Young Man. This portrait of a completely disillusioned young intellectual, subtly destroying his most significant human relationships with his wife and a close friend, was stylistically eloquent but nihilistically rebellious. In *The Entertainer* (1957) Osborne contrasted three generations in a family associated with show-business: the father, who has preserved at least the memory of his artistic integrity, the middle-aged son, a progressively unsuccessful and sleazy vaudevillian, and the latter's unsatisfactory and dissatisfied offspring. Osborne's most ambitious work *Luther* (1961) presented in a series of brief chronicle-play-like scenes not only the condition of the Roman Catholic Church in the sixteenth century but also the evolution of Luther's neurotic personality and the effect of his neuroses on his religious views. It remained to be seen whether Osborne could create enduringly interesting plays out of a temperamental rebelliousness that failed to suggest any significant positive goal.

Arnold Wesker (1932–   ) was a social realist with a sense of commitment that gave his plays a more positive quality

Arnold Wesker

that those of Osborne. In a trilogy, *Chicken Soup with Barley* (1958), *Roots* (1959), and *I'm Talking About Jerusalem* (1960), he traced the impact of leftist political ideology on a Jewish working-class family and their progressive disillusionment with it. In *Chips with Everything* (1962), he depicted a group of Royal Air Force conscripts with fidelity and vigor, and showed the persistence and triumph of class-distinctions in a public school youth who had attempted to escape them.

Another type of revolt against the limitations of English drawing-room drama was that denominated the Drama of the Absurd. The term "Absurd" achieved vogue through its use by such French Existential writers as Jean Paul Sartre and Albert Camus to suggest the essential meaningless of life and the burden on the individual of creating his own values in the midst of cosmic meaningless. The most conspicuous practitioner of the Drama of the Absurd in English literature was the Irish writer, Samuel Beckett (1906–   ), who lived in France where he was a close friend of the novelist James Joyce and one of the earliest commentators on *Finnegans Wake.* Poet, critic, novelist, and dramatist, he wrote early poems and criticism in English, but his more important novels and plays were written in French and then translated—usually by himself—into English. The most famous of his plays was *Waiting for Godot,* first produced in England in 1935, in which out of the desultory dialogue of four characters: two tramps, a callous master and his slave, he depicted disturbingly and evocatively the almost futile quest for the discovery of some meaning in life. *Endgame,* first produced in England in 1957, was even more completely negative and nihilistic. In it what seemed to be the last four human survivors on earth were a tyrannical blind man confined to a chair, his legless parents who live in ash-cans, and his slave. The slave struggled constantly to free him-self from his helpless master, but it seemed doubtful that he ever would have the courage to break his self-imposed bonds and face life on a probably lifeless earth. In 1957, *All That Fall,* a radio play that Beckett was commissioned to write for the British Broadcasting Corporation, made a powerful impres-sion. Here he appeared to counterbalance a quietly horrifying revelation of the contagiousness of evil with a compensating element of compassion not immediately evident in his earlier plays. Beckett's influence on his most gifted disciple, Harold Pinter (1930–   ), was apparent in Pinter's characters' floundering attempt to communicate with each other signifi-cantly and to give their existences some individual meaning. His most impressive plays were *The Caretaker* (1960) and *The Collection* (1962). *The Caretaker* invested with grim comedy and ominous overtones the relations between a sinisterly ad-hesive tramp and a pair of aging and contrastedly neurotic brothers. *The Collection* proved to be another study of the difficulty of meaningful communication. Here the relations among a man and his wife, a dress designer and his lower-class protégé developed complications out of explanations of their behavior that hardly coincided with the truth but served to soothe their egos. Pinter seemed equally at home in the media of radio, television, and drama, and *The Collection* was pre-sented in all three media.

POETRY

Even before the outbreak of the First World War there had been evidences of the beginnings of a poetic renaissance. The development of this revival was unquestionably quickened by the high emotions, tense anxieties, and tragic losses of four years of intensive warfare. Though a number of poets met death in battle, the more fortunate survivors and many who were not active participants found themselves moved to poetic utterance. Much of this poetry, though poignant, was transitory in its appeal, but it was followed by, even though it may not have encouraged, a wide-spread interest in poetry and manifold experiments with it.

The first of the war poets to attract attention was Rupert Brooke, who was born in 1887 and who, after a brief experience with the British Expeditionary Force in Belgium, died of blood-poisoning while he was on his way to Gallipoli. He was buried on the island of Skyros in 1915. Much of Brooke's sudden fame was due to his remarkably good looks, his winning personality, and the romantic association of his early death. Before the outbreak of the war, he had become known as a poet of youth-

The War Poets

ful romantic cynicism. Out of this mood, he was swept by the high emotions inspired by the rising wave of patriotism, and in a series of sonnets, he became the spokesman for the dedication of the English spirit to the service of the conflict. In his case, as in that of other poets who died during the war, it is idle to speculate as to the potentialities of development. There seems little doubt, however, that of these dead war poets, Wilfred Owen (1893–1918) was the most gifted. He saw enough of the warfare to penetrate beyond its adventitious glamor and, in consequence, his poems about it are scrupulously honest. Despite his youth, Owen had developed an individual technique of considerable originality; he had experimented successfully with the substitution of consonance for rhyme, and, although his poems are few, many of them are distinguished. Other poets who ended their lives in England's service were Charles Sorley (1895–1915) whose posthumous volume, *Marlborough and Other Poems* (1916), showed great lyrical promise, and Isaac Rosenberg (1890–1918), whose reputation has grown with the years that have passed since his death.

The war poets who survived the four years' agony followed different lines of development after the war. Siegfried Sassoon

Siegfried Sassoon

(1886–   ), who in *Counter-Attack* (1918) and *Picture-Show* (1920) had treated the war with horrifying realism and bitter satire, won a wider reputation by writing of his experiences before and during the war. His most charming and popular book, *Memoirs of*

a Fox-Hunting Man (1928), is a nostalgic re-creation of the
lives of the country gentry in the world the war almost destroyed. Its continuation—*Memoirs of an Infantry Officer*
(1930)—and his acknowledged autobiography—*The Old Century and Seven More Years* (1938), *The Weald of Youth*
(1942), and *Siegfried's Journey* (1946)—though naturally
less novel, were equally attractive. Sassoon continued to write
poetry in a vein of romantic melancholy, but his capacity for
conspicuous growth seemed impaired by his experiences in the
war. He turned back sadly to his pre-war memories; in the
post-war world he felt and remained alien. Sassoon did not
prove to be a prolific poet; his later poetry, however, had
qualities vastly different from the poems that made his reputation. *Sequences* (1957) communicated persuasively attitudes
and insights reminiscent of the 17th-century mystic, Henry
Vaughan. *The Path to Peace* (1960) gathered the utterances
of a quiet introspective poet, deeply moved by his conversion
to Catholicism. *The Collected Poems* (1961) showed how far
he had travelled since the bitterly satirical poems of the First
World War.

Robert Graves (1895–   ) was to grow far beyond the
lyrical Celtic fancy and the Germanic realism of the poems he
wrote before and during the war. He put behind
him his early poetic simplicities, and developed a   ***Robert***
severely intellectual style which, though difficult   ***Graves***
of interpretation, was rewarding in its honest representation of
a subtle though uncompromising mentality. Taking leave of his
early life in his autobiography, *Good-By to All That* (1929),
and setting himself definitely against the main current of
Georgian poetry in his *Survey of Modernist Poetry* (1927),
he reached his widest audience, not as a poet but as a novelist.
In a series of historical novels, of which *I, Claudius* (1934)
and *Claudius the God* (1934) are perhaps the most remarkable, he displayed not only the acute intellectuality that marked
his later verse but also rich stores of historical information
and great power in the creation of the characters of historic
personages. *Homer's Daughter* (1955) fictionized ingeniously
and robustly Samuel Butler's theory that the *Odyssey* was

written by a woman. Grave's choice was Nausicaa, and the novel gave a vivid account of the experiences out of which she was to fashion the great epic. Graves' productivity as an historical novelist and as the creator of a highly personal mythology in *The White Goddess* (1948), tended to obscure his distinction as a poet capable of continuous growth. The election of Graves as Professor of Poetry at Oxford in 1961 recognized belatedly a poet of great individuality and power. In the long decades since the First World War, he plotted his own course independent of changes in taste and style. An exciting critic of his own work, he evolved a personal style classical in its roots but modern in this tone. In his *Oxford Addresses on Poetry* (1962), he attacked "Apollonian" poets recklessly and extolled such "Dionysian" writers as Skelton, Wyatt, and Ralegh as devotees moved by the archetypal feminine principle whom he himself served under the name of the White Goddess.

On poets already prominent in 1914, the war and its aftermath made varying deep impressions. Robert Bridges, who served as Poet Laureate from 1913 to 1930, was moved to write a modest number of characteristically discreet and tasteful official poems. His later lyrical work, in the vein of classicized
Survivors   romanticism, revealed no new powers, although it showed few or no signs of decline. His most astonishing achievement in the post-war period was the publication in his eighty-fifth year of *The Testament of Beauty* (1929). Intellectually, this, the most ambitious of his poems, presents his philosophy of life, a blending of the teaching of modern science with Platonic doctrine. Technically, the poem is of great interest, since it is written in loose Alexandrines which give it at times an almost conversational quality. Despite the fact that there are long passages in which the ideas are imperfectly poeticized, there are many passages of great beauty and stirring imagination. In its kind among modern poems, it has no rival.

The war inspired John Masefield to the writing of "August, 1914," one of the finest and most restrained of the war lyrics, and of his prose account of the tragic adventure of *Gallipoli* (1916). Otherwise, he seems to have been relatively unaffected by the conflict, although he was sent to America to appeal for support for the British cause. The course of his development after 1918 was not spectacular. In fact, after the sensational realism of his early narrative poems, Masefield's art tended to revert toward conventional poetic romanticism. *Reynard the Fox* (1922), with its vivid sketches of the members of a hunt and its presentation of the hunt from the point of view of the quarry, is his last impressive long poem. The best of his later work is in the lyrical and sonnet forms; although his poetry is critically unwinnowed, it has moments of poignant feeling and intense insight. But his lapse into romanticism brought to light technical and intellectual limitations which his earlier realism had tended to conceal. After he succeeded Bridges as Poet Laureate in 1930, his official utterances were astonishingly inconsequential; at the beginning of the Second World War, however, he told in heroic vein the tale of the disaster at Dunkirk (1941), in *The Nine Days' Wonder.*

Of the surviving pre-war poets, William Butler Yeats (1865–1939) was the one to show the most remarkable development in the last two decades of his life. Yeats's reputation was made as a Celtic lyricist, but it was remade by the appearance in his art of realistic and intellectual elements which far surpass in honesty and weight the disembodied charm of his early poems. In later life, Yeats himself found in the early poems "little but romantic convention, unconscious drama." He came to the conclusion that "We should write out our thoughts in as nearly as possible the language we thought them in, as though in a letter to an intimate friend. We should not disguise them in any way; for our lives give them force as the lives of people in plays give force to their words." What then is heard in Yeats' later poems, *The Tower* (1928), *The Winding Stair* (1929), and *Last Poems and Plays* (1940), is an old man, rich in wisdom and disconcerting in his honesty, talking nobly. His cultivation of the colloquial rhythm and his elimination from his verse of the last trace of affectation or dishonesty made Yeats a leader of the new poetic generation. He was the greatest poet the post-Victorian period had produced.

But the main current of English verse in the first decade after the war was not to manifest the courage in experimentation seen in the work of such oldsters as Bridges and Yeats. Instead, a group of poets, who came to call themselves Georgians, by reason of the fact the many of them first attracted attention in a series of anthologies called *Georgian Poetry,* attempted a renovation of English poetry on lines much closer to the Victorian tradition. Although each of these poets had his unmistakably individual qualities, they were alike in their attempt to record in relatively simple metrics and diction their unsophisticated delight in simple things, the lovelier aspects of the English countryside, rural pleasures and pastimes, and the naïveté of nice children. The Georgians then were anti-urban and anti-mechanical in an urban and mechanical age. Edward Thomas (1878–1917) may serve as a measure of the normality of the Georgians. During his lifetime, his reputation depended upon the sensitive observations of nature and of country life, published in various magazines and collected posthumously in the volumes called *Cloud Castle* (1928) and *The Last Sheaf* (1928). But his poetic reputation rests on his descriptive lyrics which express what Aldous Huxley has called "a nameless emotion of quiet happiness shot through with melancholy." With W. H. Davies (1871–1940), simplicity became a cult. Between his life as a tramp, recorded in *The Autobiography of a Super-Tramp* (1908), and his poetry, the connection seems tenuous, and the limitations of his delicate lyrical gift may depend on the fact that the subject matter of his poetry is so much narrower than the experience of his life. But in the vein of simplicity and child-likeness, Davies worked with astonishing assurance. His music was deliberately restricted by the instrument he chose and the type of tune he wished to play upon it. The poetry of Harold Monro (1879–1932), who made his Poetry Book Shop in Bloomsbury the headquarters for an intense activity of publication, readings, and exhibitions, is more urban and realistic than that of the other Georgians. He attempted more strenuously then they to poeticize the circumstances of modern life, and, although his vein is a shallow one, he worked it with vigor and

The Georgian Poets

honesty. More than any of the other Georgians, he felt the need for a renovation of the technique of poetry. The realistic element in the diction of much post-war verse owes much to Monro's early experiments in such volumes as *Real Property* (1922) and *The Earth for Sale* (1928).

Walter de la Mare (1873–1956) resembles the Georgians in his cultivation of the mood of child-like wonder and in his resistance to the impingement of the contemporary world upon his imaginative life. But the childlikeness of de la Mare is never naïve, nor is his resistance to the contemporary world mere escapism. It is rather that, like William Blake, he lives in a world that is not the world of men. His world, unlike Barrie's world of fantasy, has its terrors and its agonies, no less than its delights and ecstasies. It is shrouded in eternal mystery; its tears are the tears of a child with no armor against experience, and its laughter is prankish and puckish, with touches of inhuman malice. De la Mare's most sustained expression of his view of life is his novel, *Memoirs of a Midget* (1921). The heroine is a sensitive feminine Gulliver among the Brobdingnagians. Here, by telling his story from the point of view of an exceedingly acute and psychologically quite normal dwarf, de la Mare gets an astonishing effect of the monstrous insensitiveness and coarseness of ordinary human beings. His great gift, however, is lyrical, since his characteristic mood cannot be long sustained and has to be woven like a magic spell or charm. He is a past master of the most seductive devices of poetry. His sense of rhythm is infinitely subtle, and his sensitivity to the potentialities of eerie sound patterns is, among modern poets, unequalled.

Walter de la Mare

Except for Bridges and Yeats, none of the twentieth-century poets thus far considered made any really startling extensions of the material of poetry or revolutionary modifications of its technique. And yet, no feature of modern poetry is more striking than the constant impulse it shows to experiment with subject matter, form, or metrics, or more than one of these elements. Even before 1914, there had been evidence of a widening dissatisfaction with traditional Victorian themes and modes, and the most exciting and meaningful poetry written since that date constitutes a series of more and more complex poetic experiments.

Of these experiments, the simplest was that known as Imagism. This movement was sponsored by three Americans—Ezra Pound, Amy Lowell, and H. D. (Hilda Doolittle) —and one Englishman, Richard Aldington, who issued a manifesto, published a series of anthologies, and conducted an active critical campaign for their principles and their practices. The Imagists defined poetry as the presentation of a visual situation in the fewest possible concrete words, lightened of the burdens of conventional adjectival padding, and unhampered by general ideas or philosophical or moral speculations. Form and substance were to be identical. The second part of H. D.'s poem, "Garden," may be quoted to illustrate the Imagists' tendency to use short lines, with marked cadences, little or no rhyme, precise sensory diction, and few adjectives.

*The
Imagists*

> O wind, rend open the heat,
> Cut apart the heat,
> Rend it to tatters.
> Fruit cannot drop
> Through this thick air;
> Fruit cannot fall into heat
> That presses up and blunts
> The points of pears,
> And rounds the grapes.
>
> Cut the heat:
> Plough through it,
> Turning it on either side
> Of your path.

Though the effects that could be attained by this restricted technique were very limited, and although most of the poets associated with the movement broke away from it, Imagism did modern poetry a tremendous service by pointing the way to a renovation of the vocabulary of poetry and to the necessity of ridding poetic technique of vague and empty verbiage and dishonest and windy generalities.

The early poetry of Richard Aldington (1892–1962)—
Images Old and New (1915), *Images of War and Images of
Desire* (1919), *Medallions in Clay* (1921)—illustrates both the virtues and the defects of the **Richard
Aldington**
Imagist creed. It is rich in sensitiveness and in
sensuous values, skillful in craftsmanship, but limited in scope
and appeal, and betrays the synthetic quality of verse written to
a formula. *A Fool i' the Forest* (1925), which he calls a phan-
tasmagoria, presents allegorically in a sort of jazz fantasy the
death of imagination and intellect in the post-war *débâcle*. In
later years, Aldington's fiction attracted more attention than his
poetry. His novel, *Death of a Hero* (1929), was one of the
most deeply disillusioned treatments of the purposes and the
significance of the First World War. Other novels—*The
Colonel's Daughter* (1931) and *Rejected Guest* (1939)—re-
echoed his bitter disillusionment and his violent revulsion from
the hypocrisies of bourgeois society. His autobiography, *Life for
Life's Sake* (1941), was significant not only as a contribution to
modern literary history, but also as evidence that Aldington, to
an even greater extent than Sassoon, never recovered completely
from the shock of his wartime experiences.

Chambers of Imagery: Series I and II (1912) and *Laodice
and Danae* (1916) by Gordon Bottomley (1874-1948) are not
only excellent illustrations of Imagist doctrine but
the work of an authentic poet. For, although allied   **Gordon
Bottomley**
with the Imagists, he is typically Renaissance in
feeling. Much of his work is founded on other men's creations:
Icelandic sagas, Italian tales, Shakespearean characters. He escapes any taint of academic dryness, however, by virtue of his
powerful imagination and his genuine poetic power. His poetic
dramas, which are written in the grand manner, show him more
the poet than the playwright, though some of them have been
acted. Both *King Lear's Wife* (1920) and *Gruach* (1921) deal
with the earlier life of characters from Shakespeare's plays in
such a way that their part in the Elizabethan tragedies seems
both natural and inevitable.

D. H. Lawrence's connection with the Imagists was merely a
temporary one, since he was sufficiently individual to work out

his own line of development. He did, however, share their view that the significance of poetry should be implicit rather than explicit, and that poetry should be freed from the restrictions of the traditional form. Poetry was to Lawrence the medium most appropriate to the expression of sudden intuitions, momentary glimpses of natural beauty, startling identifications with the psychology and emotions of birds and animals, moments of bitterness and exasperation with human stupidity, and both the high and low points in his own emotional and physical experience. Only rarely did Lawrence take pains to give his intuitions completely satisfactory forms; often Lawrence's verse is the raw material for poetry rather than poetry itself. But it is never dull or lifeless. Sometimes, indeed, it is extremely moving and beautiful, and always it is a completely sincere though sometimes exasperated expression of some memorable moment in his impassioned life.

D. H. Lawrence

More drastic innovations in poetic techniques than those made by the Imagists were exhibited by such diverse poets as Hopkins, the Sitwells, and Eliot.

Gerard Manley Hopkins, claimed by the young revolutionary poets of the 'twenties as their immediate ancestor, along with Owen and Eliot, and recognized as a modern poet of the first importance, was born in 1844, wrote the bulk of his poetry during the 'seventies and 'eighties, and died in the year 1889. In spite of his technical innovations and his experimentation with prosody, he was, however, spiritually and intellectually, a man of his own times. His attitudes toward man, nature, and God were very like those of most people of his day. As a convert to Catholicism during his Oxford days, and therefore more ardent in his faith than most, he did not question the accepted ultimate values. Nor did he suffer from the disillusionment and bewilderment of poets of the twentieth century, nor share their revolutionary zeal. Some critics claim that Hopkins is a modern poet, primarily because his poetry was introduced to the world by his literary executor, Robert Bridges, as late as 1918. The opposite could as easily be argued. A Victorian poet, introduced to the public thirty years after his death, would the more quietly be passed

Gerard Manley Hopkins

over if he did not offer something significant to the later generation. What is it then that makes him, though a Victorian in outlook, modern in his approach to poetry?

A primary reason, perhaps, is that his approach to poetry is
as personal as that of the younger poets of the twentieth century, who, since they do not know for what audiences they are
writing, must write, whether they will or not, for themselves.
Hopkins's dilemma sprang from purely private causes whereas
the poets of the later generation have had to face a disintegration of social values. Hopkins had chosen the calling of priest
and teacher. His profound religious beliefs and his intellectual
acceptance of the traditional doctrines of the Church drove him
to feel that his poetry must be devoted exclusively to the furtherance of his faith. But the natural man within was at war:
Hopkins was as much a pagan as an ascetic, as much a lover of
man and natural things as a lover of God and of things spiritual.
Conflict and tension came from this disharmony. His searching
honesty and integrity made him face his own double nature. He
would not publish his poems unless his Church approved them,
and he could not write the poetry that he felt his Church would
entirely like; therefore, he had to content himself with a private
audience of two or three friends, poets who, if they did not
understand, were sympathetic and appreciative.

The poetry that expresses Hopkins's inner tension, his "straining against the current," has an immediate and personal quality,
a mixture of the sensuous and the spiritual that sets it quite
apart from the usual religious and pietistic poetry. In this quality, it is comparable only with Donne's. Above everything, Hopkins wished his poetry to give the impact and immediacy of
experience itself; he wished it to have integral design or "in-
scape." Of the fifty poems completed and the forty early poems
and fragments, there are very few that do not have a singularly
individual and authentic stamp.

Within the classic and rigidly disciplinary form of the sonnet,
Hopkins attempted most of his experimenting in diction and
metre. Oddness and strain, even obscurity, sometimes resulted.
He was conscious that he was not always successful. The

"sprung-rhythm" which he developed and which he found particularly submissive to his needs was the rhythm of the nursery rhyme or of common speech, a complicated counterpointing of the metres in common poetic use. Stress was the foundation of this new rhythm also, but stress broken with runs of unaccented syllables and with rests. This free system of marked stresses alternating with varying numbers of unaccented syllables seemed to fit his purpose of suggesting counter-statements and inner tensions. Hopkins took a fierce joy in mastering words, which he hammered into curious but compelling patterns. He experimented with new usages, compound, coined, and portmanteau words. His language was made compressed and elliptical by the omission of conjunctions and relative pronouns. More than any other English poet, he used to brilliant advantage sound patterns of every variety—alliteration, assonance, inner rhymes, and repetitions which became so inextricably woven into the design he was trying to create that they seem unalterable.

All his poetry expresses an intense emotional and purely personal experience: joy, even rapture, as in "Pied Beauty" or "Hurrahing in Harvest," sheer delight in natural things in "Binsey's Poplars," tenderness in "Brothers," or spiritual anguish in the "terrible sonnets." His unflinching honesty and passion, his incomparably vivid and violent sensory imagery, his complete poetic integrity and demonic energy, make him one of the most intense and original poets of all time.

The three Sitwells, Dame Edith (1887–   ), Sir Osbert (1892–   ), and Sacheverell (1897–   ), sharply differing in certain respects, yet present marked similarities springing from their common background and purpose. From their first notoriety, with the publication of *Wheels,* a review published during the war (1916) in violent revolt against the Georgian poets, they became the emblem of intellectualized, self-conscious poetry, representing to different publics either the proper butt of attack or the banner of progress. Acting always as a close-knit trinity, occasionally publishing works together—*Twentieth Century Harlequinade* (1916), by Edith and Osbert, *One Hundred and One Harlequins* (1922) by Edith and Sacheverell, *Poor Young People* (1925) and *Trio* (1938) by Edith, Osbert, and

Sacheverell—they presented a joint challenge to conventional literary practices and judgments.

Edith, the outstanding figure of the three, is among the most successful of those who have produced highly calculated poetry. She offers the literary equivalent of modern music *Edith* and modern painting, not only in the science which *Sitwell* permeates her technique, but in the actual cadences and visual impressions which she evokes. A favorite technical device in her early poems is the transference of one sense impression to different senses, a conscious synæsthesia that refers to sounds by color adjectives or to light in terms of tactile values as in the lines

> Each dull, blunt wooden stalactite
> Of rain creaks, hardened by the light.

The method, the extravagantly imaginative "metaphysical" use of metaphor, sometimes produces remarkably fresh and beautiful results as in the lines from a later poem:

> All things have beginnings; the bright plume
> Was once thin grass, in shady winter's gloom.
> And the furred fire is barking for the shape
> Of hoarse-voiced animals; cold air agape
> Whines to be shut in water's shape and plumes.

Despite her extravagant images, few living poets have evolved more word play that is both original and right. But it does put a limit on her world, robs it of exuberant vitality, enhances its atmosphere of elegant weariness, its sense that life itself is lacking in ingenuity and nuance. The world of Dame Edith's early poems is a universe where all is brittle and bright and evanescent. Her first book, *The Mother and Other Poems* (1915), was intense and clear cut, marked by tragic irony. But with later volumes she moved toward the fantastic, artificial, yet never shallow medium which she had made her own. *Façade* (1922) is nonsense poetry which may be read for its surface amusement, but which in every case carries an elaborate pattern of form and content, *Rustic Elegies* (1927) are three complex and decorative studies which strangely and triumphantly blend the elements of satire and lyricism, erudition and dream imagery. But it is in *The Sleeping Beauty* (1924) that Dame Edith best achieves the effect for which she is striving. Casting the old fairy tale in an eighteenth-century setting, she lavishes on it her varied, subtle, often gorgeous technique, her humor, too weary to be wholly cruel, and her sense of tragedy, too jaded to be high.

Dame Edith's brilliantly idiosyncratic early poetry proved to be only a beguiling prelude to the major poetry she produced under the influence of the events of the Second World War. Her earlier poetry had been aloof, aristocratic, and a little inhuman; her later poetry was compassionate, committed, and, in the best sense, tragic. The suffering and destruction wrought by the war, the revelation of the evil of which man was capable not only aroused in her the deepest feelings of horror and compassion but moved her to create a style appropriate to the expression of great themes and powerful emotions. Her lyric, "Still Falls the Rain," inspired by the air-raids on London, is one of the most memorable of contemporary war-poems. *The Song of the Cold* (1945) and *The Canticle of the Sun* (1949), in which she cultivated a long flowing rhythm distinct from her early crisp brevity and manipulated with assurance her symbols of life and death: roses, hearts, kisses, gold, lions; bones, tombs, dust are poignant expressions of her sense of modern man's tragic plight and of her hope of his redemption through love.

Dame Edith's *Collected Poems* (1957), assembling from all her published work what she wished to preserve, firmly established her not only as an assiduous experimenter in poetic technique but as a poet with a capacity for sustained growth in depth and power. In the pungent preface to *The Outcasts* (1962), she protested against the banishment of grandeur from contemporary poetry and maintained that poetry, instead, should be "the deification of reality." Here the contrasted themes were the sense of loss and desolation in our times and the need for praising beauty and love and God. In two prose works, *Fanfare for Elizabeth* (1946) and *The Queens and the Hive* (1962), out of a profound sympathy for her heroine and the period in which she lived, she gave life to a large cast of extraordinary characters and showed them acting out their fates against the gorgeous tapestry of Renaissance England.

Though the poetic origins of T. S. Eliot (1888–   ) were complex, the line of his intellectual development became increasingly clear as the years passed. Those origins were in part English and in part continental. His major English progenitor was the seventeenth-century poet John Donne, from whom he learned to present antithetical moods in a single poem, the cultivation of metaphysical conceits, and the use upon occasion of colloquial rather than literary diction. But a more immediate influence on Eliot's technique was the poetry of such French poets as Jules Laforgue, Tristan Corbière and St. John Perse, especially the latter's *Anabase,* which Eliot translated. From the first, comes something of Eliot's early cynicism, his depressed view of modern life, and his generally deflationary temper. From Perse, especially in *The Waste Land,* Eliot borrowed the technique of projecting his themes   **T. S. Eliot** and his moods through a series of apparently incoherent images. But out of his borrowings, Eliot gradually developed a mode of expression unmistakably his own, a technique that had a profound influence on the poets that followed him.

Such early poems of Eliot as "The Love Song of J. Alfred Prufrock" and "Portrait of a Lady" show most clearly the influence of Laforgue in their somewhat self-consciously depressed tone and their sense of inadequacy in meeting the demands of a romantic imagination. In *The Waste Land* (1922), Eliot's most ambitious poem in his early period, on the basis of a theme from mediæval romance, invested with associations from a great variety of historical and legendary events, he attempted to create a sense of the sordidness and vulgarity, the moral debility and spiritual desiccation of modern life. In short compass he expressed as powerfully and completely as Aldous Huxley's *Point Counter Point* the disillusionment that attacked life and letters in the decade after the First World War. With *Ash Wednesday* (1930), Eliot disconcerted his less agile followers by reacting against the dispirited mood of the earlier poems in the direction of a tentative religious faith.[1]

If Eliot's *The Waste Land* is the most influential English poem of the twentieth century, his *Four Quartets* (1944) is perhaps the most distinguished. It consists of four meditative poems, the title of which—"Burnt Norton," "East Coker," "The Dry Salvages," and "Little Gidding"—designate places that have some significance for the poet's personal or spiritual experience. The complex design of "Burnt Norton" is fastidiously paralleled in each of the succeeding poems: it consists of five parts, and each part is distinguished in tone and mood, in form and style from each of the other parts. The parts, moreover, occur in the same order in each of the poems. Terms and phrases from one poem awaken echoes in the succeeding poems. As in music, themes are stated, repeated, and developed. The major theme of the *Four Quartets* is the antithesis between time and the timeless, between time and eternity, and the series of poems rises to its climax in a consideration of the Incarnation, the point of intersection of time and eternity. A subordinate theme of the *Quartets* is the poet's personal experience and particularly his never-ending attempt to achieve a style appropriate to his thought. The poems are compelling demonstrations of Eliot's control of styles that are in turn colloquial, meditative, and exalted. The *Four Quartets* are difficult and challenging poetry, but their repetitive structure makes them somewhat less disconcerting at first contact than the extremely elusive structure of *The Waste Land.* Seriously comparable to the later quartets of Beethoven, they are perhaps Eliot's most impressive poetic achievement.

The technical experimentation so conspicuous in the poetry of such writers as Hopkins, Dame Edith Sitwell, and Eliot is equally apparent in the work of the poets who rose after them. In these older poets, the line of experimentation was coherent; in a number of the younger poets—particularly C. Day Lewis and W. H. Auden—experimentation took on the form of the attempt to fuse such diverse technical methods as the clipped

[1] For his work as a dramatist, see pages 462–463; for a consideration of Eliot's work as a critic, see pages 501–503.

and compact utterance and the sprung rhythm of Hopkins,
the consonance of Wilfred Owen, the colloquialism and allusiveness of Eliot, the slangy bounce of the popular song, and
the concentrated succinctness of Old English poetry, the effect
of which they attempt to get in modern English by the omission of articles, conjunctions, and relative pronouns. Not all
these elements appeared in the same poem nor equally in all the
younger poets, but one or another of these elements was likely
to appear at any unlikely moment. Certain of the
younger poets were also allied in their preoc- *Poets of*
cupation with social-political problems. They all *the*
grew up during the darker stages of the great post- *'Thirties*
war economic depression, and they were all aware of its effects
on English life. As Auden wrote, their world was one of
unlovely

> Smokeless chimneys, damaged bridges, rotting wharves and
>   choked canals,
> Tramlines buckled, smashed trucks lying on their side across
>   the rails;
> Power-stations locked, deserted, since they drew the boiler fires;
> Pylons falling or subsiding, trailing dead high-tension wires.

They were all acutely aware of the deficiencies of the order that
had created the world in which they must live or die; they
abominated bourgeois society, with its repressions, creature comforts, and materialism; they felt that nothing short of a revolution would bring about a new order, basically communistic, in
which living would be decent and self-respecting. But, despite
the fact that many of these younger poets held common political
views, and utilized many of the same technical methods, they
emerged clearly, as more and more of their work appeared, as
individually gifted poets.

C. Day Lewis (1904–   ) gave perhaps the clearest expression to the revolutionary doctrines shared by a number of his
poet-friends. He first found an individual voice in *Transitional
Poem* (1929), in which he rejected the conventional technique
of his earlier volumes and strove to define his relationship to
the social and political problems that confronted his generation.

The Magnetic Mountain (1935) was his fullest attack upon the shortcomings and the weaknesses of the old order and his clearest call to revolutionary activity that would bring in the new order of things. The basic imagery of the poem—the train journey of which the inevitable destination is the magnetic mountain of the new society—is powerfully used, and the poem has brilliant satirical passages in which the adherents of things as they are mercilessly expose themselves. Since his illuminating study of the poetic origins and ideals of the new poetry in *A Hope for Poetry* (1934), his most significant volumes have been *A Time to Dance* (1935) and *Overtures to Death* (1938). In "The Conflict," a poem from *A Time to Dance* (1935), he described himself as one

> Who on a tilting deck sings
> To keep their courage up, though the wave hangs
> That shall cut off their sun . . .

> Yet living here,
> As one between two massing powers I live
> Whom neutrality cannot save
> Nor occupation cheer.

But the symbolic significance of the title *Overtures to Death* (1938) suggests that his earlier revolutionary idealism had been overshadowed by his deepening consciousness of the rising threat of a terrific conflict between the major modern political ideologies. The poetic tributes to such poets as Hardy, de la Mare, and Blunden in *Poems, 1943-47* (1948) indicated that he was orienting himself to more traditional conceptions of the subject-matter and style of poetry, and the moving sonnet-sequence, "O Dreams, O Destinations," from the volume, *Word Above All* (1943) was a tender, though searching, analysis of the nature of childhood. Here, as elsewhere in his later poetry, his preoccupations were not social and political, but personal and intimate. His long poem, *An Italian Visit* (1935), although it had its uninspired passages, not only rendered a lively modern response to familiar and unfamiliar Italian scenes but included good-natured parodies of some of his contemporaries and successors. He has also achieved a considerable reputation as the translator of Virgil's *Georgics* (1940) and *Æneid* (1952) into the modern idiom. The prose volumes, *A Hope for Poetry* (1934) and *The Poetic Image* (1947), marked clearly the stages in his thinking about the function and style of poetry. His distinguished performance in various fields related to poetry resulted in his appointment as Professor of Poetry at Oxford in 1951.

W. H. Auden (1907–   ) was one of the most restlessly experimental and unpredictable of the younger poets. Though radical political doctrine was implicit in many of his early poems, that allegiance was not so conspicuous as in the poems of Day Lewis. Nor was there any perceptible consistency in the development of Auden's *W. H. Auden* style. He ranged freely from the most cryptic and condensed utterance to a parody of music-hall rhythms, folk-ballads, and nursery rhymes. He was equally restless in his use of literary forms. Collaborating with Christopher Isherwood, he wrote a number of poetic plays—*The Dog Beneath the Skin* (1935), *The Ascent of F6* (1936), and *On the Frontier* (1938)— which moved rather disconcertingly through a variety of serious and playful styles and which suggested through satire or symbol the political views he held. With Isherwood, also, he wrote an admirable account of their observations in China in *Journey to a War* (1939), and, with Louis MacNeice, he joined in producing an unconventional guide book in verse and prose, *Letters from Iceland* (1937). Where Day Lewis was self-critical and censorious, Auden was uncritical and spontaneous. In consequence, his poetry contained a great deal of chaff, but at his best he showed an intellectual complexity and cultural richness not apparent in Day Lewis's more overt propaganda.

Auden was one of the most alert and informed intelligences among contemporary poets. He was widely read in psychology, philosophy, and religion, but his allusiveness was less overt than that of T. S. Eliot. There was something chameleon-like about his thinking and literary practice; the constant element beneath the incessant surface-changes remained elusive. His development has been complicated, and his status rendered ambiguous by the fact that he left England before the Second World War, settled in America, and became an American citizen. If the poems he published in America show some loss in immediacy and concreteness, they also had a greater depth and maturity. In *New Year Letter* (1941), perhaps the most autobiographical of his poems, he seemed to take a backward glance over the influences that have shaped his thought and work. *The Double Man* (1941) reflected his awareness of the conflict between private and public values. In *For the Time Being* (1944), "The Sea and the Mirror," a series of monologues attributed to various characters from Shakespeare's *Tempest,* constituted his richest and subtlest utterance, his ripest wisdom about human nature and human relationships. *The Age of Anxiety* (1946), a series of urban eclogues that won him the Pulitzer Prize, if not his most distinguished work, became for many readers a symbol of the dominant state of mind of the mid-century. Auden devoted himself consistently to what Stephen Spender designated as "the main task of contemporary poetry, which is to transmute the antipoetic material of modern life into transparent poetry." *Nones* (1952) showing no decline in technical virtuosity, struck a new, if uncertain, Christian note. His *Homage to Clio* (1960) sought for unity in its consideration of the relation of contemporary man to history. In a relaxed mood, the tone was familiar, the diction colloquial. An indication of Auden's critical prestige was his term as Professor of Poetry at Oxford from 1956-1961.

Louis MacNeice (1907–1963), although sympathetic with Auden's early radicalism, was essentially a romantic individualist, whose personal ideal may well be expressed in his own lines:

> All that I would like to be is human, have a share
> In a civilized articulate and well-adjusted
> Community, where the mind is given its due
> And the body is not distrusted.

To him, life and art were matters of more permanent concern than politics. Like Auden, he was inclined to indulge in too relaxed and informal poetic utterance, but his poems expressed a vigorous reaction to a world which only imperfectly administered to his needs and desires. MacNeice was by nature too witty and high-spirited to be at ease with the solemnities of leftist political and poetic doctrine. *Louis* His high spirits frequently led him into lapses of *MacNeice* taste that mar otherwise effective poems, but his humor offset audaciously but tellingly the implied horrors of the air-raid poem, "Brother Fire." His passionate individualism, however, did not mean that he was insensitive to the plight of modern man, and such a poem as "Prayer before Birth" is at once an expression of broad human compassion and satirical protest against modern political threats to personal liberty.

Although his *Collected Poems* (1949) varied widely in quality and importance, they exhibited an always engaging and lively personality. At his lightest, his poetry had the effect of witty improvisation, and he enriched the vocabulary of poetry by his free use of colloquial diction and consciously extended its range of tones. *Ten Burnt Offerings* (1952), however, showed an unsteady movement away from his earlier casual exuberance in the direction of introspection and speculation, and *Visitations* (1957), although characteristically unassuming and casual, treated wryly the problems created by the onset of middle age and the difficulties involved in the acceptance of an assured religious faith.

Although the early reputation of Stephen Spender (1909–   ) was made as one of the group of poets of the 'thirties who shared leftist political views, his essentially romantic and introspective temperament lent a special personal quality to his early radicalism. Brought up in *Stephen* a vigorously Liberal tradition and, unlike his friends, *Spender* closely in touch with European thought and culture, he always stressed, in even the most political of his poems, the import of social revolution for the individual and his values. It was not surprising, therefore, that, with the fading of the hope that Marxism had aroused in him and his associates, Spender should have faced the problem of the relationship of the highly imaginative and sensitive individual to the tensions and violences of the world of the mid-century. If the poetry he wrote in the 'forties was not clear-cut in its judgments and lacked final resolution of his problems, the reason was Spender's compulsion to preserve honesty and integrity at whatever cost against the inner and outer forces that threatened disintegration and disaster. Despite his venture into poetic drama in *Trial of a Judge* (1938) and into political narrative in *Vienna* (1934), his forte was the exploration of the individual consciousness and its attempts to clarify its relationship to itself and the world. In *World within a World* (1951) Spender told his life-story with courageous frankness and unfaltering insight. Of two critical studies, the earlier, *The Destructive Element* (1935), marked the peak of the Marxist influence on his critical thinking; the later, *The Creative Element* (1953), was a warning against the threat to the artist of other varieties of authoritarianism.

The Second World War, like the first, inevitably stimulated the production of a great mass of poetry, most of which was of merely ephemeral interest. The tone of this poetry, however, differed markedly from that produced during the earlier war. The records and recollections of the first conflict had prepared even young men to meet the second, not with a sense of shock and horror, nor with enthusiasm or romantic idealism, but with the spirit of endurance and resignation. In consequence, the poetry of the Second World War tended to express the writer's personal sense of separation from what was familiar and dear, an alert and rather objective recording of the strange sights and events he was forced to witness, and a rather stoical acceptance of whatever fate had in store for him. The global character of the war, moreover, not only enlarged *Poetry of* the bounds of the writer's experience but stimu- *the Second* lated his imagination as the First World War had *World War* not done. Men in the British Armed Forces fought not only in the Low Countires, France, and Germany, but also in North Africa, Greece, Burma, and the Far East. The mere recording of these experiences inevitably introduced a fresh and exciting stream of exoticism into twentieth-century English literature. And the interest in remote countries and strange ways of life did not terminate with the end of the conflict. The fact that the austere British fiscal program made it almost impossible for Englishmen to travel widely increased immensely the lure of the inaccessible. Finally, the government, through the British Arts Council, made grants that permitted young writers to escape the claustrophobic confines of the British Isles and allow themselves the stimulus of novel environments and peoples. Thus, the peace, no less than the war, resulted in the production of a number of distinguished works on exotic places and peoples unfamiliar to most English readers.

The Second World War, like the First, not only brought to light a considerable number of talents but also claimed its victims. The works of the three most promising poets who were casualties of the war have been preserved in *Raiders' Dawn* (1942) and *Ha! Ha! Among the Trumpets* (1945) by the Welshman Alun Lewis (1915-1944), who was killed in Burma, *Alamein to Zem-Zem* (1946) and *Collected Poems* (1951) by Keith Douglas (1920-1944), who was killed during the invasion of Normandy, and *Collected Poems* (1945) by Sidney Keyes (1922–1943), who died while a prisoner in Tunisia. Of the poets who survived the war, Roy Fuller (1912–   ), who served with the Fleet Air Arm, in *The Middle of a War* (1942) and *A Lost Season* (1944) not only recorded his experience in sharp senory images but also expressed poignantly the soldier's sense of estrangement and boredom, even in the face of peril and death. In *Counterparts* (1954) he succeeded in wresting significance from seemingly trivial aspects of contemporary urban life. Fuller also showed considerable gifts as a novelist. In *The Ruined Boys* (American title, *That Distant Afternoon*, 1959), he recounted the spiritual liberation of a sensitive boy after his disillusionment with the masters of a second-rate public school headed for dissolution. *The Father's Comedy* (1961) was an adroit study of a socially and politically ambitious father, who, in defending a son whom he feels he has misguided, is forced to face up to himself. In his *Collected Poems* (1962), the most effective were those drawn from his experiences during the Second World War and not from his rather gray and resigned life later. Lawrence Durrell (1912–   ), who had lived in Corfu before the war and was on government service in the Near East, was one of a group of English writers, with temporary headquarters in Cairo, who published a wartime literary magazine, *Personal Landscape*. In *A Private Country* (1943) and *Cities, Plains, and People* (1946) Durrell, with an almost oriental sensory delight, drew sketches of life in the Near East from his stores of intimate experience and considerable erudition.

The untimely death of Dylan Thomas (1914-1953) robbed mid-century English poetry of its most individual and indubitable talent. Although his poetic production was limited in quantity, its over-all quality was exceedingly high. Thomas's earliest poems made an immediate, if almost overpowering, impression. Here was poetry in which meaning was in danger of being drowned out by the clamor of importunate figures, in which the most extravagantly exuberant metaphors fused or clashed. The violent metaphorical juxtapositions in these early poems owed not a little to Freud's conception of the unconscious and had the effect of surrealism. Like Freud, too, Thomas seemed pre-occupied with sex as the great force manifesting *Dylan* itself in all the forms of life and linking them to-*Thomas* gether. But the metaphorical violence of the poetry had its source not only in his desire to administer to the reader a series of shocks, but in his attempt to express his highly intuitive, indeed mystical sense of the reconciliation of opposites— life and death, beauty and horror, growth and decay, Eros and Thanatos. It was not only Thomas's style that has analogies with that of metaphysical poetry; his view of life was close to that of the two Welsh mystic poets, Henry Vaughan and his brother Thomas.

Thomas announced, in the preface to his *Collected Poems* (1952) that "These poems, with all their crudities, doubts, and confusions, are written for the love of Man and in praise of God." This sentiment was, in the best sense, pious. Such a delightful lyric as "Fern Hill," for example, expresses an ecstatic sense of joy in life on the human plane, but "The Force that through the Green Fuse Drives the Flower," with its potent expression of the mystical unity of things, is essentially a religious poem:

The force that through the green fuse drives the flower
Drives my green age; that blasts the roots of trees
Is my destroyer.
And I am dumb to tell the crooked rose
My youth is bent by the same wintry fever.

"And Death Shall have no Dominion," with its biblical echoes, is saved from sentimentality by its frank facing of the grim facts of death. For Thomas, not only life but death was holy. Indeed, the intensity of his love of death may have been a condition of the intensity of his love of life. On the physical plane, the drive to self-destruction triumphed, but through his poems celebrating the equal powers of life and death, the poet lives on.

Thomas was not only a remarkable poet but a very gifted prose writer. "A Child's Christmas in Wales" is a humorously and tenderly detailed reminiscence touched with pathos. His last work, *Under Milk Wood* (1954), a radio play in highly rhythmic prose, re-creates with earthy humor and poetic gusto the life of a Welsh village from the coming of dawn to the coming of darkness. The rowdy lovers of life are shrewdly set off against the haters of life and the hapless victims they have imprisoned.

Some of Thomas' contemporaries cultivated more traditional poetic modes. Kathleen Raine (1908–   ), in *The Year One* (1952), through her penetrating insights into the character of her native Northumbria, achieved an almost atavistic interpretation of nature. Her *Collected Poems* (1956) garnered from her four earlier volumes the poems that expressed her conviction that "the ever-recurring forms of nature mirror eternal reality." *The Golden Bird* (1951) by Ann Ridler (1912–   ), though heavily weighted with mythical symbolism, showed a sustained imaginative exuberance, and *A Matter of Life and Death* (1959) reenforced the sense of her delight in human love and tenderness. *The Creation* (1951) by James Kirkup (1918–   ), a long poem in the baroque style developed by Crashaw, used metaphysical metaphor and wit tastefully, and *The Submerged Village* (1951) expressed poignantly his sense of the poet's isolation in the modern world. His autobiographical accounts of his infancy and childhood—*The Only Child* (1957) and *Sorrows, Passions, and Alarms* (1959)—recaptured vividly the sensitive observations and feelings of a growing child.

The poetry of the late 1950's made a sharp break with the major influences operative before this decade. The new poets reacted, on the one hand, against the extremely allusive, musically organized, international style of Ezra Pound and T. S. Eliot and, on the other hand, against the audaciously metaphorical surrealistic style of the spectacular Dylan Thomas. Despite differences inevitable in a literary form as individual as poetry, the writing of the younger poets marked a return to strict metrical regularity, a fairly colloquial level of diction, a conversational word-order, sobriety of tone, and a rather persistent irony. Certain, if not all, of these characteristics were apparent in *The Less Deceived* (1955) by Philip Larkin (1922–   ), *Bread Rather than Blossoms* (1956) by D. J. Enright (1920–   ), *A Word Carved on a Sill* (1956) by John Wain (1925–   ), *The Hawk in the Rain* (1957) by Ted Hughes (1930–   ), and *My Sad Captains* (1961) by Thom Gunn (1929–   ).

BIOGRAPHY AND CRITICISM

If any single literary event were to be chosen to mark the termination of the Victorian era, that event might well be the **Lytton Strachey** publication in 1918 of Lytton Strachey's *Eminent Victorians*. For the title turned out to be, not adulatory but ironical, since the purpose of the book was the removing of the halos with which a pious period had invested its heroes and heroines. To the successful fulfillment of this purpose the temperament and talent of Strachey (1880–1932) were admirably adapted. His sympathies were classical rather than romantic, French rather than English. Although he admired and appreciated the idiosyncratic individuality of the styles of such English writers as Sir Thomas Browne and William Blake, his preference was for the chilly ironies of Gibbon and the perfect polish of Racine. His sceptical critical spirit was completely antithetical to the sentimental optimism of the Victorian era, and it was easy for him to find in that period overabundant material for the free play of his irony and his love for the mock-heroic. His biographical method was a conscious reaction to the pious hagiography and the tasteless inclusiveness of the ponderous two-volume lives-and-letters characteristic of nineteenth-century biography. His aim was the creation of an honest and lifelike portrait, not a stuffed effigy. Of Strachey's honesty, there can be little doubt; of his fairness, at least in *Eminent Victorians,* there is very real question. Behind the protestation of fairness there was a spirit of mockery, not to say animosity, that threatened the fidelity of his historical portraits. But this brilliant and influential volume marked the peak of Strachey's anti-Victorianism.

When he turned to an elaborate and exceedingly artful study of the Queen who had impressed her personality upon an era, the impulse to mock and to belittle yielded to a distinctly kindly and even affectionate feeling toward his subject. In consequence, *Queen Victoria* (1921) is a more enduringly satisfying work than the earlier volume. He was not, to be sure, always able to resist the temptation to reconstruct imaginatively the psychological processes of his characters, and when he turned away from the nineteenth century to the more florid sixteenth century, he succumbed to the temptation without compunction. *Elizabeth and Essex* (1928), in consequence, comes closer perhaps to being an historical romance than a true biography; Strachey's scepticism and aloofness were put to flight by the sturdy old Queen and her handsome foolhardy favorite. But the model he had set for biography in the earlier volumes found many imitators, most of whom, however, did not have a tithe of the master's gift of style or of his discrimination in the selection of his materials.

Sir Harold Nicolson and Philip Guedalla were perhaps the most successful of the disciples of Strachey. In the work of Nicolson (1886–   ), two phases can already be distinguished. In the 'twenties, like Strachey, he was primarily concerned with the reinterpretation of problematical Victorian figures, like Tennyson and Swinburne. Perhaps the finest work of his early period is the subtly anti-romantic study in *Byron, the*

Strachey's Followers

Last Journey (1924) of the last year in the life of the most flamboyant of the English romantics. In the 'thirties, Nicolson occupied himself with biographical studies of great personages with whom he had intimate contacts during his diplomatic career: his father in *Sir Arthur Nicolson, Bart.* (1930); his patron, in *Curzon, the Last Phase* (1934); and Lord Dufferin, in *Helen's Tower* (1937). In these later works, Nicholson has made his most substantial contributions to contemporary biography. Like Strachey and Nicolson, Philip Guedalla (1889–1944) found his most fruitful subjects in nineteenth-century topics such as *The Second Empire* (1922), *Palmerston* (1926), and *The Duke* (1931), a biography of Wellington. Guedalla's work was characterized by an abundance of wit and epigram, an almost rococo delight in historical décor, a flair for pageantry, and an almost too deliberate contrivance of historical panoramas.

Long before the death of Guedalla, biographical writing had manifested a marked reaction against the method and influence of Lytton Strachey. His elegance and irony, his highly polished and witty style had tended to obscure the strong bias apparent in his attitude toward his Victorian subjects and his highhanded treatment of historical facts. The extent of the reaction is clearly evident in the impressive biographies written by Mrs. Cecil Woodham-Smith (1896–   ): *Florence Nightingale* (1950) and *The Reason Why* (1953). The earlier of these works, hailed as the definitive biography of its subject, rescued her heroine from the irony with which Strachey had treated the more pious and self-righteous aspects of Miss Nightingale's personality. *The Reason Why* was a carefully documented and coolly dispassionate study of the fantastic personalities of the British officers—Lords Cardigan, Lucan, and Raglan—who shared the responsibility for the fruitless charge of the Light Brigade.

To a field allied to biography, namely, autobiography, belongs one of the indubitably great books of the period. *Seven Pillars of Wisdom* (1926) by T. E. Lawrence (1888–1935) is probably the greatest non-imaginative narrative to appear in the interval between the two World Wars. The book, which gives an account of Lawrence's part in uniting the Arab tribes against the Turks in 1915 and in guiding them to their triumph, rises far above the spate *T. E. Lawrence* of war-memoirs of statesmen and generals. The ultimate source of the distinction of the book is the impact upon one of the most complex and problematical of personalities of a great heroic experience. The result may best be regarded as a modern prose epic, a unique example of the appearance of a heroic narrative in an era disinclined to the grand style. For anything like a full understanding of Lawrence's perverse and baffling character, one must turn to his posthumously published *Letters* (1938) and his essays in literary criticism, *Men in Print* (1940), but *Seven Pillars* has its own intrinsic merits in the painfully vivid description of the terrain over which Lawrence and the Arabs fought, accounts of primitive manners and customs that remind one of the more domestic details of the *Odyssey* and *Beowulf,* subtle analyses of the characters of the chiefs and generals of whose devious relationships Lawrence was a masterly manipulator, and the architectonics of the epic narrative itself. Twenty-five years after his death, the terms of his will made possible the publication of *The Mint,* his account of his experiences as an unidentified recruit in the Royal Air Force. Its style was frequently distinguished, if not mannered; its content, however, proved monotonous, since, aside from its sharp sketches of sadistic officers and kindly but obscene-mouthed privates, it was a masochistic record of physical discomforts and psychological distresses. Of this complex and ambiguous personality, no definitive judgment is yet possible.

Left Hand, Right Hand! (1945–1950), the autobiography in five volumes by Sir Osbert Sitwell (1892–   ), achieved a distinction utterly antithetical but equal to that of *Seven Pillars of Wisdom* and seems likely to be its brilliant and versatile author's most enduring monument. The work is autobiographical in the widest sense, since its aim is the re-creation of the social history of England as seen by this acutely observant but generally sympathetic participant. His noble birth and distinguished family heritage familiarized him with the almost feudal society of late Victorian and Edwardian England and the complex ancestral and historical roots of this now vanished way of life. Sir Osbert's unhappy experience at Eton, where he detested both boys and masters, and in the Huzzars at Aldershot is more conventional and less impressive than his superb characterization of his father, Sir George, who, although himself an eccentric in the great tradition, was baffled by the æsthetic vagaries of his gifted and rebellious children, Edith, Osbert, and Sacheverell. In the later volumes of the autobiography, the author tells how, as an officer in the Grenadier Guards stationed in London, he not only made a reputation for himself as poet and novelist but became a patron of the new French painters and of the Russian ballet. He was at home in all the literary and æsthetic circles of the period between the wars, and gives vivid life to their major personalities. For some tastes, Sir Osbert's baroque style may seem slightly effete, but with it he achieves masterly effects in landscape and portrait. In the following passage, for example, he pictures tellingly the impingement of modern industrialism on the once remote beauty and elegance of the family seat, Renishaw:

Then, as now, in the distance beyond the park, the great plumes of smoke would wave triumphantly over the pyramids of slag, down which, every now and then, crawled writhing serpents of fire, as the cinders were discharged from the trucks. After dark, this process at conjecturable intervals lit the whole night with a wild glory, so that, my father told me, standing on the lawn, he could read his watch by the light of Stavely flares three miles away, and in the woods this sudden illumination gave an added poignance to the sylvan glades that it revealed, causing the rabbits to be frozen for an instant into immobility, their eyes reflecting the glare and the terror within them, showing a shape, which might be that of an otter from the lake below, scudding through the long wet grass, and making the owl hiccup uneasily in the trees where formerly he had hooted with assurance.

No type of non-imaginative prose-writing since 1914 has been more fertile than that of literary criticism. It has, to be sure, been less rich on the theoretical than on the practical side, for English critics, since the downfall of the neoclassical doctrine, have been persistently suspicious of critical systems and have devoted a very small portion of their powers to the development of such systems. In fact, the major critical consequence of the romantic movement was the encouragement of intuition and impressionism at the expense of order and of impersonal critical standards. It is not surprising, therefore, that twentieth-century criticism should still be predominantly impressionistic in nature and that it should still manifest reluctance to evolve or to adopt a systematic æsthetic-critical theory.

Since most contemporary criticism is basically romantic in its assumptions and its procedures, it exhibits something of the protean quality of romantic imaginative literature. For example, although J. Middleton Murry (1889–1957) and Sacheverell Sitwell may both be *J. Middleton Murry* regarded as romantic critics, their methods and their results are remarkable diverse. Murry is the best contemporary example of the dithyrambic tendency in romantic criticism. His procedure is the identification of himself with the subject he is criticizing in order that he may see the work from the point of view of its creator. This method is, therefore, the carrying to its logical conclusion that sympathetic comprehension and responsiveness that is the basis of all sound critical activity. The weaknesses in criticism of this sort are its intense subjectivity and the temptation—especially acute in the case of Murry—to remake the author in his own image rather than to remould himself in the image of the author. Murry has perhaps been most successful in exploiting the relationship between Keats's mind and Shakespeare's in his *Keats and Shakespeare* (1925). When in *Son of Woman* (1931), his critical study of D. H. Lawrence, the process of identification is impeded by personal obstacles, the results are far less dependable. *Jonathan Swift* (1953) proved to be one of his happier critical performances. This impressive work not only assembled and synthesized most of the findings of modern scholarship but praised persuasively Swift's neglected early poems and gave a fresh interpretation of his subject's baffling personality and his ambiguous relations with Stella and Vanessa.

The impressionism of Sacheverell Sitwell (1897–   ) is more informed and less idiosyncratic than that of Murry. He first made his reputation as a poet by conducting technical ex-

Sache-
verell
Sitwell

periments only slightly less striking than those made by his sister Dame Edith, but his æsthetic curiosity concerning periods neglected by nine-teenth-century taste led him to devote most of his energies to sympathetic interpretations of baroque and neo-classical art. For this enterprise he has a distinguished sensibility and sympathy and a style that is as responsive to the lush exuberance of the baroque as to the correctness and restraint of the classical. A characteristic bravura passage is his metaphorical account of the controversy concerning El Greco's "St. Maurice" in *Southern Baroque Art* (1924):

The music was a force that held every vessel straining at its ropes, and very quickly the pulse of every person in the crowd was rattling like a mandoline. The martial music had power to brace up and kindle the heart of every person there. The square was as if latticed and festooned with taut wires, for every effect of marching to music is like walking a tight-rope, from which you dare not look down. The bells rolled out louder and louder, till their very metal was molten as if to beat into sword-blades, and when the whole volume of sound died away suddenly, its last breath blew away, dwindling in force till the hills at the end of the valley were reached.

A more chaste and controlled passage is that describing the effect of the Palladian bridge at Prior Park outside Bath:

It is, indeed, more of a memorial than a bridge. But its Virgilian authority and calmness, the beauty of its stilted diction, transport us into a world of peace and order. Nothing is more soothing to the spirit than the health-giving properties of this deliberate and timeless building. It has the perfection of the greatest classical music.

Despite the willful associative nature of the organization of his impressions, Sitwell's astonishing capacity for evocation goes a long distance in communicating his imaginative responses to diverse kinds of beauty.

Sir Herbert Read (1896–   ) has said that his writings on literature and the fine arts are neither critical nor historical but philosophic, and certainly among the major critics of the period he has manifested the widest of intellectual concerns. Essentially, Read is the heir to the great English tradition of romantic individualism; again and again he submits æsthetic and social movements to the test of whether they assist or hinder the individual in the full development of his potentialities. He has also described himself as "a philosophic anarchist," and the phrase may serve to suggest his impatience with systems of thought and ways of life that might inhibit the enrichment of individual life. His own restless quest for the fruition of his powers is apparent in the variety of forms in which he has expressed himself: sensitive childhood reminiscences in *The Innocent Eye* (1933), fantastic fiction in *The Green Child* (1935), poetry in the powerful *A World within a War* (1945) and other volumes, and numerous studies of the theory and practice of literature and the fine arts. His æsthetic ideal is "organic form," which is found "when a work of art has its own inherent laws, originating with its very invention, and fusing in one vital unity both structure and content." To this, he opposes "abstract form," which results when organic form has become mere pattern and the artist contents himself with adapting content to pre-determined structure. *The Philosophy of Modern Art* (1952) is perhaps the most satisfactory introduction to his methods and beliefs. *The True Voice of Feeling* (1953) is an eloquent defense of the English romantic poets whose prestige has suffered considerably from the attacks of Eliot in England and the New Critics in America.

The most influential work on the theory of literature and of criticism was contributed by the psychologist I. A. Richards (1893–   ). In this field, his basic work was *Principles of Literary Criticism* (1924). Here he was primarily concerned with analyzing the elements involved in the process of comprehending a work of art and, secondarily, with relating æsthetic value to the theory of value generally. He was more successful

I. A. Richards

in carrying out the first of these purposes, although what he had to say about the value of works of art was extremely suggestive. With *Practical Criticism* (1929), he went on to study the obstacles in the way of that accurate and sympathetic comprehension of a work of art that must precede any significant evaluation of it. Probably no earlier student of the critical process had brought out into the light such difficulties in the way of real comprehension as those he suggestively denominated as "mnemonic irrelevances," "technical preoccupations," "doctrinal adhesions," and either excess or inhibition of feeling. This study led Richards to believe that he must investigate the ways in which words acquire legitimate and illegitimate meanings, and, in later years, leaving the study of the process of criticism to such disciples as F. R. Leavis and William Empson, he concerned himself with such introductions to semantics as *Interpretation in Teaching* (1938). Richards's major service to criticism has been the demonstration of the need for the most careful study of the process of comprehension preliminary to the equally significant, if no less difficult, process of evaluation.

F. R. Leavis (1895–   ), educated at Cambridge and for many years a member of its English faculty, was the leading

F. R. Leavis

spirit in a group of critics whose activities brought about significant changes in the climate of contemporary literary opinion. As the energetic and self-sacrificing editor of the distinguished critical journal, *Scrutiny* (1932–53), he gathered about him kindred spirits whose exacting standards and close analysis of literary texts constitute an instructive parallel to those of the New Critics in America. Although his tone was frequently severe and his manner peremptory, his unfailingly serious concern and his penetrating intelligence compelled attention, if not assent. *New Bearings in English Poetry* (1932) is still a provocative guide to the movement led by Eliot and Pound. In *Revaluation* (1947), he argued vigorously for the rehabilitation of the literary reputations of Dryden, Marvell, and Emily Brontë, and pled for some modification in the prestige usually accorded Milton, Pope, and Shelley. The thesis of *The Great Tradition* (1948) was that the really major novelists of the nineteenth and twentieth centuries are George Eliot, Henry James, and Joseph Conrad. In *The Common Pursuit* (1952) he garnered the most important of his contributions to *Scrutiny*. William Empson (1906–   ), although far less productive than Leavis, has proved to be the most seminal of contemporary critics; his position on the critical scene is similar to that of Kenneth Burke in American criticism. His early books, *Seven Types of Ambiguity* (1930) and *Some Versions of Pastoral* (Am. title, *English Pastoral Poetry:* 1935) have had a profound influence in both England and America in the direction of subtilizing the perceptions and responses of critics to works chosen for close scrutiny. *The Structure of Complex Words* (1951), written, as Empson writes, "on the borderland of linguistics and literary criticism," is a major contribution to literary semantics, the total impact of which only the future will make clear. Empson is important, moreover, not only as a critic but as a poet. Characteristically, the *Collected Poems* (1949) are not voluminous, but, although oblique and cryptic, they match in subtlety his provocative critical-analytical writing.

The most influential of the practicing critics was the Anglo-American poet, T. S. Eliot (1888–   ), whose criticism, unlike that of most of his contemporaries, was based on a coherent series of principles. His theo- **T. S. Eliot** retical system, however, did not remain static, and, therefore, the direction in which his thinking moved must be noted. The source of Eliot's critical system was that movement in American criticism that was led by Professors Irving Babbitt and Paul Elmer More and was known as humanism. The movement, a modern variety of neoclassicism hostile to both the romantic and the realistic movements in literature and to unlimited democracy and to humanitarianism in politics, called for a return to classical standards in criticism and for the measurement of modern literature on the scale of the classics. On the moral side, American humanism insisted on the need for a constant awareness of man's double nature and for the domination of the

physical and the instinctive by the spiritual and the intellectual.
Eliot's critical position, in *The Sacred Wood* (1920), is practically indistinguishable from that of the humanists. He was,
however, aware of the fact that, despite the supremacy of works
of art of the first rank, there is a constant process of modification of critical estimation of works in other ranks. In an important passage in his essay, "Tradition and the Individual
Talent," he said:

The existing monuments form an ideal order among themselves,
which is modified by the introduction of the new (the really new)
work of art among them. The existing order is complete before
the new work of art arrives; for order to persist after the super-
vention of novelty the *whole* existing order must be, if ever so
slightly, altered; and so the relations, proportions, values of each
work of art toward the whole are readjusted; and this is conformity between the old and the new.

Eliot, therefore, felt that it was the function of the modern
critic, on the one hand, to define his attitudes toward the ancient
and modern classics and, on the other, to estimate modern
works in relation to such classics.

Eliot's development beyond this stage in his thinking came
about through his increasing dissatisfaction with the moral assumptions of humanism. He grew to feel that they could not be
defended unless they were sanctioned by such a theology as he
had come to accept as final. Accordingly, in such a later work
as *After Strange Gods* (1934), he felt it necessary to consider
such modern authors as James Joyce, D. H. Lawrence, and
Katherine Mansfield, not only æsthetically but morally. His
spiritual position compelled him to label them heretics.
On Poetry and Poets (1957), he collected essays and occasional
addresses on poets and dramatists who had influenced his
writing. With respect to Milton and Goethe, he attempted—
perhaps without complete success—to make amends for in-
justices he felt he had done them in his earlier criticism. In
general, the tone of this collection was less waspish and more
benign than that of *After Strange Gods* and reflected Eliot's
sense of his growing responsibility as an international man of

letters. Eliot's practical criticism is less impressive when he is concerned with modern figures than with figures from earlier periods. As a poet of the greatest distinction, he had an unusual advantage in his approach to such fellow-poets as Dante, Donne, and Dryden. As a subtle moralist, he is perhaps most illuminating in his re-definition of the significance of such figures as Tennyson and Baudelaire. His superb critical style derives from that of Matthew Arnold, but, while it has the latter's note of authority, it is less repetitious and less mannered. As an editor of the *Criterion,* he won both English and American disciples. His powers of interpretation and expression gave him a prestige beyond that of any other contemporary critic. Eliot did more than any other single writer to hasten the renaissance of criticism, in both England and America.

Although no critic who emerged in the 1950's seemed likely to attain the stature of either T. S. Eliot or F. R. Leavis, there was no mistaking the direction in which criticism was moving. It was a period of vigorous reaction, on the one hand, against the microscopic analysis advocated and exemplified by the English followers of the American New Critics and, on the other hand, against the anti-romantic bias of Eliot and the ethical dogmatism of Leavis and his numerous followers. Frank Kermode's *The Romantic Image* (1957) argued against the denigration of the romantic poets by Eliot and the New Critics. He attempted to show that certain concepts fundamental to romanticism: the alienated artist, the poetic imagination as a means of access to a world more real than that rendered by the senses, and the poem as an organism are also central to the understanding of writers like Eliot and Pound who have conventionally been regarded as anti-romantic poets. Helen Gardner in *The Business of Criticism* (1959) launched a lively attack on the excessive professionalism of much academic criticism and defended the traditional proposition that the critic's function is to assist the reader in finding the values that he believes the work to express. Graham Hough's *Image and Experience* (1960) contended that there was a need for a counter-revolution in poetry against the changes wrought by Pound and Eliot, a counter-revolution that would restore lucidity, clarity of structure, and communicativeness to poetry. C. S. Lewis' *An Experiment in Criticism* (1961) maintained that a work of art can be either "received" or "used," and objected to the Leavis school on the grounds that it used literature for moral or psychological enlightenment; on the other hand, receiving literature meant opening one's mind and heart to it and coming to an understanding of it for its own sake and not for any ulterior aim. However valid these views may prove to be, there was no doubt that literary criticism would continue to maintain the distinguished position that it had achieved in twentieth-century literature.

BIBLIOGRAPHIES

Bibliographies

Each chapter is furnished with a separate bibliography, giving first an account of general works pertinent to the period covered, and second a list of standard texts and selections as well as biographical and critical studies of individual authors. Authors are mentioned in alphabetical order. Titles are usually given in abbreviated form, and, although publisher and date of publication are cited, no attempt has been made to list the first edition of scholarly works. The abbreviations for publishers, where used, are as follows:

Alcuin: The Alcuin Press; Allen: George Allen and Unwin; Andrews: W. Andrews and Co.; Appleton: D. Appleton Co.; Archer: Denis Archer; Arnold: Edward Arnold and Co.; Banta: George Banta Publishing Co.; Barker: Arthur Barker, Ltd.; Batsford: B. T. Batsford, Ltd.; Bell: George Bell and Sons, Ltd.; Benn: Ernest Benn, Ltd.; Black: A. and C. Black, Ltd.; Blackie: Blackie and Son, Ltd.; Blackwell: B. H. Blackwell, Ltd.; Blackwood: Wm. Blackwood and Sons, Ltd.; Bles: Geoffrey Bles, Ltd.; Boivin: Boivin et cie.; Burleigh: T. Burleigh; Butterworth: T. Butterworth and Co.; C. U. P.: Cambridge University Press; Cape: Jonathan Cape, Ltd.; Cassell: Cassell and Co., Ltd.; Chambers: W. and R. Chambers; Chatto: Chatto & Windus; Chaundy: L. Chaundy and Co.; Chiswick: The Chiswick Press, Ltd.; Clarendon: The Clarendon Press; Columbia U. P.: Columbia University Press; Constable: Constable and Co., Ltd.; Cornell U. P.: Cornell University Press; Crofts: F. S. Crofts and Co.; Crowell: Thomas Y. Crowell Co.; Daniel: C. W. Daniel Co.; Davies: Peter Davies; Day: The John Day Co.; Dent: J. M. Dent and Sons, Ltd.; Dodge: Dodge Publishing Co.; Doran: George H. Doran Co.; Doubleday: Doubleday, Page and Co.; Duckworth: G. Duckworth and Co., Ltd.; Dutton: E. P. Dutton and Co., Inc.;

Etchells and Macdonald: Frederick Etchells and Hugh Macdonald; Eyre: L. Eyre & Spottiswoode; Faber: Faber & Faber; Farncombe: C. J. Farncombe and Sons; Fenland: The Fenland Press; Fifield: A. C. Fifield; Frowde: H. Frowde; Geddes: P. Geddes; Ginn: Ginn and Co.;

Gollancz: V. Gollancz; Grasset: B. Grasset; Grant: Grant and Murray; Grayson: Grayson and Grayson; Greenberg: Greenberg Publisher, Inc.; Harcourt: Harcourt, Brace and Co.;

Harmsworth: Desmond Harmsworth, Ltd.; Harper: Harper and Brothers; Harrap: George G. Harrap and Co., Ltd.; Harvard U. P.: Harvard University Press; Heath: D. C. Heath and Co.; Heffer: W. Heffer and Sons; Heinemann: William Heinemann; Hodder: Hodder & Stoughton; Hodges, Figgis: Hodges, Figgis and Co., Ltd.; Holden: R. Holden and Co.; Hollings: F. Hollings; Holt: Henry Holt and Co.; Huebsch: B. W. Huebsch; Hulbert: Hulbert Publishing Co., Hutchinson: Wilford Hutchinson; Isbister: W. Isbister; Jack: T. C. and E. C. Jack; Jenkins: Herbert Jenkins; Johns Hopkins U. P.: Johns Hopkins University Press; Joiner: Joiner and Steele; Kennerley: M. Kennerley; King: P. S. King and Son; Knopf: Alfred A. Knopf; Lahr: E. Lahr; Lane: John Lane; Laurie: T. Werner Laurie; Librairie Univ.: Librairie Universitaire; Lippincott: J. B. Lippincott Co.; Longmans: Longmans, Green and Co.; Luce: John W. Luce and Co.; Macaulay: The Macaulay Co.; MacLehose: J. MacLehose and Sons; Macmillan: The Macmillan Co.; MacVeagh: Lincoln MacVeagh; Marshall: H. Marshall and Son; Mattieson: K. Mattieson, Ltd.; Maunsel: Maunsel and Co.; Messner: J. Messner, Inc.; Methuen: Methuen and Co., Ltd.; Moxon: Edward Moxon; Murby: Thomas Murby and Co.;. J. Murray: John Murray;

Nelson: Thomas Nelson and Sons; Newton: S. Newton; Nimmo: Wm. Nimmo and Co.; Nott: Stanley Nott, Ltd.; Nutt: David Nutt; O. U. P.: Oxford University Press; Palmer: C. Palmer; Parsons: L. Parsons; Paterson: W. Paterson; Paul: K. Paul, French, Trubner; Perrin: Librairie Académique Perrin; Pickering: W. Pickering; Princeton U. P.: Princeton University Press; Putnam: G. P. Putnam's Sons; Quaritch: Bernard Quaritch; Richards: The Richards Press; Roberts: Roberts Brothers;

Routledge: George Routledge and Sons; Rudge: W. E. Rudge; S.P.C.K.: Society for the Promotion of Christian Knowledge; Sawyer: C. F. Sawyer; Scott: Walter Scott Publishing Co.; Scribner's: Charles Scribner's Sons; Secker: Martin Secker, Ltd.; Simpkin: Simpkin, Marshall, Hamilton, Kent and Co.; Sinkins: J. Sinkins; Sotheran: H. C. Sotheran and Co.; Stechert: G. E. Stechert and Co.; Stokes: Frederick A. Stokes Co.; Taylor: J. F. Taylor; Titus: E. W. Titus; Univ. of Mich. P.: University of Michigan Press; Univ. of Wash. P.: University of Washington Press; Viking: The Viking Press, Inc.; Vrin: J. Vrin; Washburn: Ives Washburn, Inc.; Webster: Webster Publishing Co.;

White: E. V. White; Wilson: H. W. Wilson Co.; Witherby: H. F. and G. Witherby; Yale U. P.: Yale University Press.

GENERAL WORKS

Among the most valuable reference books for English literature generally are H. D. Traill's *Social England* (6 vols., rev. ed., Putnam, 1901–04) and J. R. Green's *Short History of the English People* (4 vols., Harper, 1893–95), which may be used to connect literary with social and political history. Both the *Dictionary of National Biography*, which may be consulted for biographical treatment fuller than that given in the text, and the *Cambridge History of English Literature* (Putnam, 1907–16) are indispensable reference works covering the entire range of English literature. Other useful and comprehensive treatments of the subject are to be found in J. J. Jusserand's *A Literary History of the English People* (Putnam, 1925); *A History of English Literature, 650–1914,* by E. Legouis and L. Cazamian (Macmillan, 1929); and W. J. Courthope's *A History of English Poetry* (6 vols., Macmillan, 1920–26). The standard bibliography for English literature is *The Cambridge Bibliography of English Literature,* edited by F. W. Bateson (4 vols., C. U. P., 1941). Invaluable one-volume surveys of English literature are George Sampson's *The Concise Cambridge History of English Literature* (Macmillan, 1941), *A Literary History of England,* edited by A. C. Baugh (Appleton-Century-Crofts, 1948), and *A History of English Literature,* edited by Hardin Craig (Oxford, 1950).

CHAPTER I

GENERAL WORKS

Besides such standard works as the *Cambridge History of English Literature* and Traill's *Social England,* the student may wish to consult more recent works like T. Allison's *Pioneers of English Learning* (Blackwell, 1932), F. B. Gummere's *Founders of England,* with supplementary notes by F. P. Magoun (Stechert, 1930), and R. H. Hodgkin's indispensable *History of the Anglo-Saxons,* 2 vols. (Clarendon, 1935). Excellent histories are *England before the Norman Conquest* (Longmans, 1926) by R. W. Chambers and the comprehensive work by R. G. Collingwood and J. N. L. Myres entitled *Roman Britain and the English Settlements* (Clarendon, 1936). A. C. Baugh's *History of the English Language* (Appleton-Century, 1935) is admirably adapted to the non-specialist, and S. Robertson's *The Development of Modern*

English (Prentice-Hall, 1934) traces in a readable fashion the growth of the language from its origins to present-day American English. The most useful historical accounts of early English literature are to be found in J. J. Jusserand's *A Literary History of the English People,* 3 vols. (Putnam, 1895–1949), and in S. A. Brooke's two works: *The History of Early English Literature* (Macmillan, 1892) and *English Literature from the Beginning to the Norman Conquest* (Macmillan, 1898). W. P. Ker's *The Dark Ages* (Scribner's, 1904) is a classic. A more recent survey of this field is George K. Anderson's *The Literature of the Anglo-Saxons* (Princeton U. P., 1949).

SELECTIONS AND TRANSLATIONS

The student will find ample selections from Old English literature in *Select Translations from Old English Poetry* (Ginn, rev. ed., 1926) and *Select Translations from Old English Prose* (Ginn, 1908), by A. S. Cook and C. B. Tinker; and in the reliable prose translation of *Anglo-Saxon Poetry* (Everyman Lib., 1927) by R. K. Gordon. J. D. Spaeth's translation of *Old English Poetry* (Princeton U. P., 1922) is done in alliterative verse, with useful bibliography, introduction, and notes. Modern versions of *Beowulf* are available either in Gordon (above) or in the separate editions of C. G. Child, *Beowulf and the Finnesburh Fragment, Translated* (Houghton Mifflin, 1904); D. H. Crawford, *Beowulf* (Chatto and Windus, 1926), translated into English verse, with an introduction, notes, and appendices; and A. Strong, *Beowulf* (Constable, 1925) translated into modern English rhyming verse, with introduction and notes, with a foreword on "Beowulf and the Heroic Age" by R. W. Chambers. F. B. Gummere's *The Oldest English Epic* (Macmillan, 1909) remains deservedly popular because of its good introduction and notes.

CHAPTER II

GENERAL WORKS

Good historical surveys of this period are available in H. W. C. Davis's *England under the Normans and Angevins, 1066–1272* (Putnam, 11th ed., 1937), and in K. H. Vickers's *England in the Later Middle Ages* (Putnam, 2nd ed., 1919). For excellent illustrations of life and society, the reader may also wish to consult J. J. Jusserand, *English Wayfaring Life in the Middle Ages* (Putnam, 1889). W. Cunningham's *The Growth of English Industry and Commerce, During the*

Early and Middle Ages (C. U. P., 5th ed., 1922) is the standard economic history of the period; while F. H. Crossley, *The English Abbey, Its Life and Work in the Middle Ages* (Scribner's, 1936), a beautifully illustrated work, is a thorough treatment of the religious life of the time. Among the foremost literary histories are C. S. Baldwin's *Three Medieval Centuries of Literature in England, 1100–1400* (Little, Brown, 1932); W. P. Ker's *English Literature, Medieval* (Holt, 1912), a stimulating introductory book; and W. H. Schofield's *English Literature from the Norman Conquest to Chaucer* (Macmillan, 1906), a comprehensive and reliable survey with noteworthy chapters on Anglo-Latin and Anglo-Norman literature.

TEXTS AND TRANSLATIONS

One of the most comprehensive selections of texts in this period is *Middle English Metrical Romances* (Prentice-Hall, 1930) by W. H. French and C. B. Hale, with valuable introductory notes and glossaries. The reader may find the following collections of translations useful: W. A. Neilson and K. G. T. Webster, *Chief British Poets of the Fourteenth and Fifteenth Centuries* (Houghton Mifflin, 1916); J. Weston, *The Chief Middle English Poets* (Houghton Mifflin, 1914); and *Romance, Vision, and Satire, English Alliterative Poems of the Fourteenth Century* (Houghton Mifflin, 1912). Besides these standard texts, there are more recent collections like M. R. Adamson's *A Treasury of Middle English Verse, Selected and Rendered into Modern English* (Dutton, 1930); G. H. Gerould's revised and enlarged *Old English and Medieval Literature* (Nelson, 1933); and M. Schlauch's *Medieval Narrative, a Book of Translations* (Prentice-Hall, 1928).

CHAPTER III

GENERAL WORKS

Studies of CHAUCER and his period are so numerous that the general student should consult a work like R. D. French's *Chaucer Handbook* (Crofts, 1927) before making a specific choice of readings. J. M. Manly's *Some New Light on Chaucer* (Holt, 1926) is a useful supplement to the material found in the usual encyclopedias and older biographies, and other helpful introductions are: G. H. Cowling, *Chaucer* (Methuen, 1927); D. Martin, *A First Book about Chaucer* (Routledge, 1929); and Grace E. Hadow, *Chaucer and His Times* (Home Univ. Lib., Holt, 1914). R. K. Root, *The Poetry of Chaucer* (Houghton

Mifflin, rev. ed., 1922) and G. L. Kittredge, *Chaucer and His Poetry* (Harvard U. P., 1915) are both excellent but more advanced. For those who already know something about Chaucer, J. L. Lowes's *Geoffrey Chaucer and the Development of His Genius* (Houghton Mifflin, 1934) is admirable reading. More recent surveys of fifteenth-century literature are E. K. Chambers' *English Literature at the Close of the Middle Ages* (Clarendon, 1945) and Henry S. Bennett's *Chaucer and the Fifteenth Century* (Clarendon, 1947). Marchette G. Chute's *Geoffrey Chaucer of England* (Dutton, 1946) is the liveliest of the modern biographies. Briefer manuals are Nevill Coghill's *The Poet Chaucer* (Oxford, 1949), Robert D. French's *A Chaucer Handbook* (Second edition; Appleton-Century-Crofts, 1947), and John Spevis's *Chaucer the Maker* (Faber & Faber, 1951). Highly specialized studies for advanced students are Gordon H. Gerould's *Chaucerian Essays* (Princeton U. P., 1952), Kemp Malone's *Chapters on Chaucer* (Johns Hopkins Press, 1951), and John S. P. Tatlock's *The Mind and Art of Chaucer* (Syracuse U. P., 1950).

TEXTS AND SELECTIONS

The most fully annotated edition of CHAUCER's *Works* is that of W. W. Skeat in seven volumes (Clarendon, 1894–97), the first of which contains the life of Chaucer. Good one-volume editions are numerous, the best being those of Skeat (Macmillan, 1895); the "Globe" edition (Macmillan, 1898); H. N. MacCracken's *The College Chaucer* (Yale U. P., 1913); and the edition by F. N. Robinson (Houghton Mifflin, 1933), which has a good introduction and excellent notes and bibliographical aids. A volume of selections worth noting is J. M. Manly's *Canterbury Tales* (Holt, 1930); R. K. Root's edition of *Troilus and Criseyde* (Princeton U. P., 1926), though suitable only for advanced students, contains a valuable introduction.

The standard collective edition of JOHN GOWER's *Works* is by G. C. Macaulay (4 vols., Clarendon, 1899–1902), with an introduction in each volume. Further critical material on GOWER is available in W. G. Dodd, *Courtly Love in Chaucer and Gower* (Ginn, 1913) and especially in C. S. Lewis, *The Allegory of Love* (Clarendon, 1936). Although there are many editions of SIR THOMAS MALORY's *Morte d'Arthur*, including E. Strachey's abridged and modernized Globe edition (Macmillan, 1928) and A. W. Pollard's modernized version (Macmillan, 1900), the best is still that of H. Oskar Sommer (Nutt, 1889–91). Recent discoveries have brought to light new material on Malory, which is treated in Eugène Vinaver's *Malory* (Clarendon, 1929). W. W.

Skeat's *The Vision of William concerning Piers the Plowman* (Clarendon, 1886) is the standard edition of all three texts of this great Middle English poem. Among the most useful translations for the student are Skeat's *The Vision of Piers the Plowman* (Chatto and Windus, 1922) and H. W. Wells's *The Vision of Piers Plowman, Newly Rendered into Modern English* (Sheed and Ward, 1935). For recent critical discussion of this work, A. H. Bright's *New Light on Piers Plowman* (O. U. P., 1928) is recommended. Two later studies are E. Donaldson's *Piers Plowman* (Yale U. P., 1949) and Durant Robertson's *Piers Plowman & Scriptural Tradition* (Princeton U. P., 1951). Discussions of JOHN WYCLIF that should be noted include M. Deanesly, *The Lollard Bible and other Medieval Biblical Versions* (C. U. P., 1920), H. B. Workman, *John Wyclif, A Study of the English Medieval Church* (2 vols., Clarendon, 1926), and Kenneth B. McFarlane's *John Wycliffe & the Beginnings of English Nonconformity* (Macmillan, 1953). The best selections are in H. E. Winn, *Select English Writings* (O. U. P., 1929).

CHAPTER IV

GENERAL WORKS

For historical background, the reader may consult J. D. Wilson's *Life in Shakespeare's England* (C. U. P., 1911), or volumes 3 and 4 of H. D. Traill's *Social England* (Cassell, 1902–04). R. H. Tawney's *Religion and the Rise of Capitalism* (Harcourt, 1926) offers an invaluable analysis of economic conditions; while J. H. Blunt's *The Reformation of the Church of England* (2 vols., Longmans, 1878–82) and G. G. Perry's *The Reformation in England* (Longmans, 1886) give brief but important accounts of the church history of the times. Equally valuable material may also be found in such biographies as A. F. Pollard's *Henry VIII* (Longmans, 1905) and either J. B. Black's *The Reign of Elizabeth* (Clarendon, 1936) or J. E. Neale's *Queen Elizabeth* (Harcourt, 1934). A good survey of the literature of the period is E. C. Dunn's *The Literature of Shakespeare's England* (Scribner's, 1936). J. M. Berdan's *Early Tudor Poetry* (Macmillan, 1920) is a stimulating introduction to the whole literature of the early Tudor period. C. S. Lewis's brilliant, if idiosyncratic, *English Literature in the Sixteenth Century, excluding Drama* (Clarendon, 1954) is recommended for advanced students. Vivian de S. Pinto's *The English Renaissance, 1510–1688* (Dover, 1950) is a convenient historical and bibliographical manual. The intellectual background of the era may be studied in Hardin Craig's *The Enchanted Glass* (Oxford, 1936) and E. M. W. Tillyard's *The Elizabethan World Picture* (Chatto, 1948).

INDIVIDUAL WRITERS

Useful reprints of ROGER ASCHAM'S English writings may be found in Arber's *English Reprints* (Constable, 1923) and in *English Works* edited by W. Aldis Wright in the Cambridge English Classics (C. U. P., 1904). The best modern edition of THOMAS CAMPION'S works is that of P. Vivian (Clarendon, 1909), which contains a biographical introduction by the same author. There are also critical studies by T. MacDonagh, *Thomas Campion and the Art of English Poetry* (Hodges, Figgis, 1913) and Miles M. Kastendieck, *England's Musical Poet* (Oxford, 1938). The standard modern edition of GEORGE CHAPMAN is T. M. Parrott's *The Plays and Poems* (Dutton, 1910–14), and there is also a selection of the best plays edited by W. L. Phelps in the Mermaid Series (Scribner's, 1904). John W. Wieler studies the philosophical background of the playwright's work in *George Chapman, the Effect of Stoicism upon his Tragedies* (King's Crown Press, 1949). SAMUEL DANIEL'S complete works, edited by A. B. Grosart (Hazell, Watson & Viney), appeared in five volumes in 1885–96, but the most modern edition of his *Poems, together with A Defense of Ryme,* is that of A. C. Sprague (Harvard U. P., 1930).

The best edition of MICHAEL DRAYTON'S complete works is that of J. W. Hebel (Blackwell, 1931–33). The most convenient small edition is Cyril Brett's *Minor Poems of Michael Drayton* (Clarendon, 1907), which contains an excellent biographical and critical introduction. The best critical study of Drayton is Oliver Elton's *Michael Drayton* (Constable, 1905).

J. Churton Collins's *The Plays and Poems* (Clarendon, 1905) is the best modern edition of ROBERT GREENE'S work, and there is an edition of the plays by T. H. Dickinson in the Mermaid Series (Scribner's, 1909). The fullest biographical treatment of Greene is J. C. Jordan's dissertation, *Robert Greene* (Columbia U. P., 1915). Greene's prose works, edited by G. B. Harrison (Bodley Head Quartos, Dutton, 1923–24), include all the famous "conny-catching pamphlets."

The most authoritative modern life of RICHARD HOOKER is in J. Keble's standard edition of Hooker's works, which was revised by Church and Paget (3 vols., Clarendon, 1888). Books I-V of Hooker's *Of the Laws of Ecclesiastical Polity* were reprinted in the Everyman's Library edition (Dutton, 2 vols., 1907). Contemporary studies of Hooker include Ebenezer Davies' *The Political Ideas of Richard Hooker* (S. P. C. K., 1946), Peter Munz' *The Place of Hooker in the History of Thought* (Routledge, 1952), and John Shirely's *Richard Hooker & Contemporary Political Ideas* (S. P. C. K., 1949). HUGH LATIMER'S complete *Sermons and Remains* are included in the Parker Society's publications (C. U. P., 1845), but there is a useful edition of selected sermons edited by H. C. Beeching in Everyman's Library (1906). The best life of Latimer, that of R. Demaus (Religious Tract Society, 1869), has been abridged and edited by N. Watts (Religious Tract Society, 1936). A contemporary study will be found in Allan Chester's *Hugh Latimer, Apostle to the English* (Penna. U. P., 1954).

Besides the collective edition of THOMAS LODGE'S works, edited with an introduction by Sir E. Gosse (Hunterian Club, 1883), there are a dissertation by M. E. N. Frazer, *Thomas Lodge as a Dramatist* (Univ. of Penn. Press, 1898) and a biography by N. B. Paradise (Yale U. P., 1931). The best modern edition of JOHN LYLY'S works is R. W. Bond's *The Complete Works* (Clarendon, 1902), which includes a valuable biographical and critical introduction.

Unlike most of the foregoing Renaissance writers, THOMAS MORE is the subject of several important biographies, both contemporary and modern. Of the modern biographies, the standard was T. E. Bridgett's *Life and Writings of Sir Thomas More* (Burns and Oates, 2nd ed., 1892), until the appearance of R. W. Chambers's monumental work, *Thomas More* (Cape, 1935). One of the most useful selections of the English works is that of P. S. and H. M. Allen in the Clarendon Series (Clarendon, 1924). Recent studies of More will be found in W. E. Campbell's *Erasmus, Tyndale, & More* (Eyre, 1949) and Theodore Maynard's *Humanist as Hero* (Macmillan, 1947).

The standard edition of THOMAS NASHE'S works is that of R. B. McKerrow (5 vols., Sidgwick and Jackson, 1910), but there are several modern editions of Nashe's famous picaresque story, *The Unfortunate Traveller,* notably those by H. F. Brett Smith (Blackwell, 1920), S. C. Chew (Greenberg, 1926), and P. Henderson (Alcuin, 1930). The most modern complete edition of GEORGE PEELE'S works is that of A. H. Bullen (J. C. Nimmo, 1888). Numerous monographs and biographies of SIR WALTER RALEGH have been written, the best of them being E. Edward's *The Life of Sir Walter Ralegh,* together with his letters (2 vols., Macmillan, 1868), and H. de Sélincourt's *Great Ralegh* (Methuen, 1908). The standard modern edition of his poems is by Agnes M. C. Latham (Constable, 1929). Selections from Ralegh's prose works have been edited by G. E. Hadow (Clarendon, 1917).

More recent studies of Ralegh include Philip Edwards' *Sir Walter Raleigh* (Longmans, 1953), Sir Philip Magnus' *Sir Walter Raleigh* (Falcon Books, 1952), D. B. Quinn's *Raleigh & the British Empire* (Hodder, 1947), E. A. Strathmann's *Sir Walter Raleigh, a Study in Elizabethan Skepticism* (Columbia U. P., 1951), and Hugh R. Williamson's *Sir Walter Raleigh* (Faber, 1951).

The earliest life of SIR PHILIP SIDNEY, written by his friend Fulke-Greville, was reprinted in 1907 with editorial notes by Nowell Smith (Clarendon). Among various modern biographies, the fullest is that of H. R. Fox Bourne (Putnam, 1891), but there are useful studies by M. W. Wallace (C. U. P., 1915) and Mona Wilson (Duckworth, 1931). The standard modern collective edition of Sidney's works is by A. Feuillerat (4 vols., C. U. P., 1912–26).

Concerning the life and writings of EDMUND SPENSER, such a vast literature has accumulated that the reader would do well to consult first such a guide as H. S. V. Jones's *Spenser Handbook* (Crofts, 1930). Among the many separate critical studies of Spenser, the following are perhaps most significant: *Spenser* by R. W. Church (E. M. L., Macmillan, 1879), *Spenser* by E. Legouis (Dutton, 1926), *Edmund Spenser, a Critical Study* by B. E. C. Davis (C. U. P., 1933), and the very important treatment of Spenser's allegory in C. S. Lewis's *The Allegory of Love* (Clarendon, 1936). More recent studies include Leicester Bradner's *Edmund Spenser & the Faerie Queene* (Chicago U. P., 1948) and Alexander C. Judson's *The Life of Edmund Spenser* (Johns Hopkins U. P., 1945). Among the foremost editions of Spenser's works may be mentioned the excellent one-volume edition by E. de Sélincourt and J. C. Smith (O. U. P., 1909), with a valuable introduction; the Shakespeare Head edition of W. L. Renwick (1928–34); and the Variorum edition by E. Greenlaw, C. G. Osgood, and F. M. Padelford, now being published by the Johns Hopkins Press.

The first reliable account of the life of Henry Howard, EARL OF SURREY, was written by E. Bapst in his *Deux Gentils-hommes-Poètes de la Cour de Henry VIII* (Plon, Nourrit, 1891), but there is valuable biographical material in F. M. Padelford's critical edition of Surrey's *Poems* (Univ. of Wash. Press, 1920, rev. 1928). There is an excellent short life of SIR THOMAS WYATT in the introduction to E. M. W. Tillyard's *The Poetry of Sir Thomas Wyatt, a Selection and a Study* (Scholartis Press, 1929). The standard modern edition of *The Poems of Sir Thomas Wiat* is that of Miss A. K. Foxwell (Univ. of London Press, 2 vols., 1913).

CHAPTER V

GENERAL HISTORICAL AND CRITICAL WORKS

The best all-round book on early English drama is still E. K. Chambers's *The Mediaeval Stage* (2 vols., Clarendon, 1903), but *The English Folk-Play* (Clarendon, 1933) by the same author offers a valuable supplement. A. W. Ward, *A History of English Dramatic Literature* (Macmillan, 1899, rev.), and Allardyce Nicoll's two books, *British Drama, an Historical Survey from the Beginnings to the Present Time* (Harrap, 1932) and *The Development of the Theatre* (Harrap, 1927), are also highly recommended. Karl Young, *The Drama of the Medieval Church* (Clarendon, 1933), is an admirably documented work. For the later development of pre-Shakespearean drama, the standard works are *The Elizabethan Stage* (Clarendon, 1923) by E. K. Chambers and *Elizabethan Drama 1558–1642* (Houghton Mifflin, 1908) by F. E. Schelling. Useful shorter studies include C. F. Tucker Brooke's *The Tudor Drama* (Houghton Mifflin, 1911), Janet Spens's *Elizabethan Drama* (Methuen, 1922), and F. S. Boas's *An Introduction to Tudor Drama* (Clarendon, 1933). For information on CHRISTOPHER MARLOWE, the student should consult J. L. Hotson's *The Death of Christopher Marlowe* (Harvard U. P., 1925) and M. W. Eccles's *Christopher Marlowe in London* (Harvard U. P., 1934), both of which are brilliant examples of modern research that have thrown much light on Marlowe's biography. F. S. Boas's two books, *Marlowe and His Circle* (Clarendon, 1929) and *Christopher Marlowe* (Clarendon, 1940), give the most reliable summaries of biographical information. Later studies worth consulting are P. H. Kocher, *Christopher Marlowe* (U. of North Carolina Press, 1946), Harry Levin, *The Overreacher* (Harvard U. P., 1952), and F. P. Wilson, *Marlowe & Early Shakespeare* (Clarendon, 1953).

TEXTS AND SELECTIONS

The chief texts necessary for a study of this period of the drama are in J. M. Manly's *Specimens of the Pre-Shakespearean Drama* (Ginn, 1897), an extremely valuable collection; and in A. W. Pollard's *English Miracle Plays, Moralities and Interludes* (Clarendon, 8th ed., rev., 1927), which includes some useful annotated selections from the Tudor Interludes and an interesting essay on the origin of the drama. Among the best modern collections are W. A. Neilson, *The Chief Elizabethan Dramatists* (Houghton Mifflin, 1911); J. Q. Adams's very useful *Chief*

Pre-Shakespearean Dramas (Houghton Mifflin, 1924); and the two useful volumes edited by A. H. Thorndike: *Minor Elizabethan Drama,* vol. 1, *Tragedies,* and vol. 2, *Comedies* (Everyman's Lib., Dutton, 1910). There are several modern collective editions of Marlowe's works, the best being that of C. F. Tucker Brooke (Clarendon, 1910) and the Methuen Marlowe edition in six volumes under the general editorship of R. H. Case.

CHAPTER VI

Biographical and General Critical Works

Biographies of WILLIAM SHAKESPEARE deserving special mention include Sir Sidney Lee's *Life* (Macmillan, 1898, rev. ed. 1924); J. Q. Adams's (Houghton Mifflin, 1923); and Sir W. Raleigh's *Shakespeare* (Macmillan, 1907), a brilliant biographical study as well as a masterly essay in literary criticism. The standard collection of biographical material, however, is Sir E. K. Chambers's *William Shakespeare, a Study of Facts and Problems* (Clarendon, 2 vols., 1930), the first part of which is the most complete account of Shakespeare's life now available, with an authoritative study of the conditions under which his plays were produced. Of the numerous short biographical studies available, the student will find some of the most useful material in J. Bailey's *Shakespeare* (Longmans, 1929); J. S. Smart's *Shakespeare Truth and Tradition* (Longmans, 1928), an acute analysis of the data on which knowledge of Shakespeare is based; and Hazelton Spencer's *The Art and Life of Wm. Shakespeare* (Harcourt, 1940). Marchette G. Chute's *Shakespeare of London* (Dutton, 1949) gives a lively and reliable account of Shakespeare and his world, and Karl J. Holzknecht's *The Backgrounds of Shakespeare's Plays* (American, 1950) furnishes essential information concerning the theater and dramatic craft of the period. T. M. Parrott's *William Shakespeare, a Handbook* (Scribner's, 1934, 1955) and Peter Alexander's *A Shakespeare Primer* (Nesbit, 1951) are useful manuals. Mark Van Doren's *Shakespeare* (Holt, 1939) and Hardin Craig's *An Interpretation of Shakespeare* (Dryden Press, 1948) are good general introductions to his art and meaning.

Essays and Special Critical Studies

Serious criticism of Shakespeare's work began with Dryden's "character" in his famous *Essay of Dramatic Poesy* (see W. P. Ker's edition of Dryden's *Essays,* Clarendon, 1900). Other early critical views are to be found in the essays of Addison and Steele (*Tatler*, 35, 47, 188; *Spectator*, 40, 44, 235, 592); in Dr. Johnson's works, a good selection of which is in Sir W. Raleigh's *Johnson on Shakespeare* (Frowde, 1908); and in the useful collection of eighteenth-century criticism of Shakespeare entitled *Eighteenth Century Essays on Shakespeare* (Mac-Lehose, 1903) by D. Nichol Smith. The most important criticism of the romantic period is in S. T. Coleridge's *Notes and Lectures on Shakespeare,* in the modern standard edition by T. M. Raysor, *Coleridge's Shakespearean Criticism* (2 vols., Harvard U. P., 1930). W. Hazlitt's *Characters of Shakespeare's Plays,* still one of the best books of its kind, is now available in Everyman's Library (Dutton, 1907) and in The World's Classics (O.U.P., 1929); and Lamb's equally important contributions to Shakespearean criticism are collected in E. V. Lucas, *The Works of Charles and Mary Lamb* (7 vols., Methuen, 1903–05). The most notable critical studies of the twentieth century include A. C. Bradley's *Shakespearean Tragedy* (Macmillan, 1904); Sir A. T. Quiller-Couch's *Shakespeare's Workmanship* (Macmillan, 1931); H. Granville-Barker's *Prefaces to Shakespeare* (3 vols., Sidgwick and Jackson, 1927–37); E. E. Stoll's *Art and Artifice in Shakespeare* (C. U. P., 1933); and J. D. Wilson's *The Essential Shakespeare* (C. U. P., 1932) and *What Happens in Hamlet* (C. U. P., 1935). Miss C. F. E. Spurgeon's book, *Shakespeare's Imagery and What it Tells Us* (Macmillan, 1936) should also be noted. Out of Shakespeare's imagery, G. Wilson Knight has attempted to evolve elaborate symbolic patterns, in *The Crown of Life* (Methuen, 1948), *The Olive & the Sword* (Oxford U. P., 1944), and *The Shakespearian Tempest* (Methuen, 1953). Shakespeare's relationship to the literature and thought of his age are studied in Samuel Bethell's *Shakespeare & Popular Dramatic Tradition* (Staples Press, 1948), Muriel Bradbrook's *Shakespeare & Elizabethan Poetry* (Chatto, 1951), Alfred Harbage's *Shakespeare and the Rival Traditions* (Macmillan, 1952), Theodore Spencer's *Shakespeare & the Nature of Man* (Macmillan, 1945), Alwin Thaler's *Shakespeare & Sir Philip Sidney* (Harvard, 1947), and W. B. Watkins' *Shakespeare & Spenser* (Princeton U. P., 1950).

EDITIONS AND TEXTS

Of the countless editions of Shakespeare's works, it will suffice here to mention the *Warwick* edition (Blackie, 1931–36), one of the best cheap annotated editions of the separate plays; the *Yale Shakespeare* (40 vols., edited by W. L. Cross, Tucker Brooke, and others, Yale U. P., 1917–28) which is the most authoritative and fully annotated

American edition; *The New Shakespeare* (C. U. P., 1921–31) edited by Sir A. Quiller-Couch and J. Dover Wilson, and embodying some of the most recent discoveries with regard to the text; and the excellent American *Cambridge* edition (Houghton Mifflin, 1942) in one volume, a valuable conservative text based on the Folio; *Shakespeare, Twenty-Three Plays and the Sonnets* edited by T. M. Parrott, Edward Hubler, and R. S. Telfer (Scribner's, 1938), with excellent introductions and notes.

CHAPTER VII

Biographical and Critical Works

For a general treatment of Shakespeare's chief dramatic contemporaries, the student may consult T. M. Parrott and R. H. Ball's *A Short View of Elizabethan Drama* (Scribner's, 1943); F. E. Schelling's *Elizabethan Drama, 1558–1642* (Houghton Mifflin, 1908); or W. M. A. Creizenach's *The English Drama in the Age of Shakespeare* (Lippincott, 1916). Fuller accounts of the individual writers are available in other recent studies. The most important studies of Francis Beaumont and John Fletcher are A. H. Thorndike's *The Influence of Beaumont and Fletcher on Shakespere* (O. B. Wood, 1901) and Baldwin Maxwell's *Studies in Beaumont and Fletcher, and Massinger* (Univ. of N. Carolina, 1939). Later general studies include John F. Danby's *Poets on Fortune's Hill* (Faber, 1952) and Lawrence B. Wallis's *Fletcher, Beaumont & Company, Entertainers to the Jacobean Gentry* (King's Crown Press, 1947). For advanced students, Eugene M. Waith's *The Pattern of Tragicomedy in Beaumont and Fletcher* (Yale U. P. 1952) may be recommended. Another valuable work is C. M. Gayley's *Beaumont, the Dramatist, a portrait* (Century, 1914). The best modern studies of Thomas Dekker are M. L. Hunt's *Thomas Dekker* (Columbia U. P., 1911), and K. L. Gregg's *Thomas Dekker, a Study in Economic and Social Backgrounds* (Univ. of Wash. Press, 1924). There are important studies of John Ford by M. M. Sergeaunt (Blackwell, 1935) and G. F. Sensabaugh, *The Tragic Muse of John Ford* (Stanford U. P., 1944). Three helpful modern works on Thomas Heywood are O. Cromwell's *Thomas Heywood, a Study in the Elizabethan Drama of Everyday Life* (Yale U. P., 1928), A. M. Clark's *Thomas Heywood, Playwright and Miscellanist* (Blackwell, 1931), and F. S. Boas' *Thomas Heywood* (Williams & Norgate, 1950).

The most complete and authoritative account of Ben Jonson and

his works is given in volumes 1 and 2 of the monumental edition
(6 vols., Clarendon, 1925–28) edited by C. H. Herford and P. Simpson;
but the briefer *Ben Jonson* (E. M. L., Macmillan, 1919) by G. Gregory
Smith is also noteworthy. Marchette G. Chute's *Ben Jonson of West-
minster* (Dutton, 1953) gives an animated account of the poet and his
times. Two recent studies of special aspects of his work are Helena
Baum's *The Satiric & Didactic in Ben Jonson's Comedy* (U. of North
Carolina Press, 1947) and Allan Gilbert's *The Symbolic Persons in the
Masques of Ben Jonson* (Duke U. P., 1948). Good accounts of PHILIP
MASSINGER are available in *D. N. B.* and in A. H. Cruickshank's *Philip
Massinger* (Blackwell, 1920). Besides C. H. Herford's excellent article
on THOMAS MIDDLETON in *D. N. B.*, there are critical essays by Swinburne (in his *Age of Shakespeare*, Harper, 1908) and by T. S. Eliot. A
more elaborate work is that of W. D. Dunkel, *The Dramatic Technique
of Thomas Middleton in the Comedies of London Life* (Univ. of Chicago Press, 1925). The most valuable recent works on JAMES SHIRLEY
are *The Relations of Shirley's Plays to the Elizabethan Drama* (Columbia
U. P., 1914) by R. S. Forsythe and *James Shirley, Dramatist, a Biographical and Critical Study* (Nason, 1915) by A. H. Nason. For the
general reader, the best sketch of JOHN WEBSTER's life and works is
John Webster and the Elizabethan Drama (Sidgwick and Jackson,
1916) by Rupert Brooke; the most recent authoritative account is in
F. L. Lucas's standard modern edition, *The Complete Works of John
Webster* (Chatto and Windus, 1927). For a contemporary estimate of
Webster's significance, see Clifford Leech's *John Webster, a Critical
Study* (Hogarth Press, 1951). For an authoritative history of the early
seventeenth-century theatre, see G. E. Bentley's *The Jacobean and
Caroline Stage, Dramatic Companies, and Players* (2 vols., O. U. P.,
1941).

TEXTS AND SELECTIONS

The average student will find all the texts necessary for a study of
this period in the various one-volume selections from the old dramatists
published both in the Mermaid Series (Scribner's) and in Masterpieces
of the English Drama (American), as well as in W. A. Neilson's *The
Chief Elizabethan Dramatists* (Houghton Mifflin, 1911). Other separate
editions that deserve special mention are: the Everyman's Library edition
of Beaumont and Fletcher by G. P. Baker; T. M. Parrott's standard
work, *The Plays and Poems of George Chapman* (Dutton, 1910–14);
E. Rhys's selected edition of Dekker's plays (Mermaid Series, Scribner's,
1904); the edition of Ford's dramatic works by H. de Vocht (Louvain,

Librairie Univ., 1927) ; and F. E. Schelling's *The Complete Plays of Ben Jonson* (2 vols., Everyman's Lib., Dutton, 1910, reprinted 1929, 1934).

CHAPTER VIII

GENERAL WORKS

For a historical background of this period the student may consult G. M. Trevelyan's *England Under the Stuarts* (Putnam, 15th ed., 1930) or the two relevant volumes in the *Oxford History of England* entitled *The Early Stuarts* (Clarendon, 1937) by Godfrey Davies, and *The Later Stuarts* (Clarendon, 1934) by G. N. Clark. The social life of the times is ably presented in A. Bryant's *The England of Charles II* (Longmans, 1935) and Storm Jameson's *The Decline of Merry England* (Bobbs-Merrill, 1930) ; while the history of thought is traced in G. N. Clark's *The Seventeenth Century* (Clarendon, 1929) and *The Seventeenth Century Background* (Chatto and Windus, 1934) by Basil Willey. Two more specialized works are Sir Herbert Grierson's *Cross Currents in English Literature of the Seventeenth Century* (Chatto and Windus, 1929) and *Seventeenth-Century Studies* (Clarendon, 1938) presented to Sir Herbert Grierson. Cicely V. Wedgewood's *Seventeenth-century English Literature* (Oxford, 1950) furnishes an admirable brief introduction to the period, and Douglas Bush's *English Literature in the Earlier Seventeenth Century* (Oxford, 1945) will prove useful to advanced students. Joan Bennett's *Four Metaphysical Poets* (Cambridge U. P., 1934) offers an acute critical consideration of Donne, Herbert, Vaughan, and Crashaw.

INDIVIDUAL WRITERS

The main authority for the life of FRANCIS BACON is still *The Life and Times* (2 vols., Houghton Mifflin, 1880) by James Spedding, but among the shorter studies are M. Sturt's *Francis Bacon* (W. Morrow, 1932) and C. W. S. Williams's *Bacon* (Barker, 1933). Bacon's philosophy is treated in three further studies: J. Nichol, *Francis Bacon, His Life and Philosophy* (Lippincott, 1888–89), C. D. Broad, *The Philosophy of Francis Bacon* (C. U. P., 1926) and Fulton H. Anderson, *The Philosophy of Francis Bacon* (Chicago U. P., 1948). Both the *Essays* and the *Advancement of Learning* are in Macmillan's Library of English Classics, and there is a selection from all the works entitled *Selections with Essays by Macaulay and S. R. Gardiner* (Clarendon, 1927), by P. E. and E. F. Matheson. Modern studies of SIR THOMAS BROWNE are *Sir Thomas Browne* by Sir Edmund Gosse (E. M. L., Macmillan, 1905), W. P. Dunn's *Sir Thomas Browne, a Study in Religious Philosophy* (U. of Minnesota Press, 1950), Jeremiah S. Finch, *Sir Thomas Browne, a Doctor's Life of Science and Faith* (N. Y.: Schuman, 1950), and Dewey K. Ziegler, *In Divided and Distinguished Worlds, Religion & Rhetoric in the Writings of Sir Thomas Browne* (Harvard U. P., 1943). The best collective editions of Browne's works are those of C. Sayle (3 vols., Grant, 1927) and the very elaborate one by G. L. Keynes (6 vols., Golden Cockerel Press, Faber and Gwyer, 1928–31). Separate editions of the more familiar works are available in the Golden Treasury Series (Macmillan) and in Everyman's Library. The most useful modern edition of the works of WILLIAM BROWNE of Tavistock is that by Gordon Goodwin (Muses' Library, Scribner's, 1894), with an introduction by A. H. Bullen. There is an illuminating study by F. W. Moorman, *William Browne, His Britannia's Pastorals and the Pastoral Poetry of the Elizabethan Age* (K. J. Trübner, 1897).

The standard modern biography of JOHN BUNYAN is *John Bunyan, His Life, Times, and Work* by J. Brown (Hulbert, rev. ed. by F. M. Harrison, 1928); but G. B. Harrison's *John Bunyan, A Study in Personality* (Doubleday, 1928) and W. Y. Tindall's *John Bunyan, Mechanick Preacher* (Columbia U. P., 1934) are both valuable shorter studies. There are numerous editions of two or more works by Bunyan, including G. B. Harrison's edition of *The Pilgrim's Progress* and *The Life and Death of Mr. Badman* (Nonesuch Press, 1928) and the two-volume edition of the latter and *Grace Abounding* in Everyman's Library. The standard modern edition of *Pilgrim's Progress* is by J. B. Wharey (Clarendon, 1928); that of *The Holy War,* Bunyan's most elaborate allegory, is by J. Brown (Houghton Mifflin, 1887). The best modern edition of the poems of THOMAS CAREW is that of A. Vincent (Muses' Lib., Scribner's, 1899), whose introduction also contains the best account of Carew's life.

Dr. Johnson's life of COWLEY in his *Lives of the English Poets* (Everyman's Lib.), notable alike for its powerful criticism and for having first applied the term "metaphysical" to the style of poetry written by Cowley, Crashaw, and Donne, is the classic critique of the metaphysical school. There is also an interesting recent study, *Abraham Cowley, The Muse's Hannibal* (O. U. P., 1931) by A. H. Nethercot; two more general works that should be noted are *The Donne Tradition* (Harvard U. P., 1930) by G. Williamson and *Four Metaphysical Poets* (C. U. P., 1934) by Joan Bennett. The standard modern edition of Cowley's works is that of A. R. Waller (C. U. P., 1905). J. R. Lumby's edition of Cowley's prose works (C. U. P., 1909) can also be profitably consulted. The best account of RICHARD CRASHAW is by L. C. Martin in the introduction to his standard modern edition of Crashaw's complete works (Clarendon, 1927). The classic life of JOHN DONNE is that of Izaak Walton, first published in 1640 and since reprinted in all editions of Walton's *Lives*. Sir E. Gosse published his important *Life and Letters of John Donne* (Dodd, Mead) in 1889. *Donne the Craftsman* (O. U. P., 1928) by P. Legouis and *A Garland for John Donne* (Harvard U. P., 1931), edited by T. Spencer, both contain valuable criticism. The standard critical work on Donne's prose is Evelyn Simpson's *A Study of the Prose Works of John Donne* (Clarendon, 1924). Besides the Grierson edition of Donne's poems, there are other good ones by J. Hayward (Nonesuch Press, 1929) and H. I'A. Fausset (Everyman's Lib., Dutton, 1931). Although no complete edition of Donne's prose exists, there are now severel excellent volumes of selections from the sermons and other prose works. Among these should be noted that of L. P. Smith (Clarendon, 1919) ; the *Ten Sermons* (Nonesuch Press, 1923), by G. Keynes; and *Devotions on Emergent Occasions* (Simpkin, 1926), edited by W. H. Draper.

The best modern edition of the works of GILES and PHINEAS FLETCHER is by F. S. Boas (2 vols., C. U. P., 1908–09). Phineas Fletcher's *Venus and Anchises* (*Brittain's Ida*) is also available in an edition by E. Seaton (O. U. P., 1926). A study of GEORGE HERBERT AND HIS TIMES by A. G. Hyde was published in 1906 (Putnam), and there is an elaborate biographical commentary by G. H. Palmer in the introduction to his notable edition, *The English Works of George Herbert* (3 vols., Houghton Mifflin, 1905). Joseph H. Summers, *George Herbert, his Religion & Art* (Harvard U. P., 1954) gives a contemporary estimate of the poet's work, and Rosamund Tuve, *A Reading of George Herbert* (Faber, 1952), submits his poetry to intensive explication. The standard modern edition of ROBERT HERRICK is F. W. Moorman's *The Poetical Works* (Clarendon, 1915), and there is another finely printed edition in the Hesperides Series (2 vols., O. U. P., 1935). Moorman's excellent monograph, *Robert Herrick, a Biographical and Critical Study* (Lane, 1910) is the most reliable and exhaustive treatment of Herrick. All the extant poetry of RICHARD LOVELACE survives in two little volumes called *Lucasta;* the standard modern edition of these is C. H. Wilkinson's *The Poems of Richard Lovelace* (2 vols., Clarendon, 1925). This edition, containing a very full and authoritative biographical introduction, was reprinted in a cheaper one-volume edition in 1930 (O. U. P.). The standard modern edition of ANDREW MARVELL'S works is *The Poems and Letters* (2 vols., Clarendon, 1927) by H. M. Margoliouth, and there is another edition of the *Poems and Satires* by G. A. Aitken (Muses' Lib., Scribner's, 1898). Since Augustine Birrell's life (E. M. L., Macmillan, 1905) is a readable but not very accurate book, the student should also consult T. S. Eliot's essay, now included in the *Selected Essays* (Harcourt, 1932).

Among the many conflicting biographical and critical studies of JOHN MILTON the student must tread warily. He may begin by comparing Miss H. Darbishire's *The Early Lives of Milton* (Constable, 1932) with Dr. Johnson's trenchant study in his *Lives of the English Poets* (2 vols., Everyman's Lib.). The nineteenth-century attitude toward Milton, as represented in D. Masson's enormous *Life of John Milton, narrated in connexion with the Political, Ecclesiastical and Literary History of his Time* (7 vols., Macmillan, 1859–94), has been superseded to some extent by views expressed in such works as D. Saurat's *Milton, Man and Thinker* (Dial Press, 1925), J. Holly Hanford's *The Youth of Milton* (Univ. of Mich. Press, 1925), and his *John Milton, Englishman* (Crown, 1949). Excellent one-volume biographies are those by M. Pattison (E. M. L., Macmillan, 1879); R. Garnett (W. Scott, 1890); and Sir W. Raleigh (Putnam, 1900). Two very important critical studies are to be found in R. D. Havens's exhaustive account of *The Influence of Milton on English Poetry* (Harvard U. P., 1922) and E. M. W. Tillyard's *Milton* (MacVeagh, Dial Press, 1930). Later special studies of Milton include Donald Clark, *John Milton at St. Paul's School* (Columbia U. P., 1948), Robert Cawley, *Milton & the Literature of Travel* (Princeton U. P., 1951), J. M. French, *The Life Records of John Milton* (Rutgers U. P., 1949), J. E. Thorpe, *Milton Criticism* (Rinehart, 1950), and E. M. W. Tillyard, *Studies in Milton* (Chatto, 1951). J. H. Hanford's *A Milton Handbook* (Crofts, 1939) is an excellent short guide and introduction to Milton's works. *The Works of John Milton* (18 vols., Columbia U. P., 1931–38), issued under the general editorship of F. A. Patterson, is the standard modern edition; but there are many other excellent shorter editions of collected and separate works. Among the former may be mentioned the one-volume editions by H. C. Beeching (Clarendon, 1900) and W. A. Wright (O. U. P., 1903); and W. V. Moody's American Cambridge edition (Houghton Mifflin, 1899, rev. ed. 1941). The best editions of *Paradise Lost* are those by A. W. Verity (C. U. P., 1910) and G. H. Cowling (Methuen, 1926). The best selections of the prose works, for students, are in M. W. Wallace's *Milton's Prose* (World's Classics, O. U. P.,

1925) and the volume in the Riverside literature series (Houghton Mifflin, 1911) edited by L. E. Lockwood.

JEREMY TAYLOR'S *Whole Works* were first collected and edited with a life by R. Heber in 1822. C. P. Eden's revision of this work (Longman's, 1850–54) is the best modern authority. There is a biography by W. J. Brown (S. P. C. K., Macmillan, 1925), and later studies by Charles J. Stranks, *Life & Writings of Jeremy Taylor* (S. P. C. K., 1952) and Hugh R. Williamson, *Jeremy Taylor* (London, Dobson, 1952). Two modern selections have been published, one by M. Armstrong (Golden Cockerel Press, 1923) and *The Golden Grove* (Clarendon, 1930). L. P. Smith's introduction to the latter is the best critical study of Taylor. The standard modern edition of HENRY VAUGHAN'S works is by L. C. Martin (2 vols., Clarendon, 1914). Critical studies of Vaughan include R. Sencourt's *Outflying Philosophy* (Simpkin, 1925); E. Blunden's essay, *On the Poems of Henry Vaughan* (Cobden-Sanderson, 1927); Elizabeth Holmes's *Henry Vaughan and the Hermetic Philosophy* (Blackwell, 1932), and Francis E. Hutchinson's *Henry Vaughan, a Life & Interpretation* (Clarendon, 1947).

The most important work on IZAAK WALTON is S. Martin's *Izaak Walton and His Friends* (Dutton, 1904). The best modern editions of Walton's *Lives* are by A. H. Bullen (Bell, 1884); A. Dobson (Temple Classics, 1898); and G. Saintsbury (World's Classics, O. U. P., 1927). Modern editions of *The Compleat Angler* include those by Andrew Lang (Dent, 1896, now in Everyman's Lib.) and the delightfully illustrated edition by R. Le Gallienne (Lane, 1897). GEORGE WITHER'S works are available in a two-volume edition by F. Sidgwick (Muses' Lib., Scribner's, 1903), and there is a selection by H. Morley (Routledge, 1891).

CHAPTER IX

GENERAL WORKS

In addition to the works listed at the head of the preceding chapter, the student will find useful background material in R. Garnett, *The Age of Dryden* (Bell, 1895), and in Sir E. Gosse's *From Shakespeare to Pope* (Dodd, Mead, 1885), which treats of the rise of the neoclassical school. The most complete survey of Restoration drama is *A History of Restoration Drama* (C. U. P., 1923) by Allardyce Nicoll. Other stimulating critical works on this form are J. Palmer's *The Comedy of Manners* (Bell, 1913); two books by Bonamy Dobrée entitled *Restoration*

Comedy (Clarendon, 1924) and *Restoration Tragedy* (Clarendon, 1929); and J. W. Krutch's *Comedy and Conscience after the Restoration* (Columbia U. P., 1924).

INDIVIDUAL WRITERS

The standard modern edition of SAMUEL BUTLER's collected works is by A. R. Waller (C. U. P., 1905–08). For information on Butler's role as a "character" writer, the reader may consult R. Aldington's *A Book of Characters* (Dutton, 1924), which has a very valuable introduction; and Gwendolyn Murphy's *A Cabinet of Characters* (O. U. P., 1925). The fullest biographical account of WILLIAM CONGREVE is in the *Life* (Heinemann, 1888, rev. ed., 1924) by Sir E. Gosse; but there is also a good recent monograph, *William Congreve* (O. U. P., 1931), by D. C. Taylor. Congreve's *Complete Works* were edited by M. Summers (4 vols., Nonesuch Press, 1923). The best modern editions are those of *The Comedies* (Macmillan, 1927) by J. W. Krutch; of the *Works* (Davies, 1930) by F. W. Bateson; and the one-volume edition by Bonamy Dobrée (World's Classics, O. U. P., 1925). Congreve's popularity is studied in Emmett L. Avery's *Congreve's Plays on the Eighteenth Century Stage* (Modern Lang. Assn., 1951).

Since the publication of Dr. Johnson's great study of JOHN DRYDEN (in his *Lives of the English Poets*), which was the first really important biographical and critical work, many first-rate biographies have appeared. Among the shorter studies are those by G. Saintsbury (E. M. L., Macmillan, 1881), Allardyce Nicoll, *Dryden and his Poetry* (Harrap, 1923), and Alan Lubbock's *The Character of John Dryden* (L. and Virginia Woolf, 1925). Some of the best modern criticism is to be found in T. S. Eliot's *Homage to John Dryden* (in *Selected Essays*, Harcourt, 1932) and Mark Van Doren's *The Poetry of John Dryden* (Harcourt, 1920), which is specially recommended. *The Intellectual Milieu of John Dryden* (Univ. of Mich. Press, 1934) by L. I. Bredvold is a masterly work on the philosophical background of Dryden's poetry. G. R. Noyes's edition of *The Poetical Works* (Houghton Mifflin, 1909) is the best modern edition and contains one of the ablest of modern critical essays on Dryden. The best modern edition of Dryden's prose works is W. P. Ker's *Essays of John Dryden* (2 vols., Clarendon, 1900), with an extremely valuable commentary and a chronological list of Dryden's writings. A complete edition of the *Dramatic Works* (6 vols., Nonesuch Press, 1931–32) was edited by M. Summers. Among the many annotated selections, the best are D. Nichol Smith's *Poetry and Prose* (Clarendon, 1925); Bonamy Dobrée's *Poems of John Dry-*

den (Everyman's Lib., Dutton, 1934); and G. R. Noyes's *Selected Dramas of John Dryden* (Scott, Foresman, 1910).

THOMAS OTWAY'S works are available in two complete modern editions, one by M. Summers (Nonesuch Press, 1926); the other, and by far the better one, by J. C. Ghosh (Clarendon, 1932). Two useful studies of Otway are R. G. Ham's *Otway and Lee* (Yale U. P., 1931) and Olive Taylor's *Next to Shakespeare* (Duke U. P., 1950). Of the many books on SAMUEL PEPYS, the best are J. R. Tanner's introduction to the *Diary* (Bell, 1925); A Ponsonby's *Samuel Pepys* (E. M. L., Macmillan, 1928); and A. Bryant's very scholarly work, *Samuel Pepys* (3 vols., C. U. P., 1933–38). The best edition of Pepys's great *Diary* is that of Wheatley (9 vols., Bell, 1893–99; cheap ed., 1904); but there are many others, notably that of G. Gregory Smith in the Globe Series (Macmillan, 1929) and the two-volume edition in Everyman's Library (Dutton, 1908). The abridged *Everybody's Pepys* (Bell) was published in 1926, and an edition of the *Letters and Second Diary* (Dutton) by R. G. Howarth appeared in 1932. The most detailed critical biography of WILLIAM WYCHERLY is W. Connely's *Brawny Wycherly* (Scribner's, 1930). Besides the editions of the plays by W. C. Ward (Mermaid Series, Scribner's, 1896) and M. Summers (Nonesuch Press, 1924), there is an excellent edition of *The Country Wife* and *The Plain Dealer* by G. B. Churchill (Heath, 1924).

CHAPTER X

GENERAL WORKS

Abundant material on the social and political history of the period may be found in G. M. Trevelyan's *England Under Queen Anne* (3 vols., Longmans, 1930–34); in C. G. Robertson's *England Under the Hanoverians* (Putnam, 10th ed., 1930); or in the briefer accounts in Green's or Trevelyan's histories of England. A. S. Turberville's *English Men and Manners in the Eighteenth Century* (Clarendon, 1926) and J. B. Botsford's *English Society in the Eighteenth Century as Influenced from Oversea* (Macmillan, 1924) offer admirable commentaries on manners and customs of the times. Of the numerous histories of literature available, the best for the student are the exhaustive series of works by O. Elton: *The Augustan Ages* (Blackwood, 1899), *A Survey of English Literature, 1730–1780* (Macmillan, 1928), and *1780–1830* (2 vols., Arnold, 1912). Three useful manuals are John Butt's *The Augustan Age* (Hutchinson, 1950), Roger P. McCutcheon's *Eighteenth-*

century Literature (Oxford, 1949), and Alan D. McKillop's *English Literature from Dryden to Burns* (Appleton-Century-Crofts, 1948). The changing conceptions of nature during the century may be studied in Basil Willey's *The Eighteenth-century Background* (Chatto & Windus, 1940). Somewhat more limited in range of subject is Alexandre Beljame's *Men of Letters & the English Public in the Eighteenth Century* (Paul), 1948.

INDIVIDUAL WRITERS

The first notable *Life* of JOSEPH ADDISON was that by Samuel Johnson (*Lives of the English Poets*); the authoritative modern biography is Peter Smithers' *The Life of Joseph Addison* (Clarendon, 1954). Everyman's Library includes a convenient reprint of all the *Spectator* papers (4 vols., Dutton, 1907), edited with an introduction by G. Gregory Smith. The best editions of the *Spectator*, however, are the two eight-volume editions by G. Gregory Smith (Dent, 1897–98) and by G. A. Aitken (Nimmo, 1898). The latest and most thorough edition of LORD CHESTERFIELD's letters by B. Dobrée (6 vols., Viking, 1930) contains over 2600 letters, together with a full-length biography. Another good modern edition is that of C. Strachey (2 vols., Putnam, 1925) with an introduction and notes; and there is a volume of selections in Everyman's Library (Dutton, 1929). A popular introduction to Lord Chesterfield is Samuel Shellabarger's *Lord Chesterfield and his World* (Little, Brown, 1951).

Dr. Johnson's penetrating *Life* of ALEXANDER POPE (*Lives of the English Poets*) was the first in a long series of competent critical studies. The most detailed modern biography is that of W. J. Courthope (Vol. V) in the standard edition of Pope's *Works* by W. Elwin and Courthope (10 vols., J. Murray, 1871–89). Sir Leslie Stephen's biography, *Alexander Pope* (E. M. L., Macmillan, 1880) betrays a strong animus toward Pope's character; while the more recent biography by Edith Sitwell (Faber and Faber, 1930) is an uncritically flattering work. Among the recent critical studies of Pope, the most helpful are A. Warren's *Alexander Pope as Critic and Humanist* (Princeton U. P., 1929), R. K. Root's *The Poetical Career of Alexander Pope* (Princeton U. P., 1938), Norman Ault's *New Light on Pope* (Methuen, 1949), Douglas Knight's *Pope & the Heroic Tradition* (Yale U. P., 1951), W. L. MacDonald's *Pope & his Critics* (Dent, 1951), F. B. Thornton's *Alexander Pope, Catholic Poet* (Pellegrini & Cudahy, 1952), and Geoffrey Tillotson's *On the Poetry of Pope* (Clarendon, 1950). For those who already know something about Pope, *The Early Career of Alexander Pope* (Clarendon, 1934) by G. Sherburn is a fascinating scholarly treatment of Pope's activities up to the year 1728. The most satisfactory compact edition of Pope's poetry is that of H. W. Boynton (Cambridge Poets, Houghton Mifflin, 1902); but there are also excellent selections by G. Sherburn (Nelson, rev. ed., 1940) and L. I. Bredvold (Crofts, 1926). Two modern lives of SIR RICHARD STEELE have been published: that of A. Dobson (Longmans, 1888) is brief but readable; G. A. Aitken's (2 vols., Isbister, 1889) is the more thorough and scholarly. The best edition of the *Tatler* is also by Aitken (4 vols., Duckworth, 1898–99), but no edition is now in print; there never has been a collected edition of Steele's works. Selections from the *Tatler, Spectator,* and their successors are available in a recent edition by W. Graham (Nelson, 1928).

Among the extraordinarily numerous biographies of JONATHAN SWIFT, a still useful study is that of Sir Henry Craik (J. Murray, 1882), though the more recent lives by Carl Van Doren (Viking, 1930) and J. M. Murry (Cape, 1954) synthesize the modern research on Swift's problematical personality. Critical studies are likewise abundant: among the most illuminating of them are *The Mind and Art of Jonathan Swift* (O. U. P., 1936) by Ricardo Quintana, W. D. Taylor's *Jonathan Swift, a Critical Essay* (Davies, 1933), A. E. Case's *Four Essays on Gulliver's Travels* (Princeton U. P., 1945), H. J. Davis's *The Satire of Jonathan Swift* (Macmillan, 1947), Evelyn Hardy's *The Conjured Spirit* (Hogarth, 1949), and Maurice Johnson's *The Sin of Wit* (Syracuse U. P., 1950). Later editions of separate works equipped with excellent introductions and notes include *A Tale of a Tub* (Clarendon, 1920) by A. C. Guthkelch and D. N. Smith; *Gulliver's Travels* (First Edition Club, O. U. P., 1926) and the *Poems of Jonathan Swift* (3 vols., Clarendon, 1937) by Harold Williams; and *The Drapier's Letters* (Clarendon, 1935) by H. Davis. There is a convenient edition of the *Journal to Stella* (Everyman's Lib., Dutton, 1924) by J. K. Moorhead. Of a new edition of the *Prose Works* edited by H. Davis and published by Blackwell, a number of volumes have already appeared.

CHAPTER XI

GENERAL WORKS

Besides the relevant texts mentioned in Chapter X, the student will find useful material on the social and political background of the period in Paul Mantoux's *The Industrial Revolution in the Eighteenth Century* (Cape, rev. ed. trans. by M. Vernon, 1928) and in the volumes entitled *Johnson's England* (2 vols., Clarendon, 1933), edited by A. S. Turberville. Certain important aspects of the intellectual background may be found in J. B. Bury, *The Idea of Progress* (Macmillan, 1920) and C. B. Tinker, *Nature's Simple Plan* (Princeton U. P., 1922). For an understanding of the changes in literary taste and style, one may consult C. E. Vaughan, *The Romantic Revolt* (Scribner's, 1907); Herbert Read, *Reason and Romanticism* (Faber and Gwyer, 1926); and Sherard Vines, *The Course of English Classicism* (Harcourt, 1930).

INDIVIDUAL WRITERS

There are several good biographies of WILLIAM BLAKE, notably those by G. K. Chesterton (Dutton, 1910), A. Gilchrist (2 vols., Macmillan, 1863), A. C. Swinburne (Dutton, new ed., 1906), and A. Symons (Dutton, 1907). A later work, *The Life of William Blake* (Nonesuch, 1927) by Mona Wilson is also to be recommended. Among the more recent critical studies, the most useful are S. F. Damon's *William Blake, His Philosophy and Symbols* (Houghton Mifflin, 1924) and D. Saurat's *Blake and Modern Thought* (Constable, 1929). Important contemporary studies include Bernard Blackstone's *English Blake* (Cambridge U. P., 1949), Northrop Frye's *Fearful Symmetry* (Princeton U. P., 1947) and Mark Schorer's *William Blake, the Politics of Vision* (Holt, 1946). The complete *Works, Poetic, Symbolic, and Critical* (3 vols., Quaritch, 1893) were edited by E. J. Ellis and W. B. Yeats, with an elaborate critical apparatus and illustrations from Blake's *Prophetic Books*. Later and more accessible editions include those of Geoffrey Keynes, *The Writings of William Blake* (3 vols., Nonesuch, 1925) and *Poetry and Prose* (Nonesuch, 1927); and the valuable critical edition of *The Prophetic Writings* (2 vols., Clarendon, 1926) by D. J. Sloss and J. P. R. Wallis. The spectacular discovery of the private papers of JAMES BOSWELL has led to a striking increase in our knowledge of the man and estimation of his personality. Geoffrey Scott and F. A. Pottle have edited the *Private Papers of James Boswell from Malahide Castle* (18 vols., Mt. Vernon, N. Y.: Rudge, 1928–34). Portions of his extensive journals have been published: *London Journal, 1762–1763* (McGraw-Hill, 1950); *Boswell in Holland, 1763–1764* (McGraw-Hill, 1952); *Boswell on the Grand Tour: Germany and Switzerland, 1764* (McGraw-Hill, 1953). The best book on EDMUND BURKE is still the classic life (E. M. L., Macmillan, 1879) by John Morley; but recent discoveries published in A. P. I. Samuels's *The Early Life, Correspondence and Writings of Edmund Burke* (C. U. P., 1923) have resulted in fresh and more detailed studies. Among them should be noted the biographies by B. Newman (Bell, 1927) and R. H. Murray (O. U. P., 1931). E. J. Payne's *Select Works* (3 vols., Clarendon, 1874–78) is an invaluable selected edition; another good one is that of L. N. Broughton (Modern Student's Library, Scribner's, 1925). Thomas W. Copeland's *Our Eminent Friend, Edmund Burke* (Yale U. P., 1949), is a suggestive statement of current views of Burke.

Within the past two decades at least a dozen biographies of ROBERT BURNS have appeared, professing to treat him from new points of view; the best is *The Life of Robert Burns* (Macmillan, 1932) by F. B. Snyder. The standard edition of Burns is the Centenary Edition (4 vols., Jack, 1896–97) by W. E. Henley and T. F. Henderson. The text of this edition, with its brilliant introduction by Henley, is reproduced in the condensed Cambridge Poets edition. There are several good selected editions, notably those by C. L. Hanson (Ginn, 1899) and C. S. Dougall (Black, 1927). The best edition of Burns's *Letters* is that of J. DeLancey Ferguson (2 vols., Clarendon, 1931). Recent Burns studies include David Daiches' *Robert Burns* (Rinehart, 1952), Hans Hecht's *Robert Burns, the Man and his Work* (Hodge, 1950), and *Robert Burns, New Judgments* (MacLellan, 1947). The "marvelous boy," THOMAS CHATTERTON, has been the subject of several recent biographies, the most thorough of which are those by E. P. Ellinger (Univ. of Penn. Press, 1930), E. H. W. Meyerstein (Ingpen and Grant, 1930), W. M. Dixon (O. U. P., 1930), and John C. Nevill (Muller, 1948). The standard edition of *The Poetical Works* is that of W. W. Skeat (2 vols., Bell and Daldy, 1871) with an essay on the Rowley Poems. Although there is no full-length biography of WILLIAM COLLINS, H. W. Garrod's two books, *Collins* (Clarendon, 1928) and *The Poetry of Collins* (O. U. P., 1928) are valuable and penetrating critical studies. The best edition of Collins is that of E. Blunden (Etchells and Macdonald, 1929).

WILLIAM COWPER's tragic life has been variously treated by his biographers. Among the older lives, that by Goldwin Smith (E. M. L., Macmillan, 1880) is the most satisfactory; the more recent *William Cowper and the Eighteenth Century* (Nicholson and Watson, 1935) by G. Thomas, is to be recommended for its fairness and thoroughness. More recent studies are Lord David Cecil's *The Stricken Deer* (Constable, 1947), Norman Nicholson's *William Cowper* (Lehmann, 1951) and Maurice J. Quinlan's *William Cowper, a Critical Life* (Univ. of Minn. Press, 1953). The best edition of Cowper's poetry is by H. S. Milford (Clarendon, 1921), but there is also a recent cheap edition (Everyman's Lib., Dutton, 1931), with an introduction by H. I'A. Fausset. The first *Life* of GEORGE CRABBE was written by his son and has recently appeared in a new edition with a critical introduction by E. M. Forster

(O. U. P., 1932). A. Ainger's *Crabbe* (E. M. L., Macmillan, 1903) is, however, the only wholly satisfactory biography. Critical accounts of Crabbe may be found in R. Huchon's *George Crabbe and His Times* (J. Murray, 1907, trans. by F. Clarke) and in J. H. Evans, *The Poems of George Crabbe, a Literary and Historical Study* (Macmillan, 1933). The best editions of Crabbe's poems are that of A. W. Ward (3 vols., Cambridge English Classics, C. U. P., 1905–07) and the more recent one by A. J. and R. M. Carlyle (O. U. P., 1914).

That EDWARD GIBBON was his own best biographer is attested by the numerous reprints of his fragmentary *Memoirs,* which are among the most delightful of autobiographies in the English language. The most accurate edition of the *Memoirs* is J. Murray's *The Autobiographies of Edward Gibbon* (J. Murray, 1896), but the editions by O. F. Emerson (Ginn, 1898) and G. B. Hill (Putnam, 1900) are also valuable. Within recent years several good biographies of Gibbon have appeared; in addition to the *Life* by J. A. C. Morison (E. M. L., Macmillan, 1878) there are C. Dawson's *Edward Gibbon* (O. U. P., 1935), R. B. Mowat's *Gibbon* (Barker, 1936), and *Edward Gibbon* (Chatto and Windus, 1937) by D. M. Low. Innumerable reprints of Gibbon's *Decline and Fall of the Roman Empire* have been published, the best edition of which is that of J. B. Bury (Methuen, 1897–1900). Although no first-rate biography of OLIVER GOLDSMITH has yet been written, there are several good ones, notably those of A. Dobson (W. Scott, 1887, rev. ed. Dodd, Mead, 1899) and Stephen Gwynn (Butterworth, 1935). Among recent critical studies of Goldsmith, the most important are K. C. Balderston's splendid edition of the *Collected Letters* (C. U. P., 1928) and H. J. Smith's study of *The Citizen of the World* (Yale U. P., 1926). The student should not fail also to read the accounts of Goldsmith given in Boswell's *Life of Johnson.* In Everyman's Library there are convenient editions of the *Poems and Plays* (Dutton, 1910), *The Vicar of Wakefield* (1909), and of *The Citizen of the World* and *The Bee* (1934). A contemporary study worth consulting is William Freeman's *Oliver Goldsmith* (London, Jenkins, 1951). The best biography of THOMAS GRAY is that of Sir E. Gosse (E. M. L., Macmillan, 1882). Gray's *Correspondence* has been edited by P. Toynbee and L. Whibley (3 vols., Clarendon, 1935). A good selected edition is *Gray, Poetry and Prose* (O. U. P., 1926) by J. Crofts, but the most accurate modern edition of Gray's poetical works is that of A. L. Poole (O. U. P., 1917, 1937).

SAMUEL JOHNSON's greatness is of course nowhere better revealed than in Boswell's peerless *Life* (6 vols., edited by G. B. Hill; rev. by L. F. Powell, Clarendon, 1934). This great biography is supplemented by other notable contemporary portraits in Mrs. Piozzi's *Anecdotes of Dr. Johnson* (1786, modern ed. by S. C. Roberts, O. U. P., 1925) and in Fanny Burney's *Diary,* the relevant portions of which have been skillfully edited by C. B. Tinker and are included in his *Dr. Johnson and Fanny Burney* (Moffat, Yard, 1911). The standard edition of Johnson's complete works is still that of his literary executor, Sir John Hawkins (14 vols. 1787–89, and frequently reprinted) ; the most useful selected edition is C. H. Conley's *The Reader's Johnson* (American Book Co., 1940), which has an admirable introduction. Two valuable later studies are Joseph W. Krutch's *Samuel Johnson* (Holt, 1944), and Colwyn Vulliamy's *Ursa Major, a Study of Johnson & his Friends* (London, M. Joseph, 1947). The best editions of Johnson's *Letters* (2 vols., Clarendon, 1892) and of his *Lives of the English Poets* (3 vols., Clarendon, 1905) are by G. B. Hill. The only suitable biography of JAMES MAC-PHERSON is J. S. Smart's *James MacPherson, an Episode in Literature* (Nutt, 1905). *The Poems of Ossian* (Geddes, 1896) were edited by W. Sharp. A more specialized study is Derick Thomson's *The Gaelic Sources of MacPherson's Ossian* (Oliver & Boyd, 1952).

The standard edition of THOMAS PERCY's *Reliques of Ancient English Poetry* is that of H. W. Wheatley (3 vols., S. Sonnenschein, 1886), and there is also a convenient edition in Everyman's Library (2 vols., Dutton, 1906). The best biography of Bishop Percy is A. C. C. Gaussen's *Percy, Prelate and Poet* (Smith, Elder, 1908). Among the various lives of RICHARD BRINSLEY SHERIDAN, the latest and best is *Harlequin Sheridan* (Blackwell, 1933) by R. C. Rhodes, whose edition of *The Plays and Poems* (3 vols., Blackwell, 1928), though elaborate, is likewise the most satisfactory. A useful introduction is J. W. Cove's *Sheridan, his Life and his Theater* (Morrow, 1948). Sheridan's contribution to the drama of his time is most ably discussed in E. Bernbaum's *The Drama of Sensibility* (Ginn, 1915) and Allardyce Nicoll's *A History of Late Eighteenth Century Drama* (C. U. P., 1927). G. C. Macaulay's life of JAMES THOMSON (E. M. L., Macmillan, 1907) is still the best biography of the poet. The best edition of the *Complete Poetical Works* (Frowde, O. U. P., 1908) is by J. L. Robertson.

CHAPTER XII

GENERAL WORKS

By far the most extensive treatment of English prose fiction is E. A. Baker's monumental *History of the English Novel* (10 vols., Witherby,

1924–39), which traces the development of the novel from its earliest origins in the mediæval romances to the present day. An excellent brief analysis is that of R. M. Lovett and H. S. Hughes, entitled *History of the Novel in England* (Houghton Mifflin, 1932). Among various studies devoted to specific aspects of the novel, the reader will find useful information in Pelham Edgar's *The Art of the Novel from 1700 to the Present Time* (Macmillan, 1933); G. F. Singer's *The Epistolary Novel* (Univ. of Penn. Press, 1933); M. Summers's *The Gothic Quest* (Fortune Press, 1938); and R. E. Ernle's *The Light Reading of Our Ancestors* (Hutchinson, 1927).

INDIVIDUAL WRITERS

The best recent book on WILLIAM BECKFORD is *Beckford* (Scribner's, 1937) by Guy Chapman, who has also edited *Vathek,* with the *Episodes of Vathek* (2 vols., Constable, 1929), as well as Beckford's *Travel-Diaries* (2 vols., Constable, 1928) and *The Vision,* etc. (Constable, 1930). Another good biography is that of J. W. Oliver (O. U. P., 1932); and there is an important study entitled *Beckford and Beckfordism* (Duckworth, 1930) by S. Sitwell.

One of the best biographies of FRANCES BURNEY, MME. D'ARBLAY, is *Fanny Burney and the Burneys* (Stokes, 1926) by R. B. Johnson, whose edition of *Evelina* (2 vols., Dent, 1903) is probably the most thorough. Emily Hahn's *A Degree of Prudery* (Doubleday, 1950) is a spirited modern biography. Information concerning Fanny Burney's court activities may be obtained in *Fanny Burney at the Court of Queen Charlotte* (Lane, 1912) by C. Hill; and her relationship with Dr. Johnson is discussed in C. B. Tinker's study, *Dr. Johnson and Fanny Burney* (Moffat, Yard, 1911). A. A. Overman's *An Investigation into the Character of Fanny Burney* (H. J. Paris, 1933) gives a fresh and valuable insight into her personality. Besides Johnson's edition of *Evelina,* there is a good one by F. D. McKinnon (Clarendon, 1930) and another in Everyman's Library. The *Diary and Letters* have been edited by S. C. Woolsey (Roberts, 1880) and M. Masefield (Routledge, 1931); the *Early Diary,* by A. R. Ellis (2 vols., Bell, 1889).

The most important book on DANIEL DEFOE is Paul Dottin's *Daniel Defoe et ses Romans* (3 vols., Univ. of France, 1924), part of which has been translated under the title, *The Life and Strange and Surprising Adventures of Daniel Defoe* (Macaulay Co., 1929) by L. Ragan. Useful contemporary introductions to Defoe are William Freeman's *The Incredible Defoe* (London, Jenkins, 1950), James R. Sutherland's *Defoe* (Methuen, 1950), and Francis Watson's *Daniel Defoe* (Longmans,

1952). Among the many critical studies of Defoe, the most useful are W. P. Trent's *Daniel Defoe, How to Know Him* (Bobbs-Merrill, 1916) and A. W. Secord's *Studies in the Narrative Method of Defoe* (Methuen, 1937). Because of Defoe's astounding fecundity there is no complete edition of his works and probably never will be, but his most important works have been frequently reprinted. *The Novels and Selected Writings* (14 vols., Shakespeare Head, Blackwell, 1927–28) is one of the best collected editions; another noteworthy edition is that of the *Romances and Narratives* (16 vols., Dent, 2nd ed., 1900) by G. A. Aitken. *Robinson Crusoe,* the *Journal of the Plague Year,* and the *Memoirs of a Cavalier* are all in Everyman's Library, and Defoe's various *Tours* through the British Isles have been ably edited by G. D. H. Cole (2 vols., Davies, 1927) and E. B. Chancellor and M. Beeton (Batsford, 1929). Secord's selected edition of *A Journal of the Plague Year and Other Pieces* (Doubleday, 1935) may also be recommended.

W. L. Cross's biography, *The History of Henry Fielding* (3 vols., Yale U. P., 1918) is a masterly piece of scholarship that does full justice to its great subject. An elaborate contemporary study is Frederick Dudden's *Henry Fielding, his Life, Works, & Times* (2 vols., Clarendon, 1952). Among the many critical studies of Fielding, the most noteworthy are F. T. Blanchard's *Fielding the Novelist* (Yale U. P., 1926); A. Digeon's *The Novels of Fielding* (Routledge, 1925); and *Fielding's Theory of the Novel* by F. O. Bissell (Cornell U. P., 1933). The best recent edition of the *Novels* is the Shakespeare Head (Blackwell, 1926) in ten volumes. W. L. Cross's edition of *Tom Jones* (2 vols., Knopf, 1924), and that of *Jonathan Wild* by Wilson Follett (Knopf, 1926) both contain valuable introductions. *Joseph Andrews* and *Tom Jones* are also available in both Everyman's and the Modern Library editions. The fullest biographical account of WILLIAM GODWIN is still that of C. K. Paul, *William Godwin, his Friends and Contemporaries* (2 vols., King, 1876), but for subsequent critical findings one should also consult F. K. Brown's *Life of William Godwin* (Dutton, 1926), Rosalie Grylls' *William Godwin & his World* (London, Odhame, 1953), David Monro's *Godwin's Moral Philosophy* (Oxford, 1953), Allan Rodway's *Godwin & the Age of Transition* (Harrap, 1952), George Woodcock's *William Godwin* (London, Porcupine Press, 1946), and *Shelley, Godwin, and their Circle* (Holt, 1913) by H. N. Brailsford. Among the various editions of *Caleb Williams,* one may recommend those of E. A. Baker (Routledge, 1903) and Van Wyck Brooks (Greenberg, 1926). R. A. Preston has edited *An Enquiry Concerning Political Justice* (2 vols., Knopf, 1926).

The only full-length biography of MATTHEW GREGORY LEWIS is by M. Baron-Wilson (2 vols., Colburn, 1839), and the only separate recent critical study is that of I. M. Rentsch (Pöschel and Trepte, 1902), in German. Further criticism may be found in E. Railo's *The Haunted Castle* (Dutton, 1927), and in E. A. Baker's edition of Lewis's only well-known novel, *The Monk* (Dutton, 1907). The first and only competent biographical account of HENRY MACKENZIE in English is *A Scottish Man of Feeling, Some Account of Henry Mackenzie* (O. U. P., 1931) by H. W. Thompson, who has also edited *The Anecdotes and Egotisms of Henry Mackenzie* (O. U. P., 1927). The best edition of *The Man of Feeling* is by H. Miles (Scholartis Press, 1928).

Despite the acknowledged influence of MRS. ANN WARD RADCLIFFE, she has not as yet stirred the efforts of biographers, scholarly or otherwise. The only critical studies available are C. F. McIntyre's *Ann Radcliffe in Relation to Her Time* (Yale U. P., 1920) and A. A. S. Wieten's *Mrs. Radcliffe, Her Relation Towards Romanticism* (H. J. Paris, 1926). *The Mysteries of Udolpho* is now available in Everyman's Library (1931), and there is a good edition of *The Romance of the Forest*, with an introduction by H. R. Steeves (Scribner's, 1931). SAMUEL RICHARDSON has received far greater tribute from French and German biographers than from his own countrymen, for until recent years the only lives written in English were the brief ones by A. Dobson (E. M. L., Macmillan, 1902) and C. L. Thomson (Marshall, 1900). The best and most authoritative book on Richardson now available in English is A. D. McKillop's *Samuel Richardson, Printer and Novelist* (Univ. of North Carolina Press, 1936). Paul Dottin's excellent critical study, *Samuel Richardson, Imprimeur de Londres* (Perrin, 1931) has not yet been translated, but one may consult B. W. Downs's *Richardson* (Dutton, 1928) and two noteworthy studies by K. G. Hornbeak—*The Complete Letter Writer in English, 1568–1800* (1934), and *Richardson's Familiar Letters and the Domestic Conduct Books* (1937), both published by the Smith College Press. A later useful study is W. M. Sale's *Samuel Richardson, Master Printer* (Cornell U. P., 1950). *Pamela* (2 vols, 1933) and *Clarissa* (4 vols., 1932) are now available in a convenient Everyman's Library edition; and there is a good edition of the *Familiar Letters on Important Occasions,* with an introduction by B. W. Downs (Routledge, 1928).

TOBIAS SMOLLETT is another eighteenth-century worthy who has had to wait patiently for his full meed of biographical recognition. The earlier lives by D. Hannay (Great Writers, W. Scott, 1887) and O. Smeaton (Scribner's, 1897) are now supplemented by L. Melville's

Life and Letters of Tobias Smollett (Faber and Gwyer, 1926) and H. S. Buck's two works, *A Study in Smollett* (Yale U. P., 1925) and *Smollett as Poet* (O. U. P., 1927). *Humphrey Clinker* is reprinted in the Modern Library (1929) with an introduction by A. Machen; *Peregrine Pickle*, with an introduction by P. Henderson (2 vols., 1930) and *Roderick Random* (1927) are in Everyman's Library. There is also a very good edition of Smollett's *Letters* by E. S. Noyes (Harvard U. P., 1926). Three specialized studies are F. W. Boege's *Smollett's Reputation as a Novelist* (Princeton U. P., 1947), G. M. Kahrl's *Tobias Smollett, Traveler-Novelist* (Chicago U. P., 1945), and L. M. Krapp's *Tobias Smollett, Doctor of Men & Manners* (Princeton U. P., 1949).

Unquestionably the best book on LAURENCE STERNE is W. L. Cross's flavorsome *Life and Times of Laurence Sterne* (2 vols., Yale U. P., 1925), which has gone far to remove the unwarranted censures of Sterne evoked by the Victorian prudery of Bagehot and Thackeray. Among other important critical works on Sterne, the reader will find useful data in L. P. Curtis, *The Politicks of Laurence Sterne* (O. U. P., 1929) and H. Read, *The Sense of Glory* (C. U. P., 1929), which discusses the moral purpose in Sterne's chief works. Two later studies are Ludowick Hartley's *This is Lorence* (U. of N. Carolina Press, 1943) and Thomas Yoseloff's *A Fellow of Infinite Jest* (Prentice Hall, 1945). Convenient reprints of *Tristram Shandy* are included in the Modern Library and Everyman's; and there is a good edition of the *Sentimental Journey*, with an introduction by Virginia Woolf (O. U. P., 1928). Sterne's *Letters* have been ably edited by both R. B. Johnson (Dodd, Mead, 1927) and L. P. Curtis (Clarendon, 1935).

In his own flashing phrases, HORACE WALPOLE has bequeathed a more vivid and complete account of his life and background than any other man has ever recorded. The reader has but to choose among more than 3,000 of his letters, which have been carefully edited by Mr. and Mrs. Paget Toynbee (16 vols., Clarendon, 1903–05; supplement, 3 vols., 1918–25) and a host of other scholars. Since Walpole is generally acknowledged the greatest of England's letter writers, he is eminently deserving of the magnificent edition now being prepared by W. S. Lewis. In this edition there have already appeared the *Correspondence with the Rev. Cole* by W. S. Lewis and A. D. Wallace (2 vols., Yale U. P., 1937) and the voluminous *Correspondence with Madame du Deffand* (6 vols., Yale U. P., 1939) edited by W. S. Lewis and W. H. Smith. For other accounts of Walpole's life, the reader may consult A. Dobson's *Horace Walpole*, a memoir (4th ed., edited by P. Toynbee, O. U. P., 1927), and the lives by S. Gwynn (Butterworth,

1932), L. Melville (Hutchinson, 1930), and D. M. Stuart (E. M. L., Macmillan, 1927). Walpole's influence upon English fiction is shown in K. K. Mehrotra's *Horace Walpole and the English Novel, a Study in the Influence of "The Castle of Otranto,"* 1764–1820 (Blackwell, 1934), and in the excellent introduction to the edition of the *Castle of Otranto* by H. R. Steeves (Scribner's, 1931).

CHAPTER XIII

GENERAL WORKS

The student will find useful background material on the political and social aspects of the romantic movement in Traill's *Social England* (Vol. VI); C. G. Robertson's *England Under the Hanoverians* (Methuen, 1934); and in C. Brinton's *The Political Ideas of the English Romanticists* (O. U. P., 1926). For the influence of the French Revolution on the thought of the time, one may consult E. Dowden's *The French Revolution and English Literature* (Scribner's, 1897); A. E. Hancock's *The French Revolution and the English Poets* (Holt, 1899); and I. Babbitt's *Rousseau and Romanticism* (Houghton, 1919). E. de Sélincourt's *English Poets and the National Ideal* (O. U. P., 1915) is also a valuable study of changing literary points of view; while C. H. Herford's *Age of Wordsworth* (Bell, 1901) and E. Bernbaum's *Guide Through the Romantic Movement* (Second ed., rev.; Ronald, 1949) are perhaps the best brief surveys of the literature of the period. Among other useful histories of literature one may recommend O. Elton's *Survey of English Literature, 1780–1830* (Macmillan, 1920), A. Symons's *The Romantic Movement in English Poetry* (Dutton, 1909), and Malcolm Elwin's *The First Romantics* (Macdonald, 1947).

INDIVIDUAL WRITERS

Many lives of LORD BYRON have been written, particularly in recent years; but the official biography is still Thomas Moore's *Life of Lord Byron with His Letters and Journals* (J. Murray, 1830). Other noteworthy biographical studies, based largely on Moore, are K. Elze's *Lord Byron* (J. Murray, 1872); J. Nichol's *Byron* (E. M. L., Macmillan, 1880); R. Noel's *Life of Byron* (W. Scott, 1890); and E. C. Mayne's *Byron* (Scribner's, 1912). The results of recent scholarly investigations are presented in W. A. Borst's *Lord Byron's First Pilgrimage* (Yale U. P., 1948). E. J. Lovell's *Byron: the Record of a Quest* (Univ. of Texas Press, 1949), and P. G. Trueblood's *The Flowering of Byron's*

Genius: Studies in Byron's Don Juan (Stanford U. P., 1945). For recollections of Byron and his circle one may consult Leigh Hunt's *Lord Byron and Some of His Contemporaries* (3 vols., Colburn, 1828) and E. J. Trelawney's *Records of Shelley, Byron, and the Author* (Dutton, 1905). The best one-volume editions of the works are the Cambridge edition, with a biographical sketch by P. E. More (Houghton, 1905) and the Murray edition, with a memoir by E. H. Coleridge (Scribner's, 1905). The most recent edition of Byron's correspondence is that of J. Murray (Scribner's, 1922).

Of the several available lives of THOMAS CAMPBELL, the most convenient is that of J. C. Hadden (Anderson, 1899). The *Complete Poetical Works* were edited by J. L. Robertson (O. U. P., 1907). A good selected edition is that of L. Campbell (Macmillan, 1904).

Among the older biographies of SAMUEL TAYLOR COLERIDGE, that of J. D. Campbell (Macmillan, 1894) and H. D. Traill's *Coleridge* (E. M. L., Macmillan, 1884) are recommended; of the more recent ones, E. K. Chambers's *Samuel Taylor Coleridge, a Biographical Study* (Clarendon Press, 1938) is the most reliable. H. I'A. Fausset's *Samuel Taylor Coleridge* (Cape, 1926) is a penetrating critical study. I. A. Richards' *Coleridge, on Imagination* (Harcourt, 1935) is an important analysis of his critical theory. Advanced students of Coleridge will find J. L. Lowes's *The Road to Xanadu* (Houghton, 1927) one of the most fascinating pieces of scholarship in recent years. The standard edition of Coleridge's *Complete Works* is by W. G. T. Sheed (7 vols., Harpers, 1884). There are two good editions of the *Biographia Literaria:* one by J. Shawcross (2 vols., Clarendon Press, 1907); the other by J. C. Metcalf (Macmillan, 1926). Selections from Coleridge's poetry have been edited by E. H. Coleridge (Milford, 1927), A. J. George (Heath, 1902), and E. L. Griggs (Nelson, 1934); prose selections may be found in the edition by H. A. Beers (Holt, 1893) and in the Bohn and Everyman's Libraries.

The authoritative biography of THOMAS DE QUINCEY is H. A. Eaton's *Thomas De Quincey: A Biography* (O. U. P., 1936). J. H. Fowler's *De Quincey as Literary Critic* (O. U. P., 1922) also gives valuable information on De Quincey's style and methods. Two later studies are J. E. Jordan's *Thomas De Quincey, Literary Critic* (California U. P., 1952) and Sigmund Proctor's *Thomas De Quincey's Theory of Literature* (Univ. of Michigan Press, 1943). Among the various selected editions of De Quincey's works may be mentioned those of M. H. Turk (Ginn, 1902) and S. Low (Bell, 1911).

The best first-hand accounts of WILLIAM HAZLITT are in the two books written by his grandson, W. C. Hazlitt, *Memoirs of William Hazlitt* (2 vols., Bentley, 1867) and *Lamb and Hazlitt: Letters and Records* (Dodd, Mead, 1899). There is a good short biography of Hazlitt in the English Men of Letters series (Macmillan, 1902) by A. Birrell, but the more recent *Life of William Hazlitt* (Doran, 1922) by P. P. Howe and *Born under Saturn* by Catherine MacLean (Macmillan, 1944) are much more complete. There is a good edition of the *Works* in Everyman's Library (Dutton, 1906–10), and good selections have been edited by A. Beatty (Heath, 1918), P. P. Howe (Doran, 1923), and C. H. Gray (Macmillan, 1926). The most convenient selected edition of Hazlitt's critical essays on English literature is that of J. Zeitlin (O. U. P., 1913, 1926).

Biographies of LEIGH HUNT have been written by R. B. Johnson (Sonnenschein, 1896) and C. Monkhouse in the Great Writers Series (Scott, 1893). The best edition of the *Poetical Works* is that of H. Milford (O. U. P., 1923), and there is a good selection of Essays (2 vols., Dent, 1891) edited by R. B. Johnson. Hunt's *Autobiography* (2 vols., Constable, 1903) has been edited by R. Ingpen.

The standard biographies of JOHN KEATS are Sidney Colvin's *John Keats; His Life and Poetry* (Scribner's, 1925) and Amy Lowell's *John Keats* (2 vols., Houghton, 1925). Two recent biographical studies— Robert Gittings' *John Keats: the Living Year* (Harvard U. P., 1954) and Hyder Rollins's *The Keats Circle* (2 vols., Harvard U. P., 1948) contain important new material. The recent studies, *Keats, a Study in Development* (Secker, 1922) by H. I'A. Fausset; *Keats* (Milford, 1921) by E. de Sélincourt, and *The Evolution of Keats's Poetry* (2 vols., Harvard U. P., 1936) by C. L. Finney are also extremely valuable. Recent critical studies of Keats's art include Walter Bate's *The Stylistic Development of Keats* (Oxford U. P., 1945), Werner Beyer's *Keats & the Daemon King* (Oxford, 1947), James Caldwell's *John Keats' Fancy* (Cornell U. P., 1945), Richard Fogle's *The Imagery of Keats & Shelley* (Univ. of N. Carolina Press, 1949), N. F. Ford's *The Prefigurative Imagination of John Keats* (Stanford U. P., 1951), J. M. Murry's *The Mystery of Keats* (Nevill, 1949), and Earl Wasserman's *The Finer Tone* (Johns Hopkins Press, 1953). The best one-volume editions of the poems are those of H. E. Scudder (Houghton, 1899) and M. B. Forman (Frowde, 1907), but there is also a more recent edition of the *Complete Poetry* with an introduction by G. R. Elliot (Macmillan, 1927). Forman's edition of Keats's *Letters* (Milford, 1901) is the most complete.

A. Ainger's excellent *Charles Lamb* (E. M. L., Macmillan, 1882) and the more recent *Life of Charles Lamb* (2 vols., Methuen, 1921) by E. V. Lucas are the most satisfactory of the many biographical works on LAMB. Two more popular studies are Katherine Anthony's *The Lambs, a Story of Pre-Victorian England* (Knopf, 1945) and Will Howe's *Charles Lamb & his Friends* (Bobbs-Merrill, 1944). The standard edition is E. V. Lucas's *The Works of Charles and Mary Lamb* (7 vols., Methuen, 1903–05), which is supplemented by P. Fitzgerald's *The Life, Letters, and Writings of Charles Lamb* (6 vols., Navarre Society, 1924). Separate editions of the *Essays of Elia, Tales from Shakespeare,* and the *Letters* are available in Everyman's Library; and there is an important edition of *Lamb's Criticism* (C. U. P., 1923), with an introduction by E. M. W. Tillyard.

For biographical material on WALTER SAVAGE LANDOR, one may consult either the ably written life by S. Colvin (E. M. L., Macmillan, 1888) or the more recent work, *Walter Savage Landor, Last Days, Letters and Conversations* (Methuen, 1934) by H. C. Minchin. Among the more convenient editions, S. Colvin's *Selections* (Macmillan, 1902) and the volume of selections by H. Ellis in Everyman's Library (Dent, 1933), and E. de Sélincourt's edition of the *Imaginary Conversations* (World's Classics, 1931) all contain excellent critical introductions.

Within recent years two good scholarly biographies of THOMAS MOORE have appeared: *The Harp That Once* (Holt, 1937) by Howard Mumford Jones and *The Minstrel Boy* (Hodder & Stoughton, 1937) by L. A. G. Strong. Moore's *Poetical Works* have been edited by A. D. Godley (Frowde, 1910); his *Irish Melodies and Songs* have been edited by S. Gwynn (Muses' Library, Routledge, 1908), with a valuable critical introduction.

The best biography of PERCY BYSSHE SHELLEY is that by N. I. White (2 vols., Knopf, 1940). More specialized biographical studies include K. N. Cameron's *The Young Shelley* (Macmillan, 1950), C. Cline's *Byron, Shelley & their Pisan Circle* (Harvard U. P., 1952), Ivan Roe's *Shelley, the Last Phase* (Hutchinson, 1953), Hans Haüsermann's *The Genevese Background* (Routledge, 1952), and Newman White's *The Examination of the Shelley Legend* (U. of Penna. Press, 1951). C. H. Grabo has written two of the most penetrating critical studies of Shelley in recent years: they are *A Newton Among Poets* (U. of North Carolina Press, 1930) and *The Magic Plant* (U. of North Carolina Press, 1936). Contemporary critical studies of Shelley's poetry and ideas include Carlos Baker's *Shelley's Major Poetry* (Princeton U. P., 1948), Joseph Barrell's *Shelley & the Thought of his Time* (Yale U. P., 1947), Richard Fogle's *The Imagery of Keats & Shelley*

(Univ. of N. Carolina Press, 1949), A. M. Hughes's *The Nascent Mind of Shelley* (Clarendon, 1947), F. A. Lea's *Shelley & the Romantic Revolution* (Routledge, 1945), and J. A. Notopoulas's *The Platonism of Shelley* (Duke U. P., 1949). *A Shelley Primer* (Reeves and Turner, 1887) by H. S. Salt is still useful. The best one-volume editions of the poetical works are those of E. Dowden (Crowell, 1893), G. E. Woodberry (Heath, 1908) and T. Hutchinson (O. U. P., 1919). Shelley's *Essays and Letters* have been edited by E. Rhys (Camelot Classics, Scott, 1886) with a critical introduction; and there are good separate editions of the lyrical and dramatic poems by C. H. Herford (Chatto and Windus, 1918).

The most extensive biography of ROBERT SOUTHEY is the six-volume *Life and Correspondence* (Longmans, 1849–50) by C. C. Southey. E. Dowden has written a good brief life (E. M. L., Macmillan, 1906), and there are two more recent works, *The Early Life of Robert Southey, 1774–1803* (Columbia Univ. Press, 1917) by W. Haller and Jack Simmons' *Southey* (London: Collins, 1945). The most convenient edition of Southey's *Poems* is that of M. H. Fitzgerald (O. U. P., 1919), who also edited a good selection of Southey's *Letters* (O. U. P., 1912) with a critical introduction. Southey's *Life of Nelson* has been well edited by H. B. Butler (Frowde, 1911), and there is a good edition of his *Select Prose* by J. Zeitlin (Macmillan, 1916).

Among the many biographies of WILLIAM WORDSWORTH, the most incisive are those of G. M. Harper (2 vols., Scribner's, 1916), and Sir W. Raleigh (Longmans, 1913), and the three books by E. Legouis: *The Early Life* (Dent, 1897), *William Wordsworth and Annette Vallon* (Dutton, 1922), and *Wordsworth in a New Light* (Harvard Univ. Press, 1923). For reminiscences and contemporary views of Wordsworth, the best sources are Dorothy Wordsworth's *Journals* (Macmillan, 1924) edited by W. Knight, and various essays by Coleridge, De Quincey, Hazlitt, and F. Jeffrey. Of the earlier critical studies, H. W. Garrod's *Wordsworth* (O. U. P., 1923) and C. M. MacLean's *Dorothy and William Wordsworth* (C. U. P., 1927) are to be recommended. The centenary of Wordsworth's death stimulated a number of important reinterpretations and revaluations of the poet and his work: Helen Darbishire, *The Poet Wordsworth* (Clarendon, 1950), Donald E. Hayden, *After Conflict, Quiet* (Exposition Press, 1951), Henry J. F. Jones, *The Egotistical Sublime* (Chatto, 1954), Herschel Margoliouth, *Wordsworth & Coleridge, 1795–1834* (O. U. P., 1953), George W. Meyer, *Wordsworth's Formative Years* (Univ. of Michigan Press, 1943), Katherine M. Peek, *Wordsworth in England, Studies in the*

History of his Fame (Bryn Mawr, 1943), Newton P. Stallknecht, *Strange Seas of Thought* (Duke U. P., 1945). The best edition of *The Prelude* is that of E. de Sélincourt (Clarendon Press, 1926), which contains both the original and altered versions of the poem together with introduction and notes. G. M. Harper's selected edition of the *Poems* (Scribner's, 1923) contains an excellent introduction.

CHAPTER XIV

GENERAL WORKS

The background of social life and thought in Victorian England is ably discussed in such works as G. M. Trevelyan's *History of England;* D. C. Somervell's *English Thought in the Nineteenth Century* (Longmans, 1938) ; and *Early Victorian England* (2 vols., O. U. P., 1934) edited by G. M. Young, the last chapter of which, written by Young, is a brilliant survey entitled *Victorian England, Portrait of an Age.* It has been expanded to cover the whole Victorian period and published separately (O. U. P., 1936). Among various histories of the literature of the period, the most important are H. Walker's *The Literature of the Victorian Era* (C. U. P., 1910) ; A. H. Thorndike's *Literature in a Changing Age* (Macmillan, 1920) ; J. W. Cunliffe's *English Literature during the Last Half-Century* (Macmillan, rev. and enlarged ed., 1923), an excellent manual of writers with bibliographies; and *The Beardsley Period* (Lane, 1925) by O. Burdett. T. M. Parrott's and R. B. Martius *A Companion to Victorian Literature* (Scribner's, 1955) is a convenient brief manual. The more specialized studies—Jerome H. Buckley's *The Victorian Temper* (Harvard, 1951) and John Holloway's *The Victorian Sage* (Macmillan, 1953) are recommended for advanced students.

INDIVIDUAL WRITERS

The best modern biographies of MATTHEW ARNOLD are those by Edward K. Brown (U. of Chicago Press, 1948) and Lionel Trilling (Rev. ed., Columbia U. P., 1949). S. P. Sherman's *Matthew Arnold, How to Know Him* (Bobbs-Merrill, 1917) and W. C. Brownell's esssay in his *Victorian Prose Masters* (Scribner's, 1901) are recommended for their excellent critical appreciation. The most useful introduction to Arnold's poetry is that by C. B. Tinker and H. F. Lowry (O. U. P., 1940). There are good selected editions of Arnold's works in the Golden Treasury Series (Macmillan, 1904) and in Everyman's Library. A recent selection of poetry and prose is that of E. K. Chambers

(Clarendon, 1939). Most of Arnold's literary criticism may be found in the two series of his *Essays in Criticism* (MacMillan, 1st series 1865, 2nd series 1888), which are also reprinted in Everyman's Library.

The best biography of ELIZABETH BARRETT BROWNING is that by Dorothy Hewlett (Knopf, 1952). One may also consult both the life by J. H. Ingram (Roberts, 1888) and, for incidental criticism of her work, some of the books mentioned below in connection with ROBERT BROWNING. There are two good one-volume editions of her complete *Poetical Works* (Macmillan, 1900, and Houghton Mifflin, 1900). The *Letters of Elizabeth Barrett Browning* were edited by Sir F. G. Kenyon (Macmillan, 1897). There is a separate edition of *The Letters of Robert Browning and Elizabeth Barrett Browning, 1845–46* (Harper, 2 vols., 1899). *New Letters of Robert Browning* have been edited by W. C. De Vane and K. L. Knickerbocker (Yale U. P., 1950). One of the best recent books on ROBERT BROWNING is the *Browning Handbook* (Crofts, 1935, rev. ed., 1954) by W. C. De Vane, which contains biographical information and a full critical commentary on Browning's work as a whole, as well as on individual poems. Other works that should be mentioned are O. Burdett's *The Brownings* (Constable, 1928), Frances Winwar's *The Immortal Lovers* (Harper, 1950), and Betty B. Miller's *Robert Browning, a Portrait* (Murray, 1952). There are good selected editions of Browning's works by H. E. Joyce (Scribner's, M. S. L., 1922), R. M. Lovett (Ginn, 1933), W. Graham (American, 1934), and W. C. De Vane (Crofts, 1934).

THOMAS CARLYLE is another Victorian whose biographies, especially in recent years, are inseparably connected with those of his wife. The official biography of Carlyle is by J. A. Froude (2 vols., Longmans, 1882), but an even fuller work is the recently completed *Life of Carlyle* (6 vols., Dutton, 1923–34) by D. A. Wilson. For a briefer modern account, Julian Symons' *Thomas Carlyle, the Life and Ideas of a Prophet* (Gollancz, 1952) may be recommended. Emery Neff's *Carlyle and Mill* (Columbia U. P., 1926) is an excellent study of two contrasting nineteenth-century philosophies. There is a good critical edition of *Sartor Resartus* (Athenaeum Press, Ginn, 1896) by A. MacMechan, and another of the same work together with *Heroes and Hero Worship* in Everyman's Library (Dutton, 1909). For serious study the editions of *The French Revolution* by J. H. Rose (Bell, 1902) and of the *Letters and Speeches of Oliver Cromwell* (Methuen, 1904) by S. C. Lomas, should be consulted.

Although no satisfactory life of ARTHUR HUGH CLOUGH exists, one may find a good critical estimate of his work in S. A. Brooke's *Four*

Victorian Poets (Putnam, 1908). There are also memoirs by F. T. Palgrave in his edition of the *Poems* (Macmillan, 1862) and by Mrs. Clough in the *Poems and Prose Remains of Arthur Hugh Clough* (Macmillan, 1869). The *Life and Letters* of THOMAS HENRY HUXLEY (Appleton, 1900) was prepared by his son, Leonard. The most important of Huxley's writings are available in a convenient two-volume selected edition in Everyman's Library. The *Diary of the Voyage of H.M.S. Rattlesnake* has been recently edited by J. Huxley (Doubleday, 1936). One of the best biographies in English is *The Life and Letters* of LORD MACAULAY (Longmans, new ed., 1908), written by Macaulay's nephew, G. O. Trevelyan. The best edition of Macaulay's extraordinarily influential *History of England* is by C. H. Firth (6 vols., Macmillan, 1913–15).

Besides the standard biography of WILLIAM MORRIS by J. W. Mackail (2 vols., Longmans, 1899), one may consult the shorter life by A. Noyes (E. M. L., Macmillan, 1908), and *William Morris, His Art, His Writings, and His Public Life* (Bell, 1897) by A. Vallance. Selections from his poems have been edited by P. R. Colwell (Crowell, 1904). The standard *Life* of JOHN HENRY NEWMAN, by Wilfrid Ward (Longmans, 1912), may be supplemented by the earlier studies of W. Meynell (J. Sinkins, 1890) and R. H. Hutton (Houghton Mifflin, 1891). There are convenient editions of the *Apologia and Essays on University Subjects* in Everyman's Library, and of selections with an admirable introduction by L. E. Gates (Holt, 1895). The interest aroused by the centenary of Newman's conversion to Catholicism is reflected in such studies as R. D. Middleton's *Newman at Oxford* (O. U. P., 1950), John Moody's *John Henry Newman* (Sheed & Ward, 1945), Sean O'Faolain's *Newman's Way* (Devin-Adair, 1952), Eleanor Ruggles's *Journey into Faith* (Norton, 1948), and Maisie Ward's *Young Mr. Newman* (Sheed & Ward, 1948).

The most recent critical study of WALTER PATER is that of Arthur Symons (Sawyer, 1932). Besides the standard biography of Pater by T. Wright (2 vols., Putnam, 1907), there are shorter lives by A. C. Benson (E. M. L., Macmillan, 1906) and F. Greenslet (McClure, Phillips, 1903). There are convenient editions of *Marius the Epicurean* and of *The Renaissance* in the Modern Library, and a good volume of selections edited by E. E. Hale (Holt, 1901). CHRISTINA ROSSETTI'S life is closely associated with those of her elder brothers Dante Gabriel and William Michael, who edited the best edition of her poems (Macmillan, 1904). In addition to the biographies written by M. Bell (Burleigh, 1898) and by Marya Zaturenska (Macmillan, 1949) there are appreciative critical studies by A. Symons in his *Studies in Two Literatures* (Simpkin, 1897) and by D. M. Stuart (E. M. L., Macmillan, 1930). Several interesting biographies of DANTE GABRIEL ROSSETTI may be recommended; namely, those of A. C. Benson (E. M. L., Macmillan, 1904); J. Knight (Great Writers, W. Scott, 1887); and W. Sharp (Macmillan, 1882). One of the most enjoyable studies is Max Beerbohm's *Rossetti and His Circle, 1824–54* (Heinemann, 1922), with superbly witty cartoons; others are R. L. Mégroz, *Dante Gabriel Rossetti, Painter Poet of Heaven in Earth* (Faber and Gwyer, 1928), Helen Angeli, *D. G. Rossetti his Friends & Enemies* (Hamilton, 1949) and Oswald Doughty, *D. G. Rossetti, a Victorian Romantic* (Yale U. P., 1949).

Although the official biography of JOHN RUSKIN is that of Sir E. T. Cook (2 vols., Allen, 1911), his own *Praeterita* (3 vols., Allen, 1899) is the best authority for his early life; there are good, shorter lives by W. G. Collingwood (Houghton Mifflin, 1902), F. Harrison (E. M. L., Macmillan, 1902), and A. K. P. Wingate (Scribner's, 1910). A later biographical work is *The Tragedy of John Ruskin* (Cape, 1928) by Mrs. A. Williams-Ellis. Recent studies include Henry A. Ladd's *The Victorian Morality of Art* (Long and Smith, 1932), the psycho-analytic study, *John Ruskin, an Introduction to Further Study of His Life and Work* by R. H. Wilenski (Faber and Faber, 1933), Derrick Leon's *Ruskin, the Great Victorian* (Routledge, 1949) and Peter Quennell's *John Ruskin, Portrait of a Prophet* (Viking, 1949). There are several convenient volumes of selections in Everyman's Library, the Riverside Literature Series (Houghton Mifflin, 1908), and the Modern Student's Library (Scribner's, 1918). The most important book on ALGERNON CHARLES SWINBURNE is the recent study entitled *Swinburne, a Literary Biography* by Georges Lafourcade (Bell, 1932), but the biographical facts are obtainable either in the accurate but conservative *Life* by Sir E. Gosse (Macmillan, 1917) or in that by H. Nicolson (E. M. L., Macmillan, 1926). Among other effective critical accounts of Swinburne, one may consult S. C. Chew's *Swinburne* (Little, Brown, 1929) and E. Thomas's *Algernon Charles Swinburne* (Kennerley, 1912). The best recent selection of his works is by C. K. Hyder and L. Chase (Nelson, 1937).

The official biography of ALFRED, LORD TENNYSON was written by his son, Hallam (2 vols., Macmillan, 1897); the best full-length treatment is the more dispassionate biography by his grandson, Sir Charles Tennyson (Macmillan, 1949). The shorter biographies by A. C. Benson (Dutton, 1904), A. C. Lyall (E. M. L., Macmillan, 1902), and T. R.

Lounsbury (Yale U. P., 1915) are readable, however; of the more stimulating critical studies available, the student may profitably consult H. Nicolson's analysis, *Tennyson* (Houghton Mifflin, 1923), H. I'A. Fausset's *Tennyson, a Modern Portrait* (Appleton, 1923), A. Waugh's commentary, *Alfred, Lord Tennyson* (Webster, 3rd ed., 1894), and Edward D. Johnson's *The Alien Vision of Victorian Poetry* (Princeton U. P., 1952). The best one-volume editions of Tennyson's complete poems are Macmillan's Globe (1892) and the Cambridge (Houghton Mifflin, 1898), edited by W. J. Rolfe. T. S. Eliot has an introduction to the *Poems* in the Nelson Classics (1936). The latest selected edition is by W. C. and M. P. De Vane (Crofts, 1940).

CHAPTER XV

GENERAL WORKS

For works on the history of the novel and its technique, see the Bibliography to Chapter XI.

INDIVIDUAL WRITERS

The official biography of JANE AUSTEN, entitled *Jane Austen: Her Life and Letters: A Family Record* (Smith, Elder, 1913), was written by W. and R. A. Austen-Leigh. Within recent years several excellent critical studies have appeared; among them may be mentioned three bearing the title *Jane Austen* by C. L. Thomson (H. Marshall, 1929), G. Rawlence (Duckworth, 1934), and B. K. Seymour (M. Joseph Ltd., 1937); as well as *Introductions to Jane Austen* (O. U. P., 1931) by J. Bailey, and *Jane Austen: Her Life and Art* (Cape, 1932) by D. Rhydderch. Later studies include Mary Lascelles' *Jane Austen and her Art* (O. U. P., 1939), Marvin Mudrick's *Jane Austen, Irony as Defense and Discovery* (Princeton U. P., 1952), and Andrew H. Wright's *Jane Austen's Novels, a Study in Structure* (Chatto, 1953). More specialized problems are dealt with in R. W. Chapman's *Jane Austen, Facts and Problems* (Clarendon, 1949). The most recent edition of her letters is that of R. W. Chapman (2 vols., O. U. P., 1932). The most important novels are in Everyman's Library, with excellent introductions by R. B. Johnson.

Although the lives of the three BRONTË sisters, CHARLOTTE, EMILY, and ANNE, can scarcely be regarded separately, one usually thinks first of the eldest, Charlotte, who has received the most attention from biographers. The earliest and still, to some extent, the standard biography is the classic *Life of Charlotte Brontë* by Mrs. Elizabeth Gaskell (Appleton, 1857, frequently reprinted) but it would be well to consult also Margaret Lane's *The Brontë Story, a Reconsideration of Mrs. Gaskell's Life* (Heinemann, 1953), C. K. Shorter's two books, *Charlotte Brontë and Her Circle* (Dodd, Mead, 1896) and *The Brontës* (Scribner's, 1908); May Sinclair's *The Three Brontës* (Houghton, 1912); E. Dimnet's *The Brontë Sisters* (Cape, 1927, trans. by L. N. Gill); and E. F. Benson's *Charlotte Brontë* (Longmans, 1932). The most elaborate contemporary study of the Brontë family is Lawrence and E. M. Hanson's *The Four Brontës, the Lives and Works of Charlotte, Branwell, Emily, and Anne Brontë* (O. U. P., 1949). A more limited study is *Emily Brontë, her Life and Work* by Muriel Spark and D. Stanford (Owen, 1953). Among the various critical studies of the Brontës, the most useful are *A Short History of the Brontës* (O. U. P., 1929) by K. A. R. Sugden, which contains a good critical bibliography; E. M. Delafield's *The Brontës* (Hogarth Press, 1935); W. B. White's *The Miracle of Haworth* (Dutton, 1939), and H. E. Wroot's *Persons and Places: Sources of Charlotte Brontë's Novels* (Caxton Press, 1935). The most nearly complete edition of the works of all the Brontës is the Shakespeare Head (Blackwell, 1931–34), which includes the *Letters* and the *Life* by T. J. Wise and J. A. Symington. *Jane Eyre, Shirley*, and *Wuthering Heights* are available in Everyman's Library, with introductions by May Sinclair, as well as in other inexpensive editions. Biographical details concerning EDWARD BULWER, LORD LYTTON may be obtained in the *Life* written by his grandson, V. A. G. R. Lytton (2 vols., Macmillan, 1913) or in T. H. S. Escott's *Edward Bulwer, First Baron Lytton* (Dutton, 1910). Two critical studies deserving mention are M. Sadleir's *Bulwer, a Panorama* (Little, Brown, 1931) and E. G. Bell's *Introductions to the Prose Remains, Plays and Comedies of Edward Bulwer, Lord Lytton* (W. M. Hill, 1914).

The basic biography of CHARLES DICKENS is still that of J. Forster (Chapman and Hall, 1872–74); and the best recent editions of this work are those of B. W. Matz (2 vols., Baker & Taylor, 1911) and J. W. T. Ley (Palmer, 1928). The definitive modern biography is Edgar Johnson's *Charles Dickens, his Tragedy & Triumph* (2 vols., Simon & Schuster, 1952). Other modern biographies are Jack Lindsay's *Charles Dickens, a Biographical & Critical Study* (London, Dapers, 1950), Hesketh Pearson's *Dickens, his Character, Comedy, & Career* (Harper, 1949), and Dame Una Pope-Hennessy's *Charles Dickens* (London, Howell, Soskin, 1946). G. K. Chesterton's *Charles Dickens* (Dodd, Mead, 1906) is still the best brief introduction to the novelist's work. His *Letters* were published in 1880–82 (3 vols., Chapman & Hall) and the *Letters to Wilkie Collins* in 1892 (Harper). A good recent edition of his letters to Mrs. Dickens is that of W. Dexter (Constable, 1935). BENJAMIN DISRAELI's standard biography is the work of two collaborators, W. F. Monypenny and G. E. Buckle (2 vols., Macmillan, rev. ed., 1929). André Maurois's *Disraeli* (Appleton, 1928, trans. H. Miles) is briefer but more vivid and penetrating. Hesketh Pearson's *Dizzy, the Life and Personality of Benjamin Disraeli* (Harper, 1951) provides a more recent estimate. Critical accounts of Disraeli include M. E. Speare's *The Political Novel* (O. U. P., 1924); E. T. Raymond's *Disraeli: Alien Patriot* (Doran, 1925); Sir. E. G. Clark's *Benjamin Disraeli* (Murray, 1926); the two works entitled *Disraeli* by D. L. Murray (E. Benn, 1927) and H. Beeley (Duckworth, 1936); and Muriel Masefield's *Peacocks & Primroses, a Survey of Disraeli's Novels* (London, Bles, 1953). Disraeli's *Letters to Lady Chesterfield and Lady Bradford* were edited by the Marquis of Zetland (2 vols., Appleton, 1929).

The official biography of MARIA EDGEWORTH is the *Life and Letters* (Houghton, 1895) by A. J. C. Hare, but there are briefer lives by E. Lawless (E. M. L., Macmillan, 1901) and Isabel Clarke (Hutchinson, 1949). Among the more important critical studies are C. Hill's *Maria Edgeworth and Her Circle* (Lane, 1910) and the essay in M. E. Tabor's *Pioneer Women* (Sheldon Press, 1933). S. H. Romilly's edition of the *Romilly-Edgeworth Letters* (Murray, 1936) also contains a valuable introduction. Maria Edgeworth's novels, *Castle Rackrent* and *The Absentee*, are available in convenient reprints (Macmillan). GEORGE ELIOT's life as related in her *Letters and Journals* by her husband, J. W. Cross (3 vols., Harper, 1885), remains the fullest account of the life of Mary Ann Evans; but it should be supplemented by such recent studies as E. S. Haldane's *George Eliot and Her Times* (Hodder & Stoughton, 1927); A. H. Paterson's *George Eliot's Family Life and Letters* (Selwyn & Blount, 1928); A. T. Kitchel's *George Lewes and George Eliot* (J. Day, 1933); G. W. Bullett's *George Eliot, her Life and Books* (Yale U. P., 1948); and Lawrence Hanson's *Marion Evans and George Eliot, a Biography* (O. U. P., 1952). Good critical studies of George Eliot are those by J. L. May (Cassell & Co., 1930), A. Fremantle (Duckworth, 1933), B. C. Williams (Macmillan, 1936), and Joan Bennett's *George Eliot, her Mind & her Art* (Cambridge U. P., 1948).

Within recent years several good biographical and critical studies of MRS. ELIZABETH C. S. GASKELL have been written: they are A. S.

Whitfield's *Mrs. Gaskell: Her Life and Work* (Routledge, 1929);
G. De W. Sanders's *Elizabeth Gaskell* (Yale U. P., 1929) with a bibliography by C. S. Northrup; E. S. Haldane's *Mrs. Gaskell and Her Friends* (Hodder & Stoughton, 1930); and Annette B. Hopkins' *Elizabeth Gaskell, her Life & Work* (London, Lehmann, 1952).

The standard biographies of THOMAS HARDY are those by his wife, Mrs. F. E. Hardy, the *Early Life* (Macmillan, 1928) and the *Later Years of Thomas Hardy* (Macmillan, 1930), and Carl J. Weber's *Hardy of Wessex, His Life and Literary Career* (Columbia U. P., 1940). Many studies are available, of which the most noteworthy are L. Johnson's *The Art of Thomas Hardy* (Lane, 1894); L. Abercrombie's *Thomas Hardy* (Secker, 1912); S. C. Chew's *Thomas Hardy: Poet and Novelist* (Knopf, 1928); and *The Technique of Thomas Hardy* by J. W. Beach (Chicago Univ. Press, 1922). Later studies include Edmund Blunden, *Thomas Hardy* (Macmillan, 1951); Lord David Cecil, *Hardy, the Novelist* (Constable, 1943); Albert Guerard, *Thomas Hardy, the Novels & Stories* (Harvard U. P., 1949); Evelyn Hardy, *Thomas Hardy, a Critical Biography* (London, Hogarth, 1954); James G. Southworth, *The Poetry of Thomas Hardy* (Columbia U. P., 1947); and Harvey C. Webster, *On a Darkling Plain* (U. of Chicago P., 1947).

The biography of HENRY JAMES may be most readily gleaned from his own books: *A Small Boy and Others* (1913); *Notes of a Son and Brother* (1914); *The Middle Years* (1917); and the two volumes of *Letters* (Scribners, 1920) and *Letters to A. C. Benson and Auguste Monod* (Matthews & Marrot, 1930). Valuable critical studies may be found in Rebecca West's *Henry James* (Nesbit, 1916); J. W. Beach's *The Method of Henry James* (Milford, 1918); Theodora Bosanquet's *Henry James at Work* (Hogarth Press, 1924); and P. Lubbock's *The Craft of Fiction* (Cape, 1921). Later studies include Osborn Andreas, *Henry James & the Expanding Horizon* (U. of Washington P., 1948); Marius Bewley, *The Complex Fate* (Chatto, 1952); Frederick Dupee, *Henry James* (N. Y., Wm. Sloane, 1951); Frederick Dupee, ed., *The Question of Henry James* (Holt, 1945); Leon Edel, *Henry James, the Untried Years, 1843–1870* (Lippincott, 1953); Francis O. Matthiessen, *Henry James, the Major Phase* (O. U. P., 1946), Simon Nowell-Smith, ed., *The Legend of the Master* (Constable, 1947); and Elizabeth Stevenson, *The Crooked Corridor* (Macmillan, 1949).

Biographical data on CHARLES KINGSLEY are obtainable in the *Letters and Memories of His Life* by his widow (Macmillan, 1877), in the edition of *Life and Works* (19 vols., Macmillan, 1901–03) and in the modern biography by Dame Una Pope-Hennessy (Chatto, 1948). Two critical studies may be mentioned: C. W. Stubbs, *Charles Kingsley and the Social Movement* (Blackie, 1899) and C. E. Vulliamy, *Charles Kingsley and Christian Socialism* (Fabian Society, 1935). Two recent studies of Kingsley are those of S. E. Baldwin (Cornell U. P., 1934) and M. F. Thorp (Princeton U. P., 1937).

Several excellent biographies of GEORGE MEREDITH have been written, of which the fullest are M. S. Gretton's *Writings and Life of George Meredith* (O. U. P., 1926), R. E. Sencourt's *Life of George Meredith* (Scribner's, 1929), and Lionel Stevenson's *The Ordeal of George Meredith* (Scribner's, 1953). The best critical studies are G. M. Trevelyan's *The Poetry and Philosophy of George Meredith* (Constable, 1906), *The Comic Spirit in George Meredith* by J. W. Beach (Longmans, 1911) and Siegfried Sassoon's *Meredith* (Viking, 1948). J. Moffatt's *George Meredith: A Primer to the Novels* (Hodder & Stoughton, 1909) is also of value. There are convenient editions of *The Ordeal of Richard Feverel* and *Diana of the Crossways* in the Modern Library; and a good reprint of *Comedy and the Uses of the Comic Spirit* (Scribner's, 1897).

The only noteworthy biographical and critical study of CHARLES READE is by M. Elwin (Cape, 1934); but one may also consult the memoir compiled chiefly from his literary remains by C. L. and C. Reade (Chapman and Hall, 1887). *The Cloister and the Hearth* is available in both the Modern and Everyman's Libraries; the latter edition includes a good introduction by Swinburne.

J. G. Lockhart's *Memoirs* (3 vols., Houghton, 1879; 5 vols., 1901) of his father-in-law, SIR WALTER SCOTT, ranks with Boswell's *Johnson* as one of the great biographies in English literature. A classic in its own right by virtue of its careful detail and coloring, this monumental work is reprinted (though in abridged form) in Everyman's Library. Critical appreciations are to be found in such recent works as A. S. MacNalty's *The Great Unknown* (Birch & Whittington, 1932), J. A. Patten's *Sir Walter Scott* (Clarke, 1932), Una Pope-Hennessy's *The Laird of Abbotsford* (Putnam, 1932), E. Muir's *Scott and Scotland* (Routledge, 1936), Sir H. Grierson's *Sir Walter Scott, Bart.* (Constable, 1938), and the extremely important collection of essays known as the *Scott Centenary Articles* (O. U. P., 1932).

WILLIAM MAKEPEACE THACKERAY did not wish a formal biography of himself to be written, and as if in ironic retribution few good ones exist: some of the recent critical studies, like those of G. U. Ellis

(Duckworth, 1933) and M. Elwin (Cape, 1932) as well as such earlier ones as A. Trollope's (E. M. L., Macmillan, 1879) and C. Whibley's (Dodd, Mead, 1903), should be considered. The most elaborate modern biography is Lionel Stevenson's *The Showman of Vanity Fair* (Scribner's, 1947). Perhaps the most objective appraisals of Thackeray and his work are those of G. Saintsbury in *A Consideration of Thackeray* (O. U. P., 1939), L. Melville's *William Makepeace Thackeray* (2 vols., Stone, 1899), Lambert Ennis' *Thackeray, The Sentimental Cynic* (Northwestern U. P., 1950), John Y. Grieg's *Thackery, a Reconsideration* (O. U. P., 1950), and Gordon N. Ray's *The Buried Life* (Harvard U. P., 1952). *Thackeray and His Daughter,* edited by H. T. Ritchie (Harper, 1924), should be read in connection with the biographical edition of Thackeray's *Works* (13 vols., Smith and Elder, 1898–99), as the introductions to this edition, containing about all the biographical data that Thackeray would have sanctioned, were written by his daughter, Lady Ritchie.

ANTHONY TROLLOPE'S *Autobiography* (Blackwood's, 1883; ed. by H. M. Trollope), though not a remarkable piece of literature, gives a frank account of his life and methods of work. The best modern biography is Lucy Stebbins' *The Trollopes, a Chronicle of a Writing Family* (Columbia U. P., 1945). Critical studies worth consulting are S. V. B. Nichols, *The Significance of Anthony Trollope* (McMurtrie, 1925), M. Sadleir's *Trollope: A Commentary* (Constable, 1927), which examines Trollope's work in the light of the changing Victorian background, and Winifred Gregory, *A Guide to Trollope* (Princeton U. P., 1942). Of Trollope's fifty-odd novels and tales, the Barsetshire series and several others are reprinted in Everyman's Library and in the handsome Shakespeare Head edition (Blackwell, 1929).

CHAPTER XVI

GENERAL WORKS

For the social and political background of this period, the student will find ample material in R. H. Gretton's *A Modern History of the English People, 1880–1922* (MacVeagh, 1930); in E. Halevy's *A History of the English People, Epilogue* (2 vols., Benn, 1929–34); and in T. C. Meech's *This Generation, a History of Great Britain and Ireland from 1900 to 1926* (2 vols., Chatto and Windus, 1927–28). On a narrower scale and from a more personal point of view, A. Maurois's *The Edwardian Era* (Appleton-Century, 1933) and E. C. Wing-field-Stratford's *The Victorian Aftermath* (Morrow, 1934) both merit attention; and for a variety of shorter studies of the period, one may recommend *Edwardian England, A.D. 1901–1910* (Benn, 1933) edited by F. J. C. Hearnshaw, and *The Post Victorians* (Nicholson & Watson, 1933), with an introduction by W. R. Inge. The best literary histories of the time are J. W. Cunliffe's *English Literature in the Twentieth Century* (Macmillan, 1933), H. Jackson's *The Eighteen-Nineties, a Review of Art and Ideas at the Close of the Nineteenth Century* (Richards, 1913). F. Swinnerton's *The Georgian Scene, a Literary Panorama* (Farrar and Rinehart, 1934) and C. Mackenzie's *Literature in My Time* (Loring and Mussey, 1933) are of little if any critical value, but they are commendable for their admirable thumb-nail sketches of con-temporary figures.

THE NOVEL

Besides the books on the novel mentioned in Chapter XII, the reader will find useful information in E. A. Drew's *The Modern Novel, Some Aspects of Contemporary Fiction* (Harcourt, 1926) and in H. T. and W. Follett's *Some Modern Novelists, Appreciations and Estimates* (Holt, 1918). For an understanding of the changes in novel-writing technique, both J. W. Beach's *The Twentieth Century Novel, Studies in Technique* (Appleton-Century, 1932) and C. H. Grabo's *The Technique of the Novel* (Scribner's, 1928) may be recommended; while G. W. Bullett's *Modern English Fiction, a Personal View* (Jenkins, 1926) deserves attention for its fresh point of view. Another book that should be read is W. L. Myers's *The Later Realism, a Study of Characterization in the British Novel* (Chicago U. P., 1927).

THE DRAMA

Like the novel, the stage in this period underwent many changes. These are best seen against such a broad background as that offered in J. W. Cunliffe's *Modern English Playwrights* (Harper, 1927), which traces the development of English drama from 1925. T. H. Dickinson's two works, *The Contemporary Drama of England* (Little, Brown, 1931) and *The Insurgent Theatre* (Huebsch, 1917) are also valuable. For good critical insight into the significance of modern British drama, the reader may profitably consult either A. E. Morgan's *Tendencies of Modern English Drama* (Constable, 1924) or Allardyce Nicoll's *British Drama* (Harrap, 1932). The rise of the Irish drama in this period is ably discussed by both A. E. Malone, in *The Irish Drama*

(Constable, 1929), and M. McHenry, in *The Ulster Theatre in Ireland* (Univ. of Penna. Press, 1931) as well as in *The Irish Dramatic Movement* (Methuen, 1939) by Una Ellis-Fermor and *The Irish Theatre* (Macmillan, 1939) ed. by Lennox Robinson.

POETRY

In poetry, the revolt against Victorianism and the renaissance in Ireland were perhaps even more marked than in either fiction or the drama. Among the best surveys of these new movements is that of R. L. Mégroz, whose *Modern English Poetry* (Nicholson and Watson, 1933) is a useful critical treatment of developments in British poetry after 1882, and B. I. Evans' *English Poetry in the Later Nineteenth Century* (Methuen, 1933). *The Renaissance of Irish Poetry, 1880–1930* (Washburn, 1929) by D. Morton serves as a good complement to that of Mégroz.

INDIVIDUAL WRITERS

Criticism of the work of "AE" (George W. Russell) may be found not only in the general commentaries on the Irish renaissance mentioned above, but also in special studies in the following works: E. A. Boyd, *Appreciations and Depreciations* (Lane, 1918), *Ireland's Literary Renaissance* (Lane, 1916), and *Portrait, Real and Imaginary* (Doran, 1924); George Moore, *Hail and Farewell* (Appleton, 1911–14); and H. W. Nevinson, *Changes and Chances* (Harcourt, 1923). The most thorough study of "AE," however, is D. Figgis's *AE, a Study of a Man and a Nation* (Maunsel, 1916). A vivid sense of his personality may be gained from *Letters from AE,* selected and edited by Alan Denson (London, Abelard-Schuman, 1961). Many critical estimates of SIR JAMES M. BARRIE have been made: a few of the best of them would include W. A. Darlington's *J. M. Barrie* (Blackie, 1938); *Barrie, the Story of a Genius* (Dodd, Mead, 1929), by J. A. Hammerton; Denis Mackail's *The Story of J. M. B., a biography* (Scribner's, 1941); and *J. M. Barrie and the Theatre* (White, 1922), by H. M. Welbrook. A sympathetic biographical study is Lady Cynthia Asquith's *Portrait of Barrie* (London, Barrie, 1954). Among the better critical studies of MAX BEERBOHM should be mentioned B. Lynch's *Max Beerbohm in Perspective* (Heinemann, 1921). His best-known work, *Zuleika Dobson,* is available in several inexpensive editions. Definitive is *A Bibliography of the Works of Max Beerbohm,* by Albert E. Gallatin and L. M. Oliver (Harvard U. P., 1952). Variously useful is Jacob G. Reiwald's *Sir Max Beerbohm, Man and Writer; a critical analysis with a brief life and a bibliography* (The Hague, Martinus Nyhoff, 1953). Samuel N. Behrman's *Portrait of Max; an intimate memoir* is a Boswell-like record of Beerbohm's talk (N. Y., Random House, 1960).

ARNOLD BENNETT's autobiographical comments in the three series of essays entitled *Things That Have Interested Me* (1921–26) and in his posthumous *Journals* (1932–33) throw more light on his character and personality than do most of the many critical studies by his contemporaries. For varying points of view, however, one should consult Marguerite Bennett's *My Arnold Bennett* (Nicholson and Watson, 1931) and D. C. Bennett's *Arnold Bennett* (Cape, 1935), and the studies by F. J. H. Darton (Holt, 1915) and L. G. Johnson (Daniel, 1924), as well as the critical comments in G. West's *The Problem of Arnold Bennett* (Joiner, 1932) and in Rebecca West's *Arnold Bennett Himself* (Day, 1931). More recent studies are Reginald Pound's *Arnold Bennett; a Biography* (Heinemann, 1952) and James Hall's *Arnold Bennett; Primitivism and Taste* (Seattle, Univ. of Washington Press, 1959). Of great personal interest is the correspondence in *Arnold Bennett and H. G. Wells; a Record of a Personal and a Literary Friendship*, ed. by Harris Wilson (Univ. of Illinois Press, 1960).

The best full-length critical studies of ROBERT BRIDGES are by F. Brett Young (Secker, 1914), Oliver Elton (O. U. P., 1932), and Albert J. Guérard, Jr. (Harvard U. P., 1942). A biography of Bridges was written by T. H. Warren (Clarendon, 1913). A specialized study is Elizabeth C. Wright's *Metaphor, Sound, and Meaning in Bridges' 'The Testament of Beauty'* (Univ. of Penna. Press, 1951). SAMUEL BUTLER's vivid account of his life in his fictionalized autobiography, *The Way of All Flesh,* is severely criticized in Mrs. R. S. Garnett's *Samuel Butler and His Family Relations* (Dutton, 1926). Criticism of Butler is to be found in C. E. M. Joad's *Samuel Butler* (Parsons, 1924), in the study by G. Cannan (Secker, 1915), and in works by R. F. Rattray (Duckworth, 1935), M. Muggeridge (Eyre and Spottiswoods, 1936), and Philip Henderson (London, Cohen & West, 1953). The definitive bibliography is Stanley B. Harkness' *The Career of Samuel Butler, 1835–1902* (London, Bódley Head, 1955). Important light is thrown on the difficult relations between Butler and his family in *The Family Letters of Samuel Butler, 1841–1886,* ed. by Arnold Silver (Cape, 1962). Recent studies include Philip Henderson's *Samuel Butler; the Incarnate Bachelor* (London, Cohen & West, 1953) and Joseph J. Jones's *The Cradle of Erewhon; Samuel Butler in New Zealand* (Texas U.P., 1959).

For a thorough understanding of GILBERT KEITH CHESTERTON, one should read first of all his *Autobiography* (Hutchinson, 1936), then the biographical and critical studies by H. Belloc, *On the Place of Gilbert Chesterton in English Letters* (Sheed and Ward, 1940), G. W. Bullett (Palmer, 1923), E. Cammaert, *The Laughing Prophet* (Methuen, 1937), J. West (Dodd, Mead, 1916), Hugh Kenner, *Paradox in Chesterton* (Sheed & Ward, 1947), Maisie Ward, *Gilbert Keith Chesterton* (Sheed & Ward, 1943, Maisie Ward, *Return to Chesterton* (Sheed & Ward, 1952), and Garry Wills, *Chesterton, Man and Mask* (Sheed & Ward, 1961).

JOSEPH CONRAD is another writer whose autobiography, *A Personal Record* (Harper, 1912), is the best source for the most significant facts of his life, but additional information may be found in the biographies by his wife—*Joseph Conrad as I Knew Him* (Doubleday, 1926) and *Joseph Conrad and His Circle* (Dutton, 1935)—and by G. Jean-Aubry (Doubleday, 1927), as well as in the studies by R. Curle: *Joseph Conrad* (Doubleday, 1914) and *Conrad to a Friend* (Doubleday, Doran, 1928). Another valuable early work is F. M. Ford's (Little, Brown, 1924). Of the many other excellent critical studies of Conrad's technique, one may recommend the following: E. Crankshaw, *Joseph Conrad, Some Aspects of the Art of the Novel* (Lane, 1936); R. L. Mégroz, *Joseph Conrad's Mind and Method* (Faber and Faber, 1931); R. M. Stauffer, *Joseph Conrad, His Romantic Realism* (Four Seas, 1922); and W. L. Cross, *Four Contemporary Novelists* (Macmillan, 1930). Later studies include Douglas Hewitt, *Conrad, a Reassessment* (Cambridge, Eng., Bowes, 1952); Oliver Warner, *Joseph Conrad* (Longmans, 1951); Paul L. Wiley, *Conrad's Measure of Man* (Wisconsin U. P., 1954); and Walter F. Wright, *Romance & Tragedy in Joseph Conrad* (Nebraska U. P., 1949). More recent studies of Conrad include Jerry Allen, *The Thunder and the Sunshine; a Biography of Joseph Conrad* (Putnam, 1958); Osborn Andreas, *Joseph Conrad; a Study in Non-conformity* (N. Y., Philosophical Library, 1959); Georges Jean-Aubry, *The Seadreamer; a Definitive Biography* (Doubleday, 1957); Jocelyn Baines, *Joseph Conrad; a Critical Biography* (Weidenfeld & Nicolson, 1960); Richard Curle, *Joseph Conrad and His Characters; a Study of Six Novels* (Heinemann, 1957); Adam Gillon, *The Eternal Solitary* (N. Y., Bookman Associates, 1960); Albert J. Guerard, *Conrad the Novelist* (Harvard U. P., 1960); Leo Gurko, *Joseph Conrad, Giant in Exile* (Macmillan, 1962); Robert F. Haugh, *Joseph Conrad; Discovery in Design* (Oklahoma U. P., 1957); Frederick R. Karl, *Reader's Guide to Joseph Conrad* (N. Y., Noonday,

1960); Kenneth Lohf and E. P. Sheehy, *Joseph Conrad at Mid-Century; Editions and Studies, 1895–1955* (Minnesota U. P., 1957); T. Colborn Moser, *Joseph Conrad; Achievement and Decline* (Harvard U. P., 1957); Robert W. Stallman, ed., *The Art of Joseph Conrad; a Critical Symposium* (Michigan State U. P., 1960); Edward H. Visiak, *The Mirror of Conrad* (London, Laurie, 1955); Morton D. Zabel, ed., *The Portable Conrad* (Viking, 1947). JOHN DAVIDSON has been all but forgotten by modern critics and biographers, partly because he himself wished to be forgotten. The only critical study from the early part of the century is that by H. Fineman (Univ. of Penna. Press, 1916); for other critical notices, one may refer to such books as H. Jackson's dealing with the 1890's. A recent study is James B. Townsend's *John Davidson, Poet of Armagedden* (Yale U. P., 1961). ERNEST DOWSON, reputedly the most "decadent" of the mauve-decade poets, may be seen in contrasting lights, favorable and unfavorable, shed by Frank Harris and A. R. Orage. Besides the essays by these two men, in *Contemporary Portraits* (2nd series, priv. prt., 1919) and in *Readers and Writers* (Knopf, 1922), respectively, there are critical comments by A. Symons in his *Studies in Prose and Verse* (Dent, 1904) and in his memoir in the edition of Dowson's *Poems* (Lane, 1905). The modern biography of Dowson is that of Mark Longaker (Univ. of Penna. Press, 1944). The best critical estimates of LORD DUNSANY are to be found in E. Boyd's works on Irish drama and in the two books on the Irish Theatre by U. Ellis-Fermor and L. Robinson (see above). An earlier critical study of some value is E. H. Bierstadt's *Dunsany the Dramatist* (Little, Brown, 1917). A recent study is Hazel Smith's *Lord Dunsany, King of Dreams* (N. Y., Exposition, 1959).

Aside from Havelock Ellis' *My Life* (Heinemann, 1940), there are early biographical and critical accounts of HAVELOCK ELLIS by I. Goldberg (Simon and Schuster, 1926) and H. Peterson (Houghton, 1928), but many other brief critiques have been written. Some of the best of these have been collected in a book of appreciative essays with a foreword by I. Goldberg (Oriole Press, 1929). Two recent biographies are by Arthur Calder-Marshall (Hart-Davis, 1959) and by John S. Collis (Sloane, 1959). Françoise Delisle's *Friendship's Odyssey* (Heinemann, 1946) is an indispensable account of his later personal life. ST. JOHN ERVINE'S work is discussed in all the books mentioned dealing with the Irish theatre and modern drama in general. Since no formal biography of Ervine has been written, the reader will profit most from his own reminiscences in *The Theatre in My Time* (Rich and Cowan, 1933). Good critical studies of JOHN GALSWORTHY are plentiful, but the best of them is probably that by E. Gupot (Didier, 1933). Among others may be mentioned those of H. Ould (Chapman and Hall, 1935); R. H. Coats (Scribner's, 1926); Joseph Conrad (*Last Essays*, Doubleday, 1926); and Sheila Kaye-Smith (Holt, 1916). H. V. Marrot's *Life and Letters* (Scribner's, 1935) is the latest and most authoritative biography of Galsworthy, but his wife's book, *Over the Hills and Far Away* (Hale, 1937) is a useful account of his life and travels. A valuable biographical study is Ralph H. Mottram's *For Some We Loved; an Intimate Portrait of Ada and John Galsworthy* (Hutchinson, 1956). Critical appraisals of WILFRID WILSON GIBSON are included in Conrad Aiken's *Scepticism* (Knopf, 1919); *Living Authors* (Wilson, 1931); Sir H. J. Newbolt's *New Paths on Helicon* (Nelson, 1927); and C. Williams, *Poetry at Present* (Clarendon, 1930). Gibson's *Collected Poems* were published in 1926 (Macmillan).

GEORGE GISSING is the subject of a fictionalized biography by Morley Roberts entitled *The Private Life of Henry Maitland* (Doran, 1912). Critical studies of his work have been written by F. Swinnerton (Secker, 1912); S. V. Gapp (Univ. of Penna. Press, 1936); R. C. Mc-Kay (Univ. of Penna. Press, 1933); Mabel Donnelly (Harvard U. P., 1954); and by Virginia Woolf in her introduction to a selected edition of his works edited by his son (Cape, 1929). The best criticism of HARLEY GRANVILLE-BARKER'S important contributions to modern dramaturgy may be found in J. E. Agate's *The Contemporary Theatre, 1923–1926* (Parsons, 1924-27), W. Archer's *The Old Drama and the New* (Dodd, Mead, 1926), D. L. Murray's *Scenes and Silhouettes* (Cape, 1926). Further appraisals worth noting are those in A. Duke's *The Youngest Drama* (Benn, 1923), St. John Ervine's *Theatre in My Time* (Rich and Cowan, 1933), and M. Ellehauge's *Striking Figures Among Modern English Dramatists* (Williams and Norgate, 1931). More recent studies are Margery M. Morgan's *A Drama of Political Man; a Study of the Plays of Harley Granville Barker* (Sedgwick & Jackson, 1961) and Charles B. Purdom's *Harley Granville Barker, Man of the Theater, Dramatist and Scholar* (Harvard U. P., 1956). The strong influence of LADY AUGUSTA GREGORY in the Irish Renaissance can be best seen in the appreciative observations of George Moore, in his *Hail and Farewell* (Appleton, 1911–14), and of W. B. Yeats, in his two books, *The Cutting of an Agate* and *Essays* (Macmillan, 1912, 1924). The first full length biography is Elizabeth Coxhead's *Lady Gregory; a Literary Portrait* (Macmillan, 1961).

WILLIAM ERNEST HENLEY'S biography has been written by L. C. Cornford (Houghton Mifflin, 1913), Jerome H. Buckley (Princeton

U. P., 1945), and John H. Robertson (Constable, 1949). Critical studies are few; perhaps the best of them is in A. Symons's *Studies in Two Literatures* (Smithers, 1897). Early studies of ALFRED EDWARD HOUSMAN are the sketch by A. S. F. Gow (C. U. P., 1936) and *A Buried Life, Personal Recollections of A. E. Housman*, by Percy Withers (Cape, 1940). The best biographies of Alfred Edward Housman are Lawrence Housman, *My Brother, A. E. Housman* (Scribner's, 1938); Maude M. Hawkins, *A. E. Housman, Man Behind a Mask* (Chicago, Regnery, 1958); Norman Marlow, *A. E. Housman, Scholar and Poet* (Routledge, 1958); Grant Richards, *Housman, 1897–1936* (O. U. P., 1941); George L. Watson, *A. E. Housman; a Divided Life* (Hart-Davis, 1957). The best bibliography is John Carter and John Sparrow, *A. E. Housman; an Annotated Hand-list* (Hart-Davis, 1952). For information concerning WILLIAM HENRY HUDSON, the reader may consult his autobiography, *Far Away and Long Ago* (Dent, 1918), and also Morley Roberts' *W. H. Hudson, a Portrait* (Dutton, 1924), H. C. Goddard's *W. H. Hudson, Bird-Man* (Dutton, 1928), Robert Hamilton's *W. H. Hudson, the Vision of Earth* (Dent, 1946), Richard E. Haymaker's *From Pampas to Hedgerows and Downs* (N. Y., Bookman Associates, 1954), and Ruth Tolamin, *W. H. Hudson* (N. Y., Philosophical Library, 1954).

Taking the Curtain Call (Macmillan, 1930), the biography of HENRY ARTHUR JONES, was written by his daughter, Doris A. Jones (Mrs. Thorne). The part played by Jones in the development of modern English drama is best seen in R. A. Cordell's critical study, *Henry Arthur Jones and the Modern Drama* (Long and Smith, 1932). Biographical details concerning RUDYARD KIPLING are available in his own notes, *Something of Myself* (Macmillan, 1937) and in such earlier works as R. T. Hopkins' *Rudyard Kipling, the Story of a Genius* (Palmer, 1930) and J. Palmer's *Rudyard Kipling* (Holt, 1915). For further criticism of his work one may consult R. Le Gallienne, *Rudyard Kipling* (Lane, 1900); G. MacMunn, *Rudyard Kipling, Craftsman* (Hale, 1937); W. M. Hart, *Kipling, the Story-Writer* (Univ. of Calif. Press, 1918); A. Munson, *Kipling's India* (Doubleday, 1915); and Hilton Brown (Harper, 1945). More recent studies are Charles E. Carrington's *The Life of Rudyard Kipling* (Doubleday, 1955 and Joyce M. S. Tomkins' *The Art of Rudyard Kipling* (Methuen, 1959). The standard bibliography is Florence V. Livingston's (N. Y., Wells, 1927; Supplement, Harvard U. P., 1938). No one, as yet, has attempted a biography of JOHN MASEFIELD, but there are several good critical studies, notably those of C. Biggane (Heffer, 1924), W. H. Hamilton

(Macmillan, 1922), G. O. Thomas (Macmillan, 1933), I. A. Williams (Chaundy, 1921), and Muriel Spark (London, Nevill, 1953). Useful also is *John Masefield, O. M., the Queen's Poet Laureate, a Bibliography and Eighty-first Birthday Tribute* (London, Cranbrook Tower Press, 1960), ed. Geoffrey Handley-Taylor. That the stature of GEORGE MOORE continues to grow with the passing years can be readily seen in such critical studies as C. Morgan's *Epitaph on George Moore* (Macmillan, 1935) and G. Goodwin's *Conversations with George Moore* (Knopf, 1930). Another excellent study is J. Freeman's *A Portrait of George Moore* (Laurie, 1922). Besides the authorized biography by J. M. Hone (Macmillan, 1936), studies of Moore have been written by S. L. Mitchell (Dodd, Mead, 1916), I. A. Williams (Chaundy, 1921), and H. Wolfe (Butterworth, 1933, rev. ed.). The student, however, should not overlook Moore's own vastly entertaining book of reminiscences, *Hail and Farewell* (Appleton, 1911–14), a masterpiece of autobiography. More recent discussions are Malcolm J. Brown's *George Moore; a Reconsideration* (Univ. of Washington Press, 1955), Georges P. Collet's *George Moore et la France* (Geneva, Droz, 1957), and Nancy Cunard's *G. M.; Memories of George Moore* (Hart-Davis, 1956). Among the earlier critical studies of STEPHEN PHILLIPS one may consult the essays in E. E. Hale's *Dramatists of Today* (6th ed. rev., Holt, 1911), W. Archer's *Real Conversations* (Heinemann, 1904), A. Symons's *Studies in Prose and Verse* (Dent, 1904), and C. Kernahan's *In Good Company* (Lane, 1917). These should be carefully compared, however, with later estimates such as may be found in A. Nicoll's *British Drama*. Like Jones and Phillips, SIR ARTHUR WING PINERO is another Edwardian dramatist whose extraordinary life-time reputation has wilted. Criticism of his work may be found in J. W. Cunliffe's *Modern English Playwrights* (Harper, 1927); St. J. Ervine's *Theatre in My Time* (Rich and Cowan, 1933); and in C. Hamilton's edition of *The Social Plays of Arthur Wing Pinero* (Dutton, 1917–22). Fuller biographical treatment is available in two books by H. H. Fyfe: *Arthur Wing Pinero, Playwright* (Greening, 1902) and *Sir Arthur Pinero's Plays and Players* (Benn, 1930), and in Wilbur D. Dunkel, *Sir Arthur Pinero; a Critical Biography with Letters* (Chicago U. P., 1941).

GEORGE BERNARD SHAW, the greatest of the Edwardians, has been many things to many men. To see how variously he has affected his contemporaries, one has only to compare the somewhat adulatory authorized biography by A. Henderson, *George Bernard Shaw, His Life and Works* (Boni and Liveright, 1918) with those by F. Harris (Garden City,

1931), A. G. Crouch (Cleaver, 1932), and Hesketh Pearson (Harper, 1942). H. L. Stewart has exposed his *Puritanism* (Royal Soc. of Canada, 1931); A. Brinser has discussed his *Respectability* (Harvard U. P., 1931); M. Colbourne has presented *The Real Bernard Shaw* (Dent, 1939); and B. De Casseres has even attempted to lay bare his *Anatomy* (Newton, 1930). Besides these analyses, which barely graze the surface of controversial and critical dicta that Shaw's iconoclastic temperament has evoked, one may profitably consult such earlier works as G. K. Chesterton's *George Bernard Shaw*, a sympathetic introduction to the man's ideas and early works (John Lane, 1909); R. Burton's *Bernard Shaw, the Man and the Mask* (Holt, 1916); R. M. Deacon's *Bernard Shaw as Artist-Philosopher* (Lane, 1910); A. F. Hamon's *The Twentieth Century Molière* (Allen and Unwin, 1915); H. C. Duffin's *The Quintessence of Bernard Shaw* (Allen and Unwin, 1920). Two further studies that should be mentioned are M. Ellehauge's *The Position of Bernard Shaw in European Drama and Philosophy* (Williams and Norgate, 1931), and R. F. Rattray's *Bernard Shaw, a Chronicle and an Introduction* (Duckworth, 1934). The celebration of Shaw's ninetieth birthday in 1946 and his death in 1950 provoked another outburst of works: biographical: *G. B. S. 90* (Hutchinson, 1946); Blanche Patch, *Thirty Years with G. B. S.* (Dodd, Mead, 1951); Hesketh Pearson, *G. B. S., A Postscript* (Harper, 1950); Robert F. Rattray, *Bernard Shaw, a Chronicle* (London, Dobson, 1950); Stephen Winsten, *Days with Bernard Shaw* (Hutchinson, 1948); Stephen Winsten, *Shaw's Corner* (Hutchinson, 1952), and critical: Eric Bentley, *Bernard Shaw* (New Directing, 1947); William Irvine, *The Universe of G. B. S.* (N. Y., Whittlesey House, 1949); C. E. D. Joad, *Shaw* (Gollancz, 1949); Desmond McCarthy, *Shaw's Plays in Review* (N. Y., Thames & Hudson, 1951); A. H. Nethercot, *Men and Supermen* (Harvard U. P., 1954); A. C. Ward, *Bernard Shaw* (Longmans, 1951). More recent studies include Allan Chappelow, ed., *Shaw the Villager and Human Being; a Biographical Symposium* (London, Skilton, 1961); St. John Ervine, *Bernard Shaw, his Life, Work and Friends* (Constable, 1956); Archibald Henderson, *George Bernard Shaw, Man of the Century* (Appleton, 1956); Julian B. Kaye, *Bernard Shaw and the Nineteenth-Century Tradition* (Oklahoma U. P., 1958); Louis Kronenberger, *George Bernard Shaw; a Critical Survey* (Cleveland, World, 1953) Raymond Mander, *Theatrical Companion to Shaw; a Pictorial Record of the First Performances of the Plays* (Rockliff, 1954); Louis Simon, *Shaw on Education* (Columbia U. P., 1958).

There is no biography of JAMES STEPHENS, but critical estimates of his work may be found both in the books listed above dealing with the Irish Renaissance and in essays in the following: G. W. Russell's *Imaginations and Reveries* (Macmillan, 1916), T. Spicer-Simpson's *Men of Letters of the British Isles* (Rudge, 1924), and N. J. O'Conor's *Changing Ireland* (Harvard U. P., 1924). The most extensive work is Birgit Bramsbäck's *James Stephens; a Literary and Bibliographical Study* (Harvard U. P., 1959). Among the numerous biographies of ROBERT LOUIS STEVENSON, those deserving special notice are the lives by G. Balfour (Scribner's, 1901) and R. Masson (Chambers, 1922); J. A. Steuart's *Robert Louis Stevenson* (Little, Brown, 1924), which includes much matter previously ignored or minimized; J. A. Smith's *R. L. Stevenson* (Duckworth, 1937); and S. Gwynn's *Robert Louis Stevenson* (Macmillan, 1939). One may also recommend the critical studies by F. Swinnerton (Secker, 1914) and R. A. Rice (Bobbs-Merrill, 1916). Later biographies and critical studies include: David Daiches, *R. L. S.* (Norfolk, Conn., New Directions, 1947; Malcolm Elwin, *The Strange Case of R. L. S.* (London: Macdonald, 1950); Anne Fisher, *No More a Stranger* (Stanford U. P., 1946); J. C. Furnas, *Voyage to Windward* (N. Y., Sloane, 1951); Laura L. Hinckley, *The Stevensons, Louis & Fanny* (N. Y., Hastings House, 1950); Richard Aldington, *Portrait of a Rebel; the Life and Work of Robert Louis Stevenson* (London, Evans, 1957); Elise Caldwell, *Last Witness for Robert Louis Stevenson* (Oklahoma U. P., 1960); Anne Issler, *Happier for his Presence; San Francisco and Robert Louis Stevenson* (Stanford U. P., 1949); Anne Issler, *Our Mountain Heritage; Silverado and Robert Louis Stevenson* (Stanford U. P., 1950); Sister Martha M. McGaw, *Stevenson in Hawaii* (Univ. of Hawaii Press, 1950); Moray McLaren, *Stevenson and Edinburgh; a Centenary Study* (Chapman and Hall, 1950).

JOHN MILLINGTON SYNGE was so closely associated with the Irish Renaissance that he is best seen against the background of that movement in such works as M. Bourgeois, *John Millington Synge and the Irish Theatre* (Constable, 1913), F. Bickley's *J. M. Synge and the Irish Dramatic Movement* (Houghton Mifflin, 1912), and the other more general works dealing with the Irish theatre. Further biographical and critical accounts may be found in J. Masefield's *John M. Synge, a Few Personal Recollections* (Macmillan, 1915); P. P. Howe's critical study (Secker, 1912), and in essays by W. B. Yeats, in *The Cutting of an Agate* (Macmillan, 1912); by Lady Gregory, in *Our Irish Theatre* (Putman, 1913); and by L. R. Morris, in *The Celtic Dawn* (Macmillan, 1917); Daniel Corkery, *Synge and Anglo-Irish Literature* (Cork

U. P., 1931); David H. Greene and E. M. Stephens, *J. M. Synge, 1871–1909* (Macmillan, 1959); and Alan Price, *Synge and Anglo-Irish Drama* (Methuen, 1961). The standard biography of FRANCIS THOMPSON is by Everard Meynell (Scribner's, 1913), but additional biographical facts concerning him may be gleaned from Viola Meynell's life of her mother, *Alice Meynell* (Scribner's, 1929), and also from R. L. Mégroz's critical study, *Francis Thompson, the Poet of Earth in Heaven* (Scribner's, 1927). The student will also find useful Viola Meynell's *Francis Thompson and Wilfrid Meynell; a Memoir* (Dutton, 1953), John C. Reid's *Francis Thompson, Man and Poet* (Routledge, 1959), and Paul van K. Thomson's *Francis Thompson: a Critical Biography* (Nelson, 1961). The most recent account of SIR WILLIAM WATSON is in W. B. Yeats's *Letters to the New Island* (Harvard U. P., 1934). Earlier estimates may be found in L. E. Gates's *Studies and Appreciations* (Macmillan, 1900); J. C. Squire's *Books Reviewed* (Doran, 1922); and in J. C. Collins's *Studies in Poetry and Criticism* (Bell, 1905).

HERBERT GEORGE WELLS excites fewer responses nowadays than at the time when parodists and divines made him the subject of their most solemn efforts. The student will find widely varied accounts of him in J. D. Beresford's life (Holt, 1915), V. W. Brooks's *The World of H. G. Wells* (Kennerley, 1915), W. Archer's *God and Mr. Wells* (Knopf, 1917), I. J. Brown's *H. G. Wells* (Holt, 1923), R. T. Hopkins's *H. G. Wells: Personality, Character, Topography* (Palmer, 1922), J. S. Price's *The World in the Wellsian Era* (Stacy Hall, 1923) Antonina Vallentin's *H. G. Wells, Prophet of our Day* (John Day, 1950), Vincent Brome's *H. G. Wells, a Biography* (Longmans, 1951). Norman Nicholson's *H. G. Wells* (London, Barker, 1950); W. Warren Wagar's *H. G. Wells and the World State* (Yale U. P., 1961); Bernard Bergonzi's *The Early H. G. Wells; a Study of the Scientific Romances* (Manchester U. P., 1961). Lives of OSCAR WILDE have been written by L. C. Ingleby (Appleton, 1908), R. H. Sherard (Dodd, Mead, 1928), and F. Harris (Constable, 1938). A. Ransome's study, *Oscar Wilde* (Methuen, 1913) and those by B. Brasol (Scribner's, 1938) and A. Symons (Sawyer, 1930) are the most notable of several early ones. Since Frances Winwar's *Oscar Wilde and the Yellow Nineties* (Harper, 1940), a number of important studies have appeared: James E. Agate, *Oscar Wilde & the Theatre* (London, Curtain Press, 1947); Patrick Byrne, *The Wildes of Merrion Square* (London, Staples Press, 1953); St. John Ervine, *Oscar Wilde, a Present Time Appraisal* (Allen, 1951); Hesketh Pearson, *Oscar Wilde, His Life and Wit* (Harper,

1946); George Woodcock, *The Paradox of Oscar Wilde* (London, Boardman, 1949). The bitter aftermath of Wilde's tragedy is recounted in Vyvyan Holland's *Son of Oscar Wilde* (London, Hart-Davis, 1954). More recent studies include Frank Brennand, *Oscar Wilde* (London, Landsborough, 1960); Lewis Broad, *The Friendships & Follies of Oscar Wilde* (Hutchinson, 1954); Vyvyan Holland, *Oscar Wilde; a Pictorial Biography* (London, Thames and Hudson, 1960); *The Letters of Oscar Wilde*, ed. by Rupert Hart-Davis (Hart-Davis, 1962).

Among the earlier biographical and critical works on WILLIAM BUTLER YEATS may be mentioned those of J. M. Hone (Maunsel, 1916), F. Reid (Secker, 1915), C. L. Wrenn (Murby, 1920), and H. S. Krans (McClure, Phillips, 1904). More lately, many important studies appeared; those deserving special mention include H. M. Green's *The Poetry of W. B. Yeats* (Australian Eng. Assoc., 1931), *The Poetry of W. B. Yeats* (O. U. P., 1941) by L. Macneice, and J. H. Pollock's *William Butler Yeats* (Duckworth, 1935). *Letters on Poetry from W. B. Yeats to Dorothy Wellesley* came from the O. U. P. in 1940. Tributes to the memory of W. B. Yeats, ed. by Stephen Gwynn, *Scattering Branches,* appeared in 1940 (Macmillan). The authorized biography of Yeats is by J. M. Hone (Macmillan, 1943). Later important critical studies of Yeats include Richard Ellman, *Yeats, the Man & the Masks* (Macmillan, 1948); James Hall, ed., *The Permanence of Yeats* (Macmillan, 1950); Thomas R. Henn, *The Lonely Tower* (Methuen, 1950); Alexander N. Jeffares, *W. B. Yeats, Man & Poet* (Routledge, 1949); Vivienne Koch, *W. B. Yeats, the Tragic Phase* (Routledge, 1951); Virginia Moore, *The Unicorn, W. B. Yeats' Search for Reality* (Macmillan, 1954); Thomas F. Parkinson, *W. B. Yeats, Self-Critic* (U. of California Press, 1951); Margaret Rudd, *Divided Image, a Study of William Blake and W. B. Yeats* (Routledge, 1953); Donald A. Stauffer, *The Golden Nightingale* (Macmillan, 1949); Peter Ure, *Towards a Mythology* (Hodder & Stoughton, 1946). More recent studies include Hazard Adams, *Blake and Yeats; the Contrary Vision* (Cornell U. P., 1955); Richard Ellman, *The Identity of Yeats* (O. U. P., 1954); Monk Gibbon, *The Masterpiece and the Man; Yeats as I Knew Him* (Hart-Davis, 1959); D. J. Gordon and Ian Fletcher, eds., *W. B. Yeats; Images of a Poet* (Manchester U. P., 1961); Georgio Melchiori, *The Whole Mystery of Art; Pattern into Poetry in the Work of W. B. Yeats* (Routledge, 1960); V. K. N. Nenon, *The Development of William Butler Yeats,* 2nd rev. ed., (Oliver & Boyd, 1960); Benjamin L. Reed, *William Butler Yeats; the Lyric of Tragedy* (Oklahoma U. P., 1961); George B. Saul, *Prologomena to the Study of*

Yeats's Poems (Pennsylvania U. P., 1957); Amy G. Stock, *W. B. Yeats: his Poetry and Thought* (Cambridge U. P., 1961); John Unterecker, *A Reader's Guide to W. B. Yeats* (N. Y., Noonday, 1959); Francis A. C. Wilson, *W. B. Yeats and Tradition* (Gollancz, 1958); F. A. C. Wilson, *Yeats's Iconography* (Gollancz, 1960).

CHAPTER XVII

GENERAL WORKS

Certain of the general works cited in the preceding bibliography should be consulted for the period since 1914. In addition, a number of works dealing primarily with the twentieth century will prove valuable. For succinct critical surveys and bibliographies of authors, the student may be referred to Millett, Manly, and Rickert's *Contemporary British Literature* (Harcourt, 1935), Edwin Muir's *The Present Age from 1914* (Cresset, 1939), and David Daiches' *The Present Age in British Literature* (Indiana U. P., 1958). Mark Longaker and Edwin C. Bolles's *Contemporary English Literature* (Appleton-Century-Crofts, 1953), R. A. Scott-James's *Fifty Years of English Literature, 1900–1950, with A Postcript, 1951–1955* (Longmans, 1957), and A. C. Ward's *Twentieth-Century Literature, 1901–1950* (Barnes and Noble, 1957) are useful introductory manuals. More specialized studies are William Y. Tindall's *Forces in Modern English Literature, 1885–1946* (Knopf, 1947), B. I. Evans' *English Literature Between The Wars* (Methuen, 1948), Jacob Isaacs', *An Assessment of Twentieth-Century Literature* (Secker & Warburg, 1951), Kenneth Allsop's *The Angry Decade: a Survey of the Cultural Revolt of the Nineteen-fifties* (London, Owen, 1958), and Graham Hough's *Image and Experience: Studies in a Literary Revolution* (Duckworth, 1960).

For studies of the novel, the reader is referred to David Daiches, *The Novel and the Modern World*, rev. ed. (Chicago U. P., 1960), Leon Edel, *The Psychological Novel, 1900–1950* (Lippincott, 1955), W. C. Frierson, *The English Novel in Transition* (Oklahoma, 1942), James Gindon, *Postwar British Fiction; New Accents and Attitudes* (Univ. of Cal. Press, 1962), D. M. Hoare, *Some Studies of the Modern Novel,* (Chatto & Windus, 1939), Frederick R. Karl, *The Contemporary English Novel* (Farrar, Straus, and Cudahy, 1962), Arnold Kettle, *An Introduction to the English Novel II: Henry James to the Present Day* (Hutchinson, 1953), Frank O'Connor, *The Mirror in the Roadway, A Study of the Modern Novel* (Knopf, 1956), Sean O'Faolain, *The Vanishing Hero: Studies in the Novelists of the Twenties*

(Eyre and Spottiswoode, 1956), and Mark Schorer, ed., *Modern British Fiction: Essays in Criticism* (O. U. P., 1961).

For studies of the drama, the student may consult Una M. Ellis-Fermer, *The Irish Dramatic Movement*, rev. ed. (Methuen, 1954), Martin Esslin, *The Theater of the Absurd* (Doubleday, 1961), Bamber Gascoigne, *Twentieth-Century Drama* (Hutchinson, 1962), Lynton A. Hudson, *The Twentieth-Century Drama* (Harrap, 1946), Lawrence Kitchin, *Mid-Century Drama* (Faber, 1960), Frederick Lumley, *Trends in 20th Century Drama*, rev. ed. (Fairlawn, N. J., Essential Books, 1960), Lennox Robinson, *Ireland's Abbey Theater, 1899–1951* (Sidgwick and Jackson, 1951), John R. Taylor, *The Angry Theatre: New British Drama* (Hill and Wang, 1962), and John C. Trewin, *Dramatists of Today* (London, Staples, 1953).

For studies of modern poets, the student is referred to Alfred Alvarez, *Stewards of Excellence* (Scribner's, 1958), David Daiches, *Poetry and the Modern World* (Chicago U. P., 1940) Elizabeth Drew and J. L. Sweeney, *Directions in Modern Poetry* (Norton, 1940), George S. Fraser, *Vision and Rhetoric: Studies in Modern Poetry* (Faber, 1959), F. R. Leavis, *New Bearings in English Poetry,* new ed. (Univ. of Michigan press, 1960), Vivian de S. Pinto, *Crisis in English Poetry, 1880–1940* (Hutchinson, 1951), J. G. Southworth, *Sowing the Spring, Studies in British Poets from Hopkins to MacNeice* (Blackwell, 1940), Francis Scarfe, *Auden and After* (Routledge 1942), and Anthony Thwaite, *Contemporary English Poetry* (Dufour, 1961).

INDIVIDUAL WRITERS

For very few twentieth-century writers are full-length biographical or critical studies available, but below are listed without comment the most important autobiographical, biographical, or critical works.

RICHARD ALDINGTON. Autobiographical: *Life for Life's Sake* (Viking Press, 1941); critical: T. McGreevy, *Richard Aldington, an Englishman* (Chatto and Windus, 1931).

W. H. AUDEN. Critical: Joseph W. Beach, *The Making of the Auden Canon: Revisions and Eliminations in the Collected Poetry* (Minnesota U. P., 1957), Edward Callan, *Annotated Check List of the Works* (Swallow, 1958); Richard Hoggart, *Auden, an Introductory Essay* (Chatto & Windus, 1951); Francis Scarfe, *W. H. Auden* (Monaco, Lyrebird, 1949).

SAMUEL BECKETT. Critical: Ruby Cohn, *Samuel Beckett; The Comic Gamut* (Rutgers U. P., 1962); Frederick J. Hoffman, *Samuel Beckett;*

the Language of Self (Southern Ill. U. P., 1962); Hugh Kenner, *Samuel Beckett,* A Critical Study (Grove, 1961).

ELIZABETH BOWEN. Critical: William W. Heath, *Elizabeth Bowen; an Introduction to her Novels* (Wisconsin U. P., 1961).

JAMES BRIDIE. Critical: Winifred Bannister, *James Bridie and his Theatre* (London, Rockliff, 1955).

RUPERT BROOKE. Geoffrey Keynes, *A Bibliography of Rupert Brooke,* 2nd rev. ed. (Hart-Davis, 1959); biographical: Arthur Stringer, *Red Wine of Youth, a Life* (Bobbs-Merrill, 1948).

I. COMPTON-BURNETT. Critical: Robert Liddell, *The Novels of I. Compton-Burnett* (Gollancz, 1955).

NOEL COWARD. Autobiographical: *Present Indicative* (Doubleday, 1937); *Future Indefinite* (Doubleday, 1954); Critical: P. Braybrooke, *The Amazing Mr. Noel Coward* (Archer, 1933); Robert Greacen, *The Art of Noel Coward* (Hand and Flower Press, 1953); Raymond Mander, *Theatrical Companion to Coward; a Pictorial Record* (Rockliff, 1957).

W. H. DAVIES. Autobiographical. *The Autobiography of a Super-Tramp* (Fifield, 1908); critical: T. Moult, *W. H. Davies* (Butterworth, 1934).

WALTER DE LA MARE, Biographical: Walter R. Brain, *Tea with Walter de la Mare* (Faber, 1957); Critical: Leonard Clark, *Walter de La Mare* (Bodley Head, 1960).

LAWRENCE DURRELL. Robert A. Potter and Brooke Whitings, *Lawrence Durrell: A Checklist* (UCLA, 1961); biographical: Alfred Perlès, *My Friend Lawrence Durrell, an Intimate Memoir* (Northwood, Scorpian, 1961); critical: Harry T. Moore, ed., *The World of Lawrence Durrell* (Southern Ill. U. P., 1962).

T. S. ELIOT, Biographical: Richard March and Tambimutti, eds., *T. S. Eliot; A Symposium* (Editions Poetry London, 1948); critical: L. Grundin, *Mr. Eliot Among the Nightingales* (Drake, 1932); T. McGreevy, *Thomas Stearns Eliot, a Study* (Chatto and Windus, 1931); F. O. Matthiessen, *The Achievement of T. S. Eliot, an Essay on the Nature of Poetry* (Houghton Mifflin, 1935, rev. ed., O. U. P., 1947); A. Oras, *The Critical Ideas of T. S. Eliot* (Mattiesen, 1932); H. R. Williamson, *The Poetry of T. S. Eliot* (Hodder and Stoughton, 1932). Later studies include Elizabeth Drew, *T. S. Eliot, the Design of his Poetry* (Scribner's, 1949); D. C. Gallup, *T. S. Eliot, a Bibliography* (Yale U. P., 1952); Helen Gardner, *The Art of T. S. Eliot* (London, Cresset Press, 1949); D. E. S. Maxwell, *The Poetry of T. S. Eliot* (Routledge, 1952); Leonard Unger, ed., *T. S. Eliot, a Selected Critique* (Rinehart, 1948); George Williamson, *A Reader's Guide to T. S.*

Eliot (N. Y., Noonday Press, 1953); Neville Braybrooke, ed., *T. S. Eliot; A Symposium for his Seventieth Birthday* (Farrar, *et al.*, 1958); David E. Jones, *The Plays of T. S. Eliot* (Toronto U. P., 1960); Hugh Kenner, *The Invisible Poet: T. S. Eliot* (McDowell, Obolensky, 1959); Hugh Kenner, ed., *T. S. Eliot; a Collection of Critical Essays* (Prentice-Hall, 1962); Sean Lucy, *T. S. Eliot and the Idea of Tradition* (Cohen & West, 1960); Grover C. Smith, *T. S. Eliot's Poetry and Plays, a Study in Sources and Meaning* (Chicago U. P., 1956).

E. M. FORSTER. Critical: R. Macaulay, *The Writings of E. M. Forster* (Longmans, 1938); Lionel Trilling, *E. M. Forster* (Norfolk, Conn., New Directions, 1943); J. B. Beer, *The Achievement of E. M. Forster* (Chatto & Windus, 1962); Frederick C. Crews, *E. M. Forster; the Perils of Humanism* (Princeton U. P., 1962); K. W. Gransden, *E. M. Forster* (Oliver & Boyd, 1962); James McConkey, *The Novels of E. M. Forster* (Cornell U. P., 1957).

CHRISTOPHER FRY. Critical: Derek Stanford, *Christopher Fry* (London, Nevill, 1951).

ROBERT GRAVES. Autobiographical: *But it Still Goes On, an Accumulation* (Cape, 1930); *Good-bye to All That, an Autobiography* (Cape, 1929); critical: John M. Cohen, *Robert Graves* (Oliver & Boyd, 1960).

HENRY GREEN. Critical: John D. Russell, *Henry Green; Nine Novels and an Unpacked Bag* (Rutgers U. P., 1960); Edward Stokes, *The Novels of Henry Green* (Hogarth, 1959); Andrew K. Weatherhead, *A Reading of Henry Green* (Univ. of Washington P., 1961).

GRAHAM GREENE. Kenneth Allott and Miriam Farris, *The Art of Graham Greene* (Hamilton, 1951); John Atkins, *Graham Greene* (London, Calder, 1957); Francis L. Kunkel, *The Labyrinthine Ways of Graham Greene* (Sheed & Ward, 1959); Marie B. Mesnet, *Graham Greene and the Heart of the Matter* (London, Cresset, 1954).

GERARD MANLEY HOPKINS. Autobiographical: *The Correspondence of Gerard Manley Hopkins and Richard Watson Dixon*, ed. by Claude Colleer Abbott (O. U. P., 1935); *Further Letters of Gerard Manley Hopkins including his Correspondence with Coventry Patmore*, ed. by Claude Colleer Abbott (O. U. P., 1938); *The Letters of Gerard Manley Hopkins to Robert Bridges*, ed. by Claude Colleer Abbott (O. U. P., 1935); *The Note-books and Papers of Gerard Manley Hopkins*, ed. by Humphry House (O. U. P., 1937); *Journals and Papers*, ed. by Humphrey House and Graham Storey (O. U. P., 1959); *Sermons and Devotional Writings*, ed. by Christopher Devlin (O. U. P., 1959); *Robert Bridges and Gerard Hopkins, 1863–1889, a Literary Friendship,* ed. by Jean G. Ritz (O. U. P., 1960); critical; G. F. Lahey, *Gerard Manley Hopkins* (O. U. P., 1930); E. E. Phare, *The Poetry of Gerard Manley Hopkins, a Survey and Commentary* (C. U. P., 1933). Later studies include William Gardner, *Gerard Manley Hopkins* (2 vols., Secker & Warburg, 1948, 1949); The Kenyon Critics, *Gerard Manley Hopkins* (Norfolk, Conn., New Directions, 1945); Wilhelmus Peters, *Gerard Manley Hopkins, a Critical Essay* (O. U. P., 1948); Eleanor Ruggles, *Gerard Manley Hopkins, a Life* (Norton, 1944); Norman Weygand, ed., *Immortal Diamond* (Sheed & Ward, 1949); Robert Boyle, *Metaphor in Hopkins* (North Carolina U. P., 1961); David A. Downes, *Gerard Manley Hopkins; a Study of his Ignatian Spirit* (N. Y., Bookman, 1959); Alan Heuser, *The Shaping Vision of Gerard Manley Hopkins* (O. U. P., 1958); Sister Marcella M. Holloway, *The Prosodic Theory of Gerard Manley Hopkins* (Catholic U. P., 1947); John Pick, *Gerard Manley Hopkins, Priest and Poet* (O. U. P., 1942).

ALDOUS HUXLEY. Critical: A Henderson, *Aldous Huxley* (Chatto and Windus, 1935); G. Vann, *On Being Human: St. Thomas and Mr. Aldous Huxley* (Sheed and Ward, 1933); John Atkins, *Aldous Huxley; a Literary Study* (London, Calder, 1956); Shishir K. Ghose, *Aldous Huxley, a Cynical Salvationist* (London, Asia, 1962).

JAMES JOYCE. Biographical: F. Budgen, *James Joyce and the Making of "Ulysses"* (Grayson, 1935); H. S. Gorman, *James Joyce* (Farrar and Rinehart, 1939); H. S. Gorman, *James Joyce, His First Forty Years* (Huebsch, 1925); Mary and Padraic Colum, *Our Friend James Joyce* (Doubleday, 1958); .Richard Ellman, *James Joyce* (O. U. P. 1959), the definitive biography; Herbert Gorman, *James Joyce* (Rinehart, 1948); Stanislaus Joyce, *My Brother's Keeper; James Joyce's Early Years,* ed. by R. Ellman (Viking, 1958); *The Dublin Diary of Stanislaus Joyce,* ed. by George H. Healey (Cornell U. P., 1962); critical: C. Duff, *James Joyce and the Plain Reader, an Essay* (Harmsworth, 1932); L. Golding, *James Joyce* (Butterworth, 1933); Harry Levin, *James Joyce; a Critical Introduction,* rev. enl. ed, (New Directions, 1960). Other studies include Joseph Campbell and Henry M. Robinson, *A Skeleton Key to Finnegans Wake* (Harcourt, 1944); Stuart Gilbert, *James Joyce's Ulysses, a Study* (Faber, 1952); Sean Givens, ed., *James Joyce, Two Decades of Criticism* (N. Y., Vanguard, 1948); Patricia Hutchins, *James Joyce's Dublin* (London, Grey Walls Press, 1950); R. M. Kain, *Fabulous Voyager* (U. of Chicago Press, 1947); Rolf Loehrich, *The Secret of Ulysses* (McHenry, Ill., Compass Press, 1953); Alan Parker, *James Joyce* (Boston, Faxon, 1948); John J. Slocum, *A Bibliography of James Joyce* (Yale U. P., 1953); Leonard A. Strong,

The Sacred River (Methuen, 1949); William Tindall, *James Joyce, his Way of Interpreting the Modern World* (Scribner's, 1950); Robert M. Adams, *Surface and Symbol; the Consistency of James Joyce's Ulysses* (O. U. P., 1963); James S. Atherton, *The Books at the Wake, a Study of Literary Allusions in James Joyce's Finnegans Wake* (Faber, 1959); Frances Bolderoff, *Reading Finnegans Wake* (Woodward, Pa., Classic Non-fiction Library, 1959); Thomas E. Connelly, ed., *Joyce's Portrait: Criticisms and Critiques* (Appleton-Century-Crofts, 1962); Adeline Glasheen, *A Census of Finnegans Wake, an Index of the Characters and their Roles* (Northwestern U. P., 1956); S. L. Goldberg, *The Classical Temper; a Study of James Joyce's Ulysses* (Chatto & Windus, 1961); Patricia Hutchins, *James Joyce's World* (Methuen, 1957); William P. Jones, *James Joyce and the Common Reader* (Oklahoma U. P., 1955); R. M. Kain, *Dublin in the Age of William Butler Yeats and James Joyce* (Univ. of Oklahoma Press, 1962); Hugh Kenner, *Dublin's Joyce* (Chatto & Windus, 1955); A. Walton Litz, *The Art of James Joyce; Method and Design in Ulysses and Finnegans Wake* (Oxford U. P., 1961); Marvin Magalener, *Time of Apprenticeship; the Fiction of Young James Joyce* (London; Abelard-Schumann, 1959); M. Magalener, ed., *A James Joyce Miscellany, Second Series* (U. of Southern Ill. Press, 1959); M. Magalener, ed., *A James Joyce Miscellany, Third Series* (U. of Southern Ill. Press, 1962); Marvin Magalener and Richard M. Kain, eds., *Joyce, the Man, the Work, the Reputation* (New York U. P., 1956); J. Mitchell Morse, *The Sympathetic Alien; James Joyce and Catholicism* (New York U. P., 1959); Wm. T. Noon, *Joyce and Aquinas* (Yale U. P., 1957); Wm. E. Norris and Clifford A. Nault, eds., *Portraits of an Artist; a Case Book* (Odyssey, 1962); Wm. M. Schutte, *Joyce and Shakespeare; a Study in the Meaning of Ulysses* (Yale U. P., 1957); Wm. V. Tindall, *A Reader's Guide to James Joyce* (Noonday, 1959).

D. H. LAWRENCE. Biographical: D. Brett, *Lawrence and Brett, a Friendship* (Lippincott, 1933); C. R. Carswell, *The Savage Pilgrimage, a Narrative of D. H. Lawrence* (Chatto and Windus, 1932); *D. H. Lawrence, a Personal Record* by E. T. (Cape, 1935); A. Fabre-Luce, *La Vie de D. H. Lawrence* (Grasset, 1935); Frieda Lawrence, *Not I, but the Wind* (Rydal Press, 1934); H. Kingsmill, *The Life of D. H. Lawrence* (Dodge, 1938); K. Merrild, *A Poet and Two Painters, a Memoir* (Routledge, 1938); J. M. Murry, *Reminiscences of D. H. Lawrence* (Cape, 1933); J. M. Murry, *Son of Woman, the Story of D. H. Lawrence* (Cape, 1931); *Frieda Lawrence; Memoirs and Correspondence*, ed. by E. W. Tedlock (Heinemann, 1961); Harry T. Moore, ed.,

The Collected Letters of D. H. Lawrence (Heinemann, 1962); *D. H. Lawrence, a Composite Biography*, gathered, arranged, and edited by Edward Nehls, 3 vols., (Wisconsin U. P., 1957–1959); critical: R. Aldington, *D. H. Lawrence* (Chatto and Windus, 1930); F. Carter, *D. H. Lawrence and the Body Mystical* (Archer, 1932); H. Corke, *Lawrence and Apocalypse* (Heinemann, 1933); H. Gregory, *Pilgrim of the Apocalypse, a Critical Study of D. H. Lawrence* (Viking Press, 1933); A. Nin, *D. H. Lawrence, an Unprofessional Study* (Titus, 1932); S. Potter, *D. H. Lawrence, a First Study* (Cape, 1930); P. de Reul, *L'œuvre de D. H. Lawrence* (Vrin, 1937); E. A. Seillière, *David-Herbert Lawrence et les Récentes Idéologies Allemandes* (Boivin 1936); W. Y. Tindall, *D. H. Lawrence and Susan His Cow* (Columbia U. P., 1939). Later studies include Richard Aldington, *D. H. Lawrence, Portrait of a Genius, But—*(Duell, Sloan, & Pearce, 1950); Witter Bynner, *Journey with Genius* (John Day, 1951); Eliot Fay, *Lorenzo in Search of the Sun* (N. Y., Bookman Associates, 1953); Frederick Hoffman and Harry T. Moore, eds., *The Achievement of D. H. Lawrence* (Oklahoma, U. P., 1953), Harry T. Moore, *The Life & Works of D. H. Lawrence* (N. Y., Twayne, 1951); Harry T. Moore, *The Intelligent Heart* (Farrar, Straus, and Young, 1954); Father William Tiverton, *D. H. Lawrence & Human Existence* (London, Rockliff, 1951); Anthony West, *D. H. Lawrence* (London, Barker, 1950); Armin Arnold, *D. H. Lawrence and America* (London, Linden, 1958); Anthony Beal, *D. H. Lawrence* (Oliver & Boyd, 1961); Graham Hough, *The Dark Sun; A Study of D. H. Lawrence* (Duckworth, 1956); Dallas Kenmare, *Fire-bird; a Study of D. H. Lawrence* (London, Barrie, 1951); F. R. Leavis, *D. H. Lawrence, Novelist* (Chatto & Windus, 1955); C. H. Rolph, ed., *The Trial of Lady Chatterley; Regina vs. Penguin Books Limited* (Hammondsworth: Penguin, 1961); Mark Spilka, *The Love Ethic of D. H. Lawrence* (Indiana U. P., 1955); Eliseo Vivas, *D. H. Lawrence; the Failure and the Triumph of Art* (Northwestern U. P., 1960).

THOMAS EDWARD LAWRENCE. Autobiographical: *The Letters of T. E. Lawrence*, edited by David Garnett (Cape, 1938); *T. E. Lawrence to His Biographer, Liddel Hart, Information about Himself in the Form of Letters, Notes, Answers to Questions and Conversations* (Doubleday, Doran, 1938); *T. E. Lawrence to His Biographer, Robert Graves, Information about Himself in the Form of Letters, Notes and Answers to Questions* (Doubleday, Doran, 1938); *The Home Letters of T. E. Lawrence and His Brothers* (Macmillan, 1954); biographical: C. Edmund, *T. E. Lawrence* (Davies, 1935); R. Graves, *Lawrence and the*

Arabian Adventure (Doubleday, Doran, 1928); R. H. Kiernan, *Lawrence of Arabia* (Harrap, 1935); A. W. Lawrence, ed., *T. E. Lawrence by His Friends* (Cape, 1937); B. H. Liddell Hart, *Colonel Lawrence, the Man Behind the Legend* (Dodd, Mead, 1934); B. H. Liddell Hart, *T. E. Lawrence in Arabia & After* (Cape, 1943); V. Richards, *Portrait of T. E. Lawrence, the Lawrence of the Seven Pillars of Wisdom* (Cape, 1936); E. Robinson, *Lawrence, the Story of His Life* (O. U. P., 1935); C. S. Smith, *The Golden Reign, the Story of My Friendship with "Lawrence of Arabia,"* (Cassell, 1940); L. J. Thomas, *With Lawrence in Arabia* (Century, 1924); Richard Aldington, *Lawrence of Arabia, a Biographical Enquiry* (Collins, 1955), a vigorous attack on the Lawrence legend; critical: S. Rodman, *Lawrence, the Last Crusade, a Dramatic-narrative Poem* (Viking Press, 1937); Flora Armitage, *The Desert and the Stars; a Biography of Lawrence of Arabia* (Holt, 1955); Anthony Nutting, *Lawrence of Arabia; the Man and the Motive* (London, Hollis & Carter, 1961).

KATHERINE MANSFIELD. Autobiographical. *Journal of Katherine Mansfield,* ed. by J. Middleton Murry (Constable, 1927); biographical: R. E. Mantz and J. M. Murry, *The Life of Katherine Mansfield* (Constable, 1933); Sylvia Berkman, *Katherine Mansfield, a Critical Study* (Yale U. P., 1951); Anthony Alpers, *Katherine Mansfield* (Knopf, 1953).

SOMERSET MAUGHAM. Autobiographical: *The Summing Up* (Heinemann, 1938); critical: R. A. Cordell, *W. Somerset Maugham* (Nelson, 1937); P. Dottin, *Le Théâtre de W. Somerset Maugham* (Perrin, 1937); P. Dottin, *W. Somerset Maugham et ses Romans* (Perrin, 1928); C. S. McIver, *William Somerset Maugham, a Study of Technique and Literary Sources* (Univ. of Penna. Press, 1936); R. H. Ward, *William Somerset Maugham* (Bles, 1937); K. W. Jonas, *The Maugham Enigma* (N. Y.: Citadel Press, 1954); Raymond M. Stott, *The Writings of William Somerset Maugham, a Bibliography* (London, Rota, 1956); *Supplement* (1961); Richard A. Cordell, *Somerset Maugham; a Biographical and Critical Study* (Indiana U. P., 1961); Raymond Mander, *Theatrical Companion to Maugham; a Pictorial Record* (London, Rockliff, 1955); Karl C. Pfeiffer, *W. Somerset Maugham; a Candid Portrait* (Norton, 1959).

JOHN MIDDLETON MURRY. Autobiographical: *The Autobiography of John Middleton Murry: Between Two Worlds* (Messner, 1936); critical: R. Heppenstall, *Middleton Murry, a Study in Excellent Normality* (Cape, 1934); biographical: Frank O. Lea, *The Life of John*

Middleton Murry (Methuen, 1959); Mary M. Murry, *To Keep Faith* (Constable, 1959).

SEAN O'CASEY. Autobiographical: *I Knock at the Door; Swift Glances Back at Things That Made Me* (Macmillan, 1939); *Pictures in the Hallway* (Macmillan, 1942); *Drums Under the Windows* (Macmillan, 1945); *Inishfallen, Fare Thee Well,* (Macmillan, 1949); *Rose and Crown* (Macmillan, 1952); *Sunset and Evening Star* (Macmillan, 1954); critical: Robert G. Hogan, *The Experiments of Sean O'Casey* (St. Martin's, 1960); Jules Koslow, *The Green and the Red; Sean O'Casey, the Man and His Plays* (N. Y., Arts Inc., 1950).

WILFRED OWEN. Critical: Dennis S. R. Welland, *Wilfred Owen; a Critical Study* (Chatto & Windus, 1960).

JOHN COWPER POWYS AND T. F. POWYS. Autobiographical: J. C. Powys, *Autobiography* (Lane, 1937); J. C. Powys, *Confessions of Two Brothers, John Cowper Powys and Llewelyn Powys* (Manas Press, 1916); critical: R. H. Ward, *The Powys Brothers, a Study* (Lane, 1935); L. Marlow, *Welsh Ambassadors, Powys Lives and Letters* (Chapman and Hall, 1936); Henry Coombes, *T. F. Powys* (London, Barrie & Rockliff, 1960); William Hunter, *The Novels and Stories of T. F. Powys* (Cambridge, Minority Press, 1930).

SIR HERBERT READ. Autobiographical: *Annals of Innocence and Experience* rev. enl. ed. (Faber, 1946); critical: Henry Treece, ed., *Herbert Read: an Introduction to His Work by Various Hands* (Faber, 1944).

DOROTHY M. RICHARDSON. Critical: J. C. Powys, *Dorothy M. Richardson* (Joiner and Steele, 1931); Cæser R. Blake, *Dorothy Richardson* (Michigan U. P., 1960).

HENRY HANDEL RICHARDSON. Autobiographical: *Myself When Young, with an Essay on the Art of Henry Handel Richardson* by J. G. Robertson (Heinemann, 1948); critical: Nettie Palmer, *Henry Handel Richardson: a Study* (Sydney, Angus and Robertson, 1950); Edna Purdie, *Henry Handel Richardson; Some Personal Impressions* (Sydney, Angus and Robertson 1957).

LENNOX ROBINSON. Autobiographical: *Curtain Up* (London, M. Joseph, 1942).

SIEGFRIED SASSOON. Autobiographical: *The Old Century and Seven More Years* (Faber and Faber, 1938); *The Weald of Youth* (Viking, 1942); *Siegfried's Journey, 1916–1920* (Viking, 1946). Geoffrey Keynes, *A Bibliography of Siegfried Sassoon* (Hart-Davis, 1962).

EDITH, OSBERT, and SACHEVERELL SITWELL. Autobiographical: S. Sitwell, *All Summer in a Day, an Autobiographical Fantasia* (Duckworth, 1926); O. Sitwell, *Left Hand, Right Hand!: The Cruel Month* (Macmillan, 1945); *The Scarlet Tree* (Macmillan, 1946); *Great Morning* (Macmillan, 1947); *Laughter in the Next Room* (Macmillan, 1949); *Noble Essences* (Macmillan, 1950); critical: R. L. Mégroz, *The Three Sitwells, a Biographical and Critical Study* (Richards Press, 1927); Max Wykes-Joyce, *Triad of Genius* (London, Owen, 1953). José García Villased, *A Celebration for Edith Sitwell* (New Directions, 1948); Geoffrey Singleton, *Edith Sitwell: the Hymn to Life* (London, Fortune, 1960).

STEPHEN SPENDER. Autobiographical: *World within World* (Hamilton, 1951).

LYTTON STRACHEY. Critical: C. Bower-Shore, *Lytton Strachey, an Essay,* (Fenland Press, 1933); Martin Kallich, *the Psychological Milieu of Lytton Strachey* (N. Y., Bookman Associates, 1961); Charles R. Sanders, *Lytton Strachey, his Mind and Art* (Yale U. P., 1957), K. R. Srenivasa Iyengar, *Lytton Strachey, a Critical Study* (Chatto & Windus, 1939).

DYLAN THOMAS. Biographical: John M. Brinnin, *Dylan Thomas in America* (Little, Brown, 1955); *Caitlin Thomas, Leftover Life to Kill* (Putnam, 1957); critical: John M. Brinnin, ed., *A Casebook on Dylan Thomas* (Crowell, 1961); David Holbrook, *Llareggub Revisited: Dylan Thomas and the State of Modern Poetry* (Bowes and Bowes, 1962); Elder Olson, *The Poetry of Dylan Thomas* (Chicago U. P., 1954); Derek Stanford, *Dylan Thomas: a Literary Study* (London, Spearman, 1954); Ernest W. Tedlock, ed., *Dylan Thomas; the Legend and the Poet; a Collection of Biographical and Critical Essays* (Heinemann, 1960); William Y. Tindall, *A Reader's Guide to Dylan Thomas* (Farrar et al., 1962).

EDWARD THOMAS. Autobiographical: *The Childhood of Edward Thomas, a Fragment of Autobiography* (Faber and Faber, 1938); biographical: R. P. Eckert, *Edward Thomas, a Biography and a Bibliography* (Dent, 1937); J. Moore, *The Life and Letters of Edward Thomas* (Heinemann, 1939); H. Thomas, *As It Was* (Harper, 1927); H. Thomas, *World without End* (Harper, 1931); critical: H. Coombes, *Edward Thomas* (Chatto & Windus, 1956).

EVELYN WAUGH. Critical: A. A. DeVitis, *Roman Holiday, the Catholic Novels of Evelyn Waugh* (N. Y., Bookman Associates, 1956); Frederick J. Stopp, *Evelyn Waugh, Portrait of an Artist* (Little, Brown, 1958).

VIRGINIA WOOLF. B. J. Kirkpatrick, *A Bibliography of Virginia Woolf* (London, Hart-Davis, 1957); biographical: J. K. Johnstone,

The Bloomsbury Group; a Study of E. M. Forster, Lytton Strachey, Virginia Woolf, and Their Circle (Secker & Warburg, 1954); Aileen Pippett, *The Moth and the Star; a Biography of Virginia Woolf* (Little Brown, 1955); critical: F. Delattre, *Le Roman Psychologique de Virginia Woolf* (Vrin, 1932); Winifred Holtby, *Virginia Woolf* (Wishart, 1952); David Daiches, *Virginia Woolf* (New Directions, 1942); Joan Bennett, *Virginia Woolf, her Art as a Novelist* (Harcourt, 1945); R. Chambers, *The Novels of Virginia Woolf* (Oliver & Boyd, 1947); Bernard Blackstone, *Virginia Woolf, a Commentary* (Harcourt, 1949); Dorothy Brewster, *Virginia Woolf's London* (Allen & Unwin, 1959); E. M. Forster, *Virginia Woolf* (Cambridge U. P., 1942); James Hafley, *The Glass Roof; Virginia Woolf as a Novelist* (California U. P., 1954).

INDEX

Index

A

Abbey Theatre, The, 400, 455, 456, 457–458, 459
"Abou Ben Adhem," 279
Absalom and Achitophel, 178
Absentee, The, 341
Absurd, Drama of the, 466
"Abt Vogler," 316
Across the Plains, 378, 379
Actions and Reactions, 381, 382
Acts and Monuments, 72
Adam Bede, 365, 366
Addison, Joseph, 154, 194, 195–197, 198, 199, 200, 204, 217, 358
"Address to the Deil," 232
Address to the Irish People, 274
"Adonais," 215, 275, 277
Advancement of Learning (De Augmentis Scientiarum), 141
Adventurer, The, 217
Adventures of Philip, The, 359
"Æ," 415–416
Ælfric, 18
"Aella," 214
Æneid, 69, 485
Aeschylus, 275, 459
Aesthetic movement, 405–406
Affair, The, 448
Affirmations, 417
Afoot in England, 417
After Many a Summer, 432
After Strange Gods, 502
Age of Anxiety, The, 486
Alamein to Zem-Zem, 489
Alastor, or the Spirit of Solitude, 275
Albion's England, 88
Alchemist, The, 126, 127
Aldington, Richard, 474, 475
"Alexander's Feast," 180, 212
Alexandrian Quartet, 449
Alfred, King, 19–20
Alice-Sit-by-the-Fire, 393
All for Love, 180, 184
All That Fall, 467
"Allisoun," 34
Alliterative metre, 55–56
All's Well That Ends Well, 117

Almayer's Folly, 382
Alton Locke, 363
Amateur Emigrant, The, 378
Amazing Marriage, The, 369
Ambassadors, The, 374
Amelia, 244, 245
American, The, 373
Amis, Kingsley, 450
Amis and Amiloun, 27
"Amoretti," 81
Anabase, 481
Anatomy of Melancholy, 157–158
"Ancient Mariner, The," 259, 260
"And Death Shall Have No Dominion," 491
And Even Now, 418
"Andrea del Sarto," 316
Andreas, 13
Androcles and the Lion, 395
Anglo-Norman literature, 21–22
Anglo-Saxon Chronicle, 18
Angry Young Men, The, 424, 450, 465
Ann Veronica, 389
Annus Mirabilis, 178
Anouilh, Jean, 464
Anthony and Anna, 401
Antic Hay, 432
Anticipations, 389
Antiquary, The, 345
Antony and Cleopatra, 121
Aphrodite in Aulis, 425
Apologia pro Vita Sua, 301, 302
Appeal from the New to the Old Whigs, 227
Apple Cart, The, 454
"Appleton House," 154
Appreciations, 338
Arbuthnot, 201
Arcades, 161
Arcadia, 76, 77, 78, 79, 237
Areopagitica, 164
Ariosto, 70, 85, 163, 184, 278
Aristophanes, 462
Arms and the Man, 394, 453
Arnold, Matthew, 196, 277, 319–323, 329, 402, 503
Arrow of Gold, The, 425

579